DRUGS IN LITIGATION:

DAMAGE AWARDS INVOLVING PRESCRIPTION AND NONPRESCRIPTION DRUGS

1990 EDITION

Compiled by
The Editorial Staff of the Publishers of
LAWYERS' MEDICAL CYCLOPEDIA

Compilation Editor

Richard M. Patterson, J.D.

Special Consultant

Peter C. Hoyle, Ph. D.

THE MICHIE COMPANY
Law Publishers
Charlottesville, Virginia

Library of Congress Catalog Card No. 89-61443
ISBN 0-87473-451-7

CONTENTS

INTRODUCTION

The first edition of this volume appeared in 1976, to fill the need of the legal and medical professions for a compilation of personal injury cases involving untoward results of prescription and nonprescription drugs. The need for such a volume arose because of a startling increase in the number of malpractice and product liability actions against physicians, hospitals, pharmacists and drug manufacturers. At that time the problem of adverse drug reactions was deemed critical. Although vigorously challenged by some medical authorities,[1] one study suggested that as many as 140,000 hospital patients were dying each year from drug-related disorders.[2] Later studies have suggested that these figures were too high,[3] yet other reports have shown that among the causes of hospital patient injuries, adverse drug reactions ranked second only to postoperative complications.[4] Similar results were reached in a survey of claims against the federal government.[5]

If the problem of adverse drug reactions was serious in 1976, apparently it did not improve. Six years after publication of the first edition of this volume the number of drug malpractice and product liability actions being filed each year had tripled. A 1981 study suggested that in the average 300-bed hospital there still

---

[1] Letter to the *Journal of the American Medical Association* (231: 22-23, 1975) from Nelson S. Irey, M.D., Armed Forces Institute of Pathology, Washington, D.C.; Letter to same (229: 1043-1044, 1974) from C. Joseph Stetler, Pharmaceutical Manufacturers Association, Washington, D.C.; Editorial, "The ADR Numbers Game," *Journal of the American Medical Association* 229: 1097-1098, 1974.

[2] Letter to the *Journal of the American Medical Association* (229: 1043, 1974) from Robert B. Talley, M.D. and Marc F. Laventurier, Pharm.B., in which the writers revise upward their estimates of the number of annual deaths as reported in their paper "Drug Utilization and Peer Review in San Joaquin," read before the American Association of Foundations for Medical Care, Sea Island, Ga., August 28, 1972. See also Koch-Weser, J., "Fatal Reactions to Drug Therapy," *New England Journal of Medicine* 291: 302-303, 1974; and Caranasos, G. J., et al., "Drug-Induced Illness Leading to Hospitalization," *Journal of the American Medical Association* 228: 713-717, 1974.

[3] Porter, J., and Jick, H., "Drug-Related Deaths Among Medical Inpatients," *Journal of the American Medical Association* 237: 879-881, 1977.

[4] Pocincki, L. S., et al., "The Incidence of Iatrogenic Injuries," in the Appendix to *Report of the Secretary's Commission on Medical Malpractice,* January 16, 1973 (DHEW Publication No. (OS) 73-89), pp. 50-70.

[5] Welch, R. and Shear, B. W., "Malpractice Claims in the Federal Sector," Id., pp. 26-37.

were as many as 130,000 medication errors per year.[6] And in view of the many cases collected for this latest edition, there is little doubt that the number of drug claims reaching the courts is still on the increase.

For the lawyer, the traditional means of legal research into drug liability have offered a cumbersome route. Citations to decisions dealing with drugs are widely scattered throughout the classification systems and title arrangements used to locate American case law. There have been several attempts to compile drug cases, but they suffer from a common weakness—poor indexing. Compilers have failed to take into account that many drugs have both a generic and one or more brand names. The same drug may be discussed in one appellate opinion by its generic name, and in the next by a brand name. It may be involved in a third case under yet another brand name. Frequently the cases are never connected.

In compiling this volume, the editors have done more than just provide summaries of appellate drug decisions cross-indexed under generic and brand names (although perhaps to some frustrated lawyers this in itself would justify the price of the book). The volume contains many trial court decisions and jury verdicts plus, where available, settlement amounts.

Preceding the case summaries on each drug there is a short description of the drug. This has been kept brief, its main purpose being to provide the reader with background information to give more meaning to the cases. For additional data on a drug,[7] the editors recommend the latest edition of Goodman and Gilman's *The Pharmacological Basis of Therapeutics* (New York: MacMillan), which is considered the "Bible" for drug information; *Drug Information for the Health Care Provider* (Rockville, Md.: United States Pharmacopeial Convention, Inc.); *Approved Drug Products with Therapeutic Equivalents Evaluations* (U. S. Department of Health

---

[6] Shaw, J., "Medication Errors a 'Great Hidden Problem,'" *American Medical News,* January 1/8, 1982, p. 18. A 1990 report of prescribing errors in a teaching hospital was much less alarming; however, the authors concluded that such errors still demonstrate a significant risk to the patient. Lesar, T., et al., "Medication Prescribing Errors in a Teaching Hospital," *Journal of the American Medical Association* 263:2329, 1990.

[7] Since the drug information provided herein is intended as background information for the cases discussed, such information may not always reflect the latest data being provided on a particular drug by the manufacturer, the FDA, or the scientific community. For the latest drug information the reader should consult the most recent edition of the source cited or the sources named above.

& Human Services); *Physicians' Desk Reference* (Oradell, N.J.: Medical Economics Company); AMA *Drug Evaluations* (Chicago: American Medical Association); and *The Medical Letter on Drugs and Therapeutics,* a newsletter published by The Medical Letter, Inc., New Rochelle, New York.

To keep this volume from becoming unwieldy, it has been necessary to limit its scope. With a few exceptions, the case summaries are just that, summaries, and are not intended as substitutes for the entire opinions. This book is not designed to keep the lawyer out of the library, but to direct his or her search.

Cases that involve drugs only indirectly are not included. For example, actions dealing with diagnostic radiology and contrast media will not be found unless they involve possible adverse reactions to the medium. Similarly, while reactions to anesthetics, both general and local, are included, cases on cardiac arrest while under general anesthesia are not included unless the choice or method of use of a specific anesthetic agent is material to the issues involved. Also omitted are most actions against pharmacists for merely dispensing the wrong drug, since these disputes do not question quality, dosage, or judgment in prescribing or dispensing a particular drug. Actions against pharmacists are included, however, when falling within these categories. For the same reason, most cases dealing with injection injuries (needle traumatizing a nerve) are omitted.

DRUGS AND CASES

A

ACETAMINOPHEN
Tylenol

Acetaminophen is a popular over-the-counter analgesic and antipyretic indicated for a wide variety of arthritic and rheumatic conditions involving musculoskeletal pain, as well as other painful disorders such as headaches and menstrual cramps. It is also recommended for the discomfort and fever of common colds and other viral infections. The drug has rarely been found to produce any side effects, but excessive dosage can lead to liver toxicity.[1]

While the public knows the drug mainly by the popular brand name Tylenol (McNeil Consumer Products Company, Fort Washington, Pa.), the drug is contained in dozens of pain and cold remedies and in many prescription products.

Elsroth v. Johnson & Johnson (S.D. N.Y., 1988) 700 F. Supp. 151.

Retailer and manufacturer not liable for death of consumer who ingested Tylenol capsules containing potassium cyanide

In November 1982, following a series of murders in the Chicago area as a result of someone placing cyanide in bottles of Extra-Strength Tylenol capsules, the FDA ordered manufacturers of over-the-counter drugs to produce a tamper-resistant package "having an indicator or barrier to entry which, if breached or missing, can reasonably be expected to provide visible evidence to consumers that tampering has occurred." In compliance with this order, Johnson & Johnson, manufacturer of Tylenol, produced a package for the product consisting of: (1) a foil seal glued to the mouth of the container; (2) a "shrink seal" around the neck and cap of the container; and (3) a sealed box (with the end flaps glued shut) in which the container is sold.

Despite the above precautions, on February 4, 1986, the decedent, Diane Elsroth, died from potassium cyanide poisoning after ingesting two Extra-Strength Tylenol capsules purchased from a grocery store in Bronxville, New York. The murder remains unsolved, and

[1] *Physicians' Desk Reference for Nonprescription Drugs,* 8th ed., p. 592.

it was never determined conclusively how the product was tampered with.

The administrator of the decedent's estate sued the grocery store and the manufacturer, alleging negligence, breach of warranty, and strict products liability. The United States District Court for the Southern District of New York, in granting the defendants' motions for summary judgment, held that none of the plaintiffs' claims were sustainable.

Fatal hepatitis following overdose

In Bourne v. Seventh Ward General Hosp. (La. App., 1989) 546 So. 2d 197, a 20-year-old woman died from toxic hepatitis following an overdose of Darvocet-N 100 (propoxyphene napsylate), which contains acetaminophen, and Flexeril (cyclobenzaprine). The treating internist and two hospitals where the patient was treated were all sued for neligent care. The case is summarized herein under PROPOXYPHENE NAPSYLATE.

ACCUTANE

See ISOTRETINOIN

ACETAZOLAMIDE

Diamox

Acetazolamide is a diuretic used in the control of fluid secretion and abnormal fluid retention. The drug is marketed as Acetazolamide Tablets by Danbury Pharmacal, Inc. (Danbury, Conn.), and Geneva Generics, Inc. (Broomfield, Col.), and as Diamox by Lederle Laboratories (Wayne, N.J.).

Bacardi v. Holzman (1981) 182 N.J. Super. 422, 442 A.2d 617.

Manufacturer has no duty to warn user of risk of kidney stones

The plaintiff had been taking Diamox for many years because of glaucoma. The drug had been prescribed by a series of physicians and the prescriptions were readily renewable. In 1975 the plaintiff was hospitalized for kidney stones. When he was again hospitalized in 1977, Diamox was suspected as the cause, and his physicians recommended substituting another drug. On discontinuing the use of Diamox the plaintiff no longer has been troubled by stones.

The plaintiff sued one of the physicians who had prescribed Diamox and the manufacturer, Lederle Laboratories. He settled with the physician for an undetermined sum. Against the manufacturer, he alleged a duty to warn *all users* of Diamox of its potential adverse effects.

The manufacturer admitted that kidney stones were a common side effect of the drug but argued that its duty to warn ended with a notice of this fact in the product literature and in *Physicians' Desk Reference*. The trial court agreed and granted the manufacturer a summary judgment. The judgment was affirmed on appeal, with the reviewing court upholding the trial judge's decision that a drug manufacturer has no duty to warn a consumer of the product's side effects where there is an "intermediary" (physician) who "is not a mere conduit of the product, but rather administers it on an individual basis or recommends it in some way implying an independent duty to evaluate the risk and transmit relevant warnings to the user."

Patient given Diamox by mistake

In Brown v. Crews (Fla. App., 1978) 363 So. 2d 1121, the physician prescribed Dymelor for the patient, but for three weeks she received Diamox by mistake. Two days after resuming the correct medication, the patient went into a coma, and a month later she died. The case is summarized herein under ACETOHEXAMIDE.

ACETOHEXAMIDE
Dymelor

Dymelor is an oral antidiabetic agent manufactured by Eli Lilly and Company (Indianapolis, Ind.) for controlling the blood glucose in selected patients suffering from maturity-onset diabetes mellitus.

Since diabetes mellitus may be of various degrees of severity, there can be no fixed dosage. Daily oral dosage may range between 250 milligrams and 1.5 grams. Overdosage results in hypoglycemia (low blood sugar).[2]

The product is also marketed under the generic name by Barr Laboratories (Northvale, N.J.).

---

[2] *Physicians' Desk Reference,* 35th ed., pp. 1061-62.

Brown v. Crews (Fla. App., 1978) 363 So. 2d 1121.

**Evidence of adverse reaction to Dymelor—
Directed verdict for physician reversed**

A sixty-year-old female patient was placed in a hospital by her physician for tests and treatment. She was diagnosed as having diabetes. Shortly before she was discharged from the hospital, the patient was treated with Dymelor to reduce the amount of sugar in the blood. She was discharged on March 20 and given a prescription for Dymelor with instructions to see the physician in his office in two or three weeks.

On April 9 the patient saw the physician in his office. The patient said she was not feeling well and the physician recommended she return to the hospital, but she refused. It was discovered that the patient had been given the wrong medication by the pharmacist, and that for several weeks she had been taking Diamox, a diuretic. On the day she saw the physician, the patient obtained the correct medication, Dymelor, and took it until April 11 at which time she went into a coma. On that date she was again placed in the hospital in a dehydrated condition with profoundly low blood sugar. She remained in the coma until May 23 at which time she died. The physician testified that her death was secondary to profound hypoglycemia, a condition involving a marked decrease in the blood sugar level. He also testified that he would not have allowed the patient to resume taking Dymelor without strict hospital supervision if he had known she had taken the wrong medicine.

Another physician testified that resuming Dymelor after taking Diamox by mistake, and then being admitted to a hospital with a blood sugar of 29%, showed the patient reacted adversely to the Dymelor. He concluded that the Dymelor she took the last two days of her life was far more contributory to her death than the Diamox which she took by mistake for three weeks.

A directed verdict in favor of the physician was reversed.

ACETRIZOATE

See SODIUM ACETRIZOATE

ACETYLSALICYLIC ACID
See ASPIRIN

ACHROMYCIN
See TETRACYCLINE HYDROCHLORIDE

ACTHAR
See CORTICOTROPIN

ADAPIN
See DOXEPIN HYDROCHLORIDE

ADRENALIN
See EPINEPHRINE

ADRENALIN-IN-OIL
See EPINEPHRINE

ADVIL
See IBUPROFEN

AEROSEB-DEX
See DEXAMETHASONE

ALDACTAZIDE
See SPIRONOLACTONE

ALDACTONE
See SPIRONOLACTONE

ALKA-SELTZER PLUS
See CHLORPHENIRAMINE MALEATE

ALLEREST
See CHLORPHENIRAMINE MALEATE

ALLOPURINOL
Lopurin
Zyloprim

Allopurinol is capable of reducing the production of uric acid in the body, and thus is used in the treatment of gout. Lopurin is manufactured by Boots Pharmaceuticals, Inc. (Shreveport, La.) and Zyloprim by Burroughs Wellcome Company (Research Triangle Park, N.C.).

Among the adverse reactions listed by the manufacturers is bone marrow depression.[3]

Washington v. Meadows (No. 83-9062, Circuit Court, Hillsborough County, Florida, February 8, 1985).

Physician keeps patient on medication despite rash—Complications fatal—$1.2 million verdict

A sixty-year-old woman was seen for a cold. Blood tests showed evidence of gout and the defendant physician gave her Zyloprim and told her to return in two weeks. When she returned additional blood tests were performed, and although the tests revealed a low white count the medication was continued. Two days later she returned, complaining of a rash. The Zyloprim was still not discontinued. When a high fever developed the patient was hospitalized, but treatment was unsuccessful and she died of complications of the reaction. The jury returned a verdict of $1.2 million.[4]

ALPHAPRODINE HYDROCHLORIDE
Nisentil

Alphaprodine, formerly marketed by Hoffman-La Roche, Inc. (Nutley, N.J.), is an analgesic which is related chemically and pharmacologically to meperidine hydrochloride, but which is more potent on a weight basis and has a more rapid onset and shorter duration of action. The drug has been useful when rapid analgesia of short duration is desirable (e.g., in obstetrics; in urologic examinations and procedures; preoperatively in major surgery; and in minor surgery, especially orthopaedic, ophthalmologic, rhinologic, and laryngologic procedures). The most commonly observed adverse reactions include dizziness, nausea and vomiting.[5]

The product was discontinued by the manufacturer in 1986.

---

[3] *Physicians' Desk Reference,* 40th ed., p. 775.
[4] ATLA *Law Reporter* 28:323, 1985.
[5] *Drug Evaluations,* 6th ed., p. 60.

Kim v. Hoffman-La Roche (Nos. WEC 077655 & WEC 075943, Superior Court, Los Angeles County, Cal., Dec. 5, 1986).

Three-year-old child suffers cardiorespiratory failure following pre-dental injection—$300,000 settlement with manufacturer and dentist

A three-year-old child suffered cardiorespiratory failure and died after a dentist injected him with Nisentil to calm him while his cavities were filled. The child's parents brought suit against Hoffman-La Roche, the manufacturer, for strict product liability, negligence, and "conscious disregard of the public welfare." The plaintiffs claimed that the Food and Drug Administration had requested that Nisentil not be recommended for use on children, and that the manufacturer had never tested the drug to determine safe yet effective dosages for children. The parents also sued the dentist for failure to monitor and resuscitate the child. The parties settled for $300,000, with the dentist and manufacturer each contributing $150,000.[6]

Related cases.

Brain damage at birth—Use of Demerol and Nisentil questioned

In Akuly v. Suburban Medical Center (No. 81L-28824, Circuit Court, Cook County, Ill., Nov. 25, 1986), hospital personnel were charged with negligence in administering Nisentil and Demerol to an obstetrical patient, allegedly causing the patient's child to be born with brain damage. The case is summarized herein under MEPERIDINE HYDROCHLORIDE.

ALUMINUM HYDROXIDE

See MAGNESIUM CARBONATE with ALUMINUM HYDROXIDE; MAGNESIUM TRISILICATE with ALUMINUM HYDROXIDE

AMCILL

See AMPICILLIN

---

[6]ATLA *Products Liability Law Reporter* 6:74, 1987.

AMEN
See MEDROXYPROGESTERONE ACETATE

AMIKIN
See AMIKACIN SULFATE

AMIKACIN SULFATE
Amikin

Amikacin sulfate is a semi-synthetic aminoglycoside antibiotic derived from kanamycin and is used in the short-term treatment of serious infections due to susceptible strains of Gram-negative bacteria.

The manufacturer of Amikin (Bristol Laboratories, Syracuse, N.Y.) issues the following warning in the product literature:

> Patients treated with aminoglycosides should be under close clinical observation because of the potential ototoxicity and nephrotoxicity associated with their use. Ototoxicity, both auditory and vestibular, can occur in patients treated at higher doses or for periods longer than those recommended. The risk of amikacin-induced ototoxicity is greater in patients with renal damage. High frequency deafness usually occurs first and can be detected only by audiometric testing. Vertigo may occur and may be evidence of vestibular injury.[7]

Wakefield v. United States (C.A.-5 Tex., 1985) 765 F.2d 55.

Hearing loss and tinnitus—Alleged failure to obtain informed consent and monitor toxicity level—$735,000 bench verdict against government

The patient was a forty-two-year-old man hospitalized for end-stage renal disease and infection. He was administered amikacin sulfate over a six-week period as well as hemodialysis. A month later tests revealed profound bilateral sensori-neural hearing loss. Among other things the plaintiff argued that the physicians on the staff at the Veterans Administration hospital where he was confined failed to obtain his informed consent to treatment with amikacin and failed to monitor the toxicity level of the drug in his blood. He also claimed they performed no audiometric tests. The trial judge awarded $600,000 for past and future mental anguish

---

[7] *Physicians' Desk Reference,* 40th ed., p. 692.

and $135,000 for physical impairment. The judgment was upheld on appeal.

AMINOPHYLLINE
Mudrane
Somophylline

Aminophylline is a central nervous system stimulant. Because of its ability to relax smooth muscle, particularly bronchial muscle, it is a valuable therapeutic agent in treating bronchial asthma. The drug also exhibits considerable diuretic activity. Reported reactions include dizziness, faintness, nausea and vomiting, palpitations, and sudden death, all apparently due to an excessive rate of infusion.[8] In children, a special danger exists with rectal administration because of variable rates of absorption and possible cumulative effects of prolonged treatment.[9]

Numerous manufacturers produce and market the product under the generic name. Mudrane is manufactured by Poythress Laboratories, Inc. (Richmond, Va.) and Somophyllin by Fisons Corporation (Bedford, Mass.).

Batteast v. Wyeth Laboratories (1988) 172 Ill. App. 3d 114, 122 Ill. Dec. 189, 526 N.E.2d 428.

Brain damaged infant—Excessive dosage and possible synergistic action—$9 million in compensatory damages and $13 million in punitive

The patient was a two-year-old child admitted to the hospital for an upper respiratory infection, dehydration, diarrhea, vomiting, and a temperature of 102.8 degrees. He was given antibiotics and fluids intravenously, and placed in an oxygen tent. The following day, his attending physician prescribed a bronchodilator, Marax (a combination of ephedrine sulfate, theophyline, and hydroxyzine) for the respiratory problem.

On the third day, the child pulled out his I.V., and the nursing staff could not get another one started. The physician was reached by phone, and he ordered the Marax discontinued. This order was not carried out, however. The following morning, the physician, thinking the Marax had been discontinued, ordered one-half of a

---

[8] *Lawyers' Medical Cyclopedia,* § 6.10(B) (3rd ed., 1981); *The Merck Manual,* 14th ed., p. 1400.

[9] FDA Guidelines to manufacturer, May 7, 1975.

pediatric aminophylline suppository to be inserted every eight hours. The nursing staff again erred, and began giving the child a full pediatric aminophylline suppository (125 mg.), sometimes at eight-hour intervals, and at other times at six- and twelve-hour intervals. On the second day of this treatment regimen, the child began "twitching and grunting," and suffered a seizure. An examination revealed permanent brain damage attributed to constricted blood vessels of the brain caused by an excessive amount of aminophylline.

At the trial, evidence was introduced that the previous year (1975) the FDA had instructed Wyeth Laboratories, then the manufacturer of aminophylline, to update its package insert warnings because numerous studies had revealed serious problems in children who had been given the drug rectally. Wyeth, however, had not revised the warnings, nor had the company conducted any recent tests of its own relative to the drug's safety. The attending physician (who settled with the plaintiffs prior to trial) testified that if he had been warned by the manufacturer of the dangers presented by the drug, he would have carefully monitored the dosages administered to the child.

The jury returned a verdict for $9.2 million in compensatory damages against the hospital and Wyeth, and an additional $13 million in punitive damages against Wyeth.[10] Both verdicts were affirmed, the Appellate Court of Illinois finding strict liability against Wyeth for its violation of FDA regulations.

AMITRIPTYLINE

Elavil
Endep
Etrafon
Limbitrol
Triavil

[10] Wyeth counterclaimed against the hospital and the physician, seeking indemnification based upon the doctrine of equitable apportionment. The trial court dismissed the manufacturer's claim and the Appellate Court affirmed, holding that since the injuries for which recovery was sought from the manufacturer for its failure to warn of the drug's possible side effects were the same as those for which recovery was sought from the hospital and physician on the basis of negligence in failing to treat the boy properly for the side effects, the defendants were joint tortfeasors who had directly produced a single indivisible injury, and therefore equitable apportionment was not available. Batteast v. St. Bernard's Hosp. (1985) 134 Ill. App. 3d 843, 89 Ill. Dec. 561, 480 N.E.2d 1304.

Amitriptyline is an antidepressant with sedative effects. Its mechanism of action in humans is not known. It is not a monoamine oxidase inhibitor and it does not act primarily by stimulation of the central nervous system. As with all antidepressants, there are many possible adverse reactions including, but not limited to, myocardial infarction, stroke, heart block, hypotension, seizures, paralytic ileus, skin rash, bone marrow depression and testicular swelling.[11]

High doses of amitriptyline may cause temporary confusion, disturbed concentration or transient visual hallucinations. Overdosage may cause drowsiness, hypothermia, tachycardia and other arrhythmic abnormalities, bundle branch block, congestive heart failure, disorders of ocular motility, convulsions, and coma. With regard to overdosage, the manufacturer of Elavil issues the following instructions:

> All patients suspected of having taken an overdosage should be admitted to a hospital as soon as possible. *Treatment* is symptomatic and supportive. Empty the stomach as quickly as possible by emesis followed by gastric lavage upon arrival at the hospital. Following gastric lavage, activated charcoal may be administered. Twenty to 30 g of activated charcoal may be given every four to six hours during the first 24 to 48 hours after ingestion. An ECG should be taken and close monitoring of cardiac function instituted if there is any sign of abnormality. Maintain an open airway and adequate fluid intake; regulate body temperature. The intravenous administration of 1-3 mg of physostigmine salicylate is reported to reverse the symptoms of tricyclic antidepressant poisoning. Because physostigmine is rapidly metabolized, the dosage of physostigmine should be repeated as required particularly if life threatening signs such as arrhythmias, convulsions, and deep coma recur or persist after the initial dosage of physostigmine. Because physostigmine itself may be toxic, it is not recommended for routine use. Standard measures should be used to manage circulatory shock and metabolic acidosis. Cardiac arrhythmias may be treated with neostigmine, pyridostigmine, or propranolol. Should cardiac failure occur, the use of digitalis should be considered. Close monitoring of cardiac function for not less than five days is advisable.
>
> Anticonvulsants may be given to control convulsions. Amitriptyline increases the CNS depressant action but not the anticonvulsant action of barbiturates; therefore, an inhalation anesthetic, diazepam, or paraldehyde is recommended for control of convulsions.

---

[11] *Physicians' Desk Reference,* 42d ed., p. 1329.

Dialysis is of no value because of low plasma concentrations of the drug.
Since overdosage is often deliberate, patients may attempt suicide by other means during the recovery phase.[12]

Elavil and Triavil are manufactured by Merck, Sharp & Dohme (West Point, Pa.), Endep and Limbitrol by Roche Laboratories (Nutley, N.J.), and Etrafon by Schering Corporation (Kenilworth, N.J.).

Molkenbur v. Heart (Minn. App., 1987) 411 N.W.2d 249.

No negligence in treatment of Elavil overdose

In December 1980, the patient, a teenager, took 40 Elavil tablets (25 mg), after which she informed her parents that she had "overdosed." They rushed her to the hospital where the physician on duty, after consulting the medical literature for recommended treatment in such cases, prescribed Ipecac syrup to induce vomiting. The patient did vomit but later became incoherent. The physician had her transferred to a larger hospital where she received further treatment. Later, she was transferred to still a larger hospital, and while there, she suffered cardiac arrest and brain damage.

In her lawsuit, the patient offered the testimony of medical experts that the choice of treatment by the first physician to treat her (to administer Ipecac and wait) was below the recommended standard of care. According to her experts, a cardiac monitor should have been applied and she should have been given charcoal, intravenously, or gastric lavage. The plaintiff attempted to admit other evidence, including a medical journal article on "Acute Poisoning Management Protocol," but this was rejected. The defendant physician introduced evidence that the treatment the plaintiff received met acceptable standards.

Judgment was entered for the defendants, and the Court of Appeals affirmed, finding no reversible error on the part of the trial court.

Bell v. Hart (Ala., 1987) 516 So. 2d 562.

Confusion and incoherence following 300 mg. dose of Elavil—Psychologist and pharmacist not competent to testify—Summary judgment for physician

The patient, a middle-aged woman, suffered confusion and incoherence following one 300 mg. bedtime dose of Elavil. The drug was

[12] Id. at 1330.

prescribed by her physician, the defendant, for insomnia and leg cramps. In her malpractice suit, in which she alleged "wanton and reckless misconduct" on the part of the physician in prescribing the drug, the patient attempted to prove her case with the testimony of a psychologist and a pharmacist. The trial court ruled both witnesses incompetent to testify, and since the patient had no other experts, the defendant was granted a summary judgment. The Supreme Court of Alabama affirmed.

Cofnas v. Tomasas (Sup. Ct., Kings Cty., 1989) 548 N.Y.S.2d 367.

Dyskinesia—Manufacturer's warnings to physician adequate

A patient who developed dyskinesia while taking Etrafon claimed that the manufacturer of the drug, the Shering Corporation, failed to give adequate warnings of the hazards of its use. The manufacturer moved for summary judgment on the ground that the patient's physician was fully aware of the hazard, and that dyskinesia was listed as a known risk in *Physicians' Desk Reference.*

In opposing the motion, the patient's attorney argued that since the ultimate consumer of Etrafon was not supplied with a package insert containing the warning, the manufacturer had a higher degree of duty to inform a prescribing physician of the risk than otherwise would be the case; that the manufacturer should have followed the practice of a rival drug company which supplied physicians with a pamphlet setting forth a simple test to determine the presence of dyskinesia; and that the manufacturer failed to inform physicians through *Physicians' Desk Reference* that patients who were given drug-free periods were less likely to develop dyskinesia than patients who were not.

The court granted the manufacturer's motion.

AMOXAPINE
Asendin

Amoxapine is an antidepressant of the dibenzoxazepine class. It also has a mild sedative component. The drug is indicated for the relief of the symptoms of depression in patients with neurotic or reactive depressive disorders as well as endogenous and psychotic depressions, and depression accompanied by anxiety or agitation. The drug is contraindicated in patients who have shown prior hypersensitivity to dibenzoxazepine compounds, and should not be given concomitantly with monoamine oxidase inhibitors. Because of amoxapine's neuroleptic activity, the manufacturer includes a warning of the risk of tardive dyskinesia. Other possible (incidence less than 1%) adverse reactions include, but are not limited to, skin rashes, urinary retention, hypotension, hypertension, tachycardia, hepatitis, disorientation, seizures, and impotence. The drug also may cause a shift to the manic phase in manic depressive patients, increase symptoms of psychosis in schizophrenic patients, and exaggerate symptoms of paranoia in paranoid patients.[13]

Vinchiarello v. Kathuria (1989) 18 Conn. App. 377, 558 A.2d 262.

Suicide from overdose of Asendin—No evidence of negligence on part of psychiatrist or hospital outpatient clinic

The defendant psychiatrist treated the patient from 1978 until June 1983 for depression and other mental and emotional problems, both as an inpatient and outpatient. During that period, the patient attempted suicide five times. In June 1982, the defendant began prescribing Asendin on an outpatient basis. At first the prescription called for 50 mg tablets in containers of 100 units. On June 23, 1983, the defendant increased the dosage to 100 mg tablets, again in a 100-tablet container. On July 13, 1983, the patient committed suicide by swallowing an overdose of the drug.

The patient's estate sued the defendant and the hospital outpatient clinic where the defendant treated her, alleging that the patient was allowed to obtain large doses of Asendin without "proper supervision, control, and restriction" in light of the patient's "recurring severe depressive state and past history of suicide attempts." According to the plaintiff, Asendin should only have been prescribed in the hospital environment and not provided on an outpatient basis.

The jury returned a verdict for both defendants. On appeal, the Appellate Court of Connecticut affirmed, holding that the plaintiff had failed to present any evidence that the alleged substandard care provided by the defendants was the proximate cause of the patient's death, nor was any evidence presented that Asendin should have been prescribed only on an inpatient basis.

---

[13] *Physician's Desk Reference,* 43rd ed., p. 1111.

AMPHETAMINE and DEXTROAMPHETAMINE
Biphetamine

Amphetamine and dextroamphetamine, a combination of stimulant-anorexiants sold under the name Biphetamine by Pennwalt Corp. (Rochester, N.Y.), were once widely prescribed for appetite suppression and control of obesity. However, these drugs are no longer recommended by the American Medical Association's Department of Drugs for this purpose because of the risk of dependence. Also, the FDA has concluded that the amphetamines have no advantage over other safer anorexiants, and a few states have actually banned their use for weight control.[14]

In addition to the risk of dependence, Biphetamine may have a pronounced effect on the cardiovascular system and can cause marked central nervous system stimulation. Also, it should not be given to women who are pregnant or who are likely to become pregnant.[15]

Reeder v. Hammond (1983) 125 Mich. App. 223, 336 N.W.2d 3.

Birth defects—Adequacy of manufacturer's warnings questioned

In a suit on behalf of a child born with birth defects, including mental retardation and blindness, the plaintiffs claimed the child's condition was the result of the mother taking either Biphetamine or Ovral (norgestrel with ethinyl estradiol), a birth control pill, during pregnancy.

At the hearing on the defendant manufacturers' motions for summary judgment, the mother's physician stated by affidavit that he had been sufficiently alerted as to the dangers of Ovral to pregnant patients through the manufacturer's warnings, but with respect to Biphetamine, it was his opinion that "the labeling does not adequately alert any physician concerning the potential harm of the drug when used in women of child-bearing age."

In reviewing the trial court's granting of the summary judgments, the Court of Appeals of Michigan reversed as to the manufacturer of Biphetamine, holding that a genuine issue of fact existed as to the adequacy of its warning. The court added, however, that there also remained a question as to whether the mother's

---

[14] AMA *Drug Evaluations,* 6th ed., p. 929.
[15] AMA *Drug Evaluations,* 6th ed., p. 934.

physician had read the Biphetamine warnings, and thus it was for a jury to decide what effect this had on the manufacturer's liability.

AMPICILLIN
Amcill
Omnipen
Polycillin

Ampicillin is a semisynthetic penicillin derived from the basic penicillin nucleus, 6-aminopenicillanic acid. The drug is indicated primarily in the treatment of infections caused by susceptible strains of the microorganisms: Shigella, Salmonella (including *S typhosa*), *E coli, N gonorrhoeae, H influenzae,* and *P mirabilis*. It also may be indicated in certain infections caused by susceptible gram-positive organisms: penicillin G-sensitive staphylococci, streptococci, enterococci, and pneumococci.[16]

Many companies produce this drug. The Amcill brand is manufactured by Parke-Davis (Morris Plains, N.J.); Omnipen by Wyeth Laboratories (Philadelphia, Pa.); and Polycillin by Bristol Laboratories (Syracuse, N.Y.).

Ampicillin is contraindicated in patients with a history of hypersensitivity reaction to penicillin. The adverse reactions are similar to those involved in penicillin, including fatal anaphylactic shock (see PENICILLIN). When a reaction in the form of skin rash occurs, the manufacturers suggest the drug should be discontinued unless, in the opinion of the physician, the condition for which the patient is being treated is "life threatening and amenable only to ampicillin therapy."[17]

Walstad v. University of Minnesota Hospitals (C.A.-8 Minn., 1971) 442 F.2d 634.

Skin rash—Ampicillin given to patient allergic to penicillin—Directed verdict for surgeon reversed

A 33-year-old woman patient was hospitalized for a cardiac condition. Complications developed following a heart catheterization, and she and her husband filed a malpractice suit alleging numerous acts of negligence on the part of the physicians involved in her case and the hospital personnel.

---

[16] *Physicians' Desk Reference,* 35th ed., p. 1324.
[17] Id.

At the trial, all defendants were granted directed verdicts on all counts at the close of the plaintiffs' case. On appeal, these were affirmed except as to a charge that the patient was negligently administered ampicillin despite a notation on her hospital chart that she was allergic to penicillin.

The evidence had disclosed that the patient received ampicillin on at least twelve days despite the early appearance of a skin rash on her arms and back. The reviewing court felt this made a submissible case against the cardiovascular surgeon who prescribed the drug. The court said: "[I]t is within the common knowledge and experience of a layman to judge whether the drug caused the rash which appeared on [the patient's] arms and back and whether the prescription and administration of the drug under these circumstances constituted negligence." Although the surgeon neither administered the drug himself nor was he present to supervise its administration by the hospital personnel, the court felt liability could be imputed to him under the doctrine of *respondeat superior*.

Lanczki v. Providence Hosp. (1977) 77 Mich. App. 732, 258 N.W.2d 238.

Ampicillin not cause of "abnormal psychic reaction"—Physician's summary judgment affirmed

A patient underwent a laminectomy. During the postoperative period he was given ampicillin to prevent infection. On the third night he became agitated, and refused to take any more medication. The following morning he told his physician he wanted to go home. Reluctantly the physician agreed, since there had been no complications and the patient was apparently doing well physically. Unaware of his patient's mental state, the physician left him to tend to other patients. The patient, all packed and ready to leave the hospital, suddenly, for unexplained reasons, leaped out of the window and suffered serious injuries.

In his lawsuit against the physician and the hospital, the patient, among other charges, alleged that the medications he received caused an abnormal psychic reaction. But the evidence revealed that the only medications given to the patient, other than for sleeping and pain, was the ampicillin, and an undisputed affidavit of the chief of infectious diseases at the hospital stated that "there is no medical information showing that ampicillin therapy in any way creates any psychological problems."

The trial court granted the physician's motion for summary judgment, which was affirmed on appeal.

Leary v. Rupp (1979) 89 Mich. App. 145, 280 N.W.2d 466.

Allergic reaction to ampicillin—Statute of limitations not bar to action of patient who eventually developed asceptic necrosis

Because the patient was allergic to penicillin, her physician prescribed Polycillin for her fever, sore throat and headaches. However, she still suffered a reaction, and was admitted to the hospital in what the physician described as a "life-threatening situation." She was treated with prednisone, responded well, and was released in several weeks.

The patient continued to have bladder problems, however, and also pain in the back and leg for the next several years. Five years later, she learned that she was suffering from "asceptic necrosis," which she was told was probably the result of her reaction or the drugs she was given to treat it.

Suit was brought against the physician, with the patient alleging that she should not have been given Polycillin with her history of allergy, that the prednisone she received as treatment was not necessary, was given in excessive dosages, was actually contraindicated, and that once she was on prednisone, it was withdrawn in a "sudden, abrupt, and unsafe manner."

At trial, the judge granted an order accelerating judgment for the physician based on Michigan's two-year statute of limitations. On appeal, this was reversed with the court holding that while the patient knew of some of the acts of the physician at the time of her reaction and treatment (i.e., prescribing of polycillin and prednisone) and the resulting harm, reasonable minds could differ as to when she should have realized that her physician may have acted improperly.

Clark v. Medical Services of America (No. D-20539, Superior Court, Fulton County, Ga., Jan. 15, 1988).

Infant suffers cardiac and respiratory arrest following IV administration of ampicillin—Evidence that wrong drug was given—Question of adequate emergency treatment—$2.4 million structured settlement

The patient was an eleven-month-old male infant admitted to the hospital with a diagnosis of "croup." When a nurse administered an

IV injection of ampicillin, the child went into cardiac and respiratory arrest. Emergency resuscitation efforts were unsuccessful, and the child suffered extensive brain damage, resulting in blindness, spastic quadriplegia, and epilepsy.

In their lawsuit against the hospital, the parents charged failure to have personnel on duty capable of performing an emergency endotracheal intubation, which was in violation of JCAH standards. In answer to the plaintiffs' complaint, the hospital claimed that the cardiac and respiratory arrest was either an unforeseeable complication of the croup due to a laryngospasm, or the result of an anaphylactic shock reaction to the ampicillin. As to the charge of inadequate personnel, the hospital claimed that none of the hospitals in the surrounding area provided personnel with intubation capability on a seven-day, round-the-clock basis. The plaintiffs argued, however, that JCAH standards require such personnel, and that this is a nation-wide requirement.

The plaintiffs also alleged negligence on the part of the hospital nursing staff in that the wrong drug was administered. While one of the nurses testified on deposition that the ampicillin was the drug ordered by the physician, on discovery, the plaintiffs learned that the physician's order was in fact for aminophylline, a central nervous system stimulant and bronchodilator. The plaintiffs charged that either a mistake was made during the processing of the order or the ampicillin was mistakenly taken from the pharmacy shelf.

The parties agreed upon a structured settlement having a present value of $2.4 million, the limit of the available insurance coverage.[18]

Related cases

Laryngeal edema following ampicillin and penicillin G

In DiBona v. Chilton Memorial Hosp. (No. L 35391-78, Superior Court, Passaic County, N.J., Sept. 24, 1980), the patient was treated for tonsillitis with ampicillin and was later administered an injection of penicillin G. Subsequent examination revealed laryngeal edema which had blocked respiration. The case is summarized herein under PENICILLIN.

---

[18] ATLA *Professional Negligence Law Reporter* 3:72, 1988.

AMYGDALIN
Laetrile
Vitamin B-17

Amygdalin, the major component of Laetrile (also sold at times as Vitamin B-17), is derived from pulverized apricot pits. (It also can be found in lesser amounts in other foods, including lima beans, almonds and cherries.) Although amygdalin has been around for over a quarter of a century as a "cancer cure," no valid scientific evidence has ever been found indicating that it has any value in treating this disease. The FDA has warned that the product is "worthless in the prevention, treatment or cure of cancer." The substance has no therapeutic or nutritional value. Furthermore, it can be fatal for cancer patients who delay or give up regular medical treatment to take the substance and, since it contains cyanide, can cause death when taken by mouth.

Amygdalin is not routinely subject to FDA inspection for quality and purity as other drugs. It has been found to contain toxic contaminants, including mold and other adulterants which can be dangerous when injected.

Since amygdalin has not been approved by the FDA for the treatment of cancer, nor is it recognized by the American Medical Association as beneficial or effective, a medical doctor runs the risk of malpractice liability for adverse results in administering or prescribing the drug.[19]

Sullivan v. Henry (1982) 160 Ga. App. 791, 287 S.E.2d 652.

Physician charged with malpractice in prescribing laetrile—Summary judgment for defendant reversed

The defendant, the patient's family physician for many years, began treating her with laetrile and vitamin B-17 injections on December 2, 1977, after he consulted with her surgeons and was informed that she had carcinosarcoma with "probable vascular in-

---

[19] *Lawyers' Medical Cyclopedia,* §§ 38.44b, 38.44d; *FDA Drug Bulletin,* Nov.-Dec., 1977, p. 28; Moertel, C., et al., "A Critical Trial of Amygdalin (Laetrile) in the Treatment of Human Cancer," *New England Journal of Medicine* 306: 201, 1982; Relman, A., "Closing the Books on Laetrile," *New England Journal of Medicine* 306: 236, 1982. For the culmination of nearly twelve years of litigation by cancer patients and their families seeking to obtain the use of laetrile, see Rutherford v. United States (C.A.-10 Okla., 1986) 806 F.2d 1455.

vasion" which was not subject to treatment with radiation or chemotherapy. He gave her six more injections between December 5 and December 31, at which time she complained that she "had difficulty passing urine." On January 3, 1978, she died from kidney failure.

In a lawsuit brought by the patient's family for malpractice, the defendant was granted a summary judgment on the strength of his own affidavit as an "expert" that his treatment met acceptable standards. The Court of Appeals reversed, holding that while the law presumes a physician exercises his skill in an ordinarily skillful manner, a material fact existed as to whether the defendant's use of an unapproved and dangerous drug such as laetrile met appropriate standards.

ANACIN

See ASPIRIN

ANBESOL

See BENZOCAINE

ANESTACON

See LIDOCAINE HYDROCHLORIDE

ANGIO-CONRAY

See SODIUM IOTHALAMATE

ANILERIDINE

Leritine

Anileridine is an analgesic with pharmacological activity and incidence of side effects similar to meperidine hydrochloride (Demerol). It is no longer marketed.

Cardiac arrest in asthmatic surgical patient given Leritine and other drugs

In Siegel v. Mt. Sinai Hosp. of Cleveland (1978) 62 Ohio App. 2d 12, 403 N.E.2d 202, an asthmatic patient was given numerous drugs for a spinal block, including Leritine, prior to surgery. He suffered a bronchial spasm and cardiac arrest during the surgery and later died. The case is summarized herein under SODIUM THIOPENTAL.

ANSOLYSEN
See PENTOLINIUM TARTRATE

ANTABUSE
See DISULFIRAM

ANTIVENIN
Antivenin (Crotalidae) Polyvalent

Antivenin (Crotalidae) Polyvalent, manufactured by Wyeth Laboratories (Philadelphia, Pa.), is a refined and concentrated preparation of serum globulins obtained by fractionating blood from healthy horses that have been immunized with snake venoms. The preparation contains protective substances against the venoms of the crotalids (pit vipers) of North and South America, including rattlesnakes, cottonmouths and highland moccasins of the United States, and other snakes from various parts of the world.[20]

Antivenin should be administered as soon as possible after the snakebite, preferably by a physician. Because of the possibility of an allergic reaction to the horse serum, appropriate therapeutic agents, including a tourniquet, oxygen supply, and epinephrine, should be ready for immediate use. Sensitivity tests should be administered before the full dose is given. Instructions on such tests are included in the kit.[21]

The severity and character of clinical manifestations after the bite generally dictate the amount of antivenin to be used and the route of administration, which will be either intramuscularly or intravenously. For intramuscular injection, the anterolateral thigh or buttock is suggested. Injection at or around the site of the bite is not recommended.[22]

Crouch v. Most (1967) 78 N.M. 406, 432 P.2d 250.

Gangrene at site of injection in hand—Physician charged with negligence and failure to disclose risks of treatment—Verdict of no liability affirmed

The patient, an amateur snake handler, received a rattlesnake bite on the index and middle fingers of his hand while working at a

---

[20] Manufacturer's package insert Cir. 2147 (Revised May 2, 1966).

[21] Id.

[22] Id.

reptile garden. Suction cups and a tourniquet were applied immediately and he was taken to a hospital.

About thirty minutes had elapsed when the patient was first seen by a physician. He treated the man by injecting "Antivenin" into the base of the fingers and into the left deltoid area. The hand was then packed in ice and the patient was kept at the hospital for 48 hours. He was released with instructions to keep the hand on ice.

The patient was seen again in ten days. His hand and arm were swollen, discolored and odorous with dry gangrene. Another physician was brought in and he discontinued the ice treatment, put the hand on a heat pad, and commenced antibiotic shots. The hand was saved but it was necessary to amputate the tips of two fingers.

In his suit against the first treating physician, the patient, among other things, charged that the defendant had failed to observe instructions in the kit containing the snakebite serum which stated that the serum should be injected into the thigh or buttock, and not at the site of the bite. In this connection, the patient alleged that the physician failed to warn him of the possible danger of gangrene from the use of the serum; therefore, he had failed to obtain his informed consent to this method of treatment.

In affirming a verdict for the physician, the Supreme Court of New Mexico commented that:

> It would indeed be most unusual for a doctor, with his patient who had just been bitten by a venomous snake, to calmly sit down and first fully discuss the various available methods of treating snakebite and the possible consequences, while the venom was being pumped through the patient's body.

Concluding, the court commented that the case involved a situation which brings into play an exception to the basic rule requiring a physician to disclose fully the dangers of a method of treatment; i.e., where there is an emergency and the patient is in no condition to determine for himself the proper course of action.

Buck v. United States (M.D. Fla., 1977) 433 F. Supp. 896.

Improper treatment for snakebite—$185,000 award

The patient, a fourteen-year-old boy, was playing on the air force base where his father was an officer when he was bitten by a large diamondback rattlesnake on the left leg, slightly below the knee and to the left of the tibia. Having had some Boy Scout training, he administered approved first-aid to himself with the help of a friend.

The friend then flagged down a military policeman who took the patient to the emergency room of the base hospital. They arrived within fifteen to twenty minutes following the injury.

The physician in charge of the emergency room had no training or experience in the treatment of snakebite. He consulted with his superior by telephone, a surgeon who was off-duty, but he also was unfamiliar with such treatment. By now the patient had an elevated pulse and blood pressure with signs and symptoms of systemic involvement. There was a mild discoloration and slight tenderness around the area of the bite with fang marks about an inch apart. The physicians decided that the treatment of choice was to use antivenin, and injected one ampule intramuscularly in the buttock area.

Two hours following his arrival the patient was admitted to the hospital as an inpatient and thereafter attended to exclusively by nurses or corpsmen from about 8:15 p.m. until 3:45 a.m. the next morning. By that time the patient's left thigh was swollen half again its normal size and the leg above and below the knee had turned blue.

After examining the patient, the physician again prescribed antivenin intramuscularly, and this was repeated one-half hour later. Fifteen hours after his arrival, the patient was seen by the surgeon-supervisor, who ordered more antivenin, this time intravenously, as recommended in the literature contained in the package inserts.

When he did not improve, the patient was transferred to a nearby general hospital where he underwent further treatment. He eventually survived, but with residual disability, including some deformity of the leg and spinal scoliosis.

At trial, the court found that the antivenin had been administered improperly, in that the instructions contained with the medication had not been followed correctly (treatment should have been intravenously from the beginning), and the patient had not received proper care at the base hospital.

The patient was awarded $185,000.

ANTIVENIN (CROTALIDAE) POLYVALENT

See ANTIVENIN

AQUATENSEN
See METHYCLOTHIAZIDE

ARALEN
See CHLOROQUINE

ARAMINE
See METARAMINOL BITARTRATE

ARISTOCORT
See TRIAMCINOLONE ACETONIDE

ARISTOSPAN
See TRIAMCINOLONE HEXACETONIDE

ASPIRIN
Anacin
Aspirin
Bufferin
Cope
Coricidin
Ecotrin
Empirin Compound
Excedrin
Vanquish

The above trade names for aspirin (acetylsalicylic acid)-containing drugs are only the few most popular. Aspirin is incorporated into hundreds of different drug preparations sold in the United States.[1]

Bayer Aspirin, Cope and Vanquish are made by Glenbrook Laboratories (New York, N.Y.); Bufferin and Excedrin by Bristol-Myers Products (New York, N.Y.); Coricidin by Schering Corporation (Kenilworth, N.J.); Ecotrin by Manley and James Laboratories (Philadelphia, Pa.); Empirin Compound by Burroughs Wellcome Company (Research Triangle Park, N.C.); and Fiorinal by Sandoz Pharmaceuticals (East Hanover, N.J.).

Aspirin is used as an analgesic, antipyretic (for reduction of fever) and anti-inflammatory agent. Clinical studies suggest that

[1] Weiss, H. J., "Aspirin — A Dangerous Drug?," *Journal of the American Medical Association* 229:1221-1222, 1974.

aspirin may have antithrombotic properties, and controlled prospective studies on its possible value in preventing cerebrovascular thromboembolism and myocardial infarction are being carried out.[2]

The generally recommended dosage for the adult is one or two five-grain tablets which may be repeated every four hours up to twelve tablets a day. For children, the dosage is one-half that of the adult or less, depending upon the brand and other drugs in the preparation. Some brands do not include recommendations for children, and some restrict any dosage to children over age six.

Although the incidence of serious adverse reactions to aspirin is low, and it is classified as one of the safest of drugs, aspirin may be responsible for gastric hemorrhage or bronchial asthma in susceptible individuals, and it also produces a mild hemostatic defect. These adverse reactions may be serious and occasionally fatal, and suggestions that aspirin-containing drugs be available only by prescription and contain warning labels have appeared.[3] Bleeding gastritis is reported to have been induced by long-term release aspirin as well as regular,[4] and at least one researcher suggests aspirin bleedings can occur at times in anyone, regardless of susceptibility.[5] Depending upon the brand, the drug is to be used with caution in the presence of ulcer or with anticoagulant therapy.

There is also solid medical evidence linking aspirin with Reye's syndrome in children and teenagers.[6]

Holden v. United States (Civil No. 69-CV-57, U.S. District Court, N.D., N.Y., Dec. 27, 1973).

Brain damage in eight-week-old infant—Alleged excessive dosage—$200,000 settlement

An eight-week-old infant was given adult aspirin (five grains) instead of children's aspirin (1¼ grains), apparently as a result of an Army pharmacist's mistake in filling the prescription. The par-

---

[2] Id.

[3] Id.

[4] Hoon, J. R., "Bleeding Gastritis Induced by Long-Term Release Aspirin," *Journal of the American Medical Association* 229:841-842, 1974.

[5] Id., citing McCray, R., Comments at Asian-Pacific Congress of Endoscopy, Kyoto, Japan, April 3, 1973.

[6] *American Medical News,* May 1, 1987, p. 26. See also Plough, Inc. v. National Academy of Sciences (D.C. App., 1987) 530 A.2d 1152 (attempt by aspirin manufacturer to obtain academy documents reflecting closed deliberation on methodology of study which found association between aspirin and Reye's syndrome).

ents brought suit against the government, alleging that the child suffered aspirin poisoning which resulted in brain damage and mental retardation.

At the trial, the child's hospital records were introduced which showed an extremely high serum salicylate level shortly after the alleged error. The records showed further that two weeks earlier, at the child's "six-week checkup," there were no symptoms of the mental retardation apparently existing at the time of trial.

According to the attorneys for the plaintiffs, after presentation of the plaintiff's evidence, the government settled for $200,000.[7]

Hirschberg v. State (1977) 91 Misc. 2d 590, 398 N.Y.S.2d 470.

Failure to treat aspirin poisoning—$37,328 awarded

About 10 a.m. a 27-year-old male patient allegedly swallowed 100 aspirin. Later that afternoon he attempted to commit suicide by jumping in front of a school bus. He was taken to a community hospital, but did not receive medical treatment. He was then taken to his psychiatrist's office in a county mental health clinic. There a superficial examination was conducted which revealed some symptoms of salicylate poisoning, rapid pulse and complaints of nausea and ringing in the ears, but the physician did not believe the patient had taken the amount of aspirin that he claimed. Since the clinic did not have the necessary facilities to care for the patient, he was transferred to a state hospital.

He was admitted about 5:30 p.m. but was not given a physical examination because he had arrived after normal time for such procedures. The admitting physician was not licensed to practice in the state, and was participating in a psychiatric residency program at the time. This physician placed the patient on suicide alert and prescribed 100 milligrams of Thorazine, which was given at 7:00 p.m. Since the physician did not ask to be informed of any irregular reaction to the medicine, he was not informed that the patient vomited ten minutes after receiving the medicine. At 11 p.m. the patient died.

The autopsy report indicated death from aspirin poisoning. The court awarded the patient's administrator $37,328, finding the state liable for the unlicensed physician's negligence in conducting

---

[7] ATLA *News Letter* 17:68, 1974.

a cursory examination and ignoring available signs of aspirin toxicity.

Torsiello v. Whitehall Laboratories, Division of Home Products Corp. (1979) 165 N.J. Super. 311, 398 A.2d 132.

Gastrointestinal hemorrhage following prolonged use of Anacin—Jury question whether manufacturer's warning to users adequate

An adult male patient who suffered from arthritis began taking Anacin in January of 1974. He saw his physician about thirteen times over the next seven weeks and was told to continue the medication, since it appeared to give him relief, but not to exceed the manufacturer's recommended dosage of eight tablets a day. The patient continued taking six to eight tablets a day until March, 1975, when he suffered an attack of gastrointestinal hemorrhage.

In a lawsuit against the manufacturer, the patient alleged that it had failed to give adequate warning of the inherent danger of prolonged use of the product. At the close of the plaintiff's evidence, the trial court dismissed the case. On appeal, the ruling was reversed, with the Superior Court of New Jersey holding, among other things, that it was for a jury to determine whether dangers of prolonged aspirin use were generally known and understood by lay consumers, that the evidence presented a jury question as to the adequacy of the manufacturer's warning that if pain persisted for more than ten days the user should consult a physician, and that a manufacturer's duty to warn of risks of prolonged use of an over-the-counter drug cannot be discharged merely by instructing the user to consult his physician.

Himber v. Pfizer Laboratories (1981) 82 App. Div. 2d 776, 440 N.Y.S.2d 649.

Retinal hemorrhage—Ophthalmologist not negligent in prescribing Bufferin

A diabetic patient consulted an ophthalmologist on August 21, 1975, for a floater in his eye. The physician took a history, diagnosed diabetic retinopathy, and prescribed eight Bufferin tablets a day. The patient took the Bufferin for about a week but discontinued it after he experienced severe hemorrhaging in the eyes. Later he lost his sight completely, and he died on January 30, 1977, of problems related to his diabetes.

On appeal from denial of the ophthalmologist's motion for summary judgment, the appellate court said that there was no evidence that the patient's death was caused by the Bufferin. The physician was not liable for malpractice on the basis that prescribing Bufferin was contraindicated by the patient's medical history and constituted deviation from acceptable medical standards.

Chirico v. Harkrider (No. 83A-11447-3, State Court, Cobb County, Ga., Jan. 19, 1985).

Negligent treatment of aspirin poisoning—$1,037,871 wrongful death verdict against E.R. Physician— Hospital settles for $125,000

The patient was rushed to the hospital suffering from an overdose of aspirin, apparently in a suicide attempt. His stomach was pumped, but six hours later he died. The plaintiffs charged that no salicylate level test was performed to determine exactly how much aspirin had been absorbed into the bloodstream. The hospital settled for $125,000 prior to trial, and the jury returned a verdict for $1,037,871 against the physician.[8]

Fox v. Sterling Drug, Inc. (No. 687-394, Circuit Court, Milwaukee County, Wis., August 11, 1989).

Reye's syndrome—$2.4 million settlement with manufacturer for failure to warn

A ten-month-old child was given aspirin for gastric pains, fever, and diarrhea. Several days later, she began vomiting and lost consciousness. She was diagnosed as suffering from Reye's syndrome. The child survived, but is mentally retarded, blind, and suffers from cerebral palsy and seizures.

In their product liability action against the manufacturer, the parents alleged failure to warn of the possible connection between aspirin and Reye's syndrome in children and young adults. According to the parents' attorney, they were prepared to show at trial that "the salicylate in aspirin had caused mitochondria in [the child's] liver to produce enzymes that had caused the brain to swell," which is one of the complications of Reye's syndrome.

The parties settled for $2.6 million.[9]

---

[8] ATLA *Law Reporter* 28:181, 1985.

[9] ATLA *Products Liability Law Reporter* 9:6, 1990.

Related cases

Build-up of coated aspirin in stomach—Jury question as to negligence in diagnosis

In Davison v. Mobile Infirmary (Ala., 1984) 456 So. 2d 14, the evidence presented a jury question as to whether there was negligence on the part of hospital personnel in failing to diagnose a "build-up" of coated aspirin (Ecotrin) in the patient's stomach.

Death from intracranial bleeding while on Coumadin—Patient not negligent for taking aspirin

In Eiss v. Lillis (Va., 1987) 357 S.E.2d 539, a patient on Coumadin therapy was not guilty of contributory negligence in taking aspirin which worsened his condition and eventually led to his death from intracranial bleeding. The case is summarized herein under SODIUM WARFARIN.

Postoperative internal bleeding—Gynecologist fails to test for clotting deficiency—Jury question presented

In Ornoff v. Kuhn and Kogan, Chartered (D.C. App., 1988) 549 A.2d 728, a jury question existed as to whether a gynecologist was negligent in performing a laparoscopy and then prescribing buffered aspirin postoperatively for pain without previously determining that the patient suffered from a blood clotting deficiency.

ASTRAMORPH

See MORPHINE SULFATE

ATABRINE HYDROCHLORIDE

See QUINACRINE HYDROCHLORIDE

ATARAX

See HYDROXYZINE

ATROPINE SULFATE

Atropine is an antiarrhythmic agent which is used to treat certain reversible bradyarrhythmias that may accompany acute myocardial infarction, particularly marked symptomatic sinus bradycardia. The product is manufactured and marketed by numerous companies.

Therapeutic doses of atropine cause dryness of the mouth, cycloplegia (loss of power in the ciliary muscle of the eye) and mydriasis (dilation of the pupil). In rare instances, similar drugs have induced acute angle-closure glaucoma in predisposed eyes. Large doses of atropine may cause hyperpyrexia (extremely high fever), urinary retention, and central nervous system effects (e.g., confusion, hallucinations).[10]

Lowry v. Henry Mayo Newhall Mem. Hosp. (1986) 185 Cal. App. 3d 188, 229 Cal. Rptr. 620.

Fatal cardiac arrest—Choice of Atropine as initial treatment not negligent

The patient was hospitalized for injuries arising out of an automobile accident on February 1, 1983. On February 21, she suffered cardiac arrest. The hospital's Code Blue team responded and a physician administered atropine. The patient did not respond and other resuscitative efforts were made without success.

At the hearing on the hospitals' motion for summary judgment, the plaintiffs charged that the use of Atropine as the initial treatment for cardiac arrest was a deviation from the guidelines published by the American Heart Association. The plaintiffs claimed that the patient instead should have been treated initially with epinephrine, in which case, the patient's "chances of survival would have dramatically increased." The plaintiffs, however, failed to support this argument by an affidavit of a medical expert. The physician who had administered the drug submitted a deposition explaining that the American Heart Association guidelines are just that, guidelines, and that they may be altered by a physician. She further stated that she administered atropine "because it is one of the drugs used as a first line to start the heart after the monitor reveals that there is no cardiac activity."

The defense also claimed that the Code Blue team was immune under the California "Good Samaritan" statute.

The trial court granted summary judgment for the defense and this was affirmed on appeal.

Oukrop v. Wasserburger (Wyo., 1988) 755 P.2d 233.

Excessive dosage prescribed by dentist—Patient not told or monitored—Hallucinations and possible brain damage—Verdict for $751,000 affirmed

The patient, a teenage boy, was given a prescription by Dr. Oukrop, a dentist, for 1/4 grain of atropine, which is twenty-five

---

[10] AMA Drug Evaluations, 6th ed., p. 459.

times the normal adult dose. The boy was to take the drug as premedication for the removal of two wisdom teeth. On receiving the prescription, the pharmacist called Dr. Oukrop about the excessive dose, but in a "manifestation of professional arrogance," Dr. Oukrop refused to discuss the matter, and ordered the pharmacist to fill the prescription as directed.

The boy took the drug the morning of the surgery as instructed, and appeared at the office with his mother for the extraction. By then, Dr. Oukrop had discovered his mistake, but he did not tell the boy or his mother. He removed the wisdom teeth and sent the boy home.

The boy began suffering severe hallucinations. The next day he ran away from home and was found by a neighbor. He also seriously injured his knee in a fall. The mother called Dr. Oukrop several times during this period, but the dentist still did not reveal that he had prescribed an excessive dose. He kept assuring the mother that there was nothing to worry about, and he allowed the mother to believe that her son's condition could have been the result of drugs the boy had taken on his own.

At the trial, an expert (pharmacologist) for the plaintiffs testified that the boy's brain might have been affected by the atropine, and that he might have suffered an "alteration of learning and memory processes for which there is no known treatment."

The jury returned a verdict of $751,816.37 for the plaintiffs, and the Supreme Court of Wyoming affirmed.

ATTENUVAX

See MEASLES VACCINE

AUROTHIOGLUCOSE
Solganal

Aurothioglucose is an antiarthritic agent which contains approximately 50% gold by weight. Although the mechanism of action is not well understood, gold compounds are believed to decrease synovial inflammation and retard cartilage and bone destruction. There are numerous possible adverse reactions to this drug, including aplastic anemia.[11]

The product is manufactured and marketed by the Schering Corporation (Kenilworth, N.J.) under the name Solganal.

---

[11] *Physicians' Desk Reference,* 42d ed., p. 1949.

Tatum v. Schering Corp. (C.A.-11 Ala., 1986) 795 F.2d 925.

Aplastic anemia—Issue whether physician had sufficient knowledge of drug's risk—Summary judgment for manufacturer reversed

In this wrongful death suit, the patient was treated for arthritis with Solganal and Myochrysine, another drug containing gold salts. During the course of the patient's treatment her physician did not personally check tests to determine her white blood count. One of the side effects of gold salts injections is a decrease in the white blood count which can lead to aplastic anemia. On July 19, 1982, the patient's white blood count was 3,808, which indicated leukopenia, a potential forerunner of aplastic anemia. Yet, she was given her usual injection of Solganal by the physician's nurse. On August 2, 1982, her white blood count had dropped to 2,882, yet she was given another injection. By August 31, 1982, her white blood count had dropped to 1,717. In October 1982, she died from aplastic anemia.

After settling lawsuits against the physician and the manufacturer of Myochrysine,[12] the administrator of the patient's estate pursued this claim against the Schering Corporation. On motion for summary judgment, the defendant offered evidence of the warnings issued with the package insert concerning the possibility of a patient developing aplastic anemia, together with evidence that the physician was aware of this possibility. The trial court found for the defendant and sustained its motion for summary judgment.

On review, however, the Court of Appeals reversed, finding that while there was evidence that the physician was aware of the risk of aplastic anemia, there was a disputed issue of fact concerning whether he was aware of the extent of such risk. Further, the court held that according to an affidavit supplied by one of the plaintiff's experts, the manufacturer should have instructed the physician to establish a *baseline of blood values* for comparison in monitoring a patient on Solganal. Also, there was a question as to the adequacy of the *method* of the manufacturer's warning. There was evidence that the manufacturer revised its package insert to warn physicians of a higher risk of aplastic anemia than it had earlier presumed, but no letters were written to physicians and no bulletins were sent to the manufacturer's salesmen.

---

[12] See the summary of this case under GOLD SODIUM THIOMALATE.

In view of the above, the court held that there was a question of whether the manufacturer's failure to warn was the proximate cause of the patient's death.

AVAZYME
See CHYMOTRYPSIN

AVC SUPPOSITORIES
See SULFANILAMIDE

AVLOSULFON
See DAPSONE

AZMACORT
See TRIAMCINOLONE ACETONIDE

AZOLID
See PHENYLBUTAZONE

AZULFIDINE
See SULFASALAZINE

B

BACTINE
See NEOMYCIN SULFATE

BACTRIM
See TRIMETHOPRIM and SULFAMETHOXAZOLE

BELLERGAL
See ERGOTAMINE TARTRATE

BENDECTIN
See DOXYLAMINE SUCCINATE

BENZATHINE PENICILLIN G
See PENICILLIN

BENZOCAINE

Anbesol
Cetacaine
Dermoplast
Dieutrim
Hurricaine
Medicone
Therevac
Tympagesic
Vagisil

Benzocaine is a local anesthetic of low toxicity considered to be one of the safest and most widely used of the over-the-counter topical anesthetics. Temporary anesthesia is elicited by penetrating the cutaneous barriers and blocking sensory receptors for the perception of pain and itching.

Vagisil is an over-the-counter medication used for the treatment of vaginal itching. Its active ingredients are 5% benzocaine and 2% resorcinol, a mild antimicrobial. The manufacturer of Vagisil (Combe Incorporated, White Plains, N.Y.) includes a warning that the product is not for prolonged use and that some skin and membrane irritations may be caused "by internal systemic disorders." Also, the manufacturer cautions that benzocaine "has been known to occasionally cause allergic dermatitis."[13]

Griggs v. Combe (Ala., 1984) 456 So. 2d 790.

Stevens-Johnson syndrome due to uncommon allergic reaction— Manufacturer not liable

The plaintiff developed Stevens-Johnson syndrome after using Vagisil to relieve vaginal itching. It was determined that she had experienced an allergic reaction to the main active ingredient, benzocaine. Suit was filed in federal court and the trial judge certified the question of the manufacturer's liability to the Supreme Court of Alabama.

After reviewing the facts, the Supreme Court of Alabama held that the manufacturer could not be held liable for the plaintiff's condition under any of the theories of negligence, strict products liability, breach of implied warranty of merchantability or duty to

[13] *Physicians' Desk Reference for Nonprescription Drugs,* 4th ed., p. 546.

warn. The FDA had concluded that benzocaine, which had enjoyed widespread use by the medical profession since 1903, was safe and effective for use as an over-the-counter external analgesic. The plaintiff, it was concluded, had suffered an uncommon allergic reaction due to a specific hypersensitivity which the manufacturer of Vagisil had no reason to suspect might occur and, therefore, had no duty to warn against.

BENZOXAPROFEN
Oraflex

Oraflex was a nonsteroidal anti-inflammatory agent introduced in the United States in 1982 as a "breakthrough" in the treatment of arthritis. Its less serious side effects include gastrointestinal problems, tingling of the skin, pruritis, skin rash, and loose nail beds. Also, persons exposed to sunlight could develop photosensitivity reactions.

Shortly after it was introduced, there were allegations that the drug's serious side effects, a potential for kidney and liver toxicity (especially in the elderly), were not stressed by the manufacturer, Eli Lilly and Company (Indianapolis, Ind.).

Documents now in the possession of the FDA reveal at least ninety-six known deaths associated with the drug in the United States and the United Kingdom (where the drug was marketed as early as 1980). It is alleged that the manufacturer knew of at least twenty-two deaths by February, 1982, more than two months prior to the date the product was introduced in the United States.[14]

Borom v. Eli Lilly & Co. (No. 83-38-COL, U.S. District Court, M.D. Ga., Nov. 21, 1983).

Death from kidney-liver disorder—$6 million punitive verdict against manufacturer for failure to warn

The decedent, an arthritis patient, took Oraflex for approximately two months, during which time she developed a fatal kidney-liver disorder. Her survivors sued the Eli Lilly & Company, claiming that the death was caused by the drug and that the company was aware of serious kidney and liver problems associated with Oraflex, but it had failed to warn the medical profession or the public, and had failed to submit all relevant test results on the drug

---

[14] *Lawyers' Medical Cyclopedia,* § 6.15(I) (1984 Supp.).

to the FDA. The jury returned a verdict for $6 million. Because of Alabama law (the decedent and plaintiffs were Alabama residents) which prohibits the recovery of compensatory damages in wrongful death cases, the entire award was in punitive damages.[15]

Pettaway v. Eli Lilly & Co. (No. 82-0818, U.S. District Court, S.D., Ala., Mar. 7, 1985).

Hepatitis after two weeks on Oraflex—$75,000 settlement with manufacturer

The plaintiff was given Oraflex by his physician for arthritis. Within two weeks he began to notice weakness, malaise, loss of appetite and hepatitis-like symptoms. At first, the condition was diagnosed as toxic hepatitis, probably drug-induced, but later studies by pathologists changed the diagnosis to viral hepatitis.

When the plaintiff's problems first developed, his physician blamed them on the drug, but following the filing of the plaintiff's lawsuit, the doctor, on deposition, changed his position and stated that he was no longer sure of the cause of the plaintiff's complaints.

The parties settled prior to trial for $75,000.[16]

Marquez v. Eli Lilly & Co. (No. 0877 HB, U.S. District Court, D.N.M., Feb., 1986).

Death following ingestion of Oraflex—Manufacturer had no duty to warn public—"Learned intermediary" theory applied

The patient visited his physician's office and was given a prescription for Oraflex. According to the plaintiff representing the decedent's estate, the patient's ingestion of the drug caused his death. Suit was brought, alleging, among other things, that the manufacturer had failed to warn the patient of the dangers associated with the drug. In support of this contention, the plaintiff argued that the defendant had advertised the drug extensively, and by this conduct had created a duty to warn the *public* of possible risks involved.

The manufacturer moved to dismiss, arguing that where the product is a prescription drug, the manufacturer's duty to warn is fulfilled if it warns the physician. The court agreed, stating that

---

[15] ATLA *Law Reporter* 27:133, 1984.

[16] ATLA *Products Liability Law Reporter* 4:72, 1985.

where prescription drugs are involved, the prescribing physician acts as a "learned intermediary" and the manufacturer's warning need only be directed to the prescriber.

Under the "learned intermediary" theory, said the court, a prescribing physician can take into account the propensities of the drug and the peculiar susceptibilities of each patient. Knowledge of the potential risks of the medication gained from the manufacturer, together with knowledge of the particular patient, allow the physician to make a reasonable, individualized medical judgment.

Accordingly, the court found no duty on the part of the manufacturer to warn members of the general public, and that the fact that the manufacturer had engaged in advertising the drug did not warrant an expansion of the duty to warn of its risks. Consequently, the motion to dismiss was granted.[17]

Related cases

Injuries from Oraflex—No personal injury or loss of consortium actions under RICO Act—No action for battery

In Moore v. Eli Lilly & Co. (D. Mass., 1986) 626 F. Supp. 365, the court held that a patient who suffered injuries after taking Oraflex did not have an action against the manufacturer for personal injury under the Racketeer Influenced and Corrupt Organization Act (RICO) (18 U.S.C. § 1961 et seq.), nor did he have an action for battery in absence of evidence of lack of consent, nor did his wife have an action for loss of consortium under the RICO Act.

Bladder cancer—FDA's alleged failure to restrict use of Oraflex within "discretionary function" exception to F.T.C.A.

Allegations by the plaintiff, whose decedent died from bladder cancer after taking Oraflex for arthritis, that the FDA negligently failed to follow its own regulations in permitting the manufacturer of Oraflex to market the drug, and also negligently failed to take appropriate action to restrict use of the drug after deaths and injuries from its use became apparent, fell within the "discretionary function" exception to the Federal Tort Claims Act. Bailey v. Eli Lilly Co. (M.D. Pa., 1985) 607 F. Supp. 660.

---

[17] ACLM, *Legal Aspects of Medical Practice* 5:5, 1987.

BETADINE

See IODINE

BETAMETHASONE

Celestone

Betamethasone is a synthetic adrenocortical steroid (glucocorticoid), closely related to dexamethasone, and is used as an anti-inflammatory agent. It is indicated for arthritis and rheumatic disorders, allergic states, and certain endocrine, respiratory and ophthalmic diseases. Celestone is manufactured by Schering Corporation (Kenilworth, N.J.). Among numerous possible side effects are gastrointestinal disturbances, including peptic ulcer with possible perforation and hemorrhage.[18]

Robinson v. Duszynski (1978) 36 N.C. App. 103, 243 S.E.2d 148.

Internal hemorrhage—Drug combination improper—Physician subject to claim for punitive damages

An elderly patient was admitted to the hospital suffering from arthritis on January 12, 1976. Her physician prescribed a combination of Celestone, Tandearil (oxyphenbutazone) and prednisone. Early on the morning of February 7 she developed symptoms of internal bleeding. The physician was notified of this fact but was busy in the emergency room and did not see the patient until 9:30 a.m., some seven hours after he was first called. By this time the patient's condition was critical and she was transferred to a larger hospital where she died despite emergency surgery.

In his action against the physician and the hospital, the patient's husband claimed both actual and punitive damages. The trial judge granted both defendants summary judgments on the punitive issue. On appeal, this was reversed as against the physician, the Court of Appeals of North Carolina finding that affidavits submitted by the plaintiff contained testimony by an expert in hematology and internal medicine that the physician had prescribed an improper combination of drugs for the patient and that these drugs, because of their ulceragenic characteristics, had in fact caused the patient's death.

---

[18] *Physicians' Desk Reference,* 35th ed., p. 1588.

Carroll v. St. Paul Ins. Co. (La. App., 1989) 550 So. 2d 787.

Cushing's syndrome—Patient given 190 injections of Celestone over 28-month period—General practitioner held liable

In 1984, Lawrence C. Hill, M.D., a general practitioner, began treating the patient, a woman in her thirties, for various medical problems, including sinus infections, head colds, an elbow injury, and back and muscle pain. For reasons that were not specified in the report of the case, he prescribed injections of Celestone. Between May 1984 and September 1986, the patient received 190 injections; during 1986, she received injections daily. As a result, the patient developed Cushing's syndrome, a condition evidenced by hair growth on her arms and face, a 'buffalo hump' on her back, rapid and excessive weight gain, thinning of the skin on her hands, redness of her hands, a weakening of the blood vessels in her hands, panic attacks, disturbance of her menstrual cycle, sleep disturbance, and other symptoms.

The patient and her husband sued, and a trial judge, sitting without a jury, found the defendant's treatment failed to meet the applicable standard of care and awarded the plaintiffs $175,000 plus the patient's special damages. The Court of Appeal upheld the award, but reduced the general damages to $90,000.

BETAPEN-VK
See PENICILLIN

BICILLIN; BICILLIN C-R; BICILLIN L-A
See PENICILLIN

BIPHETAMINE
See AMPHETAMINE and DEXTROAMPHETAMINE

BISHYDROXYCOUMARIN
Dicumarol

This drug is an anticoagulant used for the prevention and treatment of pulmonary embolism, venous thrombosis and for treatment of certain other cardiovascular and circulatory conditions involving emboli. It is contraindicated in patients who have active bleeding or subacute bacterial endocarditis and for pregnant patients and breast-feeding mothers.[19] Dicumarol is currently manufactured by Abbott Pharmaceuticals (North Chicago, Ill.). It was formerly produced by Eli Lilly and Company (Indianapolis, Ind.).

Baker v. St. Agnes Hosp. (1979) 70 App. Div. 2d 400, 421 N.Y.S.2d 81.

Warning of birth defect risk insufficient

The patient, pregnant and suffering from phlebitis, was hospitalized and placed upon Dicumarol. She continued to take the drug following discharge several weeks later. Six months later, the patient gave birth to a child with severe and irreparable birth defects resulting in a lawsuit against the physician, the hospital and the drug's manufacturer.

Because the patient's physician stated in an examination before trial that when he prescribed Dicumarol he was not aware that it could cross the placental barrier (and thus cause damage to an unborn child) and, furthermore, that he had not consulted the package insert for such information on the drug, the manufacturer, Eli Lilly and Company, moved for summary judgment. The trial court denied the motion.

On appeal, the reviewing court held that the evidence that the drug caused the child's birth defects was undisputed, and that while the manufacturer did include on its package insert for Dicumarol a contraindication for pregnant women, this warning was insufficient in that the manufacturer published no corresponding statements of any kind in *Physicians' Desk Reference* or in any other reference work used by manufacturers to warn of the dangers of drugs. The court found also that the failure of the patient's physician to become aware of information contained in the package insert was not an intervening cause of the injury such as would insulate the manufacturer from liability.

The trial court's denial of the manufacturer's motion for summary judgment was affirmed.

---

[19] *Physicians' Desk Reference,* 35th ed., p. 1054.

BLEPHAMIDE
See SULFACETAMIDE

BLOCADREN
See TIMILOL MALEATE

BREXIN
See CHLORPHENIRAMINE MALEATE

BUFFERIN
See ASPIRIN

BUPIVACAINE HYDROCHLORIDE

Marcaine
Sensorcaine

Bupivacaine is a local and regional anesthetic used in general surgery, dental and oral surgery, diagnostic and therapeutic procedures, and obstetrics. The solution is supplied in 0.5%, 0.25% and 0.75% concentrations. Because of deaths occurring from cardiac arrest among obstetrical patients in the early 1980s, the product is now issued with a warning that the 0.75% concentration is not recommended for obstetrical anesthesia.[20]

Marcaine is manufactured by Winthrop-Breon Laboratories (New York, N.Y.) and Sensorcaine by Astra Pharmaceutical Products, Inc. (Westboro, Mass.).

Douglas v. Lombardino (1985) 236 Kan. 471, 693 P.2d 1138.

Cardiac arrest during preparation for Caesarean section —Defense claims unexpected cardiotoxic reaction

The patient was given a spinal injection of Marcaine in preparation for a Caesarean section. She immediately went into violent convulsions and ventricular fibrillation. Attempts to resuscitate were unsuccessful and she died two and one-half hours later.

The physicians and nursing staff involved were charged with negligence in administering the anesthetic and in attempts to save the patient. Expert testimony was introduced that the resuscitative measures were substandard. The defense, however, produced evidence that Marcaine could cause sudden cardiac arrest following a

[20] *Physicians' Desk Reference,* 40th ed., p. 1915.

spinal injection, and introduced two experts, one of whom had written an article describing several cases where this occurred, and the other of whom had conducted tests on sheep which produced this result. In all cases, it was the 0.75% concentration that caused the deaths. Representatives of the manufacturer testified that on December 28, 1981, the date of the patient's death, the industry and the medical profession generally were unaware of this hazard.

The jury returned a verdict for the defendants and the Supreme Court of Kansas affirmed.

Henry v. St. John's Hospital (1987) 159 Ill. App. 3d 725, 111 Ill. Dec. 503, 512 N.E.2d 1044.

Excessive dosage during labor—Child born with cerebral palsy—$10 million award affirmed

Plaintiff's mother entered the hospital for induction of labor. At 10:30 a.m., her attending obstetrician administered a paracervical block consisting of 8 cc of Marcaine bilaterally. After observing the fetal heart monitor for fifteen minutes, the physician left for his office, leaving a first-year resident in obstetrics in charge. When the patient complained that the pain was returning, the resident administered another paracervical block consisting of 6 cc of Marcaine on the left side and approximately 4 cc on the right side. This block was administered at approximately 11:00 a.m.

The plaintiff's fetal heart monitor indicated that bradycardia had developed, which is a sign of fetal distress. The child was born with brain damage and suffers from cerebral palsy.

In an action against the hospital, the resident, the drug manufacturer, the drug distributor, and the patient's physician, the plaintiff introduced evidence that it was not acceptable practice in the medical community for a second paracervical block to be given in an amount greater than 50% of the first dose without authorization from the attending physician, that it was not accepted practice for a repeat block to be given within one half-hour of the first block without such authorization, and that it was below the standard of care for a resident physician to administer any paracervical block without consultation with a senior physician.

Extensive evidence was introduced also on whether the child's cerebral palsy was the result of the excessive dosage of Marcaine, as well as whether the warnings issued by the manufacturer of the drug were adequate to prevent such an incident as occurred in this case.

The jury returned a verdict of $10 million against the hospital, the resident and the manufacturer and distributor of the drug. The verdict was affirmed on appeal.

Ramon v. Farr (Utah, 1989) 770 P.2d 331.

Birth defects—Obstetrician not liable despite manufacturer's recommendation that Marcaine not be used for paracervical block

Approximately one hour before the birth of the plaintiff's child, the defendant obstetrician administered to the plaintiff a paracervical anesthetic block by injecting Marcaine. The amount injected is not known. At birth, the plaintiff's child appeared to be normal, but several hours later he began to show symptoms of serious problems and suffered grand mal seizures. Today, he has permanent mental and physical defects and can never be expected to reach normal ranges of mental and physical development.

The plaintiff and her husband brought suit against the hospital and the defendant obstetrician. The hospital settled for an undetermined amount before trial. The case proceeded against the defendant on three theories: (1) he had directly injected the child's head with Marcaine; (2) Marcaine should not have been used for a paracervical block because that use was not recommended by the manufacturer; and (3) the defendant failed to inform the plaintiff adequately of the risks associated with the use of Marcaine for a paracervical block.

The jury found for the defendant on the first theory. The second and third theories were not given to the jury because the trial court refused to submit the plaintiff's supporting instructions.

On appeal, the Supreme Court of Utah affirmed, holding that the evidence supported the jury's verdict on the allegation that the child was injected with the anesthetic. As to the refused instructions, the court held that any error of the trial court in this regard was harmless since the plaintiffs failed to introduce sufficient evidence that injecting only the mother with Marcaine could have harmed the child. As to the manufacturer's recommendation that Marcaine not be used for a paracervical block, the court cited the majority rule in other states that manufacturers' recommendations do not by themselves establish the standard of care.

Related cases

Plaintiffs entitled to names of physicians who reported experiences with drugs involved in litigation

Plaintiffs in action against manufacturer of Marcaine were entitled to names and addresses of twelve physicians who had reported experiences with Marcaine and bupivacaine hydrochloride but were not entitled to names and addresses of all physicians and patients who participated in FDA's Drug Experience Reports project. Newsom v. Breon Laboratories (Tenn., 1986) 709 S.W.2d 559.

BUSULFAN
Myleran

Busulfan is an alkylating agent used in the treatment of chronic myelogenous (myeloid, myelocytic, granulocytic) leukemia. The manufacturer of Myleran (Burroughs Wellcome Company, Research Triangle Park, N.C.) warns under "Contraindications" that the drug should not be used "unless a diagnosis of chronic myelogenous leukemia has been adequately established and the responsible physician is knowledgeable in assessing response to chemotherapy." The most frequent, serious, toxic effect of bisulfan is myelosuppression resulting in leukopenia (abnormal decrease of white blood cells), thrombocytopenia (abnormal decrease in blood platelets) and anemia.[1]

Young v. Park (R.I., 1980) 417 A.2d 889.

Patient under treatment for polycythemia develops anemia—Alleged lack of informed consent-verdict for physician affirmed

The plaintiff was diagnosed as suffering from polycythemia, which is the abnormal production of red blood cells. The cause of the condition was not established. The defendant physician, who was the "shop doctor" for the plaintiff's employer, prescribed a course of treatment calling for daily doses of Myleran. Approximately six months later the plaintiff was hospitalized for anemia, which he claimed was caused by his treatment.

In his lawsuit against the physician, the plaintiff alleged negligence in diagnosis and treatment, and also lack of informed consent. The negligence claim was dismissed on directed verdict for

[1] *Physicians' Desk Reference,* 40th ed., p. 754.

want of expert testimony. The question of informed consent was given to the jury who found for the defendant on his testimony that he had warned the plaintiff that Myleran carried with it the risk of anemia. The Supreme Court of Rhode Island affirmed, finding no evidence to support a reasonable inference that the defendant departed from acceptable community standards.

BUTABARBITAL SODIUM
Butisol Sodium

Butabarbital sodium, also called sodium butabarbital, is a barbiturate sedative-hypnotic with an "intermediate" duration used mainly in the treatment of insomnia. Adverse effects include drowsiness and lethargy and, infrequently, skin eruptions (e.g., urticaria, angioedema, and a generalized morbilliform rash).[2]

The drug has been produced under a dozen different brand names over the past ten years. Most stayed on the market for only a few years. Butisol Sodium, manufactured by McNeil Pharmaceutical (Fort Washington, Pa.), has been around the longest.

Dermatological reaction in patient receiving Butisol Sodium and five other drugs

In Slack v. Fleet (La. App., 1970) 242 So. 2d 650, a middle-aged woman patient who complained to her physician of "pain and cramping in the stomach, nausea, vomiting and nervousness" was given prescriptions for Butisol Sodium and five other drugs. She took the drugs simultaneously as directed, and developed a severe rash. In the resulting lawsuit, a question arose over the propriety of prescribing that particular combination of drugs in a case such as the plaintiff's. The defendant physician offered two medical witnesses who testified that his choice of medication was within acceptable standards. The plaintiff offered no expert testimony. The trial court dismissed the action and was upheld on appeal. The case is summarized herein under PHENACETIN.

BUTALBITAL
Fiorinal

Butalbital is a barbiturate having sedative and muscle relaxant properties. It is marketed under the generic name by several drug companies, and is used as an ingredient in several analgesic com-

---

[2] *AMA Drug Evaluations,* 2d ed., p. 305.

pounds, including Fiorinal, in which it is combined with aspirin and caffeine. Fiorinal is used for the relief of the symptom complex of tension (or muscle contraction) headaches.[3]

Sandoz Pharmaceuticals (Hanover, N.J.), manufacturer of Fiorinal, reports that the most frequent adverse reactions are drowsiness and dizziness. Sandoz also warns the physician to exercise caution when prescribing Fiorinal for patients with a known propensity for taking excessive quantities of drugs, which is not uncommon in patients with chronic tension headaches, and that when the product is prescribed with other central nervous system depressants, the dosage of one or more of the agents may have to be reduced.[4]

Whittle v. United States (C.A.-D.C., 1987) 669 F. Supp. 501.

Death from butalbital intoxication while on Fiorinal and Nardil—Psychiatrist found negligent—$560,451 awarded

The plaintiff's wife went to Walter Reed Army Medical Center (Walter Reed) in August, 1981, for treatment of depression and chronic headaches. She had been troubled for many years by serious headaches and had sought treatment from a number of military and civilian facilities close to the Army posts where her husband was assigned. She brought with her the medical records of her treatment from at least some of these facilities. All previous efforts to determine the source of her pain and to relieve her symptoms were largely unsuccessful.

Upon arrival at Walter Reed, she was first examined at the neurology clinic, which revealed no physical basis for her distress. She was then referred to the outpatient psychiatric clinic, where she was treated by Antonio Blanco, M.D., a second year resident in psychiatry. Dr. Blanco reviewed her history on August 13, 1981, and diagnosed her condition as "dysthymic disorder or atypical depression, hystrionic personality with obsessive traits, and possible authentic migraine headaches aggravating emotional illness." He prescribed Nardil (phenelzine sulfate) and Norgesic (orphenadrine), an analgesic.

On September 2, 1981, Mrs. Whittle again saw Dr. Blanco who prescribed a drug regimen of 75 mg. per day (five tablets) of Nardil, which is an anti-depressant monoamine oxidase inhibitor (MAOI),

---

[3] *Physicians' Desk Reference,* 42d ed., p. 1867.

[4] Id.

and up to six tablets per day of Fiorinal. The maximum recommended dosage of Nardil was 75—90 mg. per day, and the maximum recommended dosage of Fiorinal was six tablets per day.

There was substantial medical evidence, which was largely undisputed, that warned of the prolongation or potentiation of the effects of barbiturates when used in combination with MAOI drugs. This is because the MAOI interferes with the ability of the liver to metabolize barbiturates, allowing the barbiturates to remain in the blood stream at higher levels for a longer period of time. As a result of this "prolongation" effect, taking Nardil in combination with a barbiturate such as Fiorinal increases the possibility that a second, supplemental ingestion of Fiorinal will push the barbiturate level in the blood to toxic levels. The MAOI can convert the non-toxic Fiorinal regimen into a potentially toxic one. Because of the "prolongation" or "potentiation" effect, the pharmacological literature recommends that barbiturates should be administered at a reduced dose when taken concurrently with Nardil. Even the defendant's psychiatric expert admitted that these drugs should be used cautiously.

Dr. Blanco's office chart and memorandum reflected his concern about the potential adverse interactions of the two drugs. Dr. Blanco testified that it was his intention, as approved by his supervisors, that the Fiorinal would be discontinued when the Nardil reached its proper therapeutic level.

Mrs. Whittle saw Dr. Blanco on October 2, 16 and 28, and on November 13 and December 2, 1981, and on one other occasion, the date of which was not noted in the medical record. She saw him a total of eight times over a period of more than 3½ months. On some of these occasions, Mrs. Whittle reported her condition as improved and that she was feeling better. During this period, Mrs. Whittle was continued on the same regimen of Nardil and the maximum recommended dosage of Fiorinal (up to six tablets per day). Specifically, she was given thirty pills of Fiorinal on October 28, 180 pills on November 13, and 120 pills on December 2. Although Mrs. Whittle initially took Nardil less frequently than prescribed in order to avoid adverse side effects, during this period, at the urging of her husband and Dr. Blanco, she took Nardil more regularly, as prescribed, despite the unpleasant side effects she had experienced.

Mrs. Whittle's informed consent as to the course of treatment prescribed by Dr. Blanco was not obtained on September 2, when the regimen of Nardil and Fiorinal was first prescribed. Dr. Blanco testified that he and Mrs. Whittle had had such a discussion, but the chart for September 2 indicated only that Dr. Blanco warned of possible abuse of analgesics. The chart of the same date did not list any discussion about the interaction of Nardil and Fiorinal. In addition, the medical record showed that Mrs. Whittle signed a "Patients Rights" form on December 2, 1981, three days before her death and three months after the original prescription for the combined use of Nardil and Fiorinal. This form stated that each patient over the age of 12 "shall be informed of ... the risks, side effects, and benefits of all medications and treatment procedures used, especially when the medications and treatment procedures are unusual or experimental." The form also provided that the patient must give written, dated, and signed informed consent to "the utilization of any unusual medication or hazardous assessment or treatment procedure." The Patients Rights form, however, only purported to be a recitation of rights. It did not purport to list the "risks, side effects, and benefits of all medications and treatment procedures" nor did it purport to be a written, informed consent to any course of treatment.

The treatment chart for the December 2 visit did not reflect any supplemental discussion of treatment risks between Dr. Blanco and Mrs. Whittle. Furthermore, the plaintiff testified that his wife never indicated any knowledge on her part of the risks associated with the use of these drugs.

Mrs. Whittle had suffered headaches on December 2, 3, 4 and 5, and had taken Fiorinal each day for relief. On December 5, shortly after 10:00 p.m., the plaintiff found his wife on the floor of their bedroom unconscious and unresponsive. When efforts to revive his wife failed, the plaintiff called the rescue squad, which responded in 10—20 minutes and transported Mrs. Whittle to the hospital, where she was pronounced dead at 11:41 p.m.

A toxicology report showed elevated levels of butalbital in the blood, liver and gastric contents. Death was listed as "butalbital poisoning." All of the plaintiff's experts were of the opinion that Mrs. Whittle died of butalbital intoxication, a respiratory depression which acts on the respiratory center of the brain, impairing the ability to breathe. While the defendant's experts did not agree with this finding, they admitted that the level of butalbital in Mrs. Whittle's blood was within the known toxic limits. There was no indication that Mrs. Whittle's death was due to an intentional overdose on her part. One of the defendant's experts, a pathologist, who examined tissue slides prepared by the medical examiner, found early ischemic heart disease, which is consistent with findings of a death caused by myocardial infarction or heart attack. The defendant, however, did not assert that Mrs. Whittle did, in fact, suffer a heart attack. It was the defendant's basic position that the cause of Mrs. Whittle's death was "undetermined."

The trial court, which heard the case without a jury, found Dr. Blanco negligent, and awarded the plaintiff $560,451. Among the court's conclusions of law were the following:

> By continuing to prescribe large volumes of Fiorinal to Mrs. Whittle at a time when she was also taking the MAOI Nardil, and by failing to take any steps to reduce or to monitor Mrs. Whittle's usage of Fiorinal at a time when she was taking a maximum or near maximum daily dose of Nardil, Dr. Blanco displayed a cavalier approach to Mrs. Whittle's treatment. Such conduct was not consistent with the warnings in the medical literature that Nardil and Fiorinal only be used together with great caution, if at all. By so acting, Dr. Blanco breached his standard of care to Mrs. Whittle.
>
> In addition, it is well-settled that a physician has the duty of warning his patient of all material risks associated with a proposed treatment and of the available alternatives. From September 2, 1981 until December 5, 1981, Mrs. Whittle was prescribed the maximum daily recommended amount of Fiorinal (6 tablets per day), along with an amount of Nardil (75 mg. per day) approaching the recommended maximum dosage for that drug as well. While it appears that Dr. Blanco, on September 2, 1981, warned her about the possible abuse stemming from the use of analgesics, there is no evidence that he gave her any warnings about Nardil and Fiorinal. In fact, it was not until December 2 that she signed the "Patients Rights" form acknowledging her right to an explanation of the "risks, side effects and benefits of all medications and treatment procedures used." This was three days before her death and three months from the time when the combined use of Nardil and Fiorinal was first prescribed. By failing to give Mrs. Whittle an explanation of the potential risks and benefits of the proposed course of treatment, Dr. Blanco also breached his duty to obtain informed consent.

BUTAZOLIDIN; BUTAZOLIDIN ALKA
See PHENYLBUTAZONE

BUTISOL SODIUM
See BUTABARBITAL SODIUM

C

CAFERGOT
See ERGOTAMINE TARTRATE

CAMPHO-PHENIQUE
See CAMPHOR and PHENOL

CAMPHOR and PHENOL

Campho-Phenique

The combination of camphor and phenol, marketed under the name of Campho-Phenique by Winthrop Consumer Products Division of Sterling Drug, Inc. (New York, N.Y.), is a pain-relieving antiseptic for sores, cuts, burns, insect bites, fever blisters and cold sores. It is for external use only.[5]

Hahn v. Sterling Drug (C.A.-11 Ga., 1986) 805 F.2d 1480.

Child accidently ingests drug—Question of adequate warning

The plaintiffs' four-year-old daughter accidently swallowed one and one-half ounces of Campho-Phenique when the plaintiffs' other daughter, a seven-year-old, left the cap off after using the solution. The child began suffering convulsions, vomited, and for a brief period stopped breathing. She was rushed to the hospital, and after a 24-hour stay in the intensive care unit, she was released with no permanent disability.

The parents sued the manufacturer for failing to label the product with an adequate warning. At the time, the label contained the following:

> WARNING: Keep this and all medicines out of children's reach. In case of accidental ingestion, seek professional assis-

[5] *Physicians' Desk Reference for Nonprescription* Drugs, 6th ed., p. 723.

tance or contact a poison control center immediately. DIRECTIONS: For external use: apply with cotton 3 or 4 times daily.

The plaintiffs introduced a professor of pediatrics who testified that this warning was "very general" and that its effect was "watered down" by the fact that the same warning appeared on numerous other products offered by the manufacturer that are not harmful.

At the close of evidence, the trial court directed a verdict in favor of the defendant. On appeal, however, the Court of Appeals reversed, holding that the question of whether the manufacturer's warning was adequate was clearly a question for the jury to decide.

CARBAMAZEPINE
Tegretol

Carbamazepine, manufactured and marketed under the brand name Tegretol by Geigy Pharmaceuticals (Ardsely, N.Y.), and under the generic name by Lederle Laboratories (Wayne, N.J.), is an anticonvulsant and analgesic. As an anticonvulsant, the drug is indicated for the following conditions in patients who have not responded satisfactorily to treatment with other agents: (1) Partial seizures with complex symptomatology (psychomotor, temporal lobe); (2) generalized tonic-clonic seizures (grand mal); and (3) mixed seizure patterns, including the above, and other partial or generalized seizures. As an analgesic, carbamazepine is indicated for the treatment of pain associated with trigeminal neuralgia. Also, it has been reported to offer beneficial results in treating glossopharyngeal neuralgia. It is not, however, a simple analgesic, and should not be used for the relief of trivial aches or pains.[6]

The manufacturer reports numerous adverse reactions, the most severe affecting the hemopoietic system (including fatal aplastic anemia, agranulocytosis, thrombocytopenia, and leukopenia), the skin (including Stevens-Johnson syndrome), and the cardiovascular system (including congestive heart failure).[7]

---

[6] *Physicians' Desk Reference,* 42d ed., pp. 989-901.

[7] Id.

Williams v. Ciba-Geigy Corp. (W.D. La., 1988) 686 F. Supp. 573.

Stevens-Johnson syndrome—Warning to physician adequate—Drug not "unreasonably dangerous"

The plaintiff developed Stevens-Johnson syndrome while taking Tegretol and brought suit against the manufacturer, charging that the drug was "unreasonably dangerous for normal use," and that the defendant was negligent in failing to adequately warn physicians and others dispensing the drug of the "dangers inherent" in the product.

The trial court granted the defendant's motion for summary judgment, holding that under Louisiana law a drug manufacturer fulfills its duty to a consumer when it informs the prescribing physician of the drug's hazards, and in this case the warning was adequate.

The court also held that Tegretol, as approved by the FDA, was not unreasonably dangerous per se, that the package insert clearly stated that one of the possible side effects was Stevens-Johnson syndrome, and that it would be inappropriate to allow the jury to apply the so-called risk-utility test to the drug in the absence of some evidence that the FDA's approval was based on erroneous data or otherwise should be questioned.

Reeves v. Geigy Pharmaceutical, Inc. (Utah App., 1988) 764 P.2d 636.

Skin loss—Fact issue presented on causation—Summary judgment for manufacturer reversed—No evidence of negligence on part of neurologist

The plaintiff, an epileptic since age twelve, was being treated with Tegretol and phenobarbital when he noticed that the "top layer of his skin had started to peel off." On examination by a dermatologist, he was found to be suffering from "toxic epidermal necrolysis" (T.E.N.), a general term used to describe dermatological disorders that result in blistering and loss of skin. A subsequent histological examination revealed that the condition was a "full thickness" injury, which meant that the plaintiff was losing the dermal layer as well. Eventually, he had to undergo skin grafts similar to those received in the treatment of severe burn injuries.

Suit was brought against the plaintiff's neurologist, who had prescribed the Tegretol and phenobarbital, and the manufacturers of the two drugs, Geigy Pharmaceutical and Eli Lilly & Company.

The neurologist was charged with negligent treatment and in failing to inform the plaintiff of the risk involved, and the manufacturers were charged with negligently releasing a defective product, breaches of warranty, and failure to warn.

The defendants moved for summary judgments with the argument that the plaintiff offered no medical evidence supporting a causative link between the drugs and the injury. They supported their motions with affidavits of experts denying any such link. The trial court granted the judgments, but the Court of Appeals reversed, pointing to the plaintiff's medical records which contained statements by a burn specialist who had treated him that T.E.N. has been associated with "seizure medication."

The Court of Appeals, however, did affirm the summary judgment for the neurologist as to the charge of negligent treatment, finding no evidence of a violation of the standard of care.

CARBRITAL

See SODIUM PENTOBARBITOL with CARBROMAL

CARBROMAL

See SODIUM PENTOBARBITOL with CARBROMAL

CARISOPRODOL

Rela

Soma and Soma Compound

Carisoprodol is a muscle relaxant used for symptomatic relief in conditions characterized by skeletal muscle spasm and mild to moderate pain. Schering Corporation (Kenilworth, N.J.) manufactures Rela; Soma and Soma Compound are produced by Wallace Laboratories (Cranbury, N.J.).

Carisoprodol is contraindicated in cases of acute intermittent porphyria (disturbance of porphyrin metabolism) and in patients with histories of allergic or idiosyncratic reactions to carisoprodol itself or related compounds such as meprobamate (Equanil, Miltown, et al.), mebutamate (Capla), and tybamate (Solacen, Tybatran).[8]

---

[8] *Physicians' Desk Reference*, 35th ed., p. 1878.

Perkins v. Park View Hosp., Inc. (1970) 61 Tenn. App. 458, 456 S.W.2d 276.

Alleged excessive medication—Possible interaction with meprobamate—Directed verdicts for defendants

A woman was admitted to the hospital just before midnight suffering from intense back pains. Pursuant to her physician's orders, she was given 400 mg. of meprobamate and a 1/32 grain of Dilaudid (hydromorphine). It was later revealed that the previous day she had also received Soma and Phenaphen.[9]

A nurse checked the patient's room at 4 a.m. and found she was not breathing. Attempts to resuscitate were unsuccessful. An autopsy report was inconclusive, but there was strong evidence that the patient had died from anaphylactic shock.

The patient's husband filed a lawsuit against the physicians and the hospital. The case went to trial, and at the close of the plaintiff's evidence, the court directed verdicts in favor of all defendants. The plaintiff appealed as to the hospital and the admitting physician. The plaintiff contended that the trial court's holding was in error, and that the case should have been submitted to the jury because of evidence that the physician had negligently prescribed an excessive amount of medication, that he should have hospitalized the patient sooner, and that he should have better supervised her care. The plaintiff argued also that there was evidence that the hospital was negligent in failing to determine the patient's condition upon admission, and in administering medication while she was there.

The Court of Appeals ruled against the plaintiff on all counts. With regard to the drugs, the court held the evidence was not conclusive that death was the result of an overdose, and even if it was, the court felt this did not indicate that the hospital or the physician had been negligent. An overdose is "more medicine than a particular person can tolerate," the court emphasized, and in the present case there was no way of anticipating that the patient was unusually sensitive to the drugs prescribed.

According to the plaintiff, the physician had been negligent in not asking the patient what drugs she had been taking before he

[9]Editor's Note: In the opinion, the reviewing court refers to the trial court record which states that the patient was given "Soma" and "Phenaphen." Phenaphen is one of the brand names for phenacetin. Possibly the patient was given Soma Compound, which contains carisoprodol, phenacetin, and caffeine.

prescribed further medication. To this argument the court said the physician could not be held liable even if he did not make adequate inquiry because this was not proven to be the cause of the patient's death. Even taking into account drugs ordered by other physicians, the total amount prescribed did not, according to the evidence, constitute an overdose, and if the patient had an unusually low tolerance to these drugs, the physician had no way of knowing it in advance.

The plaintiff had argued that there was insidious interaction between Soma and meprobamate. To this, the count pointed out that the evidence at the trial indicated that these drugs could be used interchangeably. In this regard, the plaintiff claimed that the trial court was in error in excluding testimony by a physician about an article that had appeared in the *Journal of the American Medical Association*. In that article, the authors reported a case where a patient suffered an adverse skin reaction from Soma and, after this drug was discontinued and meprobamate was administered, the same skin reaction recurred. In answer the court held that the article was not an authoritative treatise, but merely expressed the opinion of the authors.

The plaintiff had also raised the doctrine of *res ipsa loquitur* and claimed that the trial court's failure to apply it was error. The court held that the doctrine was not applicable because the patient's death, if from anaphylactic shock, could have occurred even if accepted medical practice was observed.

CEFOXITIN SODIUM

Mefoxin

Cefoxitin sodium is a semi-synthetic, broad-spectrum antibiotic recommended for the treatment of serious infections caused by a wide range of gram-positive and gram-negative organisms. It is manufactured and marketed under the brand name Mefoxin by Merck, Sharp & Dohme (West Point, Pa.).[10]

According to the manufacturer, Mefoxin is generally well tolerated. The most common adverse reactions have been local (thrombophlebitis, pain and tenderness) following intravenous or intramuscular injection. Serious adverse reactions have been infrequent, but have included anaphylaxis, pseudomembranous colitis, leukopenia, hemolytic anemia, thrombocytopenia, bone marrow depres-

[10] *Physicians' Desk Reference*, 42d ed., pp. 1358-9.

sion, and renal failure. Other reported reactions include rash (including exfoliative dermatitis) and hypotension.[11]

McDaniel v. Merck, Sharp & Dohme (Pa. Super., 1987) 537 A.2d 436.

Hemolytic anemia—Plaintiffs' expert testimony improperly excluded—Judgments for physician, hospital, and manufacturer reversed

The patient was admitted to the hospital on February 28, 1982, for strep throat and appendicitis. Her attending physician prescribed Mefoxin for the infection. Following an appendectomy, the patient developed a serious wound infection and high fever, and underwent three more operations. For over a month she received nearly continuous doses of Mefoxin. During this period she developed hemolytic anemia with bone marrow depression which contributed to her death on April 4, 1982.

In a lawsuit against the several physicians who treated the patient and the hospital to which she was confined, the plaintiffs alleged negligent treatment and failure to obtain informed consent. Against the manufacturer, the plaintiffs alleged negligence and strict liability (under Restatement (Second) of Torts § 402A) for producing a defective product and for failing to warn of its potential hazard. At the trial, the testimony of the plaintiffs' proffered experts was either excluded or limited severely in scope. Also, records acquired by the plaintiffs from the manufacturer containing reports of adverse reactions to Mefoxin were excluded from the evidence. At the close of the plaintiffs' case, the trial court granted a nonsuit in favor of the manufacturer and two of the physicians. The remaining physicians and the hospital then presented their evidence, and the jury returned a verdict in their favor.

On appeal, the Superior Court of Pennsylvania reversed, holding that four of the plaintiffs' experts (three internists and an internist who was also certified in hematology and oncology) should have been allowed to testify on the standard of care in the use of Mefoxin to treat infections. Two of these experts were also prepared to testify on the proper labeling of the Mefoxin by the manufacturer, and the drug's risk of inducing hemolytic anemia. In addition, said the reviewing court, the trial judge erred in limiting the plaintiffs' cross-examination of a defense expert on reports in the medical

[11] Id.

literature regarding Mefoxin and anemias. In concluding, the court held that the plaintiffs had pled sufficient facts to allow a punitive claim against the manufacturer.

CELESTONE

See BETAMETHASONE

CELLULOSE, OXIDIZED

Oxycel
Surgicel

Oxidized cellulose is an absorbable hemostatic agent formerly prepared by Parke-Davis (Morris Plains, N.J.) and sold under the name Oxycel. A similar product (oxidized regenerated cellulose) is sold by Johnson & Johnson Products, Inc. (New Brunswick, N.J.) as Surgicel. In appearance and texture, oxidized cellulose resembles ordinary surgical gauze or cotton. Upon contact with blood it swells, resembling an artificial blood clot, thereby creating pressure which aids in controlling capillary, venous, and small arterial bleeding. In the product literature, the manufacturer states that although Surgicel "may be left in situ when necessary, it is advisable to remove it once hemostasis is achieved." It also says to use only that amount necessary for hemostasis, and to "remove any excess before surgical closure in order to facilitate absorption and minimize the possibility of foreign body reaction."[12]

Oxidized cellulose should not be used for permanent packing or implantation in fractures because it interferes with bone regeneration and may result in cyst formation. It should not be used for surface dressing, except for immediate control of hemorrhage, as it inhibits healing of the wound. A case of fatal intestinal obstruction due to adhesions resulting from the use of oxidized cellulose gauze in abdominal surgery has been reported, and the author of the report considers use of the material in areas of the abdomen where loops of intestine are lying free "extremely dangerous."[13]

---

[12] *Physicians' Desk Reference,* 35th ed., pp. 958-59.

[13] Osol, A. and Pratt, R., *The United States Dispensatory,* 27th ed. (Philadelphia: J.B. Lippincott Company, 1973), p. 238.

Revallion v. Parke, Davis & Co. (No. 602920, Superior Court, Boston, Mass., Nov., 1972).

Patient chokes to death after tonsillectomy —Verdict for plaintiff

After removal of a twelve-year-old patient's tonsils, the physician, a general practitioner, placed two thin layers of Oxycel in the patient's throat to help stop the bleeding. The following day the Oxycel dislodged and blocked the patient's trachea, causing her to choke to death.

A lawsuit was brought against the physician and the manufacturer. The physician settled prior to trial for an unreported amount. The case against the manufacturer went to trial with the plaintiff charging that the manufacturer had failed to give adequate warning in its product literature to physicians of the dangers of Oxycel. According to the attorney for the plaintiff, an expert witness testified that the warnings issued by the manufacturer were inadequate wherein they stated that all "excess" amounts of Oxycel should be removed after surgery. The warnings, said the witness, should have stated that "all" amounts of the substance should be removed in procedures such as tonsillectomies.

The jury returned a verdict of $24,000 for the plaintiff.[14]

Brannon v. Wood (1968) 251 Ore. 349, 444 P.2d 558.

Surgicel used as emergency measure left packed against spinal cord—Verdicts for surgeons affirmed

Surgeons faced with an emergency during an operation to remove a deep chest tumor were found free from liability in leaving Surgicel packed against the patient's spinal cord, which eventually caused permanent paralysis. Despite expert medical testimony that it was bad surgical practice to pack Surgicel so tightly as to cause the spinal cord to become compressed, and in fact bad practice to leave tightly packed Surgicel in the patient's body at all, the jury, obviously impressed by the emergency situation caused by excessive bleeding, apparently concluded that under the circumstances some risk probably was justified.

In affirming the verdict for the defendants, the reviewing court said: "the uncontradicted facts in this case show that the plaintiff was bleeding internally at such a rate that his life was in danger

---

[14] ATLA *News Letter* 14:369, 1971.

unless the bleeding could be stopped. [The physicians] who assisted at the surgery, were aware of the risk of cord compression and used Surgicel as an emergency medical technique."

Christopher v. United States (E.D. Pa., 1965) 237 F. Supp. 787.

**Oxycel packed near intervertebral foramen—
Paralysis—Judgment for patient**

Near the end of an operation involving the removal of the patient's lung, a constant bleeding developed in the posterior area of the incision, behind the head of the fifth rib near the intervertebral foramen. A suture was placed around the base of the fifth rib but this did not help. Oozing was noted from the posterior angle between the fourth and fifth ribs and an examination revealed bleeding from above the posterior margin of the fifth rib. The surgeon concluded that the intercostal vein was bleeding and tried to stop it with a clamp.

Bleeding began again and the surgeon placed Oxycel gauze, three inches by three inches, in the area. This partially controlled the bleeding. He placed a second pack on top of the first and the bleeding nearly stopped. Immediately before closing, he added a third pack of gauze. He then closed the patient's chest.

Between one and two hours after the operation, the patient was found to be unable to move his legs. A lumbar puncture was performed which revealed blood in the spinal fluid. The patient was returned to the operating room and reopened by a different surgeon. He removed Oxycel gauze from the interspace between the ribs and in the region of the intervertebral foramen. He found the foramen enlarged and some of the Oxycel inside. He removed it and closed the incision.

In a resulting lawsuit under the Federal Tort Claims Act, medical testimony at trial was to the effect that packing Oxycel gauze in and around the intervertebral foramen was not good surgical practice. The court, sitting without a jury, found for the patient, awarding past and estimated future medical expenses plus $350,000 for pain and suffering.

Frost v. Mayo Clinic (D. Minn., 1969) 304 F. Supp. 285.

**Oxycel possibly involved in paralysis—Exploratory
operation delayed—Surgeon held liable**

A 46-year-old woman underwent surgery for a protruded intervertebral disc. Immediately after the operation the patient experienced extreme pain and numbness of the legs and feet. Two days later the surgeon explored and found swelling of the cauda equina and "some swelling of Oxycel" which had been placed in the area. The surgeon performed a decompression.

The decompression was not successful and the patient remained partially paralyzed. A malpractice suit was filed and a verdict was returned for the patient in the amount of $50,000, mainly on medical evidence that in light of the symptoms presented by the patient after the first operation, good medical practice would have dictated that an *immediate* operation for decompression was necessary. The verdict was upheld on appeal.

CEPHALEXIN MONOHYDRATE
Keflex

Cephalexin monohydrate is a semisynthetic antibiotic manufactured and sold by Dista Products Company (Indianapolis, Ind.) under the name Keflex, and by several other companies under the generic name. Cephalexin is the fourth member of the cephalosporin family of antibiotics, the others being cephaloglycin (Kafocin), cephaloridine (Loridine), and cephalothin (Keflin), all produced by Eli Lilly and Company (Indianapolis, Ind.).

Cephalexin is indicated in infections caused by susceptible organisms in the urinary and respiratory tracts and in skin and soft tissues. Infections which commonly respond well to treatment include cystitis, pyelonephritis, and bacteriuria due to susceptible organisms, especially strains of *Escherichia coli, Proteus mirabilis,* and species of Klebsiella; also pneumonia and bronchopneumonia due to *Diplococcus pneumoniae;* and cellulitis, subcutaneous abscesses, and wound infections due to staphylococci. *Pseudomonas aeruginosa* and *Herella* species are insensitive to cephalexin, as are most strains of indolepositive *Proteus* and *Enterobacter.*[15]

Haynes v. Baton Rouge Gen. Hosp. (La. App., 1974) 298 So. 2d 149.

Delayed healing of infection—Keflex chosen even though package insert suggested not effective —Verdict for physician upheld

The patient and her husband sued her treating surgeon (Dr. S.), his partnership and clinic, their insurer (permitted in Louisiana),

[15] *United States Dispensatory,* 27th ed., pp. 239-241.

the hospital in which she underwent surgery, and the hospital's insurer. The evidence at the trial disclosed that Dr. S. operated on the patient in July of 1966 for a fractured hip. Additional surgery was performed in January of 1967 to facilitate healing. In August of 1970, diagnostic studies indicated avascular necrosis of the femoral head. The patient was rehospitalized on December 6, 1971, and again surgery was performed.

For this last operation, the patient was administered antibiotics preoperatively and was continued postoperatively on the broad spectrum Keflin (intravenously). Later, when a routine urine report revealed a urinary tract infection, Dr. S. switched the patient from Keflin to Keflex (orally), after drug sensitivity tests indicated the organism causing the urinary infection was *Escherichia coli,* which is sensitive, among other drugs, to Keflex.

Dr. S. noted slight drainage from the surgical incision on December 23, 1971, and a specimen indicated the offending organism to be *Enterobacter*. A drug sensitivity test showed this organism was sensitive to Keflin, but because the patient was already responding satisfactorily, in Dr. S.'s opinion, to Keflex, he saw no reason to change antibiotics, even though Keflex is not recommended for *Enterobacter*.

The patient's wound-site infection eventually cleared, as did the urinary infection, and she was discharged from the hospital on December 31, 1971.

The patient made an office visit on January 18, 1972, which was uneventful. She was next seen by Dr. W. at the medical clinic (in Dr. S.'s absence) on January 25, 1972, at which time Dr. W. noted additional drainage from the surgical incision. Dr. W. again prescribed Keflex. Dr. S. next saw the patient three days later on January 28, 1972, at which time, according to Dr. S., there was no further drainage from the incision.

The patient was subsequently seen on January 31, February 2, February 8, February 25, March 10, March 29, and April 21, all of which visits were, according to Dr. S., uneventful. The patient was seen on June 14, 1972, and roentgenograms were taken. She was next seen on June 26, 1972, at which time the hip joint was aspirated, and cortisone injected into the joint. The patient was then seen on June 30, 1972, July 26, 1972, and last seen by Dr. S. on August 9, 1972.

The patient felt her case was not handled properly and she sued, alleging negligence in failing to discover a latent deep-seated infection, in ordering insufficient roentgenograms and additional blood work, and in injecting the cortisone. But the primary complaint was that Dr. S. had prescribed Keflex even though the package insert indicated that the drug was not effective against most strains of *Enterobacter*. At the trial, however, medical experts testifying for the defense said they themselves relied more on drug sensitivity tests than on drug company literature. And even the patient's own medical witness admitted that the strain of *Enterobacter* causing the wound-site infection was probably sensitive to Keflex.

The jury returned a verdict for the defendants which was affirmed on appeal. The Court of Appeal of Louisiana said:

> Our review of the record fails to demonstrate in the face of the foregoing medical evidence that [Dr. S.] deviated from the standard of care due this patient by prescribing the antibiotic Keflex and continuing to use the same, notwithstanding the admonition in the drug company literature that Keflex had not been demonstrated to be active against most species of Enterobacter. The jury was certainly justified in finding no negligence or breach of duty on the part of [Dr. S.] in this regard.... The physicians who testified on behalf of defendant [Dr. S.], all confirmed that in their opinion [Dr. S.] in no way deviated from the standard of care or acceptable medical treatment owed to a patient such as the plaintiff.

Neumeyer v. Terral (La. App., 1986) 478 So. 2d 1281.

Alleged brain damage from excessive dosage—
Pediatricians and manufacturer not liable

This lawsuit was on behalf of a child who was first treated with Keflex at the age of one month for a respiratory infection. The child immediately developed a rash and diarrhea, and his pediatrician discontinued the drug. When the child was ten months old, he was again treated with Keflex for a respiratory condition, and he again developed a rash and diarrhea. The Keflex again was discontinued. This time, however, the diarrhea persisted, and the child had to be hospitalized.

The mother changed pediatricians, and over the next several years the child was treated periodically with antibotics, but no Keflex. At times he experienced "loose bowels," but apparently no diarrhea. In the spring of 1976, his mother had him examined at both Johns Hopkins and the Mayo Clinic for what his pediatrician had diagnosed as an "irritable bowel syndrome," unrelated to the antibiotics. The diagnoses at both institutions were "loose stools caused by antibiotic overuse." The child's mother also claimed that the child had sustained permanent brain damage and had developed seizures and a learning disorder. In her lawsuit against the two pediatricians and the manufacturer of Keflex, the mother alleged that the over-administration of Keflex and the other antibiotics had caused the diarrhea which led to dehydration and a high level of sodium, which in turn caused the brain damage.

The defense produced expert testimony that for the child to have suffered dehydration sufficient to cause brain damage, he would have had to have been semicomatose and would have suffered substantial weight loss. Instead, the evidence showed that the child experienced normal weight gain and growth.

A jury found the first pediatrician negligent but that his negligence did not result in injury to the child. The other defendants were found free of negligence. The verdict was upheld on appeal.

Jacobs v. Dista Products Co. (D. Wyo., 1988) 693 F. Supp. 1029

Pseudomembranous colitis—Manufacturer's warnings on package insert adequate

The plaintiff developed pseudomembranous colitis after being treated with Keflex for an infected foot. He brought suits against his physician and Keflex's manufacturer. The physician settled for an undisclosed amount prior to trial.

In his suit against the manufacturer, the plaintiff alleged that the warning to physicians of the risk of pseudomembranous colitis was inadequate. The package insert was introduced at trial. It contained, among various "warnings," "precautions," and "adverse reactions," the following statements:

> Pseudomembranous colitis has been reported with virtually all broad-spectrum antibiotics (including macrolides, semisynthetic penicillins, and cephalosporins); therefore, it is important to consider its diagnosis in patients who develop diarrhea in association with the use of antibiotics. Such colitis may range in severity from mild to life-threatening.
>
> * * *
>
> Broad-spectrum antibiotics should be prescribed with caution in individuals with a history of gastrointestinal disease, particularly colitis.

* * *

Symptoms of pseudomembranous colitis may appear either during or after antibiotic treatment.

The manufacturer produced expert witnesses who testified that the above statements adequately warned physicians of the risk involved. The plaintiff failed to produce any experts who testified that they did not. On motion, the court granted the manufacturer a summary judgment.

Related cases

Loss of sight after Keflex and Kantrex therapy—No breach of warranty action against manufacturers

In McCarthy v. Bristol Laboratories Division of Bristol-Myers Co. (1982) 86 App. Div. 2d 279, 449 N.Y.S.2d 280, a plaintiff who suffered loss of sight following treatment of a kidney infection with Keflex and Kantrex had no cause of action for breach of warranty against the manufacturers of the drugs where there was no privity of contract between her and the defendants.

CEPHALOTHIN SODIUM

Keflin

Seffin

Keflin, manufactured by Eli Lilly and Company (Indianapolis, Ind.), is a broad spectrum antibiotic indicated for the treatment of certain serious infections caused by susceptible microorganisms.[16]

There is some evidence of partial cross-allergenicity of the cephalosporin family of antibiotics, to which this drug belongs, and the penicillins. Therefore, the manufacturer warns that hypersensitivity reactions to Keflin are most likely to occur in patients with a history of allergy, particularly those allergic to penicillin. In persons hypersensitive to Keflin, maculopapular rash, urticaria, reactions resembling serum sickness, and anaphylaxis have been reported.[17]

Seffin is manufactured by Glaxco, Inc. (Research Triangle Park, N.C.).

---

[16] *Physicians' Desk Reference,* 35th ed., p. 1074.

[17] Id.

Killeen v. Reinhardt (1979) 71 App. Div. 2d 851, 419 N.Y.S.2d 175.

Patient with possible penicillin allergy dies of respiratory complications—Evidence of negligent choice of drugs insufficient

A 39-year-old patient was admitted to the hospital complaining of breathing difficulties, coughing, and vomiting. She was given a narcotic cough suppressant, Dilaudid (hydromorphone hydrochloride).

In the early morning hours of the following day the patient's condition worsened, advancing to a critical stage of status asthmaticus and acute bronchitis. Her physicians prescribed Keflin and Adrenalin (epinephrine). Twenty-four hours later the patient died. On autopsy the cause of death was determined to be bronchial pneumonia.

In the complaint the plaintiff asserted that neither the Keflin nor the Dilaudid should have been given because the patient allegedly had a history of allergy to penicillin,[18] and that the defendant physicians failed to discover this when the patient was admitted. The evidence at trial, however, revealed that the patient's physicians may have considered the possibility of allergy before choosing the medication. Also, the evidence showed that the patient had not suffered anaphylactic shock after being given the medication as is usually the case with an allergic reaction. With regard to charges against the hospital, the reviewing court stated that from the record at trial, "it cannot be concluded that the administration of both of these drugs [Keflin and Dilaudid] was so clearly contraindicated as to cast liability upon the hospital for failing to make further inquiry or prohibit their use." The court likewise found no evidence of malpractice in the administration of the Adrenalin.

A jury verdict for the patient's administrator was overturned.

---

[18] For another case involving alleged cross-allergenicity between Keflin and penicillin, see Addison v. Health & Hosp. Governing Comm. of Cook County (1977), 56 Ill. App. 3d 533, 14 Ill. Dec. 7, 371 N.E.2d 1060, a wrongful death action in which a mother complained that physicians disregarded her daughter's earlier allergic reaction to penicillin and prescribed Keflin. The action was dismissed because the plaintiff failed to notify the defendants in writing within one year from the date of injury as required by statute for a suit against a public body.

Related cases

Loss of vision—Insufficient evidence of causal connection

In Swanson v. Williams (1975), 303 Minn. 433, 228 N.W.2d 860, the plaintiff, who lost his eyesight from inflammation of the optic nerve while being treated with Keflin and other drugs for a ruptured appendix, was unsuccessful in his claim that the drugs caused his blindness in view of uncontradicted expert testimony that the blindness was caused by a stress ulcer which developed shortly after his surgery.

Anaphylactic shock—Directed verdict for defendant reversed on procedural issue

In a wrongful death action on behalf of a seventeen-year-old boy who suffered an anaphylactic shock reaction to Keflin while undergoing eye surgery, the trial court erred in denying the plaintiff's motion for voluntary dismissal without prejudice after excluding the testimony of the plaintiff's only medical expert under Mississippi's locality rule. Shepherd v. Delta Med. Center (Miss., 1987) 502 So. 2d 1188.

CEROSE-DM

See CHLORPHENIRAMINE MALEATE

CETACAINE TOPICAL ANESTHETIC

See BENZOCAINE; TETRACAINE HYDROCHLORIDE

CHLORAFED

See CHLORPHENIRAMINE MALEATE

CHLORAMPHENICOL

Chloromycetin
Ophthochlor
Ophthocort

Chloramphenicol is a broad spectrum antibiotic which affords effective treatment for diseases caused by rickettsias, brucellae, and most of the commonly encountered pathogenic bacteria. Several venereal diseases, including syphilis, gonorrhea, granuloma inguinale, are also susceptible to the drug. It is the drug of choice in typhoid fever, and is dramatically effective in typhus and Rocky

Mountain spotted fever.[19] The drug is sold under the brand name Chloromycetin and is manufactured by Parke Davis (Morris Plains, N.J.). Parke Davis also produces the ophthalmic preparations Ophthochlor and Ophthocort.

As early as 1949 it was reported that chloramphenicol may have a toxic effect on bone marrow,[20] and in 1952 a nationwide survey of 256 persons with aplastic anemia revealed that 38.6% had received chloramphenicol.[1] The manufacturer took steps to warn the medical profession of the possible hazard (See Love v. Wolf, below). Use of the drug continued, however, and despite a relatively rare occurrence rate (depending on the study, in 1969 it was estimated that from 1 in 200,000 to 1 in 24,200 persons treated with chloramphenicol would develop aplastic anemia).[2]

There is no clear correlation between the age of the patient and chloramphenicol-induced aplastic anemia, but there is a significantly higher incidence among females.[3] Aplastic anemia itself is usually fatal and there have been reports of the disease, when associated with chloramphenicol, later terminating in leukemia.[4]

Chloramphenicol is sold with a warning to physicians that it is not to be used "when less potentially dangerous agents will be effective," and that it must not be used "in the treatment of trivial infections or where it is not indicated, as in colds, influenza, infections of the throat, or as a prophylactic agent to prevent bacterial infections." The manufacturer warns further that:

> It is essential that adequate blood studies be made during treatment with the drug. While blood studies may detect early peripheral blood changes, such as leukopenia, reticulocytopenia, or granulocytopenia, before they become irreversible, such studies cannot be relied on to detect bone marrow depression prior to development of aplastic anemia. To facilitate appropriate studies and observation during therapy, it is desirable that patients be hospitalized.[5]

---

[19] *United States Dispensatory,* 27th ed., p. 274.

[20] Id., p. 282.

[1] Moser, R. H., editor, *Diseases of Medical Progress: A Study of Iatrogenic Disease,* 3rd ed. (Springfield, Ill.: Charles C Thomas, Publisher, 1969), p. 301.

[2] Id. See also *Physicians' Desk Reference,* 35th ed., p. 1335.

[3] *United States Dispensatory,* 27th ed., p. 282.

[4] *Physicians' Desk Reference,* 35th ed., p. 1336.

[5] Id., p. 1335.

The manufacturer recommends that blood studies be done approximately every two days during treatment with chloramphenicol.[6]

Stottlemire v. Cawood (D. D.C., 1963) 213 F. Supp. 897, 215 F. Supp. 266.

Aplastic anemia—Directed verdicts for physician and manufacturer—Insufficient evidence of negligence or failure to warn

The patient was a four-year-old girl who apparently had been suffering from a number of ailments for several years. She was seen by the defendant-physician for an ear infection and given Chloromycetin. This was on June 14, 1957. The child continued to be ill, and was taken to the hospital where she died on September 26, 1957. In a lawsuit against the physician and Parke, Davis and Company the evidence established the probable cause of death as aplastic anemia due to bone marrow deficiency allegedly caused by the Chloromycetin.

Dr. Charles Rath, a specialist in blood disorders, called as an expert witness by the plaintiff, testified that it was customary to use Chloromycetin to combat a wide variety of infections, that the drug was widely used for that purpose, and that it was also used for minor infections. Also he stated that, as is true of all medicines, there was a certain risk, and the risk had to be kept in mind by the physician. The greatest threat in connection with the use of Chloromycetin, according to Dr. Rath, was the possibility of its causing aplastic anemia. However, he further testified that, according to some figures, in only one case out of 800,000 was aplastic anemia caused by Chloromycetin. In other words, the risk was one chance out of 800,000.

The District Court directed verdicts for the physician and Parke, Davis declaring:

> The crux of the case ... is whether the doctor was guilty of any negligence or improper practice in prescribing chloromycetin. This question brings us to some of the fundamental principles governing the liability of physicians and surgeons to their patients. A physician or surgeon is required by law to exercise that degree of care and skill ordinarily exercised by the profession in the same line of practice in his own or similar locality. Failure to use such care and skill constitutes negligence. On the other hand, a physician or surgeon is not an insurer of health. He is not

---

[6] Id.

required to guarantee results. If he were, very few persons would venture to enter the medical profession. He undertakes only for the standard of skill possessed generally by others practicing in his field and for the care that they would give in similar circumstances. He must have latitude for exercise of reasonable judgment. He is not liable for an error of judgment unless the error is obvious or gross according to the prevailing practice of his profession. No inference of negligence may be drawn merely from the result of the physician's or surgeon's treatment.

As to the drug company, the court said that since the drug could be obtained only by prescription, there was no reason why there should have been a warning of any dangerous possibilities given to the general public. "There is no proof whatever that no warning or caution was given to members of the medical profession" said the court. "On the contrary, the only evidence which the plaintiff sought to introduce was to the effect that such literature was issued by the defendant Parke Davis Company."

While on the stand, Dr. Rath had been asked by the plaintiff's attorney if he agreed with a statement in *New and Non-official Remedies* that "it is advisable to restrict the use of chloramphenicol to the treatment of typhoid fever and other serious infectious diseases caused by organisms controlled by chloramphenicol but resistant to other antibiotics or other forms of treatment." The defense attorneys objected to the question and were sustained by the trial judge. This issue was raised on motion for new trial and the court, in denying the motion, pointed out that such a question might be proper on cross-examination but not on direct. To bring out information in a publication in such a manner, said the court, was an attempt to defeat the rule that treatises and other publications on technical matters are inadmissible in evidence to prove the truth of the information contained therein.

Love v. Wolf (1967) 249 Cal. App. 2d 822, 58 Cal. Rptr. 42.

Aplastic anemia—Judgment against manufacturer—Verdict in favor of physician set aside

A woman patient brought suit against her physician and Parke, Davis and Company when she developed aplastic anemia following the administration of Chloromycetin.

At the trial, the evidence disclosed that in 1952, three years after the introduction of the drug, instances had been reported of association of aplastic anemia with its use. The Food and Drug Administration conducted an investigation during which it "weighed the value of the drug against its capabilities for causing harm," and decided that "it should continue to be available for careful use by the medical profession in those serious and sometimes fatal diseases in which its use is necessary." The drug was required to be manufactured in accordance with standards prescribed by the FDA and before it could be distributed it had to be tested by the FDA and certified as having such characteristics of strength, quality and purity to ensure safety and efficacy of use. A special cautionary warning for circulars or packages and labels was prescribed. Parke-Davis complied with these requirements, and it was conceded that the drug used in the present case was pure and uncontaminated.

Parke-Davis also sent letters in 1952 to 200,000 physicians advising them of the association between Chloromycetin and aplastic anemia (also other blood dyscrasias). It said the number of cases was unknown but it recognized that "many have terminated fatally." It particularly warned of dangers from intermittent therapy and "indiscriminate therapy for minor infections." It pointed to indications of a "calculated risk involved in the use of this potent antibiotic so that alert clinical observations and adequate blood studies should be made to detect any depression of bone marrow function as early as possible, and before any irreversible state occurs." This was followed by another similar letter later in the year.

The company promised: "As information accumulates from continuing studies on the relation of blood disorders to Chloromycetin it will be disseminated promptly through appropriate channels." Its letters were intended to reach all physicians and pharmacists in the United States, and they were supplemented by full-page announcements in the *Journal of the American Medical Association*.

Advertisements and promotional material distributed by the company since 1952 have contained a condensed warning similar to that on the packages and the labels.

Regarding the patient in the present case, Mrs. Love: In August of 1958 she had several teeth extracted. An infection developed in one of the sockets, and she consulted her physician. He prescribed Chloromycetin. The prescription was refilled once. On November 4, 1958, she consulted him for bronchitis. He again prescribed Chloromycetin. This prescription was refilled several times. Altogether, 96 capsules of 250 milligrams each were dispensed to the patient.

The physician last saw Mrs. Love professionally in December of 1958. In the spring of 1959 aplastic anemia was diagnosed. She was under treatment for the disorder until the time of her death, subsequent to the trial of this suit.

The jury returned a verdict for Mrs. Love against Parke-Davis but not the physician. On motion of Mrs. Love's counsel the court ordered a new trial as to the physician. This order was appealed, and the Court of Appeals of California affirmed.

Parke, Davis & Co. v. Mayes (1971) 124 Ga. App. 224, 183 S.E.2d 410.

Aplastic anemia—Manufacturer entitled to summary judgment—Warning to physician sufficient

In another action by a patient who developed aplastic anemia after taking Chloromycetin, Parke-Davis moved for a summary judgment based on affidavits containing the following facts: The company gave proper and sufficient warning to the medical profession of the potential hazards accompanying the use of Chloromycetin. The drug was available to no one except by the prescription of a qualified medical doctor. The dosages which allegedly cause the aplastic anemia were prescribed by a qualified physician. The prescribing physician had read all of these warnings issued by Parke-Davis and knew of the possible dangers involved in the use of the drug.

The Superior Court rendered judgment denying motion and Park-Davis appealed. The Court of Appeals of Georgia reversed, stating: "Under these circumstances, the company [Parke-Davis] fulfilled its duty and no liability attached. Ordinarily, in the case of prescription drugs, a warning as to possible danger in its use to the prescribing physician is sufficient."

Mulder v. Parke, Davis & Co. (1970) 288 Minn. 332, 181 N.W.2d 882, 45 A.L.R.3d 20.

Aplastic anemia—Directed verdict for manufacturer upheld—New trial ordered against physician for failure to take blood tests

The evidence disclosed that on June 24, 1965, Mrs. Mulder consulted the defendant, a general practitioner, for an infection in her left ear. She was treated with penicillin but did not improve and returned four days later. Her condition was diagnosed as "acute purulent otitis media." On that occasion, the defendant took a culture which he tested with fifteen antibiotics and found the most effective to be Chloromycetin. He thereupon prescribed one 250-milligram capsule four times daily for four days.

On July 2, Mrs. Mulder showed improvement, and her prescription was renewed. She returned on September 22 and was treated by another physician in the same clinic. It was found she had an exacerbation of the otitis in her right ear. Her prescription for Chloromycetin was renewed. Three days later when she again saw the defendant, he took a hemoglobin test and prescribed the same treatment. About a week later, her left ear gave her trouble again, and the defendant renewed the prescription for Chloromycetin.

On January 10, 1966, the last time Mrs. Mulder was seen by the defendant, he discovered she had been hemorrhaging in her arms, legs, and breast. She was sent to a hospital where she was found to be suffering from severe anemia and profound bone marrow depression. She died on January 29, 1966. Death was attributed to "gastrointestinal hemorrhage due to aplastic anemia or bone marrow depression." Suit was filed against both the physician and the manufacturer, Parke-Davis.

The warning which Parke-Davis gave in the package insert was as follows:

WARNING

Serious and even fatal blood dyscrasias (aplastic anemia, hypoplastic anemia, thrombocytopenia, granulocytopenia) are known to occur after the administration of chloramphenicol. Blood dyscrasias have occurred after both short-term and prolonged therapy with this drug. Bearing in mind the possibility that such reactions may occur, chloramphenicol should be used only for serious infections caused by organisms which are susceptible to its antibacterial effects. Chloramphenicol should not be used when other less potentially dangerous agents will be effective, or in the treatment of trivial infections such as colds, influenza, or viral infections of the throat, or as a prophylactic agent.

Precautions: It is essential that adequate blood studies be made during treatment with the drug. While blood studies may detect early peripheral blood changes such as leukopenia or granulocytopenia before they become irreversible, such studies cannot be relied on to detect bone marrow depression prior to development of aplastic anemia.

The defendant-physician testified on cross-examination that he was familiar with the information contained in the Parke-Davis warning at the time he prescribed Chloromycetin for Mrs. Mulder. Although he was aware of the dosage recommended, in this case he chose not to be governed by it. He testified he was aware of the side effects and possible complications in the use of Chloromycetin, one of which was the dyscrasia experienced by Mrs. Mulder.

There was testimony by the pathologist who performed the autopsy that Chloromycetin occasionally results in aplastic anemia and bone marrow depression and that this was the cause of Mrs. Mulder's death. In addition, he testified that blood tests would have indicated early bone marrow depression. Notwithstanding, the trial court directed verdicts in favor of Parke-Davis and the physician.

The Supreme Court of Minnesota affirmed as to Parke-Davis, but reversed and remanded for a new trial as to the physician, declaring:

> Where the dosage is prescribed by the manufacturer, testimony of the physician's failure to adhere to its recommendation is sufficient evidence to require him to explain the reason for his deviation. This is particularly true where the manufacturer's warning puts the doctor on notice of potentially lethal effects. ... We think that the testimony was ... adequate to make an issue of whether it was negligence not to take periodic blood tests where the possibility of aplastic anemia was or should have been evident to the doctor.

Incollingo v. Ewing (1971) 444 Pa. 299, 282 A.2d 225.

Aplastic anemia—Verdicts affirmed against treating pediatrician, osteopath who renewed prescription, and manufacturer

Vincent Incollingo filed suit in February of 1962 against a pediatrician, an osteopathic physician, a druggist, and Parke-Davis for aplastic anemia suffered by his daughter, Mary Ann, allegedly as a result of the "wrongful administration" of Chloromycetin. The child died the following month.

It was alleged that the pediatrician and the osteopath had caused or contributed to the child's death by negligently prescribing the drug in disregard of its possible dangerous side effects, and that Parke-Davis negligently failed to warn the parents of such side effects, failed to perform proper tests on the drug, and failed to take other necessary precautions which would have averted the tragedy.

At the trial the evidence disclosed that the pediatrician saw the child in October of 1958 and again in July of 1959 for a condition he described as "acute catarrhal rhinopharyngo tonsillitis." On the latter date he noted also a "complicating abdominal pain, possibly mesenteric adenitis." He considered her condition to be caused by a staphylococcus aureus coagulose positive infection. On both occasions he prescribed Chloromycetin, and the child responded well. On January 22, 1960, some six months later, her parents again brought Mary Ann to his office with similar symptoms, and again he prescribed Chloromycetin. The prescription was for two ounces, and could be refilled but once. At no time did he take blood tests or prepare bacteriologic cultures.

In February of 1960 Mary Ann's mother felt the child had contracted a respiratory infection (she had developed a cold and some hoarseness). Mrs. Incollingo asked her druggist to refill the January 22 prescription of Chloromycetin. One refill having already been furnished, he told her that a physician's authorization would be required. According to the pediatrician, the druggist telephoned him to ask if the prescription could be refilled, and he answered in the negative. Mrs. Incollingo then called the third defendant, the osteopath, of whom she was a patient, asking that he authorize renewal of the prescription. He testified that Mrs. Incollingo told him that the pediatrician was not available. Without seeing or examining Mary Ann, the osteopath telephoned the druggist and authorized a refill of the prescription. At least one additional refill was obtained in the same manner. Mrs. Incollingo did not administer the medicine to her daughter exactly in accordance with the prescription instructions, but as she felt Mary Ann "needed it."

In May of 1960 Mrs. Incollingo brought her daughter to the pediatrician, who found her to be suffering from aplastic anemia. His diagnosis at the time was that it was secondary to Chloromycetin. Mary Ann's condition gradually worsened until her death in March of 1962.

Although in his testimony the pediatrician qualified the causative role of the drug to "most probably" giving rise to the anemia, there was no real medical disagreement at trial that Chloromycetin was in fact the underlying cause of Mary Ann's death.

The evidence at the trial disclosed further that Chloromycetin was at the time obtainable only upon the prescription of a licensed physician, and was not advertised to the general public. Because of its therapeutic effectiveness and low incidence of side effects, such as nausea and vomiting, Chloromycetin was then a popular, widely used drug. Prior to and during the period that it was prescribed for

Mary Ann, the following language appeared on the immediate container and the outer carton:

"WARNING — Blood dyscrasias [disorders] may be associated with intermittent or prolonged use. It is essential that adequate blood studies be made."

"CAUTION — Federal Law prohibits dispensing without prescription."

In addition, the literature distributed by Parke-Davis pertaining to the drug contained the following statement:

"Chloromycetin is a potent therapeutic agent and, because certain blood dyscrasias have been associated with its administration, it should not be used indiscriminately or for minor infections. Furthermore, as with certain other drugs, adequate blood studies should be made when the patient requires prolonged or intermittent therapy."

There was testimony to the effect that a large percentage of Philadelphia physicians would have given the same course of treatment as did the defendant pediatrician, and that Chloromycetin was indeed being misused for trivial complaints by physicians who did not read or pay attention to the warnings or who allegedly had been "oversold" by Parke-Davis' detail men. The pediatrician, however, apparently did not fit into these categories: he had read the warnings, he knew of the dangers, and he had not been oversold. The dispute as to his conduct, therefore, narrowed down to the accuracy of his diagnosis, and whether it could or could not have been made clinically; to the interpretation of "intermittent" use, and whether blood tests were or were not mandated in light of three courses of treatment of the drug separated by roughly six and nine months, respectively. There was, however, no testimony that, given the same knowledge and awareness, a substantial number of physicians at the same time and place would have followed the same procedures.

The osteopath's attorneys in effect argued that he should be exonerated as a matter of law because the information disseminated by Parke-Davis concerning its drug was "ambiguous, inadequate and incomplete in the light of the knowledge possessed by Parke-Davis," and that therefore the medical profession, and particularly he himself, were caused to use Chloromycetin indiscriminately. He testified that "the drug was considered very safe, and there was no reason for me to suspect any toxicity." He stated he was aware of the warnings in the precautionary statements on the wrapper of the drug, "but the drug detail men practically ignored it. It was played down ... we didn't concern ourselves with this small inadequate description [of warnings]."

The jury returned a verdict against the two physicians and Parke-Davis, but found the druggist free of liability.

The Supreme Court of Pennsylvania affirmed, holding that the pediatrician, "rejecting the indiscriminate use of the drug which, it was said by plaintiffs, was then characteristic of the medical profession in Philadelphia, could not limit his own responsibility to the skill and knowledge of the norm; and in exercising the knowledge he himself possessed, he was required to employ the care and judgment of a reasonable man in like circumstances. This standard of care is distinctly recognized.... It was adherence to this standard which was put in issue by the testimony of plaintiffs' witnesses; this testimony was sufficient to take the case to the jury."

As to the osteopath, the Supreme Court declared: "We decline to accept the proposition that a qualified doctor can so easily turn himself into a dupe ... the Parke-Davis warnings were there to read if he would, and the dangers of the drug were by 1960 also revealed in other medical literature to which the doctor had access and which he said he read. Indeed ... the doctor at one point testified that the drug was dangerous 'to keep on using.' The court below was correct in not permitting him to take refuge behind the asserted liability of the manufacturer."

Sharpe v. Pugh (1974) 21 N.C. App. 110, 203 S.E.2d 330, aff'd 286 N.C. 209, 209 S.E.2d 456.

Aplastic anemia—Insufficient evidence of proximate cause and negligence on part of physician

A child under treatment with Chloromycetin died in May, 1964 from aplastic anemia. In a complaint against the attending pediatrician the following facts were alleged.

The defendant saw and treated the girl on numerous occasions between April 14, 1961, the date of her birth, and January 17, 1964. He prescribed Chloromycetin: June 18, 1963, for "a minor virus infection of the throat"; October 30, 1963, "for her tonsillitis"; and January 6, 1964, for a "virus infection." On January 7, 1964, although the girl had developed "red spots" or petechiae from her waist to her feet, he advised that she continue to take the Chloromycetin as previously directed.

The plaintiff charged that the defendant knew, or in the exercise of due care should have known, that Chloromycetin was a dangerous drug which on occasion produced serious and harmful side effects, including aplastic anemia, and was not recommended by its manufacturer for the purposes for which it was prescribed.

The trial court granted the defendant's motion to dismiss. On appeal, this order was reversed, with the Supreme Court of North Carolina declaring:

> [I]t would be negligence if defendant prescribed, as a remedy for illnesses for which it was neither necessary nor suited, a drug which he knew or should have known was dangerous, without advising and warning Brenda's parents of the possible or probable injurious effects from the use thereof. Under plaintiff's allegations, defendant was negligent in his treatment of Brenda by prescribing and administering chloromycetin, and such negligence proximately caused Brenda's death. Even so, accepting as true the facts alleged by plaintiff concerning chloromycetin, defendant was also negligent in failing to advise or warn Brenda's parents with reference thereto; and it may be reasonably inferred from plaintiff's allegations that, if the facts concerning chloromycetin are as alleged by plaintiff, Brenda's parents would not have consented to or permitted the use of chloromycetin in defendant's treatment of her. Under these circumstances, we cannot say as a matter of law that defendant's alleged negligence in this respect was not a proximate cause of Brenda's injuries and death.[7]

When the case was finally tried, the following additional facts were brought out: During the course of treatment, no blood tests or other tests were administered to Brenda until January 8, 1964, after she had developed the red spots over her body. The spots became worse and on January 17, 1964 Brenda was taken to Rex Hospital in Raleigh for further tests. Thereafter she was referred to Memorial Hospital in Chapel Hill where she was seen by a specialist, Dr. Campbell White McMillan, who diagnosed her illness as aplastic anemia.

Dr. McMillan treated Brenda over the course of three and a half months, during which time she was administered hormones and given several blood transfusions. On May 8, 1964, Brenda became unconscious and was taken to Memorial Hospital where she died the next morning. The post-mortem examination revealed the cause of death to have been massive intracranial bleeding, a known complication from aplastic anemia.

---

[7]See Sharpe v. Pugh (1967) 270 N.C. 598, 155 S.E.2d 108.

Concerning aplastic anemia, Dr. McMillan testified by deposition that: "Aplastic anemia should be regarded as a descriptive term rather than a specific disease process.... It is a descriptive word of a condition ... which really refers to a set of findings rather than an underlying cause." In response to a hypothetical question, Dr. McMillan testified that Chloromycetin might have caused the aplastic anemia which led to the bleeding which caused Brenda's death; however, on cross-examination, he testified:

> Based upon my experience and knowledge in the medical field, I have not been able to determine the causes of the condition described as aplastic anemia. And the general situation at the present time regarding this disease is that the fundamental causes of it have to be regarded as unknown. When I diagnose a condition of what I have described as aplastic anemia, then it would not be possible to specifically determine with certainty any particular cause for it.... I would have to say that in any case of aplastic anemia that I discovered that the cause could be from so many different sources that it would be impossible to specify a specific source.... Brenda Sharpe, might have developed or could have developed aplastic anemia from other sources.... I see no way to jump from the question of association to the question of a clear cause.

The incidence of aplastic anemia occurring as a result of the administration of Chloromycetin at the lowest estimate was one case for every 60,000 courses of therapy.

Another witness, Dr. Joseph H. Callicott, Jr., also testified by deposition that he conducted the post-mortem examination on Brenda's body. His examination revealed that the bone marrow content showed a disease in the blood-forming cells, and in his opinion, the cause of Brenda's death was intracranial bleeding resulting from aplastic anemia. In response to a hypothetical question Dr. Callicott testified that, "It is my opinion that it is possible that the aplastic anemia could have resulted from administration of chloromycetin."

At the close of the evidence the trial court granted the defendant a directed verdict and the plaintiff appealed. The Court of Appeals of North Carolina affirmed, stating:

> We are not unmindful of the statement made in the opinion in the former appeal of this case that defendant may have been negligent if he failed to advise or warn Brenda's parents with reference to the dangers inherent in the use of chloromycetin, where defendant prescribed the drug as a remedy for illness for which it was neither necessary nor suited, knowing that the drug

> was dangerous. However, we are of the opinion that while the evidence was sufficient to support a jury finding that the defendant prescribed and administered chloromycetin, knowing it *could* cause aplastic anemia, and that defendant failed to warn Mr. and Mrs. Sharpe about this dangerous side effect, the evidence was insufficient to support a jury finding that the drug was prescribed as a remedy for illnesses for which it was neither necessary nor suited. As to the appropriateness of prescribing chloromycetin to treat viral infections, there is a total paucity of expert testimony or any other testimony.

Also, referring to the deposition testimony of Dr. McMillan, the court felt the plaintiff fell short on the issue of proximate cause. Said the court:

> Assuming, *arguendo,* that plaintiff's evidence was sufficient to establish a prima facie case of negligence—that defendant was negligent in prescribing and administering chloromycetin for and to Brenda, or that he was negligent in failing to warn the Sharpes about chloromycetin—we think the evidence failed to show a causal connection between the negligence and Brenda's contraction of aplastic anemia.

On the plaintiff's application, the Supreme Court of North Carolina granted certiorari. The six members of that court who heard the case were equally divided on the question of whether the decision of the Court of Appeals should be affirmed or reversed. Under North Carolina law, an equal division requires that a decision be affirmed.

Stevens v. Parke, Davis & Co. (1973) 9 Cal. 3d 51, 507 P.2d 653, 107 Cal. Rptr. 45, 94 A.L.R.3d 1059.

Aplastic anemia—Verdicts against physician and manufacturer upheld—Manufacturer accused of overpromotion

Mrs. Stevens, the mother of three children, died shortly over a year after taking six doses of Chloromycetin. Lawsuits were filed against the attending physician, alleging negligence in prescribing the drug, and against Parke-Davis for overpromoting the drug after knowledge of its dangerous side effects.

In 1964, it was confirmed that Mrs. Stevens was suffering from a lung condition described as bilateral bronchiectasis, an anatomical derangement in the bronchial tree that increases the susceptibility to lung infection. To alleviate the disorder, her physician performed surgery on September 1, 1964. Two days after the operation, he prescribed the first of six doses of Chloromycetin to guard against infection. The final dose was administered on November 20, 1964. Mrs. Stevens failed to improve, and in June of 1965 she was referred to Dr. Kurnick, a hematologist.

Dr. Kurnick found Mrs. Stevens to be suffering from aplastic anemia. He testified at the trial that, in his opinion, the condition was caused by Chloromycetin. Mrs. Stevens died of pneumonia on December 25, 1965, as a result of her body's inability to produce the necessary blood cells to resist the infection.

The jury returned a verdict for the plaintiffs, and the Supreme Court of California affirmed, stating:

> Parke, Davis negligently failed to provide an adequate warning as to the dangers of Chloromycetin by so 'watering down' its warnings and so overpromoting such drug that members of the medical profession, including Dr. Beland, were caused to prescribe it when it was not justified.... Dr. Beland was induced to prescribe the drug for Mrs. Stevens because of Parke, Davis' overpromotion. Like many others of the profession, he had been exposed to the promotional tactics employed by Parke, Davis. It is reasonable to assume that the company's efforts consciously or subconsciously influenced him.... Dr. Beland was induced by the manufacturer's activities to prescribe the drug.... Dr. Beland's negligent prescription of chloromycetin for Mrs. Stevens was a foreseeable consequence of the extensive advertising and promotional campaign planned and carried out by the manufacturer. The record reveals in abundant detail that Parke, Davis made every effort, employing both direct and subliminal advertising, to allay the fears of the medical profession which were raised by knowledge of the drug's dangers. It cannot be said, therefore, that Dr. Beland's prescription of the drug despite his awareness of its dangers was anything other than the foreseeable consequence—indeed, the desired result—of Parke, Davis' overpromotion.

Tunnell v. Parke, Davis & Co. (Tenn. App.) [1977] Prod. Liab. Rep. (CCH) ¶8039.

Aplastic anemia—Summary judgments for manufacturer and physician affirmed

A sixteen-year-old female patient suffering from a middle ear infection was treated with 600,000 units of penicillin and ampicillin. About four days later she returned to the physician, and the infection was worse. She was given Chloromycetin for about two weeks after the physician ran tests to be certain that it would be effective against the infection. About nine months later the patient had a sore throat and treated herself with at least three capsules of

Chloromycetin from a previous prescription. A few weeks later she returned to the physician complaining of bruising, increased menstrual flow, and fever. The physician diagnosed aplastic anemia, probably secondary to Chloromycetin therapy, and transferred the patient to a university hospital under the care of a hematologist. The diagnosis was confirmed, and her treatment included the administration of male hormones. Her blood tests returned to normal. She suffered from the side effects of the male hormone treatment, but they gradually disappeared when this treatment was terminated.

The patient's lawsuit against the manufacturer of Chloromycetin and the physician who prescribed it alleged that a less dangerous drug would have been as effective, and that the manufacturer failed to warn the medical profession of its dangerous propensities.

Motions for summary judgments for the manufacturer and the physician were sustained by the trial court and affirmed on appeal.

Related cases

Aplastic anemia—Summary judgment for manufacturer reversed —Material issues of fact as to negligence

In Whitley v. Cubberly (1974) 24 N.C. App. 204, 210 S.E.2d 289, a summary judgment in favor of the manufacturer of chloramphenicol was reversed where the record revealed that issues of fact were created as to the manufacturer's negligence in improperly marketing and overpromoting the drug, and in failing to warn the medical profession of the drug's dangerous properties.

Aplastic anemia—Summary judgment for manufacturer reversed—Jury could infer inadequate warning and overpromotion

In Salmon v. Parke, Davis and Company (C.A.-4 N.C., 1975) 520 F.2d 1359, the court, in reversing a summary judgment for the manufacturer, held that a jury could infer from the evidence that warnings issued to physicians about the risk of chloramphenicol were inadequate, and that the manufacturer had overpromoted the drug.

CHLORDIAZEPOXIDE HYDROCHLORIDE
Librax
Librium
SK-Lygen

Librium is a popular tranquilizer used for short-term relief of anxiety and tension, withdrawal symptoms of acute alcoholism, preoperative apprehension, and as an adjunct in the treatment of various disease states in which anxiety and tension are manifested. The manufacturer, Roche Laboratories (Nutley, N.J.), in listing the adverse reactions to the drug, reports that the necessity of discontinuing its use because of undesirable effects has been rare. Among possible side effects are drowsiness, ataxia and confusion, particularly in the elderly and debilitated. Other reactions reported include isolated instances of skin eruptions, edema, minor menstrual irregularities, nausea, constipation, changes in EEG patterns, blood dyscrasias and liver dysfunction. The manufacturer also warns that paradoxical reactions, e.g., excitement, stimulation and acute rage, have been reported in psychiatric patients and in hyperactive aggressive children.[8]

The usual dosage is five or ten milligrams three or four times a day for adults with mild or moderate anxiety disorders and symptoms. For severe states it is 20 or 25 milligrams. For geriatric patients it is five milligrams two to four times a day.[9]

The product is also sold by several companies under the generic name, and until 1987, Manley and James Laboratories, a division of SmithKline Beckman Company (Philadelphia, Pa.), produced the product under the brand name SK-Lygen.

Fleming v. Prince George's County (1976) 277 Md. 655, 358 A.2d 892.

Choice of drugs questioned in view of patient's agitated state—Directed verdict for defendants reversed

A 67-year-old woman was admitted to the hospital with congestive heart failure, lung disease and hypertension. The following day, when she complained of nervousness and anxiety, her attending physician prescribed Librium in doses of ten milligrams, three

---

[8] Roche Laboratories, Summary of Product Information, *Journal of the American Medical Association,* 246:1140 (Sept. 4), 1981.

[9] Id.

times per day. According to the nurses' notes, the patient became disoriented at times, but this was not observed by her physician until three nights later, at which time he prescribed five milligrams of Valium (diazepam) after she was found walking in the corridor with a sheet over her, waving a dinner knife.

Later, when she again became agitated, another physician prescribed fifty milligrams of Seconal (secobarbital sodium). A nurse checked the patient ten minutes later, and found her resting quietly, but ten minutes after that, when a nurse checked again, the patient was absent from her room. It was later discovered she had attempted to climb out her window and had fallen several floors, severely injuring herself. She later died.

In a lawsuit against the hospital and the physicians involved, an expert witness testified that, among other things, the attending physician should not have continued to prescribe the Librium in such large doses because the drug was likely to contribute to the patient's problems, particularly her agitation and confusion. Also, the prescribing of Valium, a drug similar to Librium pharmacologically, was unwise.

On the strength of this testimony and other evidence suggesting that the care received by the patient was below standard, the Court of Appeals of Maryland reversed the trial court's directed verdict in favor of the defendants.

Burroughs v. Board of Trustees of Alachua General Hosp. (Fla. App., 1979) 377 So. 2d 801.

Hospital and physician not liable for patient's accident while under medication

A patient under treatment for alcoholism and depression was given a pass and allowed to drive one hundred miles by herself to another city to enter a drug rehabilitation center there. Prior to her departure she was administered Librium and Elavil (amitriptyline hydrochloride). While on the way she became disoriented, her automobile crossed the median, and she collided with the plaintiff's car.

In an action against the hospital and the patient's physician, the trial court granted the defendants' motion for summary judgment on the theory that there was no evidence that the treatment rendered failed to meet community standards. The Court of Appeals affirmed.

Related cases

Patient dies after double dose—Directed verdict for hospital reversed

In Haney v. Alexander (1984) 71 N.C. App. 731, 323 S.E.2d 430, the trial court erred in granting the defendant hospital a summary judgment in an action on behalf of a patient who died from cardiac arrhythmia after being given a double dose of Librium.

CHLORMADINONE ACETATE MESTRANOL
C-Quens

C-Quens were marketed by Eli Lilly and Company (Indianapolis, Ind.) from May 3, 1965 until February 24, 1971, at which time they were deleted from the company's price list. The product, intended for use as an oral contraceptive, was of the sequential type, in which estrogen alone is used for the first fifteen days followed by an estrogen-progestogen combination for five days. Contraception was achieved by suppression of ovulation through inhibition of pituitary gonadotropin.

Although the manufacturer never claimed 100% effectiveness for the product (see Whittington v. Eli Lilly & Co., below), it was not satisfied with its effective rate or the necessity for rigid adherence on the part of the user to the prescribed regimen. The product was permanently withdrawn from the market on October 15, 1971.[10]

Whittington v. Eli Lilly & Co. (S.D. W. Va., 1971) 333 F. Supp. 98.

Failure of product to prevent pregnancy—Summary judgment for manufacturer

The plaintiff used the defendant's oral contraceptive C-Quens from February, 1969 until January, 1970, at which time she suspected that she was pregnant. In September, 1970, she gave birth to a healthy child.

The plaintiff premised her action on an alleged breach of implied warranty, in that, according to the plaintiff, the defendant had warranted absolute efficacy of its product.

---

[10] Editor's Note: Although C-Quens were withdrawn from the market over ten years before the publication of the first edition of this volume, the Whittington case has been included because of the significance of the court's interpretation of the language used by the manufacturer in describing the effectiveness of its product.

The company's attorneys moved for summary judgment and filed affidavits of the marketing vice-president, senior research physician and staff counsel. These affidavits, together with copies of advertising brochures and instructions for the use of the product, stated that when taken as directed, the pills "offer virtually 100% protection." Information showing the results of tests on the product was also submitted which demonstrated that in clinical trials the pregnancy rate of women using the drug "never exceeded 1.9 per 100 woman years when calculated on the basis of Pearl's Formula which is the number of pregnancies multiplied by 1200 (100 women completing 12 cycles) divided by the total number of treatment cycles." All affiants stated that at no time did the defendant company ever advertise that its product was "totally effective to prevent conception."

The court, in granting the summary judgment, stated that a review of the defendant's affidavits "indicates clearly that there was no warranty either express or implied, made by Eli Lilly and Company that 'C-Quens' would absolutely prevent pregnancy." The court added that "virtually" is clearly not synonymous with "absolutely."

The court likened the case to those in which a patient's allergy causes a harmful reaction to a drug. It said:

> Courts have been extremely reluctant to permit recovery on the theory of warranty wherein hypersensitivity or allergy produces harmful results from an otherwise safe drug. No manufacturer of an oral contraceptive guarantees the 100% effectiveness of its product. In actions by a buyer against a seller for breach of warranty to recover damages for injury resulting from the use of the product, there is generally no liability upon a seller where the buyer has been unusually susceptible to injury from the product.

The court went on to comment that by the nature of its intended action, the oral contraceptive is likely to fail on occasion, just as the processes of the female reproductive system themselves "do not reach absolute perfection in their functions."

CHLOROMYCETIN

See CHLORAMPHENICOL

CHLOROQUINE
Aralen

Chloroquine is an anti-infective developed during World War II to treat malaria. It was found to have other therapeutic properties, and subsequently was used in extraintestinal amebiasis, discoid lupus erythematosus, disseminated lupus erythematosus, photosensitivity eruptions, sarcoidosis, skin tumors and rheumatoid arthritis. Its precise mechanisms of action are not yet clearly known.[11]

It has been found that in the treatment of lupus erythematosus and rheumatoid arthritis, side effects may be frequent and severe, but it is not known whether this has been due to prolonged administration of the drug or a greater susceptibility of the patient to its toxicity. Side effects include blurred vision, skin reactions, toxic psychoses, blood dyscrasias, neuromyopathies and nerve-type deafness. Retinal damage, apparently permanent, has occurred in some patients.[12]

Chloroquine is manufactured and sold by Winthrop Laboratories (New York, N.Y.) as Aralen Hydrochloride, Aralen Phosphate, and Aralen Phosphate with Primaquine Phosphate. The manufacturer's current package inserts state that Aralen Hydrochloride is indicated only for "the treatment of extraintestinal amebiasis and for treatment of acute attacks of malaria due to *P. vivax, P. malariae, P. ovale,* and susceptible strains of *P. falciparum* when oral therapy is not feasible"; Aralen Phosphate is indicated only for "the suppressive treatment and for acute attacks of malaria due to *P. vivax, P. malariae, P. ovale,* and susceptible strains of *P. falciparum*" and for extraintestinal amebiasis; and Aralen Phosphate with Primaquine Phosphate is indicated "solely for use in the prophylaxis of malaria, regardless of species, in all areas where this disease is endemic."[13]

These preparations are issued with extensive warnings. Aralen Hydrochloride and Aralen Phosphate include warnings that if there are any indications, past or present, of visual abnormalities, including abnormalities in visual acuity or visual field, or symptoms of

---

[11] *United States Dispensatory,* 27th ed., p. 294.

[12] Id., p. 295.

[13] *Physicians' Desk Reference,* 35th ed., pp. 1895-97. Winthrop Laboratories also produce Plaquenil (hydroxychloroquine sulfate), a variation reportedly safer than chloroquine, which is indicated for the treatment of malaria, lupus erythematosus and rheumatoid arthritis. It is, however, issued with similar warnings on side effects. Id., pp. 1905-06.

"light flashes and streaks," which are not fully explainable, the drug should be discontinued immediately and the patient closely observed for possible progression, even after cessation of therapy. In addition, the Aralen Phosphate literature warns that during prolonged therapy, initial (baseline) and periodic ophthalmologic examinations (including visual acuity, expert slit-lamp, funduscopic, and visual field tests) should be performed.[14]

Oppenheimer v. Sterling Drug, Inc. (1964) 7 Ohio App. 2d 103, 219 N.E.2d 54.

Damage to retina—Company free of liability—"Intervening causal influence of physician, patient and druggist"

In May, 1958, the patient was given chloroquine (Aralen) for skin changes comparable to lupus erythematosus. The patient's physician directed a pharmacy by telephone to supply the drug to the patient. The prescription was to be refillable for six months; however, it was refilled about twenty times over a period of more than two years. There was no evidence that the prescribing physician had ordered these renewals.

In October, 1960, the patient consulted an ophthalmologist who recommended discontinuance of the drug. In February, 1961, the ophthalmologist found the patient to have a remarkably reduced field of vision. Chloroquine retinopathy was the eventual diagnosis.

The patient brought suit against the manufacturer alleging negligence in selling a harmful product, in failing to discover its defects, and failing to warn the patient of these defects. The patient also asserted breach of warranty. The manufacturer generally denied the allegations and raised the defenses of contributory negligence and assumption of risk.

At the close of evidence, the court ordered the jury to return a verdict for the defendant. A motion for a new trial was overruled, and the patient appealed. The Court of Appeals of Ohio, Franklin County, affirmed the judgment. In applying a standard of ordinary care to the manufacturer, the reviewing court found no negligence. The court characterized chloroquine as basically a "good medicine and in no sense a dangerous drug," and said the manufacturer "did what was reasonably proper in view of all the phases of the use of the drug, taking into account its usefulness as well as its possible

[14] Id., pp. 1895-97.

unfavorable effects, by advising the medical and drug world concerning it."[15]

Furthermore, in the view of the court, the intervening causal influence of the doctor, the patient and the druggist would have relieved the manufacturer from liability if it had been negligent. The court found nothing to indicate that the physician had relied upon data furnished by the manufacturer in prescribing the drug; instead, it found that the physician had relied upon his own experience and upon data gathered at medical meetings. As to the patient, the court said it was her responsibility to report any side effects to her physician which, according to the record, she did not do. With regard to the druggist, the court felt the irregularities in the refills of the prescription were an intervening cause in the patient's disorder.

The claim of breach of warranty was disposed of by the court by reference to the failure of the record to show any reliance by the patient or by her doctor upon anything published or said by the manufacturer.

Basko v. Sterling Drug, Inc. (C.A.-2 Conn., 1969) 416 F.2d 417.

Damage to retina—Verdict for manufacturer reversed on erroneous instructions—History of development of Aralen

From 1953 to 1961 a patient was treated with three different drugs for lupus erythematosus. The drugs were Aralen, Atabrine, and Triquin, all manufactured by the defendant company, and prescribed by physicians at the Yale-New Haven Hospital. In 1956 the patient began experiencing a blurring of vision (she had complained of seeing "butterflies" as early as 1954). From 1961 to 1965 her vision deteriorated quite badly, and she became almost totally blind.

At the trial, the patient called a number of medical experts who testified that she was suffering from "chloroquine retinopathy." According to the prevalent theory, chloroquine had a special affinity for the melanin pigment cells of the eye. Once absorbed by the pigment cells, the chemical inhibited the flow of nutrients to the nervous tissue of the overlaying retina (a second theory, somewhat

---

[15] Editor's Note: For the historical development of Aralen and the steps taken by the manufacturer on receiving early reports of retinopathy, see Basko v. Sterling Drug, Inc., *infra.*

discredited, was that chloroquine constricted the blood vessels in the retinal part of the eye).

The patient's first witness was the chief ophthalmologist at the Yale-New Haven Hospital. He had examined the patient in December, 1962, and stated quite emphatically that she was suffering from an "irreversible" case of chloroquine retinopathy. He based his conclusion on the fact that the patient had taken chloroquine in amounts sufficient to cause this condition, and added, "I can't think of any other disease or drug that could do it."

Similar testimony was given by a second witness who had done extensive research on chloroquine retinopathy at the National Institute of Health in Bethesda, Maryland, and who had examined the patient in July, 1966. He likewise said that the patient's retinal damage was probably due to long-term treatment with chloroquine drugs, and based his conclusion on the facts: (1) the dosage and duration of treatment were sufficient to cause retinopathy, (2) the retinal appearance was similar to other cases of chloroquine retinopathy he had observed, and (3) progressive loss of visual acuity was characteristic of this condition.

The evidence showed that of the three drugs involved in this case, only Aralen and Triquin contained chloroquine ingredients. Atabrine (quinacrine) was not made from chloroquine, and there was no evidence to indicate that it produced damage to the retina.

There was lengthy testimony introduced on the history of Aralen, which had been developed as a substitute for quinine during World War II. The drug had been extensively tested on animals and humans before being placed on the market. The tests were conducted by both the drug company and a wartime Board for the Coordination of Malarial Studies, and involved the administration of chloroquine to over 5,000 human patients under close clinical observation. The tests showed that chloroquine was highly effective in the treatment of malaria, and that it produced no serious side effects when taken in the normally prescribed quantity.

The most commonly observed side effects were nausea, abdominal cramps, diarrhea, and occasional vomiting. There were also some instances of temporary blurring of vision. Similar blurring had been observed in patients receiving treatment with quinine and other anti-malarial drugs, and the available evidence at the time strongly suggested that the condition was due to a side effect associated with the eye muscles. Upon further investigation it was found that the blurring disappeared when treatment with chloroquine was discontinued, and investigators concluded that the condition was reversible and "transitory." Several instances of corneal opacities were also reported, but these were found to clear up when chloroquine was discontinued.

In 1946 Aralen was approved by the Food and Drug Administration for the treatment of malaria. By 1953 a considerable number of investigators had used Aralen with good results in the treatment of lupus erythematosus and rheumatoid arthritis, and in 1957 the drug was approved for these additional uses. The drug company subsequently prepared a promotional booklet on the treatment of these diseases. The booklet listed "temporary blurring of vision due to weakness of accommodation" as a side effect of Aralen, and indicated the "untoward effects are limited in type and, with rare exceptions, are insignificant." For prolonged treatment the booklet recommended a "maintenance dose" of 250 milligrams daily.

Triquin was made from a combination of Aralen, Atabrine, and Plaquenil, being composed of chloroquine phosphate, quinacrine, and hydroxychloroquine sulfate. It was approved by the Food and Drug Administration in 1958, and was placed on the market shortly thereafter.

There was evidence that from the beginning the drug company knew of reports of some blurring of vision and corneal opacities in patients treated with chloroquine, and this much was conceded by the vice-president and medical director of the drug company. He insisted, however, that the early investigators failed to disclose any instances of damage to the retina, and he testified quite emphatically that there was not even the slightest evidence of retinal damage produced by chloroquine at least until 1957. His testimony was substantially corroborated by the chief ophthalmologist at Yale-New Haven Hospital who testified that clinical ophthalmologists did not begin to suspect some connection between chloroquine and retinal complications until around 1957. This witness made reference to a 1957 article by a Dr. Amerigo Cambiaggi entitled "Unusual Ocular Lesions in a Case of Systemic Lupus Erythematosus," and said that this was the first article to attribute retinal damage to chloroquine therapy. Prior to this publication, there was not a single mention of retinal damage in cases where blurring of vision had been reported. It appeared from even the latest literature that no investigator had been able to induce chloroquine retinopathy in rats, rabbits, or monkeys.

The article by Dr. Cambiaggi was rather confusing. It described the case of a patient who was treated with chloroquine phosphate and developed unusual fundus lesions. "This case is reported," he wrote, "because I found no report in the literature of fundus lesions caused by lupus erythematosus similar to those of the patient." Dr. Cambiaggi indicated that chloroquine treatment "was discontinued because of the suspicion that it might have caused ocular disturbances," but then he said he thought that the fundus lesions "were due to lupus erythematosus because of the simultaneous presence of other fundus lesions commonly related to lupus erythematosus and also because of concurrent appearance of the ocular alterations and recurrences of lupus erythematosus.... I think that chloroquine can be ruled out as a causative factor, since discontinuation of this drug did not result in improvement."

An associate medical director of the drug company testified that she had read Dr. Cambiaggi's article shortly after its publication, and said she thought that the author had reached the conclusion that the fundus lesions were not due to chloroquine therapy. The New Haven ophthalmologist, however, was of the opinion that the article supported the opposite conclusion.

The next significant date was October, 1959, when a team of British investigators published an article entitled "Retinopathy Following Chloroquine Therapy." The investigators reported three cases of retinal lesions in patients who had been treated with chloroquine for lupus erythematosus and rheumatoid arthritis, and definitely concluded that the retinal lesions were due to chloroquine therapy. On the evidence presented, they wrote, "the retinopathy here described results from treatment with chloroquine compounds." In all three cases the patients had been taking chloroquine for approximately three years, and the severity of retinal damage seemed to show some correspondence to the dose used. When chloroquine treatment was discontinued, their conditions did not improve, although the retinal lesions "ceased to progress." Significantly, the investigators indicated that retinal changes similar to those seen in the patients under study had not been previously reported in the literature. This article was referred to as the "Hobbs Report."

The Hobbs Report was read and discussed by members of the drug company's medical research department, and in the summer of 1960 the company advised the Food and Drug Administration that it wished to revise its literature on Aralen and Triquin. Various promotional materials, including product cards and package inserts, were subsequently rewritten, although it was not clear whether the promotional booklet mentioned earlier remained in circulation.

In 1959 the product card on Aralen warned of "temporary blurring of vision due to interference with accommodation," as well as corneal opacities, and advised periodic eye examinations. In addition to this warning, the 1960 product card referred to the Hobbs Report by name, and indicated the "retinal vascular response" had been observed in three patients. "Macular lesions and narrowed retinal vessels, and the scotomatous vision and field defects to which they gave rise, although evidently irreversible, ceased to progress on discontinuation of therapy." The card advised periodic eye examinations, and added, "Lowering of dosage or continuing the drug is a matter for the physician to decide and depends on such factors as ophthalmologic progression, and severity and clinical response of the disorder under treatment." The same warning was given in 1961. In 1962 the card was changed to warn that "retinal changes, consisting of narrowing of the retinal arterioles, macular lesions (areas of edema, atrophy and abnormal pigmentation), pallor of the optic disc, optic atrophy and patchy retinal pigmentation, have been reported as rarely occurring within several months to several years of chloroquine therapy.... Retinal changes were found to be practically irreversible and like the accompanying visual defect may progress on discontinuation of therapy." The card advised tri-monthly examinations. For the same years identical warnings were given on the product cards for Triquin. The package inserts and other descriptive literature for both drugs were similarly worded.

In 1963 investigators at the National Institute of Health completed a study of various cases of chloroquine-induced retinopathies and reported that "the appearance of a similar retinopathy in patients with different underlying diseases, all having in common long-term chloroquine therapy, almost certainly implicates chloroquine as the etiologic agent." Shortly thereafter the drug company mailed "Dear Doctor" letters to 248,000 physicians warning of the possibility of "impairment of vision or retinal change during or subsequent to the administration of chloroquine" and recommending periodic ophthalmologic examination.

On completion of the evidence from both sides, the jury returned a verdict in favor of the drug company. The District Court entered judgment accordingly, and the patient appealed. The United States Court of Appeals for the Second Circuit reversed the judgment and remanded the case to the District Court for a new trial.

The Court of Appeals declared:

> We find reversible error ... in the way the jury was instructed on the issue of causation. On this issue, the jury was instructed to consider simply whether plaintiff's blindness resulted from her taking one or more of defendant's drugs. More specifically,... [the District Court] told the jury that it should decide whether plaintiff's blindness 'was caused by Aralen or by Atabrine or by Triquin, or by any two of these, or by all three of them, or by none.... If you find that the damage was caused by one or more of these drugs, then you will go on to consider [the question of duty to warn].'... We believe that plaintiff was entitled to more detailed instructions on the law of multiple causation. Suppose, for example, that the jury found (1) that plaintiff's blindness was caused by a combination of Aralen and Triquin, and (2) that the risk of chloroquine retinopathy did not become known until 1959. Suppose also that the jury found (3) that there was no breach of the duty to warn with respect to Aralen, but (4) that defendant gave inadequate warnings with respect to Triquin. On these facts, plaintiff would be entitled to recover if the jury found that either Aralen or Triquin alone would have been sufficient to produce chloroquine retinopathy, and that Triquin was a 'substantial factor' in producing her injury. The jury should have been so instructed, and indeed, the court's failure to give explicit instructions may have created the erroneous impression that defendant would not be liable under such circumstances unless there was a breach of the duty to warn *with respect to both drugs* .... We conclude, therefore, that the jury should have been instructed on the 'substantial factor' test of multiple causation. We also find plain error in the court's repeated references to 'appreciable number of users' in stating the duty to warn test. The manufacturer is obligated to warn in cases where the drug may affect only a small number of idiosyncratic or hypersensitive users, and the obligation to warn attached regardless of whether the number of persons affected can fairly be said to be 'appreciable.'... '[D]uties to warn are not in all cases, measured by quantitative standards.'... A manufacturer may in some circumstances have a duty to warn 'those few persons who it knows cannot apply its product without serious injury'.

Cochran v. Brooke (1966) 243 Ore. 89, 409 P.2d 904.

Damage to retina—Judgments for prescribing physician and company affirmed—Journal articles excluded from evidence—Strict liability rejected

The patient was given chloroquine (Aralen) in 1958 by an orthopedist for severe arthritis of the spine (ankylosing spondylitis). The drug was discontinued in 1961 when the patient's vision began to fail. The patient brought suit against the orthopedist for malpractice and charged the manufacturer with negligence, strict liability, and breach of warranty.

The trial judge (sitting as trier of fact on motions for directed verdicts by all parties) found that neither the physician nor the manufacturer was negligent, and that the drug, as manufactured by Sterling, "contained no impurities, that its chemical content was as represented and that the drug was reasonably safe for the treatment of ankylosing spondylitis." The judge refused to apply strict liability (Restatement, Torts 2d, Section 402A) because the plaintiff failed to show the product was defective.

On appeal the patient's attorneys argued that the judge erred in refusing to admit in evidence numerous brochures, pamphlets and publications which contained reports of doctors who had observed loss of vision by users of chloroquine. In upholding the trial judge's rulings, the Supreme Court of Oregon stated:

> Some of the unadmitted documents were published after [the defendant-physician] had terminated plaintiff's use of chloroquine and thus were irrelevant to the test of care to be applied in this case. Some of the documents were admitted as against one of the defendants and refused as to the other. When the exhibits were presented the court exercised careful judgment in admitting the offered exhibits that met the test of Eckleberry v. Kaiser Foundation et al., 1961, 226 Or. 616, 359 P.2d 1090, 84 A.L.R.2d 1327 [admissibility of extracts from medical books and treatises as independent evidence of the statements contained therein] (and similar cases) and rejecting the others. We can find no error in the court's rulings.

Whether the manufacturer had failed to give adequate and timely warning to physicians dispensing chloroquine when it (the manufacturer) first learned that its use could cause permanent eye damage, was, said the Supreme Court, "a question for the trier of facts," and it refused to disturb the findings.

On being asked to impose strict liability on the manufacturer, the reviewing court said:

> It is, indeed, easy for compassion to dictate an absolute liability against the makers of a product that can cause blindness. But once the liability is imposed, it could not be judicially limited only to cases involving disastrous consequences. An upset stomach caused by taking aspirin would, as well, entitle the user to his measure of damages. We can agree with the plaintiff that social justice might require that the price of the drugs should

include an amount sufficient to create a fund to compensate those who suffer unanticipated harm from the use of a beneficial drug. But this kind of a system of compensation is beyond the power of a court to impose.

The judgment in the trial court was affirmed.

Sterling Drug, Inc. v. Cornish (C.A.-8 Mo., 1966) 370 F.2d 82.

Damage to retina—No intervening negligence on doctor's part—Cause of action did not begin on patient noticing "small golden light"

The patient took chloroquine (Aralen) daily from November, 1958 to December, 1962 for an arthritic condition, and extensive and permanent visual impairment resulted. In an action against the manufacturer the patient's attorney contended that it knew or should have known that some people would suffer visual losses from the use of chloroquine, and was negligent in failing to warn physicians to be on the lookout for such symptoms. The jury returned an award of $110,000 for the patient which the District Court remitted to $80,000.

On appeal, the United States Court of Appeals, Eighth Circuit, found the evidence supported the District Court's refusal to direct a verdict for the manufacturer on the questions of whether the manufacturer was aware of the relationship between the drug and retinal damage in time to warn physicians and whether the warning which was made was timely and sufficient.

The case did not present a question of the doctors' negligence intervening to proximately cause the patient's injury. According to the reviewing court, regardless of the impact of the doctors' actions, the sole issue was whether the manufacturer "negligently failed to make reasonable efforts to warn" the patient's doctors.

On the question of the commencement of the action, the reviewing court determined that the applicable statute of limitations began to run at the time the patient suffered irreversible impairment of vision, and rejected the manufacturer's contention that the injury occurred when the patient first noticed a small "golden light" which did not interfere with the patient's vision. The court noted that transient visual disturbances are not uncommon in patients being treated with chloroquine.

Krug v. Sterling Drug, Inc. (Mo., 1967) 416 S.W.2d 143.

Damage to retina—Company should have known of "dangerous potentiality"—Statute began to run when patient told of possible cause of condition—No "intervening negligence" on physician's part

The patient was given Aralen from 1953 through 1957 for lupus erythematosus. In July, 1957, she noticed occasionally "fuzzy" vision, and her doctor switched to Plaquenil and Triquin. But by 1961 she had lost almost all central vision. In 1961 an eye specialist suspected chloroquine retinopathy, having read of the condition in the medical literature. In March, 1962, the patient was examined by a research physician studying the chloroquine problem, and he concluded that she had suffered irreversible retinal degeneration as a result of the drug.

An action against the drug manufacturer and the dispensing pharmacy was brought in April, 1963. The manufacturer raised Missouri's five-year statute of limitations on tort actions but was unsuccessful; the pharmacy, however, obtained a directed verdict. The jury was given the issue of whether the manufacturer knew or should have known of the "dangerous potentiality" of chloroquine and "failed to give a timely and adequate warning to the doctor who was prescribing said drugs." It returned a verdict for the patient in the amount of $125,000.

On appeal the Supreme Court of Missouri upheld the trial court as to the applicability of the statute of limitations, holding that the jury could find negligence continuing until 1961 when the chloroquine was discontinued and the patient informed of the probable cause of her visual problems. In so doing it rejected the manufacturer's contention that the statute should have begun to run in 1955, the date the patient first noticed her vision blurring.

The reviewing court rejected also the manufacturer's argument that the negligence of the prescribing doctor was an intervening cause in the patient's injury. Pointing to the manufacturer's duty to warn the medical profession of the drug's side effects, the court said a failure in this duty created liability regardless of anything the doctor may or may not have done. In this regard the court noted a letter in 1956 from the doctor to the company in which he mentioned his patient's gradual loss of sight and inquired about a possible connection with the chloroquine. To this letter the company answered that there had been reports of blurred vision but that it was reversible on reduction in dosage.

The company's claim that it had no duty to warn a small group of patients of the possibility of an idiosyncratic reaction also was rejected by the court which viewed the argument as an evidentiary matter for the consideration of the jury, and one with which it would not interfere.

The judgment in the lower court was affirmed.

Bine v. Sterling Drug, Inc. (Mo., 1968) 422 S.W.2d 623.

Damage to retina—Company held liable on virtually same evidence as in Krug case

The patient took Aralen for systemic lupus erythematosus from late 1954 until November, 1960. In February, 1961 he was placed on Plaquenil which was continued until September, 1961. His visual difficulties began in 1959 and by November, 1965 he was virtually blind in one eye and had a "ring blind spot" in the other. A lawsuit against the manufacturer resulted in a $175,000 jury verdict which was reduced to $125,000 by the trial court.

On appeal the Supreme Court of Missouri noted that the evidence introduced at trial was similar to that offered in the Krug case (see above) and was sufficient to permit a finding that the company knew or by the exercise of ordinary care should have known that serious visual damage would result to users of its drug. The judgment was affirmed.

Sterling Drug, Inc. v. Yarrow (C.A.-8 S.D., 1969) 408 F.2d 978.

Damage to retina—Detail men should have warned physicians

The patient began taking Aralen daily for arthritis in 1958. Visual difficulties began in August, 1964. In a subsequent lawsuit against the manufacturer, the main issue was whether the company's method of warning the physicians in the field was sufficient.

The warnings of the side effects of Aralen generally, and of retinal damage in particular, were given to doctors in the Aralen product cards, in the *Physicians' Desk Reference,* and in "Dear Doctor" letters sent to the profession in February, 1963. Both the trial court (sitting without a jury) and the United States Court of Appeals, Eighth Circuit, felt that the manufacturer's detail men presented the most effective method of warning. When the evidence showed they were not used for this purpose, the manufacturer was held liable. The patient was awarded $180,000 for the 80% blindness she suffered.

In answer to the manufacturer's argument that the treating physician was adequately informed of the drug's dangers by the methods that were used, the court said:

> There was ample direct evidence from Dr. Olson [the patient's physician], and opinion evidence from qualified professional witnesses, to support the findings that Dr. Olson (and other general practitioners) receive so much literature on drugs that it is impossible to read all of it; that Dr. Olson relied on detail men, medical conventions, medical journals and conversations with other doctors for information on drugs he was prescribing; that Dr. Olson was inundated with literature and product cards of various manufacturers; that a change in literature and an additional letter were insufficient to present new information to Dr. Olson; that detail men visit physicians at frequent intervals and could give an effective warning which would affirmatively notify the doctor of the dangerous side effects of chloroquine phosphate on the retina.

Kershaw v. Sterling Drug, Inc. (C.A.-5 Miss., 1969) 415 F.2d 1009.

Damage to retina—Verdict for patient upheld— Warning by company insufficient

At the trial, the evidence disclosed the patient was afflicted with chloroquine retinopathy, which resulted in the permanent degeneration of a portion of the retina of each eye. The disease did not produce total blindness but left the patient without the use of her central vision. By using her "side vision," she was able to discern various forms and shapes. Her field of vision and depth perception were markedly impaired and could not be aided by the use of eyeglasses. She was not able to sew, read effectively, or identify individuals.

The patient took Aralen as treatment for rheumatoid arthritis for a substantial period prior to her affliction with chloroquine retinopathy pursuant to her physicians' prescriptions.

The jury returned a verdict for $150,000 in favor of the plaintiffs, and the District Court entered judgment accordingly. The company appealed, contending that it gave proper notice to physicians after learning of Aralen's potential side effects and that it was, therefore, not chargeable with negligence.

The company's contention was rejected by the Court of Appeals which affirmed the judgment. The court declared: "The plaintiffs offered abundant evidence that Sterling reasonably should have known of Aralen's properties several years before it issued warnings. Moreover, the plaintiffs introduced evidence showing that the warnings, when issued, were insufficient. We find that adequate and timely warning was not given."

Schenebeck v. Sterling Drug, Inc. (C.A.-8 Ark., 1970) 423 F.2d 919.

Damage to retina—Verdict for patient upheld

A patient and her husband filed suit against Sterling for blindness allegedly resulting from taking Aralen over a five-year period. At the trial the evidence disclosed that an internist in Hot Springs, Arkansas first prescribed Aralen in 1958 for the patient's chronic rheumatoid arthritis. He initially prescribed the usual dose of one 250-milligram tablet to be taken each day. He mailed her a second similar prescription in July of 1962. Both prescriptions were refillable. He did not personally see her between November of 1961 and May of 1963. The patient took Aralen tablets almost daily until May 7, 1963, when she reported that she had experienced blurring of her vision. The physician recommended that she stop taking the drug until she had been checked by an ophthalmologist. The patient underwent eye examinations by two ophthalmologists in Little Rock. Neither discovered any disease in her eyes.

The patient, however, continued to have difficulties with her vision. On November 16, 1963 she wrote the Mayo Clinic at Rochester, Minnesota, inquiring whether Aralen could cause her eyes to fail. She complained, "They are failing more and more all the time until I am half blind. Eye specialists find no disease, no cause. I stayed off the tablet [Aralen] for 3 months with no change." A Mayo staff specialist wrote in reply:

> If you have been taking Chloroquine (Aralen) constantly over this period it is indeed possible that your visual defect is related to the use of the medication. I would advise that you stop the medication completely until this can be definitely settled. I think you should discuss this with your general doctor and with your eye specialist who can answer this question.

The patient showed this letter to her internist who thereafter wrote to the Mayo physician on December 6, 1963: "Her vision has not improved and I fear it is permanently impaired. If you have any suggestions concerning her condition, I would appreciate hearing from you." The Mayo physician responded that he knew of no effective remedy for retinopathy related to anti-malarials and he recommended that the patient take no more of this type of medication. The internist then wrote the patient advising that she cease using chloroquine. The patient took no additional chloroquine-type drugs.

No actual pathology was discovered in the patient's eyes until September 2, 1964. There were observations of fine clumps of pigment in the macula of both eyes. Her vision, which had been characterized as "good" the prior October, had deteriorated to "industrial blindness." The patient was again referred to the Mayo Clinic where the ophthalmological staff diagnosed her condition as chloroquine retinopathy.

At the trial, the following facts were established. The drug company's literature on Aralen available generally to the medical profession between 1958 and February of 1963 stressed the relative safety of its use. Among other things the literature recited that physicians need not concern themselves with "precautions or preventive measures ... before, during or after the use of... Aralen" nor "frequent patient checkups." In the *Physicians' Desk Reference,* the company advertised between 1958 and 1961 that Aralen's side effects included "headache, visual disturbances.... Often transient, or subsides on withdrawal or reduction of dosage." The drug company's Aralen "product card" distributed to physicians by its detail men mentioned retinal vascular response in the context of an idiosyncrasy.

Information circulated in the medical community before and during 1961 reported serious ocular side effects in patients utilizing chloroquine therapy. For example, a 1961 American Medical Association publication on drugs called attention to permanent eye damage incurred by a "few" patients as a result of the use of Aralen.

A "medical information letter" dated December 21, 1962, published by Drug and Therapeutic Information, Inc., of New York City, which analyzed anti-malarial drugs, including chloroquine Aralen), noted that frequent toxic effects had been reported from the use of such drugs, and suggested caution in their dispensation. It advised that ophthalmological examinations that include plotting of the visual fields should be considered mandatory when the drug "is to be given over a period of months." The letter further indicated that usual doses of chloroquine "... can be given with reasonable safety for at least a year — longer on an intermittent schedule." The patient's internist had received this letter.

Thereafter, in February of 1963, the company radically changed its medical literature concerning side effects attributable to chloroquine and, by a special letter to almost every physician in the United States, specifically warned of the risk of chloroquine retinopathy and cautioned that prolonged therapy must be accompanied by initial and frequent ophthalmological examinations.

The jury returned a verdict in favor of the plaintiffs, and the District Court entered judgment accordingly. The company appealed, contending that the letter from Drug and Therapeutic Information, Inc., sent December 21, 1962, adequately warned the patient's internist of the dangers incident to long-term Aralen therapy; that this warning was timely since the patient then had reported no ill effects from the use of Aralen; that this physician nevertheless continued her on Aralen therapy; and that any failure to timely warn played no part in producing the patient's injury. The Court of Appeals disagreed, and affirmed the judgment of the District Court.

The Court of Appeals stated:

> We examine the appellant's [company's] contentions in the light of the continuous duty cast upon the manufacturer of an ethical drug to warn physicians of the dangers incident to prescribing the drug, to keep abreast of scientific developments touching upon the manufacturer's product and to notify the medical profession of any additional side effect discovered from its use.... A drug manufacturer's compliance with such rule enables physicians to balance the risk of possible harm against benefits to be derived by their patients' use of such drugs. In considering the alternatives of treatment, the prescribing physician is entitled to make an informed choice.... Sterling ought to have recognized and generally warned the medical profession that permanent eye damage could result from the use of this product in 1961 or, perhaps, even earlier. However, Sterling's literature continued muted until 1963 in acquainting the medical profession generally with the hazards of long-term Aralen therapy, the earlier literature affirming that the drug could be prescribed without specific precaution. Thus, Sterling breached its legal duty to the medical profession and vicariously to this plaintiff.

The court went on to say that the evidence established that the toxic effect which chloroquine produces upon the retina is one of gradual and even delayed onset with later progression. In this case, the deterioration of the patient's eyes continued for years after she ceased using the drug. In the Mayo ophthalmologist's opinion, the drug's toxic effect was not "idiosyncratic," but followed as a concomitant of prolonged use. A "timely and effective warning concerning Aralen's dangerous propensities" communicated to her internist prior to his issuing a second refillable prescription for this drug in July of 1962 would have afforded him the opportunity to change the nature and course of her treatment. Thereafter, her physician did not see her until May of 1963, when he directed her to stop using the drug until she had been examined by an ophthalmologist. After that visit, he did not direct her to resume Aralen therapy. She assumed she might resume taking the drug after receiving a report from the ophthalmologist that her eyes appeared undamaged. Thus, the court felt the plaintiff presented sufficient evidence for the jury to find that the company's failure to timely warn constituted "an omission on its part which operated through a natural sequence of events to proximately cause or contribute to plaintiff's harm."

Withers v. Sterling Drug, Inc. (S.D. Ind., 1970) 319 F. Supp. 878.

Damage to retina—Patient failed to sue when damage thought reversible—Statute of limitations applied

The patient took chloroquine (Aralen) from December, 1957 to September, 1963 for an arthritic condition. Her eye troubles began in June, 1962, and she was first seen by an eye specialist in September, 1963. The specialist linked the problems to the chloroquine but told her that the condition was reversible. Over five years later, however, in May, 1969, he changed his opinion and informed her the damage was permanent.

The patient consulted an attorney and filed suit against the manufacturer on May 26, 1969, alleging negligence, strict liability, and breach of implied warranty. The manufacturer moved for summary judgment, contending the action was barred by Indiana's two-year statute of limitations governing personal injury actions. The District Court sustained the summary judgment, rejecting the patient's attorney's contention that the cause did not accrue until the patient's physician advised her that the condition was irreversible. The court held that the cause accrued in September, 1963 when the patient became aware that she had sustained visual difficulties as a result of taking the drug.

The patient's attorney raised the question of concealment as a means of defeating the application of the statute, but the court said any such concealment, which apparently was based on evidence involving correspondence between the patient's physician and the manufacturer, occurred after the patient's cause accrued in 1963.

The patient's attorney also attempted to characterize her breach of warranty claim as one of contract, and thus take advantage of the six-year statute of limitations applicable to contract actions. This was rejected by the court on the ground that privity between the patient and the manufacturer was not shown.

Christofferson v. Kaiser Foundation Hospitals (1971) 15 Cal. App. 3d 75, 92 Cal. Rptr. 825, 53 A.L.R.3d 292.

Damage to retina—Strict liability rejected

The patient suffered from severe lupus erythematosus. From October of 1954 to January 7, 1960 she was given Aralen. She developed a severe limitation of vision, diagnosed as irreversible. Attributing this impairment to the drug, she filed suit against the drug company, drug retailer, and the physicians and health plan involved.

The issue was whether the company's duty to warn depended upon its having knowledge or some means of knowing of possible harmful side effects. The drug company viewed its duty to be to warn of side effects of its drug when such effects should or could have been foreseen, while the patient's attorneys argued for absolute liability in its strict form.

At the trial the evidence disclosed that the adverse effect was not immediate, but eventuated only over a period of years, and was an extremely rare result of use of a medication which had distinct value to mankind in the treatment of serious ailments, e.g., malaria.

Motions for nonsuit were granted for all but the drug company, and the jury returned a verdict in its favor. The trial court entered judgment accordingly, and the patient appealed. The Court of Appeals of California affirmed, stating: "... [W]e do not ... extend ... [the] rule [of absolute liability] to liability for long delayed and unforeseeable side effects unrelated to the ailment designed to be treated, from a drug which has real value in the treatment of serious ailments. We are unwilling to so broaden the rule."

Singer v. Sterling Drug, Inc. (C.A.-7 Ill., 1972) 461 F.2d 288.

Damage to retina—Patient not negligent in doubling dosage in view of label information—Strict liability established

In 1957 Aralen was prescribed for the patient for discoid lupus erythematosus. She took the drug until 1964 when she was notified by a pharmacist of possible adverse side effects. When an examination disclosed visual damage, the patient filed suit against the manufacturer on theories of negligence and strict liability.

At the trial the defendant charged contributory negligence in that the patient had misused Aralen by taking excessive dosages (twice the daily "maintenance dose" of one 250 mg. tablet) during a seven-month trip to Europe. The patient's attorneys moved to withdraw this issue from the jury's consideration but was overruled. The jury returned a verdict for the defendant.

On appeal, the United States Court of Appeals, Seventh Circuit, held that evidence that the patient was guilty of contributory negligence was insufficient. The court pointed to proof that some bottles of Aralen contained labels stating that the "usual dosage" was *two 250 mg. tablets per day,* the amount the patient took while on her trip.

Furthermore, the reviewing court held that the patient had established a case of strict liability when she introduced evidence that the manufacturer, with knowledge of the risk of Aralen causing chloroquine retinopathy, had failed to warn physicians. In this regard, the court said the trial judge had erred in instructing the jury on the theory of strict liability when he used the terms "willful and intentional misconduct." Such conduct is not required under Indiana law, said the court, to find strict liability. Judgment was reversed and the matter was remanded for new trial. In March, 1973, the case was retried, and after four days of trial was settled for $1,007,000.[16]

Hoffman v. Sterling Drug, Inc. (C.A.-3 Pa., 1973) 485 F.2d 132.

Damage to retina—Verdict for patient upheld

This case involved another lawsuit for chloroquine-related eye damage. At the trial the evidence disclosed that the patient's relevant medical history dated back to the early 1950's, when, while consulting his family physician for a gastric condition and arthritic pains, the doctor recommended that the patient see a dermatologist about a rash on his face. The patient was referred to an osteopath specializing in dermatology who diagnosed the patient's condition as lupus erythematosus, and in May of 1957 he prescribed Aralen

[16] Settlement reported in AMA *The Citation* 27:153, 1973, and ATLA *News Letter* 16:160, 1973.

as treatment. This doctor treated the patient for thirteen months, from April of 1957 to May of 1958, until the family physician referred the patient to an M.D. dermatologist. He treated the patient from June of 1958 until March of 1964, and he too prescribed Aralen. This dermatologist testified at the trial that he had informed the patient of the possibility of eye damage from the prolonged use of chloroquine, that he questioned the patient about his sight on each visit, and on several occasions suggested to the patient that he see an ophthalmologist for a "slit-lamp examination," but that he did not know that any eye damage would be irreversible. The patient stopped seeing the dermatologist in March of 1964 and continued taking Aralen under a refillable prescription until June of 1965, when another physician he was seeing for his arthritic pain advised him to stop taking the drug.

It was in 1965 or 1966 that the patient began to experience problems with his eyesight. His optometrist testified at the trial that prior to 1966 the patient's vision was correctible to 20/20, but that in June of 1966 his eyesight had deteriorated to approximately 20/30 in each eye, and it continually worsened. An ophthalmologist examined the patient in December of 1965 and found that his vision was 20/30 in each eye and could not be corrected to 20/20. In 1970 he concluded that the patient suffered from chloroquine retinopathy, and in 1971 he found his vision to be 10/200 in each eye, which rendered him legally blind under Pennsylvania law.

The testimony at the trial was along the lines of that received in the earlier Basko case. Aralen had been approved by the Food and Drug Administration for the treatment of malaria. Commonly observed side effects noted in the 1940's and early 1950's included nausea, abdominal cramps, and some instances of blurring of vision. Visual disturbances disappeared when chloroquine treatment was discontinued. By 1953 reports of the successful use of Aralen in rheumatoid arthritis and lupus erythematosus began to appear. In 1955 the company distributed a pamphlet which discussed Aralen as treatment for lupus erythematosus. In the same year the company submitted for publication in the *Physicians' Desk Reference* similar information. Finally, on July 25, 1957, the company filed a supplemental new drug application with the FDA seeking approval to advertise and sell Aralen for use in the treatment of rheumatoid arthritis and purportedly for lupus erythematosus. Conditional FDA approval was obtained three weeks later, with final approval on October 2, 1957.

Suspicion that chloroquine use might permanently damage the retina began to arise circa 1957. An article by Drs. Goldman and Preston, entitled "Reactions to Chloroquine Observed During Treatment of Various Dermatologic Disorders," stated that chloroquine was suspected of severe fundal (retinal) changes but this could not be proved. In 1959 the suspicion was strengthened by an article entitled "Retinopathy Following Chloroquine Therapy" by Hobbs, Sorsby, and Freedman. This report explained that "in the doses used to suppress or treat malaria, the toxic effects of chloroquine and its derivatives are only minor.... Since in both lupus erythematosus and rheumatoid arthritis the effective dose commonly exceeds that used for malaria, and the drug is administered for much longer periods, it is not surprising that toxic effects have been reported.... Recently we have seen changes of a much graver character, with visual damage which, in some cases at least, is evidently irreversible. These patients ... were under treatment with chloroquine compounds for lupus erythematosus and rheumatoid arthritis."

The article concluded, after a discussion of certain case reports, "On present evidence, the retinopathy here described results from treatment with chloroquine compounds." The drug company's doctor testified that this article made "it very likely, or quite likely, that chloroquine might be involved in the production of retinopathy. This I say 'likely' because the drug that they used was not Chloroquine Phosphate as sold by Winthrop but was Chloroquine Sulfate and which might have an entirely different toxicity than Chloroquine Phosphate." Numerous letters were also received by the company from physicians during this period (1956-1960) reporting loss of vision, field changes, and fundus changes in patients being treated with Aralen and inquiring into the possibility that Aralen might be the cause. The company made reference to the Hobbs, Sorsby, and Freedman article in its 1960 product literature, and, after numerous reports in medical literature of irreversible retinal damage following chloroquine treatment, it included in its 1962 product literature a warning that retinal changes "have been reported as rarely occurring within several months to several years of chloroquine therapy" and pointed out "the necessity of periodic visual field examinations in order to detect early changes during prolonged treatment with the drug." In February of 1963 the company sent out letters to physicians, 248,000 in all, warning of ocular complications from the use of the drug and of the need for initial and periodic ophthalmologic examinations of the patient.

The jury returned a verdict of $437,000 in favor of the patient, and the District Court entered judgment accordingly. The company appealed, contending that the evidence was not sufficient to permit the District Court to submit to the jury the issue whether Aralen was sold for use in the treatment of lupus erythematosus without adequate testing to determine possible harmful side effects. "A review of the record more than satisfies us of the sufficiency of evidence in this regard," stated the United States Court of Appeals for the Third Circuit in rejecting the company's contention as to liability.

The Court of Appeals continued:

> ... whether adequate testing would have disclosed potentially harmful side effects from the long-term use of Aralen and whether the studies made by defendants [Sterling] were in fact adequate were properly questions for the jury.... In view of the number of letters, beginning in 1956, from physicians reporting visual disturbances and retinal changes in patients using Aralen, and medical literature appearing in the late 1950's and early 1960's, we think it at least open to question whether Sterling used 'foresight appropriate to [its] enterprise.'

The court did, however, reverse the lower court's judgment on the amount of damages (compensatory and punitive), and ordered a new trial on these issues.[17]

Morse v. Hardinger (1976) 34 Ill. App. 3d 1020, 341 N.E.2d 172.

Damage to retina—Possible wrong diagnosis—Questionable prescribing practice

A female patient was given Aralen for rheumatoid arthritis by her family physician. Eleven years later she was diagnosed by eye specialists as having chloroquine retinopathy. By that time she had taken 1885 grams of the drug, which was eighteen times the limit set by the Food and Drug Administration. At the trial, the patient's eye condition was described as permanent and progressive.

There was also testimony that the patient suffered from osteoarthritis (rather than rheumatoid arthritis), for which Aralen has never been recommended.

---

[17] See Hoffman v. Sterling Drug, Inc. (M.D. Pa., 1974) 374 F. Supp. 850.

Furthermore, there was evidence that the defendant-physician had prescribed the drug by phone without the patient's record in front of him, that he had never noted the prescriptions in his records, that he could not recall the number of tablets prescribed or their strength, and that he had received complaints from the patient about visual problems as early as four years prior to her condition being discovered by another physician.

A jury verdict for the defendant was reversed on appeal.

Malloy v. Shanahan (1980) 280 Pa. Super. 440, 421 A.2d 803.

Damage to retina—Prescriptions refilled without physician's knowledge

The patient was diagnosed as having rheumatoid arthritis in 1958. Her physician prescribed chloroquine: one bottle of 100 tablets, to be taken at the rate of one tablet per day. The prescription did not call for a refill.

The patient did not receive another prescription until 1965, at which time the physician again prescribed 100 tablets. He issued another prescription for the same amount in 1967.

Unknown to the physician, the patient had found two pharmacies which refilled her prescriptions continuously; thus she took one tablet a day from 1959 until 1971. Because of this prolonged use of the drug, she developed retinopathy.

At trial, judgment was entered in favor of the physician. On appeal, the Superior Court of Pennsylvania affirmed, holding that the proximate cause of the patient's condition was her independent prolonged use of the drug, and that the physician was not liable, regardless of whether he told the patient of any possible side effects associated with its use.

CHLORPHENIRAMINE MALEATE

Alka-Seltzer Plus
Allerest
Brexin
Cerose-DM
Chlorafed
Chlor-Trimeton
Codimal
Comtrex
Contac
Coricidin

CoTylenol
Deconamine
Dristan
Extendryl
Fedahist
Histafed
Histalet
Histaspan
Naldecon
Novafed
Novahistine
Ornade
Quelidrine
Rhinolar
Sinulin
Sinutab
Sudafed
Teldrin
Triaminic
Tussar

Chlorpheniramine maleate is a popular antihistamine used for both therapy and prophylaxis. It is frequently administered by injection for prevention of reactions from penicillin, allergenic extracts, and other drugs. It is also contained in the over-the-counter remedies listed above and in many more.

The incidence of side effects of chlorpheniramine maleate is low. They include: moderate drowsiness, loss of appetite, restlessness, dry mouth, dizziness, weakness, nausea, headache, heartburn, double vision and dermatitis.[18] The drug is contraindicated for newborns and nursing mothers.[19]

Nelson v. Bridge (No. 313413, Superior Court, San Diego County, Cal., March 2, 1973).

Encephalitis claimed to be caused by Chlor-Trimeton—
Action against physician unsuccessful

The patient was a thirteen-year-old girl who claimed to have suffered a reaction to Chlor-Trimeton which eventually resulted in

---

[18] *United States Dispensatory,* 27th ed., p. 302.
[19] *Physicians' Desk Reference,* 43rd ed., p. 2059.

encephalitis, causing speech impairment, impairment in coordination and in her ability to concentrate.

In a negligence action against the physician, the patient and her mother testified that they had told the defendant that the girl had previously suffered a reaction to Chlor-Trimeton. At the trial, the defendant denied this and introduced as evidence the patient's chart which did not show a history of drug reaction or allergy. The defendant also offered medical testimony that it was not possible for a patient to suffer encephalitis as a result of treatment with Chlor-Trimeton.

A jury returned a verdict for the defendant.[20]

Goulet v. Smith Kline & French Laboratories (No. 43 03 94, Superior Court, Orange County, Cal., June 2, 1989).

Child suffers brain damage following mother's use of Ornade while breastfeeding—Manufacturer agrees to structured settlement

The plaintiff took Ornade and several other antihistamines in 1973 while nursing her apparently normal newborn infant. When she was five days old, the child experienced three periods of cyanosis. The plaintiff discontinued taking the medication, and the baby's symptoms disappeared. When she was five-months old, however, the child suffered a series of seizures. The child is now brain-damaged, mentally retarded, and a quadriplegic.

The parents brought suit against the manufacturer of Ornade, alleging failure to warn nursing mothers not to take the medication. According to their attorney, the plaintiffs were ready to show that in 1972 the FDA considered a proposed labeling change that would recommend against taking the drug while breastfeeding. Thus, they claimed, the defendant was on notice of the hazard. (The warning was placed on the label in 1980.)

The parties entered into a structured settlement agreement with a present value of $800,000, designed to pay $310,000 cash and $3,675 monthly for twenty years.[21]

---

[20] AMA *The Citation* 28:53, 1973.

[21] ATLA Products Liability Law Reporter 8:170, 1989.

CHLORPROMAZINE
Thorazine

Chlorpromazine is used as an antiemetic, to overcome motion sickness, as a mild sedative, to reinforce the action of other drugs, and as a tranquilizer.[22] Chlorpromazine HCL tablets are manufactured by several companies under the generic name and Thorazine by Smith Kline & French Laboratories (Philadelphia, Pa.).

One of the adverse reactions listed by the manufacturer of Thorazine is jaundice. The current package insert states:

> Over-all incidence has been low, regardless of indication or dosage. Most investigators conclude it is a sensitivity reaction. Most cases occur between the second and fourth weeks of therapy. The clinical picture resembles infectious hepatitis, with laboratory features of obstructive jaundice, rather than those of parenchymal damage. It is usually promptly reversible on withdrawal of the medication; however, chronic jaundice has been reported.[1]

Also, fatal toxic hepatitis following treatment with chlorpromazine has been reported.[2]

Montalto v. Smith Kline & French Laboratories, Inc. (No. 24212/72, Superior Court, New York County, N.Y., 1973).

Liver damage—Failure to warn alleged—Case settled

A patient undergoing psychiatric treatment was administered three oral doses of Thorazine. She suffered liver damage and brought suit against the manufacturer, claiming that it had inadequately tested the drug and had failed to warn that as little as three doses could cause liver damage. The patient's attorneys charged that tests had shown a substantial number of cases of liver damage in laboratory animals injected with Thorazine and that later clinical tests on humans were hurriedly performed without adequate time for proper evaluation or follow-up.

According to the patient's attorney, the case was settled for $9,000.[3]

---

[22] *Physicians' Desk Reference,* 35th ed., p. 1691.

[1] Id., p. 1692.

[2] Rodin, A. E. and Robertson, C. M., "Fatal Toxic Hepatitis Following Chlorpromazine Therapy: Report of a Case with Autopsy Findings," *Archives of Pathology* 66:170-175, 1958.

[3] ATLA *News Letter* 17:73, 1974.

Kosberg v. Washington Hosp. Center, Inc. (1968) 129 App. D.C. 322, 394 F.2d 947.

Fatality after electroshock therapy, Thorazine and Levophed—Conflicting testimony on cause of death—Directed verdict for psychiatrist reversed

A 22-year-old woman patient being treated by a general practitioner for apparent pregnancy was referred to a psychiatrist because of possible emotional problems. She was given electroshock therapy and chlorpromazine (Thorazine), and when she suddenly turned critical, various other drugs, including levarterenol bitartrate (Levophed), were administered. She died two days later.

Suit was brought against the general practitioner, the psychiatrist and the hospital where she had received treatment. At the trial, an internist testifying for the plaintiff said death was caused by the administration of shock therapy and chlorpromazine to a person in the patient's weakened condition. The pathologist who performed an autopsy on the patient testified that death was due to an infarcted bowel, brought on by a combination of the shock therapy, chlorpromazine and Levophed. It was his opinion that the shock therapy and the chlorpromazine, alone, would not have been fatal.

A directed verdict in favor of the psychiatrist was reversed on appeal. Directed verdicts in favor of the general practitioner and the hospital were upheld.

Brown v. City of New York (1978) 63 App. Div. 2d 635, 405 N.Y.S.2d 253.

Thorazine-induced jaundice misdiagnosed—Patient awarded $50,000

The patient was admitted to the hospital suffering from jaundice. Her condition was diagnosed as an "extra-hepatic obstruction" (a gallstone), and she underwent exploratory surgery. It was then discovered that her condition was caused instead by the drug Thorazine which she had been taking under a prescription issued by a physician at the same hospital.

At trial the plaintiff introduced a copy of *Physicians' Desk Reference* which advises physicians that Thorazine may cause jaundice, and "to withhold exploratory laparotomy until extra-hepatic obstruction is confirmed."

The patient was awarded $482,000 in damages for her "unnecessary surgery," which was reduced to $50,000 on appeal.

Brown v. State (1977) 56 App. Div. 2d 672, 391 N.Y.S.2d 204, affd. 44 N.Y.2d 1006, 408 N.Y.S.2d 502, 380 N.E.2d 328.

Unattended patient dies following administration of Thorazine—Judgment for claimant affirmed

A 35-year-old male patient was admitted to the state hospital because of "withdrawn and aggressive" behavior. After spending the night, he became "violent and assaultive," and was given some 200 mg. of Thorazine, after which he was left unattended for over an hour. He was later found dead.

At the trial, the Court of Claims held that the evidence showed that the patient should have been carefully watched following administration of the drug because of its possible side effects. Further, the evidence showed that Thorazine should be administered while the patient is in a prone position, and that in the present case, the patient was "upright" when the drug was given.

A judgment for the patient's administratrix was affirmed on appeal.

Stone v. Smith, Kline & French Laboratories (C.A.-11 Ala., 1984) 731 F.2d 1575.

Hepatitis—Warning to physician of possible side effect sufficient

The plaintiff developed hepatitis on being treated with Thorazine for "brief reactive psychosis." In her action against the manufacturer, the plaintiff charged that its warning of such a side effect had to be communicated to the ultimate consumer, and not just the prescribing physician, to be effective. This question was certified to the Supreme Court of Alabama which ruled that an adequate warning to the physician is sufficient (Stone v. Smith, Kline & French Laboratories (Ala., 1984) 447 So. 2d 1301). On receiving this answer, the United States Court of Appeals for the Eleventh Circuit affirmed the District Court's summary judgment for the defendant.

Kirk v. Michael Reese Hospital & Medical Center (1987) 117 Ill.2d 507, 111 Ill. Dec. 944, 513 N.E.2d 387.

Cause of action for failure to warn of adverse reactions not extended to passenger injured in accident

The plaintiff was a passenger in an automobile being driven by a person who recently had been given Proloxin (fluphenazine hydrochloride) and Thorazine. The driver then consumed an alcoholic beverage. According to the plaintiff, the combined effects diminished the driver's mental and physical abilities, causing him to lose control of the automobile and hit a tree, injuring the plaintiff.

In a suit against the driver's physicians, the hospital where he had been administered the drugs, and the manufacturers of the drugs, the defendants' motions for dismissal were granted, but the appellate court reversed, holding that all of the defendants owed a legal duty to warn adequately of the adverse effects of the drugs the driver had been given, that this duty implicitly extended to members of the public who may be injured as the proximate cause of a failure to so warn, and that the hospital was open to an action for strict liability. The Supreme Court of Illinois, however, reversed the Appellate Court and affirmed the trial court's dismissals, holding that the manufacturers could not have reasonably foreseen the injury to the plaintiff; that the hospital could not be held strictly liable since the plaintiff was not a patient nor a user of a product supplied by the hospital; and that neither the driver's physicians nor the other defendants owed a duty to the plaintiff, being a third party, to warn him that the driver might be impaired by the medication he was taking.

Tisdale v. Johnson (1986) 177 Ga. App. 487, 339 S.E.2d 764.

Nerve disorder and possible brain damage—Physician not informed by patient of side effects

The plaintiff began taking Thorazine in 1970 for a "nervous breakdown." The defendant physician continued to treat her with various medications, including Thorazine, following her recovery. In 1975 she began to complain of her neck "pulling to one side and jerking involuntarily." She did not mention the problem to the defendant, but in 1978, the plaintiff did tell her family physician about her condition, and he told her it probably was a "natural side effect" of the Thorazine. The plaintiff still did not tell the defendant about her problem, but shortly thereafter she ceased taking all medications that he had prescribed for her.

In 1984, the plaintiff filed suit, claiming that the drug had caused permanent brain damage. The trial court granted a summary judgment for the defendant on a finding that the plaintiff, by failing to inform the defendant of her neck problem, had failed to exercise ordinary care for her own protection. The Court of Appeals of Georgia affirmed.

Frasier v. Department of Health & Human Resources (La. App., 1986) 500 So.2d 858.

Tardive dyskinesia—Allergic reaction—Insufficient evidence of negligence against state psychiatrist

The patient, a sixty-two-year-old woman, had a long history of mental illness. In 1980, suit was filed against the state of Louisiana for alleged negligence associated with the patient's care and treatment at East Louisiana State Hospital during 1977-1980. The patient alleged that she was misdiagnosed as a schizophrenic and negligently subjected to sustained therapy with antipsychotic drugs and other medications against her will and "in disregard of a developing condition of tardive dyskinesia."

The trial court held that the patient failed to prove her case by a preponderance of the evidence and rendered judgment in favor of the defendant. On appeal, the trial court's decision was upheld. The Court of Appeals did, however, find one instance in which the administration of medication to the patient was not "reasonable, prudent and skillful." The record showed that on February 26, 1977, Thorazine was administered to the patient and thereafter she suffered an allergic reaction to the drug. Yet, on October 30, 1978, the patient was again administered Thorazine "in complete disregard to her noted allergy to the drug," which resulted in another reaction. The court held that the physicians in charge of the patient's case failed to use "reasonable care and diligence" in this particular instance and that their treatment fell below the standard of care required of a physician. The court noted, however, that the patient had not filed her cause of action alleging such negligence within the required one-year statutory period.

With regard to the defendants' failure to discontinue treating the patient with antipsychotic drugs when it was discovered that she had developed tardive dyskinesia, the court noted that in so doing the defendants were not necessarily negligent, despite reports in the current medical literature that such drugs could cause the disorder from which the patient suffered. The court cited a task force report of the American Psychiatric Association published in 1979 which stated that the withdrawal of such drugs on evidence of tardive dyskinesia was only a "suggested" practice and by no means was the only "accepted" practice.

Related cases

Cardiorespiratory arrest following administration of Thorazine and other drugs

In Allen v. Kaiser Foundation Hospital (1985) 76 Or. App. 5, 707 P.2d 1289, a jury verdict of no negligence was upheld in an action by the husband of a psychiatric patient who suffered cardiorespiratory arrest and severe brain damage after being given Haldol (haloperidol), Thorazine and Benadryl (diphenhydramine hydrochloride).

Psychologist not qualified to testify on physician's use of Thorazine in treating patient

Where a psychologist had never worked with physicians "who have dealt with the question of when and under what circumstances to prescribe Thorazine to their patients," he was not qualified to give opinions on the standard of care required of a physician in a medical malpractice action brought by a patient who suffered adverse reactions to the drug. Lundgren v. Eustermann (Minn., 1985) 370 N.W.2d 877.

Tardive dyskinesia—Patient's claim barred by statute of limitations

North Carolina's four-year statute of limitations barred the claim of a patient who alleged that she developed tardive dyskinesia as the result of the negligence of the psychiatric unit at Duke University Medical Center in treating her with Haldol and Thorazine without monitoring the side effects of the drugs. Lackey v. Bressler (N.C. App., 1987) 358 S.E.2d 560.

CHLORPROPAMIDE
Diabinese
Glucamide

Chlorpropamide is one of five drugs that, when given orally, can successfully lower the blood glucose level in selected diabetic patients. The others are acetohexamide (Dymelor), tolazamide (Tolinase), tolbutamide (Orinase), and phenformin (DBI, Metrol).[4]

---

[4]*AMA Drug Evaluations*, 2d ed., p. 129.

Pfizer, Inc. (New York, N.Y.) markets chlorpropamide under the name Diabinese, and Lemmon Company (Sellersville, Pa.) produces Glucamide.

In 1970 and 1971, a special study group, the University Group Diabetes Program (UGDP), released reports that the oral hypoglycemics tolbutamide and phenformin may be related to an increase in cardiovascular disease.[5] As a result, several clinics discontinued use of the agents and there was a slight dip in the sale of these drugs. Sales increased the following year, however, and then steadily climbed. This has been explained as the result of "a strong desire of both physicians and patients for a way to treat diabetes that does not involve injections" and "a natural reluctance to accept any possibility that the drugs might be harmful."[6]

Several studies on a small scale were performed subsequent to the UGDP report, three of which confirmed the 1970-71 findings.[7] Then, in February, 1975, a report by the prestigious Biometric Society, from a study sponsored by the National Institutes of Health, contained conclusions that the UGDP trial "raised suspicions that cannot be dismissed on the basis of other evidence presently available," and that "the evidence of harmfulness [is] moderately strong."[8]

---

[5] University Group Diabetes Program, "A Study of the Effects of Hypoglycemic Agents on Vascular Complications in Patients with Adult-Onset Diabetes": "I. Design, Methods and Baseline Results," *Diabetes (Suppl. 2)* 19:747, 1970; "II. Mortality Results," *Diabetes (Suppl. 2)* 19:787, 1970; "III. Clinical Implications of UGDP Results," *Journal of the American Medical Association* 218:1400, 1971; "IV. A Preliminary Report on Phenformin Results," *Journal of the American Medical Association* 217:777, 1971.

[6] Chalmers, T. C., "Settling the UGDP Controversy" (Editorial), *Journal of the American Medical Association* 231:624, 1975. The UGDP studies were criticized by practicing physicians, statisticians, and other investigators, who claimed, inter alia, that patient selection was inappropriate, that mortality in the tolbutamide group was not significantly different from that in the placebo group, and that the use of tolbutamide and phenformin was terminated prematurely, before definitive results were obtained. For a brief summary of the criticisms of the report, see "FDA Ponders Oral Hypoglycemics Label," *Journal of the American Medical Association* 234:263, 1975.

[7] Boyle, D., et al., "Ischemic Heart Disease in Diabetics: A Prospective Study," *Lancet* 1:338, 1972; Hadden, D. R., et al., "Myocardial Infarction in Maturity-Onset Diabetics: A Retrospective Study," *Lancet* 1:335, 1972; Marble, A., "Pharmacology of Antihyperglycemic Drugs," *New York State Journal of Medicine* 72:2174, 1972.

[8] "Report of the Committee for the Assessment of Biometric Aspects of Controlled Trials of Hypoglycemic Agents," *Journal of the American Medical Association* 231:583, 1975.

The 1975 study has initiated a heated controversy within the medical profession. In an editorial in the Journal of the American Medical Association, Thomas C. Chalmers, M.D., of the Mount Sinai Medical Center, stated "... if the drugs do cause premature death from cardiovascular disease, one might estimate that 10,000 to 15,000 such unnecessary deaths occur each year in the United States alone."[9] But in a letter to The Upjohn Company, a leading manufacturer of oral hypoglycemics, AMA Executive Vice-President James H. Sammons, M.D., said:

> Diabetic patients should not be influenced by press reports, and should continue on whatever diabetic management program their own physician has prescribed. Physicians have been fully aware of the UGDP reports for over four years, are informed of the substantial differences between the opinions of diabetes experts and practicing physicians have continued to manage their own patients according to their own wide experience and carefully considered judgments on the published literature.[10]

The Food and Drug Administration proposed a labeling requirement, warning patients that they run an increased risk of cardiovascular death, and advising physicians that diet is the preferred method of reducing blood glucose levels in diabetics and that oral compounds should be used only when diet alone, or a combination of diet and insulin, are unsuccessful.[11]

In 1977 a group of scientists and physicians calling itself "The Committee for the Care of the Diabetic" (CCD) challenged the UGDP report and attempted to obtain the raw data upon which the study was based. They were unsuccessful, but the controversy caused the FDA to launch an independent audit of its own of the data.

While the government was studying this data, critics of the UGDP began charging that the program had suffered from "scandalous mismanagement, clinical neglect, and — at best — questionable record-keeping."[12] Diabetologists who examined the records of

---

[9] Chalmers, T. C., "Settling the UGDP Controversy" (Editorial), *Journal of the American Medical Association* 231:624, 1975.

[10] "AMA Leader Assails Report's Inferences," *American Medical News,* July 14, 1975, p. 7.

[11] "New Warning Proposed for Oral Hypoglycemics," *American Medical News,* July 14, 1975, p. 7; "FDA Ponders Oral Hypoglycemics Label," *Journal of the American Medical Association* 234:263, 1975.

[12] Gregory, D. R., "Oral Hypoglycemic Controversy," *Legal Aspects of Medical Practice,* March, 1979, p. 16.

some of the patients studied by the UGDP suggested there was a "pattern of erroneous reporting."[13] A physician who had participated in the UGDP study came forth and allegedly "blew the whistle" on the program, calling it a "Medical Watergate." He claimed he reviewed 60% of the patient records in the study, and found many discrepancies.[14]

In 1978 the Food and Drug Administration completed its audit of the UGDP study. It found that although certain errors and discrepancies did mar the study, none appeared to invalidate the conclusions on tolbutamide and phenformin.

The audit team, composed of physicians, statisticians, and field investigators from the FDA staff, addressed two main questions: (1) Did the scientific paper published by UGDP accurately reflect the data which the coordinating center received from the physicians participating in the study? and (2) Do any discrepancies found by the auditors affect the conclusions of the study?

The audit examined the cases of all 129 patients who died in the course of the tolbutamide and phenformin portions of the study, plus 21 surviving patients, for a total of 150. Selected data on these patients (e.g., blood pressure, fasting blood sugar, assigned treatment, history of digitalis use, and history of angina) sent in by the clinical investigators on case report forms were compared with the data stored in the computer file and with the summary tables published in the UGDP's reports. The frequency of errors in these data transfer steps was very low. For technical reasons, the determination of error frequency was not feasible for certain items as cholesterol.

Baseline electrocardiograms for all but three of the 150 patients were interpreted on a blinded basis by an outside consultant. There were five cases in which the FDA consultant's and the UGDP's readings differed and the overall classification would have been changed from nonsignificant to significant. In three cases the FDA reading would have changed the classification from significant to nonsignificant, and in the remainder of cases the final classification would not have been affected.

The audit report found that of the 150 patients, 44 changed hypoglycemic medication at some time during the course of the study. Some, but not all, of the switches occurred in accordance with the

---

[13] Id.

[14] Id.

protocol rule, which allowed medically necessary switches from diet alone or from one of the oral agents. Because of the potential for bias as a consequence of this switching, the audit examined in detail its possible effects on the findings of the study.

In analyzing results of the study, the UGDP included each patient in the treatment group to which he or she was originally assigned, whether or not the patient later switched to another group. The audit concluded that the UGDP decision was conservative from a statistical point of view; i.e., this procedure would tend to minimize rather than exaggerate any differences found between treatment groups.

The audit reported that this lends credence to the finding that cardiovascular mortality was increased in the tolbutamide and phenformin groups, because the switching of patients would make it more difficult, not less difficult to detect such a positive finding.

The overall conclusion of the audit was that:

> ... while there are certain errors and discrepancies between the data file on the UGDP study and the published reports, none of these appears of sufficient frequency or magnitude to invalidate the finding that cardiovascular mortality was higher in the groups of patients treated with tolbutamide plus diet and phenformin plus diet compared to the groups treated with placebo or insulin.[15]

Heart failure

In March, 1978, a New Jersey widow brought a wrongful-death action for her husband who died in January, 1975 from heart failure. He had been taking chlorpropamide for diabetes and the plaintiff claimed his death was related to the drug's side effects. The matter was disposed of by summary judgment under the limitations provision of the state's Wrongful Death Act. See Presslaff v. Robins (1979) 168 N.J. Super. 543, 403 A.2d 939.

Cholestatic jaundice

Cholestatic jaundice is another possible side effect of several of the hypoglycemics, including chlorpropamide,[16] which is marketed under the name Diabinese by Pfizer Laboratories (New York, N.Y.). In Trogun v. Fruchtman (1973) 58 Wis. 2d 596, 207 N.W.2d 297, a patient taking Diabinese for borderline diabetes, isoniazid for inac-

---

[15] "Audit Confirms Conclusions of UGDP Study on Oral Diabetes Drugs," *FDA Drug Bulletin,* December/January, 1978-79, p. 34.

[16] *AMA Drug Evaluations,* 2d ed., p. 130.

tive tuberculosis, and clofibrate (Atromid-S), a hypercholesterolemic agent, developed jaundice and noninfectious hepatitis. In a malpractice suit against the treating physician, the propriety of his choice of treatment, particularly with regard to the isoniazid, was a primary issue. The case is summarized herein under ISONIAZID.

Reaction to excessive dose

In Galvan v. Fedder (Tex. Civ. App., 1984) 678 S.W.2d 596, the Court of Appeals of Texas held that a jury's finding of no damages was an arbitrary denial of recovery in an action against a physician who prescribed 1,000 milligrams of Diabinese a day (four times the recommended dose) for a patient who reacted to the medication and later suffered acute inflammatory bowel disease which led to his death.

CHLOR-TRIMETON

See CHLORPHENIRAMINE MALEATE

CHYMORAL

See CHYMOTRYPSIN

CHYMOTRYPSIN

Avazyme
Chymoral
Orenzyme

Chymotrypsin is a proteolytic enzyme crystallized from an extract of the pancreas of an ox.[17] It has been used as a physiologic agent to aid in removal of necrotic tissue, pus, blood and such material from areas of burns, infected wounds, gangrene, empyema, abscesses, and similar conditions. Administration may be topical, oral or intramuscular.[18]

Chymoral was manufactured by Armour Pharmaceutical Company (Scottsdale, Ariz.); Avazyme by Wallace Laboratories (Cranbury, N.J.); and Orenzyme by Merrell Dow Pharmaceuticals (Cincinnati, Ohio), but as of January 1986, only Avazyme is listed as available in *Physicians' Desk Reference*.

---

[17] *United States Dispensatory,* 27th ed., p. 317.
[18] Id., p. 318.

Anaphylactic reactions to intramuscular injections have been reported.[19]

Moore v. Guthrie Hosp., Inc. (C.A.-4 W. Va., 1968) 403 F.2d 366.

Grand mal seizure after alleged intravenous injection—Jury question presented

A hospital patient who suffered a grand mal seizure after a combined injection of penicillin and chymotrypsin brought suit against the hospital and the physician who had prescribed the drugs.

The patient underwent a successful hernia repair on November 30. The hospital records showed that he was to be given penicillin on November 30 through December 4 and chymotrypsin on December 3 and 4. All injections were to be given intramuscularly. Immediately on receiving the December 4 injection, he suffered the seizure.

The basis of the patient's lawsuit was that the injection had been given intravenously instead of intramuscularly. He introduced expert testimony that an intravenous injection of chymotrypsin could bring on an immediate reaction or seizure such as that suffered by the patient, but that an intramuscular injection of the same drug would not cause such a reaction for five or ten minutes. Another expert for the patient testified that an intramuscular injection would not produce a reaction for from one to three hours. It was the opinion of at least one of the patient's experts that the hospital records indicated that the injection was given improperly (intravenously) and that this was the cause of the patient's seizure.

Notwithstanding the above evidence, the District Court granted directed verdicts for both the physician and hospital. The patient appealed and the United States Court of Appeals for the Fourth Circuit reversed as to the hospital, finding that the evidence presented a question of fact for a jury.

The defendants had argued that the patient's seizure could have resulted from an anaphylactic reaction to the penicillin injected intramuscularly. The Court of Appeals said this argument should

---

[19] Newman, S. and Wallace, J. F., "Hypersensitivity and Connective Tissue Disorders," in *Diseases of Medical Progress: A Study of Iatrogenic Disease,* 3rd ed., R. H. Moser, editor (Springfield, Ill.: Charles C Thomas, Publisher, 1969), p. 419 (citing Austen, K. F., "Systemic Anaphylaxis in Man," *Journal of the American Medical Association* 192:108, 1965; Watson, P. G., "Anaphylactic Reaction Caused by Intramuscular Injection of Lyophilized Alpha-Chymotrypsin," *British Journal of Ophthalmology* 48:35, 1964).

not foreclose the jury from consideration of the patient's case for two reasons:

> First, Moore's doctor testified that an anaphylactic reaction could not result from one injection of penicillin. It could result from a second injection, but in his opinion an interval of about ten days between the first injection and a following injection was required to allow the production of antibodies leading to a reaction. He added that a reaction had been reported after an interval of five or six days. Moore's seizure occurred only four days after his initial injection. Secondly, the anaphylactic reaction from successive intramuscular injections would not be instantaneous. If the penicillin were given intramuscularly, at least five or ten minutes, and possibly as long as one to three hours, would be required for absorption and reaction. On the basis of this testimony, a reasonable inference can be drawn that Moore's seizure was not caused by successive intramuscular injections of penicillin.

CIMETIDINE HYDROCHLORIDE
Tagamet

Cimetidine hydrochloride is a histamine H receptor antagonist which inhibits gastric acid secretion and therefore is used to treat ulcer patients. Menley and James Laboratories, a subsidiary of Smith, Kline and French (Philadelphia, Pa.), manufactures the drug under the brand name Tagamet.

The manufacturer reports no contraindications to the drug, except for certain precautions in the case of pregnant, nursing or pediatric patients. There are possible adverse reactions, but most are reversible. The manufacturer does state that symptomatic response to Tagamet therapy "does not preclude the presence of gastric malignancy," and that there have been "rare reports of transient healing of gastric ulcers despite subsequently documented malignancy."[20]

Chaney v. Smithkline Beckman Corp. (C.A.-8 Ark., 1985) 764 F.2d 527.

Stomach cancer—Insufficient evidence that Tagamet was responsible

The plaintiff's husband took Tagamet for stomach ulcers from July, 1979 to December, 1980. In October 1981 he died from stom-

---

[20]*Physicians' Desk Reference,* 40th ed., pp. 1725-26.

ach cancer. The plaintiff brought suit against the manufacturer, alleging that it failed to warn physicians that Tagamet (1) caused cancer, or (2) masked the symptoms of cancer, thereby precluding a timely diagnosis.

The trial court refused to let the jury consider whether Tagamet caused the patient's cancer. It did allow it to decide the issue of whether the drug masked the cancer symptoms, and a verdict was returned for the manufacturer.

The Court of Appeals upheld the lower court's decision to withhold the causation issue from the jury, citing testimony by the plaintiff's expert witness that the probability that the Tagamet was responsible for the cancer was "probably greater than 20 percent and probably less than 80 percent." This evidence, said the Court of Appeals, constituted a mere "possibility" of causation and was insufficient to take the case to the jury.

The Court affirmed the judgment without commenting on the verdict regarding the "masking of symptoms" issue.

Ashman v. SK & F Lab Co. (N.D. Ill., 1988) 702 F. Supp. 1401.

Alleged mental confusion from interaction between drugs—Action based on inadequate warning unsuccessful

In 1984, the patient was given a prescription by his physician for Tagamet, apparently for acid stomach. The following year, the physician also prescribed Ativan (lorazipam), a sleeping pill. The patient took both drugs without any problems.

In April 1986, while the patient was still taking Tagamet, the physician changed his sleeping pill to Halcion (triazolam). Before writing the prescription, the physician consulted the package insert for Halcion and the *Physicians' Desk Reference*, both of which contained a statement that there was a potential for interaction between the two drugs, in that the Tagamet could cause a delay in the elimination from the body of Halcion. There was no such warning on the Tagamet package insert or in *PDR* under Tagamet (neither of which the physician consulted). Despite the Halcion statement, the physician went ahead and wrote the prescription.

One evening about three weeks later, the patient took a Tagamet, and about four hours later, took a Halcion. The next morning, he also took some Ativan pills which he had left over from his earlier prescription. Apparently he took too many, became unconscious, and was rushed to the hospital.

At the hospital, the patient's physician suspected a stroke and ordered a lumbar puncture to confirm his diagnosis. As a result of negligence in the performance of the puncture, the patient became partially paralyzed. In addition to a negligence action against the physician, which was settled out of court, the patient sued the manufacturer of Tagamet, claiming that the company inadequately warned of the interactive propensities of Tagamet and Halcion, and that this interaction of the drugs caused him to become confused and led to his accidental overdose of Ativan, which in turn led to the negligent lumbar puncture and his paralysis.

Prior to trial, the defendant drug manufacturer moved for summary judgment on the grounds that it was relieved from any liability under the learned intermediary doctrine, because the physician, the learned intermediary, had been made aware (by the Halcion statement) of the possible interaction between the two drugs. Also, the defendant claimed that the negligence involved in the patient's lumbar puncture which led to his paralysis could not have been foreseen by the defendant, and was thus too remote to establish liability. The court agreed, holding that either ground was a sufficient basis for granting the motion.

CINONIDE

See TRIAMCINOLONE ACETONIDE

CLEOCIN HYDROCHLORIDE

See CLINDAMYCIN HYDROCHLORIDE

CLINDAMYCIN HYDROCHLORIDE

Cleocin Hydrochloride

Clindamycin hydrochloride is a semi-synthetic antibiotic similar to lincomycin, its parent compound. Both are manufactured by The Upjohn Company (Kalamazoo, Mich.); clindamycin under the name Cleocin Hydrochloride.

Clindamycin therapy has been found to be associated with severe colitis, sometimes fatal. As a result, the manufacturer warns that the drug "should be reserved for serious infections where less toxic antimicrobial agents are inappropriate." The colitis is usually characterized by severe, persistent diarrhea and severe abdominal cramps, possibly accompanied by the passage of blood and mucus ("pseudomembranous colitis").[1]

Agents used to control diarrhea, such as opiates and diphenoxylate with atropine (Lomotil) may prolong or worsen the condition, and the manufacturer warns against their use.[2]

Wolfgruber v. Upjohn Co. (1979) 72 App. Div. 2d 59, 423 N.Y.S.2d 95, affd. (1980) 52 N.Y.2d 768, 436 N.Y.S.2d 614, 417 N.E.2d 1002.

Physician suffers diarrhea and colitis following self-treatment—Manufacturer's warning sufficient—Summary judgment granted

A physician used Cleocin Hydrochloride on himself for an infection. He eventually developed diarrhea and colitis and brought suit against the manufacturer of the drug.

The plaintiff conceded that he knew about the drug's possible side effects, so he based his action on strict liability and breach of warranty of fitness. The defendant moved for a summary judgment, but it was dismissed by the trial court. On appeal, the Appellate Division reversed, holding that the plaintiff had no basis for his action in view of the warning given by the manufacturer which, according to the court, "was adequate by any standard." Further, said the court, "the plaintiff as a doctor knew the risks of taking this particular drug whose side effects were those specifically warned against as fully as defendant was able."

Timm v. Upjohn Co. (C.A.-5 La., 1980) 624 F.2d 536.

Patient and husband awarded $310,000 following patient's pseudomembranous colitis and colectomy—Warning to physician found insufficient

The plaintiff in this suit was given a prescription for Cleocin Hydrochloride as treatment for sinusitis. She used the drug as directed, and shortly after discontinuing its use, she developed severe pseudomembranous colitis, resulting in the removal of her colon. In a lawsuit against the manufacturer, the defendant argued that its warning to the plaintiff's physician about the drug's possible side effects was adequate, and that he was aware of the dangers. The physician's testimony on this issue, however, was equivocal, and

---

[1] *Physicians' Desk Reference* 35th ed., p. 1805.

[2] Id.

the plaintiff was awarded $195,000, with her husband receiving an additional $115,000. Both judgments were upheld.

Werner v. Upjohn Co. (C.A.-4 Md., 1980) 628 F.2d 848.

Pseudomembranous colitis—$400,000 judgment vacated on erroneous admission of manufacturer's later warning

A patient who developed diarrhea and pseudomembranous colitis in December, 1974, after taking Cleocin Hydrochloride, sued his physician and the manufacturer. There was conflicting testimony regarding whether or not the physician, after consulting the 1973 package insert, warned the plaintiff that he might experience some nausea, vomiting or diarrhea on taking the drug. He did not consult the most recent drug information, issued in the summer of 1974.

A jury found that the physician, an ophthalmologist, was negligent in prescribing the drug and that this proximately caused or contributed to the plaintiff's injury, which included the removal of a large part of his colon. The jury also found that the manufacturer was negligent in marketing Cleocin Hydrochloride, that it failed to warn properly of the dangerous side effects, and that it was guilty of breach of warranty. The plaintiff was awarded $400,000.

At trial, evidence was introduced that prior to 1974, the incidence of colitis in Cleocin Hydrochloride users was thought to be quite low, but in late 1973 a study was published which found signs of the disease in 10% of a test group who took the drug. As a result of this study and other information gathered on the drug, a new warning was issued on the package inserts in the summer of 1974. In addition, "Dear Doctor" letters were sent out to every physician in the nation notifying them of the newly discovered information. In March, 1975, the warning was expanded even further.

On the introduction of this evidence (over the defendants' objections), the trial judge instructed the jury that it was to consider the manufacturer's 1975 warning only "on the issue of feasibility" (obviously referring to Federal Rule of Evidence 407, which excludes subsequent remedial measures to prove negligence, but permits such to prove "the feasibility of such measures" if feasibility is controverted by the defendant). On appeal, the reviewing court held the admission of this evidence was error, despite the trial judge's instruction.

The judgment was vacated and the cause remanded.

Bluestein v. Upjohn Co. (1981) 102 Ill. App. 3d 672, 58 Ill. Dec. 548, 430 N.E.2d 580.

Inflammatory bowel disease—Jury finds Cleocin not proximate cause

The plaintiff developed inflammatory bowel disease after being treated with Cleocin for six months for acne. In a suit against the manufacturer for failure to warn adequately of the risk, the plaintiff offered one expert witness who testified that the condition was caused by the drug, and that the manufacturer "fell below the requisite standard of care" by marketing the product without a warning that one of its adverse reactions could be severe inflammatory bowel disease.

The defendant's experts testified that there were three separate "inflammatory bowel diseases," "ulcerative colitis," "Crohn's disease" and an "antibiotic-associated colitis," and that the plaintiff's condition was Crohn's disease, which was unrelated to the effects of Cleocin. The plaintiff's expert, however, testified that in recent years the medical profession has tended to categorize all three conditions as "inflammatory bowel disease" because "a physician cannot distinguish among them in many cases."

The jury returned a general verdict for the plaintiff, but answered "no" to a special interrogatory that asked if Cleocin was the "proximate cause" of the plaintiff's injuries. The trial court entered judgment for the defendant and the Appellate Court affirmed.

Muilenberg v. The Upjohn Co. (1988) 169 Mich. App. 636, 426 N.W.2d 767.

Colitis—Insufficient warning by manufacturer—$750,000 verdict for plaintiff reversed for procedural errors—Verdict for defendant on retrial affirmed

The patient was given Cleocin for acne. He developed severe colitis and had to undergo a colectomy and ileostomy. In his suit against the manufacturer for failure to warn of this side effect, the jury returned a verdict for the patient in the amount of $750,000. But the Court of Appeals of Michigan reversed, finding that the trial judge's curative instruction failed to negate the prejudicial effect of the plaintiff's counsels' reference in his argument to the court's denial of the defendant's motion for directed verdict (320 N.W.2d 767). The Court of Appeal also held that the trial judge erred in admitting a compilation of the manufacturer's drug experience reports.

The Court of Appeals, however, did agree with the patient that his physician was not forewarned by the defendant of the dangers of the side effect of colitis, and that there was sufficient evidence to permit the jury to find that if he had been adequately warned the patient's injury could have been avoided.

On retrial of the case in January 1986, a jury returned a verdict of no cause of action. The Court of Appeals affirmed.

Stavro v. Upjohn (No. 77-1761, U.S. District Court, E.D. Mich., Mar. 17, 1982).

Protracted colitis requiring colectomy and ileostomy—Manufacturer accused of failing to warn—$500,000 settlement

The plaintiff, a Canadian citizen, was a thirty-five-year-old bookkeeper who developed protracted colitis after taking clindamycin over a prolonged period. In his lawsuit against the manufacturer, the plaintiff, who underwent a total colectomy and a permanent ileostomy, accused the defendant of failing to warn its Canadian subsidiary of the high rate of colitis and deaths associated with use of the drug, reports of which began as early as 1965. The plaintiff claimed that while the package insert for the product marketed in the United States carried a "weak warning" of the risk of colitis, its Canadian counterpart made no mention of colitis at all. (In Canada, clindamycin is marketed under the trade name Dalacin-C.) The parties reached a $500,000 settlement.[3]

Mauldin v. Upjohn Co. (C.A.-5 La., 1983) 697 F.2d 644.

Ulcerative colitis following treatment with Cleocin and Lincocin—$570,000 verdict against manufacturer for inadequate warning affirmed

The plaintiff was given both Lincocin and Cleocin to guard against infection following a severe hand injury. He soon experienced diarrhea and eventually developed ulcerative colitis, requiring extensive surgery and hospital confinement. He filed suit against the Upjohn Company, manufacturer of both drugs, for failure to warn adequately of the side effects he experienced. The jury awarded him $570,000.

On appeal the defendant argued that the evidence on causation was strictly circumstantial, and that the plaintiff's physician testi-

---

[3]ATLA *Law Reporter* 25:322, 1982.

fied that he would have prescribed the same two medications despite a stronger warning. In affirming the award, the Court of Appeal pointed out that proof of causation can be established by circumstantial evidence, and that the plaintiff's physician also testified that if he had known of the possible severity of the side effects, he would have followed a "different regimen" in using the drugs.

Sanderson v. Upjohn Co. (D. Mass., 1984) 578 F. Supp. 338.

Colitis—Adequacy of warning questioned—Plaintiff also took ampicillin—Manufacturer denied summary judgment

The plaintiff developed colitis after taking Cleocin Hydrochloride. In her suit against the manufacturer for failure to warn adequately of the risk, the defendant moved for summary judgment on two grounds: (1) the plaintiff also took ampicillin which could have caused her condition, and (2) the defendant had warned the medical profession of the risk of "severe and persistent diarrhea, abdominal pain and nausea," exactly the side effect of which the plaintiff complained.

The District Court denied the defendant's motion. As to the ampicillin, the court pointed to an affidavit of the plaintiff's dermatologist that she had taken ampicillin before without an adverse reaction. As to the warning, the court reminded the defendant that the question was one of fact which is usually determined by a jury.

Related cases

Gastrointestinal problems—Action against pharmacy barred by medical malpractice statute of limitations

In Faser v. Sears, Roebuck & Co. (C.A.-11 Ga., 1982) 674 F.2d 856, a pharmacy which had filled prescriptions for a patient who suffered severe gastrointestinal problems after taking Cleocin was entitled to a summary judgment under Georgia's statute of limitations for medical malpractice actions since "medical malpractice" as defined by statute (Ga. Code Ann. § 3-1101(a)(3)), includes a "medical ... prescription ... rendered by a person authorized by law to perform such service."

Pharmacy not liable for failing to warn patient of side effects—No breach of warranty

A patient who suffered side effects after taking Cleocin had no case against the pharmacy where she purchased the drug for failing to warn her of such side effects or for breach of warranty. Javitz v. Slatus (1983) 93 App. Div. 2d 830, 461 N.Y.S.2d 44.

CLINORIL
See SULINDAC

CLOMID
See CLOMIPHENE CITRATE

CLOMIPHENE CITRATE
Clomid
Serophene

Clomiphene citrate is a "fertility agent" used to induce ovulation and promote fertility in anovulatory women who have potentially functional pituitary-hypothalamic and ovarian systems. It is manufactured by Merrell Dow Pharmaceuticals (Cincinnati, Ohio) under the name Clomid, and by Serono Laboratories, Inc. (Randolph, Mass.) under the name Serophene. It is a potent drug that should be used only in carefully selected patients who can be closely supervised.[4]

In tests with animals, it has shown teratogenic effects, and therefore may adversely affect the human fetus. For this reason, it is not to be given during pregnancy, and before it is administered the patient should be carefully observed to determine if ovulation has occurred.[5]

Breimhorst v. Richardson-Merrell, Inc. (No. SWC 19125, Superior Court, Los Angeles County, Cal., April 15, 1974).

Birth defects—$65,000 settlement with physician—$570,000 verdict against manufacturer

A woman patient who complained of being unable to become pregnant was given Clomid. After taking the drug twice, she conceived. The pregnancy appeared normal, but the baby was born with facial palsy, impaired and deformed eyes, knock-knees, club feet, and no hands. A lawsuit was filed against the manufacturer and the physician who prescribed the drug.

---

[4] *United States Dispensatory,* 27th ed., p. 327.
[5] Id., p. 328.

Prior to trial, the physician settled with the plaintiffs for $65,000. The case against the manufacturer went to trial with the defendant contending that the infant's condition could have resulted merely by chance, since such birth defects are found in the general population. Much conflicting evidence was introduced on whether the drug could have caused the problem, with eight medical experts testifying for the plaintiffs and five for the defendant. A jury verdict was returned for the plaintiffs: $530,000 to the child and $40,000 to the mother.[6]

CODIMAL
See CHLORPHENIRAMINE MALEATE

COMOXOL
See TRIMETHOPRIM and SULFAMETHOXAZOLE

COMPAZINE
See PROCHLORPERAZINE

COMTREX
See CHLORPHENIRAMINE MALEATE

CONJUGATED ESTROGENS
See ESTROGENS (CONJUGATED)

CONRAY-60/400
See SODIUM IOTHALAMATE

CONTAC
See CHLORPHENIRAMINE MALEATE; PSEUDOEPHEDRINE HYDROCHLORIDE and CHLORPHENIRAMINE MALEATE

COPE
See ASPIRIN

---

[6] AMA *The Citation* 29:114, 1974; ATLA *News Letter* 17:301, 1974.

CORICIDIN

See ASPIRIN; CHLORPHENIRAMINE MALEATE

CORTISONE ACETATE

See CORTISONE

CORTICOTROPIN

Acthar
Cortophin
H.P. Acthar Gel

Corticotropin (ACTH) is a hormone prepared from animal pituitaries. Acthar and H.P. Acthar Gel are manufactured by Armour Pharmaceutical Company (Scottsdale, Ariz.), and Cortophin by Organon, Inc. (West Orange, N.J.).

Deaths from gas gangrene

In Croft v. York (Fla. App., 1971) 244 So. 2d 161, a patient died from gas gangrene after receiving separate injections of H.P. Acthar Gel and Adrenalin-in-oil (epinephrine). Suit was filed against the attending physician, the hospital, and Parke-Davis, the manufacturer of Adrenalin-in-oil. Armour Pharmaceutical Company was not named as a defendant. Parke-Davis obtained a summary judgment, but was reversed on appeal, the court holding that there were genuine issues of material facts, including the question of which, if either, of the drugs contained the contaminating bacteria. The case is summarized herein under EPINEPHRINE.

Cataracts and osteoporosis

In Hill v. Squibb & Sons, E. R. (Mont., 1979) 592 P.2d 1383, a patient took ACTH and several other drugs over a period of years, and eventually developed cataracts and osteoporosis. The case is summarized herein under TRIAMCINOLONE ACETONIDE.

CORTISONE

Cortisone Acetate
Cortone Acetate

Cortisone is an adrenal corticosteroid (glucocorticoid) secreted by the adrenal cortex. It is also produced synthetically,[7] by The Upjohn Company (Kalamazoo, Mich.) and Purepac Pharmaceutical Com-

---

[7] *United States Dispensatory,* 27th ed., p. 343.

pany (Elizabeth, N.J.) in tablet and injection form under the name Cortisone Acetate. Merck, Sharp & Dohme (West Point, Pa.) produces Cortone Acetate. Cortisone primarily affects protein, fat, and carbohydrate metabolism, and is used in the treatment of a variety of conditions, including allergies (particularly asthma), certain infections and arthritis.[8]

The adverse reactions of cortisone and other corticosteroids are many; they include, but are not limited to, muscle weakness, peptic ulcer, pancreatitis, and bone deterioration (osteoporosis).[9] There also may be withdrawal manifestations.[10]

With regard to adrenal corticosteroids and osteoporosis (increased porosity and softening of bone), Newman states:

> The diagnosis is frequently made only after pathological fractures have occurred. When periodic roentgenograms are obtained routinely, osteoporosis has been recognized in 10 per cent of asthmatics receiving corticosteroids, in 16 per cent of arthritics on small doses and 50 per cent on large doses of corticosteroids. Although fractures may occur within a few months, they usually become manifest only after several years of corticosteroid therapy. Compression fractures of the vertebral bodies are most common, but the femoral neck, ribs or pelvis are frequently involved.[11]

Mueller v. Mueller (1974) 88 S.D. 446, 221 N.W.2d 39.

Patient kept on cortisone for seven years—Alleged addiction and bone deterioration—Jury verdict for one dollar set aside

This malpractice case arose out of the effects of prolonged treatment with cortisone. In her complaint, the patient charged that the defendant-physician had subjected her to "an intense administration of steroids over an extended period of years [seven] without using the reasonable skill and care required in the use of this

---

[8] For a detailed list of therapeutic uses, see *United States Dispensatory,* 27th ed., pp. 348-352; for indications, warnings, precautions, adverse reactions and dosage and administration pertaining to cortisone and other oral glucocorticoids (as required by the Food and Drug Administration after evaluation of reports issued by the National Academy of Sciences — National Research Council), see *United States Dispensatory,* 27th ed., pp. 33-36.

[9] Id., p. 35.

[10] Id., p. 352.

[11] Newman, S., "Hormone-Induced Diseases," in *Diseases of Medical Progress: A Study of Iatrogenic Disease,* 3rd ed., R. H. Moser, editor (Springfield, Ill.: Charles C Thomas, Publisher, 1969), p. 361.

drug." The patient claimed that she became addicted to the drug, and that its use resulted in a "deterioration of her bone structure" which led to the collapse of her right hip.

At the trial, medical witnesses appearing for the patient testified that the defendant had not exercised the required standard of skill in administering the drug. Evidence was introduced also, in the form of the manufacturer's literature which accompanied the drug, showing that the defendant had deviated from the manufacturer's recommendations. There was also evidence, although conflicting, that the defendant had not warned the patient sufficiently as to the possible risks involved in prolonged cortisone therapy.

The jury returned a verdict for the patient, but for only $1.00 in damages. On motion of the patient's attorneys, the trial judge granted a new trial. The defendant's attorney appealed the order, claiming that the $1.00 verdict was tantamount to a verdict for the defendant, and alleged numerous other errors, including the admission of the drug manufacturer's product literature. The Supreme Court of South Dakota affirmed the new trial order.

Commenting on the admissibility of the drug literature, the court acknowledged the long established general rule that medical books or treatises are not admissible to prove the truth of statements contained therein, but questioned the propriety of including drug literature under this principle. Said the court:

> New drugs are coming on the market daily; before they are allowed on the market they are put to stringent tests as to their usefulness, and as to possible side effects. Drug manufacturers must make the tests and put these drugs on the market only after they are considered safe when used according to the drug manufacturers' recommendations. The drug manufacturers are being held accountable in courts of law for injuries caused by these drugs only when these recommendations are followed. The busy doctor has no alternative but to prescribe these drugs according to the recommendations of the drug manufacturers. No one would expect him to stop his practice and conduct tests and experiments so that he could prescribe the drug solely from his own independent findings on its usefulness and possible side effects. Every doctor who testified in this trial admitted to the use of the drug manufacturers' recommendations as a guide in prescribing drugs. Under these circumstances, it is not surprising that various state jurisdictions are now deviating from the previous rule....
>
> This all leads us to the conclusion that these manufacturers' recommendations on the use of drugs are not only admissible but essential in determining the possible lack of care of a doctor where the issue involved is injury from the administration of a

drug. We see no reason for the courts to hesitate to use a standard so widely and favorably used in the medical profession.

Dupuy v. Tilley (La. App., 1979) 380 So. 2d 634.

Cortisone-induced Cushing's Syndrome—Verdict for physicians on conflicting medical testimony

The plaintiff in this case had been treated for acne since he was a teenager. The medication that seemed to have the most effect was cortisone. Since the drug can have serious side effects, the physicians who treated him claim they told the plaintiff of this fact and informed him of the signs to watch for.

Despite this warning, and while he was still under treatment, the plaintiff developed Cushing's Syndrome, an adrenal gland condition that can be caused by excessive cortisone in the body.

In a lawsuit against the physicians, both dermatologists, the expert witnesses differed as to whether or not cortisone should be prescribed in such cases, and when prescribed, as to how much should be used and how frequently it should be given. There was also evidence that on occasion the plaintiff may have taken more cortisone than his doctors recommended.

A jury returned a verdict for the defendants and the Court of Appeals affirmed.

Buckner v. Allergan Pharmaceuticals, Inc. (Fla. App., 1981) 400 So. 2d 820.

Aseptic necrosis of femoral heads—No duty on part of manufacturer to warn patients

A patient was given corticosteroids for eye disorders and was not warned of adverse reactions. Aseptic necrosis began in her femoral heads, which was one of the known side effects.

In a suit against six manufacturers of steroid drugs, the patient alleged that the companies knew of the adverse reactions and gave adequate warnings to the medical profession, but that they were aware that the medical profession was not adequately relaying those warnings to patients. A trial court dismissed the complaint for failure to state a cause of action.

Affirming the decision, the District Court of Appeals of Florida followed the accepted rule that a manufacturer of prescription drugs has no duty to warn the patient of harmful side effects. The manufacturer's duty to warn is satisfied by warning the physician whose duty it is to inform the patient.

CORTISPORIN
See HYDROCORTISONE; NEOMYCIN SULFATE

CORTONE ACETATE
See CORTISONE

CORTOPHIN
See CORTICOTROPIN

COTRIM
See TRIMETHOPRIM and SULFAMETHOXAZOLE

COTYLENOL
See CHLORPHENIRAMINE MALEATE; PSEUDOEPHEDRINE HYDROCHLORIDE and CHLORPHENIRAMINE MALEATE

COUMADIN
See SODIUM WARFARIN

C-QUENS
See CHLORMADINONE ACETATE MESTRANOL

CROTALINE ANTIVENIN
See ANTIVENIN

CRYSTICILLIN
See PENICILLIN

CRYSTODIGIN
See DIGITOXIN

CUPRIMINE
See PENICILLAMINE

CURRETAB
See MEDROXYPROGESTERONE ACETATE

CYANTIN
See NITROFURANTOIN

CYCLOMETHYCAINE
Surfacaine

Cyclomethycaine is a topical anesthetic manufactured under the name Surfacaine by Eli Lilly and Company (Indianapolis, Ind.), and is used on the skin and the mucosa of the rectum, vagina, urethra, and urinary bladder in the treatment of dermatologic conditions and burns.[12]

An untoward effect of the drug is a transitory stinging or burning before the onset of the anesthetic effect, and there has been at least one report of an anaphylactoid reaction following the use of a suppository in a patient with a history of multiple allergies.[13] Under "Precautions" in the product literature, the manufacturer states "Avoid application to extensive skin areas. If prolonged or indefinite use of Surfacaine is undertaken, observe periodically to detect possible development of allergic reaction. Increase in redness, itching, papules, or vesicles suggests possible allergy. Discontinue use if irritation or allergy develops."[14]

Stokes v. Dailey (N.D., 1959) 97 N.W.2d 676.

Reaction to Surfacaine—Physician not negligent for failing to give patch test

The patient, a lawyer, consulted his physician in April of 1952, complaining of a skin irritation which had plagued him for years. The physician prescribed Histadyl with Surfacaine in the form of an ointment. The patient used the prescription only once: the first application caused a severe burning sensation, and he returned to a home remedy consisting of rubbing alcohol, Pragmatar (a coal-tar and sulfur over-the-counter drug) and a cologne.

About eighteen months later, in November, 1953, the patient ran out of his home remedy and again tried the physician's prescription.

[12] *Physicians' Desk Reference,* 35th ed., p. 1094.

[13] *United States Dispensatory,* 27th ed., pp. 363-64.

[14] *Physicians' Desk Reference,* 35th ed., p. 1094.

Again it caused a burning sensation, but he continued to use it until successive applications appeared to cause the irritation to spread. Less than a month later, on December 14, the patient went to the physician's office for a physical check-up. He asked the physician to look at the irritation, and the physician did so, saying "I will give you a prescription." The patient claimed he said "Don't give me the same stuff you gave me before because that drives my skin wild." The physician denied at the trial the patient said this.

In any event, the physician wrote out another prescription and the patient had it filled. When he applied it, he said the burning returned. Nevertheless, he applied it again eight hours later, and again it caused the condition to spread. The irritation gradually became worse, and after seeing him again, the physician gave the patient "two injections." The afternoon of the same day, the patient fainted at his home. He was hospitalized and eventually was placed under the care of a dermatologist.

At the trial, the dermatologist testified that the aggravation of the patient's skin condition was caused by contact with the Surfacaine, but he added that the physician's prescribing of the ointment without first giving the patient a "patch test" was not in violation of good medical practice.

The jury returned a verdict for the physician, and the trial court entered judgment accordingly. The patient's attorney appealed, contending there was insufficient evidence to justify the verdict, in that the physician should have given him a patch test to determine whether he was allergic to the Surfacaine. This contention was rejected by the Supreme Court of North Dakota, which affirmed the judgment of the trial court.

The Supreme Court said:

> Under the circumstances, we do not believe the defendant was obligated to give a patch test since he was asked only to look at the plaintiff's affliction.... Surely, where the plaintiff's own medical expert testified that the giving of the prescription without first giving a patch test is in conformity with the rules of the medical profession, the plaintiff cannot now complain because the jury failed to find the defendant guilty of negligence for failure to give him a patch test under the circumstances under which the defendant examined the plaintiff in this case.

CYCLOSERINE
Seromycin

This drug is a broad-spectrum antibiotic used in the treatment of active pulmonary and extrapulmonary tuberculosis, usually after failure of the more common anti-tuberculosis drugs such as streptomycin, isoniazid and ethambutol. The drug is also effective in the treatment of acute urinary tract infections caused by susceptible strains of gram-positive and gram-negative bacteria. It is manufactured by Eli Lilly and Company (Indianapolis, Ind.) under the name Seromycin.

As with most antibiotics, there are numerous possible side effects, most of which involve the nervous system, or are manifestations of hypersensitivity. Among these side effects are convulsions, tremor, vertigo, confusion with loss of memory, and major and minor (localized) clonic seizures.[15]

Moncrief v. Fuqua (Tenn. App., 1979) 610 S.W.2d 720.

Possible "drug-induced encephalitis"—Action dismissed for want of expert medical testimony

The plaintiff was treated with Seromycin for prostatitis in 1967. After taking the first dose he allegedly suffered adverse effects, later claimed to be "drug-induced encephalitis." He was admitted to the hospital for "a severe illness, including mental confusion," which became progressively worse, resulting eventually in confinement to a Veterans' Administration Hospital.

Suit was brought against both the physician and the manufacturer. The plaintiff alleged that the physician prescribed the drug "without first determining whether the plaintiff was susceptible to its toxic effects," and the manufacturer was charged with "wrongfully manufacturing and selling" the drug. After numerous delays the action was dismissed when the plaintiff failed to come up with expert medical testimony in opposition to the defendants' motion for summary judgment. The dismissal was affirmed on appeal.

---

[15] *Physicians' Desk Reference,* 35th ed., p. 1093.

CYSTOKON

See SODIUM ACETRIZOATE

D

DALMANE

See FLURAZEPAM HYDROCHLORIDE

DAPSONE

Avlosulfon

Dapsone is an antibacterial found satisfactory in the treatment of leprosy and a skin disorder called dermatitis herpetiformis. Jacobus Pharmaceutical Company (Princeton, N.J.) manufactures Dapsone USP, and Ayerst Laboratories (New York, N.Y.) also has marketed the drug under the name Avlosulfon.

The drug is potent and can cause serious side effects. The manufacturer warns that any patient taking the drug should be advised to report to the physician any signs of sore throat, fever, pallor, purpura (discoloration of skin or mucous membrane), or jaundice. Deaths associated with the administration of dapsone have been reported from agranulocytosis, aplastic anemia and other blood dyscrasias. The drug has also been found to cause cancer in rats and mice.[16]

Burgon v. Kaiser Foundation Hospitals (1979) 93 Cal. App. 3d 813, 155 Cal. Rptr. 763.

Peripheral neuropathy—Action not filed within statutory period

In August of 1968 the plaintiff developed a skin condition and sought treatment at the defendant-hospital. He was treated with several drugs and then put on Avlosulfon "late in 1968" along with Diasone (sodium sulfoxone), a related antibacterial of the sulfone class. The plaintiff took the two drugs until December, 1970, at which time the Diasone was discontinued.

In May or June of 1971, the plaintiff noticed a "weakness" developing in his right hand. He was seen at the Kaiser Hospital walk-in clinic where a physician on duty commented on "the bluish or purplish color" of the plaintiff's lips. He returned three times over the

---

[16] Id., p. 951.

next eighteen months for tests, but the cause of the weakness was not determined.

In November, 1972 the plaintiff collapsed at work and was taken to Kaiser. By then the muscles in his legs, hands and feet "were wasting away and he could barely walk or stand." After several more tests he was sent home.

A month later he was called by one of the physicians on his case and told that the pills (Avlosulfon) were the cause of his condition, now diagnosed as "peripheral neuropathy," and that he was to change to another antibacterial. In about six months he began to regain partial use of his muscles.

The plaintiff did not file suit until January, 1974, claiming in his complaint that he did not discover or have reason to discover the negligence of the defendants until April, 1973, when he consulted other doctors. The defendants moved to dismiss the action under California's one-year statute of limitations, and the trial judge entered judgment in their favor. On appeal, the judgment was affirmed, the Court of Appeal holding that the trial judge was correct in concluding that when the plaintiff was told that Avlosulfon was the cause of his problem, he was constructively on notice that the drug was either negligently prescribed or administered, or that his condition was negligently diagnosed, and at that time the statute of limitations commenced.

DARVON; DARVON COMPOUND; DARVON COMPOUND-65

See PROPOXYPHENE HYDROCHLORIDE

DECADRON

See DEXAMETHASONE

DECASPRAY

See DEXAMETHASONE

DECLOMYCIN

See DEMECLOCYCLINE HYDROCHLORIDE

DECONAMINE
See CHLORPHENIRAMINE MALEATE

DELALUTIN
See HYDROXYPROGESTERONE CAPROATE

DELTASONE
See PREDNISONE

DEMECLOCYCLINE HYDROCHLORIDE
Declomycin

Demeclocycline hydrochloride is one of the tetracycline antibiotics manufactured and sold under the name Declomycin by Lederle Laboratories (Wayne, N.J.).

Although all tetracyclines are of relatively low toxicity at recommended dosage levels,[17] they can be responsible for numerous adverse reactions.[18] In the case of demeclocycline hydrochloride, a photosensitivity reaction is one of the most frequent.[19] Apparently this reaction, which may be brought on by either direct sunlight or a sunlamp, is a true toxicity and not an allergy.[20] Frequency of occurrence and severity of reaction are dose-dependent. It is more likely to occur at higher altitudes and in desert regions of high sun intensity. Having previously tanned skin does not help, but window glass does provide some protection.[1]

See also TETRACYCLINE.

Physicians and pharmacists have been advised by the manufacturer to caution patients about exposure to the sun while on the medication and to warn them that the drug remains in the system

---

[17] *AMA Drug Evaluations,* 2d ed., p. 542.

[18] Id. See also *United States Dispensatory,* 27th ed., pp. 1169-76.

[19] *AMA Drug Evaluations,* 2d ed., p. 544.

[20] "Photoallergic reactions" to drugs are delayed in a manner similar to other allergies. Only small concentrations of the drug are necessary, but relatively few people are susceptible. "Phototoxicity," on the other hand, generally requires larger amounts of drug and more persons are subject to it. The mode of action is not allergic and consequently requires no sensitizing period. As the skin absorbs ultraviolet light the drug becomes activated and emits energy which damages the adjacent tissue. The clinical picture is usually that of severe sunburn in distinction to the greater variety of lesions encountered in drug photoallergy. Fisher, W. C., "Dermatologic Diseases," in *Diseases of Medical Progress: A Study of Iatrogenic Disease,* 3rd ed., R. H. Moser, editor (Springfield, Ill.: Charles C Thomas, Publisher, 1969), p. 196.

[1] *United States Dispensatory,* 27th ed., p. 396.

for 72 to 96 hours or more after cessation of treatment.[2] The product literature states: "Patients apt to be exposed to direct sunlight or ultraviolet light should be advised that this reaction [phototoxic] can occur, and treatment should be discontinued at the first evidence of skin erythema."[3]

The manufacturer warns also that the use of demeclocycline hydrochloride and other tetracyclines during the period of tooth development (including the last half of pregnancy) may cause permanent discoloration of the teeth.[4]

Rowland v. Lederle Laboratories (No. 365072, Superior Court, Alameda County, Cal., 1970).

Phototoxic reaction—Failure to warn—Actions against manufacturer and physician dismissed

A 38-year-old woman, at the time a resident of Virginia, was given Declomycin for ear and kidney infections. While under treatment, she visited California where she obtained the prescription for the same drug from another physician. Sometime later, the woman began suffering a phototoxic reaction and was hospitalized for severe sunburn.

Claiming that her condition was caused by the drug, she brought suit against the manufacturer, the hospital where she was treated and the three California physicians who treated her, including the physician she first saw on arriving in the state. Among other charges, she claimed that this physician failed to warn her of the side effects of Declomycin, namely phototoxic reaction. Against the other physicians and the hospital she alleged improper prescribing and administering of several medications.

The trial court dismissed the action against Lederle Laboratories prior to trial. On the first day of trial, the hospital was granted a judgment on the pleadings. The plaintiff's attorneys then dismissed against the physicians.[5]

---

[2] Id.

[3] *Physicians' Desk Reference,* 35th ed., p. 997.

[4] Id.

[5] AMA *The Citation* 23:39, 1971.

Moore v. Lederle Laboratories (1974) 392 Mich. 289, 220 N.W. 2d 400.

Teeth permanently stained blue-black—Evidence that drug was necessary because of patient's condition—Directed verdict for manufacturer upheld

The patient was born with cystic fibrosis. From shortly after birth until late 1964 he was treated with tetracycline (Declomycin) to prevent infections, especially respiratory infections. As a side effect of the drug the child's teeth became permanently stained blue-black, and the child's father brought suit against the manufacturer, alleging negligence in failing to discover this fact and warn the medical profession.

At the trial a dentist offered testimony for the plaintiff by way of deposition on the tooth-staining effects of tetracycline, but on cross-examination he was questioned about use of the drug on his own children.

"Q. Have you yourself, as a family man, have you used the tetracycline drugs or administered them to your children?

"A. Well, my children have been prescribed tetracycline drugs. My son, who has otitis media, or did have otitis media, which is a mild ear infection, quite frequently as an infant was given tetracycline drugs. Penicillin did not seem to touch this infection. My daughter who had bronchial pneumonia while in Japan, was given large doses for a considerable period of time of this drug. My children in their primary teeth did exhibit some of the staining. Fortunately, it was of a very low degree, not an objectionable level. And their permanent teeth now are in the area of non-objectionable level.

***

"Q. So far as your daughter was concerned, you say the disease for which she was given a tetracycline drug was what?

"A. Bronchial pneumonia.

"Q. How sick was she with that?

"A. She could have died within 24 hours had she not been placed on it immediately.

"Q. Therefore, you realized—

"A. I realized—

"Q. —the tetracycline drug in that situation saved her life?

"A. Right.

"Q. And I am sure you have no hesitation in saying that it was worth the tooth staining to save her life, is that right?

"A. Yes, I would say so.

"Q. That would be consistent with your opinion in regard to these other cases which you studied if there were a life saving situation, isn't that true?

"A. Many of the cases that I have observed are cases where it was a life saving situation, particularly in children who had congenital heart defects in which they were placed on this to reduce their potential for blood infection, which might cause their life to be lost."

An instructor in the Department of Pediatrics and Communicable Diseases at the University of Michigan was also called by the plaintiff. As the former director of the university's Cystic Fibrosis Care, Research, and Training Center, he had been involved in treating the plaintiff's child. His testimony, however, was rather damaging to the plaintiff's case. On direct examination he stated that his own daughter had "rather massive" amounts of tetracycline between the ages of one and three and did not have any staining. On cross-examination he admitted that he would not expect most cystic fibrosis youngsters to live very long if untreated; that if such a child developed pneumonia it would be a "serious matter" unless he was given an antibiotic; and that at the time tetracycline was administered to the plaintiff's child, tooth staining "was not a severe enough indication" not to use the drug. On redirect examination he did testify that in the present case the tetracycline probably prolonged the child's life, but he could not say with any degree of certainty whether his life was "saved."

The trial judge found no cause of action, and was upheld by both the Court of Appeals and the Supreme Court of Michigan.

Dalke v. Upjohn Co. (C.A.-9 Wash., 1977) 555 F.2d 245.

Discoloration of teeth—Adequacy of warnings questioned—Summary judgment for manufacturers reversed

A young girl suffering from chronic upper respiratory infections was treated with tetracycline-based drugs, including Declomycin, by her family physician from January 7, 1965 to March 22, 1973. Following such treatment she developed permanent discoloration of her teeth.

Predicating liability on failure to warn, the child's mother sued The Upjohn Company, manufacturer of Panalba (since withdrawn from the market), Pfizer Laboratories, manufacturer of Terramycin (oxytetracycline), and Lederle Laboratories, manufacturer of Declomycin.

In connection with the defendants' motion for summary judgment, the parties' affidavits disclosed that the Food and Drug Administration notified the three companies in 1962 that their drugs had tooth-staining propensities in young children. As of 1965, the following warning appeared in the package inserts of all three drugs, and in *Physicians' Desk Reference* under "Side Effects":

> [Tetracyclines] may form a stable calcium complex in any bone forming tissue with no serious harmful effects reported thus far in humans. However, use of [any tetracycline drug] during tooth development (= last trimester of pregnancy, neonatal period and early childhood) may cause discoloration of the teeth (= yellow-gray-brownish). This effect occurs mostly during long-term use of the drug, but it has also been observed in usual short treatment courses.

Then, in 1971, for reasons that do not appear in the record, some of the package inserts were changed to read, under the heading "Warnings":

> The use of drugs of the tetracycline class during tooth development (last half of pregnancy, infancy and childhood to the age of 8 years) may cause permanent discoloration of the teeth (yellow-gray-brown).
>
> This adverse reaction is more common during long-term use of the drugs but has been observed following repeated short-term courses. Enamel hypoplasia has also been reported. Tetracycline drugs, therefore, should not be used in this age group unless other drugs are not likely to be effective or are contraindicated.

Thus, from 1965 to 1971 there were these changes: the information was moved from the "Side Effects" heading to the "Warning" heading, the word "permanent" was inserted in front of the word "discoloration," the danger of "enamel hypoplasia" was added, and a caveat as to limited use was added.

The child's treating physician stated that he read the package inserts and PDR as they came out, or at least he was aware of the warnings contained therein. He also stated, however, that had he received more stringent warnings at an earlier date, he would "in all likelihood" have chosen a drug other than the tetracyclines to treat the child. The trial judge concluded that this statement created a factual conflict not properly resolved on a motion for summary judgment, but ruled that this conflict was immaterial because the warnings were adequate in that they gave the doctor reasonable notice of the potential harm.

The Court of Appeals disagreed, holding, in effect, that the defendants may have had knowledge of the additional side effect of "enamel hypoplasia" earlier than 1971, and if they had included this information in the package inserts and PDR earlier, the physician may have changed his course of action. Thus, there was a question of the adequacy of the warnings, which the court could not resolve unless it knew when the defendants first learned of enamel hypoplasia as a possible side effect.

Feldman v. Lederle Laboratories (1989) 234 N.J.Super. 559, 561 A.2d 288.

Discoloration of teeth—Manufacturer failed to warn—Critical issues preempted by federal law—Verdict for plaintiff reversed applied

The plaintiff was administered Declomycin by her father, a physician, during the first three years of her life as routine treatment for infections. When the child's teeth became discolored, suit was filed against the manufacturer for strict liability due to failure to warn.

In reversing the Superior Court, Appellate Division, which had affirmed a jury verdict for the manufacturer, the Supreme Court of New Jersey held that, in general, the principle of strict liability is applicable to manufacturers of prescription drugs, and that in the present case the evidence overwhelmingly demonstrated that the defendant knew of the danger by the end of 1962 (the plaintiff was born in 1960), but continued to market the drug in 1963, during which time the plaintiff ingested it.

The case was remanded for new trial (479 A.2d 374).

On retrial, the jury found in favor of the plaintiff. On appeal, however, the Superior Court, Appellate Division reversed, holding that while federal regulation of the drug industry does not warrant a finding of implied federal preemption of all state tort claims grounded in strict liability for failure to warn, under certain circumstances federal law may preempt a discrete issue upon which liability is predicated because compliance with state decisional law would require federal law to be violated. In this case, said the court, the theory of liability not preempted was decided adversely to the plaintiff by the jury and was not challenged on appeal, while the theory of liability which 'undergirded' the jury verdict against the manufacturer, the issue of whether the manufacturer complied with state law requiring it to warn upon becoming aware of the drug's side effects without first seeking FDA approval, was preempted by federal law requiring it to seek approval.

Related Cases

Child born with discolored teeth has cause of action against mother for taking drug during pregnancy

In a case arising in Michigan, the Court of Appeals held that a child had a cause of action against his mother for negligently permitting him to be born with damage to his teeth, allegedly caused by taking a tetracycline during pregnancy. See Grodin v. Grodin (1980) 102 Mich. App. 396, 301 N.W.2d 869.

DEMEROL
See MEPERIDINE HYDROCHLORIDE

DEMI-REGROTON
See RESERPINE

DEMULEN
See ETHYNODIOL DIACETATE with ETHINYL ESTRADIOL

DEPEN
See PENICILLAMINE

DEPO-PROVERA
See MEDROXYPROGESTERONE ACETATE

DEPROL
See MEPROBAMATE

DERMOPLAST
See BENZOCAINE

DES
See DIETHYLSTILBESTROL

DESYREL

See TRAZODONE HYDROCHLORIDE

DEXAMETHASONE

Aeroseb-Dex
Decadron
Decaspray
Hexadrol

Dexamethasone is a synthetic adrenocortical steroid (glucocorticoid) used primarily as an anti-inflammatory agent. Aeroseb-Dex is manufactured by Herbert Laboratories (Irvine, Cal.); Decadron and Decaspray by Merck Sharp & Dohme (West Point, Pa.), and Hexadrol by Organon Pharmaceuticals (West Orange, N.J.).

The adverse reactions of dexamethasone and other adrenocortical steroids are many.[6] Included among the precautions suggested by the manufacturer of Decadron is that the drug (and all steroids) should be used with caution in nonspecific ulcerative colitis (if there is a probability of impending perforation) and in the presence of active or latent peptic ulcer.[7] Dexamethasone decreases the protective gastric mucous barrier, interferes with tissue repair, and in some patients increases gastric acid and pepsin production. Furthermore, the symptoms of peptic ulcer may be masked by the effects of the drug.[8] Routine prophylactic use of antacids and periodic examination of stools for occult blood are recommended.[9]

Listed among adverse reactions are aseptic necrosis of femoral and humeral heads, and ophthalmic disorders, including glaucoma.[10]

Burnside v. Golden State Memorial Hosp. (No. NWC 10962, Superior Court, Los Angeles County, Cal., July 13, 1972).

**Ulcer patient treated with Decadron—
Verdicts for physician and hospital**

A fifteen-year-old boy was admitted to the hospital after a motorcycle accident. He was unconscious and suffering from a cerebral contusion. Seventeen days later he died, and the autopsy showed

---

[6] *United States Dispensatory,* 27th ed., p. 35.
[7] *Physicians' Desk Reference,* 35th ed., p. 1183.
[8] *AMA Drug Evaluations,* 2d ed., p. 387.
[9] Id.
[10] *Physicians' Desk Reference,* 35th ed., p. 1183.

perforated gastric ulcers and peritonitis. The patient had received Decadron during the hospitalization and the parents filed a malpractice suit, alleging that the hospital personnel had been negligent in administering the drug because it is contraindicated in a patient with stomach ulcers. Charges against the hospital also included mismanagement and failure to supervise the boy's care properly. The attorneys for the hospital and the attending physician based their defense on evidence that treatment was within acceptable standards.

A jury held both the hospital and physician free of liability.[11]

Niblack v. United States (D. Colo., 1977) 438 F. Supp. 383.

Aseptic necrosis following treatment with Decadron—Action barred by statute of limitations—No negligence on part of VA physicians

On December 30, 1970, the patient was admitted to the Veterans' Administration Hospital at Denver, Colorado suffering from severe visual impairment, nausea and headaches. His illness was diagnosed as "pseudotumor cerebri," a swelling of the brain that mimics a tumor. Treatment was commenced, consisting of Decadron in decreasing doses. It was discontinued on January 2, 1971.

On January 11, 1971 treatment was reinstituted at the rate of two mg. of Decadron three times a day. This was continued until February 22, at which time the dosage was reduced to one mg. three times daily. On March 3, the dosage was further reduced to one half a milligram three times daily, and treatment was discontinued on March 6.

During the summer of 1971, the patient complained of pain in his knees. This condition was first diagnosed as arthritis, and later, some form of bone cancer. Unsatisfied with this diagnosis, the patient conducted his own research at a local medical library and on March 15 confronted the physician who had treated him at the VA hospital with allegations that his problem might be "aseptic necrosis," possibly caused by the treatment with Decadron. The VA physician doubted such a connection, but did refer the patient to other physicians, who eventually confirmed the diagnosis.

On November 6, 1974, the patient filed suit under the Federal Tort Claims Act against the government, and also named as a defendant Merck & Company, manufacturer of Decadron. Against the

[11] AMA *The Citation* 26:119, 1973.

government, the patient charged negligence on the part of the VA physician in administering the drug and in failing to inform the patient of the risk of aseptic necrosis.

Merck & Company was dismissed from the case on May 26, 1977 on stipulation of the parties. The government denied all charges and also defended on the ground that the patient had not filed within the two-year statute of limitations.

On August 24, 1977, the District Court ruled in favor of the defendant. As to the statute of limitations, the court held that the patient had clearly understood the causal connection between the administration of Decadron and his aseptic necrosis as early as the spring of 1972, more than two years prior to the filing of his lawsuit. As to negligent administration of the drug, the court held that the evidence showed that the patient was still in danger of vision loss and of renewed brain swelling when treatment was reinstituted in January, 1971. (The patient did not dispute the fact that he was properly treated with Decadron upon admission to the hospital.) As to the charge that the risk of aseptic necrosis was not discussed with the patient, the court held that the evidence showed that the risk of that side effect "was only a remote possibility in comparison to the immediate probability of Plaintiff's permanent loss of vision or even of his life."

Thompson v. Weiss (No. 1684/81, Supreme Court, Ulster County, N.Y., Nov. 27, 1986).

Stroke misdiagnosed as multiple sclerosis—Patient given Decadron which allegedly caused further arterial occlusion—$705,000 settlement

The plaintiff, age 37, was seen by the defendant, a neurosurgeon, because of numbness on the left side of his body, loss of dexterity, and difficulty in walking. The defendant diagnosed multiple sclerosis and hospitalized the plaintiff for tests. A CAT scan and angiogram were read as normal by hospital radiologists and the defendant, and the plaintiff was discharged on steroid therapy, including Decadron. Three weeks later, the plaintiff underwent another CAT scan, and the radiologist found a lesion in the right portion of the brain, and interpreted it as a stroke or a slow-growing tumor. During the next six days, the plaintiff's condition deteriorated and he was readmitted to the hospital. Another CAT scan and radionuclide brain scan were read as showing a stroke, but the defendant continued to diagnose multiple sclerosis and prescribe Decadron. During the following month, the plaintiff continued to suffer pain and coldness in the left foot. He was readmitted to the hospital, where a complete occlusion of the femoral artery in the left thigh was found. An embolectomy and bypass were performed with marginal results; the plaintiff's leg continued to deteriorate and had to be amputed above the knee. The plaintiff's left arm was also affected, and at the time of trial lacked fine motor dexterity.

The plaintiff alleged the defendant and the hospital radiologists misread test results, leading to the misdiagnosis of multiple sclerosis. He claimed that had they been correctly read, the proper diagnosis of stroke could have been made, and he would not have received the contraindicated Decadron, which carries with it side effects of hypercoagulability and spontaneous formation of thromboemboli. He contended that the Decadron was a significant factor in causing further occlusion of the carotid artery, leading to the stroke and the occlusion of the leg artery.

The case was settled during trial for $705,000. The neurosurgeon contributed $675,000, and the hospital, $30,000.[12]

Related cases

Decadron as cause of glaucoma

In Oakes v. Gilday (Del., 1976) 351 A.2d 85, the plaintiff alleged that the physician prescribed Decadron without warning of its propensity to cause glaucoma. It was further alleged that the physician failed to use proper precautions in treating with this medication and failed to check ocular pressure constantly, which resulted in the patient developing the disease. An amendment was proposed to include the allegation that the physician administered Decadron without the informed consent of the patient, and the physician moved to dismiss on the basis of the statute of limitations. The motion was denied.

Glaucoma following prolonged treatment with Neodecadron

In Aetna Cas. & Sur. Co. of Illinois v. Medical Protective Co. of Ft. Wayne, Indiana (N.D. Ill., 1983) 575 F. Supp. 901, a child developed glaucoma following a two-year period of treatment with Neodecadron, a combination of neomycin and dexamethasone. The case is summarized herein under NEOMYCIN SULFATE and DEXAMETHASONE SODIUM PHOSPHATE.

---

[12] ATLA *Professional Negligence Law Reporter* 2:26, 1987.

Mental illness claimed caused by Decadron and other drugs

In Bayless v. Philadelphia Nat. League Club (C.A.-3 Pa., 1979) 615 F.2d 1352, a former pitcher for the Philadelphia Phillies had no civil cause of action against his club for negligence in the administration of massive amounts of Decadron, Exlocaine, and Butazolidin to treat his pain, which allegedly resulted in mental illness.

Decadron not drug of first choice in treating penicillin reaction

In Wright v. United States (E.D. La., 1981) 507 F. Supp. 147, the patient suffered an anaphylactic reaction to oral penicillin and was given Decadron which, according to the evidence, was not the drug of first choice in treating such a reaction. The court awarded the plaintiff $750,000.

DEXTROAMPHETAMINE SULFATE

Dexadrine

Dextroamphetamine sulfate is a central nervous system stimulant used in treating narcolepsy, hyperactive persons with attention deficit disorders, and exogenous obesity. The drug is contraindicated in persons with advanced arteriosclerosis, symptomatic cardiovascular disease, moderate to severe hypertension, hyperthyroidism, known hypersensitivity or idiosyncrasy to the sympathomimetic amines, glaucoma, persons in an agitated state, persons with a history of drug abuse, and during or within 14 days following the administration of monoamine oxidase inhibitors. There can be numerous possible adverse reactions, including elevation of blood pressure, tachycardia, psychotic episodes, dyskinesia, Tourette's syndrome, gastrointestinal disturbances, urticaria, and impotence.[13]

Dexadrine is manufactured by SmithKline Consumer Products (Philadelphia, Pa.).

---

[13] *Physicians' Desk Reference*, 43rd ed., p. 2047.

Ratkovich v. SmithKline & French Laboratories (N.D. Ill., 1989) 711 F. Supp.

Plaintiff claims brain-damage from Dexadrine in utero—28-year delay in filing warranty claims under Illinois Sales Act not "reasonable" notice

On March 5, 1988, the plaintiff, who was 28 years old, filed a 32-count complaint against SmithKline & French Laboratories, charging it with liability for brain damage she suffered *in utero* when her mother ingested Dexadrine during pregnancy. Included in the plaintiff's complaint were claims for recovery under the Illinois Sales Act for breaches of implied warranties of merchantability and fitness for a particular purpose.

The defendant moved to dismiss these counts, arguing that the Act requires a plaintiff to notify the defendant of a breach within a reasonable time after the plaintiff discovered or should have discovered the breach, and that the plaintiff should have discovered the breach and notified the defendant sooner than 28 years after the plaintiff's birth. The plaintiff argued that this provision does not apply because the claim is for personal injury and is not a commercial case. The court rejected the plaintiff's argument.

The plaintiff next asserted that the provision should not apply because it requires the "buyer" to notify the "seller," and the drug was purchased by the plaintiff's mother from someone other than the seller. The court also rejected this argument.

The court then considered whether the plaintiff adequately alleged that she notified the defendant within a reasonable time, and concluded that she did not. The court found it 'virtually impossible' to believe that the plaintiff's parents were unaware of the possibility of the defendant's breach of its implied warranties until 28 years after she was born with brain damage. Surely, said the court, the plaintiff's parents "must have been considering the various possible causes of plaintiff's injury from the moment she was born."

DIABINESE

See CHLORPROPAMIDE

DIAMOX

See ACETAZOLAMIDE

DIATRIZOATE MEGLUMINE
Reno-M-60

Reno-M-60 is a radiopaque contrast agent supplied as a sterile aqueous solution for use in diagnostic radiography. Following intravascular injection, Reno-M-60 is rapidly transported through the bloodstream to the kidneys and is excreted unchanged in the urine. The agent, injected in this way, permits visualization of the kidneys and urinary passages.[14] The product is manufactured by E.R. Squibb & Sons, Inc. (Princeton, N.J.).

Severe, life-threatening reactions to the agent suggest hypersensitivity in some persons. According to the manufacturer, a patient with a history of bronchial asthma or allergy, a family history of allergy, or a previous reaction to a contrast agent "warrant special attention."[15]

Pauscher v. Iowa Methodist Med. Center (Iowa, 1987) 408 S.W.2d 355.

**Fatal adverse reaction during IVP—
Hospital and physician not liable**

In preparation for an intravenous pyelogram, a 26-year-old female hospital patient was injected with Reno-M-60. Soon thereafter she complained of chest pains. The technician administering the test called a physician, but the patient went into anaphylactic shock and died.

At the trial, evidence was introduced that the patient had not been seen by a radiologist prior to the test to discuss the risks involved. Two of the shift nurses who had attended the patient testified that they separately told the patient that she was to undergo an IVP and briefly described its purpose. One nurse told her that a patient would get a "mild reaction, like hives, or a severe reaction, like difficult breathing." The other nurse described only the possibility of a mild reaction, "just the warmth of the dye, that sort of thing." Neither nurse was acting upon the direction of the radiologist. In view of this evidence, the plaintiff charged that the procedure was performed without the patient's informed consent.

The defense introduced evidence that with intravenous pyelograms, statistics show that only one person in 100,000 to 150,000

---

[14] *Physicians' Desk Reference,* 36th ed., p. 3028.
[15] Id.

will die from a reaction. The plaintiff presented no expert testimony as to whether the patient's physicians deviated from professional standards in failing to inform the patient of this risk.

At the close of evidence, the court directed a verdict for the defense. On appeal this was affirmed, with the Supreme Court of Iowa holding that the information a physician must disclose to a patient prior to a medical procedure is measured by the amount of information the patient needs to make a truly informed and intelligent decision concerning the procedure. Information that a patient faces only a one in 100,000 chance of dying as a result of a reaction to the contrast material used with an IVP would not have been significant to a decision by a reasonable person in the patient's circumstances, and thus the defendants were not liable for the patient's death under the theory of lack of informed consent.

DIATRIZOATE SODIUM

See SODIUM DIATRIZOATE

DI-ATRO

See DIPHENOXYLATE HYDROCHLORIDE with ATROPINE SULFATE

DIAZEPAM

T-Quil
Valium
Valrelease

Diazepam is a minor tranquilizer recommended for the management of anxiety disorders, or short-term relief of symptoms of anxiety. It is also used as an adjunct in the relief of skeletal muscle spasm. For adults, the usual dosage is 2 to 10 mg. two to four times a day for symptoms of anxiety or skeletal muscle spasm. The drug is also indicated for symptomatic relief of acute agitation, tremor, delirium tremens and hallucinosis due to acute alcohol withdrawal, for which the dosage is 10 mg. three or four times in the first 24 hours, then 5 mg. three or four times a day as needed.

The drug is a benzodiazepine derivative developed through original research by Roche Laboratories (Nutley, N.J.) which markets it under the trade names Valium and Valrelease. Legere Pharmaceuticals (Costa Mesa, Cal.) produces T-Quil.

Side effects listed by the manufacturer include the following:

Drowsiness, confusion, diplopia, hypotension, changes in libido, nausea, fatigue, depression, dysarthria, jaundice, skin rash, ataxia, constipation, headache, incontinence, changes in salivation, slurred speech, tremor, vertigo, urinary retention, blurred vision. Paradoxical reactions such as acute hyperexcited states, anxiety, hallucinations, increased muscle spasticity, insomnia, rage, sleep disturbances, stimulation have been reported; should these occur, discontinue drug. Isolated reports of neutropenia, jaundice; periodic blood counts and liver function tests advisable during long-term therapy.

The manufacturer also issues the following warnings and precautions:

Not of value in psychotic patients. Caution against hazardous occupations requiring complete mental alertness. When used adjunctively in convulsive disorders, possibility of increase in frequency and/or severity of grand mal seizures may require increased dosage of standard anticonvulsant medication; abrupt withdrawal may be associated with temporary increase in frequency and/or severity of seizures. Advise against simultaneous ingestion of alcohol and other CNS depressants. Withdrawal symptoms similar to those with barbiturates and alcohol have been observed with abrupt discontinuation, usually limited to extended use and excessive doses. Infrequently, milder withdrawal symptoms have been reported following abrupt discontinuation of benzodiazepines after continuous use, generally at higher therapeutic levels, for at least several months. After extended therapy, gradually taper dosage. Keep addiction-prone individuals under careful surveillance because of their predisposition to habituation and dependence. Usage in Pregnancy: Use of minor tranquilizers during first trimester should almost always be avoided because of increased risk of congenital malformations as suggested in several studies. Consider possibility of pregnancy when instituting therapy; advise patients to discuss therapy if they intend to or do become pregnant.

If combined with other psychotropics or anticonvulsants, consider carefully pharmacology of agents employed; drugs such as phenothiazines, narcotics, barbiturates, MAO inhibitors and other antidepressants may potentiate its action. Usual precautions indicated in patients severely depressed, or with latent depression, or with suicidal tendencies. Observe usual precautions in impaired renal or hepatic function. Limit dosage to smallest effective amount in elderly and debilitated to preclude ataxia or oversedation.[16]

---

[16] Roche Laboratories, Summary of Product Information, *Journal of the American Medical Association,* 246:Cover 3 & 4 (Sept. 11), 1981.

Watkins v. United States (C.A.-5 Ala., 1979) 589 F.2d 214.

Excessive amount of Valium prescribed for psychiatric patient involved in automobile accident—Government physician found negligent

This action arose out of an automobile accident involving a member of the United States Air Force. The injured parties sued the government under the Federal Tort Claims Act, alleging that a government physician negligently prescribed an excessive supply of Valium for the airman, and as a result he was unfit to operate a motor vehicle, thereby causing the accident.

The airman had been a patient at the Redstone Arsenal Psychiatric Clinic where he was diagnosed as suffering from "an acute and chronic situational reaction manifested by hysteria, anxiety, and depression." About a month after his release he was seen at the Redstone Outpatient Clinic where a physician prescribed 100 5 mg. tablets of Valium. The evidence revealed that the physician prescribed the drug without taking a medical history or checking the airman's records at the psychiatric clinic. At the trial, the physician testified that had he known that the patient was suffering from depression and had recently been treated for psychiatric problems, he would not have prescribed the Valium.

The trial court found in favor of the plaintiffs. The amount of damages was not reported. The judgment was affirmed on appeal.

Mohr v. Jenkins (La. App., 1980) 393 So. 2d 245.

Phlebitis and thrombosis following preoperative injection of Valium—Charge that nurse anesthetist injected drug too rapidly not supported by evidence

This malpractice action arose out of alleged negligence on the part of a nurse anesthetist whom the plaintiff charged improperly injected Valium into his arm, causing phlebitis and thrombosis, during a preoperative procedure.

According to the plaintiff, the defendant injected the drug too rapidly. The manufacturer's recommendation on the package insert stated that the drug should be administered "slowly, taking at least one minute for each 5 mg. (1 ml.) given."

At the trial, the plaintiff testified that the entire procedure occurred in less than one minute. The defendant, on the other hand, testified that she always administered Valium in conformity with the manufacturer's recommendations, and that she did not administer the drug to the plaintiff any faster than she did to any other patient. She admitted she did not use a watch, but expert testimony revealed that it is not standard practice to use a watch in such cases.

After hearing the evidence the trial judge dismissed the plaintiff's suit. The Court of Appeal affirmed, noting that the expert testimony indicated also that Valium has amnesic qualities, and that this might have affected the plaintiff's ability to recall exactly how long it took the defendant to administer the injection.

Libertelli v. Hoffman-La Roche, Inc. (No. 80 Civ. 5626, U.S. States District Court, New York, N.Y., Feb. 20, 1981).

Addiction—Publisher of Physicians' Desk Reference not liable

A patient who allegedly became addicted to Valium filed suit against the manufacturer and the publisher of the *Physicians' Desk Reference (PDR)*. She claimed that the publisher was grossly negligent in publishing information on Valium furnished by the manufacturer without first performing its own independent tests on Valium.

On its motion to dismiss the action, the publisher argued that it was merely a conduit for the information and that it had no obligation to test the drug. It also contended that it could not be held liable for the patient's condition because it was not malicious, or reckless nor intended harm. Finally, it claimed that it had no duty under the First Amendment to test the drug.

Agreeing with the publisher's arguments, the trial court said that the descriptions of drugs carried in the *PDR* were advertisements. Libel and defamation cases decided by the U.S. Supreme Court held that a publisher was not liable for an advertisement unless the publisher showed reckless disregard for the truth. The publisher explicitly stated in the *PDR* that it published information furnished by manufacturers and did not advocate the use of any drugs. Moreover, the material published in the *PDR* was exactly the information approved for Valium by the Food and Drug Administration, the court said.

Since there was no allegation that the publisher knew of the addictive nature of Valium or acted in reckless disregard of the truth, the motion to dismiss was granted.[17]

---

[17] AMA *The Citation* 44:21, 1981.

Simon v. Hoffman-LaRoche (No. CJ-81-1267, District Court, Oklahoma County, Okla., Sept. 9, 1982).

Valium taken during pregnancy—Child born with brain damage—Structured settlement valued at $700,000

During her last two months of pregnancy the plaintiff's mother took Valium as prescribed by her physician. The plaintiff, six-years-old at the time of trial, was born with brain damage. In a suit against the manufacturer, the plaintiff charged that there were insufficient warnings to the prescribing physicians concerning the possible dangers to a fetus if the drug was taken during pregnancy. The defendant argued that no case of brain damage induced by Valium had ever been reported in the medical journals, and that the plaintiff also suffered from other birth defects that could not be drug-induced. The parties agreed to a structured settlement with a present value of $700,000.

Munsell v. Lynk (No. 80-58801-NI, Circuit Court, Genesee County, Mich., June 1, 1983).

Psychiatrist named party in accident case for prescribing Valium for driver—All defendants settle for $410,000

The plaintiff was a nineteen-year-old truck mechanic whose motorcycle was struck by an automobile being operated by a driver under the influence of beer and Valium. The Valium had been prescribed by his psychiatrist. The injuries included burns to the chest, neck and shoulders, a comminuted fracture of the right femur and a fracture of the right radius. The psychiatrist had prescribed fifty Valium (10 mg.) for the driver the day before the accident. The plaintiff charged that he had breached his duty to the public by negligently prescribing the medication for a patient likely to misuse drugs. The plaintiff also sued the driver's insurance carrier, the manufacturer of his own motorcycle, and the motel in which the psychiatrist maintained an office. The case was settled for $410,000 with all defendants contributing.[18]

Ingram v. Hook's Drugs (Ind. App., 1985) 476 N.E.2d 881.

Adverse reaction—Pharmacy has no duty to warn customer

The plaintiff received a prescription for Valium from his physician and he took it to be filled at the defendant pharmacy. Later,

[18] ATLA *Law Reporter* 26:36, 1983.

while at work, the plaintiff experienced an adverse reaction to the drug and fell from a ladder, fracturing his leg. He filed suit against the pharmacy, alleging that the pharmacist failed to warn him of the side effects of the Valium which included dizziness, drowsiness, and fainting.

At the hearing on the defendant's motion for summary judgment, the plaintiff argued that under the Indiana statute defining the "practice of pharmacy" it is stated that the practice includes "the proper and safe storage and distribution of drugs and devices, the maintenance of proper records thereof, and the responsibility for *advising, as necessary, as to the contents, therapeutic values, hazards, and appropriate manner of use of drugs or devices.*" (Emphasis added.) The plaintiff contended that this language created a mandatory duty on the part of a pharmacist to include his own warnings on the label of a prescription drug. The defendant argued, however, that the statutory language requires advising a customer only "as necessary," and that under the law only certain specific information is required on a drug label, and that the duty to warn a purchaser of a drug of its side effects falls upon the prescribing physician.

The trial court granted the defendant's motion for summary judgment and the Court of Appeals affirmed, holding that:

> The decision of weighing the benefits of a medication against potential dangers that are associated with it requires an individualized medical judgment. This individualized treatment is available in the context of a physician-patient relationship which has the benefits of medical history and extensive medical examinations. It is not present, however, in the context of a pharmacist filling a prescription for a retail customer. The injection of a third party in the form of a pharmacist into the physician-patient relationship could undercut the effectiveness of the ongoing medical treatment. We perceive the better rule to be one which places the duty to warn of the hazards of the drug on the prescribing physician and requires of the pharmacist only that he include those warnings found in the prescription.

Horney v. Lawrence (1988) 189 Ga. App. 376, 375 S.E.2d 629.

Extravasation at site of I.V.—Tissue damage—Jury verdict for patient affirmed

During a gastroscopy performed by the defendant physician, the patient was administered Valium intravenously. Although the defendant had difficulty sedating the patient (the patient was given 30 mg. of Valium instead of the normal 15 mg.), the defendant did not check the I.V. needle on the back of the patient's hand which would have revealed that the solution was escaping into the tissues instead of going into the vein. As a result, the patient suffered tissue destruction and had to undergo surgery, which was only partially successful in correcting the condition.

A jury returned a verdict in favor of the patient, and the Court of Appeals affirmed, holding that the evidence established that the defendant failed to meet the proper standard of care which required that he visually inspect the needle site at the time of injection.

Adkins v. Mong, (1988) 168 Mich. App. 726, 425 N.W.2d 151.

Pharmacy has no duty to warn of risk of addiction nor to identify "over-prescribing physicians"

The plaintiff brought this action against various physicians and pharmacies for negligence in prescribing and supplying him with excessive amounts of drugs, including Valium, during the years 1978 through 1984. According to the plaintiff, he became addicted to the Valium and several of the other drugs. One of the defendants, Motor City Prescription Centers, moved for summary judgment on grounds that the plaintiff failed to state a claim against it. The trial court denied the motion, and the defendant appealed.

The Court of Appeals reversed, holding that the pharmacist had no duty to warn the plaintiff of the possible side effects of a prescribed medication if the prescription was proper on its face and neither the physician nor the manufacturer of the drug required that any warning be given by the pharmacist. The court also rejected the plaintiff's argument that a pharmacy has a duty to maintain detailed customer records and identify addicted customers and their "over-prescribing physicians."

Related cases

Evidence possibly linking Valium to patient's death wrongfully excluded

In a wrongful-death action against a New York hospital, a patient's administratrix was awarded $100,000 for the defendant's alleged premature discharge of the deceased following his collapse from an apparent methadone overdose. The judgment was reversed, however, for the court's refusal to admit evidence offered by the defendant that the deceased had ingested Valium following his release which contributed to his death. See Galiardo v. St. Vincent's

Hosp. & Medical Center of New York (1979) 70 App. Div. 2d 563, 417 N.Y.S.2d 60.

Choice of drugs questioned in view of patient's agitated state

In Fleming v. Prince George's County (1976) 277 Md. 655, 358 A.2d 892, a 67-year-old woman hospital patient fell or leaped from her window following treatment with Librium (chlordiazepoxide hydrochloride) and Valium. A jury question was presented regarding the proper choice of drugs. The case is summarized herein under CHLORDIAZEPOXIDE HYDROCHLORIDE.

Reaction during preparation for tooth extraction—Brain damage

In Strickland v. Board of Supervisors of Louisiana State University (La. App., 1983) 432 So. 2d 964, the plaintiff experienced an adverse reaction when she was administered Valium in preparation for extraction of her wisdom teeth. She lost consciousness and suffered brain damage. A settlement was reached with the dentist and the L.S.U. School of Dentistry. Hoffman-La Roche, the manufacturer of Valium, was granted a summary judgment when the plaintiff failed to refute its affidavit that there was no defect in the literature disseminated with the product and that no inadequate warnings were given.

Fatal reaction during preparation for CT scan following injury in hospital fall—Wrongful death action fails on proximate cause issue

In Hodge v. Crafts-Farrow State Hospital (S.C., 1985) 334 S.E.2d 818, a 61-year-old hospital patient suffered injury in a fall while being bathed. She was taken to another hospital for a CT scan to determine the extent of her injuries, and on being sedated with 5 mg. of Valium for the test she suffered a fatal reaction to the drug. A jury returned a verdict on behalf of the patient's estate against the hospital where she fell, but the Supreme Court of South Carolina reversed, finding insufficient evidence of proximate cause.

Addiction—Defendants prevented from compelling plaintiff to reveal sexual history

In an action against her psychiatrist and the manufacturer of Valium for malpractice and negligence in causing her to become addicted to the drug, the plaintiff was entitled to an order preventing the defendants from compelling her to submit to examination on details of her sex life, family history and other embarrassing facts unrelated to the nature of her lawsuit. Gordon v. Roche Laboratories, Division of Hoffman-La Roche (1981) 116 Misc.2d 688, 456 N.Y.S.2d 291.

Emergency room outpatient dies after taking Valium and alcohol—Question of proper treatment

In Stewart v. Bay Minette Infirmary (Ala., 1986) 501 So. 2d 441, a patient was seen at a hospital emergency department after having taken six 5 mg. Valium capsules and three mixed alcoholic drinks. The emergency department physician gave him a stimulant (caffeine benzoate sodium) and a combined pain killer and muscle relaxer (30 mg. of Talwin and 25 mg. of Phenergan). Five hours later the patient died. The Supreme Court of Alabama reversed a lower court summary judgment for the defendants, holding that there was a genuine issue of material fact as to whether the physician's treatment had met minimum acceptable standards.

Valium blamed for cerebral damage in alcoholic patient—Proximate cause not established

In Crooks v. Greene (1987) 12 Kan. App. 2d 62, 736 P.2d 78, a plaintiff's claim that prescribing Valium to a known alcoholic was the proximate cause of the patient's cerebral damage could not be established without expert medical testimony. Neither the package insert nor *Physicians' Desk Reference* suggested that cerebral damage would result from combining Valium and alcohol.

Coma and paralysis following treatment with Valium and other drugs—Action not barred by statute

Where a patient was rendered paralyzed, blind and virtually unable to speak, allegedly as a result of negligently prescribed combination of Valium, Placidyl, Dalmane and Methadone, the patient's conservator's discovery of the cause of the patient's injury did not trigger the one-year prescriptive period in California's medical malpractice statute of limitations. Getty v. Hoffman-La Roche (Cal. App., 1987) 235 Cal. Rptr. 48.

Excessive administration of Valium and other drugs during office surgery

In Kemble v. Antonetti (No. 87-1002-B, 44th Judicial District Court, Dallas County, Tex., January 29, 1988), a plastic surgeon administered excessive Valium and other drugs during breast augmentation surgery. The case is summarized herein under FENTANYL.

DICUMAROL

See BISHYDROXYCOUMARIN

DIENESTROL

See DIETHYLIDENEETHYLENE

DIETHYLIDENEETHYLENE

Dienestrol

This synthetic estrogen is very similar to DES (diethylstilbestrol) and therefore carries with it a significant association between maternal ingestion during pregnancy and the occurrence of vaginal cancer years later in offspring.[19] The drug was once used to prevent miscarriages. Later it was available only as a cream or suppository for the treatment of atrophic vaginitis and kraurosis vulvae. It has now been discontinued. Manufacturers included Merrell Dow Pharmaceuticals (Cincinnati, Ohio) under the brand name DV and Ortho Pharmaceutical Corporation (Raritan, N.J.) under the brand name Dienestrol Cream. Both preparations were issued with warnings regarding use during pregnancy and other possible links with cancer. (See herein under DIETHYLSTILBESTROL.)

Needham v. White Laboratories, Inc. (C.A.-7 Ill., 1988) 847 F.2d 355.

Vaginal cancer in offspring—$800,000 judgment against manufacturer affirmed on second trial—Manufacturers should have known that Dienestrol could have harmed fetus

The plaintiff's mother took Dienestrol in 1952 during pregnancy to prevent a miscarriage. In early 1974, the plaintiff learned that she had "clear cell adenocarcinoma" of the vagina, a rare form of cancer. She brought suit against the manufacturer of the drug, claiming that it was the proximate cause of her disease.

The case was trifurcated. A jury was impaneled to determine whether the Illinois statute of limitations barred the action. The verdict was that it did not. A second jury was then impaneled to decide the question of liability. That jury returned a verdict for the

[19] *United States Dispensatory,* 27th ed., p. 418.

plaintiff. Trial was then had on damages, and a verdict of $800,000 was returned.

On the liability issue, the jury was instructed that the plaintiff had the burden of proving that the defendant knew, or reasonably should have known, that in 1952 Dienestrol "could cause cancer to the female offspring of a person who was using it to prevent a miscarriage, or that Dienestrol was not apparently useful and desirable in 1952 in preventing miscarriages." On appeal, this instruction was held improper on the ground that it implied that a product that is merely "ineffective" is "defective" for purposes of a product liability action (639 F.2d 394).

Also, the reviewing court held that the district court abused its discretion in admitting a list of summaries of medical articles written prior to 1952 for the purpose of showing that the manufacturer should have known that the drug caused cancer in the female offspring of pregnant women. On introducing the list, the foundational witness had admitted that he had not read some of the articles. Thus, said the court, he was unable to testify that the summaries accurately reflected what was contained in the original articles.

On retrial (on the liability issue only), a verdict was again returned for the plaintiff, and the Court of Appeals affirmed, holding that the plaintiff established that the manufacturer should have known at the time that synthetic estrogen could cause *some* harm to a fetus (it was immaterial whether the harm took the form of cancer).

DIETHYLSTILBESTROL
DES

Diethylstilbestrol, or DES as it is commonly called, is an estrogen, an ovarian hormone, which has been synthetically produced by an assortment of drug companies over the past 25 years.

The drug is indicated for use in connection with moderate to severe vasomotor symptoms associated with menopause, atrophic vaginitis, kraurosis vulvae, female hypogonadism, female castration, primary ovarian failure, breast cancer (in certain cases) and carcinoma of the prostate.[20]

In April, 1971, it was reported that ingestion of DES during pregnancy appears to increase the risk of vaginal adenocarcinoma years

[20] *Physicians' Desk Reference*, 35th ed., pp. 1056-57.

later in female offspring. Eight cases of adenocarcinoma of the vagina in patients born between 1946 and 1951 were studied.[21] In seven of these, there was a history of maternal use of DES. Four months later other researchers reported five more cases of the same form of cancer in females whose mothers used DES during pregnancy.[1] A later report turned up fifteen more cases.[2] As a result, the Food and Drug Administration issued a requirement that a warning be included in the drug literature and on labels.[3] The warning now reads:

> *ESTROGENS SHOULD NOT BE USED DURING PREGNANCY*
>
> The use of female sex hormones, both estrogens and progestogens, during early pregnancy may affect the offspring. It has been reported that females exposed *in utero* to diethylstilbestrol, a nonsteroidal estrogen, may have an increased risk of developing later in life a rare form of vaginal or cervical cancer. This risk has been estimated to be no greater than 4 per 1000 exposures. Furthermore, from 30 to 90 percent of such exposed women have been found to have vaginal adenosis and epithelial changes of the vagina and cervix. Although these changes are histologically benign, it is not known whether they are precursors of malignancy. Even though similar data are not available with the use of other estrogens, it cannot be presumed that they would not induce similar changes.[4]

These synthetic estrogens have also been linked to congenital anomalies in children of women who have taken them during pregnancy, which has prompted the following warning:

> Several reports suggest that there is an association between intrauterine exposure to female sex hormones and congenital anomalies, including congenital heart defects and limb-reduction defects. One case-control study estimated a 4.7-fold increased risk of limb-reduction defects in infants exposed *in utero* to sex hormones (oral contraceptives, hormone withdrawal tests for preg-

---

[21] Herbst, A. L., et al., "Adenocarcinoma of the Vagina: Association of Maternal Stilbestrol Therapy with Tumor Appearance in Young Women," *New England Journal of Medicine* 284:878-881, 1971. (Abstracted in *Drug Therapy* 2:85, 1972.)

[1] Greenwald, P., et al., "Vaginal Cancer After Maternal Treatment with Synthetic Estrogens," *New England Journal of Medicine* 285:390-392. (Abstracted in *Drug Therapy* 2:84, 1972.)

[2] "Drug's Use Linked to Adenocarcinoma in the Offspring," *Drug Therapy* 2:118, 1972.

[3] Id.

[4] *Physicians' Desk Reference,* 35th ed., p. 1055.

> nancy, or attempted treatment for threatened abortion). Some of these exposures were very short and involved only a few days of treatment. The data suggest that the risk of limb-reduction defects in exposed fetuses is somewhat less than 1 per 1000.
>
> In the past, female sex hormones have been used during pregnancy in an attempt to treat threatened or habitual abortion; however, their efficacy was never conclusively proved or disproved.
>
> If diethylstilbestrol is administered during pregnancy, or if the patient becomes pregnant while taking this drug, she should be apprised of the potential risks to the fetus and of the advisability of pregnancy continuation.[5]

Still another warning was issued on the prolonged use of these hormones and an increase in the risk of endometrial carcinoma in patients taking the drug:

> Three independent case-control studies have reported an increased risk of endometrial cancer in postmenopausal women exposed to exogenous estrogens for prolonged periods. This risk was independent of other known risk factors for endometrial cancer. These studies are further supported by the finding that, since 1969, the incidence rate of endometrial cancer has increased sharply in eight different areas of the United States which have population-based cancer reporting systems.
>
> The three case-control studies reported that the risk of endometrial cancer in estrogen users was about 4.5 to 13.9 times greater than in nonusers. The risk appears to depend on both the duration of treatment and the dose of estrogen. In view of these findings, the lowest dose that will control symptoms should be utilized when estrogens are used for the treatment of menopausal symptoms, and medication should be discontinued as soon as possible. When prolonged treatment is medically indicated, a reassessment should be made on at least a semiannual basis to determine the need for continued therapy. Although the evidence must be considered preliminary, one study suggests that cyclic administration of low doses of estrogen may carry less risk than does continuous administration; it therefore appears prudent to utilize such a regimen.
>
> Close clinical surveillance of all women taking estrogens is important. In all cases of undiagnosed persistent or recurring abnormal vaginal bleeding, adequate diagnostic measures should be undertaken to rule out malignancy.
>
> At present, there is no evidence that 'natural' estrogens are more or less hazardous than 'synthetic' estrogens at equivalent estrogenic doses.[6]

---

[5] Id.

[6] Id.

DES also has been used as a postcoital contraceptive ("morning-after pill"). Ralph Nader's Health Research Group once reported to have found many university student health centers prescribing DES for college women without telling them of the vaginal cancer risk to female offspring should they become pregnant. The investigators charged "college women have been used as guinea pigs without even the most rudimentary observation of professional standards and informed consent."[7]

Today, the product is sold with the additional warning that *it should not be used as a postcoital contraceptive.*

Lawsuits against the manufacturers of DES began in the early 1970's, shortly after the discovery of the relationship between administration of the drug during pregnancy and cervical or vaginal cancer in female offspring (or "DES daughters" as the group has become to be called).

An early problem encountered by the plaintiffs was identification of the brand of DES taken and its manufacturer. Many of the cases that have reached the appellate courts deal with this issue, with the plaintiffs relying on an assortment of joint liability theories. (See "Related cases," *infra.*)

Mink v. University of Chicago (N.D. Ill., 1978) 460 F. Supp. 713.

Women who unknowingly participated in DES experiments had cause of action under theory of battery

The plaintiffs were a group of women who were given DES as part of a medical experiment conducted by the University of Chicago and Eli Lilly and Company between September, 1950 and November, 1952. The drug was administered during the plaintiff's prenatal care at the University's Lying-In Hospital as part of a double blind study to determine the value of DES in preventing miscarriages. The women were not told that they were taking part in an experiment, nor were they told that the pills they were receiving were DES. The plaintiffs claim that as a result of their taking DES, their daughters have developed abnormal cervical cellular formations and are exposed to an increased risk of vaginal or cervical cancer, and that their sons have suffered reproductive tract and other abnormalities and have likewise incurred an increased risk of cancer.

---

[7] "Drugs—DES Revisited," *Trial,* March/April, 1973, p. 44.

They allege that although the relationship between DES and cancer in offspring was known to the medical community as early as 1971, the defendants made no effort to notify them of their participation in the experiment until late 1975 or 1976, when the University sent letters to the participants suggesting that their sons and daughters undergo medical examinations.

The complaint sought recovery on three causes of action: that the defendants committed a series of batteries on the plaintiffs by conducting the experiment without their knowledge; that Lilly was strictly liable because DES is a defective and unreasonably dangerous drug, and that the defendants breached a duty to notify the plaintiffs that they had been given the drug and that their offspring should consult a medical specialist.

The defendants moved to dismiss the complaint for failure to state a claim. The court denied this motion as to the first charge, holding that the complaint sufficiently alleged a cause of action under the battery theory, but granted it as to the second and third charges, on the theory that the defendants could not be held strictly liable or guilty of failure to notify in the absence of evidence that the plaintiffs themselves suffered physical injury.

Bichler v. Willing (1977) 58 App. Div. 2d 331, 397 N.Y.S.2d 57.

DES daughter had no cause of action against pharmacist

While the plaintiff's mother was pregnant with the plaintiff, she ingested DES dispensed by the defendant pharmacist. Later, when the plaintiff developed vaginal cancer, suit was filed against the defendant under the theories of negligence, breach of warranty and strict liability.

At the trial level, the judge denied the pharmacist's motion for summary judgment, and the pharmacist appealed. The New York Supreme Court, Appellate Division, reversed, holding that the plaintiff could not recover under any of the theories where the record failed to show that the pharmacist did anything to change the prescription, make any warranty, express or implied, regarding the drug's safety, offer any advice as to its purpose or use, or was aware of any dangerous ingredient or side effects of the product.

Gray v. United States (S.D. Tex., 1978) 445 F. Supp. 337.

DES daughter fails to identify manufacturer—Government not liable for FDA's approval of drug

The daughter of a mother given DES while pregnant sued Eli Lilly and Company and the federal government, the latter under the Federal Tort Claims Act on the theory that the Food and Drug Administration approved the sale of the drug without warning of its adverse effects.

Lilly moved for summary judgment when the plaintiff failed to show that it was the manufacturer of the drug in question. The motion was granted. The government likewise moved for summary judgment, arguing that the FDA's actions in approving DES were discretionary, and thus could not be the basis of a claim under the FTCA. This motion was also granted.

Bichler v. Eli Lilly & Co. (1981) 79 App. Div. 2d 317, 436 N.Y.S.2d 625, aff'd (1982) 55 N.Y.2d 571, 450 N.Y.S.2d 776, 436 N.E.2d 182.

Manufacturer liable under "concerted action" theory—Plaintiff awarded $492,842

A daughter of a woman given DES during pregnancy underwent a radical hysterectomy removal of her ovaries, removal of both fallopian tubes, and removal of two-thirds of her vagina following a diagnosis of carcinoma of the cervix and vagina. In her lawsuit for damages against Eli Lilly and Company, the hospital to which her mother had been confined, and her mother's physician, she was awarded $492,842.39 against Lilly. On appeal, the Supreme Court of New York, Appellate Division, affirmed the judgment despite a jury finding that Lilly was not the manufacturer of the drug ingested by the plaintiff's mother. In upholding the judgment against Lilly, the court held that since the evidence showed that Lilly was one of twelve manufacturers who agreed to cooperate with each other in the approval process of DES by the Food and Drug Administration, that these manufacturers agreed on the same basic chemical formula for DES, and that Lilly's drug literature for DES was used as a model for package inserts jointly submitted to the FDA, Lilly was engaged in "concerted action" with the other manufacturers from which liability could be imposed.

The Court of Appeals affirmed, holding that the "concerted action theory"[8] became the law of the case when the defendant manufacturer did not move to dismiss the complaint for failure to state a cause of action, or move for partial summary judgment limiting the plaintiff's recovery to a percentage amount of her injuries which corresponds to the defendant's market share, or move to join other DES manufacturers as necessary parties. The court also held that the evidence sustained the finding of a "conscious parallel conduct" among DES manufacturers and that the defendant's decision not to run animal tests for effects of the drug on offspring encouraged other DES manufacturers to omit such tests. The court also found the evidence sufficient to support a finding that cancer in offspring was a "foreseeable risk" of taking DES during pregnancy.

Payton v. Abbott Labs. (1982) 386 Mass. 540, 437 N.E.2d 171.

No action for emotional distress for increased likelihood of cancer—Daughters who probably would not have been born except for mother's use of DES barred from recovery—Right of action exists for injury in utero — "Market share" theory possible in future cases

In a DES daughter case the Supreme Judicial Court of Massachusetts held: (1) absent physical harm there is no right of action for emotional distress allegedly resulting from an increased statistical likelihood that a plaintiff will develop cancer in the future; (2) if a plaintiff would probably not have been born except for her mother's ingestion of DES, she is barred from recovering damages from ingesting the drug; (3) there is a right of action for injury to a plaintiff, in utero, resulting from the mother's ingestion of a drug and that right is not limited to prospective application; and (4) recovery might be allowed from manufacturers, if shown to be negligent, to the extent of their participation in the DES market even though the daughters could not identify the particular source of the DES taken by their mothers, but this question could not be answered on the record presented in the case at hand.[9]

---

[8] Editor's Note: Other cases involving the inability of a plaintiff to identify a specific DES manufacturer, resulting in an assertion of a "collective responsibility" theory of action, are listed under "Related cases," *infra*.

[9] See *supra* note 8.

Axler v. E.R. Squibb & Sons, Inc. (No. 2888, Court of Common Pleas, Philadelphia County, Pa., Mar. 25, 1982).

DES daughter settles for $2.25 million

The twenty-one-year-old plaintiff's mother had used DES while pregnant. When the plaintiff was seventeen years old she was diagnosed as having clear cell adenocarcinoma of the vagina. As the result of radiation therapy she is unable to bear children. In her action against the manufacturer, she introduced the prescription given to her mother which specifically called for the Squibb brand of diethylstilbestrol. The jury returned a verdict of $1,750,000 to which a $500,000 penalty was added under Pennsylvania's procedural rule for failure of the defendant to make a reasonable settlement offer.[10]

Watson v. Eli Lilly & Co. (No. 82-0951, U.S. District Court, D. D.C., Feb. 10, 1983).

DES daughter settles for $600,000

The plaintiff's mother took DES while pregnant, and nineteen years later the plaintiff developed vaginal cancer which was removed by surgery. The manufacturer and plaintiff entered into a structured settlement agreement having a present value of $600,000. The plaintiff received $250,000 cash and will receive $30,000 per year for life.[11]

McMahan v. Eli Lilly & Co. (C.A.-7 Ill., 1985) 774 F.2d 830.

Reproductive abnormalities in DES daughter—Jury case presented on manufacturer's knowledge of risk—Evidence of knowledge of precise injury not required

In reversing a directed verdict for the manufacturer, the U.S. Court of Appeals, Seventh Circuit, held that a DES daughter who claimed her difficulties in achieving full-term pregnancy and normal delivery were caused by her prenatal exposure to DES offered sufficient evidence from which a jury could have found that in 1955 the manufacturer knew or should have known that DES might cause reproductive abnormalities, such as prematurity, in female offspring of women exposed to the drug during pregnancy.

---

[10] ATLA *Law Reporter,* 25:276, 1982.
[11] Id., 26:374, 1983.

The court held also that the plaintiff need not prove that the manufacturer should have anticipated the *precise* injuries allegedly suffered, so long as the injuries lay within the scope of the known dangerous propensities of DES.

Payton v. Abbott Labs (C.A.-1 Mass., 1985) 780 F.2d 147.

DES daughter blames drug for tubal and uterine deformities—$50,000 award for ectopic pregnancies and miscarriage—Verdict set aside for trial court's error

The plaintiff claimed that DES ingested by her mother while pregnant in 1953 caused her, the plaintiff, to have a deformed fallopian tube and uterus which resulted in two ectopic pregnancies and a miscarriage following a uterine pregnancy. A jury found for the plaintiff and awarded her $50,000. The trial judge struck the jury finding regarding one of the ectopic pregnancies, but allowed the award to stand.

The Court of Appeals reversed, holding that a new trial was required because the trial judge's action "eliminated one of the legs on which the damage award rested." The reviewing court did hold, however, that the evidence was sufficient that "25 mg. of DES were a contributing cause of the woman's injuries" and that the drug in question was manufactured by the defendant company.

Doe v. Eli Lilly & Co. (No. 82-3515, U.S. District Court, D. D.C., June 28, 1985).

Genitourinary malformations in male offspring—$400,000 verdict against manufacturer for failure to warn—$100,000 settlement with physician and second supplier of DES

The plaintiff, a genetically normal male, alleged that as the result of his mother taking DES during her pregnancy in 1961 he suffered from hypospadias, micropenis and testicular hypoplasia, which required that he undergo bilateral surgical excision of the testes. In his lawsuit against Eli Lilly & Co., one of the manufacturers of DES, he charged that the company negligently failed to warn the medical profession of animal studies conducted in the late 1930s which demonstrated teratogenic effects of the drug and a 1959 human case report of genital malformations.

Eli Lilly & Co. was also accused of negligence in failing to advise against a high dosage of DES and against prophylactic use of the product. Further, the plaintiff claimed Lilly had breached implied warranties of merchantability and fitness for a particular purpose.

A jury found against Lilly on all of the above charges and awarded the plaintiff $400,000. The plaintiff also reached a pretrial settlement of $100,000 with the prescribing physician and Emons Industry, another company who supplied DES taken by the plaintiff's mother.[12]

Jacobi v. Rexall (No. 636-624, Circuit Court, Milwaukee County, Wis., Aug. 21, 1986).

Cervical clear-cell carcinoma in DES daughter—$350,000 settlement

The plaintiff, age 20, developed cervical clear-cell carcinoma, and was required to undergo a hysterectomy and radiation therapy. It was discovered that her mother had taken DES while pregnant with the plaintiff in 1961-62. Because the exact prescription and manufacturer of the DES could not be identified, the plaintiff sued fourteen companies which had manufactured or distributed the product during 1961-62. Under Wisconsin's contribution-to-risk theory (any party who could have contributed to the risk faced by the plaintiff can be named as a defendant), the burden is on the defendants in such cases to resolve their proportion of liability. The parties settled for $350,000.[13]

Bouillion v. Eli Lilly & Co. (W.D. La., 1988) 672 F. Supp. 467.

Gynecological injuries—Insufficient evidence that mother was given DES—Type of injuries not exclusive to DES exposure—Summary judgment for manufacturer

The plaintiff claimed that she sustained certain congenital injuries and deformities of her reproductive organs ("t-shaped uterus, a non-filling right fallopian tube, and a partial filling and no spillage of the left fallopian tube") as a result of her mother taking DES during pregnancy. The plaintiff could not, however, offer evidence that her mother actually received DES.

The mother's medical records were incomplete: there was no record of a physician having prescribed DES, but there was a record of her having been prescribed another drug (Hesper-C) to prevent

[12] ATLA *Law Reporter* 29:42, 1986.

[13] ATLA *Products Liability Law Reporter* 6:7, 1987.

miscarriage. Also, the manufacturer introduced the affidavits of two of the plaintiff's physicians which stated that the type of injuries sustained by the plaintiff has occurred in women who were not exposed to DES in utero.

The court granted the manufacturer's motion for summary judgment.

Medics Pharmaceutical Corp. v. Newman (1989) 190 Ga. App. 197, 378 S.E.2d 487.

Adenocarcinoma in DES daughter—Supplier could not avoid liability on ground that drug was not sold to prevent miscarriage—$811,692 verdict affirmed

The plaintiff, whose mother was given DES by her physician while pregnant with the plaintiff to prevent miscarriage, developed adenocarcinoma in 1980 at age sixteen and had to undergo the removal of her uterus, cervix, and vagina.

The defendant was a supplier of the DES which it purchased from the manufacturer. The defendant sold the product to the plaintiff's mother's physician under its own label under the brand name Diastyl. At the time, the package insert that accompanied each stock bottle listed several uses for Diastyl, but did not mention use for the prevention of miscarriage.

The plaintiff's case went to the jury which awarded the plaintiff $811,692 in damages. On appeal, the defendant claimed that the trial court erred in denying its motion for directed verdict on the ground that the defendant could not have foreseen the harm caused the plaintiff's mother, in that the defendant had not recommended or marketed its product for the reason that it was given to the plaintiff's mother — to prevent miscarriage. The Court of Appeals of Georgia did not agree, however, and affirmed the verdict, holding that evidence was presented from which the jury could have concluded that the defendant knew or should have known that physicians were regularly prescribing DES to prevent miscarriages, and that whether a manufacturer or distributor of DES should have foreseen that it would be used for that reason was a question for the jury.

The court also held that there was sufficient evidence for the jury that the defendant breached its general duty to use reasonable care to provide a product which is reasonably safe for those purposes for which it could be foreseeably used.

Enright v. Eli LIlly & Co., ___ N.Y.S.2d ___ (App. Div., 1989).

Granddaughter of DES user has cause of action for injuries attributable to mother's in utero exposure

Patricia Enright's mother took DES while pregnant with Patricia. Allegedly because of exposure to the drug, Patricia developed abnormalities of the reproductive system that prevented her from carrying her daughter, Karen, to term, and as a result of being born prematurely, Karen suffers from severe disabilities. Patricia and her husband brought suit on behalf of themselves and Karen against several drug companies that manufactured DES at the time the drug was taken by Patricia's mother, alleging strict liability for failure to warn of the drug's hazard. The trial court granted the defendants' motion for summary judgment as to Karen. The appellate court reversed, holding that an individual has a cause of action for personal injuries attributable to injury to his or her mother while the mother was in utero. The reviewing court noted prior legislative and judicial action favoring the availability of remedies in such situations. Also, the court held that to create a generational limitation on a manufacturer's liability in such a case would dilute economic incentives for drug manufacturers to produce safe products, which is an underlying purpose of strict liability.[14]

Related cases

Pharmacy not subject to strict liability—Manufacturer's share of market not sufficient for application of theory

A pharmacy that sold DES to the plaintiff's mother could not be subject to an action for strict liability, and a DES manufacturer with only a ten percent share of the DES market did not have a "substantial share" necessary to make the "market share" theory of liability applicable.[15] Murphy v. E.R. Squibb & Sons (1985) 40 Cal. 3d 672, 221 Cal. Rptr. 447, 710 P.2d 247.

Strict liability unavailable—State of the art evidence admissible—Market share theory not applicable to fraud or breach of warranty—No joint liability

In a "complex litigation" ruling, the California Court of Appeal upheld a lower court decision that (1) DES manufacturers could not

---

[14] *ATLA Products Liability Law Reporter* 9:85, 1990.

[15] Editor's Note: Other cases involving the inability of a plaintiff to identify a specific DES manufacturer, resulting in an assertion of a "collective responsibility" theory of action, are listed under "Related cases," *infra*.

be held strictly liable for injuries caused by design defects in the drug; (2) DES manufacturers are entitled to introduce "state of the art" evidence to show dangers complained of were not known or "reasonably knowable" at the time the product was produced and sold; (3) the "market share" approach to liability[16] does not apply to product actions based on fraud or breach of warranty; and (4) DES manufacturers may be held severally liable, based upon their "market share" of the product, but cannot be jointly liable for DES injuries. Brown v. Superior Court (1986) 183 Cal. App. 3d 1125, 227 Cal. Rptr. 768. The Supreme Court of California also affirmed, holding that if strict liability were imposed in such cases, it could stifle medical research and testing, and have an adverse effect on the availability and cost of prescription drugs. As to the fraud and warranty claims, the Court held that the market share theory was not applicable because the plaintiffs' mothers, not the plaintiffs, were the persons who relied upon the manufacturers' representations. Also, the plaintiffs could not ascribe a fraudulent intent to someone who could not be identified. As to joint liability, the Court held that such a finding would be unfair because a defendant manufacturer could be held responsible for the entire judgment even though its market share may have been comparatively insignificant. Brown v. Superior Court (1988) 245 Cal. 3d 412, 751 P.2d 470.

Strict liability available in Rhode Island—Application of Comment (k) under Restatement § 402A defined

A DES daughter was awarded damages in the U.S. District Court for the District of Rhode Island, with the manufacturer being held strictly liable in tort and also for breach of implied warranty of merchantability. After the verdict, the judge, pursuant to Rhode Island Supreme Court Rules, certified the pertinent liability questions to the state supreme court. In response, the state court recognized the theory of strict liability in Rhode Island, and held that under the Restatement (Second) of Torts, the § 402A Comment (k) exemption from strict liability for unavoidably unsafe drugs was a defense to a contract theory of breach of implied warranty of merchantability and to allegations of design defect, but not to allegations of failure to warn. Castrignano v. E. R. Squibb & Sons (R.I., 1988) 546 A.2d 775.

---

[16] *Id.*

Clarification of Washington law governing DES liability

In George v. Parke-Davis (1987) 107 Wash. 2d 584, 733 P.2d 507, the Supreme Court of Washington was asked to clarify the law governing DES litigation in that state involving successor corporate liability and "market share" liability.[17] In so doing, the court held that: (1) successor liability is limited to those cases in which the transferor and transferee both manufacture DES; (2) the traditional rules of successor liability still apply; (3) national figures may be admitted on the question of market share if local data is not available and if the trial judge determines that they are sufficient to establish a reasonable approximation of the drug companies' shares; (4) in the case at bar, the number of pills sold by the defendants should be used rather than the total milligrams sold; (5) defunct corporations should be figured into market share calculations if their actual market shares can be calculated. (Viable defendants, however, cannot implead defunct corporations to reduce their liability.); (6) there is no vertical liability between raw drug manufacturers and tablet manufacturers; and (7) settlements between the plaintiff and drug manufacturers should be ignored when calculating both actual and presumptive liability.

Eli Lilly & Co. may not relitigate liability issue in New York

In a New York DES daughter's action against Eli Lilly & Company, the Supreme Court, Appellate Division, held that the earlier case of Bichler v. Eli Lilly & Co. (see above) precluded the defendant manufacturer from relitigating the issue of its liability for marketing the product without adequate testing. Schaeffer v. Eli Lilly & Co. (1985) 113 App. Div. 2d 827, 493 N.Y.S.2d 501.

The fact that a DES daughter did not suffer from cancer, nor claim that her ailment (gross tissue and organ abnormality of the cervix and vagina) would become cancerous, did not prevent her from using the doctrine of offensive collateral estoppel to preclude Eli Lilly & Company from relitigating the issue of whether it was negligent in testing DES before it made the product available to the public. Rubel v. Eli Lilly & Co. (S.D.N.Y., 1987) 681 F. Supp. 151.

Manufacturer permitted to relitigate liability issue in New Jersey

The doctrine of offensive collateral estoppel did not bar Eli Lilly & Co. from relitigating questions of its negligence in testing and

---

[17] *Id.*

marketing DES and whether the product was defective. The New Jersey courts are not required to give full faith and credit to decisions rendered in other states on the issue of the manufacturer's liability. Kortenhaus v. Eli Lilly & Co. (1988) 228 N.J. Super. 162, 549 A.2d 437.

Plaintiff unsuccessful basing claim on violation of Food, Drug and Cosmetic Act

In Keil v. Eli Lilly & Co. (E.D. Mich., 1980) 490 F. Supp. 479, a DES daughter was unsuccessful in basing her action on allegations that the manufacturer failed to place adequate warning labels on the product in violation of the misbranding provisions of the Food, Drug and Cosmetic Act. The court held that no private cause of action lay under the Act and, although a rebuttable presumption of negligence would arise on proof of an FDCA violation, a Michigan product liability statute required that the plaintiff's prima facie case be made without benefit of any presumption.

Drugstore owner not liable for predecessor's sale of DES to plaintiff's mother

The purchaser of a drugstore that had sold DES to the plaintiff's mother sixteen years prior to the date the store changed hands was not liable to the plaintiff under the "successor liability doctrine." Lemire v. Garrard Drugs (1980) 95 Mich. App. 520, 291 N.W.2d 103.

Plaintiff not entitled to certification of class

In McElhaney v. Eli Lilly & Co. (D. S.D., 1982) 93 F.R.D. 875, the plaintiff was not entitled to certification of a proposed class consisting of all people in South Dakota who had been exposed to DES as unborn children where the class was not adequately defined, the members not readily identifiable, and the plaintiff's claim was not typical of the claims of the class.

In Mertens v. Abbott Laboratories (D.N.H., 1983) 99 F.R.D. 38, the plaintiff's action could not be maintained as a class action where a general determination of a right to recover could not aid any particular DES plaintiff until liability and damages to that plaintiff also were determined, because the common questions did not predominate over individual issues, and a class action was not superior to other available methods.

Hospital can join DES manufacturer in malpractice claim

A hospital being sued by a DES daughter for malpractice in connection with treatment of her vaginal cancer could join the DES manufacturer under the statute permitting tortfeasors to claim contribution where two or more persons are subject to liability for the same personal injury. Helmrich v. Eli Lilly & Co. (1982) 89 App. Div. 2d 441, 455 N.Y.S.2d 460.

DES daughter necessary party to manufacturer's declaratory judgment action against insurers

A DES daughter who was suing a manufacturer for vaginal cancer had an interest in a declaratory judgment action against the manufacturer's insurers to establish liability coverage, and therefore she was required to be joined as a party to the action. Vale Chemical Co. v. Hartford Acc. & Indem. Co. (Pa., 1986) 516 A.2d 684.

Origin of cause of action — Applicable law

The causes of actions of two DES daughters did not originate in the state where the plaintiffs were exposed to DES in utero, but in the states where their cancer developed and became capable of ascertainment. Renfroe v. Eli Lilly & Co. (C.A.-8 Mo., 1982) 686 F.2d 642.

Where a DES daughter's cancer manifested while she was a resident of Tennessee and she incurred medical bills there, public policy warrants application of Tennessee law. Trahan v. E.R. Squibb & Sons, Inc. (M.D. Tenn., 1983) 567 F. Supp. 505.

Testicular cancer in male offspring—Plaintiff allowed to change domiciles to bring action

In an action by a man who claimed his testicular cancer was due to his mother taking DES during pregnancy, the trial court properly applied the statute of limitations of New Jersey, even though the plaintiff did not establish his domicile in that state until the statute had run in New York, his previous domicile. Pine v. Eli Lilly & Co. (1985) 201 N.J. Super. 186, 492 A.2d 1079.

Plaintiff must show manufacturer knew of or should have foreseen side effects

A DES daughter had to prove that the manufacturer knew of or should have foreseen the side effects of which the plaintiff complained in order to recover under the theory of strict liability. McElhaney v. Eli Lilly & Co. (C.A.-8 S.D., 1984) 739 F.2d 340.

Physicians' affidavits on cause of cancer defeats motion for summary judgment

Affidavits of two doctors that in their opinion the "changes" in the plaintiff's vaginal tissue were caused by her mother's ingestion of DES while pregnant were sufficient to defeat the manufacturer's motion for summary judgment. Bulthuis v. Rexall Corp. (C.A.-9 Cal., 1986) 789 F.2d 1315.

DES daughter has jury case against manufacturer

In Bogorad v. Eli Lilly & Company (C.A.-6 Mich., 1985) 768 F.2d 93, a DES daughter's claims for negligence and breach of warranty against the manufacturer should have been allowed to go to the jury where the record showed that at the time the manufacturer recommended the drug to the plaintiff's mother's doctor, it was known in the scientific community that DES could adversely affect a fetus, and that it was being given to animals as a carcinogen to study resulting cancers.

DES mothers not entitled to damages for emotional distress

The mothers of DES daughters are not entitled to recover damages from the drug's manufacturers for emotional distress brought on by the increased risk of their daughters developing cancer. Plummer v. Abbott Laboratories (D. R.I., 1983) 568 F. Supp. 920.

Evidence of physical injury sufficient to allow consideration of damages for fear of developing cancer

Under the law of Illinois, if a DES daughter establishes a physical injury caused by the exposure to DES, such injury will sufficiently establish the genuineness of her mental injury so as to allow a jury to consider compensating her for a reasonable fear of developing cancer. McAdams v. Eli Lilly & Co. (N.D. Ill., 1986) 638 F. Supp. 1173.

Punitive damages not recoverable in market share liability case

A DES daughter was not entitled to recover punitive damages from the manufacturer where the claim was being pursued under the "market share" liability theory.[18] Magallanes v. Superior Court (1985) 167 Cal. App. 3d 878, 213 Cal. Rptr. 547.

Manufacturer's advertised use of DES not significant

That a DES manufacturer marketed its product only for use as palliative treatment of prostate cancer in males did not entitle it to a summary judgment in an action by a DES daughter. Miles Laboratories v. Superior Court of Orange County (1982) 133 Cal. App. 3d 587, 184 Cal. Rptr. 98.

Wisconsin law unclear on strict liability and negligence issues—Questions certified to state supreme court

Finding the law of Wisconsin unclear on key strict liability and negligence issues in a claim by a DES daughter against the manufacturer, the Seventh Circuit Court of Appeals certified the following questions to the state supreme court: 1. Can the reasonableness of a prescription drug manufacturer's decision to produce and market a drug, assessed on the basis of information that was available at the time that decision was made, establish that a drug is not defective under Wisconsin's law of strict liability? 2. Assuming that ex ante reasonableness can be relevant to whether a drug is defective, as suggested by Comment (j) to section 402A of the Second Restatement, does the filing of a supplemental new drug application create a separate product for purposes of determining whether Comment (i) or Comment (j) controls? 3. Do Wisconsin's public policies require courts to protect DES manufacturers from negligence judgments awarded under a failure to warn theory, where the evidence demonstrates only that the manufacturer responded negligently to information suggesting the potential for injuries different from the injury suffered by the plaintiff? Shirkey v. Eli Lilly & Co. (C.A.-7 Wis., 1988) 852 F.2d 227.

DES manufacturer not required to warn franchisee or consumer of risk

A manufacturer of DES that had a franchisee agreement with a retail pharmacy did not have a duty to warn the pharmacy or consumers of the dangers associated with the product. Its obligation to warn extended only to physicians. Hofherr v. Dart Industries (C.A.-4 Md., 1988) 853 F.2d 259.

---

[18] Editor's note: Other cases involving the inability of a plaintiff to identify a specific DES manufacturer, resulting in an assertion of a "collective responsibility" theory of action, are listed under "Related cases," *infra.*

Defective product exception to successor liability rule not applicable to action based upon negligence

The successor corporation to a defunct manufacturer of DES could not be held liable under the defective product exception to the rule of successor liability where the action was based upon negligence and not upon strict liability. Maloney v. American Pharmaceutical Co. (1989) 207 Cal. App. 3d 285, 255 Cal. Rptr. 1.

Insufficient evidence that plaintiff's mother took DES during pregnancy

Where a DES daughter's mother could remember only that during her pregnancy her physician had prescribed some "little red cinnamon drops or pills" to prevent miscarriage, the plaintiff failed to demonstrate a "nonspeculative connection" between her injuries and the defendant's product. Shields v. Eli Lilly & Co. (D.D.C., 1988) 697 F. Supp. 12. See also Shields v. Eli Lilly & Co. (D.D.C.., 1988) 704 F. Supp. 224.

Husband of DES daughter has no claim for loss of consortium

In Clark v. Eli Lilly & Co. (N.D. N.Y., 1989) 725 F. Supp. 130, the court held that a husband could not recover damages for loss of consortium based upon the injuries his wife suffered as a result of her in utero exposure to DES.

Inability to identify manufacturer—Assertion of "collective responsibility" theories

Numerous drug manufacturers produced DES in the 1950s and 1960s, and many daughters who claim injury from their mothers having taken the product during pregnancy have had difficulty in identifying the particular manufacturer involved in their claim. In an attempt to overcome this obstacle, a number of these plaintiffs have asserted an assortment of theories based upon one form or another of joint or collective responsibility (e.g., "concert of action," "enterprise liability," "market share liability," "alternative liability," etc.). See the following:

California: McCreery v. Eli Lilly & Co. (1978) 87 Cal. App. 3d 77, 150 Cal. Rptr. 730; Sindell v. Abbott Laboratories (1980) 26 Cal. 3d 588, 163 Cal. Rptr. 132, 607 P.2d 924; Mertan v. E.R. Squibb & Sons (1983) 141 Cal. App. 3d 511, 190 Cal. Rptr. 349; Magallanes v. Superior Court (1985) 167 Cal. App. 3d 878, 213 Cal. Rptr. 547; Brown v. Superior Court (1988) 245 Cal. 3d 412, 751 P.2d 470.

District of Columbia: Tidler v. Eli Lilly & Co. (C.A.-D.C., 1988) 851 F.2d 418.

Florida: Morton v. Abbott Laboratories (M.D. Fla., 1982) 538 F. Supp. 593; Conley v. Boyle Drug Co. (Fla. App., 1985) 477 So. 2d 600; Wood v. Eli Lilly Co. (S.D. Fla. 1989) 723 F. Supp. 1456.

Illinois: Morrissy v. Eli Lilly & Co. (1979) 76 Ill. App. 3d 753, 32 Ill. Dec. 30, 394 N.E.2d 1369; Smith v. Eli Lilly & Co. (1988) 173 Ill. App. 3d 1, 122 Ill. Dec. 835, 527 N.E.2d 333.

Iowa: Mulcahy v. Eli Lilly & Co. (Iowa, 1986) 386 N.W.2d 67.

Massachusetts: Payton v. Abbott Labs (D. Mass., 1981) 512 F. Supp. 1031; Payton v. Abbott Labs (1982) 386 Mass. 540, 437 N.E.2d 171; McCormack v. Abbott Laboratories (D. Mass., 1985) 617 F. Supp. 1521.

Michigan: Abel v. Eli Lilly & Co. (1979) 94 Mich. App. 59, 289 N.W.2d 20, aff'd (1984) 418 Mich. 311, 343 N.W.2d 164.

Missouri: Zafft v. Eli Lilly & Co. (Mo., 1984) 676 S.W.2d 241.

New Jersey: Lyons v. Premo Pharmaceutical Labs (1979) 170 N.J.Super. 183, 406 A.2d 185; Ferrigno v. Eli Lilly & Co. (1980) 175 N.J.Super. 551, 420 A.2d 1305; Namm v. Charles E. Frosst & Co. (1981) 178 N.J.Super. 19, 427 A.2d 1121; Pipon v. Burroughs-Wellcome Co. (D. N.J., 1982) 532 F. Supp. 637, aff'd (C.A.-3 N.J., 1982) 696 F.2d 984.

New York: Bichler v. Eli Lilly & Co. (1981) 79 App. Div. 2d 317, 436 N.Y.S.2d 625, aff'd (1982) 55 N.Y.2d 571, 450 N.Y.S.2d 776, 436 N.E.2d 182; Kauffman v. Eli Lilly & Co. (1985) 65 N.Y.2d 449, 492 N.Y.S.2d 584, 482 N.E.2d 63; Schaeffer v. Eli Lilly & Co. (1985) 113 App. Div. 2d 827, 493 N.Y.S.2d 501; Tigue v. E.R. Squibb & Sons (N.Y. Misc., 1987) 518 N.Y.S.2d 891, aff'd (1988) 139 App. Div. 2d 431, 526 N.Y.S.2d 825.

Pennsylvania: Burnside v. Abbott Laboratories (1985) 351 Pa. Super. 264, 505 A.2d 973.

South Carolina: Ryan v. Eli Lilly & Co. (D. S.C., 1981) 514 F. Supp. 1004; Mizell v. Eli Lilly & Co. (D. S.C., 1981) 526 F. Supp. 589.

South Dakota: McElhaney v. Eli Lilly & Co. (D. S.D., 1983) 564 F. Supp. 265.

Washington: Martin v. Abbott Laboratories (1984) 102 Wash. 2d 581, 689 P.2d 368; George v. Parke-Davis (1987) 107 Wash. 2d 584, 733 P.2d 507.

Wisconsin: Collins v. Eli Lilly & Co. (1984) 116 Wis. 2d 166, 342 N.W.2d 37.

Discoverability or admissibility of evidence

For claims on behalf of DES daughters involving questions on the discoverability or admissibility of evidence, see:

California: Jones v. Superior Court for City of Alameda (1981) 119 Cal. App. 3d 534, 174 Cal. Rptr. 148.

District of Columbia: Tidler v. Eli Lilly & Co. (Dist. Ct. D.C., 1982) 95 F.R.D. 232; Doe v. Eli Lilly & Co. (Dist. Ct. D.C., 1983) 99 F.R.D. 126.

Illinois: Wetherill v. University of Chicago (N.D. Ill., 1981) 518 F. Supp. 1387; Andrews v. Eli Lilly & Co. (N.D. Ill., 1983) 97 F.R.D. 494; Wetherill v. University of Chicago (N.D. Ill., 1983) 565 F. Supp. 1553; Wetherill v. University of Chicago (N.D. Ill., 1983) 570 F. Supp. 1124; Deitch v. E.R. Squibb & Sons, Inc. (C.A.-7 Ill., 1984) 740 F.2d 556.

Louisiana: Schneider v. Eli Lilly & Co. (E.D. La., 1983) 556 F. Supp. 809.

Statutes of limitation

A New York statute permitting the revival of time-barred claims based on exposure to DES and four other specific substances, but not providing for the revival of other time-barred claims, did not violate the equal protection clause of the United States Constitution. Hymowitz v. Eli Lilly & Co. (Misc., 1987) 518 N.Y.S.2d 996, aff'd (1989) 73 N.Y.2d 487, 539 N.E.2d 1069.

Under Wisconsin's three-year statute of limitations, a DES daughter's cause of action against the manufacturer arising out of the death of her infant daughter, which she alleged was caused by her own in utero exposure to DES, accrued at the time of her daughter's death. As to her own alleged "physiological changes," her cause of action commenced to run when she was informed of such changes, and as to problems associated with her pregnancy with her second child her cause of action commenced to run when she learned that her pregnancy problems with her first child were probably caused by DES. Keith-Popp v. Eli Lilly and Co. (W.D. Wis., 1986) 639 F. Supp. 1479.

Pursuant to New Jersey's "tolling for infancy statute," a DES daughter's cause of action accrued when she reached age 21 even though she discovered her cause of action at age 20, which was after she had reached the age of majority. Hadden v. Eli Lilly & Co. (1986) 208 N.J. Super. 716, 506 A.2d 844.

In Burnside v. Abbott Laboratories (Pa. Super., 1986) 505 A.2d 973, a substantial issue of material fact existed as to whether a DES daughter acted reasonably when she decided to forego immediate pursuit of her claim on being assured by physicians that her condition was not related to the DES ingested by her mother.

For additional DES claims barred by statutes of limitation, see:

California: Pomeranz v. Abbott Laboratories (1987) 191 Cal. App. 3d 1331, 236 Cal. Rptr. 906; Jolly v. Eli Lilly & Co. (1988) 44 Cal. 3d 1103, 751 P.2d 923, 245 Cal. Rptr. 658.

Kansas: Lester v. Eli Lilly & Co. (D. Kan., 1988) 698 F. Supp. 843.

Michigan: Thomas v. Ferndale Laboratories, Inc. (1980) 97 Mich. App. 718, 2296 N.W.2d 160.

Nebraska: Brown v. Eli Lilly & Co. (D. Neb., 1988) 690 F. Supp. 857.

New Hampshire: Mertens v. Abbott Labs (D. N.H., 1984) 595 F. Supp. 834.

New York: Manno v. Levi (1983) 90 App. Div. 2d 628, 456 N.Y.S.2d 219. Greene v. Abbott Laboratories (1987) 137 Misc. 2d 424, 521 N.Y.S.2d 382, aff'd (1989) 148 App. Div. 2d 403, 359 N.Y.S.2d 351.

Pennsylvania: Obrien v. Eli Lilly & Co. (C.A.-3 Pa., 1982) 668 F.2d 704; Johnson v. Eli Lilly & Co. (W.D. Pa., 1983) 577 F. Supp. 174, aff'd (C.A.-3 Pa., 1984) 738 F.2d 422; Holder v. Eli Lilly (E.D. Pa., 1989) 708 F. Supp. 672.

Rhode Island: Swiss v. Eli Lilly & Co. (D. R.I., 1982) 559 F. Supp. 621.

Tennessee: Mathis v. Eli Lilly & Co. (C.A.-6 Tenn., 1983) 719 F.2d 134.

For additional DES claims not barred by statutes of limitation, see:

California: Kensinger v. Abbott Laboratories (1985) 171 Cal. App. 3d 376, 217 Cal. Rptr. 313; Leveque v. Abbott Laboratories (1987) 194 Cal. App. 3d 178, 240 Cal. Rptr. 278.

District of Columbia: Dawson v. Eli Lilly & Co. (D. D.C.) 543 F. Supp. 1330.

Florida: Diamond v. E.R. Squibb & Sons, Inc. (Fla., 1981) 397 So. 2d 671; Wood v. Eli Lilly Co. (S.D. Fla., 1989) 723 F. Supp. 1456 (statute of repose held unconstitutional).

Kansas: Colby v. E.R. Squibb & Sons, Inc. (D. Kan., 1984) 589 F. Supp. 714.

Massachusetts: Errichiello v. Eli Lilly & Co. (D. Mass., 1985) 618 F. Supp. 484.

Michigan: Yustick v. Eli Lilly & Co. (E.D. Mich., 1983) 573 F. Supp. 1558.

Missouri: Renfroe v. Eli Lilly & Co. (E.D. Mo., 1982) 541 F. Supp. 805.

Ohio: Harper v. Eli Lilly & Co. (N.D. Ohio, 1983) 575 F. Supp. 1358.

Rhode Island: Anthony v. Abbott Laboratories (R.I., 1985) 490 A.2d 43.

Tennessee: Tate v. Eli Lilly & Co. (M.D. Tenn., 1981) 522 F. Supp. 1048.

Vermont: Cavanaugh v. Abbott Laboratories (1985) 145 Vt. 516, 496 A.2d 154.

DIEUTRIM

See BENZOCAINE

DIGITOXIN

Crystodigin

Digitoxin is a cardiac glycoside obtained from *Digitalis purpurea* and indicated in the treatment of heart failure, atrial flutter, atrial fibrillation, and supraventricular tachycardia. Crystodigin is manufactured by Eli Lilly and Company (Indianapolis, Ind.).

Side effects include anorexia, nausea and vomiting, abdominal discomfort and diarrhea. Overdosage can cause the same reactions plus mental depression, premature heart beats, complete heart block, ventricular tachycardia, ventricular fibrillation, disorientation and delirium. Digitalis poisoning may simulate almost any known type of arrhythmia seen clinically.[19]

Brosseau v. Children's Mercy Hospital (No. CV-83-11343, Circuit Court, Jackson County, Mo., Aug. 3, 1984).

Child given fatal overdose following surgery—Hospital agrees to structured settlement worth $375,000— Physician settles for $110,000

A one-year-old girl developed tachycardia (rapid heart beat) following surgery for a congenital heart defect. A surgical resident,

[19] *Physicians' Desk Reference,* 40th ed., p. 1040.

after consulting with a cardiologist, ordered digitoxin in dosages of .1 milligrams with two follow-up doses of .55 milligrams each. On receiving the medication the child developed profound bradycardia (slow heart beat) and died. In their wrongful death action the plaintiffs charged that the resident physician ordered an overdose of the drug, that the proper dose for a one-year-old infant is no more than .05 milligrams per kilogram of body weight, and that the hospital nurses were negligent in failing to recognize the overdose. The plaintiffs also claimed the hospital pharmacy failed to obtain adequate information on the patient prior to dispensing the drug in violation of the American Society of Hospital Pharmacists minimum standards.

The physician settled for a lump sum payment of $110,000, and the hospital entered into a structured settlement agreement calling for $123,000 in cash, $1,000 monthly for twenty years, and a final payment of $250,000 at the end of twenty years.[20]

DIGOXIN
Lanoxin

Digoxin is a purified digitalis preparation derived from the leaves of *Digitalis lanata*. It is used to treat heart conditions, especially ischemic, hypertensive, valvular, and congenital heart disease. The correct dosage is important, and doses should be individualized in terms of therapeutic response.[21]

Several companies manufacture and market digoxin under the generic name. Lanoxin is produced by Burroughs Wellcome Co. (Research Triangle Park, N.C.).[22]

Cazes v. Raisinger (La. App., 1983) 430 So. 2d 104.

Excessive dosage—Insufficient evidence that drug caused death—$40,000 award reduced to $7,500

The decedent, a 71-year-old heart patient who also suffered from diabetes, was admitted to the hospital because of an overdose of Lanoxin. It was discovered that on filling a prescription for the decedent, the defendant pharmacist had typed on the label "One tablet four times a day" instead of one tablet a day as prescribed by the decedent's physician.

---

[20] ATLA *Law Reporter* 127:473, 1984.

[21] AMA *Drug Evaluations,* 6th ed., pp. 420, 424.

[22] *Physicians' Desk Reference,* 41st ed., p. 749.

The incident occurred on August 2, 1980. On August 25, the decedent was seen by a psychiatrist because she was afraid to take her medicine. She was seen again on September 3. On December 22, she was hospitalized for congestive heart failure. She was released two days later but was again hospitalized on January 4, 1982, and on January 16 she died. According to the death certificate, the cause of death was myocardial infarction as a consequence of coronary artery disease and chronic pulmonary disease. No autopsy was performed.

In their suit against the pharmacist, the decedent's survivors alleged that the decedent died as a result of "an irregular heart beat caused by the overdose of Lanoxin which aggravated a preexisting heart and circulatory condition." The case was tried without a jury and the plaintiffs were awarded a wrongful-death judgment of $40,000.

On appeal, the judgment was amended, the Court of Appeal of Louisiana holding that the medical testimony did not establish that the overdose of Lanoxin produced any lasting effects on the decedent's heart. The medical evidence, said the court, showed only that the overdose caused the decedent to become weak, and to suffer nausea, loss of appetite, vomiting, diarrhea and visual disturbances. In accordance, the court reduced the award to $7,500 for pain and suffering.

Bradley v. Burroughs Wellcome Co. (1986) 116 App. Div. 2d 548, 497 N.Y.S.2d 401.

Alleged excessive dosage—Time to sue runs from date of last exposure

The plaintiff's mother was administered Lanoxin continuously from 1965 through October, 1978. She died in March, 1981. The plaintiff commenced her action in September, 1981, alleging that the defendant manufacturer was negligent in failing to warn that her mother's dosages of Lanoxin should have been reduced, and that as a result, she continued to ingest an excessive dosage which ultimately caused her death.

The defendant moved for summary judgment, claiming the action was barred by the statute of limitations, and submitted documents showing that the patient first suffered her alleged injuries as early as 1972. The trial court dismissed the complaint.

The New York Supreme Court, Appellate Division, reversed, holding that the time to sue for injuries resulting from the ingestion of chemical substances runs from the *last exposure* to the substance rather than from the first exposure or the discovery of the injury.

Kehr v. Simfam RX, Inc. (No. N39746, Superior Court, San Diego County, Cal., June 16, 1989).

Excessive dosage—Label incorrectly typed at pharmacy—$175,000 settlement

The plaintiff, who was 88 years of age, was given a prescription for digoxin by her physician. The instructions called for a dosage of "qd." or once per day. The pharmacist wrote this on the order, but the owner of the pharmacy, who was typing the labels that day, misinterpreted the symbol to be "qid," or four times per day. When the label was returned to the pharmacist, she failed to notice the mistake.

Two weeks later, the plaintiff was taken to the hospital suffering from a "minor stroke." While there, she was given the proper daily dosage of digoxin, and her condition improved. After three days she was released in the care of her daughter.

At home the plaintiff began taking the excessive dosage again, and a week later she was rushed to the hospital in a semi-comatose state. This time the diagnosis was an overdose of digoxin. Laboratory reports revealed that her blood contained more than ten times the safe amount of the drug. She recovered, but had to have a pacemaker installed.

The plaintiff sued the pharmacy owner and the pharmacist, alleging negligence in filling the prescription. The plaintiff's daughter also sued, claiming negligent infliction of emotional distress from having witnessed her mother's "near death," and from having "unwittingly given her mother an overdose" when she administered the incorrect amount of digoxin.

The defendants moved for summary judgment as to the daughter's claim, which the trial court granted. The defendants then settled with the plaintiff for $175,000.[23]

[23] ATLA Professional Negligence Law Reporter 4:194, 1989.

p-DIISOBUTYLPHENOXYPOLYETHOXYETHANOL
Ortho-Gynol Contraceptive Jelly

p-Diisobutylphenoxypolyethoxyethanol is a spermicide used in Ortho-Gynol Contraceptive Jelly which is manufactured by Ortho Pharmaceutical Corp. (Raritan, N.J.). As a contraceptive, the product is designed for use with a vaginal diaphragm. The manufacturer warns of occasional "burning and/or irritation of the vagina or penis," but reports no serious adverse reactions.[23]

Wells v. Ortho Pharmaceutical Corp. (C.A.-11 Ga., 1986) 788 F.2d 741.

Birth defects—$4.7 million award affirmed against spermicide manufacturer

This action was brought on behalf of an infant born with severe birth defects, allegedly as a result of her mother using Ortho-Gynol Contraceptive Jelly at the time of conception.

After a lengthy bench trial involving numerous experts on both sides, the court held that the plaintiff had established that the spermicide caused the child's defects and that the defendant manufacturer had negligently failed to warn of this risk. The combined award to mother and child exceeded $5.1 million.

On appeal, the reviewing court acknowledged that the trial court admitted that it "found the studies to be inconclusive" on the ultimate issue of whether the product caused the birth defects (missing left arm, partial development of left clavicle and shoulder, cleft lip, nostril deformity, and an optic nerve defect), but noted that the law did not require the plaintiff "to produce scientific studies showing a statistically significant association between spermicides and congenital malformations in a large population." What matters, said the reviewing court, was that the trial court "found sufficient evidence of causation in a legal sense in this particular case."

As to the manufacturer's warning, the only warning on the label was that the spermicide "might cause irritation to the female or male genitalia, is not 100 percent effective, and should be kept out of the reach of children." Yet, evidence established that prior to the date the plaintiff purchased the product, the manufacturer "had actual or constructive knowledge that Ortho-Gynol might cause

[23] *Physicians' Desk Reference for Nonprescription Drugs,* 6th ed., p. 628.

birth defects" and thus it was under a duty to warn purchasers, including the plaintiff, of this risk.

The trial court's decision on liability was affirmed, but the reviewing court found a portion of the damages duplicative, and reduced the final award to $4,736,030.

Related cases

Birth defects—Action against manufacturer revived by amendment to statute

In Renzulli v. Ortho Pharmaceutical Corp. (Docket No. 82-0469B, U.S. District Court, D. R.I., July 5, 1983), it was held that an amendment to the Rhode Island wrongful-death statute which provided for the application of the discovery rule revived an action by a plaintiff who had used Ortho-Gynol contraceptive spermicidal jelly in 1975 while pregnant, and who later gave birth to a child with Down's syndrome and heart defects. The child died in May, 1977 at the age of nine months.[25]

DILANTIN

See PHENYTOIN SODIUM

DILAUDID

See HYDROMORPHONE HYDROCHLORIDE

DIMENHYDRINATE

Dramamine

Dimenhydrinate is the chlorotheophylline salt of the antihistamine diphenydramine. It is manufactured by Searle Laboratories (Chicago, Ill.) and sold under the name of Dramamine for the prevention and treatment of motion sickness and nausea. The product comes in ampules, vials, liquid, suppositories and tablets. In the 1981 product literature,[26] under "Dosage and Administration," the manufacturer describes the dosage for "intramuscular administration" and "intravenous therapy." No mention is made of subcutaneous injection.

---

[25] ATLA *Products Liability Law Reporter* 3:37, 1984.

[26] *Physicians' Desk Reference,* 35th ed., pp. 1645-46.

Barnes v. St. Francis Hosp. & School of Nursing, Inc. (1973) 211 Kan. 315, 507 P.2d 288.

Fat necrosis after subcutaneous injection—Nurses found negligent

On October 27, 1967 a patient was admitted to the hospital for a hemorrhoidectomy. She was operated on the next day. Following surgery she developed a painful indurated area in the left buttock, which was medically diagnosed as "fat necrosis." She was dismissed from the hospital on November 6, but was returned to the emergency room the next day where an incision was made under local anesthesia. On November 9 the patient was readmitted to the hospital and additional conservative treatment was begun. She was discharged and returned home November 28. The patient was again admitted on December 8; surgery was performed once more, and the patient remained hospitalized until January 2, 1968.

In a negligence action against the hospital, the patient's evidence tended to show that the fat necrosis, which denotes the death of fatty tissue, was caused by an injection of Dramamine improperly administered subcutaneously in the area of the left hip; that the correct way to administer the drug hypodermically would have been to inject it into the muscle, where the absorption would be better; that Dramamine could not safely be injected into the subcutaneous tissue, since it was an irritating substance and would cause damage to the tissue; and that the injection of the drug subcutaneously was not "good nursing procedure."

The physician's order, placed over the telephone, was for Dramamine to be given hypodermically. The evidence showed that "hypodermically" means either subcutaneously or intramuscularly; that the nurses involved were familiar with how different drugs were administered, and that nursing judgment had to be used in determining whether an injection should be given subcutaneously or intramuscularly where it had not been spelled out by the physician. Various nurses employed at the hospital testified that Dramamine, if given by needle, was to be administered deep, that is, intramuscularly; that it could not be given subcutaneously because it was irritating; and that the physician's order was given in the ordinary way, where the drug was as well known as Dramamine.

The jury returned a verdict in favor of the patient, and the trial court entered judgment accordingly. The hospital appealed, and the Supreme Court of Kansas affirmed, declaring:

We believe there is abundant evidence to establish knowledge on the part of the nursing staff that [D]ramamine, if administered hypodermically, rather than orally, must be given intramuscularly, even though the doctor's order may not be specific on this point.... [W]e are forced to conclude there was sufficient evidence to take the case to the jury and to support the jury's verdict.

DINOPROST TROMETHAMINE

Prostin F2 Alpha

Dinoprost tromethamine is a prostaglandin used to stimulate the uterus and induce abortion. It is usually injected through the abdomen into the amniotic sac. Possible dangerous adverse reactions include cervical or lower uterine laceration or rupture, retention of the placenta, and hemorrhage. Fever, hypotension and fainting, hypertension, headache, and pain and irritation at the site of the injection are also sometimes seen. The drug should be used with caution in women who have a history of cesarean section, hysterotomy, uterine fibroids, or cervical stenosis.[27]

Prostin F2 Alpha is manufactured by the Upjohn Company (Kalamazoo, Mich.).

Northern Trust Co. v. Upjohn Co. (No. 80 L 1539, Circuit Court, Cook County, Ill., April 14, 1989).

Cardiopulmonary arrest following Prostin-induced abortion—$9.5 million verdict against physician, hospital and manufacturer

The patient, 39 years of age, was admitted to the Illinois Masonic Medical Center for an intra-amniotic injection of Prostin F2 Alpha to induce a second-trimester abortion. Immediately after the injection, she experienced a sudden abnormal elevation in blood pressure. Her physician considered the conditions transient and left the department, and although the patient's symptoms persisted, and her condition worsened, she was not monitored by the nursing staff on a constant basis. Thirty minutes later she suffered cardiopulmonary arrest, resulting in brain damage, dementia and transcortical speech aphasia.

The patient's estate brought suit against the physician, the hospital, and the manufacturer of Prostin F2 Alpha. The physician was charged with negligence in failing to follow the manufacturer's es-

[27] AMA *Drug Evaluations,* 6th ed., p. 818.

tablished protocol for injecting Prostin F2 Alpha, failing to recognize and evaluate symptoms that required assessment and intervention to prevent cardiopulmonary arrest, and failing to remain at the patient's bedside. The hospital staff was accused of failing to abide by the manufacturer's drug protocol for the immediate availability of intensive care and acute surgical services, failing to require a thorough evaluation of the patient's post-injection symptoms by the defendant physician or another physician, failing to inform another physician of the patient's symptoms after the defendant physician left the department, and failing to properly handle the emergency that arose.

The Upjohn Company was charged with negligence, strict liability, and breach of implied warranty of merchantability in, among other things, failing to warn that transient complications of Prostin F2 Alpha could mask more serious problems, failing to warn that a physician should investigate each patient and determine if complications are transient or potentially catastrophic, and failing to warn that patients have sustained cardiopulmonary arrest and death after an injection of Prostin F2 Alpha. As to the claim of strict liability, the plaintiff alleged that although Upjohn knew or should have known that the drug was unreasonably dangerous and defective, it had failed to warn of its effect on patients in general, and especially on persons with hypertension or those using other medications. Also, Upjohn was charged with failing to specify treatment for cardiopulmonary arrest induced by the drug.

During the discovery stage of the case, the plaintiff's attorneys found that seven years earlier, Upjohn had received several reports documenting a relationship between Prostin F2 Alpha and cardiac arrest.

Upjohn claimed that their drug had not caused the patient's death, that she had suffered an amniotic fluid embolus, a rare complication of pregnancy. The physician claimed that Upjohn's package insert had misled him, that it had caused him to believe that the patient's symptoms were transient, and that if it had warned him of the possibility of cardiopulmonary arrest, he would have "approached [the patient's] injection differently" by using a smaller dose of the drug. The hospital was expected to defend on the ground that the patient was not suffering from organic brain damage, but a hysterical conversion reaction to her abortion (because she was Catholic).

The jury returned a verdict for the plaintiff against all defendants in the total amount of $9.5 million, which included $1.5 million for past and future pain and suffering.[1]

DIMETHISTERONE

See ETHINYL ESTRADIOL with DIMETHISTERONE

DIPHENOXYLATE HYDROCHLORIDE with ATROPINE SULFATE

Di-Atro

Lomotil

Diphenoxylate hydrochloride is a drug chemically related to the narcotic meperidine, and is used as adjunctive therapy in the treatment of diarrhea. The atropine sulfate has been added to discourage deliberate overdosage. It acts as a mild stimulant.

Purepac Pharmaceutical Company (Elizabeth, N.J.) produces the drug under the generic name, Legere Pharmaceuticals (Costa Mesa, Cal.) produces Di-Atro, and Searle & Company (San Juan, P.R.) manufactures the product under the Lomotil label.

Searle warns that the drug is not innocuous, and that dosage recommendations should be strictly adhered to, especially in children. For several years the company's product information has listed the drug as contraindicated in children of less than two years of age.[2]

Dunaway v. Raney (No. 7048, Circuit Court, Marion County, Miss., Jan. 13, 1977).

**Lomotil contraindicated in child of three weeks—
$25,000 settlement with physician**

The three-week-old female infant was diagnosed as having severe infant diarrhea and the physician prescribed Lomotil every three hours while awake. The child became cyanotic after one and one-half doses. The physician was unable to diagnose the cause of the cyanosis and referred the infant to a pediatrician who determined that the condition was due to drug depression caused by the Lomotil.

---

[1] ATLA *Law Reporter* 32:305, 1989.

[2] *Physicians' Desk Reference,* 35th ed., pp. 1661-62.

The plaintiff complained that the physician negligently prescribed Lomotil since *Physicians' Desk Reference* did not at the time recommend it for children under three months of age, and that he failed to recognize the error and administer an antidote.

According to the attorney for the infant, the physician settled for $25,000.[3]

DIPHENYLHYDANTOIN SODIUM

See PHENYTOIN SODIUM

DIPHTHERIA and TETANUS TOXOIDS with PERTUSSIS VACCINE (DTP)

Tri-Immunol

This combination of toxoids and vaccine provides for the simultaneous immunization against diphtheria, tetanus and pertussis. It is indicated for infants and children through six years of age. Because the incidence and severity of pertussis decrease with age, routine pertussis immunization is not recommended for persons seven years of age or older.

The manufacturer of Tri-Immunol (Lederle Laboratories, a division of American Cyanamid Company, Wayne, N.J.) cautions that immunization should be deferred during any acute illness, and that the "occurrence of any type of neurological symptoms or signs, including one or more convulsions (seizures) following administration of this product is a contraindication to further use." The product is also contraindicated if the child has a personal or family history of central nervous system disorders, and the "presence of any evolving or changing disorder affecting the central nervous system is a contraindication to administration of DTP regardless of whether the suspected neurological disorder is associated with occurrence of seizure activity of any type."

Significant adverse reactions attributed to the pertussis vaccine component have been: "high fever of 40.5 C (105 F), a transient shock-like episode, excessive screaming (persistent crying or screaming for three or more hours duration), somnolence, convulsions, and encephalopathy."

---

[3] ATLA *Law Reporter* 20:328, 1977.

Mild to moderate temperature elevations frequently follow DTP and are often accompanied by "fretfulness, drowsiness, vomiting, and anorexia."[4]

Piefer v. Devitt (No. 590-343, Circuit Court, Milwaukee County, Wis., Feb. 1, 1984).

Infant suffers seizures, mental retardation—Third injection given despite reaction—$3 million verdict against pediatrician

The patient, a three-month-old infant, received her first DTP injection in July. That evening her mother called the defendant pediatrician and reported that the child had a rectal fever of 106 degrees and was irritable. A month later, after her second injection, the child suffered projectile vomiting and a rash. She received her third injection in October, and that night she went into seizures. Although the child experienced further seizures, the defendant did not prescribe anticonvulsants until six months later. A month after that, the girl suffered a seizure which lasted over two hours and left her mentally retarded. She has an IQ of 52 and requires round-the-clock custodial care.

The jury awarded $3.05 million which included $1.3 million for future medical care, $1.25 million for past and future pain and suffering, and $500,000 for impairment of future earnings.[5]

Cannon v. Strauss (No. 49428, Superior Court, Suffolk County, Mass., January 4, 1985).

Wrong vaccine administered—Physician settles for $400,000

A forty-two-year-old nurse's aide applying for nurses' training visited her physician's office for an inoculation of diphtheria and tetanus vaccine which was required of all nursing school applicants. But instead of administering the "DT" vaccine, the physician gave the patient "DTP" which is not recommended for persons over six years of age. The patient began to suffer cramping, vomiting and nausea within hours after the injection. She called the physician, but he only advised her to chew on ice and drink no food or water. On the eighth day she suddenly died from a seizure. The case was settled for $400,000.[6]

---

[4] *Physicians' Desk Reference,* 40th ed., pp. 1031-32.

[5] ATLA *Law Reporter* 27:235, 1984.

[6] Id., 28:225, 1985.

Triplett v. Lederle Laboratories (No. 82-4618, Circuit Court, Broward County, Fla., Mar. 12, 1985).

Seizures, brain damage and mental retardation—Plaintiff, unable to identify manufacturer, names several companies—$300,000 settlement

At age two months the infant plaintiff received a routine DTP vaccination from her pediatrician. She immediately screamed, and a lump developed at the injection site. She developed a high fever and began to have seizures, which eventually numbered over 200 per day. Brain damage resulted, and the child is now retarded and will require custodial care for the remainder of her life.

The child's parents were unable to identify the particular manufacturer of the vaccine and, therefore, brought suit against several drug companies that produced DTP. The parties agreed to a $300,000 settlement, with all defendants participating.[7]

Toner v. Lederle Laboratories (C.A.-9 Idaho, 1987) 828 F.2d 510.

Paralysis—Manufacturer negligent in failing to market safer vaccine—$1.1 million verdict affirmed

In 1979, the plaintiff, a three-month-old child, was vaccinated with Tri-Immunol. Shortly thereafter he developed transverse myelitis resulting in permanent paralysis from the waist down.

The basis of the lawsuit against the manufacturer was that it could have marketed a safer vaccine (Tri-Solgen). The jury returned a verdict for $1.1 million, but the Ninth Circuit Court of Appeals found that the law was not clear on the controlling questions of liability, and it certified these questions to the Supreme Court of Idaho. (See Toner v. Lederle Laboratories (C.A.-9 Idaho, 1986) 779 F.2d 1429.) The primary question concerned whether Comment k of § 402A of the *Restatement (Second) of Torts* excepting from strict liability unavoidably unsafe products applied to strict liability claims based on an allegedly defective design of a product and, more particularly, whether the principles of the *Restatement* comment applied to the claim in this suit. The Supreme Court of Idaho ruled that the comment did apply and that the fact that a product was excepted from strict liability under the unavoidably unsafe products doctrine did not shield a manufacturer from a negligence

[7] ATLA *Products Liability Law Reporter* 4:90, 1985.

claim. The court further ruled that the warnings given in the present case were adequate. (See Toner v. Lederle Laboratories (1987) 112 Idaho 328, 732 P.2d 297.)

In light of the decision of the Supreme Court of Idaho, the Ninth Circuit Court of Appeals affirmed the jury verdict, holding that under Idaho Law, Lederle Laboratories was not strictly liable for the plaintiff's paralysis, because the vaccine was an unavoidably unsafe product, but there was no error in the jury finding that Lederle was negligent in failing to develop and market the safer vaccine, and that this negligence was the proximate cause of the plaintiff's injury.

Percival v. American Cyanamid Co. (W.D. Okla., 1987) 689 F. Supp. 1060.

Brain damage—Manufacturer's warning to physician adequate—No duty to warn consumer

The parents of a child who suffered brain damage after receiving three doses of DPT vaccine alleged, among various other theories, that the manufacturer was negligent in failing to warn them directly of the possible adverse reactions to the vaccine, and in failing to adequately warn the physician who administered the vaccine.

On granting the manufacturer's motion for summary judgment on these two specific charges, the trial court held that under Oklahoma law a prescription drug manufacturer need only warn the prescribing physician of the potential hazards of a drug. As to such warning, the court found that the following information, contained in the package insert, adequately informed the physician of the risk involved.

> ADVERSE REACTIONS
> Adverse reactions may be local and include pain, erythema, tenderness and induration at the site of injection. Significant reactions attributed to the pertussis vaccine component have been high fever (greater than 39°C), a transient shock-like episode, excessive screaming, somnolence, *convulsions, encephalopathy* and thrombocytopenia. Such reactions almost always appear within 24 to 48 hours after injection but have been thought to occur after an interval as long as seven days. A small nodule may develop at the site of the injection and remain for a few weeks before being completely absorbed. Sterile abscesses have been reported. Systemic reactions include mild to moderate transient fever, chills, malaise, and irritability.

Neurological disorders such as encephalopathy, possibly due to the pertussis component, have been reported to occur rarely following the injection of this product and they *may be fatal, or result in permanent damage to the central nervous system.*

***

Should symptomatology referable to the central nervous system develop following administration, no further immunization with this product should be attempted.

Routine immunization should be postponed or avoided in patients with acute infections, or a personal or family history of neurological disturbances.

Bock v. Yoder (La. App., 1988) 518 So. 2d 1139.

Infant's foot-drop noticed 16 days after injection—No causal connection

The plaintiff's child was born on June 1, 1982. On September 3, he received a DPT injection. On October 25, he was diagnosed as having a "left foot-drop." In a lawsuit against the physician, the plaintiff claimed that the injection was improperly administered.

At the trial, the evidence established that the mother did not notice the child's foot-drop until sixteen days after the injection. The defendant's experts testified that because of this, the injection could not have been the cause of the disorder. Also, the plaintiff's expert, who testified that in his opinion the injection had caused the foot-drop, admitted on cross-examination that when he gave this opinion he thought the mother had noticed the foot-drop "several days" after the injection.

The trial judge dismissed the suit, and the Court of Appeal affirmed.

White v. Wyeth Laboratories (1988) 40 Ohio St. 3d 390, 533 N.E.2d 748.

Brain damage—Verdict for plaintiffs reversed—Manufacturer not liable under Restatement Comment k exception applicable to "unavoidably unsafe products"

In 1983, the plaintiffs' four-year-old son was given two injections of the DTP vaccine. He experienced no reaction to the first injection, but following the second, two months later, he suffered a severe convulsion and was rushed to the hospital. He was discharged after two days and appeared to be in good health; however, a month later he suffered more convulsions and eventually was diagnosed as having a permanent seizure disorder and mental retardation.

The plaintiffs' suit against the manufacturer alleged negligence and strict liability, and sought punitive damages. They claimed the defendant: (1) failed to test the vaccine adequately to determine whether it caused severe adverse reactions; (2) failed to warn the medical profession and the public adequately of the propensity of the vaccine to cause such adverse reactions; and (3) failed to manufacture a safer alternative vaccine.

At the close of the plaintiffs' case, the trial court directed a verdict in favor of the manufacturer on the issue of punitive damages, finding no evidence that it acted maliciously, recklessly or willfully. At the close of all the evidence, the court directed a verdict in favor of the manufacturer as to the negligence claims, but not as to strict liability. The jury returned a verdict for the plaintiffs in the amount of $2.1 million.

On appeal, the Court of Appeals of Cuyahoga County reversed, holding that because DTP is an "unavoidably unsafe product," under Comment k of the *Restatement (Second) of Torts* Wyeth could not be held strictly liable by the vaccine's inherent dangers. The court further held that the warning accompanying the product adequately informed the medical profession of the risk of such a reaction, and there was no evidence that Wyeth could, at the time, offer a safer alternative vaccine.

The case was certified to the Supreme Court of Ohio which affirmed the Court of Appeals, holding that a product is unavoidably unsafe if, when it is distributed, no alternative design existed that would have effectively accomplished the same purpose with less risk. The Supreme Court found that Wyeth's license application to market a safer, fractionated cell vaccine had been rejected by the FDA, and thus it could not have legally marketed an equally effective product with less risk.

Williams v. City of New York (No. 23503/83, Supreme Court, New York County, N.Y., September 7, 1988).

Brain damage—Clinic administers vaccine despite child's earlier seizures—$2.1 million settlement

The plaintiff's three-year-old child had received her first DTP injection at a city clinic without incident. Three hours after her second injection, however, she was rushed to the hospital suffering from a seizure disorder, which the physicians determined was probably due to the vaccine. She was treated with phenobarbital and appeared to recover.

Two months later, during a routine check-up at the clinic, the plaintiff informed the staff of the child's seizure following the second injection. Despite this information, the staff administered a third injection. Several hours later the child again developed seizures and was rushed to the hospital. This time treatment was unsuccessful, and today the plaintiff's daughter remains severely retarded and will suffer seizures for the rest of her life.

If this case went to trial, the plaintiff was prepared to introduce the clinic's manual of procedure which stated that if a child suffers seizures following an injection of DTP vaccine, only a vaccine not containing pertussis should be given thereafter. According to the plaintiff's attorney, the parties settled for $2.1 million, plus waiver of unpaid medical bills totaling $250,000.[8]

Wallace v. Khorram (No. 87-CI-167, Circuit Court, Bell County, W. Va., January 24, 1989).

Pediatrician orders third DTP injection despite neurologist's finding of prior toxin-induced brain damage

The defendant, a Dr. Khorram, ordered an injection of DTP vaccine for the plaintiffs' child at age two months. Several hours after the injection, the child's temperature soared to 106 degrees, and he cried "inconsolably." During the following weeks, he became "increasingly agitated" and developed irregular sleeping patterns. Two months later, even though the child's mother informed Dr. Khorram of this reaction, the physician ordered a second DTP injection. Within several hours the child again spiked a fever, and this time suffered seizures.

During an examination of the child two weeks later, Dr. Khorram suspected neurological problems, and referred him to a neurologist. The neurologist informed the mother that the child had suffered brain damage from having been "exposed to a toxic substance at age two months." Two months later, however, without consulting the neurologist, Dr. Khorram ordered a third DTP injection for the child. The child is now permanently brain-damaged and continues to suffer seizures.

---

[8] ATLA *Professional Negligence Law Reporter* 4:49, 1989.

The plaintiffs and Dr. Khorram agreed to a structured settlement with a present value of $313,276.[9]

Leuzinger v. Berk (No. 680-162, Circuit Court, Milwaukee County, Wis., May 4, 1989).

Brain damage—Pediatrician administers second vaccination despite apparent adverse reaction—$1.54 million jury verdict—Manufacturer settles for $1.3 million

The plaintiff's three-month-old son received a DTP vaccination from his pediatrician. The following day he cried "inconsolably" for four hours, and on several occasions "jerked his head" and "clenched his fists." The child continued to exhibit "occasional jerking movements" over the next two weeks, which the pediatrician assured the plaintiff were only "startle reactions." A month later, the pediatrician administered a second DTP injection. The child developed seizures and was rushed to the hospital. He is now brain-damaged, borderline mentally retarded, and must take medication to prevent seizures.

The plaintiff and her husband sued the pediatrician, claiming that he was negligent in administering the second vaccination after what later was determined to be an adverse reaction to the first. They also sued Wyeth Laboratories, manufacturer of the vaccine, on the grounds that the vaccine was unnecessarily and unreasonably dangerous. Wyeth settled before trial for $1.3 million, and a jury returned a verdict against the pediatrician for $1.54 million, to which the trial court added $480,000 in prejudgment interest.[10]

Abner v. Pediatric Care, P.S.C. (No. 87-CI-729, Circuit Court, Kenton County, Ky., June 27, 1989).

Brain Damage—Clinic employees failed to warn of adverse reaction—No history taken on second visit—$5.6 million verdict

Following her first DTP injection, the two-month-old patient cried inconsolably and developed a high fever, then became excessively sleepy. Not realizing that these symptoms suggested an adverse reaction, the child's mother brought her back to the defendant clinic for her second injection two months later. Six hours after this injection, the child began to suffer seizures and went into a coma.

---

[9] ATLA *Professional Negligence Law Reporter* 4:111, 1989.
[10] ATLA *Professional Negligence Law Reporter* 4:190, 1989.

At the time of trial, she was profoundly retarded and required nearly total care.

The parents charged the clinic with negligence in failing to warn of the possibility of an adverse reaction, and in failing to take a history on the second visit to determine if there was an adverse reaction to the first injection. At the trial, a former clinic employee testified that it was not the general practice of the clinic's physicians or employees to warn of the possibility of adverse reactions nor to take patient histories before subsequent PTP injections.

The jury returned a verdict of $5.6 million.[11]

Gatts v. Lederle Laboratories (No. 255505, District Court, Plymouth County, Iowa, June 27, 1989).

Pediatricians disregard child's seizures following first injection—Brain damage—$375,000 structured settlement

A four-month-old child's pediatrician informed his mother that he should have his DTP vaccine. Several hours after the vaccination, the child suffered a seizure. His parents took him back to the office, where the pediatrician's partner diagnosed "febrile convulsion." The parents took the child home, but he continued to suffer seizures, which they reported to the physicians.

Two months later, the pediatrician administered "split doses" of the vaccine over a two-week period. The child's seizures continued, and he was eventually diagnosed as brain-damaged.

The parents filed suit against the pediatrician, alleging negligent administration of the vaccine, and against the manufacturer of the vaccine, alleging failure to warn of the hazard. The pediatrician entered into a structured settlement which had a present value of $375,000. The parents also settled with the manufacturer, but the amount remains confidential.[12]

Rohrbough v. Wyeth Laboratories, Inc. (N.D. W. Va., 1989) 719 F. Supp. 470.

Brain damage—Plaintiffs' experts fail to attribute Lennox-Gastaut syndrome to vaccine—Manufacturer granted summary judgment

The plaintiffs' child suffered a seizure following her second dose of DTP. Even though she had to be hospitalized, she was given

---

[11] ATLA *Professional Negligence Law Reporter* 5:11, 1990.

[12] ATLA *Professional Negligence Law Reporter* 5:12, 1990.

another half dose the following month. She experienced another seizure and today is profoundly retarded and suffers from a seizure disorder which some physicians have designated Lennox-Gastaut syndrome.

In the plaintiffs' suit against the manufacturer, in which they claim strict liability, breach of express and implied warranties, and failure to warn, the trial court granted the defendant's motion for summary judgment, holding that the plaintiffs' failed to establish causation. The plaintiffs offered the opinions of three experts, but none were willing affirmatively to attribute the child's injuries to the vaccine. One of the experts, a pathologist, did file a later affidavit stating that in his opinion the vaccine "caused the neurological injuries from which [the plaintiffs' child] has suffered and continues to suffer," but the court refused to accept it under the rule that if a statement in an affidavit contradicts earlier deposition testimony "constitutes an attempt by the nonmoving party to create a sham issue of fact," it may be disregarded.

Related cases

DTP and other immunizations administered to ill child—Death occurs three days later —Settlement allegedly $400,000

In Gonzales v. Lovelace Medical Center (No. CV-84-02215, District Court, Bernalillo County, N.M., Feb. 2, 1986), a pediatrician gave a two-year-old child DTP vaccine and, at the same time, vaccinated him for measles, mumps, rubella, polio and tuberculosis, despite the fact that the child showed symptoms of fever, wheezing and a runny nose when he was brought in. The following day the child became lethargic and pale, and on the third day he was hospitalized where he allegedly received negligent care. Later that day he died. The pediatrician was accused of gross negligence in administering the multiple immunizations which were contraindicated because of the child's apparent illness. The hospital was sued for negligent treatment. The parties settled, but by the terms of the agreement could not disclose the amount. Local newspaper accounts, however, reported the sum to be $400,000.[13]

Brain damage—Manufacturer not required to warn mother, but whether physician's warning was adequate and whether it would have averted injury were questions for jury

In an action on behalf of a child who suffered brain damage following a DTP injection, the learned intermediary doctrine relieved

[13] ATLA *Law Reporter* 29:323, 1986.

the manufacturer of the duty to warn the mother directly of the risk of receiving the vaccine, but the trial court erred in failing to permit the jury to consider whether the physician adequately warned the mother, and whether such a warning might have averted the injury. Neimiera v. Schneider (1989) 114 N.J. 550, 555 A.2d 112.

Brain damage—Punitive damages available under "market share" theory

Under the "market share" theory of liability as established in California, the parents of a child who suffered brain damage following a reaction to DTP vaccine could claim punitive damages. Morris v. Parke Davis & Co. (C.D. Cal., 1983) 573 F. Supp. 1324.

Brain damage—New Jersey rejects "risk-modified market share" liability," "concert-of-action," and "alternative liability" theories

In an action on behalf of a brain-damaged child who had been given DTP vaccine supplied by an unidentified manufacturer, the Superior Court of New Jersey, Appellate Division, held that a "risk-modified market share" theory was appropriate to determine the collective responsibility of the defendant drug companies (219 N.J. Super. 601, 530 A.2d 1287); however, on appeal to the Supreme Court of New Jersey, that court reversed, holding that the state should not modify traditional tort theories. The Court also rejected the "concert of action" theory, citing the lack of allegations that the DTP manufacturers had a tacit understanding or common plan to produce a defective product or not conduct adequate tests, and the "alternative liability" theory, since not all of the culpable defendants were joined in the action. Shackil v. Lederle Laboratories (1989) 116 N.J. 155, 561 A.2d 511.

Brain damage—"Alternate liability" theory rejected in Oregon—Manufacturers not insulated from liability because vaccination mandated by government

In a DTP case in which the plaintiff could not identify the manufacturer of the vaccine, the Supreme Court of Oregon rejected the theory of "alternative liability," but also rejected the argument that the defendants were insulated from liability because the plaintiff had received the vaccine as part of a government-mandated vaccination program. Senn v. Merrell Dow Pharmaceuticals (1988) 350 Or. 256, 751 P.2d 215.

Fatal reaction—"Alternative liability" theory not available in Georgia, but manufacturer identified as supplier of vaccine

In Chapman v. American Cyanamid Co. (C.A.-11 Ga., 1988) 861 F.2d 1515, the parents of a six-week-old infant who died after being given DTP vaccine sued two manufacturers (American Cyanamid Co. and Wyeth Laboratories) which had possibly supplied the vaccine to the pediatrician who administered it. Both defendants moved for summary judgment, claiming that under Georgia law a products liability plaintiff must prove that a specific manufacturer's product was the proximate cause of injury to proceed either under the theory of negligence or strict liability. The trial court sustained the defendants' motions, but the Court of Appeals reversed as to defendant American Cyanamid, finding that while in Georgia the theory of alternative liability is not available, the plaintiffs produced substantial circumstantial evidence from which a jury could conclude that the vaccine administered to their child was manufactured by that company.

Brain damage—Plaintiff not entitled to instruction that manufacturer's compliance with FDA regulations not a defense

In Malek v. Lederle Laboratories (1984) 125 Ill. App. 3d 870, 81 Ill. Dec. 236, 466 N.E.2d 1038, in which the parents of a four-month-old child who suffered brain damage following vaccination with DTP vaccine (Tri-Immunol) charged the manufacturer with inadequate warnings, the plaintiffs were not entitled to a jury instruction that it was not a defense that the manufacturer complied with FDA regulations in producing and marketing the product. See also Malek v. Lederle Laboratories (1987) 152 Ill. App. 3d 493, 105 Ill. Dec. 608, 504 N.E.2d 893 (alleged newly discovered evidence).

Fatal reaction—State tort action not preempted by federal laws

A wrongful-death claim for a DTP-related death was not preempted by FDA regulations, the Public Health Service Act nor the National Childhood Vaccine Injury Act of 1986, and the action was permissible not withstanding the manufacturer's compliance with federal regulations. Patten v. Lederle Laboratories (D. Utah, 1987) 655 F. Supp. 745.

Brain damage—Claim not time-barred by statute nor preempted by federal law

Under Ohio's discovery rule, a fact issue existed as to when the claim of the parents of a DTP-injured child arose. Also, the savings clause of the statute of limitations tolled the running of the statute because the manufacturer was not registered in the state and did not have a statutory agent there. Furthermore, the plaintiffs' claim in state court for defective design, failure to warn, and punitive damages was not preempted by FDC regulations nor by the Public Health Service Act. Wack v. Lederle Laboratories (N.D. Ohio, 1987) 666 F. Supp. 123.

Brain damage—FDA regulations do not preempt state law claims against manufacturer—DTP vaccine not "unavoidably unsafe" drug

In Graham v. Wyeth Laboratories (D. Kan., 1987) 666 F. Supp. 1483, a DTP manufacturer was not entitled to a summary judgment based on the argument that FDA regulations of prescription drugs preempted state law in claims against manufacturers, and that DTP vaccine was, as a matter of law, an "unavoidably unsafe" prescription drug which contains an adequate warning. The court also held, however, that the manufacturer could not be held strictly liable on the failure to warn theory where the plaintiffs admitted that they received warnings.

FDA regulations do not preempt state strict product liability law

Comprehensive FDA regulations for marketing and design of DTP vaccine and other drugs do not preempt New Mexico's strict product liability law for defective design of vaccine. MacGillivray v. Lederle Laboratories (D. N.M., 1987) 667 F. Supp. 743.

Brain damage—State court claim not preempted by federal law—Market share theory applicable to design defect claims and breach of express warranty—Implied warranty action not available under design defect theory

Claims by the parents of a brain-damaged child were not preempted by the National Childhood Vaccine Injury Act of 1986, and California's market share theory was available to claims based on design defect and breach of express warranty. A claim of breach of implied warranty, however, could not be asserted on the design defect theory. Morris v. Parke, Davis & Co. (C.D. Cal., 1987) 667 F. Supp. 1332.

FDA regulations do not preempt state claims—Issue of fact exists on adequacy of warning and questions of negligence and breach of warranty

In Martinkovic v. Wyeth Laboratories (N.D. Ill., 1987) 669 F. Supp. 212, a DTP manufacturer was denied summary judgment, the court holding that FDA regulations did not preempt state tort claims arising out of injury caused by the vaccine and that genuine issues of material fact existed as to the adequacy of the warning contained in the package insert, and as to whether the manufacturer was negligent or whether it breached warranty in producing and packaging the vaccine.

Brain damage—No federal preemption of state law—Whether vaccination was contraindicated and weight of expert testimony on safer vaccine both questions for jury

In Knudsen v. United States (M.D. Fla., 1987) 691 F. Supp. 1346, the court held that Congress did not intend, through granting the FDA authority to test and license vaccine, to preempt state law governing claims for DPT vaccine-related injury. It also held that whether the package insert suggested that the infant's vaccination was contraindicated, and whether the plaintiff's expert had an adequate scientific basis for his opinion that the manufacturer could have developed a safer vaccine, were questions for the jury.

Brain damage—Availability of less toxic vaccines at time of injection precludes summary judgment—Claim not preempted by federal law

Evidence that at the time the plaintiff's brain-damaged child was injected with DPT less toxic pertussis vaccines were available raised a fact issue as to whether the vaccine used was a defective product and precluded a summary judgment for the manufacturer. Also, the plaintiff's claim was not preempted by federal law. Jones v. Lederle Laboratories (E.D. N.Y., 1988) 695 F. Supp. 700.

Brain damage—Federal law does not preempt Virginia's common law on liability for defective design or failure to warn

In Abbot v. American Cyanamid Co. (C.A.-4 Va., 1988) 844 F.2d 1108, the court held that federal law does not preempt Virginia's common law on liability for a DTP manufacturer's defective design or failure to warn. Virginia's coexisting law on liability for the defective design of a vaccine, or for a manufacturer's failure to warn, would not frustrate the federal interest in vaccine safety or availability. The court went on to hold that under Virginia law, a manufacturer's allegedly adequate warning as to a vaccine does not foreclose a design defect claim in either warranty or tort. And in the case at hand, a question of fact precluded a summary judgment for the manufacturer as to the adequacy of the warning.

Brain damage—Federal law does not preempt Texas product liability action—"Mass immunization" exception to learned intermediary doctrine inapplicable—Fact issue exists as to whether manufacturer withheld information from FDA

In this Fifth Circuit case, the Food, Drug and Cosmetic Act did not implicitly preempt a Texas product liability action against a DPT manufacturer for failure to warn, but the "mass immunization" exception to the learned intermediary doctrine did not apply to the plaintiff's claim. However, a fact issue did exist as to whether the manufacturer withheld material information from the FDA so as to render the agency-approved warning inadequate. Hurley v. Lederle Laboratories Division of American Cyanamid Co. (C.A.-5 Tex., 1989) 863 F.2d 1173.

Brain damage—City health department not subject to liability under commonwealth agency waiver of immunity

Where a child suffered brain damage following a DTP vaccination by a city health department physician, the city was not subject to liability as a "Commonwealth party" under a statute waiving sovereign immunity with respect to medical malpractice committed by health care employees of commonwealth agency medical facilities. Matteo v. City of Philadelphia (1986) 99 Pa. Commw. 152, 512 A.2d 796.

Strict liability not available under Iowa Tort Claims Act

In Hoctel v. State (Iowa, 1984) 343 N.W.2d 832, the Supreme Court of Iowa held that the Iowa Tort Claims Act does not permit an action on behalf of a child injured after receiving an immunization shot provided by the state that is based solely on the theory of strict liability.

Fatal reaction—Restatement Comment k applied

Under Utah law, Comment k of the *Restatement (Second) of Torts* § 402A, which provides an exception to strict liability in tort for "unavoidably unsafe" products, applied to a claim by the parents of a two-month-old infant who died the day after he received DTP vaccine. Patten v. Lederle Laboratories (D. Utah, 1987) 676 F. Supp. 233.

Brain damage—Manufacturer not granted immunity by statutes

Neither the California statute requiring every child in the state to receive DTP vaccine before being admitted to school (Health & Safety Code §§ 3380-3390) nor the statute providing that "no person shall be liable for any injury caused by an act or omission in the administration of a vaccine or other immunizing agent to a minor ... if such immunization is required by state law ...." (Health & Safety Code § 429.36) grants immunity to the manufacturer of a vaccine. Flood v. Wyeth Laboratories (1986) 183 Cal. App. 3d 1272, 228 Cal. Rptr. 700.

Fatal reaction—Two-year medical malpractice statute applies

Illinois' two-year statute of limitations applicable to medical malpractice actions, rather than the four-year statute for U.C.C. claims, governed a breach of warranty action against a physician who administered a fatal DTP injection. Desai v. Chasnoff (1986) 146 Ill. App. 3d 163, 100 Ill. Dec. 138, 496 N.E.2d 1203.

Brain damage—Malpractice action not timely filed—Claim against manufacturer did not interrupt running of statute

A malpractice claim against a physician who administered a DTP injection was properly dismissed for the plaintiff's failure to file the action within Louisiana's statutory three-year prescription period. The fact that the plaintiff filed a claim against the manufacturer within the required period did not interrupt prescription as to the malpractice claim. Cheramie v. Terral (La. App., 1988) 516 So. 2d 1329.

Brain damage—Four-year statute of limitations applied to breach of warranty claim—Summary judgment precluded by physician's inconsistent statements as to cause of child's seizures

In a breach of warranty and negligence action by the mother of a child who suffered brain damage following a DTP vaccination, the four-year statute of limitations, measured from the date of the last vaccination, applied to the warranty claim, rather than the two-year statute applicable to personal injuries, measured from the time of the discovery of the harm. However, the manufacturer's summary judgment was precluded by a material question of fact as to whether a physician's statement that the child's post-vaccination seizures were not caused by the vaccine, made after an earlier statement that the seizures were caused by the vaccine, excused the mother from diligently inquiring as to the possible connection between the vaccine and the seizures, and thus, under the discovery rule, tolled the running of the statute. Connaught Laboratories, Inc. (Pa. Commw., 1989) 557 A.2d 40.

Litigation involving former DTP vaccines

In an action by the mother of an infant who contracted encephalopathy following vaccination with either Quadrigen or Compligen (DTP vaccines which included Salk polio vaccine, neither of which product is marketed today), the evidence introduced by the plaintiff made out a prima facie case as to negligence of the manufacturer of Quadrigen (in designing the drug and in the decision to market it) and as to the negligence of the physician who administered the vaccine, but not as to the defective nature of Compligen. Ezagui v. Dow Chemical Corp. (C.A.-2 N.Y., 1979) 598 F.2d 727.

In Parke-Davis and Co. v. Stromsodt (C.A.-8 N.D., 1969) 411 F.2d 1390, the evidence supported the finding that the manufacturer of Quadrigen was negligent in testing the product and in warning of the risk of brain damage in certain patients.

Claims under the National Childhood Vaccine Injury Act

In 1986 Congress enacted the National Childhood Vaccine Injury Act (42 U.S.C. § 300aa-10 et seq.) to compensate children or their parents for injury or death attributable to DTP or similar vaccines. If the requirements of the Act are met, the petitioner is awarded a specified amount ($250,000 in case of death) plus reasonable attorney's fees. The Act sets forth the nature and extent of the medical evidence which must be submitted, including a list of injuries or conditions which, if found to occur within a prescribed time period following the administration of the vaccine, create a rebuttable presumption that the injuries and conditions were vaccine-related. For DTP-related claims decided under this Act, see: Rochester v. United States (Cl. Ct., 1989) 18 Cl. Ct. 379; Lolley v. United States (Cl. Ct., 1989) 18 Cl. Ct. 498; Matthews v. Secretary of Dept. of Health & Human Serv. (Cl. Ct., 1989) 18 Cl. Ct. 514; Ciotoli v. Secretary of the Dept. of Health & Human Serv. (Cl. Ct., 1989) 18 Cl. Ct. 576.

DISULFIRAM
Antabuse

Disulfiram is used in the treatment of alcoholism. The drug produces a sensitivity to alcohol which results in a highly unpleasant reaction when the patient ingests even small amounts. The drug is indicated in the management of selected chronic alcoholic patients who want to remain in a state of enforced sobriety so that supportive and psychotherapeutic treatment may be applied to their best advantage.[14]

The initial dosage of disulfiram is a maximum of 500 mg. daily for two weeks. The average maintenance dose is then 250 mg. daily, not to exceed 500 mg. Ayerst Laboratories (New York, N.Y.), manufacturer of Antabuse, warns that the drug should never be administered to a patient when he is in a state of alcohol intoxication, or administered without his full knowledge. The drug also is contraindicated in the presence of certain diseases, including severe myocardial disease, coronary occlusion and psychoses. There are also a number of adverse reactions.[15]

The product is also manufactured by Danbury Pharmacal, Inc. (Danbury, Conn.) and Par Pharmaceutical, Inc. (Spring Valley, N.Y.) under the generic name.

Rothering v. DePaul Rehabilitation Hospital (No. F1-1785, Wisconsin Patient's Compensation Panel, June 28, 1985).

Fatal hepatoxicity—Alleged failure to perform follow-up lab studies while on Antabuse—$600,000 settlement

A 31-year-old police officer with a fifteen-year history of alcoholism voluntarily admitted himself to the defendant hospital for treatment. Laboratory studies were determined to be normal, and he was put on an outpatient Antabuse program. Four weeks later he began to suffer from nausea and developed pain in the upper right abdominal quadrant. The Antabuse was discontinued and three days later further lab studies were done. The patient's SGOT level was found to be elevated to 2548 (top of the normal range is 40). He was immediately hospitalized for a liver transplant but died of hepatoxicity.

---

[14] *Physicians' Desk Reference,* 41st ed., pp. 632-3.
[15] Id.

The patient's surviving spouse alleged that the hospital staff failed to conduct proper follow-up testing when the patient was first placed on Antabuse. (The package insert for Antabuse suggested testing within 10-14 days after initiation of the drug; there apparently was no specific hospital policy regarding such testing.)

According to the attorneys for the plaintiff, the parties settled for $600,000.[16]

Mampe v. Ayerst Laboratories (D.C. App., 1988) 548 A.2d 798.

Brain damage—Warnings on package insert and in *PDR* would not have altered psychiatrist's treatment—Summary judgment for manufacturer affirmed

The plaintiff brought suit against the manufacturer of Antabuse, claiming that the warnings on the package insert and in *Physicians' Desk Reference (PDR)* inadequately represented the severity of the drug's adverse effects when the user also consumes alcohol. The plaintiff's physician, a psychiatrist, had prescribed Antabuse for the plaintiff's drinking problem in March 1982. The drug apparently had no immediate effect, and the plaintiff continued to consume alcohol from time to time. Near the end of May, the plaintiff suffered a "physical collapse" and was rushed to the hospital in critical condition. She was later diagnosed as suffering from brain damage, probably the result of the effects of the drug.

On the manufacturer's motion for summary judgment, both parties submitted affidavits of experts containing opinions on the adequacy of the warnings. The plaintiff's psychiatrist, however, stated that he had not relied on the warnings in treating the patient, and that even if he had read the warnings, it would have had no effect on his method of treatment. (The psychiatrist said that his decision to prescribe Antabuse was based on knowledge acquired from "a variety of different kinds of communications," including medical journals, lectures, and personal contact with his peers.)

The trial court granted the summary judgment on this issue, and the Court of Appeals affirmed. The psychiatrist, not a party to this action, settled with the plaintiff for an undisclosed sum.

---

[16] ATLA *Law Reporter* 29:35, 1986.

DIUPRESS
See RESERPINE

DIUTENSEN
See METHYCLOTHIAZIDE

DIUTENSEN-R
See RESERPINE

DOLENE
See PROPOXYPHENE HYDROCHLORIDE

DONNAGEL
See SCOPOLAMINE HYDROCHLORIDE

DONNATEL
See SCOPOLAMINE HYDROCHLORIDE

DONNAZYME
See SCOPOLAMINE HYDROCHLORIDE

DOPAMINE HYDROCHLORIDE
Intropin

Dopamine is used to increase cardiac output, and is therefore sometimes given to patients suffering from the effects of myocardial infarction or other conditions which result in hemodynamic imbalances present in the so-called "shock syndrome." These conditions include severe trauma, open heart surgery, renal failure and chronic cardiac decompensation as in congestive heart failure.[17]

Because the drug improves performance of the heart at the expense of peripheral circulation, the manufacturer of Intropin (American Critical Care, McGaw Park, Ill.) advises that patients with occlusive vascular diseases, for example arteriosclerosis, arterial embolism, diabetic endarteritis or Buerger's disease, should be closely monitored for any changes in color or temperature of the skin in the extremities. If a change appears, and it is believed that it is caused by compromised circulation, "the benefits of continued Intropin infusion should be weighed against the risk of possible necrosis," which can lead to gangrene.

[17] *Physicians' Desk Reference,* 35th ed., p. 578.

The product also is marketed by several companies under the generic name.

Erickson v. United States (D. S.D., 1980) 504 F. Supp. 646.

Choice of drug and amount of dosage questioned after patient loses feet to gangrene—$500,000 awarded under FTCA

The patient was a 48-year-old male admitted to a VA hospital for knee surgery. On the second day after his operation he began to feel poorly. His condition deteriorated and on the fourth day he showed symptoms of a pulmonary embolism, but received no treatment. Four days after that he suffered a heart attack, at which time he was administered dopamine hydrochloride at the rate of 15.52 micrograms per minute. Fifteen minutes later the dosage was doubled to 31.05 micrograms per minute. He was also given heparin for the embolism.

The dopamine was continued for eighty hours, during which time the patient's hands and feet became "cold and white." He also complained of "tingling and numbness in his legs and toes."

The second day he had to be given morphine for pain in his feet. On the third day after the drug therapy was commenced, the patient's feet and lower legs became "mottled and more cyanotic," and no pulse could be found in the ankles. The condition worsened, and the patient eventually lost both feet through amputation for gangrene.

Suit was brought under the Federal Tort Claims Act. An expert witness testified that the patient's condition did not call for treatment with dopamine because it had not been determined that the patient was suffering from hypovolemia (diminished blood volume). Also, if the patient had been suffering from hypovolemia, and dopamine had been the drug of choice, the amount given was excessive, approximately six times the correct amount.

The patient was awarded damages totaling $500,000.

Macon-Bibb County Hospital Authority v. Ross (1985) 176 Ga. App. 221, 335 S.E.2d 633.

Infiltration into tissue—$27,000 award against hospital affirmed

The defendant hospital was sued by a patient who suffered a severely scarred arm from the sloughing off of skin caused by the infiltration of Dopamine during intravenous administration of the drug into a small vein in her wrist. At the trial, a registered nurse appearing as an expert for the plaintiff testified that hospital personnel did not follow the instructions set out in *Physicians' Desk Reference* which stated that Dopamine should be infused into a large vein whenever possible to prevent the possibility of infiltration into surrounding tissue. The information in *PDR* specifically recommended the large vein at the bend of the patient's elbow for intravenous administration, and stated that less suitable infusion sites should be used only if the patient requires immediate attention, and then the IV should be moved to a larger vein as soon as possible.

The witness testified that in her opinion the hospital personnel did not follow proper standards in choosing the smaller vein or, at the least, in failing to document why the infusion was not placed in the recommended site either initially or subsequently. Also, the witness suggested the hospital should have used an IV infusion pump rather than a "drip chamber" because the pump would have better regulated the flow. Furthermore, the witness criticized the hospital personnel's failure to notify promptly the attending physician that the plaintiff had a "swollen and blistered" arm.

The jury awarded the plaintiff $27,000 and the Court of Appeals of Georgia affirmed, rejecting the hospital's argument that the plaintiff's expert should not have been allowed to testify because she had never worked in a hospital in the Macon area. The "locality rule," did not apply, said the court, because the question at issue concerned "professional judgment" of the hospital staff rather than the adequacy of the facilities of "a small hospital."

DORIDEN

See GLUTETHIMIDE

DOXEPIN HYDROCHLORIDE

Adapin
Sinequan

Doxepin is a heterocyclic antidepressant used to treat the major depressive episodes of major depression, mixed bipolar disorder and depressed bipolar disorder. It also may be effective in the depressive periods of dysthymic disorder and in atypical depression.[18] The most common adverse reactions are flushing, diaphoresis, dryness of the

[18] AMA *Drug Evaluations,* 6th ed., p. 144.

mouth, blurred vision, constipation, tachycardia, and hypotension.[19]

Adapin is manufactured by Pennwalt Corporation (Rochester, N.Y.), and Sinequan by Roerig, a division of Pfizer Pharmaceuticals (New York, N.Y.). The product is also marketed under the generic name by Danbury Pharmacal, Inc. (Danbury, Conn.) and Geneva Generics, Inc. (Broomfield, Col.).

Hermes v. Pfizer, Inc. (C.A.-5 Miss., 1988) 848 F.2d 66.

Facial dystonia—$800,000 jury verdict against manufacturer for failure to warn affirmed

Sinequan was prescribed for the plaintiff, age 50, when she experienced difficulty in sleeping. While taking the medication, she developed permanent facial dystonia and dyskinesia. Her face is now disfigured; she is unable to control the movement of her jaw, mouth, and tongue and cannot talk or eat without supporting her jaw. She incurred medical expenses of $3,000. She has been too embarrassed by her condition to return to work as a bookkeeper.

The plaintiff sued Pfizer, the manufacturer, alleging strict liability, negligence, and breach of implied warranty. Specifically, she argued that Pfizer's description of Sinequan in *Physicians' Desk Reference* did not adequately warn the prescribing physician that the drug could cause permanent facial dystonia or dyskinesia. Pfizer's warning stated only that Sinequan could cause "extrapyramidal symptoms." Pfizer's expert testified that the manufacturer's warning of extrapyramidal symptoms, which referred to numerous body parts, included the risk of facial dystonia. He also testified that Sinequan could cause only a *temporary* dystonia. Two neurologists testified for the plaintiff that her condition was permanent. The jury returned a verdict of $800,000.[20]

On review, the Court of Appeals affirmed, rejecting Pfizer's arguments that the evidence of the drug's potential side effects was insufficient to trigger a duty to warn, and that there was insufficient evidence that the drug was a cause of the plaintiff's injury.

---

[19] Id., p. 137.
[20] ATLA *Products Liability Reporter* 6:71, 1987.

Wozniak v. Lipoff (1988) 242 Kan. 583, 750 P.2d 971.

Patient with Graves' disease takes overdose—$584,000 verdict against physician affirmed

In July 1984, the patient developed symptoms of Graves' disease, a severe form of hyperthyroidism. At the time she was employed by the defendant, an internist. The defendant prescribed propylthiouracil (PTU), a drug commonly used to treat such conditions. The treatment was not successful, however, and the patient began suffering from depression and anxiety, and showed other symptoms of serious mental problems, all of which are common in advanced cases of Graves' disease.

The defendant, who was not experienced in treating patients with serious thyroid disease, consulted a psychologist in regard to the patient's deteriorating mental condition, but did not keep him informed as to the patient's failure to progress. By December, the patient's thyroid function had slowed to a normal range, and the defendant reduced the dosage of PTU. He also gave the patient a prescription for Sinequan (75 mg. daily) for her depression. The prescription called for sixty pills with three refills. On January 7, the patient committed suicide by swallowing fifty-five of the pills.

In the resulting malpractice suit by the patient's family, the plaintiffs alleged numerous acts of negligence on the part of the defendant, including failure to call in specialists to treat a condition with which he was not familiar. Also, the plaintiffs accused the defendant of negligence in making so many Sinequan pills available to the patient, and introduced into evidence the manufacturer's package insert which warned that because of the risk of suicide in depressed patients, "prescriptions should be written for the smallest feasible amount."

The jury returned a verdict that the defendant was 80% at fault and the patient, 20%, and awarded the plaintiffs $584,000. The Supreme Court of Kansas affirmed.

DOXYLAMINE SUCCINATE

Bendectin

Until discontinued, Bendectin, a combination of doxylamine succinate and pyridoxine hydrochloride, was used for nausea and vomiting during pregnancy. Adverse reactions reported by the manufacturer, Merrell Dow Pharmaceuticals (Cincinnati, Ohio), included drowsiness, vertigo, nervousness, epigastric pain, headache, heart palpitations, diarrhea, disorientation and irritability.[21]

Drug-related birth defects

In response to charges the drug may also cause birth defects, the manufacturer reported that studies on rats and rabbits revealed no suggestion of drug-induced fetal abnormalities at doses of up to ninety times the maximum human dose, and that several studies on women who received Bendectin during pregnancy have shown that the incidence of birth defects in their offspring is no higher than in women not taking the drug during pregnancy.

Although additional independent studies of pregnant women who took Bendectin during pregnancy seemed to clear the drug of any relationship to birth defects,[22] in the wake of additional claims the FDA requested the manufacturer to narrow the indications for the drug in the product labeling and then initiated proceedings to require a patient package insert.[1]

The claims alleging birth defects continued to pile up, however, and in June 1983 the manufacturer ceased production of Bendectin.

While only a fraction of the total Bendectin claims on file have been tried, an extensive amount of scientific evidence and expert testimony has been introduced in these cases. In September 1987, the United States Court of Appeals, First Circuit, in the case of Lynch v. Merrell-National Laboratories (C.A.-1 Mass., 1987) 830 F.2d 1190,[2] summarized this evidence:

---

[21] *Physicians' Desk Reference,* 36th ed., p. 1290.

[22] Cordero, J. F., et al., "Is Bendectin a Teratogen?" *Journal of the American Medical Association* 245:2307-2310, 1981; Mitchell, A. A., et al., "Birth Defects Related to Bendectin Use in Pregnancy, I, Oral Clefts and Cardiac Defects," Id., 2311-2314; Jick, H., et al., "First-Trimester Drug Use and Congenital Disorders," Id., 246:343-346.

[1] "Indications for Bendectin Narrowed," *FDA Drug Bulletin,* March, 1981, p. 1.

[2] In the Lynch case, the parents of a child suffering from birth defects allegedly caused by mother taking Bendectin during pregnancy were estopped from relitigating the issue of causation because that issue had been fully litigated in a consolidated trial in which the plaintiffs had chosen not to participate. The plaintiffs' criticism of methods used in the earlier studies in which no significant association was shown between effects of drug and birth defects was insufficient to establish causation. The trial court found that none of the animal studies submitted by the plaintiffs provided evidence of teratogenicity at doses comparable to human therapeutic doses of the drug. On appeal, the Court of Appeals affirmed, holding that the expert medical testimony offered by the plaintiffs was properly rejected by the trial court. The first such testimony involved animal studies and "analogous" chemicals,

1. Human development in the womb carries a substantial risk of death or abnormality. Disasters of deformation, fatal fetal accidents occur. Fifteen percent of all clinically recognized pregnancies result without human intervention in death before birth. Three to six percent of children born have malformations. Beckman and Brent, *Mechanism of Known Environmental Teratogens: Drugs and Chemicals,* 13 Clinics in Perinatology 649, 652 (1986).

2. For most of these disasters there is no one to blame. The cause of sixty-five percent of malformations observable in the first year of life is unknown. Another twenty to twenty-five percent are due to genetic factors. Seven percent are due to maternal conditions such as rubella, syphilis, nutritional deficiencies, and narcotics addiction. One to two percent are due to mechanical difficulties in delivery. The known impact of "chemicals, drugs, radiation, and hyperthermia" is a causal factor in less than one percent of the deformations. These estimates come from impartial pediatricians. *Id.,* 650. The plaintiffs' own witness, Alan Kimball Done, had a very similar opinion. According to him, the cause of 75 to 80 percent of all birth defects is unknown. *Lynch* at 863.

3. According to Murray G. Feingold, Physician-in-Chief at the National Birth Defects Center, deposed by the plaintiff, the incidence of limb reduction in the population at large is less than 1 per 1,000 live births. Limb reductions, then, are relatively rare and so are particularly shocking. They are a subspecies of the larger class of all birth defects whose incidence is more common. In ninety-five percent of the cases of limb reduction, Doctors Done and Feingold agree, the cause is unknown.

4. After the Thalidomide-caused catastrophe of the 1960's, popular suspicion found it easy to link any birth defect with a drug taken during pregnancy. Limb reduction, in particular, acted as a red flag. Wilson, *Misinformation About Risks of Congenital Anomalies,* in Marois, *Prevention of Physical and Mental Congenital Defects: Part C* (1985) 165, 167. Under the name Debendox in Australia and Britain and under the name Lenotan in Germany, Bendectin — widely used in pregnancy — was an object of such suspicion, as it was in the United States. Stimulated by the suspicion, extensive epidemiological studies were undertaken. Researchers examined Bendectin in relation to birth defects and attempted to determine if there was a correlation between the use of Bendectin and the defects from which a conclusion of causation might be drawn. These studies were conducted by Australians, Americans, Englishmen, and Germans. The researchers were specialists in a variety of fields from gynecology, public health, embryology, and teratology, to epidemiology proper. The

---

neither of which furnished a foundation for the expert's opinion. A second expert offered by the plaintiffs would have testified from studies of questionable validity which had never been published in a scientific journal or elsewhere.

researchers had every motive to detect a malignant drug inflicting horrible injuries. The first studies began in 1963; studies are still being published in 1986. No correlation, much less a causal connection, has been demonstrated between the use of Bendectin and limb reduction. Beckman and Brent, *supra* at 653.

5. A study by Dr. Steven H. Lamm shows that, while Bendectin usage declined from 1 million new therapy starts in 1979 to zero in 1984, there has been no change in the incidence of birth defects. *Lynch* at 864. Lamm holds an M.D. from the School of Medicine of the University of Southern California, 1956, and a diploma in Tropical Public Health from the London School of Hygiene and Tropical Health, 1974. He is the president of Consultants in Epidemiology and Occupational Health, Inc. and first became involved in the Bendectin litigation when asked to prepare a report by the guardian ad litem for a plaintiff in the multidistrict litigation. This report reflected this non-relation between the use of Bendectin and limb reduction.

6. On the basis of the epidemiological evidence to date, Bendectin is as likely as aspirin to cause limb reduction. Because many mothers take aspirin during pregnancy, as they once took Bendectin, there will always be some children whose mothers took aspirin who were then born with defects including limb reduction. The coexistence of the defect and the taking of aspirin does not prove that one caused the other. Rather, the connection is one of "happenstance." Wilson, *Misinformation About Risks of Congenital Abnormalities, supra,* at 167. To blame aspirin or to blame Bendectin would be an "aberration of reason." *Id.* at 168. The association of Bendectin with limb reduction is in the view of the health-care community an instance of popular delusion and error. Beckman and Brent, *supra* at 653.

The evidence summarized above has some plaintiffs' lawyers worried about the success of future Bendectin cases. Thus far, the defense has prevailed in approximately two-thirds of the cases that have gone to trial. New York plaintiffs' attorney Paul Rheingold of Rheingold & Golomb, P.C., a specialist in prescription drug cases, has put his Bendectin claims "on hold." On November 1, 1987, he was quoted as saying "I wouldn't take on a new one. I still think it would be very difficult to win." Other attorneys disagree. Detroit plaintiffs' lawyer, Thomas Bleakley, believes Bendectin cases will become even easier to win as treating doctors begin to accept the evidence. "Both sides have their experts, and juries perceive that each are paid for their testimony," he says. "Give me the neutral treating physician and put him on my side and we're going to win."[3] Bleakley serves as lead counsel in the multi-district litigation involving about 1,150 Bendectin plaintiffs.

Albertson v. Richardson-Merrell, Inc. (Fla. App., 1983) 441 So. 2d 1146.

Alleged birth defects—Plaintiff has cause of action against manufacturer and its detail man for misrepresentation

The plaintiff took Bendectin during pregnancy for nausea and vomiting. When her child was born with severe birth defects she sued the manufacturer and its detail man, alleging in her complaint that Richardson-Merrell negligently marketed the drug without conducting tests to determine if it caused birth defects in test animals, and later, when it did have a study performed, concealed the true findings and submitted a rewritten version to the FDA. As to the detail man, the plaintiff charged that he intentionally misrepresented the safety of the drug to the plaintiff's physician, causing him to prescribe the drug for the plaintiff during her pregnancy.

The trial court found no cause of action and dismissed the complaint. The Court of Appeal reversed, holding that the plaintiff's charges did state a cause of action. As to the detail man's conduct, the court offered the following comment:

> It is eminently clear that Merrell's and its detail man's purpose in allegedly misinforming physicians about the safety of taking Bendectin was not to persuade physicians (unless they had morning sickness) to buy and ingest that preparation. Obviously they not only expected but desired these physicians to prescribe the drug for their pregnant patients to ingest. Any effect could hardly be said to stop with the mothers in light of the dependency of their embryos. While the universe of potential detrimental reliers may have been indefinite in number and the individuals making it up were not preidentifiable, nevertheless, the characteristics of the class were crystal clear. Appellant allegedly knew those characteristics and inferentially knew not only that such persons would rely but also that their dependent embryos would be affected as a result of such reliance.

---

[3] Moss, D.C., "Bendectin Tide Turning?" *A.B.A. Journal,* Nov. 1, 1987, p. 18.

In re Bendectin Litigation (C.A.-6 Ohio, 1988) 857 F.2d 290.

Birth defects—Verdict for manufacturer in consolidated litigation affirmed

In this consolidated case involving more than 800 claims[4] that Bendectin caused birth defects in children of mothers who took the drug during pregnancy, the court, in denying the claimants' motions for judgment n.o.v. and new trial, held that the evidence supported the jury's verdict that the claimants had failed to establish causation.

At issue, among other things, was the trial court's decision that, during the causation phase of the trial, only testimony from expert witnesses should be received, and evidence offered by individual claimants should be excluded, the reasoning being that to do otherwise would confuse the jury and invite prejudice.

Also, children who were the alleged victims of the drug were excluded from the courtroom on grounds that their presence also would be prejudicial.

Other issues raised by the claimants in their motions included: (1) improper trifurcation of causation and liability issues; (2) failure to allow the claimants' counsel to cross-examine the defendant's expert witnesses using learned treatises to the extent permitted under the Federal Rules of Evidence; (3) admission into evidence of the so-called Lamm Charts, the results of a study offered by the defense on the alleged link between Bendectin and birth defects; (4) exclusion of evidence of alleged fraud by the defendant drug company in conducting and reporting on animal and human tests on the hazards of Bendectin; (5) exclusion of evidence that drugs chemically related to Bendectin contained pregnancy warnings and were contraindicated in the treatment of premature infants; and (6)

---

[4]In 1982, the Judicial Panel on Multidistrict Litigation ordered that all actions involving Bendectin pending against Merrell in the federal courts be transferred to the Southern District of Ohio for consolidation. (In re Richardson-Merrell, Inc. (Jud. Pan. Mult. Lit., 1982) 533 F. Supp. 489.) In 1984, when 568 cases had accumulated in the Southern District of Ohio court and another 149 cases were pending in various state courts, a class action was certified for settlement purposes. Merrell made a settlement offer of $120 million and a hearing was set for determining proper allocation of this sum. Several attorneys for plaintiffs appealed this ruling, however, and the U.S. Court of Appeals for the Sixth Circuit issued a writ of mandamus vacating the order on grounds that the district judge erred in determining that the class met the requirements of Fed. R. Civ. Pro. 23(b)(1)(A). In re Bendectin Products Liability Litigation (C.A.-6 Ohio, 1984) 749 F.2d 300.

denial of claimants' access to material information in the possession of the defendant company and the FDA.

On appeal, the plaintiffs argue that the federal district court did not have jurisdiction over actions brought by Ohio plaintiffs, over actions originally filed in state courts, or over actions originally filed in the federal district courts in any of the fifty states and later transferred to the United States District Court for the Southern District of Ohio. Other issues raised on appeal concerned various aspects of the trial, including certain evidentiary rulings and the district court's decision to create the Plaintiffs' Lead Counsel Committee, to prevent withdrawal from the common issues trial while permitting new transfers into the case, to apply Ohio law to all plaintiffs, to trifurcate on the causation question, and to exclude visibly deformed plaintiffs.

The Court of Appeals directed the dismissal without prejudice of those thirteen actions brought by Ohio citizens in federal court in which Merrell Dow conceded that no federal question jurisdiction was invoked and that the district court was therefore without jurisdiction to render judgment on the merits against those plaintiffs. As to all other suits brought by Ohio citizens in federal courts and subject to this appeal, the court held that the district court did have federal question jurisdiction, and thus the adverse jury verdict is binding on those plaintiffs. In all other respects, the Court of Appeals affirmed the lower court's decision.*

Oxendine v. Merrell Dow Pharmaceuticals (D.C., 1986) 506 A.2d 1100.

Birth defects—$750,000 award reinstated and case remanded for consideration of punitive damages

A mother claimed that her child's deformed arm and hand were caused by Bendectin which she took during pregnancy. At trial, the plaintiffs' medical expert, a specialist in teratology, testified that he concluded from four separate sources of information (*in vivo* studies; *in vitro* studies; pharmacological studies; and epidemiological studies) that Bendectin did cause birth defects. He admitted, however, that the individual results of *each* of these four studies were inconclusive on that question.

*Editor's note: the decision of Court of Appeals ran thirty pages, and should be consulted.

The jury returned a verdict of $750,000 for the plaintiffs, but the trial court held the evidence was insufficient and awarded the plaintiffs a judgment n.o.v. The District of Columbia Court of Appeals reversed, holding that the individual studies may have "showed little or nothing when viewed separately from one another, but they combined to produce a whole that was greater than the sum of its parts." The case was remanded for consideration of punitive damages.

Richardson v. Richardson-Merrell (C.A.-D.C., 1988) 857 F.2d 823.

Birth defects—$1.16 million jury verdict overturned by trial court

Following an eight-week trial, a District of Columbia jury returned a $1.16 million verdict in favor of ten-year-old girl who claimed Bendectin ingested by her mother during pregnancy caused her severe birth defects (missing right leg and badly deformed left leg and arm). The trial judge, however, overturned the award, ruling that on the basis of the evidence presented, "no reasonable jury could find ... [that the] birth defects were more likely than not to have been caused by" prenatal exposure to the drug (649 F. Supp. 779). The judge added that there is "now a nearly universal scientific consensus that Bendectin has not been shown" to cause birth defects.[5]

The trial judge gave the following summary of the evidence on whether the drug was responsible for congenital anomalies [footnotes have been omitted].

> Expert witnesses for both sides generally agreed that congenital birth defects are present in approximately two to four percent of all live births; that limb reduction defects, specifically, occur at a rate of approximately three per thousand; that genetic or chromosomal abnormalities account for from 10 to about 15 percent of all birth defects, and maternal illnesses, e.g. diabetes, or viral or bacterial infections, will explain perhaps three to five percent more; and that there is a large category — a majority — to which no cause can be ascribed with certainty. They are also agreed that "environmental" factors can and do cause some of the remainder, including substances ingested by the mother. Plaintiffs assert that Carita Richardson's afflictions were caused by the

---

[5] *National Law Journal,* Jan. 19, 1987; *American Medical News,* Jan. 16, 1987, p. 23.

Bendectin her mother took in the summer of 1975. Defendant denies it, but, being without evidence to implicate another of the known causes of birth defects, places Carita in the "unknown" category for which science has yet to find an explanation.

Unable to prove directly how Bendectin actually (or could have) affected Carita while in her mother's womb, plaintiffs here proceeded (as did the plaintiff in *Oxendine [See supra.])* with circumstantial evidence. Through the testimony of experts in several disciplines — pharmacology, embryology, veterinary medicine, and the like — they established the similarity of the chemical structure of doxylamine to that of other antihistamines known to be teratogenic in animals. Witnesses described the effects of Bendectin components in solution in *in vitro* experiments upon frog nerve fibers and the mesenchyme cells of mouse limb buds, postulating that other effects might occur in the human intra-uterine environment, when Bendectin is infused *via* the mother, which could inhibit the development of fetal organs. And they criticized the animal experiments conducted by Merrell in 1963 and 1966, suggesting that Merrell's raw data had been misassessed, and the number of tests and dosage levels had been insufficient to dispel doubts about Bendectin's safety. Moreover, when such observations as Merrell had made were properly interpreted, they said, the studies did indicate Bendectin's teratogenic potential in animals which raised suspicions of a similar effect in humans.

Defendant's case consisted, in part, of discipline-by-discipline retorts to plaintiffs' witnesses, supplemented by the testimony of several clinicians with extensive experience in prescribing Bendectin for pregnant women or in treating malformed children, all of whom were certain no connection existed between the medication and the malformations. At least equally well-qualified defense experts asserted that a structural chemical resemblance does not import similar chemical activity; that *in vitro* studies on animal tissues have never been scientifically validated as predictors of physiological effects upon living human beings, and, indeed, are generally regarded as useless for the purpose; and that Merrell's animal tests had been, in fact, both properly conducted and properly interpreted, reflecting precisely the conclusions Merrell had drawn from them. Moreover, they declared, animal studies, too, are of limited usefulness in assessing a drug's teratogenic potential in humans; of some 600 known animal teratogens, only a small fraction of them have been shown to have such an effect upon human embryos. All defense witnesses, as might be expected, were of the opinion that Bendectin is not a human teratogen.

There appeared to be some confusion on the part of the jury in that it found that Bendectin had caused the girl's birth defects and that the manufacturer had failed to give adequate warning regarding the risks involved in taking the drug, yet the jury absolved the manufacturer of any negligence and determined that the drug was not "unreasonably dangerous for its intended purpose" and that there had been no breach of warranty.[6]

The Court of Appeals affirmed, holding that in view of overwhelming contradictory epidemiological evidence, the plaintiff's expert testimony, based on chemical structure activity analysis, various other laboratory tests, and animal studies, did not furnish the necessary foundation for the conclusion that Bendectin caused the child's injuries.

Will v. Richardson-Merrell, Inc. (S.D. Ga., 1986) 647 F. Supp. 544.

Birth defects—Jury finds for manufacturer on conflicting evidence

The plaintiffs brought suit against the manufacturer of Bendectin, alleging that the mother's use of the product during pregnancy caused their nine-year-old daughter to be born with birth defects (fingers missing from one hand). After a nine-day trial and much conflicting evidence on whether the product was teratogenic and whether it caused the injuries in question, the six-member jury found in favor of the manufacturer. The trial court denied the plaintiffs' motions for judgment n.o.v. and new trial.[7]

Blum v. Merrell Dow (No. 82-1027, Superior Court, Philadelphia County, Pa., Jan. 20, 1987).

Birth defects—Jury awards $1 million compensatory and $1 million punitive damages against manufacturer

In an action by a child who claimed that Bendectin taken by his mother during pregnancy for nausea caused him to be born with severely deformed feet, a state court jury in Philadelphia returned a verdict of $1 million in compensatory damages and $1 million in punitive damages against the manufacturer, Merrell Dow Pharmaceuticals, Inc.

Despite what the defense claimed to be over 35 published epidemiologic studies or reports "well-supporting" the safety of

---

[6] *National Law Journal,* Oct. 13, 1986, p. 10.

[7] ATLA *Products Liability Law Reporter* 5:14, 1986; *American Medical News,* July 25, 1986, p. 30.

Bendectin, the jury found that the child's birth defects were caused by the drug. The punitive damage award stemmed mainly from testimony that Merrell Dow's researchers had discovered as early as 1962 that the offspring of test animals that had been administered Bendectin had an increased incidence of mutation, but that the company had failed to report these findings to the FDA.[8]

Ramirez v. Richardson-Merrell (E.D. Pa., 1986) 628 F. Supp. 85.

Birth defects—Pharmacy has no duty to warn patient of hazard

The parents of a child born with deformities claimed that they were the result of the mother taking Bendectin during pregnancy. In a suit against the manufacturer and the pharmacy where the drug was purchased, the pharmacy was charged with negligence and with strict liability in failing to warn the plaintiffs of the potential hazards associated with the product. The pharmacy moved for summary judgment, contending that it had no duty to issue such a warning.

The court granted the pharmacy's motion, holding that the duty to warn of a prescription drug hazard runs from the manufacturer to the physician and not to the patient through the pharmacy. "To impose a greater duty on the pharmacist would be anomalous and would create an unduly high burden on the pharmacists," said the court. In the case of a prescription drug, the "weighing of benefits of medication against potential dangers that are associated with it, which is the basis of the prescription drug system, requires an individualized medical judgment which only the physician can provide."

Ealy v. Richardson-Merrell, Inc. (No. 83-3504, U.S. District Court, D.C., July 14, 1987.

Birth defects—Jury awards $20 million compensatory and $75 million punitive damages against manufacturer—Trial judge strikes punitive portion

The plaintiff's mother took Bendectin during pregnancy, and the plaintiff was born with bilateral radial displasia, missing fingers, and fused elbows. At the time of trial, at age eight, he had trouble

---

[8] *National Law Journal,* Feb. 2, 1987, p. 44.

holding and throwing things, and performing simple activities such as scratching his back, combing his hair, and swinging a baseball bat.

The drug company was charged with negligent manufacture, negligent failure to warn, negligent marketing and testing, and breach of the implied warranty of fitness for a particular purpose. The defendant argued that the drug does not cause birth defects and that it was approved by the Food and Drug Administration.

The jury returned a verdict of $95 million: $20 million in compensatory damages and $75 million in punitive. However, the trial judge ordered remittitur of the punitive award, finding "no clear and convincing evidence that defendant Merrell Dow acted with conscious and deliberate disregard of plaintiffs' rights when it produced, manufactured and distributed Bendectin prior to 1978, the year minor plaintiff's mother ingested Bendectin."[9]

Raynor v. Richardson-Merrell, Inc. (No. 83-3506, U.S. District Court, D. D.C., May 20, 1987).

Birth defects—$300,000 jury verdict against manufacturer

After adverse rulings on alleged fraud, grounds for punitive damages, and collateral estoppel (Raynor v. Richardson-Merrell, Inc. (D. D.C., 1986) 643 F. Supp. 228, summarized *infra*), the plaintiff in this action, an infant alleging Bendectin-related birth defects, received a jury verdict for $300,000. The plaintiff claimed that the drug was defective, that the manufacturer failed to warn the medical profession of the risks involved, and that it was negligent in testing the drug.[10]

Hull v. Merrell Dow Pharmaceuticals (S.D. Fla., 1988) 700 F. Supp. 28.

Birth defects—Manufacturer granted summary judgment on strength of medical evidence

The parents of a child born with deformities of the left leg and foot claimed the condition was caused by the mother taking Bendectin during pregnancy. The district court, however, pointing

---

[9] ATLA *Products Liability Law Reporter* 6:140, 1987; *ABA Journal,* Dec. 1, 1987, p. 41.

[10] ATLA *Products Liability Law Reporter* 6:140, 1987.

to the "extensive and overwhelming" scientific literature "demonstrating the safety of Bendectin" which has been introduced in previous litigation against the manufacturer, granted the manufacturer's motion for summary judgment. The court, in reaching its decision, also relied upon an affidavit of an expert for the defense that stated that the child's mother first took Bendectin too late in her pregnancy (seventh week) for the drug to be implicated in the child's deformities.

Thompson v. Merrell Dow Pharmaceuticals, Inc. (1988) 229 N.J.Super. 230, 551 A.2d 177.

Birth defects—No evidence that obstetricians deviated from standard of care—Pharmacologist not qualified to testify on causation issue—Expert testimony from earlier trial not admissible

The plaintiff brought suit against her obstetricians and the Merrell Dow company, claiming that her child was born with birth defects because she ingested Bendectin during the early stages of her pregnancy.

The trial court entered summary judgment in favor of the obstetricians after the plaintiff conceded that she had no medical expert who could testify that the defendants had deviated from acceptable standards of medical care in prescribing the drug. Trial was begun against Merrell Dow, but when the court refused to qualify the plaintiff's only expert witness, a pharmacologist, and refused to allow the plaintiff to introduce into evidence transcripts or videotaped testimony of twelve expert witnesses who had testified at an earlier proceeding against the manufacturer, Merrell Dow successfully moved for involuntary dismissal.

On appeal, the Superior Court of New Jersey, Appellate Division, affirmed, holding that the plaintiff's pharmacologist witness, who was to testify that the plaintiff's ingestion of Bendectin caused the birth defects, was properly rejected because he had never performed research concerning the drug, had never studied developing embryos, and had never examined nor was qualified to examine the plaintiff's child. As to the plaintiff's request to introduce testimony from the previous trial, the reviewing court held that the trial court properly rejected this request because the testimony dealt with the causation issue generally, and there was a question as to whether the defendant, in the earlier trial, had a fair opportunity and adequate motive to cross-examine these witnesses concerning the specific defects suffered by the plaintiff's child.

Brock v. Merrell Dow Pharmaceuticals, Inc. (C.A.-5 Tex., 1989) 874 F.2d 307.

Birth defects—Jury verdict for plaintiffs reversed for lack of conclusive proof of drug's teratogenicity

The plaintiffs' child was born with Poland's syndrome, a birth defect, which they claimed was the result of the mother taking Bendectin during pregnancy. At trial, extensive conflicting medical evidence was presented on the possible cause of the child's condition, and the jury found for the plaintiffs. On appeal, however, the U.S. Court of Appeals reversed, holding that while there was a wealth of published epidemiological data on Bendectin, none reached the conclusion that the drug was teratogenic, and while, traditionally, courts would not question the reasoning of medical experts, when confronted with difficult questions, they will look behind the conclusions of the experts in determining the sufficiency of the evidence.

Daubert v. Merrell Dow Pharmaceutical, Inc. (S.D. Cal., 1989) 711 F. Supp. 546.

Birth defects—Summary judgment denied manufacturer on claims of unreported and flawed studies on drug's relationship to congenital malformations

In 1972, on the advice of her obstetrician, the plaintiff took Bendectin for nausea during the 34th through the 41st day of her pregnancy. Her child was born with a limb-reduction defect of his arm and hand.

In the suit against the manufacturer, based on strict liability and breach of warranty, Merrell Dow moved for summary judgment, claiming that it could not be held liable because the drug was properly prepared, and the company had no knowledge of any dangerous propensities, if any, at the time of distribution. In countering this argument, the plaintiff and her husband contended that as early as 1962, Merrell Dow began receiving information suggesting a relationship between Bendectin and limb defects. Furthermore, claimed the plaintiffs, a study upon which the company relied, the "Staples/Carl" test, showed a significant relationship between the drug and congenital malformation, "yet they were never reported to company officials, the Food and Drug Administration or the public." Also, said the plaintiffs, a second study upon which the company relied, the "Bunde-Bowles" study, was flawed, in that it was "plagued with unscientific procedures and inaccuracies." According to the plaintiffs, in this study patients were administered Bendectin, yet the data used in the results claimed they did not receive the drug, and also patients who were documented as receiving Bendectin during pregnancy received the drug at a time when exposure was irrelevant.

In view of the above, the court held that there existed a genuine issue of material fact as to the plaintiff's strict liability claim, and the defendant's motion for summary judgment was denied.

Wilson v. Merrell Dow Pharmaceuticals, Inc. (C.A.-10 Okla., 1990) 893 F.2d 1149.

Birth defects—Jury verdict for manufacturer affirmed on epidemiological evidence of lack of causation

The plaintiffs' child was born with a finger missing from each hand, which the plaintiffs claimed was caused by his mother having been prescribed Bendectin during pregnancy. The plaintiffs sued the manufacturer, alleging product liability, fraud and misrepresentation, breach of express and implied warranty, strict liability, and negligence.

At trial, the plaintiffs produced three geneticists, all of whom testified that the birth defect suffered by the plaintiff's child was not genetically induced. The manufacturer failed to present a geneticist to testify that the child's defect was genetic, as its attorney promised to do in his opening argument; however, the defense did present uncontradicted expert testimony that of approximately forty epidemiological studies conducted on Bendectin, none showed a statistically significant association between ingestion of the drug and birth defects of the limbs or birth defects generally.

The jury returned a verdict for the manufacturer, and the U. S. Court of Appeals, Fifth Circuit, affirmed.

Related cases

Birth defects—$20,000 verdict set aside—Jury finds for manufacturer in second trial and plaintiff ordered to pay costs

In Mekdeci v. Merrell-National Laboratories (Civil No. 77-255, U.S. District Court, Middle District, Florida, April 9, 1981), a mother whose infant son was born with a sunken chest and arm and hand deformities following her use of Bendectin during pregnancy was awarded $20,000 for medical expenses. The award, however, was set aside by the court which ruled it a compromise verdict. A new trial was ordered, and this time the jury found for the defendant manufacturer, with an unusual ruling by the trial judge that the defendant could be allowed to recover its "taxable costs," which the company fixed at $206,122.65. This was appealed by the plaintiffs' lawyers who claimed that it was an unfair "attack in part on plaintiffs' access to the courts"[11] but the Court of Appeals affirmed. (Mekdeci v. Merrell-National Laboratories (C.A.-11 Fla., 1983) 711 F.2d 1510.)

Birth defects—Claimants in consolidated case not entitled to information on manufacturer's experience with earlier drugs

In a preliminary decision arising out of the consolidated Bendectin products liability litigation, the court held that the claimants were not entitled to obtain information through discovery pertaining to the experiences of the manufacturer with two earlier products, Thalidomide and MER-29, because the probative value of such evidence likely would be outweighed by its potential prejudice, and because the claimant's request appeared to be calculated to produce information that would portray the manufacturer in a damaging light with regard to past activities rather than to produce admissible evidence. In re Richardson-Merrell, Inc. "Bendectin" Products Liability Litigation (S.D. Ohio, 1983) 624 F. Supp. 1271.

Birth defects—Claims by residents of United Kingdom

In Dowling v. Richardson-Merrell, Inc. (C.A.-6 Ohio, 1984) 727 F.2d 608, the U.S. District Court, invoking the doctrine of forum non conveniens, properly dismissed claims against Richardson-Merrell that involved Debendox (the British version of Bendectin), when it was established that the Debendox in question was manufactured and marketed in the United Kingdom by British companies under a British license, that the alleged injuries (birth defects) all occurred in either England or Scotland, that the plaintiffs were all residents of those countries, and that the claimants' allegations included charges that the defendant concealed reports of adverse

[11]*National Law Journal,* July 27, 1981, p. 6.

test results on the drug from the national health authorities in England.

In a similar case, it was held that while claims filed in the United States against the Merrell company by British and Scottish residents were properly dismissed under forum non conveniens, an action against two of the company's employees (a medical director and a test supervisor) could not be so dismissed because the employees did not show that they would be subject to jurisdiction in the United Kingdom. Watson v. Merrell Dow Pharmaceuticals (C.A.-6 Ohio, 1985) 769 F.2d 354.

Also, an action in state court by British plaintiffs involving fifteen claims for birth defects allegedly resulting from pregnant mothers taking Debendox was properly dismissed on grounds of forum non conveniens. Chambers v. Merrell Dow Pharmaceuticals (1988) 35 Ohio St. 3d 123, 519 N.E.2d 370.

Birth defects—Illinois parents have cause of action for loss of child's "society and companionship"

Under Illinois law, the parents of a child who was born with deformities attributed to Bendectin taken by his mother during pregnancy were entitled to bring an action against the manufacturer for loss of the child's "society and companionship." Dralle v. Ruder (1986) 148 Ill. App. 3d 961, 102 Ill. Dec. 621, 500 N.E.2d 514.

Birth defects—Allegation that violation of FDCA constituted negligence did not raise federal question

An action brought in state court on behalf of a child born with birth defects, based in part on the theory that Bendectin manufacturer's alleged violation of Federal Food, Drug and Cosmetic Act constituted negligence, did not raise a federal question. Merrell Dow Pharmaceuticals v. Thompson (1986) 478 U.S. 804, 106 Sup. Ct. 3229, 92 L. Ed. 2d 650.

Birth defects—Manufacturer's motion for collateral estoppel denied—No grounds for fraud or punitive damages—Pharmacy not liable for failure to warn

In Raynor v. Richardson-Merrell, Inc. (D. D.C., 1986) 643 F. Supp. 238, the U.S. District Court for the District of Columbia held that collateral estoppel is not appropriate in an action for damages for birth defects allegedly caused by Bendectin where there have been prior inconsistent verdicts against the manufacturer of the drug. On the defendants' motions for summary judgment, the court ruled that it would be abuse of discretion to use one decision as a basis for offensive collateral estoppel while ignoring other contrary decisions. The court also held that the manufacturer could not be liable under the theory of fraud in absence of evidence that it knew the drug could cause the harm claimed or that it lacked sufficient knowledge of the drug's safety. Also, it was held that punitive damages were not available in absence of clear and convincing evidence of outrageous conduct on the part of the manufacturer, and that the pharmacy that filled the prescription for Bendectin could not be held liable for failure to warn of the risk to pregnant users.

Birth defects—Claim by daughter of mother in Air Force barred by *Feres* doctrine

In Heath v. United States (E.D. Cal., 1986) 633 F. Supp. 1340, an action against the government on behalf of a child born with birth defects whose mother, while on active duty in the U.S. Air Force, had taken Bendectin during pregnancy was barred under the *Feres* doctrine as derivative of injuries suffered by the mother.

Birth defects—Pharmacy cannot be held strictly liable for failure to warn of risks associated with drug

In an action against a pharmacy that sold the plaintiffs Bendectin which allegedly caused the plaintiffs' child to be born with certain congenital abnormalities, it was held that the implied warranty of merchantability did not apply to the sale, and that the pharmacy could not be held strictly liable for failing to warn of risks associated with use of the drug. Makripodis v. Merrell-Dow Pharmaceuticals (1987) 316 Pa. Super. 589, 523 A.2d 374.

In Coyle v. Richardson-Merrell, Inc. (Pa. Super., 1988) 538 A.2d 1329, the pharmacy where the mother purchased the Bendectin could not be held strictly liable for failure to warn of the risk of injury to the fetus of a pregnant consumer of the product.

Birth defects—Plaintiff's claim time-barred

In Urland v. Merrell Dow Pharmaceuticals (C.A.-Pa., 1987) 822 F.2d 1268, a jury found that the parents of a child who claimed to have suffered birth defects as a result of her mother taking Bendectin during pregnancy had not filed their action against the manufacturer within two years of learning of the injury. According to the evidence, the couple became aware of their possible cause of action against the defendant on being interviewed by a reporter for the *National Enquirer* in connection with an article on an alleged cover-up by the manufacturer of the drug's potential side effects.

Birth defects—Expert's affidavit establishes cause of action against manufacturer—No evidence of fraud

In view of the plaintiffs' expert's unequivocal statements as to causation, material issues of fact existed as to whether a mother's ingestion of Bendectin during pregnancy caused her child's hands to be congenitally deformed. The plaintiffs failed, however, to submit any evidence supporting an action against the manufacturer for fraud in the development, testing or marketing of the drug. Hagen v. Richardson-Merrell, Inc. (N.D. Ill., 1988) 697 F. Supp. 334.

Birth defects—"Timing of ingestion" defense—Mother's contradictory affidavit properly rejected on summary judgment

In Martin v. Merrell Dow Pharmaceuticals (C.A.-3 Pa., 1988) 851 F.2d 703, on the manufacturer's motion for summary judgment, the district court properly disregarded a mother's affidavit with regard to the date she first took Bendectin. The affidavit was submitted only after the mother faced almost certain defeat on the summary judgment, and flatly contradicted eight of her previous sworn statements. The manufacturer had sought summary judgment on the basis of a "timing of ingestion" defense in which it submitted affidavits of experts showing that the child could have suffered Bendectin-induced birth defects only if the mother had taken the drug during a specified "critical period" of her pregnancy.

DPT

See DIPHTHERIA and TETANUS TOXOIDS with PERTUSSIS VACCINES

DRAMAMINE

See DIMENHYDRINATE

DRISTAN

See CHLORPHENIRAMINE MALEATE

DROPERIDOL and FENTANYL
See FENTANYL and DROPERIDOL

DTP
See DIPHTHERIA and TETANUS TOXOIDS with PERTUSSIS VACCINES

DURACILLIN
See PENICILLIN

DURAMORPH
See MORPHINE SULFATE

DYAZIDE
See TRIAMTERENE

DYDROGESTERONE
Duphaston

Dydrogesterone, formerly marketed by Philips Roxane Laboratories (now Roxane Laboratories, Columbus, Ohio) as Duphaston, is a synthetic steroidal compound structurally related to naturally occurring progesterone. The product was used to treat menstrual disorders, especially amenorrhea and abnormal uterine bleeding due to hormonal imbalance.[12] The product is no longer offered.

Glass v. Philips Roxane (No. C0270-762, Superior Court, Los Angeles County, Cal., Dec. 12, 1983).

Birth defects—Manufacturer accused of failing to disclose risk—Jury verdict for $1,250,000

The plaintiff's mother took Duphaston for three months during her pregnancy in 1971 to prevent miscarriage. The plaintiff was born with five underdeveloped and deformed fingers on one hand. In the lawsuit against the manufacturer, Philips Roxane Laboratories, Inc. (now Roxane Laboratories, Inc., Columbus, Ohio), it was alleged that the defendant company falsified studies on laboratory rats, did not conduct proper clinical testing, and failed to warn the medical profession and consumers of the risk of birth defects in children of mothers who used the product, even though such evi-

[12] *Physicians' Desk Reference,* 31st ed., p. 1257.

dence, according to the plaintiff, was available as early as 1967. (The drug was removed from the market in 1979, two years after the FDA ordered the defendant to place warnings on the package insert concerning the danger of birth defects.)

Prior to trial, the plaintiff offered to settle for $500,000. At the beginning of trial, the defendant offered $150,000. The case went to the jury, which returned a verdict for the plaintiff in the amount of $1,250,000, including $750,000 in punitive damages.[13]

DYMELOR

See ACETOHEXAMIDE

DYRENIUM

See TRIAMTERENE

E

ECHOTHIOPHATE IODIDE

Phospholine Iodide

Ayerst Laboratories (New York, N.Y.) manufactures echothiophate iodide under the brand name Phospholine Iodide as an ophthalmic preparation (miotic) for the treatment of certain forms of glaucoma.

Under "Duration of Treatment" in the product literature the manufacturer states that "there is no definite limit so long as the drug is well tolerated."[14] Among common local side effects, however, are "twitching of the eyelids, brow ache, headache, ocular pain, ciliary and conjunctival congestion, accomodative myopia, and poor vision in dim light." Also, localized allergy occasionally develops, manifested by conjunctivitis and contact dermatitis.[15]

Serious adverse effects include the possibility of detached retina. The manufacturer states: "Although the relationship, if any, of retinal detachment to the administration of Phospholine Iodide has not been established, retinal detachment has been reported in a few cases during the use of Phospholine Iodide in adult patients without

---

[13] ATLA *Products Liability Law Reporter* 2:9, 1983.

[14] *Physicians' Desk Reference,* 35th ed., p. 621.

[15] *AMA Drug Evaluations,* 2d ed., p. 677.

a previous history of this disorder."[16] Periodic examination for this possibility is desirable during treatment.[17]

The manufacturer also reports that lens opacities (cataracts) have occurred in patients under treatment for glaucoma with Phospholine Iodide, and that similar changes have been produced experimentally in monkeys.[18]

Fykes v. Chatow (No. 976896, Superior Court, Los Angeles County, Cal., Oct. 29, 1974).

Detached retina—Charges of failure to warn and unnecessary delay in treatment—$2,500 settlement with manufacturer—Verdict for $65,000 against physician and hospital

A 49-year-old male patient had been treated for glaucoma for eight years. On April 9, 1969 his physician prescribed Phospholine Iodide for his left eye. Three weeks later, because of spots before his eyes, and because of a need for a general physical examination, the patient was seen by an internist at the same clinic. After the examination the internist advised him to consult an ophthalmologist. Apparently the internist offered to arrange for the appointment, but since the patient already had an appointment with an ophthalmologist in two months, he declined the offer.

Four days later the patient began to suffer loss of vision in his eye. He attempted to obtain an earlier appointment with an ophthalmologist but was unsuccessful. Three days later he tried again, and was advised to return in two weeks. The patient then returned to the clinic where he had first been treated and *demanded* to see an ophthalmologist. He was not examined, but he was advised to discontinue use of the Phospholine Iodide, and to return to have his eyes dilated for an examination three days later. It was discovered at that time that he had a detached retina.

The patient underwent eye surgery two days later but suffered a redetachment. He filed suit against the two physicians who had treated him, the clinic, the hospital where he underwent the operation, and the manufacturer of Phospholine Iodide. In his complaint, the patient alleged that the first physician who saw him failed to advise him of the risk of retinal detachment in using Phospholine

---

[16] *Physicians' Desk Reference,* 35th ed., p. 621.

[17] *The Merck Manual of Diagnosis and Therapy,* 12th ed. (Rahway N.J.: Merck Sharp & Dohme Research Laboratories, 1972), p. 1025.

[18] *Physicians' Desk Reference,* 35th ed., p. 621.

Iodide. He also charged that this physician had caused a delay in the diagnosis and treatment of his condition. The suit was defended on the grounds that there was no causal relationship between use of the drug and the patient's retinal detachment. As to the delay in diagnosis and treatment, it was argued by the defense that this had no bearing on the outcome of the patient's condition.

Prior to trial, the drug company settled with the patient for $2,500. The case against the remaining defendants went to the jury which returned a verdict for the patient in the amount of $65,000 against one physician and the hospital.[19] The second physician (Dr. Chatow) was found free of liability.[20]

Winkjer v. Herr (N.D., 1979) 277 N.W.2d 579.

Cataracts following treatment of two months' duration—Summary judgment for physician affirmed

During an examination for contact lenses, the defendant, an ophthalmologist, discovered that the plaintiff had an elevated intraocular pressure which suggested glaucoma. The plaintiff was given pilocarpine (Ocusert) in the form of eyedrops, but this caused him discomfort and blurred his vision, so the prescription was changed to Phospholine Iodide. This was sometime in October, 1974.

The plaintiff was checked again in November, and was told to return for an examination in January, because "there was evidence that Phospholine Iodide could cause the formation of cataracts." The plaintiff did return on January 17, at which time the defendant told him that the cataracts had already begun developing.

In his lawsuit, the plaintiff charged the defendant with negligence in prescribing the Phospholine Iodide. On motion for summary judgment, however, the plaintiff failed to submit affidavits refuting uncontradicted testimony by the defendant's experts that his diagnosis and treatment of the plaintiff's condition was reasonable and proper.

The plaintiff argued that it was eventually discovered that he did not in fact have glaucoma but a less serious condition known as "ocular hypertension." The defendant's experts pointed out, however, that in the beginning the two conditions are not distinguishable, and the treatment is the same. Furthermore, the defendant's experts testified that at the time the plaintiff was given

[19] AMA *The Citation* 30:120, 1975.
[20] Id., 31:13, 1975.

Phospholine Iodide there was no evidence that the drug could cause cataracts "in the levels and lengths of time prescribed by the defendant." In fact, in the words of the court it was "highly unlikely and actually unheard of."

The defendant's motion for summary judgment was granted by the trial judge and affirmed on appeal.

Mowery v. Crittenton Hosp. (1986) 155 Mich. App. 711, 400 N.W.2d 633

Detached retina—Manufacturer not liable for failure to warn patient—Warning to physician, if inadequate, not proximate cause of injury

In August 1981, the patient underwent surgery for removal of a cataract and the implantation of an intraocular lens. Two weeks after the operation, it was discovered that the lens had become partially detached. To prevent complete dislocation of the lens, the patient's surgeon prescribed Phospholine Iodide. In doing so, the surgeon warned that one of the drug's side effects was retinal detachment.

The patient's intraocular lens became dislocated the following month and the surgeon discontinued the Phospholine Iodide. After several unsuccessful attempts to reposition the lens medically, the surgeon operated again, using Phospholine Iodide during the procedure. On November 13, 1981, the patient was diagnosed as suffering a retinal detachment. This was corrected by surgery, but the patient claimed that she experienced some permanent vision loss.

In the patient's lawsuit against the hospital, the surgeon and Ayerst Laboratories, the manufacturer of Phospholine Iodide, she charged that Ayerst breached its express or implied warranty of the drug and was strictly liable because the product was defective. She charged also that the manufacturer misrepresented the safety of the drug. In moving for summary judgment, Ayerst claimed that it did adequately warn the patient's surgeon of the risks of retinal detachment in using the drug. It offered the deposition of the surgeon who testified that she was aware of the association of retinal detachment with the drug and that despite this risk she chose to prescribe the drug for the patient because the risk was worth taking to avoid repeated intraocular lens dislocation.

The trial court granted the manufacturer's motion for summary judgment, finding that since the surgeon was aware of the drug's risks, but chose to prescribe it anyway, any inadequacy regarding the manufacturer's warning could not be the proximate cause of the patient's injury. The Court of Appeals affirmed, holding that it appeared that even if the surgeon had been given additional warnings by the manufacturer of the risk of retinal detachment, she still would have chosen to prescribe Phospholine Iodide for the patient.

ECOTRIN

See ASPIRIN

EDROPHONIUM CHLORIDE

Enlon

Tensilon

Edrophonium chloride is a short and rapid-acting cholinergic drug manufactured under the name Enlon by Anaquest (Madison, Wis.) and the name Tensilon by Roche Laboratories (Nutley, N.J.). It is used in the diagnosis and evaluation of treatment of myasthenia gravis, and to reverse the neuromuscular block produced by certain adjuncts to anesthesia such as curare, tubocurarine, gallamine triethiodide and dimethyl-tubocurarine.[1]

Apparently at one time there was divided opinion as to whether edrophonium chloride should also be used to reverse the action of the neuromuscular blocking agent succinylcholine chloride (Anectine; Quelicin).[2] But under "Indications" in the product literature, the manufacturer of Tensilon states that it is not effective against this blocking agent,[3] and Osol and Pratt report that it may actually prolong the action of succinylcholine chloride.[4]

The effects of edrophonium chloride on the patient who has been given succinylcholine chloride is discussed further in the following case.

---

[1] *Physicians' Desk Reference,* 35th ed., p. 1528.

[2] See Chapman v. Argonaut-Southwest Ins. Co., *infra.* Succinylcholine chloride is used primarily to produce brief relaxation for procedures such as endotracheal intubation, endoscopy, orthopedic manipulation, and electroconvulsive therapy. *AMA Drug Evaluations,* 2d ed., p. 245. Anectine is manufactured by Burroughs Wellcome Company (Research Triangle Park, N.C.) and Quelicin by Abbott Pharmaceuticals (North Chicago, Ill.).

[3] *Physicians' Desk Reference,* 40th ed., p. 1504.

[4] *United States Dispensatory,* 27th ed., p. 1111.

Chapman v. Argonaut-Southwest Ins. Co. (La. App., 1974) 290 So. 2d 779.

Death of three-year-old child following surgery—Giving of Tensilon to counteract Anectine questioned—Judgment for defendants affirmed

A three-year-old girl was undergoing dental restoration of massive tooth decay. The surgery was extensive and general anesthesia was required. Preoperative medication consisted of Demerol 25 mg., Vistaril $12\frac{1}{2}$ mg. and Atropine $\frac{1}{250}$ grain, which were administered at approximately 8:20 a.m. At about 9 a.m. the child was taken to surgery and anesthetized through a face mask with a mixture of halothane and oxygen. At about 9:30 she was injected intravenously with $1\frac{1}{2}$ c.c. of Anectine to aid in nasal intubation. She was then placed on assisted respiration which continued for an undetermined period, following which she resumed spontaneous breathing. The assisted respiration was then discontinued.

The operation proceeded under general anesthesia. At the onset, the child's heartbeat was approximately 140 per minute. At about 10 a.m. the heartbeat rose to 160 per minute. Twenty minutes later the anesthesiologist noted that the child's spontaneous breathing was insufficient, and he renewed assisted respiration by means of a manually operated squeeze bag attached to the nasal tube.

The operation was completed at approximately 11:15. When the child still required assisted respiration at 11:40, she was given one-fourth of one cubic centimeter of Tensilon, intravenously, to restore breathing. Immediately her heartbeat dropped to 84 per minute and her breathing improved. Within five to ten minutes, spontaneous breathing returned, and her heartbeat rose to approximately 124. The surgeon then observed her for about fifteen to twenty minutes during which time she continued to breathe normally. The anesthesiologist removed the nasal tube, placed the child on a rolling stretcher, and proceeded to the recovery room. On the way, the anesthesiologist noted that the child no longer appeared to be breathing properly. He felt her abdomen and detected no sign of respiration. She was rushed to the recovery room and again placed on assisted respiration. She failed to improve and medication was administered to restore pulse and respiration. This also was unsuccessful and she died in the recovery room at approximately 12:50 p.m.

An autopsy was performed and the pathologist reported death was due to "adrenal insufficiency" which was based on a finding that the child's adrenal glands were "1/5th normal size, and were therefore hypofunctioning." The pathologist later explained that "the abnormally small glands were incapable of producing sufficient adrenal fluids to sustain life under surgical stress."

The parents filed suit against all concerned, alleging: (1) negligence in improperly administering the Tensilon while the child was in respiratory distress after surgery, and (2) negligence in prematurely removing the child from the operating room after the administration of the Tensilon.

It was contended by the plaintiffs that the Tensilon aggravated a condition of impaired respiration which had been deliberately induced at the start of the operation by the administration of the drug Anectine, a drug which produces neuromuscular paralysis to facilitate intubation of the general anesthetic. It was further contended that failure or deficiency in respiration was to be expected following the administration of Tensilon, and therefore the child should have been kept under observation in the operating room where emergency equipment was readily available.

At the trial extensive medical testimony was presented, the primary issue being the use of the two drugs, Anectine and Tensilon, and their particular interrelationship. Testimony established that Anectine is a synthetic drug which produces effects similar to curare, namely, the capacity to relax a patient by paralyzing the neuromuscular system. Anectine produces almost instant relaxation and muscular paralysis, lasting, in most cases, from three to five minutes. During this period, a patient is unable to breathe spontaneously, or at least spontaneous breathing is difficult, and respiration must be assisted. Anectine molecules are immediately attacked by an element in the blood plasma known as cholinesterase which breaks down Anectine into its components and destroys its efficacy. In most cases, total dissipation of Anectine is achieved within ten to fifteen minutes, after which the patient breathes spontaneously. This initial effect of Anectine is known in the medical profession as "Phase I Block." Although the advisability of giving Anectine in surgery is disputed by some anesthesiologists, it is used by others at the commencement of an operation to relax the patient sufficiently for intubation.

The evidence further showed that anesthesiologists agree that assisted respiration is necessary following the administration of Anectine until the initial effects (Phase I Block) wear off. A Phase I Block may turn into a Phase II Block which is different "mechanically." A Phase II Block is a "desensitizing" block. It is generally agreed that Tensilon should not be used to counteract Anectine during a Phase I Block but there is divided opinion as to whether it can be used during a Phase II Block.

The plaintiffs produced an anesthesiologist who testified that, in his opinion, the premedication given the child was rather strong, and that it was then unnecessary, in the child's case, to administer Anectine to aid in intubation. He said he considered Anectine a "dangerous drug" which sometimes produces prolonged paralysis. He also said there is a "wrong and right way to administer medication" and the giving of Anectine followed by Tensilon "was gross error." He said when Anectine is used it is better practice not to give Tensilon to reverse a Phase II Block, but he conceded that Tensilon might be given "cautiously, slowly, and in small dosage" to test for the presence of a Phase II Block. He said that Tensilon "breaks down the cholinesterase which inhibits Anectine thereby prolonging the effects of Anectine." In this expert's opinion, the anesthesiologist in the instant case mistakenly gave the patient Tensilon to reverse or cure what he considered to be a Phase II Block. He then mistakenly assumed the Phase II Block was permanently reversed, and when the effects of Tensilon wore off after fifteen or twenty minutes, the blockage resumed. This witness disagreed with the autopsy report, and attributed death to the administration of Anectine, followed by Tensilon, and the failure to keep the patient under sufficient observation.

A second expert testifying for the plaintiff, a professor of pharmacology, stated that Anectine and Tensilon "should never be given during the same operation," and that Tensilon "should never be employed to overcome the effects of Anectine." He admitted that there is a wide divergence of opinion on this issue in the medical profession, however. He added that, in his opinion, the only treatment for a patient suspected of continued respiratory distress due to Anectine is to "breathe for the patient," keep him warm, and wait "for hours" if necessary.

The defendants also produced several medical experts, among them Dr. John Adriani, a well-known expert in anesthesiology and pharmacology. Dr. Adriani was acknowledged by the court as "world renowned in his field," and one who "has probably done more drug research than any other individual." Dr. Adriani testified that he considered Tensilon as a "good and useful drug." He conceded that it should not be used to counteract a Phase I Block brought on by Anectine, but that it is "properly used to diagnose the presence or reverse the effects of a Phase II Block." Dr. Adriani reviewed the patient's entire record and found no criticism whatsoever of any drug or procedure employed. He said he believed the child was in a Phase II Block when the Tensilon was administered, and that the anesthesiologist was justified in giving the Tensilon when he did. He added that, in his opinion, the anesthesiologist waited "a sufficient time" before removing the child from the operating room, and although he conceded that had the anesthesiologist waited longer, the emergency might have occurred in the operating room, he said that "it is purely a matter of individual judgment of the observer which is all any anesthesiologist can do." Dr. Adriani agreed with the pathologist that the child's death was induced by an adrenal deficiency.

The trial court entered judgment for the defendants. On appeal the reviewing court affirmed. Regarding the use of the two drugs in question, the Court of Appeals said:

> We gather from the record that there is a vast difference of opinion among recognized experts concerning the use of Tensilon following Anectine. Plaintiffs have failed to establish that the profession in general considers the use of Tensilon improper under the circumstances involved herein. In this regard, we note that, based upon the reputation and credentials of the various experts, those of Dr. Adriani appear to be the most widely accepted in the profession.

Later in the opinion, the court said:

> The record, in this instance, discloses that neither the giving of Tensilon, the amount given, nor removal of the patient from the operating room constituted medical malpractice. On the contrary, the clear preponderance of evidence is to the effect that both actions were proper and in keeping with local standards of care practiced by anesthesiologists and surgeons in the Baton Rouge area. Moreover, it appears the procedures were in accord with the teachings and writings of certain well known authorities in the field whose views are respected and followed in other areas of the state as well as throughout the United States. Granted some authorities are in disagreement. Nevertheless, the procedure followed herein is sanctioned by authorities equally as qualified and as highly regarded as plaintiffs' experts, if not more so.

ELAVIL
See AMITRIPTYLINE

EMBOLEX
See HEPARIN SODIUM; LIDOCAINE HYDROCHLORIDE

EMPIRIN COMPOUND
See ASPIRIN

ENARAX TABLETS
See OXYPHENCYCLIMINE HYDROCHLORIDE with HYDROXYZINE HYDROCHLORIDE

ENDEP
See AMITRIPTYLINE

ENDURON
See METHYCLOTHIAZIDE

ENDURONYL
See METHYCLOTHIAZIDE

ENLON
See ENDROPHONIUM CHLORIDE

ENOVID; ENOVID-E
See NORETHYNODREL with MESTRANOL

EPHEDRINE
See THEOPHYLINE and EPHEDRINE

EPINEPHRINE
Adrenalin
Adrenalin-in-Oil
EpiPen
Primatine
Sus-Phrine

Epinephrine is an active principle of the adrenal medulla, circulates in the bloodstream, and has many actions in the body, including vasoconstriction and an increase in blood pressure. It may be obtained by extraction from adrenal glands or by synthesis. It is recommended for a number of conditions, including bronchial asthma, and other allergic conditions, shock, cardiac and respiratory failure, and to prolong action of local anesthetics.[5]

Adrenalin-in-oil was manufactured by Parke-Davis (Morris Plains, N.J.). An advantage of the oil suspension is its prolonged duration of action;[6] however, the American Medical Association's Department of Drugs has advised that the use of this route "is unwise because bioavailability is not uniform and fatal cases of gas gangrene due to *Clostridium perfringens* have been reported."[7] EpiPen is produced by Center Laboratories (Port Washington, N.Y.), Primatine by Whitehall Laboratories (Long Island, N.Y.), and Sus-Phrine by Forest Pharmaceuticals (St. Louis, Mo.).

Croft v. York (Fla. App., 1971) 244 So. 2d 161.

Gas gangrene after injections—Drug possibly contaminated—Summary judgment for manufacturer reversed

The widow of a deceased patient brought suit against her husband's physician, the hospital to which he had been confined, and Parke-Davis for his death from gas gangrene following an injection of allegedly contaminated Adrenalin-in-oil produced by Parke-Davis.

Parke-Davis filed a motion for summary judgment supported by an affidavit of the manager of the company's "Plant Regulatory Affairs of the Quality Control Division" which recounted the general procedures and regulations followed by the company in the production, handling and distribution of its drugs. The affiant stated that production and distribution at all times were under such sanitary and sterile conditions that there was no likelihood of contamination and that during the years he served as manager he had never heard of any incident in which the company's Adrenalin-in-oil was found to be contaminated or to cause gas gangrene to develop in a patient's body. Attached to this affidavit was the package insert for the solution.

Based on further pleadings, exhibits, depositions and affidavits the following undisputed facts emerged: The patient suffered a sinus congestion and consulted his physician who had an office in the defendant hospital. In addition to the Adrenalin-in-oil, the physi-

---

[5] *United States Dispensatory,* 27th ed., p. 476.
[6] *AMA Drug Evaluations,* 2d ed., p. 459.
[7] Id.

cian prescribed an injection of Acthar-gel, a corticotropin produced by Armour Pharmaceutical Company (Phoenix, Ariz.). Both drugs were obtained from the hospital pharmacy and were given by a nurse employed by the hospital. The Adrenalin-in-oil was injected into one hip and the Acthar-gel into the other, but there was no record as to which drug was injected into which hip.

The patient suffered discomfort and pain during the night and returned to the physician's office the next day complaining of fever and a painful swelling of the left buttock. An emergency operation revealed gas gangrene. Although every effort was made to save the patient, he died the following day.

By deposition the defendant-physician at first expressed the opinion that the gangrene did not result from a contaminated drug but was caused by a spore on the patient's skin which entered the body through the opening caused by the hypodermic needle. Later, however, he executed an affidavit in opposition to the drug company's motion for summary judgment in which he stated that since giving his deposition he had further studied the case and concluded that the probable cause was a spore in one of the drugs.

The trial court sustained Parke-Davis' motion for summary judgment. The plaintiff appealed, contending that the pleadings, exhibits, depositions, and affidavits created genuine issues of material facts.

The District Court of Appeals agreed, reversed the judgment, and stated:

> Can it be said from the pleadings, exhibits, depositions and affidavit on file in the case subjudice that Parke-Davis, the moving party, has sustained the burden assumed by it of conclusively establishing the nonexistence of any genuine issue of fact? We clearly think that it has not. It is true that the evidence leaves unresolved the critical question of whether the drug injected in the decedent's left hip was the drug manufactured by Parke-Davis or was the drug manufactured by Armour and Company. In order for Parke-Davis to prevail on its motion, however, it would be required to conclusively establish that either (1) the gas gangrene which caused the decedent's death did not result from the injection administered by the hospital in the decedent's left hip, or (2) that the drug injected in the decedent's left hip was not the [A]drenalin in oil produced and sold by it. A careful examination of the record clearly reveals that Parke-Davis has failed to carry the burden of conclusively establishing either of the two above-enumerated hypotheses. Because of this failure it is not entitled to a summary final judgment despite the fact that the evidence is not such as would support a judgment for the plaintiff

if the case was submitted to the jury solely on the basis of the evidence now in the record.

Ayres v. United States (C.A.-5 Tex., 1985) 750 F.2d 449.

Excessive dose of epinephrine administered with spinal anesthetic—Government liable

The patient was to undergo surgery at the V.A. hospital in Dallas, Texas. When the first injection, containing twelve milligrams of tetracaine and "some amount" of epinephrine, did not appear to induce anesthesia, the anesthesiologist administered a second injection, again containing both tetracaine and epinephrine. The patient immediately began experiencing difficulty in breathing, and within minutes temporarily ceased breathing. After the surgery the patient was left with weakness below the waist, impotence, and incontinence. At the time of trial he was confined to a wheelchair.

Evidence was introduced that epinephrine, which is added to an anesthetic to prolong its duration, should not have been included in the second injection. The district court held that the anesthesiologist was negligent in administering the second injection containing the epinephrine and a resident physician who was assisting him was negligent in not calling the error to his attention.

The Court of Appeals affirmed.

Garron v. State of New York (No. 68209, Court of Claims, N.Y., Dec. 15, 1986).

Choice of drug questioned after alleged mismanagement of accident victim's fluid status and airway—$600,000 settlement

The plaintiff, age ten, was admitted to Stony Brook Hospital's pediatric intensive care unit for head injuries following an automobile accident. The physicians tried to insert a Swan-Gans catheter but were unsuccessful. When the plaintiff's blood pressure began to drop, an attempt was made to place an endotracheal tube in her airway. The physician missed the trachea and blocked off a lung, and she was administered epinephrine. This was continued until the fifth day of hospitalization, when her toes and fingers became discolored and gangrenous, resulting in amputations of portions of her toes, fingers, and left foot.

In her lawsuit, the plaintiff claimed mismanagement of her fluid status and negligence in establishing the airway. She alleged that the inability to insert the catheter and the tube into the trachea was due to inexperience and this led to the administration of epinephrine. This decision was also negligent, she claimed, because there were drugs less dangerous than epinephrine that could have been used. The parties settled for $600,000.[8]

Related cases

Reaction to anesthetic containing epinephrine

In LeBeuf v. Atkins (1980) 28 Wash. App. 50, 621 P.2d 787, a dental patient who apparently suffered from hypertension reacted to Xylocaine (lidocaine hydrochloride), a local anesthetic containing epinephrine. The case is summarized herein under LIDOCAINE HYDROCHLORIDE.

Fatal cardiac arrest—No negligence in administering atropine sulfate instead of epinephrine

In Lowry v. Henry Mayo Newhall Memorial Hospital (1986) 185 Cal. App. 3d 1-8, 229 Cal. Rptr. 620, a hospital code blue team physician was not negligent in administering atropine sulfate to a cardiac arrest victim rather than epinephrine as suggested in guidelines published by the American Heart Association. The case is summarized herein under ATROPINE SULFATE.

EPIPEN
See EPINEPHRINE

EQUAGESIC
See MEPROBAMATE

EQUANIL
See MEPROBAMATE

ERGOMAR
See ERGOTAMINE TARTRATE

---

[8] ATLA *Professional Negligence Liability Reporter* 2:42, 1987.

ERGOSTAT
See ERGOTAMINE TARTRATE

ERGOTAMINE TARTRATE
Bellergal
Cafergot
Ergomar
Ergostat
Gynergen
Migral
Wigraine

Ergotamine tartrate is a crystalline alkaloid derived from ergot, a fungus which grows on rye. The drug has several uses, but mainly it is prescribed as an analgesic, primarily for vascular or migraine headaches. Cafergot, which also contains caffeine, is produced by Sandoz Pharmaceuticals (East Hanover, N.J.), as are Bellergal and Gynergen. Ergomar is manufactured by Fisons Corporation (Bedford, Mass.), Ergostat by Parke-Davis (Morris Plains, N.J.), Migral by Burroughs Wellcome (Research Triangle Park, N.C.), and Wigraine by Organon Pharmaceuticals (West Orange, N.J.).

Sandoz warns that vasoconstrictive complications may occur with the use of Cafergot, at times of a serious nature. These include the loss of pulse, weakness, muscle pains and numbness of the extremities. The product literature also states that although these effects occur most commonly with long-term therapy at relatively high doses, they also have been reported with short-term or normal doses. Other adverse reactions may include transient tachycardia or bradycardia, nausea, vomiting, localized edema and itching.[9]

Tridente v. Crozer-Chester Medical Center (No. M79-0539, Court of Common Pleas, Delaware County, Pa., Jan. 4, 1982).

Overdose of Cafergot causes partial leg paralysis—
Hospital settles for $650,000

The plaintiff, a forty-one-year-old woman, was admitted to the defendant hospital and treated with Cafergot for vascular headaches which were believed to be due to a carotid artery aneurysm. The plaintiff was given the medication orally and in suppository

[9] *Physicians' Desk Reference,* 35th ed., p. 1571.

form, but the total dosage was five times greater than that recommended by the manufacturer. As a result of the overdose, the plaintiff suffered partial leg paralysis and had to undergo a sympathectomy which resulted in a permanent "foot drop." The defendant hospital entered into a structured settlement with a present value of $650,000.[10]

Bergen v. Salant (No. C303315, Superior Court, Los Angeles County, Nov. 11, 1982).

Patient suffers reaction to Cafergot—Residual impairment—Physician's directions questioned—Structured settlement worth $512,196

The patient was a fifteen-year-old girl. Her mother took her to the defendant physician for treatment of cold symptoms — headaches and general malaise. The defendant suspected migraine and prescribed Cafergot. His instructions to the pharmacist for the label were "Take one as needed for headache." To the patient his instructions were: "Take one tablet every four hours with two aspirins in between doses." The patient took twenty tablets over five days, at which time she developed numbness and tingling in her lower legs. She was hospitalized and diagnosed as suffering an acute allergic reaction to ergotamine overdose. Despite vasodilation to increase the circulation in her legs she suffers residual bilateral heel contractions, calf atrophy, equinus deformity of the ankles and a limp. According to the attorney for the plaintiff, the parties agreed to a structured settlement with a present value of $512,196.[11]

Hemingway v. Ochsner Clinic (C.A.-5 La., 1984) 722 F.2d 1220.

Cafergot given to patient with possible Buerger's disease, worsening condition—$15,000 awarded

A male patient in his twenties underwent gastrointestinal surgery at the defendant-clinic for pancreatitis. Following the operation, he became diabetic.

On June 10, 1973, the patient was seen as an outpatient for an injury to his foot in a motorcycle accident. The injury was minor, and he was treated and released. It was noted on the examining physician's report, however, that the foot was "cold and blue," that

---

[10] ATLA *Law Reporter* 25:282, 1982.

[11] Id., 26:282, 1983.

it was without a pulse, and that there appeared to be "acute arterial insufficiency." The condition worsened, and on June 17, the patient returned for an arteriogram.

The diagnosis was now possible venous occlusion and a sympathectomy was recommended to increase circulation to the area. It seemed to help, but on July 7, the patient returned again to the emergency room with his foot once more blue and cold. This time the examining physician, who had assisted in the operation, noted that possibly the patient had Buerger's disease. The patient was admitted, given a continuous epidural block to relieve his pain, and put on medication designed to dilate the blood vessels in order to promote circulation.

On the morning of July 9, the patient awoke with a severe headache. A resident asked him what he usually took for it, and he told him Cafergot, that he had taken it for years. The resident gave him a Cafergot suppository. Two hours later his foot began to turn blue again. It was then concluded that the patient was hypersensitive to ergotamine tartrate.

At the trial, evidence was introduced that this was not the first time the patient had been given Cafergot, that the clinic physicians had prescribed it in May for the patient's headaches, and again in June. This was after it was determined that the patient was a diabetic.

On examination by the plaintiff's attorney, the clinic physicians admitted that the literature which accompanies Cafergot and the pharmaceutical textbooks state that the drug is contraindicated for patients suffering from certain types of vascular disease, including Buerger's disease.

Eventually an award of $15,000 was approved.

Riff v. Morgan Pharmacy (1986) 353 Pa. Super. 21, 508 A.2d 1247.

Excessive dosage—Nerve damage—Physician and pharmacy jointly liable

The plaintiff suffered from migraine headaches. During a severe attack in January 1979, her physician gave her a prescription for a package of twelve Cafergot suppositories with instructions to insert one in her rectum "every four hours for headache." The prescription did not authorize a refill. The defendant pharmacy filled the prescription, with the pharmacist typing on the label "insert one every

4 hours for headache." The plaintiff took "three or four" of the suppositories, one every four hours, until she obtained relief. Two months later, she suffered another migraine attack and took the remaining suppositories. Over the next several months, she suffered more attacks, and her husband obtained a total of five refills of the original prescription.

On August 31, 1979, the plaintiff began experiencing discomfort with her right foot. The condition worsened, and on being hospitalized it was found that the effects of the Cafergot had severely restricted circulation in the foot, causing permanent nerve damage. As a result, "her foot tends to drag and is in a constant state of discomfort."

In her suit against the pharmacy and the physician, the plaintiff introduced evidence that the maximum dosage for Cafergot suppositories as specified in the medical literature is "one suppository, with a permissible second suppository in one hour if necessary." The dose is not to exceed *two per attack,* and in no event should the user administer *in excess of five in one week.*

The physician admitted he was aware of this "uniformly accepted" maximum dosage and that his instructions should have reflected this information. The pharmacist claimed the physician had authorized the five refills by telephone, but the physician denied this.

A jury found the defendants jointly liable and the Superior Court of Pennsylvania affirmed, holding that the pharmacist had a duty to warn the patient or notify the physician of the "obvious inadequacies" appearing on the face of the prescription.

ERYTHROMYCIN ESTOLATE
Ilosone

Erythromycin belongs to the macrolide group of antibiotics. Ilosone is manufactured by Dista Products Company, a division of Eli Lilly and Company (Indianapolis, Ind.). The product is also produced under the generic name by Danbury Pharmacal, Inc. (Danbury, Conn.), Lederle Laboratories, a division of American Cyanamid Company (Wayne, N.J.), and Schein Pharmaceuticals (Port Washington, N.Y.).

Included in the product literature is a special box warning that hepatic dysfunction with or without jaundice has occurred, chiefly in adults, in association with erythromycin estolate administration. Other side effects include abdominal cramping and discomfort, vomiting and diarrhea. Also, during prolonged or repeated therapy, there is a possibility of overgrowth of nonsusceptible bacteria or fungi, and there have been isolated reports of reversible hearing loss occurring chiefly in patients with renal insufficiency and in patients receiving high doses of the drug.[12]

Penny v. St. Paul Fire & Marine Ins. Co. (La. App., 1976) 329 So. 2d 833.

Hepatitis—Evidence of causal connection insufficient

The plaintiff had suffered viral hepatitis in April, 1971. By July, her liver tests were normal. The following December she developed a sore throat, sinus infection and general congestion. Her physician prescribed Ilosone and several other drugs. Three days later the plaintiff developed a rash, abdominal pains and nausea, which eventually was diagnosed as hepatitis.

At trial the plaintiff argued that both *Physicians' Desk Reference* and the American Medical Association's *Drug Evaluations* state that Ilosone is contraindicated for patients with pre-existing liver conditions. However, the plaintiff's own expert witness, a specialist in anatomical clinical pathology, admitted that many cases of drug-induced hepatitis cannot be distinguished from viral hepatitis, and that the plaintiff's problem was probably a flare-up of her earlier viral condition. The defense's experts naturally offered strong testimony to this effect, and the jury returned a verdict for the defendant. The Court of Appeal affirmed.

ESTOMUL

See MAGNESIUM CARBONATE with ALUMINUM HYDROXIDE

ESTROGENS (CONJUGATED)
PMB 200/400
Premarin

Conjugated estrogens are a mixture of the sodium salts of the sulfate esters of estrogenic substances, principally estrone and equilin.[13] They are recommended for treatment of abnormal uterine

---

[12] *Physicians' Desk Reference,* 40th ed., p. 838.
[13] *United States Dispensatory,* 27th ed., p. 500.

bleeding due to hormonal imbalance in the absence of organic pathology.[14]

Both PMB 200/400 (which also contains meprobamate) and Premarin are manufactured by Ayerst Laboratories (New York, N.Y.), and Geneva Generics, Inc. (Broomfield, Colo.) markets the product under the generic label.

Chumbler v. McClure (C.A.-6 Tenn., 1974) 505 F.2d 489.

Use of Premarin for treating cerebral vascular insufficiency questioned—Directed verdicts for defendants—Evidence of two schools of thought

A negligence action was brought against a physician and Ayerst Laboratories, manufacturer of Premarin, by a patient who alleged that he suffered impotence because of the physician's use of the drug in treating his cerebral vascular insufficiency. The plaintiff charged that the physician was experimenting, that Premarin was not an accepted means of treatment for his condition, and that he had not given his informed consent to such treatment.

At the close of evidence the trial court directed verdicts for both the drug company and the physician's estate (the physician having died prior to trial). These were affirmed on appeal. As to the drug company, the reviewing court agreed that the plaintiff failed to prove that it had participated in any alleged experiments with the drug, or that it had overpromoted Premarin, or that it had not issued sufficient warnings concerning the drug's side effects. As to the physician, the court pointed to testimony at trial from various physicians that, although the deceased, Dr. McClure, was alone among neurosurgeons in Nashville, Tennessee in using Premarin for cerebral vascular insufficiency, there were some physicians elsewhere who did use it for that purpose. Thus, concluded the court, there were "two schools of thought" regarding such treatment.

On the issue of lack of informed consent, the reviewing court held the trial court did not err in excluding all testimony offered by the plaintiff in this regard, in view of Tennessee's "Dead Man's Statute."

---

[14] *Physicians' Desk Reference,* 35th ed., p. 628.

Beal v. Hamilton (Tex. Civ. App., 1986) 712 S.W.2d 873.

Thrombophlebitis—Lack of informed consent—$250,000 judgment upheld against physician

In February 1979, the plaintiff sought treatment from the defendant physician because of abdominal pain, headaches, and nervousness. The defendant diagnosed the plaintiff's condition as "gastritis, artificial menopause, and anxiety," and prescribed Premarin. Four days later, the plaintiff was admitted to the hospital suffering from thrombophlebitis, a known side effect of Premarin. The emergency room physician immediately discontinued the drug. On visiting the plaintiff, however, the defendant again prescribed Premarin.

The plaintiff filed suit, alleging the defendant was negligent in failing to diagnose the plaintiff's condition in the first place, in failing to inform the plaintiff of the hazards of Premarin, specifically thrombophlebitis (and thus failed to obtain the plaintiff's informed consent), and in failing to discontinue the use of Premarin after the plaintiff was diagnosed as having thrombophlebitis.

The defendant was late in filing pleadings, particularly answers to requests for admissions, and when the case came to trial, neither the defendant nor his attorney appeared. The plaintiff was granted a default judgment for $250,000 which was affirmed on appeal. The Court of Appeals of Texas held that the plaintiff's evidence established Texas' statutory requirements for a malpractice suit based on lack of informed consent, *i.e.*, that thrombophlebitis was an inherent risk in taking Premarin, and that this risk was material enough to influence the plaintiff in her decision to give or withhold her consent.

ETHAMBUTOL HYDROCHLORIDE
Myambutol

Myambutol is an antibacterial used for the treatment of pulmonary tuberculosis. It is produced by Lederle Laboratories (Wayne, N.J.).

The product literature states under adverse reactions that the drug may produce decreases "in visual acuity which appear to be due to optic neuritis and to be related to dose and duration of treatment. The effects are generally reversible when administration of the drug is discontinued promptly." The statement goes on to say, however, that "in rare cases recovery may be delayed for up to one year or more and the effect may possibly be irreversible in these cases."[15]

Oksenholt v. Lederle Laboratories (1981) 51 Ore. App. 419, 625 P.2d 1357, aff'd (1982) 294 Ore. 213, 656 P.2d 293.

Permanent vision loss—Physician has cause of action against manufacturer following $100,000 settlement with patient

In 1973 the plaintiff, a physician, treated a patient with Myambutol. Four months later the patient began experiencing problems with her vision, and shortly thereafter suffered permanent loss of sight, apparently due to the effects of the drug.

The patient sued the plaintiff who settled for $100,000. He then brought this action against the manufacturer charging negligence and fraud in failing to warn him that the drug could cause permanent loss of vision. (The drug literature did warn of possible temporary loss.) On appeal of the trial court's granting of the defendant's motion to strike the plaintiff's complaint, the Court of Appeals of Oregon held that while there was insufficient evidence to establish an action for fraud, the plaintiff did have a cause of action based on charges that the defendant violated its duty to inform the plaintiff of the hazards of the drug, and its duty to protect the plaintiff from foreseeable harm to his reputation, earning capacity and income as a result of a patient's claim for damages.

The manufacturer appealed to the Supreme Court of Oregon which affirmed, but held that while the plaintiff did state a cause of action against the defendant for fraudulent misrepresentation, he could not recover the amount of his settlement with the patient. The plaintiff did, however, have a cause of action for special damages, i.e., loss of income, loss of earning capacity due to harm to his reputation, etc. The plaintiff also had a cause of action for punitive damages.

Bass v. Barksdale (Tenn. App., 1984) 671 S.W.2d 476.

Permanent vision loss—Family physician negligent in not supervising treatment of T.B. patient

The plaintiff was found to be suffering from tuberculosis. Since her family physician had not treated a patient with T.B. for over three years he turned her over to the local public health depart-

[15] *Physicians' Desk Reference,* 35th ed., pp. 1011-12.

ment. Included in her medication was ethambutol. During therapy she noticed her vision was "declining" and informed the family physician, but he did not refer her to an ophthalmologist until eight weeks later. By then she had suffered permanent vision loss.

The jury found negligence on the part of the family physician, the public health nurse to whom the plaintiff was referred, and the public health physician in charge of the T.B. control unit. The plaintiff was awarded $300,000.

On appeal the Court of Appeals found procedural errors and reversed, but held that the evidence was sufficient to sustain the verdict against the family physician. Included in the opinion was a summary of the testimony of the public health physician, a specialist in preventive medicine, which established the standard of care at the time for a physician prescribing ethambutol.

> (1) Know or obtain a medical history including a history of visual abnormalities before prescribing the drug; (2) make a physical examination of the patient, including finger perimetry and testing of color discrimination before prescribing the drug; (3) know the contraindications, the risks, the precautions and the adverse reactions of the drug before prescribing it; (4) give or cause to be given a test of visual acuity using a Snellen eye chart before prescribing the drug; (5) test or cause to be tested each of the patient's eyes separately as well as both eyes together before prescribing the drug; (6) weigh the risks and benefits of ethambutol therapy on patients with visual defects such as cataracts before prescribing the drug, (7) give or cause another to give warnings of the risks of treatment of tuberculosis with ethambutol before the patient begins to take the drug, including the risk of loss of vision and temporary loss of vision; (8) tell or cause another to tell the patient who is to receive the ethambutol about what symptoms to watch for that may indicate a decrease in visual acuity and, if the symptoms occur, the course of action to take. The reasons for the precautions with regard to the patient's vision is that a known side effect of ethambutol is an adverse effect on vision and initial testing must be done to be sure that any variations in visual acuity during the drug therapy are not due to underlying disease conditions such as cataracts or optic neuritis.

Ross v. Jacobs (Okla. App., 1984) 684 P.2d 1211.

Loss of vision—Manufacturer's warning ambiguous —Summary judgment reversed

After taking Myambutol for four months the patient's vision began to deteriorate. On discontinuing the drug his condition did not improve, and at the time of trial his vision had reduced to 20/400.

In a suit against the physician who prescribed the drug and the manufacturer, the trial court granted the manufacturer's motion for a summary judgment on the ground that it had adequately warned the medical profession of Myambutol's possible side effects. The warning read:

> MYAMBUTOL may produce decreases in visual acuity which appear to be due to optic neuritis and to be related to dose and duration of treatment. The effects are generally reversible when administration of the drug is discontinued promptly. In rare cases recovery may be delayed for up to one year or more and the effect may possibly be irreversible in these cases.

The Court of Appeals disagreed, holding that the language of the warning was ambiguous. According to the Court "There seems little commitment to admit a true danger of permanent visual loss, even though the manufacturer appears to have known of a growing number of cases of permanent visual loss or blindness."

Related cases

Permanent vision loss—Brazil proper forum for action by Brazilian consumer

In De Melo v. Lederle Laboratories (C.A.-8 Minn., 1986) 801 F.2d 1058, the Court of Appeals, Eighth Circuit, upheld dismissal of an action by a Brazilian citizen who suffered permanent loss of sight after being treated with Myambutol. The court held that even though Lederle Laboratories developed, tested, patented and manufactured Myambutol, the drug was marketed by a Brazilian corporation (a subsidiary of American Cyanamid, which also owns Lederle Laboratories), and therefore Brazil was a more appropriate forum for a product liability action.

ETHCHLORVYNOL

Placidyl

This drug is classified as a hypnotic agent and is used to treat anxiety and sleep disorders. Adverse reactions include hypotension, nausea, vomiting, blurred vision, dizziness, facial numbness, urticaria and dimness of vision. Also, long-term use of larger than usual doses may result in psychological and physical dependence. A daily dose of 1.5 grams may be sufficient to induce the latter.[16]

Placidyl is manufactured and marketed by Abbott Laboratories (North Chicago, Ill.).

Jones v. Irvin (S.D. Ill., 1985) 602 F.2d 399.

Over-medication—Pharmacy has no duty to warn patient or physician of possible drug abuse

The plaintiff and her husband brought suit against the plaintiff's physician and the pharmacy that filled the plaintiff's prescriptions for injuries sustained as a result of her "consumption of an excessive amount of a prescription drug [Placidyl] over a period of time and its reaction with other drugs." The plaintiff specifically charged that the pharmacy knew or should have known that Placidyl "is a drug of abuse and that it was being prepared in massive amounts" and that it should have notified either the plaintiff or the physician that "something was amiss."

The plaintiff charged also that the pharmacy should have known that the plaintiff was being "over-medicated" and that the quantities in which the drugs were being prescribed could "have adverse reactions," and that the pharmacy was negligent in not notifying the plaintiff or her physician of this fact.

The pharmacy moved for dismissal of the charges against it, arguing that it had no duty to warn the plaintiff or the physician of any of the dangers enumerated. The district court granted the pharmacy's motion, holding as follows:

> [A] pharmacist has no duty to warn the customer or notify the physician that the drug is being prescribed in dangerous amounts, that the customer is being over medicated, or that the various drugs in their prescribed quantities could cause adverse reactions to the customer. It is the duty of the prescribing physician to know the characteristics of the drug he is prescribing, to know how much of the drug he can give his patient, to elicit from the patient what other drugs the patient is taking, to properly prescribe various combinations of drugs, to warn the patient of any dangers associated with taking the drug, to monitor the patient's dependence on the drug, and to tell the patient when and how to take the drug. Further, it is the duty of the patient to notify the physician of the other drugs the patient is taking. Finally, it is the duty of the drug manufacturer to notify the physician of any adverse effects or other precautions that must be

---

[16] AMA *Drug Evaluations,* 6th ed., p. 106.

taken in administering the drug. [citation omitted] Placing these duties to warn on the pharmacist would only serve to compel the pharmacist to second guess every prescription a doctor orders in an attempt to escape liability.

The court emphasized, however, that its holding was a narrow one, and that a pharmacist still owes the customer the "highest degree of prudence, thoughtfulness and diligence."

Related cases

Coma and paralysis following treatment with Placidyl and other drugs— Action not barred by statute

Where a patient was rendered paralyzed, blind and virtually unable to speak, allegedly as a result of a negligently prescribed combination of Valium, Placidyl, Dalmane and Methadone, the patient's conservator's discovery of the cause of the patient's injury did not trigger the one-year prescriptive period in California's medical malpractice statute of limitations. Getty v. Hoffman-LaRoche (1987) 189 Cal. App. 3d 1294, 235 Cal. Rptr. 48.

ETHINYL ESTRADIOL with DIMETHISTERONE
Oracon

Ethinyl estradiol with dimethisterone is an estrogen-progestagen oral contraceptive of the "sequential" type; that is, the estrogen hormone (ethinyl estradiol) is used by itself during the first fifteen to sixteen days followed by a combination with a progestagen (dimethisterone) for the last five days. The mechanism of action underlying the use of these drugs is believed to be primarily suppression of anterior pituitary function in its release of gonadotropins, which, in turn, prevents ovulation.[17] This particular contraceptive was manufactured by Mead Johnson & Company (Evansville, Ind.) under the name Oracon until the mid-1970's.

For an extensive discussion of the possible side effects of oral contraceptives, see NORETHINDRONE with MESTRANOL.

---

[17] *United States Dispensatory,* 27th ed., pp. 807, 809.

Needham v. Mead Johnson (No. 584435, Superior Court, San Francisco County, Cal., June 12, 1972).

Fatal pulmonary thromboembolism—No liability on part of manufacturer or physicians

In 1966 an unmarried eighteen-year-old girl sought treatment for irregular menstrual periods. Her physicians, specialists in obstetrics and gynecology, prescribed Oracon. Although the girl was living at home, the physicians did not obtain the consent of her parents to this treatment, nor did they warn the girl or her parents of any possible risks in taking Oracon.

In January, 1967, the girl began developing chest pains and shortness of breath. On one occasion, she experienced abdominal spasms. According to the parents, they called one of the physicians and informed him of the symptoms. The girl was seen on January 9. Details of this examination were not given.

On January 23, 1967, the girl died suddenly from a pulmonary thromboembolism. In the subsequent lawsuit against Mead Johnson and the physicians, the parents claimed the Oracon caused the girl's death through the formation of blood clots. They charged that the physicians were negligent in prescribing the pills, and in failing to warn of the risks involved.

At the trial, the parents offered medical witnesses who testified that blood clots can cause the condition from which the girl died and that early symptoms of these clots would be similar to those suffered by the girl prior to her death. The physicians contended that in prescribing the Oracon, they followed the appropriate standard of care as it existed in 1966, pointing out that at that time medical research had not disclosed that birth control pills could cause potentially dangerous blood clots. The defendants also argued that the parents had introduced no direct evidence that the Oracon had caused any such clots. The defendants also denied that they had been informed of the girl's symptoms as the parents claimed, and they introduced their medical records which contained no reference to any such complaints. One of the physicians, however, stated that the girl's parents had told him of such symptoms after the girl's last visit to the office.[18]

---

[18] AMA *The Citation* 26:113, 1973.

Burleson v. Mead Johnson & Co. (C.A.-5 Tex., 1972) 463 F.2d 180.

No causal relationship between Oracon taken at time of conception and birth defects

An infant was born without arms and legs, a deformity known medically as phocomelia. A lawsuit was filed on his behalf alleging that the condition was caused by the effects of Oracon, taken by the child's mother immediately prior to pregnancy.

At the trial the evidence disclosed that the drug was prescribed by the mother's gynecologist for the regulation of her menstrual cycle. Apparently, she took it over a period of six weeks, during which time she became pregnant.

There was unanimity of opinion among the expert medical witnesses at the trial that there was no "reasonable medical probability" that the Oracon could have been the cause of the phocomelia. The plaintiff produced no facts, nor inferences that could be drawn from facts, that controverted the drug manufacturer's showing of a lack of causal relationship. Furthermore, uncontroverted evidence offered by the mother's obstetrician, gynecologist, and attending pediatrician, virtually ruled out the drug as the cause of the defects.

The trial court rendered a summary judgment in favor of the manufacturer, and the United States Court of Appeals, finding no genuine issue of fact for trial, affirmed.

Jorgensen v. Meade Johnson Laboratories, Inc. (C.A.-10 Okla., 1973) 483 F.2d 237.

Mongoloid child has cause of action against manufacturer

This complaint, brought against the manufacturer of Oracon by a husband and wife on behalf of their two children, alleged that from May, 1966 through October, 1966 the wife had used Oracon for contraceptive purposes. She had discontinued the pills around November 1, 1966, and had become pregnant. On July 17, 1967, she gave birth to Mongoloid twins. According to the plaintiffs, the Oracon had altered the chromosome structure of the mother's body to produce the deformity in the children.

The manufacturer moved to dismiss the suit, but the trial judge overruled the motion. Then, on reconsideration, the court dismissed the action, declaring:

> It is general knowledge that birth control pills have been merchandised for several years. Likewise it is general knowledge that articles by medical authorities respecting dangers incident to such use have appeared in the medical publications. Any right of a child arising out of injury to the chromosome of its mother through the use of such pills prior to its conception should be created by the Legislature and not by judicial decision. [See 336 F. Supp. 961.]

The decision was appealed to the Court of Appeals, Tenth Circuit, which disagreed with the trial judge. Said the court:

> If the view prevailed that tortious conduct occurring prior to conception is not actionable in behalf of an infant ultimately injured by the wrong, then an infant suffering personal injury from a defective food product, manufactured before his conception, would be without remedy. Such reasoning runs counter to the various principles of recovery which Oklahoma recognizes for those ultimately suffering injuries proximately caused by a defective product or instrumentality manufactured and placed on the market by the defendant.

The court went on to say: "We are persuaded that the Oklahoma courts would treat the problem of the injuries alleged here as one of causation and proximate cause, to be determined by competent medical proof. Such personal injury cases raise factual issues turning on the medical evidence."

A petition for rehearing was denied, the judgment in the lower court was vacated, and the case was remanded for trial.

ETHINYL ESTRADIOL with NORETHINDRONE ACETATE

See NORETHINDRONE ACETATE with ETHINYL ESTRADIOL

ETHYNODIOL DIACETATE with ETHINYL ESTRADIOL

Demulen

Demulen is one of the combination oral contraceptives which act primarily through the mechanism of gonadotropin suppression due to the estrogenic and progestational activity of their components. The product is manufactured by Searle & Company (San Juan, P.R.).

For an extensive discussion of the possible side effects of oral contraceptives, see NORETHINDRONE with MESTRANOL.

Goodson v. Searle Laboratories (D. Conn., 1978) 471 F. Supp. 546.

User suffers stroke—No duty on part of manufacturer to warn patient

On November 15, 1972 the plaintiff's physician issued her a prescription for Demulen. On November 19, 1973 she suffered a cerebrovascular accident (stroke) which resulted in partial blindness and some permanent loss of dexterity in one hand. She brought suit against the manufacturer of the drug, charging that the product was defective and unreasonably dangerous. The manufacturer contended that it warned the medical profession prior to the plaintiff's use of Demulen of the risk of cerebral thrombosis (the likely cause of the plaintiff's stroke) in using the drug, and that it had no legal duty to warn the plaintiff. The court agreed, citing several of the leading decisions to that effect, and granted the defendant's motion for summary judgment.

ETHYNODIOL DIACETATE with MESTRANOL
Ovulen

Ethynodiol diacetate with mestranol is an estrogen-progestagen oral contraceptive which acts to prevent ovulation by inhibiting the output of gonadotropins from the pituitary gland. It is manufactured under the names Ovulen, Ovulen-21 and Ovulen-28 (the numbers indicate the number of tablets in the package and thus the particular dosage schedule) by Searle & Company (San Juan, P.R.).[19]

For an extensive discussion of the possible side effects of oral contraceptives, see NORETHINDRONE with MESTRANOL.

Hickok v. G. D. Searle & Co. (C.A.-10 Colo., 1974) 496 F.2d 444.

Blood clots—Contents of article on cause-and-effect relationship inadmissible—Verdict for manufacturer upheld

The patient took Ovulen-21 over a period of several months in late 1967 and early in 1968. She developed epileptic seizures which she attributed to side effects of the drug. She filed suit against the manufacturer, alleging that its product caused blood clots in her brain which resulted in scar tissue and the epilepsy.

---

[19] *Physicians' Desk Reference,* 35th ed., p. 1650.

The case was tried before a jury in April, 1973. At the trial the manufacturer introduced strong medical evidence that there was a lack of sufficient proof that oral contraceptives, including Ovulen-21, caused blood clots. During testimony by one of the manufacturer's experts, the plaintiff's attorney cross-examined with regard to one current study suggesting a cause-and-effect relationship between oral contraceptives and strokes. The study was reported in an article in the current issue of the *New England Journal of Medicine.* The witness admitted he was aware of the article.

The plaintiff's attorney then called a medical expert of his own and attempted to have him testify concerning the contents of the article, but the court refused to allow any detailed reference to the material.

The trial was concluded, the case went to the jury, and a verdict was returned for the drug manufacturer. On appeal, the exclusion of the testimony concerning the journal article was the major issue. The United States Court of Appeals, in affirming the judgment of the lower court, held that the trial judge properly refused the proffered testimony under the well-established principle that, in view of the hearsay rule, medical textbooks and professional articles are not freely admissible in evidence to prove the substantive or testimonial facts stated therein. Said the court: "It is not as if Dr. Altshuler [plaintiff's witness] played some part in the preparation of the New England Journal article or the studies upon which it was based. Moreover, its publication only days prior to his testimony precluded the possibility that it substantially contributed to the formation of his own opinion concerning the relationship of birth control pills to blood clotting."

Hamilton v. Hardy (1976) 37 Colo. App. 375, 549 P.2d 1099.

Stroke victim who complained of headaches had jury case against doctor—Also entitled to strict liability instruction against manufacturer

A woman on Ovulen began having headaches. Her doctor assured her that there was no problem, and that she should continue using the drug. Eleven months later she suffered a stroke.

In her suit against her doctor and the manufacturer she alleged negligence on the part of the doctor in not taking her off the drug and in not informing her of the risks involved. Against the manufacturer she charged failure to warn, breach of implied and express warranty, negligent testing, and intentional misrepresentation.

The trial court dismissed as to the doctor, finding no violation of "an objective standard of care applicable to the situation presented" and no failure to obtain the plaintiff's informed consent. The court also granted the manufacturer's motion for dismissal on the theories of breach of warranty, negligent testing, and intentional misrepresentation. The remaining charge was given to the jury but the court refused to instruct on strict liability. The jury found in favor of the manufacturer.

On appeal, the Colorado Court of Appeals reversed, finding that there was sufficient evidence for a jury to decide the issues of the doctor's negligence and lack of informed consent, and that the jury should have been instructed on the strict liability theory.

Goldstein v. G. D. Searle & Co. (1978) 62 Ill. App. 3d 344, 19 Ill. Dec. 208, 378 N.E.2d 1083.

Stroke victim's claim under U.C.C. not barred for failing to notify manufacturer within reasonable time

The plaintiff, who had taken Ovulen in 1966 and 1967, and who suffered a stroke in October of 1967, did not file an action against the manufacturer until October, 1971. Her claim was based upon breach of implied warranty and the manufacturer argued that she had not complied with the Uniform Commercial Code requirement that she give notice of an alleged breach "within a reasonable time." The trial court entered summary judgment for the defendant.

On appeal, the Appellate Court of Illinois reversed, holding that a summary judgment was precluded by the existence of a genuine issue of fact as to whether the plaintiff's notice was in fact "reasonable." (The plaintiff claimed she first learned of Ovulen's potential for causing strokes when she read of Senate Committee hearings on oral contraceptives in 1970.)

Klink v. G. D. Searle & Co. (1980) 26 Wash. App. 951, 614 P.2d 701.

Stroke victim given Ovulen for failure to menstruate—Not informed of risks involved—$1.1 million awarded against physician

A nineteen-year-old patient was given Ovulen by her physician presumably because she had never experienced a normal menstrual period (a condition known as primary amenorrhea). Approximately seventeen months later she suffered a massive bilateral stroke.

Evidence at the trial revealed that an oral contraceptive such as Ovulen can be used as a diagnostic tool to establish whether the uterus "can in fact bleed," but that when used in this manner it should not be prescribed for a period in excess of six months. Also, although he testified that he did inform the plaintiff of some "alternative methods of birth control," her physician admitted that he did not inform her of any possible side effects from taking birth control pills, or that in view of her condition her chances of becoming pregnant were "slight," or that the Ovulen was not a treatment for the underlying cause of her failure to menstruate. At trial she testified that if she had been informed of these facts, she would not have consented to taking the pills.

A jury returned a verdict in the amount of $1.1 million against the physician (the manufacturer, originally named a defendant, apparently settled with the plaintiff or was dismissed from the action prior to trial). On appeal the judgment was affirmed, the Court of Appeals of Washington holding that while the size of the award was indeed large, the court could not properly substitute its judgment for that of the jury.

Drew v. G. D. Searle & Co. (Civil No. 1969-192, U.S. District Court, W.D. N.Y., May, 1970).

Thrombophlebitis—Settlement—Amount not disclosed

A nineteen-year-old patient who took Ovulen-21 for a period of six weeks in 1968 developed thrombophlebitis. Prior to such time, she had no medical history of either a blood or circulatory disorder. A lawsuit was filed against the manufacturer of the drug. According to the attorney for the plaintiff, immediately after service of the plaintiff's interrogatories, the case was settled. The amount was not revealed pursuant to the terms of the settlement agreement.[20]

Urban v. G. D. Searle & Co. (Civil No. 1970-39, U.S. District Court, W.D. N.Y., May, 1971).

Pulmonary embolus—Settlement—Amount not disclosed

A 23-year-old patient took Ovulen for a period of eight months in 1969. During this period she developed a pulmonary embolus. Prior

[20] ATLA *News Letter* 14:292, 1971.

to such time she had no history of a blood or circulatory problem. A lawsuit was filed against the manufacturer and the case was settled prior to trial. The amount was not revealed pursuant to the terms of the settlement agreement.[1]

Seley v. G. D. Searle & Co. (1981) 67 Ohio St. 2d 192, 21 Op. 3d 121, 423 N.E.2d 831.

Stroke—Patient failed to inform physician of history of hypertension—Verdicts for manufacturer and physician affirmed

The plaintiff was a twenty-six year-old stroke victim who had been taking Ovulen for approximately eight months. When she obtained the prescription for the product she failed to inform the defendant physician that during a prior pregnancy she had suffered toxemia with blood pressure readings as high as 196/130.

In her action against the manufacturer she alleged failure to warn and strict liability, and against the physician, failure to warn and negligence. A jury found for both defendants. On appeal, the Court of Appeals reversed as to the manufacturer, finding several errors including ambiguous and contradictory jury instructions. On review by the Supreme Court of Ohio, however, that court reversed the Court of Appeals, holding, among other things that while certain instructions may have been unclear, specific interrogatories to the jurors indicated that in view of their consideration of the evidence that the plaintiff had failed to inform her physician of her prior history of hypertension, it was unlikely that they would not have reached the same conclusion had the court's instructions been more clear.

Stephens v. G. D. Searle & Co. (E.D. Mich., 1985) 602 F. Supp. 379.

Stroke—Manufacturer of oral contraceptives has duty to warn consumer

The plaintiff suffered a stroke while taking Ovulen-21. In finding that a substantial issue of material fact existed as to the adequacy of the manufacturer's warnings, the court denied the defendant's motion for summary judgment and held that under the law of Michigan a manufacturer is under a duty to warn the patient directly,

---

[1] Id.

and not just the prescribing physician, of the risk and side effects of oral contraceptives.

Stafford v. Nipp (Ala., 1987) 502 So. 2d 702.

Stroke—Issue whether physician prescribed Ovulin for over nine years or whether pharmacist dispensed product without authorization—Summary judgments for defendants reversed

The plaintiff alleged that she was given a prescription for Ovulin-21 for birth control in October 1971, and that her physician continued to renew the prescription for over nine years, until, in December 1980, she suffered a stroke which she claimed was caused by the product. The physician, on the other hand, on motion for summary judgment, submitted an affidavit that he had prescribed only a six-month supply of Ovulin-21.

The pharmacist whom the plaintiff claimed dispensed the Ovulin-21 was also named a defendant. In answer to the affidavit that the physician had prescribed only a limited supply of the product, the pharmacist submitted an affidavit that he would not have dispensed the product without the prescription being renewed, but that he had no records for the period in question.

The trial court sustained the summary judgments of both defendants, but the Supreme Court of Alabama reversed, finding that there were material issues of disputed fact as to whether the physician did indeed write a limited prescription and whether the pharmacist dispensed the product without authority. The court further found that there was a fact issue raised as to whether the pharmacist warned the plaintiff concerning taking the product over a nine-year period without prescriptive authority from the physician and without periodical physical examinations. In this regard, the court stated that a drug manufacturer's warnings accompanying the product at the time of sale by pharmacy does not "as a matter of law, shield the pharmacist from liability based on breach of warranty where the pharmacist continues to fill the prescription without authorization from a doctor."

Related cases

United Kingdom proper forum for products case

The United Kingdom, rather than Illinois, was the proper forum for a product liability case involving Ovulen and related birth control products where all of the plaintiffs were U.K. residents, where all of the products were manufactured, marketed and used there, and where most of the evidence and the majority of witnesses were located there. Jones v. Searle Laboratories (1983) 93 Ill. 2d 366, 67 Ill. Dec. 118, 444 N.E.2d 157.

ETRAFON

See AMITRIPTYLINE; PERPHENAZINE

EUCALYPTUS OIL AND MENTHOL

Halls Mentho-Lyptus

Eucalyptus oil is distilled from the leaves of the *Eucalyptus globulus* or some other species of the eucalyptus tree. It is used as an antiseptic, stimulant, and expectorant. Menthol is an alcohol either obtained from mint oils or prepared synthetically, which is used as an antipruritic, topical anesthetic, and as a flavoring agent. The two ingredients are combined in several over-the-counter remedies for the temporary relief of minor throat irritation and cough due to colds or allergies. The Warner-Lambert Company (Morris Plains, N.J.), manufacturer of Halls Mentho-Lyptus Cough Tablets, issues few warnings with the product except that persons with high fever or persistent cough should use it only as directed by a physician.[2]

Burlison v. Warner-Lambert Co. (C.A.-8 Iowa, 1988) 842 F.2d 991.

Anaphylactic reaction—No evidence that manufacturer knew of possibility of allergy to product—Summary judgment affirmed

The plaintiff claimed that she suffered an anaphylactic reaction after taking three Hall's Mentho-Lyptus cough tablets. In her negligence action against the manufacturer, based on the failure to warn, the plaintiff failed to offer evidence that the manufacturer knew or had reason to know that some consumers of Hall's tablets might be allergic to the product. The trial court concluded that there was no submissible jury issue, and the Court of Appeals affirmed.

---

[2]*Physicians' Desk Reference for Nonprescription Drugs,* 3d ed., p. 663.

EUTRON
See METHYCLOTHIAZIDE

EXCEDRIN
See ASPIRIN

EXTENDRYL
See CHLORPHENIRAMINE MALEATE

F

FEDAHIST
See CHLORPHENIRAMINE MALEATE

FENOPROFEN CALCIUM
Nalfon

Nalfon is manufactured by Dista Products Company, a division of Eli Lilly and Company (Indianapolis, Ind.). The drug is a nonsteriodal anti-inflammatory, antiarthritic agent that also possesses analgesic and antipyretic activities. Its exact mode of action is unknown, but it is thought that prostaglandin synthetase inhibitation is involved. The product is indicated for the relief of the symptoms of rheumatoid arthritis and osteoarthritis, and is recommended for acute flares and exacerbations as well as for the long-term management of these diseases.[3]

The most common adverse reactions are gastrointestinal and, according to clinical studies conducted by the manufacturer, have occurred in about 14% of the patients. These reactions include dyspepsia, constipation, nausea, vomiting, abdominal pain, anorexia, occult blood in the stool, diarrhea, flatulence, and dry mouth. The drug is contraindicated in patients who have shown a hypersensitivity to it, and to patients with a history of significantly impaired renal function. Also, it should not be given to patients in whom aspirin and other nonsteroidal anti-inflammatory agents induce symptoms of asthma, rhinitis or urticaria.[4]

---

[3]*Physicians' Desk Reference,* 42d ed., p. 911.
[4]Id., pp. 911-12.

Burnham v. Tabb (Miss., 1987) 508 So. 2d 1072.

Death following asthma attack and respiratory arrest—Insufficient evidence that Nalfon cause

The patient, a sixty-five-year-old woman, suffered from chronic allergies, hayfever and asthma. And, on at least three occasions, the patient had experienced allergic reactions to aspirin. In 1983, she was seen by the defendant ophthalmologist for cataract surgery. Prior to the operation, the defendant noted the patient's allergy to aspirin on her chart.

During the patient's first postoperative visit to the defendant's office, he gave her a prescription for Nalfon (600 m.g.) to combat swelling in her eye. On returning home, the patient had the prescription filled and took her first dose that afternoon. Shortly thereafter she began having difficulty breathing, and her husband took her to the hospital. She improved upon being administered oxygen but later went into respiratory arrest and a coma. Four weeks later she died from bacterial septicemia, respiratory failure and renal failure.

At the trial, the defendant admitted that he had failed to exercise reasonable care in prescribing Nalfon to the patient in light of her history of allergy to aspirin. (In the *Physicians' Desk Reference* it is stated that Nalfon should not be given to patients in whom aspirin or other nonsteroidal anti-inflammatory drugs induce symptoms of asthma.) The defendant denied, however, that the Nalfon was the cause of the patient's attack.

Both sides introduced extensive medical testimony which was in conflict on whether the patient's reaction was caused by the Nalfon. The jury returned a verdict in favor of the defendant which was affirmed on appeal.

FENTANYL
Sublimaze

Sublimaze is a narcotic analgesic with actions similar to those of morphine and meperidine. It is recommended for analgesic action of short duration during the anesthetic periods, premedication, induction, and maintenance, and in the immediate postoperative period (recovery room) as the need arises.

The manufacturer, Janssen Pharmaceutica Inc. (New Brunswick, N.J.), in the product literature under "Dosage and Administration," states that dosage should be individualized, and that some of the factors to be considered in determining the dose are: age, body weight, physical status, underlying pathological conditions, use of other drugs, type of anesthesia to be used, and the surgical procedure involved. Also, vital signs should be monitored routinely.[5]

According to the product literature, these are the usual dosage requirements:

Usual Adult Dosage:

I. *Premedication* (to be appropriately modified in the elderly, debilitated, and those who have received other depressant drugs) — 0.05 to 0.1 mg. (1 to 2 ml.) may be administered *intramuscularly* 30 to 60 minutes prior to surgery.

II. *Adjunct to General Anesthesia*

Induction — 0.05 to 0.1 mg. (1 to 2 ml.) may be administered initially intravenously and may be repeated at 2 to 3 minute intervals until desired effect is achieved. A reduced dose as low as 0.025 to 0.05 mg. (0.5 to 1 ml.) is recommended in elderly and poor-risk patients.

Maintenance — 0.025 to 0.05 mg. (0.5 to 1 ml.) may be administered intravenously or intramuscularly when movement and/or changes in vital signs indicate surgical stress or lightening of analgesia.

III. *Adjunct to Regional Anesthesia* — 0.05 to 0.1 mg. (1 to 2 ml.) may be administered intramuscularly or slowly intravenously when additional analgesia is required.

IV. *Postoperatively (recovery room)* — 0.05 to 0.1 mg. (1 to 2 ml.) may be administered intramuscularly for the control of pain, tachypnea and emergence delirium. The dose may be repeated in one to two hours as needed.

Usual Children's Dosage: For induction and maintenance in children two to 12 years of age, a reduced dose as low as 0.02 to 0.03 mg. (0.4 to 0.6 ml.) per 20 to 25 pounds is recommended.

Wagner v. Kaiser Foundation Hospitals (Docket No. 422-258, Circuit Court, Multnomah County, Ore., July 14, 1977).

**Visual and memory loss following surgery—
Excessive dosage alleged—$750,000 verdict**

A 44-year-old male patient, a private school teacher, was anesthetized with Sublimaze for tear duct surgery. When he awoke, he had "spatial disorientation, defects in both visual fields (peripheral vision) and a marked reduction in his ability to learn new material." He could remember things he learned in school, but could not

[5] *Physicians' Desk Reference,* 35th ed., pp. 956-57.

easily remember people's names or material recently discussed in a class or meeting.

The patient contended that during his surgery the anesthetists used excessive amounts of Sublimaze. On the maintenance dosages of the drug, they used increments of 3 to 2 ml. while *Physicians' Desk Reference* and the package insert specified maintenance increments should be from .5 to 1 ml. The patient further alleged that his respiration was not monitored in the recovery room.

According to the attorney for the patient, he obtained a jury verdict of $750,000.[6]

Swayze v. McNeil Laboratories (C.A.-5 Miss., 1987) 807 F.2d 464.

Excessive dose during surgery administered by unsupervised nurse anesthetist—Directed verdict for manufacturer on issue of adequacy of warning

This action was brought on behalf of a child who died three years after receiving an overdose of fentanyl during surgery. During the operation, a nurse anesthetist erroneously determined what dosage to administer the child. An earlier lawsuit was brought against the surgeon, the hospital and the nurse anesthetist. This was settled for an undisclosed but substantial sum.

In her action against the manufacturer of fentanyl, the child's mother alleged that the defendant knew or should have known that fentanyl was frequently administered by nurse anesthetists without proper supervision and that because of this the defendant had a duty to warn consumers of the risk of excessive dosage. The plaintiff further charged that the manufacturer had a duty to put pressure on the medical community to avoid such practices, and if the medical community failed to do this, the manufacturer had a duty to remove the product from the market.

The trial court granted a directed verdict for the manufacturer which was affirmed on appeal.

Kemble v. Antonetti (No. 87-1002-B, 44th Judicial District Court, Dallas County, Tex., Jan. 29, 1988).

Excessive anesthesia administered by plastic surgeon during office breast surgery — $500,000 settlement

The patient, age 65, was scheduled for breast augmentation surgery in her plastic surgeon's office. A nurse anesthetist was en-

[6] ATLA *Law Reporter* 20:380, 1977.

gaged to administer the anesthesia, but she did not appear, and the surgeon, assisted by two hospital residents, administered the anesthesia.

During the operation, the surgeon gave the patient 10 cc. of Sublimaze, 10 mg. of Valium, and 100 cc. of Xylocaine. At least once, the patient experienced a drop in blood pressure, and the procedure had to be interrupted. Following surgery, the patient suffered a period of hypoxia from respiratory depression, and she remained comatose for three days.

At the date of the filing of her malpractice action, the patient still suffered mental confusion and a speech impairment, was confined to a wheelchair, and required constant care of an attendant. According to the patient's attorney, the surgeon has settled for $500,000, the limit of his liability policy.[7]

Franklin v. Gupta (No. 85242052/CL39375, Circuit Court, Baltimore, Md., March 3, 1988).

Respiratory arrest during surgery—Excessive dosage—$375,000 verdict set aside

The patient, age 43, was scheduled for surgery for carpal tunnel syndrome. The night before his operation, he was seen by an anesthesiologist who ordered pre-anesthesia medication. The anesthesiologist did not, however, perform an anesthesia evaluation. The following morning, because he was needed for another operation, the anesthesiologist turned the patient over to a nurse anesthetist. Without consulting the surgeon, this anesthetist administered a brachial plexus block and 3 cc. of Sublimaze. When the block was unsuccessful, the anesthetist left the operating room to consult with the anesthesiologist. When she returned, the patient was in respiratory arrest.

The patient survived, but claimed to have suffered an "out-of-body experience" and "post-traumatic stress syndrome." He says he experiences recurring nightmares and has developed a fear of doctors and hospitals, which prevents him from undergoing the surgery for his carpal tunnel syndrome. In his malpractice suit against the anesthesiologist, anesthetist, surgeon, and hospital, the patient charged that the anesthesiologist was negligent in failing to perform a pre-anesthesia evaluation and implement an anesthesia plan, and, in view of the patient's condition, in failing to be present

---

[7] ATLA *Professional Negligence Law Reporter* 3:74, 1988.

during the surgery. Also, the patient alleged that the anesthetist administered an excessive dose of Sublimaze, in that the PDR recommended only .05 to .10 mg. of Sublimaze as an adjunct to regional anesthesia.

The jury awarded the patient $375,000 against all defendants except the surgeon, but the trial judge granted the defendants' motions for judgment n.o.v. on the grounds that the patient did not show sufficient proof of alternative treatment and psychological injury.[8]

FENTANYL and DROPERIDOL
Innovar

Innovar is a combination of the morphine-like analgesic, fentanyl, and droperidol, a butyrophenone derivative used to produce sedation and reduce the incidence of nausea and vomiting. The combination, formerly manufactured by McNeil Laboratories, Inc. (Fort Washington, Pa.) and now by Janssen Pharmaceutica, Inc. (New Brunswick, N.J.), is used as an adjunct to anesthesia, chiefly for premedication and induction, because fentanyl alone has a very short duration of action, while the action of droperidol is prolonged.[9]

For premedication, 0.5 to 2 ml. of Innovar is administered intramuscularly 45 to 60 minutes preoperatively, according to the physical status, age, and weight of the patient. The intravenous dosage for induction of anesthesia is 0.1 ml./kg. of body weight.[10]

Fentanyl may cause muscle rigidity, especially involving the muscles of respiration, and may produce signs of bronchoconstriction.[11]

McDaniel v. McNeil Laboratories, Inc. (1976) 196 Neb. 190, 241 N.W.2d 822.

Cardiac arrest during surgery—Anesthesiologist settles—Verdict for manufacturer affirmed on question of drug's safety

A 47-year-old woman suffered cardiac arrest during a hemorrhoid operation. The evidence disclosed that the anesthesiologist

---

[8] Id., p. 119.

[9] *AMA Drug Evaluations,* 2d ed., p. 241.

[10] Id.

[11] *Physicians' Desk Reference,* 35th ed., p. 953.

had administered double the maximum dosage of Innovar when the patient complained that she could "still feel what they are doing." Suit was brought against the hospital, attending physician, anesthesiologist and the manufacturer of the drug. Prior to trial the hospital and attending physician were dismissed. On the third day of trial the anesthesiologist settled for an undisclosed sum, and the case proceeded against the manufacturer.

The plaintiff produced experts who testified that in their opinion the drugs fentanyl and droperidol, combined in a 1 to 50 fixed ratio to form Innovar, were an "unreasonably dangerous" combination, and in this regard they believed that the warnings on the package insert were inadequate. Despite this evidence, which was disputed by the manufacturer, the jury returned a verdict for the defendant.

On appeal, the verdict was affirmed, with the Supreme Court of Nebraska holding that while approval of a drug by the Food and Drug Administration is not necessarily conclusive as to its safety, Innovar was approved by the FDA for use as an anesthetic, and the FDA's determination should not be subject to challenge simply because experts may differ in their opinions as to whether the drug is safe, unless there is some proof of fraud or nondisclosure of relevant information by the manufacturer at the time approval was obtained.

McKinley v. Vize (Mo. App., 1978) 563 S.W.2d 505.

Patient with history of asthma suffered cardiac arrest during dental surgery—Choice of anesthetic questioned—$28,000 award affirmed against dentist

This action was brought by the parents of an eighteen-year-old boy who died from cardiac arrest during the removal of two wisdom teeth. The boy had suffered from asthma as a child, but prior to the dental surgery his family physician had pronounced him "in good health" and no mention was made of asthma or allergy.

The patient was given Innovar, which experts at the trial testified causes a constrictive action upon the bronchial tubes. Just prior to his surgery, the patient's blood test showed a high eosinophil count which is found in persons who are allergic. Also, on admission to the hospital, it was noted on the patient's "Progress Notes" that he had a "history of childhood asthma"; however, this information was not made a part of the patient's medical chart and neither the dental surgeon nor the nurse anesthetist saw the entry.

The nurse anesthetist testified that had she known about the patient's history she would have used an anesthetic other than Innovar, one which dilated the bronchial tubes rather than constricted them.

During the trial, the hospital and the nurse anesthetist settled with the plaintiffs for an undetermined amount. A jury returned a verdict against the dental surgeon for $28,000 which was affirmed on appeal.

Related cases

Choice of combination questioned

In Harris v. Doe (Superior Court, San Mateo County, California, 1972), an anesthesiologist was charged with negligence in choosing the combination of halothane and Innovar as the anesthetic agent for an eleven-year-old child who suffered from a bone disease and weighed only 36 pounds. The case is summarized herein under HALOTHANE.

FIBRINOGEN
Parenogen

Fibrinogen is the sterile human plasma fraction, dried from the frozen state, which in solution is capable of being converted into insoluble fibrin on addition of thrombin. As administration of fibrinogen involves the risk of transmitting the virus of serum hepatitis, the substance should be used only in conditions where hemorrhagic complications are or may be serious and intravenous use of fibrinogen may be lifesaving.[12]

The product has been marketed by Cutter Laboratories, Inc. (Berkeley, Cal.) under the name Parenogen and by several other suppliers under the generic name. At present it is not on any manufacturer's list.

Hodge v. Fenderson (Superior Court, Kern County, California, 1974).

Physician charged with failure to determine if risk of hepatitis necessary—Also failure to keep proper records —$150,000 settlement

An obstetrical patient underwent a successful delivery. About ten days later, however, she began to suffer post-partum bleeding. Her

[12] *United States Dispensatory* 27th ed., p. 521.

regular obstetrician was not available, and she was seen by an associate who ordered her hospitalized and prescribed three units of whole blood and two units of Parenogen. The bleeding stopped, and it appeared that the patient would have no more trouble, but approximately three months later she became ill, and unable to keep food down. She returned to her obstetrician's office, but again he was not available, and she saw another associate. He had no knowledge of her previous hospitalization for bleeding, as apparently the incident had not been entered on her record, and he diagnosed her ailment as flu syndrome. Ten days later she died from fulminating hepatitis.

A lawsuit was filed against the two associates. It was alleged among other things that there was no showing in her hospital record that the patient had been tested prior to being given the Parenogen to determine whether it was warranted under the circumstances. Such tests were necessary, it was claimed, in view of warnings by the drug's manufacturer that the presence or absence of hepatitis virus in the solution could not be proven with absolute certainty, and therefore its use should be weighed against the medical consequences of withholding it.

The plaintiff charged that the first doctor was negligent in administering Parenogen, and in failing to keep an accurate record of the patient's hospitalization and treatment, which prevented the second doctor from properly diagnosing and treating her hepatitis.

According to the attorney representing the plaintiff, the defendants settled prior to trial for $150,000.[13]

FIORINAL
See BUTALBITAL

FLAGYL
See METRONIDAZOLE

FLEET PHOSPHO-SODA
See SODIUM PHOSPHATE

---

[13] ATLA *News Letter* 18:69, 1975.

FLUOGEN
See INFLUENZA VIRUS VACCINE

FLUORESCEIN SODIUM
See SODIUM FLUORESCEIN

FLUOTHANE
See HALOTHANE

FLUPHENAZINE HYDROCHLORIDE
Permitil
Proloxin

Fluphenazine hydrochloride is a member of the phenothiazine group of tranquilizers and is used in the management of manifestations of psychotic disorders, especially schizophrenia. As with most tranquilizers, there are many possible adverse reactions, including sudden, unexplained death.[14]

Permitil is manufactured by Schering Corporation (Kenilworth, N.J.) and Proloxin by E.R. Squibb & Sons, Inc. (Princeton, N.J.).

Moon v. United States (D. Nev., 1981) 512 F. Supp. 140.

Treatment with Proloxin not proximate cause of mental patient's death from drowning

The patient, under treatment for schizophrenia at the Reno Veteran's Administration Hospital, drowned during a hospital outing. As one of the charges of negligence, the patient's parents accused the psychiatric staff of overprescribing Proloxin (one of the side effects of which is hypothermia) which they claimed caused the patient, a good swimmer, to drown. At the trial the plaintiffs introduced evidence that the manufacturer of Proloxin recommended daily doses of from two to ten milligrams, and that doses above twenty milligrams should be given only with "precautionary measures." According to the patient's records, he was receiving daily doses substantially in excess of twenty milligrams.

Although the medical evidence was conflicting, the court held that it failed to establish that the administration of Proloxin was unreasonable, and that the manufacturer's limitation on dosage appeared to be "merely cautionary for physicians and not to present

---

[14]*Physicians' Desk Reference,* 40th ed., p. 1749.

any absolute limits for the amounts of such medication which may be safely prescribed." The Court further held that even if the defendants were negligent in prescribing the drug, under Nevada law such conduct could not be said to be the proximate cause of the patient's death. In arriving at this decision, the court was impressed by evidence that other patients at the same hospital who were being treated with Proloxin had been taken on skiing trips in the mountains without any ill effects from hypothermia.

Kirk v. Michael Reese Hospital & Medical Center (1987) 117 Ill.2d 507, 111 Ill. Dec. 944, 513 N.E.2d 387.

Cause of action for failure to warn of adverse reactions not extended to passenger injured in accident

The plaintiff was a passenger in an automobile being driven by a person who recently had been given Proloxin and Thorazine (chlorpromazine). The driver then consumed an alcoholic beverage. According to the plaintiff, the combined effects diminished the driver's mental and physical abilities, causing him to lose control of the automobile and hit a tree, injuring the plaintiff.

In a suit against driver's physicians, the hospital where he had been administered the drugs, and the manufacturers of the drugs, the defendants' motions for dismissal were granted, but the appellate court reversed, holding that all the defendants owed a legal duty to warn adequately of the adverse effects of the drugs the driver had been given, that this duty implicitly extended to members of the public who may be injured as the proximate cause of a failure to so warn, and that the hospital was open to an action for strict liability. The Supreme Court of Illinois, however, reversed the Appellate Court and affirmed the trial court's dismissals, holding that the manufacturers could not have reasonably foreseen the injury to the plaintiff, that the hospital could not be held strictly liable since the plaintiff was not a patient nor a user of a product supplied by the hospital; and that neither the driver's physicians nor the other defendants owed a duty to the plaintiff, being a third party, to warn him that the driver might be impaired by the medication he was taking.

Related cases

Tardive dyskinesia—Informed consent doctrine available to involuntarily committed mental patient

In an action on behalf of patient confined to a state hospital for a manic-depression disorder who developed tardive dyskinesia while being treated with Proloxin and Mellaril (thioridazine), the Supreme Court of Alabama held that absent a finding of incompetency or an emergency situation, a person involuntarily committed to a mental hospital is not *ipso facto* barred from the invocation of the "informed consent" doctrine. Nolen v. Peterson (Ala., 1989) 544 So. 2d 863.

FLURAZEPAM HYDROCHLORIDE
Dalmane

Flurazepam hydrochloride is a hypnotic agent used for the treatment of insomnia characterized by difficulty in falling asleep, nocturnal awakenings, or early morning awakenings. Several companies manufacture and market the drug under the generic name, and Roche Products, Inc. (Manati, P.R.), produces Dalmane.[15]

The product is issued with the usual precautions for sleep-inducing medications, including the fact that the risk of oversedation, dizziness, confusion or ataxia increases substantially with larger doses in elderly and debilitated patients.[16]

Laboy v. United States (D. P.R., 1985) 626 F. Supp. 105.

Evidence fails to establish fatal overdose

The survivors of a veteran found dead after ingesting Dalmane brought suit against the Veterans Administration for alleged negligence in the treatment he received as a patient in the V.A.'s Mental Hygiene Clinic. The plaintiffs alleged that the defendant's medical personnel were negligent in not hospitalizing the decedent, in not treating him as a potential suicidal patient, and in entrusting him with a medication such as Dalmane.

The plaintiffs, however, failed to establish a prima facie case when the medical evidence revealed that on examination at death the decedent's urine showed that he had consumed only 34 milli-

---

[15] *Physicians' Desk Reference,* 41st ed., p. 1688.

[16] Id.

grams of Dalmane, which amounted to slightly over one capsule. According to evidence introduced by the defense, it would have taken 100 such capsules to produce a lethal dose.

It was also established that the decedent showed no particular signs of noncompliance with the treatment he was receiving, and that four days before his death he was responding well to his medication.

Related cases

Coma and paralysis following treatment with Dalmane and other drugs— Action not barred by statute

Where a patient was rendered paralyzed, blind and virtually unable to speak, allegedly as a result of a negligently prescribed combination of Valium, Placidyl, Dalmane and Methadone, the patient's conservator's discovery of the cause of the patient's injury did not trigger the one-year prescriptive period under California's medical malpractice statute of limitations. Getty v. Hoffman-LaRoche (1987) 189 Cal. App. 3d 1294, 235 Cal. Rptr. 48.

FLUZONE

See INFLUENZA VIRUS VACCINE

FOLEX

See METHOTREXATE

FURADANTIN

See NITROFURANTOIN

FUROSEMIDE

Lasix

Lasix is a potent diuretic produced by Hoechst-Roussel Pharmaceuticals Inc. (Somerville, N.J.) for the treatment of edema associated with congestive heart failure, cirrhosis of the liver, and kidney disease. It is also indicated as adjunctive therapy in acute pulmonary edema.

The manufacturer warns that if given in excessive amounts, the drug can lead to profound diuresis with water and electrolyte depletion.[17]

The product also is marketed by several companies under the generic name.

Mackey v. Greenview Hosp., Inc. (Ky. App., 1979) 587 S.W.2d 249.

Cardiac arrest—Patient failed to disclose prior use of Lasix—Verdict for defendants upheld

The patient, while undergoing a breast biopsy, suffered cardiac arrest, resulting in extensive brain damage. It was later learned that she had been using Lasix prior to admission which likely lowered her potassium level to the point whereby her physicians were unable to restore normal heart function in time to prevent permanent impairment.

The physicians and anesthesiologists involved in the patient's case denied knowledge of her use of the drug, yet there was evidence that she informed the floor nurse that she was using Lasix, and that the nurse entered this fact on the patient's hospital form entitled, "Admission Information and Nursing Care Data." The evidence was in dispute, however, as to whether this form was in the patient's chart which accompanied her to the operating room. Also, the patient's surgeon and one of her anesthesiologists both testified that they took separate preoperative histories from her the night prior to the surgery, and that she failed to inform them that she was using the drug, and, furthermore, that she suffered from a heart condition and had used nitroglycerine tablets on occasion.

The jury returned a verdict for all defendants and the reviewing court affirmed.

G

GAMULIN Rh

See Rh_o (D) IMMUNE GLOBULIN (HUMAN)

---

[17]*Physicians' Desk Reference,* 35th ed., p. 938.

GARAMYCIN
See GENTAMICIN SULFATE

GAVISCON
See MAGNESIUM TRISILICATE with ALUMINUM HYDROXIDE

GELUSIL
See MAGNESIUM TRISILICATE with ALUMINUM HYDROXIDE

GENTAMICIN SULFATE

Garamycin
G-myticin

Gentamicin sulfate is a water soluble antibiotic of the aminoglycoside group derived from a strain of *Micromonospora purpurea.* In the injectable form (intramuscularly) it is used in treating *Pseudomonas aeruginosa, Proteus species, E. coli,* and *Klebsiella, Enterobacter, Serratia, Citrobacter* and *Staphylococcus species.*

Patients treated with gentamicin sulfate should be under close observation because of the potential toxicity associated with the drug. Eighth cranial nerve damage (ototoxicity, both vestibular and auditory) can occur, primarily in patients with preexisting renal damage, when treatment is prolonged or when dosage is higher than recommended. In patients with impaired renal function, dosage must be adjusted. The Schering Corporation (Kenilworth, N.J.), manufacturer of Garamycin, includes in the product literature a table showing the approximate adult dosage based on the patient's renal function. This dosage is reduced accordingly in the presence of renal impairment.[18]

Pedinol Pharmacal, Inc. (Farmingdale, N.Y.) markets the product under the name G-myticin, and several companies produce it under the generic label.

---

[18] *Physicians' Desk Reference,* 40th ed., pp. 1622-24.

Bishop v. Tsai (Docket No. 81-307, U.S. District Court, W.D. Pa., April, 1982).

Overdose of gentamicin results in eighth cranial nerve damage—Permanent equilibrium disturbance—Hospital settles for $250,000

The patient was a fifty-nine-year-old engineering contractor. During hospital confinement for lower lobe pneumonia he was given gentamicin for thirty-four days without pretherapy tests or monitoring of toxicity levels or urea nitrogen blood levels. Although he experienced dizziness and roaring in his ears during therapy he did not report these symptoms because he had not been warned that they might be drug-related. He suffered irreversible eighth cranial nerve damage which resulted in a permanent equilibrium disturbance and inability to walk without assistance. The hospital settled for $250,000.[19]

Siehr v. Stern (No. 82-16527 F, Circuit Court, Hillsborough County, Fla., Jan. 31, 1984).

Internist allegedly negligent in prescribing drug—$300,000 settlement for permanent vertigo

The defendant internist was treating the plaintiff, a seventy-one-year-old housewife, for rheumatoid arthritis. When she became ill with chills, nausea and a high fever, he admitted her to the hospital and prescribed gentamicin. When she was discharged eight days later he renewed the prescription. Not long afterward she began developing vertigo, which eventually became permanent. In the plaintiff's suit she alleged the defendant had improperly administered the drug, that the dosage was too high, and that he had failed to monitor the toxicity level in her blood. The parties settled for $300,000.[20]

Mitchell v. Parker (1984) 68 N.C. App. 458, 315 S.E.2d 76.

Kidney damage—Question of proper monitoring—Evidence sufficient for jury

The patient had undergone a gastric segmentation for obesity. On the second day after surgery she developed a serious infection for which her surgeon prescribed Garamycin and other medication.

---

[19] ATLA *Law Reporter* 25:376, 1982.

[20] Id., 27:282, 1984.

The Garamycin was administered from October 10 to October 24. On the 17th, serum creatine and blood urea nitrogen (BUN) tests were performed. The BUN was thirteen. Two days later it was nineteen. No more tests were performed until November 1, at which time the BUN was over 200. By then the patient had suffered permanent kidney damage.

The trial judge directed a verdict for the surgeon and his assistant, but the Court of Appeals reversed, holding the evidence of negligence was sufficient for the jury.

Mielke v. Condell Memorial Hosp. (1984) 124 Ill. App. 3d 42, 79 Ill. Dec. 78, 463 N.E.2d 216.

Ototoxicity—Damage to labyrinth—Verdicts for physicians and hospital affirmed for want of expert testimony

The patient was administered gentamicin on admission to the hospital for a perforated duodenal ulcer and later, after gastric surgery, was given gentamicin and furosemide. She developed ototoxicity, causing destruction of her labyrinth and at the time of trial could walk only with assistance.

The patient's medical evidence consisted mainly of a physician who offered to testify by reading summaries of articles from medical literature regarding the ototoxicity of gentamicin and its interaction with furosemide. The trial court refused to allow this testimony.

The trial court directed a verdict in favor of the hospital and entered judgment on jury verdicts in favor of the patient's physicians. The Appellate Court affirmed, holding that exclusions of the patient's expert's testimony was not error, and that the patient had failed to establish a prima facie case against the hospital.

Hansen v. Garbaccio (No. 83-41235-NM, Circuit Court, Kent County, Mich., February 5, 1985).

Permanent vertigo and hearing loss following excessive administration of Garamycin—$203,500 verdict against nephrologist

The patient was a sixty-one-year-old woman with kidney disease who was on continuous ambulatory peritoneal dialysis. While on a vacation trip to Florida she developed symptoms of a peritoneal infection and stopped at a hospital. The emergency room physician called her nephrologist who prescribed Garamycin. She took the drug four times daily for two and one-half days and the symptoms disappeared, but on a follow-up visit to a Florida nephrologist it was discovered that the prescription from her physician called for a dosage five times higher than that recommended by the manufacturer. The dosage was immediately reduced, but two weeks later she began to experience severe vertigo and significant hearing loss in both ears. At time of trial she suffered a permanent 70% hearing loss in the left ear and 45% in the right. She also suffered continuous vertigo and required a cane to walk. The jury returned a verdict for $203,500.[1]

Albers v. Aycinena (No. 170062, Superior Court, San Mateo County, Cal., Aug. 16, 1974).

Hearing impairment and renal damage—Patient placed on high gentamicin dosage prior to renal function test —Verdicts for physicians

A hospital patient being treated with gentamicin sulfate for a severe kidney infection suffered hearing impairment and renal damage from the side effects of the drug. On being admitted to the hospital, the patient had been given cultures and sensitivity tests, but no renal function test. He was started on 240 mg. per day of gentamicin sulfate. A renal function test was finally performed on the third day, and the dosage was reduced.

The patient filed a malpractice suit based on charges that the renal function test should have been performed before he was placed on the gentamicin sulfate. (Patients with impaired renal function are more likely to suffer from the side effects of gentamicin sulfate.) According to the patient's complaint, this was the procedure recommended by the manufacturer of the drug. As the result of the failure to run this test, the patient alleged that he was given six times the dosage recommended by the manufacturer for patients with renal function similar to his.

Named in the lawsuit were the patient's admitting physician (a urologist) and a consulting nephrologist. The nephrologist had seen the patient only once, and apparently had not commented on the administration of the drug. He had, however, recommended that the patient be transferred to another hospital where there were better facilities for the patient's type of case.

---

[1] ATLA *Law Reporter* 28:277, 1985.

At the trial, the patient introduced several medical witnesses, including a nephrologist (not the defendant) who had been called in on the case after the patient's complications had developed. He testified that the defendant urologist had violated acceptable standards of care in the community when he had failed to order renal function tests before administering the gentamicin. Also, this witness testified that the risks of the drug should have been fully explained to the patient, which apparently had not been done. A second witness, an ear, nose and throat specialist, testified that it was also his opinion that the urologist had failed to meet acceptable standards of care when he failed to perform audiometric tests before and during the administration of the drug. He also agreed that renal function tests should have been performed before treatment was commenced and that the risks of the drug should have been more fully explained. This witness testified further that the defendant-nephrologist was also guilty of violating acceptable standards of care by failing to advise the urologist to discontinue use of the drug.

A third witness for the patient, another urologist, testified that he likewise thought standards of care had been violated by the urologist in failing to perform the renal function test and in giving too large a dosage of gentamicin.

In defending their actions the urologist and nephrologist both argued that they had followed acceptable standards. The nephrologist testified that when he was first brought into the case, the patient was obviously dying of his kidney infection, and that the high dosage of gentamicin was necessary to save his life, and that the patient was in no condition to discuss the possible risks in the use of the drug. Another urologist testifying for the defendants stated that, in his opinion, the dosage was proper, although he admitted on cross-examination that he probably would have performed more renal function tests if he had been in charge of the case.

After a lengthy trial the jury returned verdicts for both defendants.[2]

---

[2] AMA *The Citation* 30:52, 1974.

Schering Corp. v. Giesecke (Tex. Civ. App., 1979) 589 S.W.2d 516.

**Hearing loss—Physicians settle for $265,000—
Manufacturer guilty of failing to warn**

A patient underwent surgery on October 22, 1971 for a ruptured diverticulum of the colon. Along with other antibiotics, the patient's physicians prescribed Garamycin postoperatively. His condition worsened, however, and a second operation was necessary because of peritonitis. A partial colectomy was performed, and the patient's abdomen was "washed" with kanamycin, an antibiotic similar to Garamycin. During this time the patient was also being given injections of Garamycin.

On October 31, the patient suffered acute kidney failure. He went into a coma from severe uremic poisoning and eventually became totally deaf.

In his complaint, the plaintiff attributed his hearing loss to the excessive use of antibiotics, particularly Garamycin. The plaintiff's physicians settled for $265,000 prior to trial. A jury returned a verdict of $200,000 against the manufacturer of Garamycin on evidence that prior to marketing the product it had information that the drug's side effects could lead to permanent hearing loss, but it did not adequately warn the medical profession of this fact.

On appeal, however, the verdict was set aside, the reviewing court holding that the defendant should be entitled to a credit for any amount of the $265,000 paid by the doctors that was related to the plaintiff's loss of hearing.

Grassis v. Retik (1988) 25 Mass. App. 595, 521 N.E.2d 411.

**Hearing loss—Issue whether blood serum
tests should have been performed—
Verdict for physicians upheld**

The patient, a two-year-old infant, was hospitalized for a severe kidney infection. Over a period of a week, she received nineteen doses of gentamicin. Each dose contained 25 mg. of the drug, and the doses were given every eight hours. Six months after the child was released from the hospital, her parents noticed that she was suffering from a hearing impairment. On being tested, she was found to have lost 65% of her hearing in both ears.

The physicians who had treated the child during her hospitalization were charged with negligence and with failure to obtain the parents' informed consent to the treatment selected. At the trial, the plaintiffs offered expert testimony that during her treatment the child's blood serum should have been tested periodically for evidence of gentamicin toxicity. The defense countered with medical testimony that such tests are done only if the patient has impaired kidney function, and in the Grassis child's case, there was no such impairment. Furthermore, the defense expert suggested that the hearing loss could have been due to the infection itself, another infection, hypertension, or a genetic problem. (The child was born with a double ureter, a sixth digit on her right hand, and an "intoed" alignment of her feet. Also, her mother was born with three kidneys.)

The jury returned a verdict for the defendants, and the Appeals Court of Massachusetts affirmed.

Related cases

Hearing loss—Error to admit editorial on practice of exceeding manufacturer's recommended dosage

In O'Brien v. Angley (1980) 63 Ohio St. 2d 159, 407 N.E.2d 490, the patient suffered hearing loss following injections of Garamycin in excess of the manufacturer's recommended dosage. At trial the defendants introduced over objections by the plaintiff an editorial from *The Journal of the American Medical Association* expressing the opinion that best medical practice often requires that a physician ignore the manufacturer's recommendations in prescribing a drug, often at the peril of being confronted later in court by such recommendations. A judgment for the defendants in trial court was reversed on appeal because of the admission of this evidence.

Heart attack following injection—Jury award overturned

In Berwald v. Kasal (1980) 102 Mich. App. 269, 301 N.W.2d 499, an injection of Garamycin was blamed for causing the patient to suffer a heart attack, allegedly because of an adverse reaction to the drug. A jury awarded the patient $125,000 and his wife $4,500, but the verdict was overturned for insufficient evidence of negligence and procedural errors.

GLUCAMIDE

See CHLORPROPAMIDE

GLUCOSE POLYMERS

Polycose

Polycose, manufactured by Ross Laboratories (Columbus, Ohio), is a caloric supplement derived solely from carbohydrate for persons with increased caloric needs or those unable to meet their such needs with a normal diet. It is designed to be added to tube-feeding formulas and to most foods and beverages, or mixed in water, in amounts determined by taste, caloric requirement and tolerance. The manufacturer cautions that the product is not to be fed undiluted, and is to be used only as directed by a physician.[3]

Ross Labs v. Thies (Alaska, 1986) 725 P.2d 1076.

Retailer and manufacturer liable for selling undiluted product in container resembling baby bottle

The plaintiff's infant daughter became severely dehydrated when her mother gave her an undiluted solution of Polycose which the infant's aunt had purchased from a local retailer. The container in which the solution was purchased had a plastic nipple and resembled a baby bottle.

After considerable pretrial discovery, the trial court granted the plaintiff's motion for summary judgment, holding that the defendant retailer and Ross Laboratories, manufacturer of Polycose, were strictly liable for the child's injuries. The court based its findings on evidence that the defendants had sold the product in a container which resembled a "nipple-ready" baby bottle without a warning that the solution was undiluted. On appeal, the trial court's findings were affirmed, the Supreme Court of Alaska holding that the nipple-ready bottle, taken together with the similarity in name, label, and contents with recognized products to be consumed by infants, required the defendants to foresee that some consumers would mistakenly believe that Polycose was a product to be fed directly to babies. Thus, held the court, there was no genuine issue of fact to be decided on this point.

---

[3] *Physicians' Desk Reference,* 42d ed., p. 1833.

The reviewing court did, however, reverse the trial court's ruling that the question of punitive damages should be submitted to a jury. In the opinion of the reviewing court, no punitive damages were justified against either the retailer or the manufacturer.

GLUTETHIMIDE
Doriden

Glutethimide is a nonbarbiturate sedative and hypnotic recommended for short-term use. It is not indicated for chronic administration.[4] Under "Adverse Reactions" the manufacturer of Doriden, USV Pharmaceutical Corporation (Tuckahoe, N.Y.), has stated in advertisements to physicians:

> Withdraw glutethimide if a generalized skin rash occurs. Rash usually clears spontaneously within a few days after withdrawal. Occasionally, a purpuric or urticarial rash may occur; exfoliative dermatitis has been reported rarely. With recommended doses, there have been rare reports of nausea, hangover, paradoxical excitation, and blurring of vision. Rarely, acute hypersensitivity reactions, porphyria, and blood dyscrasias (thrombocytopenic purpura, aplastic anemia, leukopenia) have been reported[5]

The drug has been frequently abused, and has led to many cases of chronic and acute intoxication, with a number of fatalities, and also to dependence and addiction.[6]

Finley v. United States (N.D. Ohio, 1970) 314 F. Supp. 905.

Skin rash and depigmentation suffered by black patient taking Doriden—No liability on part of physicians

A Negro male employee of the Veterans Administration Hospital in Cleveland sought treatment for a service-connected peptic ulcer at the downtown VA outpatient facility. While obtaining medicine for the ulcer, the patient mentioned he also was having difficulty sleeping. The physician in attendance asked him whether he had previously taken any sleeping pills, and the patient said that he had. The physician then wrote a prescription for Doriden which the patient had filled at the pharmacy section of the facility.

---

[4] *Physicians' Desk Reference,* 40th ed., p. 1812.

[5] U.S.V. Pharmaceutical Corporation, Product Information, *Journal of Legal Medicine* 3:5, 1975.

[6] *United States Dispensatory,* 27th ed., p. 560.

The patient had taken the ulcer medicine and the Doriden for a week when he noticed small bumps and a rash appearing on his arm. According to the patient, while at work he stopped at the outpatient department of the VA hospital where the physician on duty told him that he appeared to have heat rash. This physician, said the patient, did not prescribe any treatment or medication.

The patient said that several days later, when the rash appeared to be getting worse, he returned to the outpatient department and saw another physician who likewise told him the rash was probably due to heat, or possibly measles. Again, the patient said he was given no medication. Both of these physicians later denied examining the patient.

The patient's rash worsened, and he was seen by a private physician who told him that he was probably suffering a drug reaction. He was told to stop taking the Doriden and to seek treatment at a private hospital the following day. The patient had difficulty getting treatment at the private hospital and returned to the VA hospital. After a dermatological examination, which disclosed he was indeed suffering from a "drug eruption," he was advised to discontinue taking all drugs and was given medication to take home to relieve the itching caused by the rash. The patient later said he asked to be hospitalized but was told by the VA physician that the hospital was in the process of moving and that only emergency cases were being admitted.

When his rash did not improve after two weeks, he returned to the VA hospital and was admitted as an inpatient. The diagnosis was "Dermatitis medicamentosa, possibly due to Doriden." There was also in the records a reference to an anemic condition which a resident physician in hematology later stated "could possibly be related to Doriden intake, although I am unaware of this side-effect."

The patient's rash apparently improved and he was discharged from the hospital. Within several weeks, however, he noticed that his skin was beginning to lighten; then all the hair on his head and body fell out. The skin lightened further until all pigmentation was gone, leaving his body white. His hair grew back in, but it was white rather than black as it previously had been. This all developed over a period of from one to two months.

A malpractice suit was filed against the government alleging negligence on the part of the VA physicians. At the trial the patient's attorneys introduced two dermatologists. The first testified that the patient was suffering from "leukoderma," which he explained was a depigmentation brought on by a reaction to the Doriden. The second dermatologist agreed substantially as to the patient's condition but testified that it could have been caused by several things, one of which was the effects of Doriden. Because he said he had never seen any reports that a drug could produce depigmentation, which he termed "vitiligo," this expert preferred to consider the Doriden as a possible but not probable cause of the condition. Both experts agreed that Doriden could not have been the *direct* cause of the depigmentation, and that a patient would have to have had a predisposition to the condition which was somehow triggered by the drug. Both experts agreed that if the Doriden had directly produced the depigmentation, the condition would have improved on withdrawal of the drug.

The specifications of negligence presented by the patient's attorneys were (1) that the physician who prescribed Doriden was negligent in doing so; (2) that the two physicians in the VA outpatient department who (according to the patient) examined the patient for the skin rash were negligent in not taking steps to treat him; and (3) that the physician who eventually diagnosed the patient's case as a drug reaction was negligent in not having him admitted immediately to a hospital as an inpatient.

After hearing the evidence, the trial judge held that although the patient's medical experts offered sufficient evidence to support a finding of proximate cause, there was no proof that the physicians departed from recognized medical standards in their dealings with the patient. The patient failed, said the court, to prove by a preponderance of evidence that there was malpractice.

The patient's attorneys had raised a specific charge that the physician who had prescribed the drug was negligent in failing to warn that skin rash was a known side effect. As evidence, they showed that skin rash was mentioned in the manufacturer's information on the drug as published in the *Physicians' Desk Reference.* In commenting on this, the trial judge said:

> While there is evidence that Doriden is known to produce skin rash, there is no proof as to the incidence of such side-effect in relation to the use of the drug. If it appeared from the evidence that there was an abnormally high proportion of skin disorder reaction to the use of Doriden, the Court might be in a position to conclude, applying common knowledge and experience, that a warning was called for. However, from common knowledge and experience the Court is aware of the fact that many drugs do

carry warnings of possible side-effects in their descriptive literature, even though the possibility of such reaction occurring is remote.

Related cases

Numerous side effects following six years of therapy— No cause of action against manufacturer

In Fellows v. USV Pharmaceutical Corp. (D. Md., 1980) 502 F. Supp. 297, the plaintiff complained that he suffered numerous side effects from taking Doriden from 1970 to 1976. His action against the manufacturer was dismissed upon motion for summary judgment, the court finding no cause of action for negligence, breach of warranty, strict liability or misbranding.

G-MITICIN

See GENTAMICIN SULFATE

GOLD SODIUM THIOMALATE

Myochrysine

Myochrysine is a sterile aqueous solution of gold sodium thiomalate which is itself a mixture of the mono- and disodium salts of gold thiomalic acid. Myochrysine is manufactured by Merck, Sharp and Dohme, a division of Merck and Company, Inc. (West Point, Pa.) and is supplied for intramuscluar injection in the treatment of selected cases of active rheumatoid arthritis, both adult and juvenile type. In past years gold sodium thiomalate also has been produced by other manufacturers under the generic name.

Adverse reactions listed in the Myochrysine package insert include dermatitis, pruritis, stomatitis, nephrotic syndrome, anaphylactic shock, hepatitis, and numerous other side effects. Under "Hematologic reactions," the manufacturer states: "Blood dyscrasia due to gold toxicity is rare, but because of the potential serious consequences it must be constantly watched for and recognized early by frequent blood examinations done throughout treatment. Granulocytopenia; thrombocytopenia, with or without purpura; hypoplastic and aplastic anemia; and eosinophilia have all been reported."[7]

---

[7]*Physicians' Desk Reference,* 40th ed., pp. 1205-06.

Tatum v. Karst (Docket No. CV-83-988-G, Circuit Court, Montgomery County, Ala., October 30, 1984).

Fatal aplastic anemia following gold injections—Physician settles for $400,000, manufacturer for $50,000

A fifty-five-year-old housewife developed aplastic anemia and died following eight months of treatment with gold sodium thiomalate for rheumatoid arthritis. Her survivors alleged that her physician, a general practitioner, failed to perform sufficient diagnostic tests before placing her on gold therapy, failed to try safer and more conservative therapy, failed to monitor the effects of the treatment through proper blood tests, and allowed his nurses to perform blood tests that he should have performed. Against the manufacturer, Merck, Sharp & Dohme, the plaintiffs charged failure to warn adequately of the risk of aplastic anemia.

The physician settled for $400,000 prior to trial, and during trial Merck, Sharp & Dohme settled for $50,000. An action against a second manufacturer, Schering Corporation, which also supplied a product used by the patient which contained gold compounds, was transferred to federal court.[8]

GYNERGEN
See ERGOTAMINE TARTRATE

H

HALDOL
See HALOPERIDOL

HALLS MENTHO-LYPTUS
See EUCALYPTUS OIL and MENTHOL

HALOPERIDOL
Haldol

Haloperidol is the first of the butyrophenone series of major tranquilizers and is indicated for use in the management of manifestations of psychotic disorders, including the control of tics and vocal utterances of Tourette's Disorder in children and adults, and for the

[8] ATLA *Law Reporter,* 28:181, 1985. The lawsuit against Schering Corporation is summarized herein under AUROTHIOGLUCOSE.

treatment of severe behavior problems in children involving "combative, explosive hyperexcitability."[9]

The drug is manufactured by several companies under the generic label, and by McNeil Pharmaceutical, a division of McNeilab, Inc. (Spring House, Pa.) under the brand name Haldol. The product literature lists many adverse reactions and includes a special warning regarding tardive dyskinesia (a syndrome consisting of potentially irreversible, involuntary movements) and bronchopneumonia, some of which cases have been fatal. The manufacturer also warns that "[c]ases of sudden and unexpected death have been reported in association with the administration of Haldol," although it has not been determined what role the drug has played in these.[10]

Moran v. Botsford General Hospital (No. 81-225-533 NM, Circuit Court, Wayne County, Mich., Oct. 1, 1984).

Accident victim continued on Haldol despite respiratory problems—Respiratory arrest and death—$437,000 settlement from hospital and physicians

The patient was a twenty-one-year-old tool and die maker who was being treated in the defendant hospital following an automobile accident. Because of the patient's increasing fear of doctors, a psychiatrist was called in and prescribed Haldol. After the third dose, the patient suffered a "respiratory compromise" and required oxygen. Although Haldol was noted in the record as the probable cause of the patient's difficulty it was readministered by another physician. The following day the patient suffered respiratory arrest, irreversible brain damage and became comatose. He died, still in a coma, six months later. The hospital settled for $225,000, the psychiatrist for $67,500, an internist for $90,000 and a surgeon for $55,000.[11]

Faigenbaum v. Oakland Medical Center (1985) 143 Mich. App. 303, 373 N.W.2d 161, aff'd (1986) 426 Mich. 223, 393 N.W.2d 847.

Failure to diagnose tardive dyskinesia—Condition worsened by continued treatment—$378,000 settlement—$1 million award set aside

The patient was diagnosed as having Huntington's Chorea, when in fact she was suffering from drug-induced tardive dyskinesia.

---

[9] *Physicians' Desk Reference,* 40th ed., pp. 1089-90.

[10] Id.

[11] ATLA *Law Reporter* 28:136, 1985.

Although she was admitted to and discharged from several hospitals and examined by numerous physicians, the misdiagnosis was not discovered for over three years, and the patient's condition was made worse by continuing treatment with Haldol.

Prior to trial the patient's representative settled with four doctors, two hospitals and three drug companies for $278,000, and during trial two more doctors settled for $100,000. A judgment was entered against the Oakland Medical Center, the remaining defendant, for $1 million, but the Court of Appeals reversed, finding the defendant free of liability under the doctrine of governmental immunity because it was functioning under the authority of the Michigan Department of Mental Health. The Supreme Court of Michigan affirmed.

Leal v. Simon (App. Div., 1989) 542 N.Y.S.2d 328.

Patient's dosage reduced by internist, worsening condition and causing equino-varus deformities—$2.5 million jury verdict reduced on appeal to $1.1 million

The plaintiff, age 35, was blind and severely retarded, and had an I.Q. of 30. Although he was severely handicapped and institutionalized, he could walk, dress himself, and converse to some extent in both English and Spanish. In 1978, after exhibiting self-abusive behavior, he was put on a dosage of 4 mg. of Haldol daily. A year later, he was moved to a United Cerebral Palsy (UCP) Intermediate Care Facility, where the defendant, an internist, reduced his dosage to 2 mg. daily because, according to the plaintiff's complaint, of an impending state audit of the facility. There was no change in the plaintiff's behavior to warrant this change in his medication.

The plaintiff soon became hyperactive and agitated. He was transferred to another hospital where he was placed on Mellaril, with an increasing dosage of up to 150 mg. three times daily. He became more agitated, and the defendant switched him back to Haldol, with increasing doses ranging from 20 to 60 mg. daily for several months. Eventually, the plaintiff became unable to feed or dress himself and developed limited and slurred speech and recurring self-abusive behavior. He also developed equino-varus deformaties of the feet and flexion contractures of the knees that prevent him from straightening his legs.

In the lawsuit against the defendant internist and UCP, the defendant was charged with negligence in changing the Haldol dosage, in failing to consult with other physicians before altering the dosage, and in failing to research medical history more thoroughly. The defendant contended that he was merely trying to wean the plaintiff from drug dependence.

The jury awarded $2.5 million, finding the defendant 55% liable and UCP, 45%.[12] On appeal, the liability of the defendant was affirmed, but the court held that the jury had deviated from the verdict form as to UCP's negligence, which rendered invalid that portion of the verdict that found UCP actively negligent. The court also found the award excessive, and ordered a new trial unless the plaintiff agreed to remittitur to $1.1 million.

Daniels v. Universal Health Services (No. A 233563, District Court, Clark County, Nev., Apr. 23, 1987).

Excessive administration of Haldol to institutionalized patient—Failure to monitor—Renal failure and brain damage—$724,000 jury verdict

The patient was a 54-year-old institutionalized mentally retarded woman with cerebral palsy and a kidney disorder. During treatment of her physical problems, she became agitated and was transferred without family consent to the psychiatric ward of the defendant hospital. There she was locked up, restrained, given doses of Haldol, and left unattended. Six days later she developed renal failure and was moved to intensive care. She spent most of the next three months in the hospital, much of the time in intensive care and on kidney dialysis.

In a lawsuit by her guardian, it was alleged that the defendant hospital and its physicians failed to monitor the patient, did not take a proper history nor conduct a physical exam, and administered excessive Haldol without taking into account its toxicity or ascertaining the cause of the patient's agitated behavior. At the time of trial, the patient was unable to walk or feed herself, activities which she previously could perform.

The jury returned a verdict for $724,000: $108,000 for past damages, $542,000 for future damages, and the balance for costs and interest.[13]

---

[12] ATLA *Professional Negligence Law Reporter* 2:91, 1987.

[13] Id., 2:141.

Sagor v. Beverly Enterprises (No. C 449288, Superior Court, Los Angeles, Cal., Jan. 27, 1988).

Excessive dosage given to nursing home patient—Insufficient care—$199,781 jury verdict

The patient, age 80, was confined to an extended-care facility with diabetes, circulatory insufficiency, and organic brain syndrome. When his mental state deteriorated further, the staff medicated him with Haldol and placed him in restraints. He developed decubitus ulcers and gangrene, and a leg had to be amputated. His condition worsened following the amputation, and he died from sepsis brought on by additional infected decubitus ulcers.

In a wrongful-death action on behalf of the patient's estate against the extended-care facility, the plaintiff charged that the patient was over-medicated with the Haldol and improperly attended. A jury awarded the estate $199,781.[14]

Dixson v. University of Chicago Hosps. (1989) 190 Ill. App. 3d 369, 137 Ill. Dec. 829, 546 N.E.2d 774.

Death following a five-milligram injection of Haldol—Jury verdict for defendant hospital affirmed

In March 1977, a 64-year-old male was admitted to the defendant hospital because he was experiencing "strange feelings" and having hallucinations. No physical problems were found, and he was sent to the psychiatric ward for an examination there. The following day, he became violent and had to be restrained. A nurse administered an injection of five milligrams of Haldol. Shortly thereafter, the patient appeared to suffer a cardiac arrest, and thirty minutes later he died.

An autopsy was performed, and tests were made for traces of drugs. All results were negative. The medical examiner concluded that the patient died from "sickle-cell crisis." The family filed suit, however, charging that the real cause of death was the injection of Haldol. At trial, the toxicologist who performed the tests at the patient's autopsy testified that while his tests did not reveal any trace of Haldol in the patient's body, it was unlikely that the instruments used in 1977 would detect such a small quantity of Haldol in the blood.

---

[14] Id., 3:58, 1988.

The assistant head nurse on duty at the time testified that according to her notes the patient was given the five milligrams of Haldol intramuscularly. A witness for the plaintiff, however, a pharmacologist, pharmacist, and nutritionist who specializes in testifying as an expert in drug-related cases, was of the opinion that the patient died from an *intravenous* injection, more specifically, an "intravenous push," which meant that the drug was put into the vein all at once, rather than slowly over a matter of minutes. This witness also said that in his opinion, five milligrams of Haldol administered by an intravenous push could kill a person. On cross-examination, however, this witness admitted that he had never encountered any medical journal articles mentioning sudden death as a result of an intravenous injection of Haldol. He said there were articles describing intravenous injections of Haldol, but they did not say whether the drug was administered as a "push."

The defendant's expert, an internist who had published several papers on Haldol, testified that he was unaware of any reported cases where a five-milligram intravenous push of the drug caused death. He stated further, that in his opinion, the patient's death was associated with sickle-cell trait; that he had read of instances of the sudden death of young black persons from sickle-cell trait following extreme exertion. The jury returned a verdict in favor of the defendant hospital, and the Appellate Court of Illinois affirmed.

Related cases

Cardiorespiratory arrest following administration of Haldol and other drugs

In Allen v. Kaiser Foundation Hospital (1985) 76 Or. App. 5, 707 P.2d 1289, a jury verdict of no negligence was upheld in an action by the husband of a psychiatric patient who suffered cardiorespiratory arrest and severe brain damage after being given Haldol, Thorazine (chlorpromazine), and Benadryl (diphenhydramine).

Tardive dyskinesia—County health clinic psychiatrist immune under statute

A Michigan community mental health psychiatrist's decision to treat a paranoid schizophrenic patient with Haldol and Mellaril, which allegedly caused the patient to develop tardive dyskinesia, was a discretionary act and thus immune from any claim of malpractice under the state's governmental immunity statute. Coen v. Oakland County (1986) 155 Mich. App. 662, 400 N.W.2d 614.

Tardive dyskinesia—Patient's claim barred by statute of limitations

North Carolina's four-year statute of limitations barred the claim of a patient who alleged that she developed tardive dyskinesia as the result of the negligence of the psychiatric unit at Duke University Medical Center in treating her with Haldol and Thorazine without monitoring the side effects of the drugs. Lackey v. Bressler (1987) 86 N.C. App. 486, 358 S.E.2d 560.

No claim against manufacturer under Mental Health Patient "Bill of Rights" Act

The plaintiff, a mental patient given Haldol by medical personnel, had no private cause of action under the Mental Health Patient "Bill of Rights" Act (42 U.S.C. § 10841) on grounds that the manufacturer of the drug "suppressed the fact that Haldol has ... approximately 350 ... serious and deadly side effects." Brooks v. Johnson and Johnson (E.D. Pa., 1988) 685 F. Supp. 107.

HALOTHANE
Fluothane

Halothane is a potent, nonflammable, halogenated hydrocarbon anesthetic that provides rapid induction of anesthesia. When used in high concentrations, it causes circulatory depression, and therefore is generally given with nitrous oxide.[15] Halothane is manufactured under the name Fluothane by Ayerst Laboratories (New York, N.Y.).

Halothane has caused reversible alterations in the results of liver function tests after a single administration, the changes being similar to those observed following administration of other anesthetics.[16] In 1973, the American Medical Association's Department of Drugs, in evaluating the anesthetic, stated:

> Although fatal liver necrosis has been reported after such use, the incidence is probably no higher than that associated with other general anesthetic techniques. However, it has been suggested that serious liver damage may follow repeated administration of halothane. Although insufficient controlled data have been accumulated to prove this hypothesis, the development of hepatitis in two anesthesiologists, and its recurrence following administration of a subanesthetic concentration of halothane, in-

[15] *AMA Drug Evaluations,* 2d ed., p. 229.
[16] Id., p. 230.

dicates that the drug is capable of acting as a hepatic sensitizing agent in rare individuals. On this basis, halothane probably should not be given to patients who are known to have developed jaundice and unexplained fever following a prior exposure.[17]

In the product literature, the manufacturer warns: "When previous exposure to Fluothane was followed by unexplained jaundice, consideration should be given to the use of other agents."[18]

In Osol and Pratt's *The United States Dispensatory,* the authors state:

> While recognizing that death from liver failure after halothane occurs in less than 1 out of 10,000 halothane administrations, it is recommended that any patient who has had hepatitis after halothane, or any patient receiving halothane in whom an unexplained second temperature elevation in the immediate postoperative period develops, should not receive halothane again.[19]

Ganczewski v. Smith (No. 52055, Superior Court, Ventura County, Cal., 1971).

Death from massive liver damage after two operations in twelve days under halothane—$150,000 verdict against surgeon—Anesthesiologist, hospital and drug company not liable

A 45-year-old female patient underwent a hysterectomy. Eleven days after the operation she was readmitted to the hospital with a temperature of 105, nausea, lack of appetite, and dark and concentrated urine. The diagnosis was hemorrhage in the vaginal area, and the same surgical team that had performed the earlier operation performed corrective surgery. In both operations, halothane was the anesthetic used.

Two days after the second operation the patient died. An autopsy revealed massive liver damage. The halothane was suspected, and the patient's husband filed suit against the surgeon, anesthesiologist, hospital, and the manufacturer of the anesthetic. The plaintiff's complaint charged that the patient had showed some evidence of liver damage after the first operation, and that therefore the defendants were negligent in administering halothane a second time in view of reports in the medical literature that halothane can cause liver damage in some patients. The plaintiff also contended that the defendants should have called in a specialist.

---

[17] Id.

[18] *Physicians' Desk Reference,* 40th ed., p. 621.

[19] *United States Dispensatory,* 27th ed., p. 575.

At the trial, the evidence suggested that the patient showed no indications of jaundice after her first operation, and the defense stressed that this ruled out the presence of liver damage at that time. The plaintiff argued that despite this, the defendants should have performed a liver function test before halothane was used again. The anesthesiologist testified that he suspected no liver damage after the first operation, and if he had, he would not have given halothane a second time.

The defendants also attempted to show that the cause of death was not actually due to halothane, but infectious hepatitis which probably had been present prior to the first operation.

At the conclusion of the trial, the jury returned a verdict for $150,000 against the surgeon. The remaining defendants were found free of liability.[20]

Pedigo v. Cleveland Clinic Foundation (No. 881140, Common Pleas Ct., Cuyahoga County, Ohio, 1973).

Total disability from cirrhosis of liver after four operations under halothane—$800,000 awarded

A male patient underwent four operations in which halothane was used as the general anesthetic. He eventually became totally disabled from cirrhosis of the liver brought on, it was alleged, by chronic hepatitis caused by the anesthetic. A jury awarded the patient $700,000 and his wife $100,000.[21]

Vasquez v. Galehouse (Superior Court, Los Angeles County, Cal., 1971).

Liver damage fatal after second dental operation under halothane—$225,000 verdict

A female dental patient was given halothane as the general anesthetic during the extraction of seven teeth. A week later she had five more teeth extracted, again, according to the patient's husband, with halothane as the anesthetic. Nine days later she died, the cause of death being established as hepatic necrosis (liver damage) with a secondary diagnosis of infectious hepatitis. The patient's husband brought suit against the dentist and anesthesiologist, alleging that they should have suspected that his wife had

[20] AMA *The Citation* 24:163, 1972.
[21] ATLA *News Letter* 16:367, 1973.

developed a sensitivity to halothane and that they were negligent in using it a second time. The defendants denied that they had used halothane during the second extraction.

The jury returned a verdict of $225,000 against the defendants.[1]

Harris v. Doe (Superior Court, San Mateo County, Cal., 1972).

Negligence charged in use of halothane and Innovar in surgery on frail child—Case settled for $712,500

An eleven-year-old child failed to regain consciousness after an operation to replace a metal rod in the child's leg. At the time of trial, the child still remained in a coma. It was alleged that the anesthesiologist was negligent in choosing the combination of halothane and Innovar as the anesthetic agents for a child of the patient's size and physical condition. (The patient was only 32 inches tall, weighed 36 pounds and had suffered since birth from osteogenesis imperfecta, sometimes called "brittle bone disease.") The anesthesiologist was also charged with choosing inadequate premedications, and in using inadequate monitoring devices during the operation.

Prior to trial, it was reported that the anesthesiologist was prepared to present evidence that halothane and Innovar were often used in combination, but before the case was tried, it was settled for $712,500.[2]

Cornfeldt v. Tongen (Minn., 1977) 262 N.W.2d 684.

Liver failure following second operation under halothane—Cause of death in question—Verdicts for anesthesiologist and manufacturer upheld

The patient, a fifty-year-old woman, underwent emergency surgery for a perforated ulcer. During a follow-up examination a pathology report indicated some suspicious cells, possibly cancerous, and a gastrectomy was ordered. In preparing for this surgery, a routine preoperative laboratory report suggested that the cancer may have spread to the liver.

For the first operation the anesthesiologist had used halothane. The patient seemed to do well on it, and it was ordered again for the gastrectomy.

---

[1] AMA *The Citation* 24:114, 1972.

[2] Id., 26:116, 1973.

The operation was performed, and to the surgeons' surprise, no cancer was found. During recovery, however, the patient became jaundiced. Her liver began to malfunction, and despite treatment by specialists and a liver transplant, the patient died of hepatitis about two months later.

Suit was brought against the surgeons, anesthesiologist, hospital, and the manufacturer of halothane. The surgeons were charged with negligence in proceeding with the gastrectomy in the presence of questionable test results and failure to obtain the patient's consent, and the anesthesiologist with choosing halothane a second time and failing to inform the patient of the increased risk involved. The drug manufacturer was accused of inadequately warning the medical profession of the risk of hepatitis associated with the use of halothane.

The court directed verdicts for the assistant surgeon, the hospital and the drug manufacturer, and a jury returned verdicts for the surgeon and the anesthesiologist. The Supreme Court of Minnesota reversed only as to the surgeon, holding that the trial court erred in refusing to instruct the jury on his and the anesthesiologist's duty to secure the patient's informed consent to the operation.

Whether the patient died of halothane hepatitis was never fully established. Only the hospital records reflected this diagnosis, and the trial court refused to admit it when the plaintiff's expert admitted that there was no scientific proof that the halothane was the causative agent.

Lindquist v. Ayerst Laboratories, Inc. (1980) 227 Kan. 308, 607 P.2d 1339.

Death from liver failure—No violation of community standard—Manufacturer also free of wrongdoing

A male patient underwent surgery on his right testicle on August 13, 1969. The anesthetic used was halothane. Due to a staph infection, the patient remained in the hospital longer than usual. A routine laboratory report on August 24 revealed a highly malignant form of cancer had spread into his pelvic area, and on August 29 a second operation was performed, a retroperitoneal node dissection. A different anesthesiologist administered the anesthetic, again halothane.

Four days later the patient developed extreme jaundice, lapsed into a coma and died on September 8 of liver failure.

At trial the patient's widow sought to prove negligence on the part of the two anesthesiologists for using halothane twice on her husband within sixteen days, and negligence on the part of the second anesthesiologist for failing to inform the patient fully about the risk attendant with the use of halothane. The plaintiff introduced the package insert which warned that the anesthetic should not be given in "multiple administrations" when a patient suffers from jaundice or an unexplained high fever.

The plaintiff also charged the manufacturer of halothane with failing to test the product adequately, with attempting to hide the fact that it could cause liver damage, and with breach of warranty of fitness.

A jury returned verdicts for both defendants, and the Supreme Court of Kansas affirmed, finding that the expert testimony revealed that the standard of practice in the community at the time did not "discourage multiple doses of Fluothane." As to the manufacturer's warning about multiple administrations in the presence of an unexplained fever, the court pointed out that the patient's fever was the result of his staph infection. As to failure to inform the patient of the risk, the court noted that the second anesthesiologist testified that he had discussed "significant risks involving the use of Fluothane." He admitted that he had not discussed possible liver damage but only "because the risk was too remote."

The court found that the plaintiff had failed to submit evidence sufficient to show that tests by the manufacturer "would have produced more conclusive results regarding repeated use of Fluothane within short periods of time." Likewise, there was insufficient evidence of the manufacturer's intentional withholding of information on the drug and of breach of warranty.

Related cases

Death from liver failure—Surgeon accused of failing to take proper history which would have disclosed earlier halothane reaction

In Moore v. Francisco (1978) 2 Kan. App. 2d 526, 583 P.2d 391, the plaintiff had a jury case against an orthopedic surgeon who allegedly was negligent in failing to take a proper prior medical history of a patient which would have disclosed that she had once suffered fever and jaundice following an operation in which halothane was used. Halothane was used again, and the patient died, presumably from liver failure attributable to the anesthetic.

Death from liver failure—Trial court errs on limiting expert testimony and in instructing on manufacturer's duty to warn

In another wrongful-death case in which halothane was used for a second consecutive operation, despite a report that the patient had run a high fever following the first operation, verdicts for the physicians and manufacturer were set aside where the trial court had limited all expert medical testimony to knowledge possessed by experts in the year in which the death occurred, and where the court instructed the jury that a manufacturer has a duty to warn users of its anesthetic only if it knew or should have known that it had a tendency to affect injuriously an "appreciable number of people." Tomer v. American Home Products Corp. (1976) 170 Conn. 681, 368 A.2d 35.

Fatal cardiac arrythmia on administration of Neo-Synephrine while under halothane anesthesia

In Laurence v. Ambulatory Surgical Facility, Inc. (Docket No. 82-418-CY, Circuit Court, Broward County, Fla., Jan. 11, 1983), a three-year-old boy suffered fatal cardiac arrythmia while under halothane anesthesia when two drops of Neo-Synephrine were placed in each nostril. The case is summarized herein under PHENYLEPHRINE HYDROCHLORIDE.

Hospital's failure to perform eosinophil test not proximate cause of hepatitis

In Coffran v. Hitchcock Clinic, Inc. (C.A.-1 N.H., 1982) 683 F.2d 5, the jury could have found that the plaintiff, who developed hepatitis following two hernia operations under halothane anesthesia, failed to carry the burden of proving that the hospital's failure to perform an eosinophil test was the cause of her hepatitis, and therefore the trial court abused its discretion in granting the plaintiff a new trial on grounds that the verdict in favor of the hospital was against the great weight of evidence.

Nurse anesthetist exposed to Fluothane during pregnancy—Child born with neurological disorder—No recovery against manufacturer

In Helminski v. Ayerst Laboratories, a Division of American Home Products Corp. (C.A.-6 Mich., 1985) 766 F.2d 208, a nurse anesthetist was unsuccessful in claiming that her child's neurological disorder was caused by her exposure to Fluothane during pregnancy.

Malignant hyperthermia—Jury case against manufacturers for failure to warn

In an action on behalf of a patient who suffered oxygen deprivation and brain damage due to malignant hyperthermia which occurred during elective knee surgery, genuine issues of material fact existed as to whether the negligence of the manufacturers of Fluothane and Anectine (succinylcholine chloride) was the proximate cause of the patient's injuries in view of an affidavit of a pharmacologist stating that failure of the patient's anesthesiologist and other medical personnel to recognize and immediately treat the malignant hyperthermia was due in part to the manufacturers' inadequate warnings and overpromotion of the products. Holley v. Burroughs Wellcome Co. (N.C. 1986) 348 S.E.2d 772.

Fatal liver necrosis—Choice of halothane as anesthetic and failure to advise patient of risk not negligence

An anesthesiologist's choice of halothane and her failure to advise a tonsillectomy patient of the risk of liver disease in using the anesthetic was not negligence under the medical standards in effect at the time (1972). Granado v. Madsen (Tex. App., 1987) 729 S.W.2d 866.

Patient hypersensitive to halothane—Fatal reaction—Physicians and manufacturer not liable

In McQuaid v. Burlington County Memorial Hospital (1986) 212 N.J. Super. 472, 515 A.2d 796, an appellate court affirmed the jury's verdict that the death of a surgical patient who was hypersensitive to halothane was not caused by negligence on the part of his physicians, and that the manufacturer of halothane had not failed to give adequate warnings concerning the risk associated with use of the anesthetic.

HEPARIN SODIUM

Embolex
Hep-Lock
Liquaemin

Heparin sodium is a potent anticoagulant used in the prevention and treatment of thromboembolic disorders, including acute thrombophlebitis, pulmonary embolism, and thromboembolic complications of myocardial infarction and congestive heart failure. The possibility of hemorrhage is the most dangerous complication of heparin therapy.[3]

Several companies market heparin under the generic label. Embolex is produced by Sandoz Pharmaceuticals (East Hanover, N.J.), Hep-Lock by Elkins-Sinn (Cherry Hill, N.C.), and Liquaemin by Organon, Inc. (West Orange, N.J.).

Zeigert v. South Chicago Community Hosp. (1981) 99 Ill. App. 3d 83, 54 Ill. Dec. 585, 425 N.E.2d 450.

Heparin administered without gas studies and venogram—No monitoring for internal bleeding—Verdicts for hospital and physician upheld

The patient had undergone saphenous vein stripping. When she developed a severe pain behind her knee and in her chest the defendant physician suspected a blood clot and ordered heparin. Although a pulmonary scan was normal the heparin was continued and the patient also was given a painkiller. When both legs began to swell, however, it was discovered the patient was suffering from internal bleeding. The heparin was discontinued immediately and blood transfusions were ordered.

In addition to charges of improperly diagnosing the patient's problem, the defendant physician was accused of negligence in ordering heparin without further tests. The patient's expert testified that in view of the negative lung scan it was below acceptable standards to order the anticoagulant without first performing blood gas studies and a venogram. Also, he testified that the defendant deviated from the standard of care when he continued to administer an anticoagulant without tests to monitor the possibility of internal bleeding.

The defendant physician's expert testified that to continue the anticoagulant was not below standard practice because there was an error factor in the lung scan of from fifteen to twenty percent, that a venogram was not advisable because of the risk, and that blood tests could have given "inaccurate results which could be misleading in treating a pulmonary embolism." He added that "clinical observation" is an acceptable method of monitoring a patient being treated with anticoagulants.

The jury returned a verdict for the defendants which was affirmed on appeal.

[3] *United States Dispensatory,* 27th ed., pp. 1058-61.

Belmon v. St. Frances Cabrini Hosp. (La. App. 1983) 427 So. 2d 541.

Negligence in drawing blood from heparinized patient—Insufficient monitoring by nurse—$57,376 award affirmed

The patient was hospitalized for a suspected pulmonary embolus and given 7,500 units of heparin in the emergency room. She was later transferred to the intensive care unit and put on a continuous heparin I.V. drip at a rate of 2,000 units per hour. Early the following morning she developed pain in her right arm near where a technician had drawn blood. This was reported to a nurse, but she did not call a physician. The pain worsened and the arm began to swell. The nurse checked it occasionally but did not call a physician until almost noon. When he saw the arm he reduced the heparin and later discontinued it when a lung scan ruled out the presence of an embolus. The patient suffered damage to the median and radial nerves, causing permanent weakness of her arm and hand.

The evidence disclosed that the technician, in drawing blood, had treated the patient's case as a "routine matter" which, according to expert testimony, was below acceptable standards. Where a patient is on heparin, "extra precautions" should be taken to avoid "extra sticks" in locating the vein. Also, on completion, the puncture site should be compressed longer than usual. This was not done.

The court found also that the nursing staff did not "diligently monitor" the patient as is required in heparin therapy. The patient was awarded $57,376 which was affirmed on appeal.

Rosenstein v. St. Peter's Hospital (No. 14834/83, Supreme Court, Albany County, N.Y., Dec. 9, 1986).

Bleeding during heparin therapy undiagnosed—Permanent nerve damage—$909,000 jury award

The plaintiff, age 53, was placed on heparin therapy for thrombophlebitis in her right calf. Five days later she developed pain in the left upper thigh. The next day her symptoms worsened and included intensified pain, faintness, and pallor. A physical medicine rehabilitation specialist was called in to consult, and he ordered blood studies to be done over the next two days to rule out heparin-induced bleeding. The test results from the first day were normal and indicated no bleeding. On the second day, the blood tests were not done.

The plaintiff's symptoms continued, and on the third day a nurse noted ecchymosis in her left upper thigh and groin. The heparin was discontinued and emergency hemoglobin and hematocrit studies were done. When the tests indicated significant blood loss, the plaintiff was given four units of blood. Repeat blood studies the next day indicated that her condition had stabilized, and she was discharged eight days later. Subsequently, however, a CAT scan of the upper left leg and back area disclosed a large hematoma, and further studies showed damage to the femoral nerve.

Despite twenty-two months of physiotherapy, the plaintiff, previously a very active woman, had diminished quadriceps muscle function, permanent scarring, a chronic sensation of pressure in the leg, and permanent hypersensitivity. She could not sit or stand in one position for more than half an hour at a time.

At trial, the plaintiff charged the hospital personnel with failure to (1) supervise and monitor her care and condition; (2) notify the physician of her complaints during the heparin therapy; (3) discontinue the heparin therapy on symptoms of bleeding; and (4) timely and adequately treat the bleeding. The plaintiff claimed that the bleeding, which continued over four days, was so slow that it did not show up on any test results. Nonetheless, blood had collected in the retroperitoneal space, consolidated, formed a hematoma, and compressed the left femoral nerve causing permanent damage.

The jury awarded $750,000 to the plaintiff and $204,000 to her husband for loss of consortium.[4]

Barraza v. Vazquez (No. 85-485, Law Court, El Paso County, Feb. 16, 1987).

Occluded femoral artery—Failure to administer full dosage of heparin—Leg amputated—$726,000 jury verdict against cardiologist

The plaintiff, age 45, was being treated for a myocardial infarction by the defendant, a cardiologist. The defendant ordered "mini-heparin" therapy but did not order an echogram or a ventriculogram. Ten days later, the plaintiff complained of pain and numbness in his left leg. An occluded femoral artery was found; three embolectomies were unsuccessful, and the leg had to be amputated above the knee. The plaintiff is now totally disabled.

---

[4]ATLA *Professional Negligence Liability Reporter* 2:24, 1987.

At trial, the plaintiff charged that the defendant was negligent in failing to order a full dosage of heparin in a high-risk patient, to use an echogram or ventriculogram, to respond promptly to complaints of pain and numbness, and to call in a vascular surgeon for consultation. The defendant claimed that the plaintiff had a preexisting history of hypertension and possible pericarditis which precluded full heparin treatment.

The jury awarded the plaintiff $726,000, plus prejudgment interest. The hospital settled for $20,000.[5]

Leenheer v. Feliciano (No. L-071788-85MM, Superior Court, Passaic County, N.J., June 14, 1988).

Patient suffers fatal intracerebral hemorrhage while on heparin and Coumadin—$338,000 verdict against physicians

The patient, age 68, was admitted to the hospital suffering from bilateral pulmonary emboli. His family practitioner and his internist prescribed Heparin and Coumadin (sodium warfarin) to "thin his blood." The patient was in the hospital for two weeks. After his release, during a follow-up appointment with the family physician, the patient underwent a prothrombin evaluation. The test suggested that his blood was "too thin"; a laboratory report, however, indicated that the results were in the normal range, and apparently the medication was continued.

About three weeks later, the patient returned to the physician's office, complaining of severe headaches. He was rushed to the hospital, but died five days later from an intracerebral hemorrhage.

In her suit against the two physicians, the patient's wife alleged failure to perform weekly prothrombin tests of his blood. At trial, the defendants each blamed the other for the patient's death. The jury returned a verdict of $338,000.[6]

Related cases

Intracranial bleeding—Verdict for defendant

In Vecchione v. Carlin (1980) 111 Cal. App. 3d 351, 168 Cal. Rptr. 571, a hospital nurse was accused of using an excessive dose of heparin sodium as an adjunct in administering sodium bicarbonate to a premature newborn infant suffering from oxygen deficiency. A

---

[5] Id., 2:57.

[6] ATLA *Professional Negligence Law Reporter 4:48, 1989.*

jury verdict for the defendants was affirmed because of conflicting evidence as to whether the cause of death, intracranial bleeding, was the result of overheparinization or intrauterine problems during pregnancy.

Fatal pulmonary thrombosis—$2 million settlement

In O'Conner v. Shortz (No. 82-5975 CA (L) O1B, Circuit Court, Palm Beach County, Fla., Oct. 21, 1983), a $2 million settlement was made by an orthopaedic surgeon and an internist who were accused of administering insufficient doses of heparin and improperly monitoring its effects in treating a forty-two-year-old man for a deep vein thrombosis following knee surgery. The patient "threw the clot" which lodged in his pulmonary artery, causing death.[7]

HEP-LOCK

See HEPARIN SODIUM

HEXADROL

See DEXAMETHASONE

HEXYLRESORCINOL

Jayne's P-W Vermifuge

Hexylresorcinol is used in the treatment of roundworm (*Ascaris lumbricoides*) and whipworm (*Trichuris trichiura*) infections. It is useful in some mixed infections and, although less effective than other drugs, is used also for hookworm, pinworm, and dwarf tapeworm.[8] It has been marketed by Glenbrook Laboratories (New York, N.Y.) under the name Jayne's P-W Vermifuge, a nonprescription item.

The principal untoward effect of hexylresorcinol is burning sensation of the skin and oral and anal mucous membranes. It is recommended, therefore, that the tablets be swallowed without chewing and, when administration is by enema, that the perianal region be protected by a careful application of petrolatum. The drug is contraindicated in patients with ulcerative diseases of the gastrointestinal tract.[9]

---

[7] ATLA *Law Reporter* 27:139-40, 1984.

[8] *AMA Drug Evaluations,* 2d ed., p. 634.

[9] Id.

Holbrook v. Rose (Ky. App., 1970) 458 S.W.2d 155.

Child dies after receiving three Vermifuge tablets—Traces of Darvon also found—Directed verdicts for pharmacist and drug company affirmed

A three-year-old girl apparently was suffering from a parasitic infestation ("worms"). The child's father consulted a retail pharmacist who mentioned a worm medicine called "Jayne's P-W Vermifuge." This medicine, the main ingredient of which was hexylresorcinol, was a nonprescription item sold over the counter. The father purchased two bottles, one containing regular dosage tablets for persons over six years of age, and another containing tablets for children under six.

The following morning the child's 25-year-old sister placed three of the children's tablets in the girl's mouth. The label on the bottle contained a warning that the tablets must be swallowed whole, and not chewed or crushed. Although the child was instructed not to chew the pills, she did so. Later, her lips became parched and her mouth sore and raw.

The child continued to play and eat her meals, but not as much as she usually did. Periodically she would indicate that her mouth was still bothering her. On the afternoon of the next day, she began vomiting, and by the following morning was acutely ill. According to her parents, she was given "half of an aspirin" and taken to the emergency room of a local hospital. By then she was semicomatose, and a pediatrician who examined her found her respiration "fast and labored." Her condition steadily deteriorated and she died the following morning. Death was attributed to respiratory failure preceded by convulsions.

The child's parents filed a lawsuit against the pharmacist and the manufacturer of Jayne's P-W Vermifuge. The action was based on the alternative claims of negligence, breach of warranty and strict liability. At the trial a pathologist testified that in his opinion hexylresorcinol could cause death if ingested in sufficient quantity, but that he did not know of any specific case of human death attributed to the drug. The pediatrician who had examined the child at the hospital also testified that he had made an extensive review of the medical literature and had also found nothing to indicate that hexylresorcinol was regarded as a dangerous drug. This was confirmed by the medical researcher who had been responsible for introduction of the drug on the market in 1933.

Apparently during cross-examination of the pediatrician, it was disclosed that a toxicologist's report indicated that traces of another drug, Darvon (propoxyphene hydrochloride), were found in the child's stomach. The witness admitted that this drug, if given in sufficiently large doses or over a long period of time, could cause the symptoms from which the child suffered just prior to her death. Also included in the toxicologist's report was a statement that he failed to find evidence of any drug in a quantity sufficient to cause death, and that the child's death could not be determined from the evidence submitted to him.

At the close of the plaintiff's case, the pharmacist was granted a directed verdict. A similar motion by the drug manufacturer was denied and the defense presented its case. The jury returned a verdict in the amount of $15,400. Attorneys for the manufacturer moved for a judgment notwithstanding the verdict, which was sustained by the trial judge, and the plaintiff appealed.

On appeal, the court commented that the evidence failed to establish that it was "probable" that the ingestion of the Jayne's P-W Vermifuge was the legal cause of death. The court observed that the only expert who testified that the death could have been the result of the hexylresorcinol was the pathologist who based his opinion on the original medical history of the case. This history, said the court, was inaccurate, since it did not include the toxicologist's report that there were traces of Darvon in the child's stomach. Also, the history on which the pathologist based his opinion suggested that the child became ill immediately after taking the worm medicine, when in fact later testimony showed that it was the next day before she became sufficiently ill to warrant the concern of her parents.

The judgment in the lower court was affirmed.

HISTAFED

See CHLORPHENIRAMINE MALEATE

HISTALET

See CHLORPHENIRAMINE MALEATE

HISTASPAN

See CHLORPHENIRAMINE MALEATE

H.P. ACTHAR GEL
See CORTICOTROPIN

HURRICAINE
See BENZOCAINE

HYDROCHLOROTHIAZIDE
Hydrochlorothiazide is a diuretic and antihypertensive marketed under many brand names by many pharmaceutical companies. The drug is used for the management of hypertension, both as the sole therapeutic agent and to enhance the effect of other antihypertensives in the more severe forms of hypertension. It also is used as adjunctive therapy in edema associated with congestive heart failure, hepatic cirrhosis, and corticosteroid and estrogen therapy. It has been found useful in edema caused by various forms of renal dysfunction, such as nephrotic syndrome, acute glomerulonephritis, and chronic renal failure.[10]

Adverse reactions to hydrochlorothiazide are usually reversible upon reduction of dosage or discontinuation of the drug. Adverse reactions that have been reported include pancreatitis, jaundice, orthostatic hypertension, transient blurred vision, dizziness, muscle spasm, and hyperglycemia. More serious reactions include aplastic anemia and Stevens-Johnson syndrome.[11]

Geibel v. United States (W.D. Pa., 1987) 667 F. Supp. 215, aff'd (C.A.-3, Pa., 1988), 845 F.2d 1011.

Alleged excessive dosage by VA hospital physician—Emotional injury—Judgment for defendant

The patient, a 60-year-old woman, was being treated at a veteran's administration hospital for "high blood pressure, tearfulness, and anxiety." Her physician, a Dr. Preston, prescribed several antihypertensive drugs, including Inderal (propranolol hydrochloride) and hydrochlorothiazide. When the patient appeared to react to the medication, Dr. Preston concluded that she had a "sensitivity" to drug therapy generally, and he discontinued all drugs. The patient was kept on a low sodium diet, and when her blood pressure dropped to near normal, she was discharged from the hospital and advised to return periodically for check-ups. As an outpatient, how-

---

[10] *Physicians' Desk Reference,* 43d ed., p. 841.
[11] Id.

ever, Mrs. Geibel could not keep her blood pressure down, and Dr. Preston placed her on hydrochlorothiazide (25 mg. daily) and Inderal (10 mg. in the morning and 20 mg. at bedtime).

A month later, Mrs. Geibel returned to the hospital complaining of abdominal pain. On examination, she was found to have three duodenal ulcers and a hiatal hernia. She was treated successfully for these conditions and released with instructions to continue her antihypertensive therapy. Several months later she returned again, this time suffering from high blood pressure and vertigo. She also complained of a mild rash on her arms that the admitting physician thought might be a reaction to the hydrochlorothiazide. But when she was seen by an attending physician, a Dr. Marwaaha, he saw no such rash and told her that she probably was merely "scratching herself." When Dr. Marwaaha also told her that she had "dirty feet," the patient became very upset. She and Dr. Marwaaha apparently got into an argument, causing her blood pressure to rise. At the completion of the examination, Dr. Marwaaha ordered her hospitalized and doubled her dosage of hydrochlorothiazide and Inderal.

Mrs. Geibel remained in the hospital for two weeks, during which time she complained to the hospital officials about the care she received from Dr. Marwaaha. When the matter was not resolved to her satisfaction, she filed suit under the FTCA, claiming that she had been "negligently over-drugged" during her hospitalization.

At the trial, Mrs. Geibel offered testimony by a psychiatrist who stated that the treatment she received by Dr. Marwaaha was "inappropriate," and that as a result she suffered emotional injury. The defense introduced expert testimony that the treatment was proper. As to the charge of overdosage, the defense experts testified that even when the patient's dosage of hydrochlorothiazide and Inderal was doubled, she was still receiving what were considered "very low doses" of the medication. As to the claim for emotional injury, the defense introduced evidence that Mrs. Geibel had been treated for emotional problems long before she was first seen by Dr. Marwaaha.

The district court judge, who tried the case without a jury, found no evidence that Dr. Marwaaha deviated from the required standard of care.

Addison v. Emfinger (Ala., 1989) 551 So.2d 375.

Fatal pancreatitis following prolonged treatment with hydrochlorothiazide—Plaintiff has jury case against general practitioner

The defendant physician, a general practitioner, began treating the patient in 1978, at which time he prescribed hydrochlorothiazide for a blood pressure problem. Sometime in 1980, while still taking the drug, the patient began complaining of intermittent abdominal pain and tenderness. In August 1983, gallbladder X-rays were ordered, and the defendant advised the patient that she might require gallbladder surgery. The patient objected to the idea of an operation, however, and nothing more was done.

In January 1985, while still taking the drug, the patient's pain became more severe and she was hospitalized. She was treated by the defendant who apparently did not connect her complaints with her continued use of hydrochlorothiazide. She was released from the hospital, but three days later she returned to the emergency room with even more severe pain. This time the defendant called in a surgeon who performed exploratory surgery and discovered acute necrotizing pancreatitis. The patient's pancreas was removed, but the infection was widespread, and she died ten days later.

The administrator of the patient's estate sued the defendant, charging that either (1) he was negligent in failing to consider the possibility that the hydrochlorothiazide caused the pancreatitis, or (2) he was negligent in treating the patient's gallbladder condition which allowed the disease to develop into pancreatitis.

At trial, an expert for the plaintiff testified that when the patient first complained of abdominal problems in 1980, the standard of care would have required the defendant to test her for pancreatitis, especially in light of her continued use of hydrochlorothiazide. The defendant's expert, however, who was the surgeon who operated on the patient in 1985, testified that the drug, which the patient was taking in "minimal" doses, "played no role" in the development of pancreatitis, and that the gallbladder disease caused the pancreatitis. Furthermore, he testified that the defendant had given the patient the proper treatment, both for the gallbladder disease and the pancreatitis.

At the close of evidence, the trial judge directed a verdict in favor of the defendant. On appeal, however, the Supreme Court of Alabama reversed, holding that the testimony of the plaintiff's expert not only furnished a scintilla of evidence for submission of the case to the jury, but, if believed by the jury, was adequate to support a verdict in the plaintiff's favor.

HYDROCORTISONE
Cortisporin

Cortisporin is only one of many popular anti-inflammatory agents containing hydrocortisone used in ophthalmology. (For a complete list, see the latest edition of *Physicians' Desk Reference.*) Cortisporin is manufactured by Burroughs Wellcome Company (Research Triangle Park, N. C.).

Hydrocortisone is an adrenocortical steroid which can be isolated from adrenal glands or produced synthetically. Other adrenocortical steroids available as drops or ointments for topical ophthalmic use include cortisone, dexamethasone, fluorometholone, medrysone and prednisolone.[12]

Cortisporin, the preparation involved in the first case below, also contains polymyxin B, bacitracin, and neomycin, all antibacterials. Hydrocortisone, while reducing inflammation, does not fight infection; it actually lowers resistance to infection, and can mask the symptoms of serious ocular disease. The same applies to the other adrenocortical steroids.[13]

Generally, the severe adverse reactions associated with the systemic use of adrenocortical steroids, among which are electrolyte imbalance, osteoporotic changes and peptic ulcer, do not occur when the agents are applied topically. Serious local complications can occur, however, evidenced by discomfort, burning sensation, and tearing.[14] One of the most serious risks is glaucoma. Patients with open angle glaucoma show a further increase in intraocular pressure during steroid therapy, and offspring of patients with glaucoma may have an excessive rise in intraocular pressure after application. Glaucoma induced by the use of these agents, however, usually regresses when the medication is stopped.[15]

---

[12] *AMA Drug Evaluations,* 2d ed., p. 714.

[13] Id.

[14] Id.

[15] Newman, S., "Hormone-Induced Diseases," in *Diseases of Medical Progress: A Study of Iatrogenic Disease,* 3rd ed., R. H. Moser, editor (Springfield, Ill.: Charles C Thomas, Publisher, 1969), p. 371.

Kong v. Clay-Grant Pharmacy (No. 619350, Superior Court, San Francisco County, Cal., 1972).

Glaucoma in ten-year-old treated with Cortisporin for fifteen months—$105,000 settlement

A ten-year-old boy was suffering from a rash around the eyelids. An ophthalmologist prescribed Cortisporin. The drug had been administered for about fifteen months when glaucoma was discovered. The boy suffered loss of vision in one eye and severe impairment in the other.

The child's parents brought suit against the ophthalmologist and the pharmacy that had supplied the drug. The defendants argued that the glaucoma was not caused by the drug, and that it had preexisted the treatment. They contended that any increased intraocular pressure caused by Cortisporin would have decreased as soon as use of the drug was terminated.

The case was settled before trial for $105,000.[16]

Related cases

Glaucoma in patient treated with steroid for three years—Cause of action against doctors, pharmacist and pharmacy

A Georgia plaintiff had a cause of action against two doctors, a pharmacy and a pharmacist as a result of developing glaucoma over a three-year period during which she used a steroid, believed to be hydrocortisone. The defendants raised the statute of limitations as a defense but were unsuccessful under the "doctrine of continuing tort." Piedmont Pharmacy, Inc. v. Patmore (1977) 144 Ga. App. 160, 240 S.E.2d 888.

HYDROMORPHONE HYDROCHLORIDE
Dilaudid

This is a narcotic analgesic and antitussive related to morphine. The cough syrup form is indicated for the control of persistent, exhausting cough or dry, nonproductive cough.[17] Dilaudid is manufactured by Knoll Pharmaceutical Company (Whippany, N.J.). The product is also manufactured and sold under the generic name by

---

[16] AMA *The Citation* 26:122, 1973.

[17] *Physicians' Desk Reference,* 35th ed., p. 967.

Elkins-Sinn, Inc. (Cherry Hill, N.J.) and Wyeth Laboratories (Philadelphia, Pa.).

Knoll Pharmaceutical warns in the product literature that Dilaudid may produce dose-related respiratory depression in susceptible individuals or when used in excessive doses.[18]

Death from respiratory complications

In Killeen v. Reinhardt (1979) 71 App. Div. 2d 851, 419 N.Y.S.2d 175, a patient with possible penicillin allergy died of respiratory complications after receiving Dilaudid and later Keflin (cephalothin sodium). She had been admitted to the hospital complaining of breathing difficulties, coughing and vomiting. The case is summarized herein under CEPHALOTHIN SODIUM.

HYDROMOX

See RESERPINE

HYDROPRES

See RESERPINE

HYDROSERPINE

See RESERPINE

HYDROXYPROGESTERONE CAPROATE

Delalutin

Prodrox

This drug is a derivative of the hormone progesterone, is said to be about seven times as potent, and has been recommended for all conditions for which progesterone is used, including prevention of miscarriage.[19] The product is manufactured by E.R. Squibb & Sons, Inc. (Princeton, N.J.) as Delalutin, and by Legere Pharmaceuticals (Scottsdale, Ariz.) as Prodrox.

Barson v. E.R. Squibb & Sons, Inc. (Utah, 1984) 682 P.2d 832.

Birth defects—Manufacturer failed to warn—
$1.5 million verdict affirmed

The plaintiff was born in March, 1973 with severe birth defects, including total absence of arms, abnormally small tongue, atresia

[18] Id.

[19] *United States Dispensatory,* 27th ed., p. 598.

of the ear canal, scoliosis and a rectal tag. During her pregnancy the plaintiff's mother had been given Delalutin to prevent miscarriage. It was the only drug she took.

In their action against the manufacturer, the plaintiff and her parents alleged that Squibb had represented that the drug was safe when in fact it had knowledge that it could cause birth defects. At the trial the plaintiffs introduced evidence that scientific information and literature relative to progesterones causing birth defects existed prior to 1972, which should have made a prudent drug manufacturer conduct tests for such side effects on any derivative of progesterone, including Delalutin.

The jury returned a verdict for the plaintiffs in the amount of $1.5 million and the Supreme Court of Utah affirmed.

Related cases

Birth defects

In Vaccaro v. Squibb Corp. (1979) 71 App. Div. 2d 270, 422 N.Y.S.2d 679, a New York Appellate Court held that a mother of a child born without arms and legs and with other severe defects, allegedly as a result of the mother taking Delalutin while pregnant, stated a cause of action for mental and emotional damages. The child's father, said the court, had no such action. On further appeal, however, the Court of Appeals reversed, holding that the mother had no claim for independent physical injuries, and thus could not recover for emotional and psychic harm. Vaccaro v. Squibb Corp. (1980) 52 N.Y.2d 809, 436 N.Y.S.2d 871.

HYDROXYZINE
Atarax
Vistaril

Hydroxyzine is a tranquilizer used to alleviate anxiety, tension and agitation. Pfizer Laboratories (New York, N.Y.) manufactures the product under the brand name Vistaril, and several companies market the drug under the generic name.

Pfizer reports that side effects associated with Vistaril are "usually mild and transitory in nature." Dry mouth and drowsiness have been reported, as have "involuntary motor activity including rare instances of tremor and convulsions," but usually "with doses considerably higher than those recommended."[20]

With regard to the intramuscular solution, Pfizer cautions that as with all intramuscular preparations, Vistaril should be injected "well within the body of a relatively large muscle," and that "inadvertent subcutaneous injection may result in significant tissue damage."[21]

Miller v. United States (S.D. Miss., 1976) 431 F. Supp. 988.

Urinary difficulty—History of possible allergy to "antihistamine properties" of Vistaril—$20,000 award under FTCA

The patient was a veteran of World War II and a former prisoner of war who, in January of 1971, entered the Gulfport Veterans' Hospital for the treatment of his nerves and for bronchitis. He informed two physicians and a nurse that he had previously taken antihistamines and thought that he was allergic to them, that they affected his ability to urinate. The patient was discharged in February and given a month's supply of prescribed drugs which included Vistaril and Stelazine (trifluoperazine) which, according to medical experts, have antihistamine properties. Thereafter, the patient had problems urinating, and in April his physician changed the medicine to other tranquilizers. The patient continued to complain and all medication was discontinued in May.

Soon thereafter the patient went to a private physician who diagnosed a serious infection of the prostate or epididymitis and prescribed a sulfa drug. The patient returned to the Veterans' Hospital, and in June of 1971 an indwelling catheter was inserted which remained in place for over four and one-half years. During this period of time it caused the patient severe problems.

In March of 1976 the patient developed a severe infection in his right testicle area. The private physician called in a urologist, surgery was performed, the catheter was removed, and the patient's condition improved.

The patient filed his administrative claim in April of 1974, and the complaint in February of 1975. Defendant contended that the claim was barred by the statute of limitations, but the evidence was uncontroverted that the patient did not know the physicians for the Veterans' Hospital had prescribed a drug "with antihistaminic ef-

---

[20] *Physicians' Desk Reference,* 35th ed., p. 1422.

[21] Id., p. 1423.

fects" until his wife, a licensed practical nurse, discovered it in June of 1972 when "she read of Vistaril's effects in the *Physicians' Desk Reference."*

The patient's urologist, whose operation resulted in the removal of the catheter, testified "that Vistaril probably caused the bladder damage...."

The defendant's motion for summary judgment was denied, and the patient was awarded $20,000.

Pfizer, Inc. v. Jones (1980) 221 Va. 681, 272 S.E.2d 43.

Necrosis following injection—Manufacturer's warning sufficient—Judgment for $100,000 reversed

In August, 1975, an obese woman patient was hospitalized for a gallbladder condition. During her stay she received four injections of a combined solution of Vistaril and Demerol (meperidine hydrochloride).

Immediately following the third injection (in the right buttock) the patient complained of a "very bad pain" in her hip. The following morning the site was inflamed and there was hardening under the skin. Blisters soon developed, and over a period of a week the inflammation spread to a very large area, with raised blisters and dark discoloration. Over two months later, when she was finally released from the hospital, the patient had a "large concave hole" in her hip, the result of necrosis of the tissue.

In her lawsuit against Pfizer, Inc., the patient charged that the defendant did not sufficiently warn her attending physicians nor the nurses who administered the injections regarding the dangers of injecting the solution into subcutaneous tissue rather than deep muscle, which the patient alleged caused her injury. A medical expert testifying for the patient was of the opinion that a special warning should have appeared on the package insert "to ensure that extra care be taken in the injection of obese patients." (The nurse who administered the injection testified that the patient was a "very large woman" which would make injection deep within the muscle more difficult.)

The patient's attorney argued that although Pfizer gave explicit instructions as to how the drug should be administered, it negligently failed to warn that necrosis might result if the drug were improperly injected into an obese person.

A jury returned a verdict of $225,000, which the trial court reduced to $100,000.

On appeal, the Supreme Court of Virginia reversed, holding that Pfizer's warning was sufficient, that it did not have to specify exactly what danger might result from a violation of its instructions on the package insert.

McWain v. Tucson General Hosp. (1983) 137 Ariz. 356, 670 P.2d 1180.

Sciatic nerve damage—Plaintiff offers no expert testimony—Res ipsa loquitur not applicable

The plaintiff suffered damage to the sciatic nerve following an injection of Vistaril into her hip. She alleged negligence on the part of the physician who prescribed the drug and the nurse who administered the injection. When the plaintiff offered no expert testimony on the required standard of care, the trial court granted the defendants' motion for summary judgment.

The Court of Appeals affirmed, holding that the doctrine of res ipsa loquitur did not apply since there was no evidence that the alleged negligent acts of the physician and/or nurse were more likely to cause the injury than any other possible cause.

Fleming v. Baptist General Convention of Oklahoma (Okla., 1987) 742 P.2d 1087.

Injection administered subcutaneously rather than intramuscularly—Tissue erosion and necrosis—$60,000 jury award affirmed

The plaintiff had been suffering from chronic back pain and migraine headaches for many years and for three years had been receiving intramuscular injections of a combined prescription for Atarax and Talwin at least twice weekly. On the occasion in question, she received an injection as an emergency room patient in the defendant's hospital. The nurse mistakenly gave the injection subcutaneously rather than intramuscularly. The skin at the injection site in the plaintiff's left thigh became discolored, eroded and eventually gangrene set in. The plaintiff required two skin grafts to close the wound. The plaintiff sued both her physician and the hospital. She charged the physician with negligence in prescribing an excessive number of injections which allegedly contributed to her injury. She charged the hospital with liability for the negligence of the nurse.

Both defendants alleged that the patient had been guilty of contributory negligence in that: (1) having received more than three hundred injections over a three-year period, she was fully aware that she was receiving an excessive amount of medication; and (2) when she received the injection, she "flinched" which indicated that she knew the injection had been administered improperly and yet she did nothing about it.

Neither defense was accepted, and the jury returned a verdict for $60,000 for the plaintiff, which was affirmed on appeal.

Love v. Park Lane Medical Center (Mo., 1989) 737 S.W.2d 720.

Drug injected subcutaneously instead of intramuscularly—Necrotic ulcer develops at site—Patient awarded $69,500 less 49% for comparative negligence in failing to seek treatment

While the patient was being treated in the defendant hospital for an ear infection, she was given an injection of Vistaril and Nubaine in her hip. On insertion of the needle, she felt "an excruciating pain," and screamed for the nurse either to stop or speed up the injection. After the injection, the pain continued, and was so severe that the patient could neither lie or sit on her hip. The site of the injection became red and swollen, and eleven days later she showed it to her family physician. He ordered an electromyogram, which indicated no nerve damage.

A week after the patient was discharged from the hospital, the injection site had turned black and covered approximately a four-inch area. The patient believed that this was a sign that the lesion was healing, and she did not mention it again to her physician until over seven weeks later. By then the pain had become severe, a necrotic ulcer had formed, and the site was draining. Two operations were required to remove the dead tissue and close the wound.

At trial, an assistant professor from the University of Kansas School of Nursing testified for the plaintiff that the nurse who administered the injection had failed to meet acceptable standards of practice, suggesting that she had administered a subcutaneous rather than intramuscular injection as was required with a drug such as Vistaril. The plaintiff also called as an expert witness the director of nursing at the University of Kansas Medical Center who testified that if a patient "screamed in pain" during an injection, prior to the release of the medication, she would stop the injection.

A third expert, a physician, testified that a subcutaneous injection of Vistaril could cause a hematoma and tissue destruction such as that experienced by the plaintiff.

The jury returned a verdict of $69,500 for the plaintiff, but assessed 49% of the fault against her for her delay in consulting her physician. The verdict was upheld.

Long v. St. Vincent's Hosp. (No. CV-86-6832, Circuit Court, Jefferson County, Ala., June 29, 1989).

Drug injected subcutaneously instead of intramuscularly—Tissue necrosis and nerve damage—$250,000 verdict against hospital

The patient, age 52, was administered an injection of Vistaril and Demerol (meperidine hydrochloride) into her hip, in an area other than a muscle, which is contrary to instructions contained in the Vistaril package insert. The patient immediately experienced pain, and later suffered tissue necrosis and nerve damage. Despite treatment with steroids, she still has "burning pain" and tenderness in her thigh, and numbness in her leg and foot. She must "protect her hip from contact," is unable to sit for long periods, and has some limited range of motion. At the time of trial, she was wearing a transcutaneous electrical stimulator unit for her pain.

According to the plaintiff's attorney, the jury returned a verdict of $250,000 against the hospital, which included $10,000 for loss of consortium.[1]

Related cases

Skin lesion at site of injection—Verdict for hospital affirmed

In Sassar v. Humana of Florida, Inc., (Fla. App., 1981) 404 So. 2d 856, the plaintiff was unsuccessful in showing that a skin lesion that developed at the site of an injection of Vistaril was caused by a nurse's negligence in injecting the drug into the subcutaneous area of the plaintiff's thigh rather than deep within the muscle.

Blood clot and partial paralysis blamed on Vistaril and Demerol

In Tolman v. Memorial Hosp. of Natrona County (No. 59428, District Court, Natrona County, Wyo., May 9, 1988), a spinal surgery patient claimed excessive administration of Vistaril and

[1] ATLA *Professional Negligence Law Reporter* 5:12, 1990.

Demerol (meperidine hydrochloride) following her operation caused a blood clot to form on her spinal cord which resulted in partial paralysis. The case is summarized herein under MEPERIDINE HYDROCHLORIDE.

HYPAQUE; HYPAQUE-50; HYPAQUE SODIUM

See SODIUM DIATRIZOATE

I

IBUPROFEN

Advil
Motrin
Nuprin
Rufen

Ibuprofen is a nonsteroidal anti-inflammatory agent used in treating the signs and symptoms of rheumatoid arthritis and ostearthritis. It is also indicated for the relief of mild to moderate pain in general. There are numerous side effects, and anaphylactoid reactions have been reported in a few hypersensitive patients. Visual disturbances include diminished vision, scotomata, changes in color vision, conjunctivitis, diplopia, optic neuritis and cataracts.[2]

Advil is produced by Whitehall Laboratories, a division of American Home Products (New York, N.Y.), Motrin by The Upjohn Company (Kalamazoo, Mich.), Nuprin by Bristol Myers (New York, N.Y.), and Rufen by Boots Pharmaceuticals (Shreveport, La.). Also, the drug is produced under the generic name by Danbury Pharmacal, Inc. (Danbury, Conn.).

Nichols v. Upjohn Co. (C.A.-5 Tex., 1980) 610 F.2d 293.

Permanent loss of vision—Alleged failure to warn—
Verdict for manufacturer affirmed

The plaintiff claimed he suffered permanent loss of vision in his right eye after taking Motrin. In his lawsuit against the manufacturer, The Upjohn Company, he alleged that the company's warnings regarding this side effect were inadequate and that the defendant's advertising material contained misrepresentations.

---

[2] *Physicians' Desk Reference,* 40th ed., pp. 1854-55.

After a three-day trial the jury deliberated fifty minutes and returned a verdict for the defendant. The Court of Appeal affirmed.

Permanent visual impairment—"Qualified expert rule" satisfied

Where a patient claimed that she suffered permanent visual impairment as a result of taking Motrin prescribed by her physicians, her attorney's affidavit that he had contacted "a licensed medical practitioner in the State of Oregon" who was willing to testify that the defendants deviated from the reasonable standard of care, satisfied the Oregon statute requiring that a party opposing a motion for summary judgment provide an affidavit that a "qualified expert" has been retained to establish a genuine material fact. Starr v. Wasner (1988) 93 Or. App. 48, 760 P.2d 900.

ILOSONE

See ERYTHROMYCIN ESTOLATE

IMIPRAMINE HYDROCHLORIDE

SK-Pramine
Tofranil

This drug, the original tricyclic antidepressant, is a member of the dibenzazepine group. It is prescribed for the relief of the symptoms of depression, and may also be useful as temporary adjunctive therapy in reducing enuresis (bed-wetting) in children ages six years and older.

Until 1986, Smith Kline & French Laboratories (Philadelphia, Pa.) produced imipramine under the brand name SK-Pramine, and Geigy Pharmaceuticals (Ardsley, N.Y.) manufactures Tofranil. The drug is also produced by several companies under the generic name.

Geigy lists numerous adverse reactions for Tofranil in its product literature, including "confusional states (especially in the elderly) with hallucinations, disorientation, delusions; anxiety, restlessness, agitation; insomnia and nightmares; hypomania; exacerbation of psychosis." Also, the manufacturer cautions:

> It should be kept in mind that the possibility of suicide in seriously depressed patients is inherent in the illness and may persist until significant remission occurs. Such patients should be carefully supervised during the early phase of treatment with imipramine hydrochloride, and may require hospitalization. Prescriptions should be written for the smallest amount feasible.

Haggerty v. New York (No. 60065, Court of Claims, N.Y., April 27, 1979).

Suicide following treatment with Tofranil—Drug prescribed despite warning in medical record—$100,000 awarded

The patient's admission diagnosis and medical record disclosed that he had been previously hospitalized for suicidal tendencies and indicated that Tofranil exacerbated his suicidal state of mind. Despite this information, the patient was given Tofranil and placed in an open ward. While the ward attendant was asleep, the patient hanged himself with his belt which the hospital failed to remove.

The lawsuit was brought by the patient's former wife, as administratrix of decedent's estate, and included the allegation that the hospital was negligent in administering a contraindicated drug to a suicidal patient.

According to the attorney for the plaintiff, she obtained a verdict from the court in the amount of $100,000.[3]

Docken v. Ciba-Geigy (1987) 86 Ore. App. 277, 739 P.2d 591.

Child dies after taking drug prescribed for brother—Cause of action stated against physician, pharmacy and manufacturer

In 1983, a child, age unknown, took several Tofranil tablets which had been prescribed for his older brother. The child died. In reversing a dismissal of actions against the physician, pharmacy and the manufacturer of the drug, the Oregon Court of Appeals held that a jury could find that the boy's death was forseeable by all three defendants, and that for purposes of an action for strict liability, a person other than the person for which a drug is prescribed may be considered a "user or consumer" under Oregon's statutory version of § 402A of the *Restatement (Second) of Torts* which uses the terms "user, consumer or *injured party* in describing a claimant."

Stebbins v. Concord Wrigley Drugs (1987) 164 Mich. App. 204, 416 N.W.2d 831.

"Impaired" patient involved in automobile accident—Summary judgments for physician and pharmacy affirmed

After taking Tofranil at bedtime as prescribed by his physician, the following morning the patient ran a red light and struck the

[3] ATLA *Law Reporter* 23:285, 1980.

plaintiff's automobile. In addition to suing the patient for negligence, the plaintiff sued the physician and the pharmacy where the patient purchased the drug, charging that they failed to warn the patient adequately of the drug's side effects, in that they caused "psychological as well as physical impairments" that brought about the accident.

The patient settled with the plaintiff prior to trial, and the physician and pharmacy moved for summary judgments, which the trial court granted. On appeal, the Court of Appeals of Michigan affirmed, noting that the physician, in his affidavit, stated that he had warned the patient of the possibility of "drowsiness" while taking Tofranil, and of the risk of operating an automobile. The physician stated also that the patient had never complained of drowsiness or any other side effect from the drug, even when he was taking twice the dosage that he was taking when he was involved in the accident. The physician also offered the affidavit of an expert witness who stated that the dosage taken by the patient the night before the accident would not have affected his ability to drive the following morning.

In affirming the pharmacy's summary judgment, the reviewing court held that the pharmacy had no duty to warn the patient of possible side effects of the drug if the prescription was proper on its face and neither the physician nor the manufacturer had requested that any such warning be given.

IMOVOX
See RABIES VACCINE

INDERAL
See PROPRANOLOL HYDROCHLORIDE

INDERIDE
See PROPRANOLOL HYDROCHLORIDE

INDOCIN
See INDOMETHACIN

INDOMETHACIN
Indocin

Indomethacin is an anti-inflammatory, antipyretic (reduces fever) and analgesic agent useful in the management of arthritic disorders. It is recommended for moderate to severe rheumatoid arthritis, including acute flare-up of chronic disease; moderate to severe rheumatoid (ankylosing) spondylitis; and moderate to severe degenerative joint disease of the hip (osteoarthritis). The drug has also been found effective in relieving pain and reducing fever, swelling, and tenderness in acute gouty arthritis in selected patients.[4]

Numerous adverse effects of indomethacin have been reported, including those involving the gastrointestinal system. Among these are single or multiple ulcerations, including perforation and hemorrhage of the esophagus, stomach, duodenum, or small intestine. Fatalities have been reported.[5]

Indomethacin is produced under the name Indocin by Merck, Sharpe & Dohme (West Point, Pa.), and under the generic name by numerous companies.

Webb v. Claus (No. SEC 4312, Superior Court, Los Angeles County, Cal., Feb. 9, 1973).

Upper gastrointestinal bleeding in patient on Indocin for four years—Mallory-Weiss syndrome implicated—Verdict for physicians

The plaintiff in this case was a 53-year-old male patient who had been treated with Indocin for four years for arthritis. One day he fainted and was rushed to the hospital in early shock from upper gastrointestinal bleeding.

The patient blamed the Indocin for his condition and filed a negligence action against his family physician who had prescribed the drug, and against a second physician who took calls for the patient's physician and who on two occasions had renewed prescriptions for the drug. At the trial the patient produced a medical witness who testified that in his opinion the Indocin had indeed caused the intestinal bleeding and that the defendants' treatment of the patient was below standard.

---

[4] *United States Dispensatory,* 27th ed., p. 616.
[5] Id., p. 617.

The defense disputed this, and the family physician took the stand and testified that his treatment was within acceptable standards, and that in his opinion the patient's problem was Mallory-Weiss syndrome, a perforated esophagus brought on by forceful vomiting.[6] The jury agreed, and returned verdicts for the two defendants.[7]

Wilkins v. Rueger (No. 76-630-889NM, Circuit Court, Wayne County, Mich., May 8, 1980).

Gastrointestinal bleeding—$10,000 settlement

A 55-year-old male patient was given Indocin by an internist in 1968 for his arthritis. He took the drug until 1974, when he suffered massive gastrointestinal bleeding and was hospitalized for a vagotomy and subtotal gastrectomy.

The patient brought the lawsuit against the internist and the manufacturer of the drug.

According to the patient's attorney, prior to trial the drug manufacturer settled for $10,000.[8]

Ferguson v. Williams (1988) 92 N.C. App. 336, 374 S.E.2d 438.

Patient allergic to aspirin suffers fatal anaphylactic reaction to Indocin—Plaintiff has cause of action against pharmacist for bad advice

The plaintiff's husband was given a prescription by his physician for Indocin and took it to the defendant pharmacist to have filled. According to the plaintiff, her husband told the pharmacist that he was allergic to aspirin, Percodan, and penicillin, and that the defendant wrote on the prescription form, "allergic to Percodan." The plaintiff then claimed that the defendant told her husband that it was safe to take the Indocin even though "the medical literature specifies that the use of the drug Indocin is contraindicated in persons who suffer aspirin allergies or aspirin sensitivities." The plaintiff's husband took the Indocin, suffered an anaphylactic reaction, and died.

---

[6] The following etiology has been given for Mallory-Weiss syndrome: "Retching or vomiting causing esophageal arterial laceration, associated with chronic alcoholism, hiatus hernia, atrophic gastritis, esophagitis." *Current Medical Information and Terminology,* 4th ed. (Chicago: American Medical Association, 1971), p. 247.

[7] AMA *The Citation* 28:71, 1973.

[8] ATLA *Law Reporter* 23:474, 1980.

When the plaintiff filed her complaint, the trial judge granted the defendant's motion to dismiss, and the plaintiff appealed. The Court of Appeals reversed, holding that the complaint stated a claim upon which relief could be granted. Under the law of North Carolina, said the court, while a pharmacist has no duty to advise a customer about a drug "absent knowledge of the circumstances," once a pharmacist is alerted to the specific facts and undertakes to advise a customer, he or she has a duty to advise the customer correctly.

Related cases

Nerve damage following treatment with Indocin and Sterazolidin—Physician found negligent

In Cooper v. Bowser (Tex. Civ. App., 1980) 610 S.W.2d 825, the Court of Civil Appeals of Texas affirmed a jury verdict in favor of a 45-year-old patient who suffered loss of hearing, eyesight and motor control following the use in 1975 of Sterazolidin (a combination of phenylbutazone and prednisone which is no longer marketed) and Indocin to reduce swelling in an injured leg. The patient's physician was found negligent for ignoring warnings on the package insert and in *Physicians' Desk Reference* regarding prolonged treatment with Sterazolidin.

INFLUENZA VIRUS VACCINE
Fluogen
Fluzone

Influenza vaccine is prepared from formalin-killed influenza virus grown in eggs. Vaccines may contain either the whole virus particle or portions of the virus coat antigens; the latter are called subunit vaccines. Influenza vaccine usually contains antigens of both the major influenza types, A and B.

There are two antigenic components on the surface of the virus: the hemagglutinin and the neuraminidase. A numbering system for each of these antigens is used to designate influenza subtypes. Vaccine administration stimulates antibody to both the hemagglutinin and the neuraminidase antigens. Antibody to the hemagglutinin is considered of primary importance in resistance to infection. There is no single level of this antibody that can be considered protective in a given individual, but a titer of 1:40 or greater is used as a general indication of the presence of immunity. For maximum effectiveness, annual administration of the vaccine is recommended. This is necessary because vaccine-induced immunity is short-lived and frequent changes in the antigenic character of the virus require almost continuous updating of the vaccine.

The effectiveness of influenza vaccines is a subject of continuing debate, but the majority of experts in the field believe that influenza vaccine is approximately 80% effective, i.e., prevents approximately 80% of the cases of influenza which would occur in a nonvaccinated population during an influenza epidemic. Vaccine is usually administered by intramuscular or subcutaneous injection. Intradermal administration has been used but has not been as thoroughly investigated as the other routes of administration.[9]

Fluogen is manufactured by Parke-Davis (Morris Plains, N.J.); Fluzone by Connaught Laboratories, Inc. (Swiftwater, Pa.), and Wyeth Laboratories (Philadelphia, Pa.) produces a vaccine under the generic name.[10]

In general, influenza vaccine has an excellent safety record; however, the swine influenza vaccination program of 1976 disclosed a previously unknown and serious complication. Approximately one in 100,000 persons who received swine influenza vaccine developed Guillain-Barre syndrome (polyneuritis), a form of ascending paralysis which usually requires hospitalization, and in approximately 5% of cases is fatal. Guillain-Barre syndrome was seen five to six times more often in vaccinated than in unvaccinated persons in the ten weeks following the swine influenza vaccination program. The association of Guillain-Barre syndrome with other influenza vaccines has not been established, but is assumed to exist.

Other complications of influenza vaccination which may be serious are severe allergic reactions, including angioneurotic edema, bronchospasm, and anaphylaxis. These reactions, which are rare and were not a serious problem during the swine influenza program, probably result from sensitivity to egg protein or some other nonviral component of the vaccine. Known hypersensitivity to eggs is considered a contraindication to receiving influenza vaccine.

Minor side reactions to influenza vaccine occur in 5-10% of vaccinees and are thought to result from toxicity of the virus antigen itself. These reactions begin six to twelve hours after vaccina-

---

[9] *Lawyers' Medical Cyclopedia,* § 6.25(E) (3rd ed., 1981).

[10] Under the swine flu program sponsored by the federal government in 1976, the cooperating manufacturers were Parke-Davis, Wyeth, Merrell-National Laboratories (Cincinnati, Ohio), and Merck, Sharpe & Dohme (West Point, Pa.).

tion and are most severe within the first 24 hours after vaccination. They rarely last more than 48 hours. Minor reactions may be systemic in nature and include fever, chills, malaise, and muscle aches or local with pain, tenderness, redness and induration at the vaccination site. Systemic or local reactions of this type are not contraindications to subsequent influenza vaccination.

Because reliable killing of the virus is easily achieved during production, influenza vaccines carry no risk of causing active influenza infection. There is however, a widespread misconception that this occurs. Also, because influenza vaccine contains inactivated virus, it does not pose a risk to fetuses of pregnant women who receive the vaccine or to fetuses of pregnant women who are exposed to persons who have been vaccinated.[11]

Swine flu claims

Under the 1976 National Swine Flu Immunization Program,[12] in order to induce vaccine manufacturers, health providers and local agencies to participate in administering swine flu vaccine to the adult population of the United States, the government agreed to substitute itself as the sole defendant in any claims for personal injury or death arising out of the use of the vaccine. When the first of these claims arose, this provision of the act was challenged, but was found constitutional.[13]

The majority of claims arising under the program involved Guillain-Barre syndrome (GBS) or similar symptoms. Most of the actions were settled promptly by the government. In some cases, the amount of the damages was disputed.[14] Of the remaining GBS

---

[11] *Lawyers' Medical Cyclopedia,* § 6.25(E) (3rd ed., 1981).

[12] 42 U.S.C. 247b(j)-(*l*).

[13] Sparks v. Wyeth Laboratories, Inc. (W.D. Okla., 1977) 431 F. Supp. 411; Ducharme v. Merrell-National Laboratories (C.A.-5 La., 1978) 574 F.2d 1307; Jones v. Wyeth Laboratories, Inc. (C.A.-8 Ark., 1978) 583 F.2d 1070.

[14] Draisma v. United States (W.D. Mich., 1980) 492 F. Supp. 1317; Lee v. United States (E.D. Tenn., 1980) 499 F. Supp. 307; Overton v. United States (C.A.-8 Mo., 1980) 619 F.2d 1299; Funston v. United States (M.D. Pa., 1981) 513 F. Supp. 1000; Barnes v. United States (W.D. Pa., 1981) 516 F. Supp. 1376, aff'd (C.A.-3 Pa., 1982) 685 F.2d 66; Barnes v. United States (M.D. Ala., 1981) 525 F. Supp. 1065; Gallimore v. United States (E.D. Pa., 1982) 530 F. Supp. 136; Pretre v. United States (E.D. Mo., 1981) 531 F. Supp. 931; Sulesky v. United States (S.D. W.Va., 1982) 545 F. Supp. 426; McDonald v. United States (M.D. Pa., 1983) 555 F. Supp. 935; Fraysier v. United States (S.D. Fla., 1983) 566 F. Supp. 1085, aff'd (C.A.-11 Fla., 1985) 766 F.2d 478; Manko v. United States (C.A.-8 Mo., 1987) 830 F.2d 831.

claims that were resisted, most centered on the question of proximate cause.[15]

While the government conceded liability in many Guillain-Barre cases, claims for anaphylactic shock have been resisted because of the following written precautions issued at the time of vaccination: "As with any vaccine or drug the possibility of severe or potentially fatal reactions exists. However, flu vaccine has rarely been associated with severe or fatal reactions. In some instances people receiving vaccine have had allergic reactions." In reversing a judgment

[15] In re [Swine Flu Immunization] Products Liability Litigation (D. Colo., 1980) 495 F. Supp. 1188; Parham v. United States (E.D. Tenn., 1980) 503 F. Supp. 70; Hixenbaugh v. United States (N.D. Ohio, 1980) 506 F. Supp. 461; Gicas v. United States (E.D. Wis., 1981) 508 F. Supp. 217; Terrell v. United States (N.D. Tex., 1981) 517 F. Supp. 374; Warner v. United States (M.D. Fla., 1981) 522 F. Supp. 87; Adleson v. United States (N.D. Cal., 1981) 523 F. Supp. 459; MacEwen v. United States (M.D. Ala., 1981) 525 F. Supp. 1063; Rein v. United States (E.D. N.Y., 1982) 531 F. Supp. 67; Marneef v. United States (E.D. Mich., 1981) 533 F. Supp. 129; Robinson v. United States (E.D. Mich., 1982) 533 F. Supp. 320; Simonetti v. United States (E.D. N.Y.,1982) 533 F. Supp. 435; Bean v. United States (D. Colo., 1980) 533 F. Supp. 567; Thompson v. United States (N.D. Okla., 1981) 533 F. Supp. 581; Montoya v. United States (D. Colo., 1981) 533 F. Supp. 586; Lung v. United States (E.D. N.Y., 1982) 535 F. Supp. 100; Kubs v. United States (E.D. Wis., 1982) 537 F. Supp. 560; Latinovich v. United States (E.D. Wis., 1982) 537 F. Supp. 671; Baum v. United States (M.D. Pa., 1982) 541 F. Supp. 1349; Cook v. United States (N.D. Cal., 1982) 545 F. Supp. 306; Sulesky v. United States (S.D. W.Va., 1982) 545 F. Supp. 426; McDonald v. United States (M.D. Pa., 1983) 555 F. Supp. 935; O'Gara v. United States (E.D. Pa., 1983) 560 F. Supp. 786; Stich v. United States (D. N.J., 1983) 565 F. Supp. 1096, aff'd (C.A.-3 N.J., 1984) 730 F.2d 115 (1984); Varga v. United States (N.D. Ohio, 1983) 566 F. Supp. 987; Fraysier v. United States (S.D. Fla., 1983) 566 F. Supp. 1085, aff'd (C.A.-11 Fla., 1985) 766 F.2d 478; Beall v. United States (M.D. Pa., 1983) 567 F. Supp. 131, aff'd (C.A.-3 Pa., 1984) 735 F.2d 1347; Spencer v. United States (W.D. Mo., 1983) 569 F. Supp. 325; Peterson v. United States (D. Idaho, 1983) 569 F. Supp. 676; May v. United States (W.D. Mo., 1983) 572 F. Supp. 725; Gates v. United States (C.A.-10 Okla., 1983) 707 F.2d 1141; Lima v. United States (C.A.-10 Colo., 1983) 708 F.2d 502; Cohen v. United States (S.D. N.Y., 1983) 571 F. Supp. 589, aff'd (C.A.-2 N.Y., 1983) 729 F.2d 1442; Saxe v. United States (N.D. Ohio, 1983) 577 F. Supp. 135, aff'd (C.A.-6 Ohio, 1984) 751 F.2d 386; Hasler v. United States (C.A.-6 Mich., 1983) 718 F.2d 202; Grubbs v. United States (N.D. Ind., 1984) 581 F. Supp. 536; Gaul v. United States (D. Del., 1984) 582 F. Supp. 1122; Smith v. United States (C.A.-8 Ark., 1984) 726 F.2d 428; Gundy v. United States (C.A.-10 Colo., 1984) 728 F.2d 484; Hockett v. United States (C.A.-11 Fla., 1984) 730 F.2d 709; Unthank v. United States (C.A.-10 Utah, 1984) 732 F.2d 1517; Kress v. United States (E.D. Pa., 1984) 587 F. Supp. 397, aff'd (C.A.-3 Pa., 1985) 762 F.2d 993; Gassmann v. United States (C.A.-11 Fla., 1985) 768 F.2d 1263; Benedict v. United States (C.A.-6 Ohio, 1987) 822 F.2d 1426; Brazzell v. United States (C.A.-8 Iowa, 1986) 788 F.2d 1352; Manko v. United States (W.D. Mo., 1986) 636 F. Supp. 1419.

for the survivors of an anaphylactic shock victim, the U.S. Court of Appeals, Fifth Circuit held that it did not feel that "any greater detail of the pathology of anaphylactic shock was required to put [the victim] on notice of the risk of this rare reaction." Mills v. United States (C.A.-5 La., 1985) 764 F.2d 373.

Non-swine flu claim

A Mississippi man developed "transverse myelitis," a condition closely related to Guillain-Barre syndrome (GBS), five days after receiving a non-swine influenza vaccine (Trivalent, Types A & B, 1982-83 formula). A jury returned a verdict of $200,000 against the manufacturer for failure to warn. The Supreme Court of Mississippi reversed, holding that the manufacturer's warning was adequate. On the package insert there was a statement warning physicians that although the connection between the vaccine and GBS was not clear, persons considering the vaccine "should be made aware of the benefits and possible risks, including GBS." The plaintiff's physician, whom the jury found free of negligence, had warned the plaintiff that he might have a sore arm and run a slight fever, but he did not warn him of the risk of GBS because he believed "the risk to be minimal and remote and therefore a warning, which would scare his patients, was not required." Wyeth Laboratories v. Fortenberry (Miss., 1988) 530 So. 2d 688.

INH

See ISONIAZID

INNOVAR

See FENTANYL and DROPERIDOL

INSULIN

There are many insulin preparations available in the United States for treatment of diabetes mellitus. Generally, these preparations differ in concentration, time of onset, duration of action, purity, and species of origin. Also, they are classified into three major groups: rapid-, intermediate-, and long-acting.

Although patients treated with insulin develop antibodies to the insulin, serious allergic problems are rare. Allergic reactions to insulin can be either systemic or local. The latter occurs about ten times more frequently than the former, but both forms may be seen in some patients.[16]

E. R. Squibb & Sons v. Cox (Ala., 1985) 477 So. 2d 963.

Brain damage, memory loss—Manufacturer not responsible for plaintiff taking wrong insulin

The plaintiff was a diabetic who regularly used a diluted, modified insulin manufactured by the defendant company under the brand name N-U-100 insulin. In August 1981 he went to his local pharmacist to purchase a bottle. He was given a box which he assumed contained the type of insulin he ordered. He returned home and put it in the refrigerator. Four days later he took the bottle out of the refrigerator and threw away the box and the package insert without looking at either. He did notice that the insulin in the bottle was *clear,* rather than *cloudy,* like his previous insulin, and that the label on the bottle said R-U-100 insulin instead of N-U-100, which he was used to seeing on the label. (R-U-100 is full-strength, unmodified insulin.)

The plaintiff claimed he took the bottle back to his pharmacist and was told that the insulin was "okay," that it was clear because "Squibb was in the process of removing impurities from its insulin preparations." The pharmacist told a different story: he claimed the plaintiff called him at home, and that he told the plaintiff that he should bring in the insulin so he could look at it. He said the plaintiff never came in. An employee of the pharmacist told still a different story: she said the plaintiff did come in and she compared his bottle with two others in the store marked R-U-100. He then said he would return, but didn't.

In his suit against Squibb (he settled with the pharmacist for an undetermined amount), the plaintiff claimed he took the R-U-100 insulin and suffered permanent brain damage, memory loss and personality change. He charged Squibb with mispackaging the product and with inadequately warning of the consequences of taking undiluted, unmodified R-U-100. A jury awarded him $300,000.

The Supreme Court of Alabama reversed, holding that there was no evidence of mispackaging introduced at the trial. (The plaintiff claimed the box containing the R-U-100 insulin bottle was marked N-U-100, but the deposition of the pharmacist, who agreed, was not offered into evidence.) As to the charge of inadequate warning, the

---

[16] AMA *Drug Evaluations,* 6th ed., p. 775.

court held that such warning, if inadequate, could not have been the proximate cause of the plaintiff's injury because he did not read the package insert, and thus it would not have altered his course of action and prevented his injury.

Edmondson v. Central DuPage Hospital (No. 83L 1452, Circuit Court, DuPage County, Ill., Oct. 27, 1986).

Non-diabetic given insulin following stroke—
Severe insulin shock and brain damage—
$350,000 settlement

The plaintiff was a 59-year-old male with a history of coronary artery disease. During coronary bypass surgery, he suffered a severe cerebral infarction. While recovering from the stroke, he was fed by hyperalimentation. Due to elevated glucose levels, he was administered insulin pursuant to a standing hospital order. He was not, however, a diabetic. He was later discovered comatose and in severe insulin shock. Subsequent tests revealed permanent brain damage.

On being sued, the defendant hospital contended that the insulin shock and coma had minimal effect upon plaintiff's condition, and that his neurological symptoms were the result of the stroke. The parties settled for $350,000.[17]

Related cases

Wrong type of insulin dispensed by pharmacy—Action barred by statute of limitations

In Moon v. Harco Drugs (Ala., 1983) 435 So. 2d 218, a cause of action against a pharmacy for alleged negligence in selling a diabetic patient's husband the wrong type of insulin did not accrue when the patient discovered for the first time that she had been furnished the wrong insulin, but accrued instead when she first became ill from using the product, and the limitations period could not be extended on the theory of a "continuous tort" because there were no repeated acts of negligence.

"Lente" insulin given to customer instead of
"Semilente"—$250,000 awarded
against pharmacy

In Pressler v. Irvine Drugs (1985) 169 Cal. App. 3d 1244, 215 Cal. Rptr. 807, a pharmacy was held liable for the negligence of a phar-

---

[17] ATLA *Professional Negligence Law Reporter* 2:12, 1987.

macist who gave a customer "Lente" insulin instead of "Semilente," a less potent product, but the award of $325,000 in general damages was reduced to $250,000 under California's statute limiting noneconomic loss recovery against health care providers.

INTRAVENOUS SOLUTIONS

Intravenous feeding (parenteral nutrition) is used to provide fluid, nutrients, and electrolytes when oral or tube feeding is not feasible or must be supplemented. Initially, the proportion is usually two parts of 5 to 10% dextrose in water to one part isotonic saline. If feeding is continued for several days, it is often necessary to supply sodium, potassium, magnesium, and calcium, and therefore a balanced electrolyte solution may be used.[18]

There are over one hundred commercially available intravenous solutions: varying strengths of carbohydrates in water, single and multiple electrolyte solutions, protein and vitamin solutions, and combinations of all of these. Most are marketed under the generic names, and the leading manufacturers are: Abbott Pharmaceuticals (North Chicago, Ill.), Cutter Laboratories, Inc. (Emeryville, Cal.), McGaw Laboratories (Glendale, Cal.), and Travenol Laboratories, Inc. (Deerfield, Ill.).

Epling v. Sutter Gen. Hosp. (No. 219418, Superior Court, Sacramento County, Cal., Oct. 4, 1973).

Infiltration of solution—Verdict for hospital

The patient filed suit against the defendant-hospital for alleged negligence of hospital personnel in allowing the infiltration of an intravenous solution into the tissues of her arm, resulting in "adhesive capsulitis." The patient, a 57-year-old woman hospitalized for gallbladder removal and hernia repair, claimed that she suffered excruciating pain and swelling as a result of the infiltrated solution.

At the trial, the hospital admitted that the solution had infiltrated, but argued that this was a normal risk in such cases, and that in administering the solution the hospital personnel followed the proper standard of care. The hospital also introduced a physician who testified that, in his opinion, the patient's pain and suffer-

---

[18] *The Merck Manual of Diagnosis and Therapy*, 12th ed. (Rahway, N.J.: Merck, Sharpe & Dohme Research Laboratories, 1972), pp. 1661-1662.

ing were due to an unrelated neurological condition. The jury returned a verdict for the hospital.[19]

For additional cases involving tissue infiltration of intravenous solutions, see LEVARTERENOL BITARTRATE and PROMAZINE HYDROCHLORIDE herein.

Priolo v. Baxter (No. 187882, Superior Court, Sacramento County, Cal., 1971).

Contaminated solution—$850,000 judgment against supplier—Hospital not liable

A 22-year-old woman hospital patient died 26 hours after receiving an intravenous solution subsequent to gallbladder surgery. Tests revealed that the solution, Dextrose-Saline, was contaminated by bacteria which had entered the bottle through a hairline crack.

A suit was filed against the hospital and the company which supplied the solution. The supplier, against charges that the bottle was defective, argued that the bottle had cracked after it had been shipped, and that it was the responsibility of the hospital personnel to inspect such bottles before administering the solution to a patient.

Prior to trial, the defense offered $400,000 to settle but the plaintiff refused. The case was tried and a jury returned a verdict against the supply company in the amount of $900,000 in general damages, $1,000 in special damages, and $1,000,000 in punitive damages. The hospital was found free of liability. On motions for new trial and judgment n.o.v. on grounds of excessiveness, the trial judge ruled the verdict would be set aside as to damages unless the plaintiffs accepted a remittitur to $350,000 in general and $500,000 in punitive damages. The plaintiffs complied, leaving a total judgment of $850,000.[20]

Thompson v. Narvades (No. 82-12, Circuit Court, Gadsden County, Fla., July 25, 1986).

Infiltration of solution—Volkmann's contracture and partial permanent disability—$385,000 jury award

The patient, a 2-year-old child, was hospitalized for gastroenteritis. During the administration of intravenous solutions, the fluids

---

[19] AMA *The Citation* 29:29, 1974.

[20] Id. ATLA *News Letter* 14:409, 1971.

infiltrated the child's right forearm causing severe swelling in the immediate area. The defendant physician elevated the arm and applied warm soaks, but this did not relieve the swelling, and the child suffered compromised circulation resulting in a Volkmann's ischemic contracture of the right hand. Several corrective procedures had to be performed and the child now has only 60 to 65% normal hand function.

At trial, the child's parents alleged the physician failed to recognize the compromised circulation and failed to consult with an orthopedic surgeon to determine whether conservative measures were appropriate or whether a fasciotomy should have been performed.

The jury awarded $385,000, holding the hospital and physician equally responsible.[21]

Wilabay v. Herbeck (No. 86-2751-A, 188th Judicial District Court, Gregg County, Tex., June 13, 1988).

Brain damage—Alleged excessive administration of solution—$4.6 million settlement

The patient, a nine-month-old child, underwent surgery for an intestinal blockage. Three hours after the operation, she suffered severe seizures, resulting in extensive, permanent brain damage, which left her unable to walk, talk, and control her bowels and bladder.

In their suit against the surgeon, hospital, and the admitting pediatrician, the child's parents claimed that: (1) the defendants negligently administered intravenous solutions in excess of three times the proper amount, thereby causing cerebral edema, which in turn caused the seizures; and (2) the surgeon and pediatrician failed to diagnose the child's condition and prescribe the necessary medication to control the seizures.

According to the plaintiffs' attorney, shortly after selecting the jury, the parties settled for $4.6 million, with the hospital contributing $3 million, the pediatrician $1.5 million, and the surgeon, $100,000.[1]

Related cases

Septicemia outbreaks linked to contaminated IV bottles

In December, 1970, the Center for Disease Control (CDC) of the United States Public Health Service launched an investigation into

---

[21] ATLA *Professional Negligence Law Reporter* 2:13, 1987.
[1] ATLA *Professional Negligence Law Reporter* 4:12, 1989.

a sudden increase in the incidence of blood poisoning (septicemia) among hospital patients receiving intravenous fluids. On completion of the study, the CDC concluded that between October, 1970 and March 1, 1971, 150 cases of blood poisoning, including nine deaths, had occurred in eight hospitals among patients who had received intravenous fluids and intravenous fluid systems manufactured by Hospital Products Division of Rocky Mount, North Carolina, a division of Abbott Laboratories. The investigators reported contamination of cap liners in unopened Abbott IV bottles, from which they postulated "the organisms [could] enter the fluid from the plastic liners when the caps are opened and replaced while the bottle is held for later use."[2]

The manufacturer issued a nationwide recall of the bottles on March 22, 1971. Later, however, the Food and Drug Administration recommended to the Department of Justice that criminal charges be brought against the manufacturer and those of its employees "responsible" for distribution of the bottles, to resolve allegations that certain company officials had been aware of the possibility of contamination, but had delayed in bringing about the recall order. The matter was given to a grand jury in North Carolina, and an indictment was returned on May 29, 1973. This indictment was dismissed by the trial court on the grounds of prejudicial publicity. However, the trial court's ruling was reversed on appeal.[3]

As would be expected, numerous civil lawsuits were filed containing claims for punitive damages. A joint effort by plaintiffs' lawyers, called the "Abbott IV" group, was formed to carry on this litigation.[4]

A second outbreak of septicemia associated with suspected contaminated intravenous solutions occurred in March, 1973. The cases arose in Wisconsin and Ohio, and involved at least four hospital patients. There was one death. Although it had not been established that its product was the source, Cutter Laboratories voluntarily recalled the unused portion of approximately 66,000 units of Lactated Ringer's with Dextrose 5% (D5LR) as a precautionary measure. All the patients involved had received infusions of this solution.[5]

---

[2] United States v. Abbott Laboratories (C.A.-4 N.C., 1974) 505 F.2d 565.

[3] Id.

[4] Rheingold, P. D., "Drug Litigation: 6th Edition — 1972 Developments" (Mimeographed), American Trial Lawyers Convention, St. Louis, Mo., July, 1972.

[5] *American Medical News,* April 2, 1973, p. 13.

INTROPIN

See DOPAMINE HYDROCHLORIDE

IODINE

Ioprep

Iodine is used primarily in the treatment of goiter, which is caused by an iodine deficiency, and also as a germicide. It is considered by many as one of the best wound disinfectants, and is used extensively to sterilize the skin prior to surgery. It is also of value in treating fungus infections and is effective against some viruses.[6]

As a wound disinfectant, iodine should not be applied in concentrations higher than 2 or 3%. The common iodine solution used for superficial lacerations contains approximately 2% iodine and 2.5% sodium iodide. It is toxic if taken internally. A less toxic solution, providone-iodine, is an organic iodine and polyvinylpyrrolidone complex which slowly releases the iodine. This product, sold under the name Betadine by The Purdue Frederick Company (Norwalk, Conn.), comes in various forms, including a gargle.[7]

Nickolai v. Washington Hosp. (Superior Court, Alameda County, Cal., Dec. 26, 1972).

Patient swallowed iodine solution during preparation for operation—Solution not intended for internal use—$600,000 settlement

The patient, a forty-year-old male, was scheduled for maxillary sinus surgery. The surgeon ordered that the patient's mouth be prepared with a 1% iodine solution called "Ioprep." An endotracheal tube with an inflatable cuff to seal off the trachea was placed in his mouth, into which the antiseptic was poured, to be kept there for five minutes. During this time the patient apparently coughed, and swallowed the solution. He died eight days later.

In the subsequent lawsuit, it was alleged that the surgeon had never before performed this preoperative procedure using the solution "Ioprep," and that the container from which the solution was taken was clearly marked "for external use only." It was charged that when he had previously prepared patients in this manner, he had used the antiseptic "Betadine."

---

[6] *United States Dispensatory,* 27th ed., pp. 625-27.

[7] Id.

The case was settled for $600,000.[8]

IOPREP

See IODINE

ISONIAZID

INH

Laniazid

Rifamate

Isoniazid is regarded as the mainstay of drug therapy of tuberculosis.[9] Of the three drugs commonly used in tuberculosis-isoniazid, aminosalicylic acid, and streptomycin-isoniazid is the most effective when used by itself, but resistance to it develops very rapidly. For this reason it is generally given simultaneously with one or both of the other drugs.

The drug is recommended for all forms of active tuberculosis in which the organisms are susceptible, and as preventive treatment in persons who have a high risk of developing active tuberculosis.

Isoniazid is marketed under the generic name by Danbury Pharmacal, Inc. (Danbury, Conn.). INH is marketed by CIBA Pharmaceutical Company (Summit, N.J.); Laniazid by Lannett Company, Inc. (Philadelphia, Pa.); and Rifamate by Merrell Dow Pharmaceuticals (Cincinnati, Ohio).

In humans, isoniazid has been relatively free from toxic reactions when taken in therapeutic doses, but some untoward effects have been reported, generally due to central nervous system stimulation. Symptoms most frequently encountered from isoniazid are dryness of mouth, constipation, vertigo, muscular twitching, difficulty in urination, headache, exaggerated reflexes, sudden drop in blood pressure, insomnia, weakness, tingling sensations, tinnitus, toxic hepatitis, allergic reactions, fever, jaundice, paresthesias of the feet and legs, weakness and paralysis with loss of reflexes of ankles and knees, and convulsions.[10]

More recently, hepatitis became of particular concern, and the manufacturers began including the following warning in their product literature:

---

[8] AMA *The Citation* 27:68, 1973.

[9] *United States Dispensatory,* 27th ed., pp. 641, 642.

[10] Id.

Severe and sometimes fatal hepatitis associated with isoniazid therapy may occur and may develop even after many months of treatment. The risk of developing hepatitis is age related. Approximate case rates by age are: 0 per 1,000 for persons under 20 years of age, 3 per 1,000 for persons in the 20-34 year age group, 12 per 1,000 for persons in the 35-49 year age group, 23 per 1,000 for persons in the 50-64 year age group, and 8 per 1,000 for persons over 65 years of age. The risk of hepatitis is increased with daily consumption of alcohol. Precise data to provide a fatality rate for isoniazid-related hepatitis is not available; however, in a U.S. Public Health Service Surveillance Study of 13,838 persons taking isoniazid, there were 8 deaths among 174 cases of hepatitis.

Therefore, patients given isoniazid should be carefully monitored and interviewed at monthly intervals. Serum transaminase concentration becomes elevated in about 10-20 percent of patients, usually during the first few months of therapy but it can occur at any time. Usually enzyme levels return to normal despite continuance of drug but in some cases progressive liver dysfunction occurs. Patients should be instructed to report immediately any of the prodromal symptoms of hepatitis, such as fatigue, weakness, malaise, anorexia, nausea, or vomiting. If these symptoms appear or if signs suggestive of hepatic damage are detected, isoniazid should be discontinued promptly, since continued use of the drug in these cases has been reported to cause a more severe form of liver damage.

Patients with tuberculosis should be given appropriate treatment with alternative drugs. If isoniazid must be reinstituted, it should be reinstituted only after symptoms and laboratory abnormalities have cleared. The drug should be restarted in very small and gradually increasing doses and should be withdrawn immediately if there is any indication of recurrent liver involvement.

Preventive treatment should be deferred in persons with acute hepatic diseases.

Trogun v. Fruchtman (1973) 58 Wis. 2d 596, 207 N.W.2d 297.

Hepatitis—Propriety of INH treatment of "low-risk" tuberculosis patient—Judgment for physician affirmed

The patient was seen by the defendant, an internist, in November, 1966. Based upon his prior medical record, and certain tests which revealed a premature arteriosclerotic condition, the defendant diagnosed the patient as "possibly a diabetic" and placed him on 1,500 calories per day. Later this was increased to 2,000 calories. In October 1967 the defendant put the patient on Diabinese (chlorpropamide) 100 mg. daily.

In July of 1968, isoniazid hydrazate (INH) was prescribed. This came about as a result of the defendant receiving a report from the City of Milwaukee Tuberculosis Control Center that the patient had been examined on February 1, 1968 and had been found to have "Primary TB, inactive." The dosage was 300 mg. daily. Approximately seven weeks later the patient became jaundiced, was hospitalized and underwent an exploratory laparotomy. This resulted in the lawsuit.

At the trial the patient's first witness was Dr. K., a specialist in internal medicine and pulmonary diseases. He testified that the patient had suffered from "obstructive jaundice" or "noninfectious hepatitis" which was "probably due to drugs." He said when the patient was examined he had actually been taking three drugs: the Diabinese, INH, and Atromid-S (the latter to lower the fat and cholesterol count). He said he was not prepared to say for certain which drug caused the jaundice, but that it probably was not the Atromid-S. Also, according to the witness, Diabinese was "directed to the pancreas" rather than the liver, which was the organ involved in the patient's case. On cross-examination, however, Dr. K. admitted that Diabinese has been known to cause jaundice, but pointed out that such cases were "very rare."

On the other hand, said Dr. K., the drug INH was known to cause side effects since its inception in the early 1950's and it "could" have been a "substantial factor" in the patient's hepatitis. However, on cross-examination, the witness admitted that he had given INH to "thousands" of patients and it had caused only "a few" cases of hepatitis. When asked about disclosure of this risk to patients, he said that in 1968 he was not telling his patients of the possibility of contracting jaundice from the drug, and that it was not standard practice among internists in the community to do so. The cross-examination of Dr. K. concluded with his agreeing that a person who has had a positive TB skin test (such as the patient) should be put on INH pursuant to the recommendations of the State Board of Health.

On the patient's attorney's redirect examination of Dr. K., he testified that despite the rarity of instances of INH causing jaundice, he felt that it, rather than the Diabinese, caused the jaundice in the patient. One reason for this, he said, was that the patient had been taking Diabinese for a year whereas he had taken INH for only six to eight weeks before showing symptoms.

The patient's third and final witness was Dr. M., a specialist in tuberculosis and medical director of the Milwaukee TB Control Center. He testified that in 1964 the State Public Health Service was instituting a program of prophylaxis in larger metropolitan areas using the drug INH as the agent in inactive cases. He stated that the use of INH increased significantly after 1964 and private physicians utilized the Public Health Service guidelines for the use of such drug "inasmuch as Public Health Service communications are available to the local physicians." He further stated that under the customary procedure of his department a specific recommendation as to whether the patient was a suitable candidate for INH would have been made. He also stated it was the customary practice of physicians in the Milwaukee area in 1968 to follow his department's recommendations. Those recommendations, he stated, were based upon the guidelines of the Public Health Service.

Dr. M. testified that the first tuberculosis roentgenogram done by his department upon the patient was on April 22, 1957 and at that time there existed a "calcification" (i.e., a previously infected but presently healed area) in the "second interspace on the left." The last roentgenogram taken of the patient was in 1968. No discernible change had occurred in the interim, and this indicated "stability." According to Dr. M. this stability placed the patient in a relatively low-risk group in terms of developing active TB. He was then asked by counsel whether his department would have advised prophylaxis with INH. He answered: "As a relatively low-risk individual, he would not be advised to be prophylaxed," and that it was a departure from customary practice to so prophylax with INH a person in the patient's low-risk category.

On cross-examination Dr. M. did acknowledge that in July of 1967 the State Board of Health modified their previous recommendations with respect to the use of INH in chemoprophylaxis. This modification enlarged the previous recommendations with respect to the use of INH in the treatment of inactive cases of TB.

Dr. M. was also asked the following question:

> And if I understand correctly, you would agree that the family doctor, when he has a patient who has a positive skin test, who is reported to have, I think it's primary TB inactive, who has a spot on his lung for a period of at least 12 years, you would agree that that doctor would be acting in conformance with the accepted practice as practiced by doctors in Milwaukee County, by putting that man on INH, if he in his judgment ... would you agree that that doctor would be acting in conformance with the accepted

standards of medicine as practiced in Milwaukee County, if he put that patient on INH prophylactically?

Dr. M.'s response was: "If in his professional judgment it warranted it," and added that it was "common knowledge" that those physicians engaged in the treatment of TB would like to see all persons who had a positive skin test at some point or another placed on INH. Since there were not enough public funds to support such treatment, said the witness, it was the practice of TB public health departments to treat the most severe cases first and thereafter the less severe cases. The nationwide public TB control strategy was to "prophylax" approximately two million persons per year on the assumption that in twelve years approximately 24 to 25 million persons would be covered. Dr. M. further testified it was the intention of the public health authorities in this country to treat everyone having a positive TB result with INH prophylactically.

At this juncture in the trial the court conducted a conference with Dr. M. in chambers. In this conference, on the record, the court indicated that it was confused with respect to the physician's testimony as to the community standard relating to the use of INH, and not the practice of the State Board of Health or the Milwaukee TB Control Center. The physician indicated that his organization operated under the Public Health Service standards and put persons with inactive TB into certain prophylactic categories. As to what was done by physicians in the community, Dr. M. stated he had nothing precisely to judge it by.

Continuing under cross-examination, Dr. M. read part of the report of the ad hoc committee on chemoprophylaxis, entitled "Chemoprophylaxis for the Prevention of Tuberculosis" — specifically, the first paragraph of the section which related to persons recommended for chemoprophylaxis: "Every positive reactor is at some risk of developing active disease. Thus, any person found to have a reaction of 10 mm. or more to the Mantoux test, using 5 TU of PPD, should receive chemoprophylaxis whenever he is identified."

Dr. M. admitted that the patient in the instant case was a positive reactor and did have a reaction of ten millimeters or more to the Mantoux test. Dr. M. also admitted that, in his opinion, the "ideal" treatment of persons having a positive reaction of ten millimeters or more to the Mantoux test was chemoprophylaxis with INH. He also said that treatment of persons with inactive TB (such as the patient) reduced the risk of the TB becoming active and affecting other persons. The witness was then asked the following question:

> Now, doctor, do you agree that a private physician in July of 1968, who had a private patient who had a positive reaction of 10 millimeters or more on the skin test, should in the exercise of the practice of medicine as practiced by competent skilled practitioners, practicing in this community, give such a person INH for chemoprophylaxis?

The witness responded in the affirmative.

Dr. M. also admitted that it was not until 1970 that his organization began routinely advising patients of the possible hepatitis side effect of INH; that this side effect was not generally known by physicians until 1970; and, at least to his knowledge, that a private-practicing physician in July of 1968 would not warn a patient of a side effect such physician did not know of.

On redirect examination, Dr. M. testified that the *Physicians' Desk Reference* was a reliable and accurate source of information which physicians in the community customarily purchase and keep for reference in their offices. He also stated that this book in 1967 did, under the section denominated "Adverse Reactions," state that one of the adverse reactions to the drug isoniazid was hepatitis. With respect to the patient, the witness acknowledged that a lesion such as the patient's could have been caused by another source, such as histoplasmosis — "a disease caused by histoplasma capsulatum, which simulates tuberculosis in its end-healing process, inasmuch as it does deposit calcium in the lungs."

Also during the redirect examination of Dr. M., he testified regarding the publication *Crusader* which he stated was published by the Respiratory and Thoracic Disease Association of Wisconsin. The publication itself listed its publisher as the Wisconsin Anti-TB Association. The July, 1967 issue of this publication, as testified to by Dr. M., listed several categories of persons who, having a ten millimeter reaction on a five TU intradermal test, ought to be considered for chemoprophylaxis. Dr. M. stated again that, in terms of risk, the patient was a relatively low-priority risk.

Asked whether the consent forms used by the Milwaukee TB Control Center contained any warnings of adverse effects to chemoprophylaxis with INH, Dr. M. gave the following list: "Rash, fever, nervousness, ticks, delay in micturition, pregnancy, nephritis, neuritis; if not mentioned, dermatitis, if not mentioned, dizziness, excitement — they would be in one category." When asked to compare the compilation with the 1967 *Physicians' Desk Reference,* Dr. M. read from the book:

> ... Adverse reactions: peripheral neuritis is most often observed; central nervous system effects, insomnia, headache, restlessness, mental confusion, toxic psychoses, increased reflexes, muscle twitching, paresthesias; optic neuritis and optic atrophy have been reported; extremely high dosages have produced convulsions in apparently normal individuals; urinary disturbance in the male, constipation and dryness of mouth; allergic reactions occur infrequently; hepatitis, agranulocytosis and exfoliative dermatitis have occasionally been reported.

The final question on redirect examination of Dr. M. was whether, in his opinion, most competent and skillful physicians in Milwaukee in 1968 generally followed the recommendations of the Public Health Service with respect to when patients with positive skin tests should get INH treatment. He responded that "inasmuch as they were promulgated" they would.

On recross-examination Dr. M. testified that persons such as the patient with positive reactions of ten millimeters and abnormal roentgenograms fell within the recommendation set forth in the *Crusader* and, therefore, should receive treatment with INH. He elaborated this to mean that of the four categories of inactive TB patients — primary, minimal, moderately advanced, and far advanced — the patient fell within the "primary" category, or least serious.

Also elicited on recross-examination was the full statement in the *Physicians' Desk Reference* with respect to adverse reactions of INH. This sentence read: *"Side effects are infrequently encountered and are rarely serious."* (Emphasis added.) Dr. M. acknowledged that in his long experience in the field of TB control, this statement, in 1968, was correct.

On further redirect examination Dr. M. read part of his signed statement:

> It is my opinion that Mr. Trogun was not in any category of persons who in 1968 in Milwaukee were given I.N.H. therapy in the customary practice in effect at that time by competent and skillful physicians exercising due care and for that reason, he being not in such category, I did not recommend to his physician that he be given I.N.H. therapy.

On further recross-examination the witness admitted that his department's regulations, from the Public Health Service, were not necessarily the same as those governing when a private physician gave INH.

At the close of evidence the trial court granted the defendant's motion for nonsuit and dismissal of the case, and the patient appealed. The Supreme Court of Wisconsin affirmed the order and judgment of the trial court, stating:

> In granting defendant's motion for nonsuit, the trial court correctly concluded (1) the record was 'totally devoid' of any evidence establishing a breach of the requisite standard of care with respect to the treatment with Diabinese; (2) with regard to the INH, such drug was called for under the circumstances; and (3) 'there was absolutely no potentiality of drawing any reasonable inference that there was a substandard method of care by the defendant.' The trial court did not err in granting the nonsuit motion. Even viewing the credible evidence most favorably to the plaintiff, it is clear that a substandard standard of care was not established in [the defendant's] treatment of plaintiff with INH. This course of treatment was not a deviation from the standard of care customarily practiced by skilled and competent physicians in the Milwaukee area.

Brick v. Barnes-Hind Pharmaceutical Co. (D. D.C., 1977) 428 F. Supp. 496.

Death from hepatitis and cirrhosis—Warning on label sufficient

A patient was treated with isoniazid at a Veterans' Administration hospital over an eighteen-month period. During this time she developed hepatitis and cirrhosis, which eventually caused her death. In a wrongful-death action against the supplier of the drug, it was alleged that the drug had not been properly tested for the "dangerous and harmful side effects it would produce," and that the defendant "had breached the implied warranty of merchantability, safety and fitness of such drug for medicinal use," which the court concluded to mean that the defendant allegedly did not sufficiently warn doctors of isoniazid's side effects.

The complaint was dismissed upon summary judgment, with the court holding that since it was well known that liver damage was among the adverse effects of prolonged use of isoniazid, and the defendant's label and warning complied fully with the requirements of the Food and Drug Administration, clearly stating that an occasional side effect of the drug was hepatitis, the defendant could not be held liable.

Santoni v. Moore (1982) 53 Md. App. 129, 452 A.2d 1223.

Fatal hepatitis—Clinic doctors allegedly negligent in not discovering patient's reaction to isoniazid

Mario Santoni, a 56-year-old naturalized citizen from Italy, applied for a maintenance job with the city of Baltimore. As a prerequisite to his employment, he was required to undergo a medical examination which included a tuberculin skin test and a chest X-ray. The skin test was positive, but the X-ray showed that his chest was clear, which indicated that he did not have active tuberculosis, but that he did have live bacilli in his body. This meant that he had a greater than ordinary risk of developing tuberculosis.

He was put on an isoniazid program jointly sponsored by the city of Baltimore and the United States Public Health Service. He was to report once a month for a thirty-day supply of medication and, on each visit, was to report any adverse reactions, particularly signs of hepatitis, which had recently been linked with prolonged use of isoniazid. The protocol required that each participant in the program was to be asked specifically about any "jaundice, dark urine, sustained loss of appetite, marked fatigue or prolonged nausea or vomiting." If there was any indication of hepatitis, the isoniazid was to be discontinued immediately.

Mr. Santoni went on the program on January 20, 1972. In March, he began to experience fatigue and decreased appetite. By April, he noticed "fullness, abdominal discomfort and increased flatulence." By May, "his stools became lighter, and his urine became darker." By early June, he began to look worse and to feel more tired." Despite his symptoms, apparently Mr. Santoni mentioned nothing to the nurses whom he saw monthly at the health clinic. His last visit there was on June 12.

On June 22, 1972, Mr. Santoni entered the hospital where his condition continued to deteriorate. He died on July 3 from liver failure.

In her lawsuit against the directors of the tuberculosis program, Santoni's widow charged negligence on the part of the program personnel in failing to discover her husband's hepatitis in time to save his life. At trial it was revealed that twelve other patients on the tuberculosis program had died of liver disease during 1972, although there was no evidence that any of them complained of any adverse reactions to isoniazid. The defense, however, argued that Mr. Santoni was aware of his symptoms, and that he was guilty of contributory negligence in not informing the clinic of his deteriorating condition.

The jury returned a verdict for the defendants, finding evidence of negligence on the part of two clinic doctors, but also that the patient's own negligence caused or contributed to his death. On appeal, the Court of Special Appeals of Maryland reversed, holding that there was no evidence of contributory negligence as a matter of law, and that the trial court erred in submitting this issue to the jury. The case was remanded for retrial on the issue of damages.

The Court of Appeals, however, took the case on certiorari and reversed the Court of Special Appeals, holding that the issue of Mr. Santoni's contributory negligence was indeed a question for the jury, which could infer from the evidence that he failed to heed instructions by clinic personnel with respect to reporting symptoms that might be indicative of hepatitis. But on remand to the Court of Special Appeals, that court held that hearsay evidence consisting of a conversation between Mr. Santoni and his wife to the effect that he did not know of any risk involved in taking isoniazid was admissible, and the trial court's exclusion of this evidence was prejudicial error. The case, therefore, was once again reversed and a new trial was ordered.

Jackson v. State (La. App., 1983) 428 So. 2d 1073.

Hepatitis—State-sponsored health unit not liable for failure to warn

The plaintiff was a cook in the public school system. When a skin test for tuberculosis showed positive, the local parish health unit physician prescribed isoniazid for her as a "preventative" measure. Two months later the plaintiff developed hepatitis.

In her lawsuit against the state, the plaintiff claimed that parish health unit personnel had failed to warn her of the risks in taking isoniazid, especially the possibility of hepatitis. But the trial judge ruled that the plaintiff failed to show that had she been informed of this risk, she would not have submitted to the treatment. The judge dismissed her action and the Court of Appeals affirmed.

Banda v. Danbury (La. App., 1985) 469 So. 2d 264.

Hepatitis—Physician not negligent in his monitoring of patient on INH

Because of a positive skin test for tuberculosis, the plaintiff was placed on INH by the defendant physician, an employee of the local parish health unit. Three months later the plaintiff complained of "occasional nausea and headaches." She was instructed not to take INH on an empty stomach. A month later she complained of "diarrhea and nausea," and was told to discontinue the treatment for several days until the diarrhea stopped. If the symptoms persisted, she was to see a physician. Three days later the plaintiff notified the parish health unit that her eyes appeared jaundiced. She was hospitalized and found to be suffering from hepatitis, secondary to the INH.

In her suit against the defendant physician and the state, the plaintiff accused the defendant of failing to monitor her treatment properly. The trial court held that the plaintiff's evidence failed to establish this allegation and entered judgment for the defendant.

The Court of Appeal of Louisiana affirmed, noting that expert testimony on behalf of the defendant established that he was diligent in his care. The court noted also that in addition to the advice the plaintiff received each time she called the defendant's office to inform them of her complaints, the plaintiff or her husband, when they came in monthly to pick up her medicine, were always asked numerous questions regarding any side effects she may have been experiencing.

ISOTRETINOIN
Accutane

Isotretinoin, manufactured and marketed as Accutane by Roche Laboratories (Nutley, N.J.), is a dermatologic preparation used for the treatment of acne. There are numerous side effects, including but not limited to benign intracranial hypertension (pseudotumor cerebri), decreased night vision, inflammatory bowel disease, hepatotoxicity, headaches, insomnia, elevated triglyceride levels, and exacerbation of arthritis. The drug is teratogenic, and it is contraindicated during pregnancy.[11]

In May 1988, the Association of Trial Lawyers of America (ATLA) announced the formation of a support group for plaintiffs' attorneys in cases involving Accutane. As of that date, ATLA reported that just under forty claims had been filed against the manufacturer. Side effects alleged in these suits included loss of vision, birth defects, and suicide. According to a spokesperson for the

---

[11] *Physicians' Desk Reference,* 42d ed., p. 1705; AMA *Drug Evaluations,* 6th ed., p. 1009.

group, the drug has been given to one out of twenty-three Americans since its introduction in 1982. Also, according to the ATLA group, the FDA has received reports of sixty-six babies born with severe birth defects after their mothers took the drug. (An FDA internal report, however, is said to contain an estimate that between 252 and 1,369 such births occurred between 1982 and 1986.)[12]

At the time of Accutane's approval by the FDA in 1982, the drug was a known animal teratogen, and human teratogenicity was suspected but not verified. The original labeling of the drug instructed physicians to inform women patients of the risk of birth defects, and to prescribe it for women of childbearing age only if pregnancy was excluded and the woman was using an effective method of contraception. When Accutane's human teratogenicity was later confirmed, the labeling was revised, and included instructions that therapy should begin not earlier than two or three days after the beginning of the woman's menstrual period. Despite the warnings, the manufacturer continued to receive reports of birth defects. In addition, a specific embryopathy associated with first trimester exposure to the drug was identified.

The characteristic group of birth defects associated with isotretinoin include external ear malformations, cleft palate, micrognathia, conotruncal heart defects, ventricular septal defects, aortic arch malformations, and certain brain malformations.

There is some evidence that over-prescribing (i.e., prescribing for patients who do not have severe, recalcitrant cystic acne) may be partly responsible for the problem.[13]

Felix v. Hoffmann-LaRoche, Inc. (Fla., 1989) 540 So. 2d 102.

Birth defects—Manufacturer's warning adequate

The mother of the plaintiff in this action received a prescription from her family physician for Accutane for an acne problem. It is unclear from the record whether she was pregnant at the time the physician prescribed the drug, but the plaintiff was born with severe birth defects which were attributed to the Accutane ingested by his mother during pregnancy.

---

[12] ATLA *Products Liability Law Reporter* 7:90, 1988; *National Law Journal,* May 16, 1988, p. 3.

[13] FDA *Drug Bulletin* 18:27 (Nov.), 1988.

In a lawsuit against the manufacturer of Accutane, it was alleged that the defendant breached a duty to the plaintiff by failing to provide an adequate warning that the drug could cause birth defects. The manufacturer defended with the argument that the package insert accompanying the drug warned that "women of child-bearing potential should not be given Accutane unless an effective form of contraception is used, and they should be fully counseled on the potential risk to the fetus should they become pregnant while undergoing treatment. Should pregnancy occur during treatment, the physician and patient should discuss the desirability of continuing the pregnancy period." A similar warning was listed in *Physicians' Desk Reference*.

It was disputed whether the mother's family physician, who was not a defendant in this action, had warned her of the risk involved. The physician did testify, however, that the time he prescribed Accutane, he was aware of the dangers it posed to pregnant women.

The trial court granted the manufacturer's summary judgment, and the District Court of Appeal affirmed (513 So. 2d 1319), holding that the manufacturer's warning regarding possible birth defects was adequate, and that the prescribing physician's knowledge of the drug's propensity to cause birth defects was sufficient to establish that even if the manufacturer's warning was inadequate, it could not have been the proximate cause of the plaintiff's injuries. The Supreme Court of Florida reviewed the case for direct conflict of decisions, and approved the finding of the Court of Appeal.

Noland v. Lichten (No. CV 87-11-3973, Court of Common Pleas, Summit County, Ohio, August 3, 1989).

Severe birth defects—Plaintiff pregnant when drug prescribed—Dermatologist agrees to $2 million structured settlement

The plaintiff consulted the defendant, a dermatologist, about her acne problem. He told he would like to prescribe Accutane, but he explained the risk involved with women patients of child-bearing years, and had her sign a consent form stating that she was not pregnant. Although at the time, the plaintiff had not had a menstrual period for sixty days, she signed the form. Several days later, she discovered that she was indeed pregnant. The plaintiff's child was born with heart and brain defects, and is now profoundly mentally retarded and suffers from generalized spasticity and truncal hypotonia.

In her malpractice action against the defendant, the plaintiff alleged that he was negligent in failing to perform a pregnancy test before prescribing the drug, and that he could have prescribed a less potent drug for her acne. The defendant contended that the plaintiff was herself negligent for failing to inform him of her missed menstrual periods.

According to the plaintiff's attorney, the parties agreed to a structured settlement with a present value of $2 million, compounded at 5% annually, calling for $875,000 in cash, periodic lump sum payments totaling $775,000, and monthly payments of $5,000 for the life of the child.[14]

Simi v. Hoffmann-LaRoche (No. A8605 02536, Circuit Court, Multnomah County, Ore., July 29, 1988).

Cataracts—Spectroscopic studies establish Accutane as cause—Manufacturer settles with plaintiff

A dermatologist prescribed Accutane for the plaintiff's acne. Two months after he stopped taking the drug, the plaintiff noticed that his vision had become impaired. Tests revealed severe bilateral subcapsular cataracts. In his lawsuit against the manufacturer, the plaintiff introduced the results of spectroscopic studies on the lens matter that had been removed during his lens implant procedure. These studies established that the plaintiff's use of Accutane was a substantial factor in causing his cataracts. During trial, the parties agreed to a confidential settlement.[15]

J

JAYNE'S P-W VERMIFUGE

See HEXYLRESORCINOL

K

KANAMYCIN

Kantrex

Kanamycin, manufactured under the name Kantrex (kanamycin sulfate) by Bristol Laboratories (Syracuse, N.Y.), is a bactericidal

[14] ATLA *Professional Negligence Law Reporter* 5:32, 1990.
[15] ATLA *Products Liability Law Reporter* 8:7, 1989.

antibiotic indicated for treatment of serious infections caused by susceptible strains of various microorganisms.[16] The drug has an antibacterial spectrum similar to gentamicin and neomycin.[17]

The major toxic effect of kanamycin is its action on the auditory portion of the eighth cranial nerve. High frequency deafness usually occurs first and can be detected by audiometric testing. Tinnitus or vertigo may occur and are evidence of impending bilateral, irreversible deafness. In patients with impaired kidney function, this risk is sharply increased, and in such cases the daily dosage should be reduced and the interval between doses lengthened. If there is evidence of progressive renal dysfunction during therapy, audiometric tests and discontinuation of the drug should be considered. Older patients should also be observed closely.[18]

Because of the possible effects of kanamycin on the eighth cranial nerve and the kidneys, other drugs capable of eliciting these responses can compound the problem and should be avoided during or in close sequence following systemic administration of kanamycin.[19] Antibiotics in this group include streptomycin, neomycin, paromomycin, gentamicin, and polymyxins.[20]

Marsh v. Arnold (Tex. Civ. App., 1969) 446 S.W.2d 949.

Hearing loss—Question of proper drug and disclosure of risk—Verdict for urologist upheld

The patient was admitted to the hospital on March 23, 1963 because of urinary bleeding. The defendant-physician, a urologist, examined the patient's bladder with a cystoscope, and found an inflamed area near the prostate. A biopsy and X-ray examination were done, the X-rays disclosing a rare condition — calcified seminal vesicles. This did not explain the bleeding or rule out cancer, however, and the examination was extended to the kidneys.

Because of the apparent inflammatory condition and because of an expected "cystoscopic reaction," the defendant decided on antibiotic therapy. Tests indicated bacteria from the prostate area were sensitive to four antibiotics, Dimocillin (methicillin), Chloromycetin (chloramphenicol), Declomycin (demelhylchlortetracy-

[16] *Physicians' Desk Reference,* 35th ed., p. 711.
[17] *AMA Drug Evaluations,* 2d ed., p. 570.
[18] *Physicians' Desk Reference,* 35th ed., p. 710.
[19] *United States Dispensatory,* 27th ed., p. 654.
[20] Id.

cline), and Kantrex. Declomycin was tried first, but after a day the patient turned worse, and was given Terramycin (oxytetracycline) by injection, intravenous fluids and other supportive measures. A day and a half later, when his fever again rose, he was started on Kantrex. Two days following this, the defendant irrigated the patient's seminal vesicles with a solution containing neomycin.

The patient began to improve and was eventually discharged. In all, he had received fifteen grams of Kantrex during his seven and one-half days of hospitalization.

At home he soon began to develop "equilibrium problems" and he was referred to an ear, nose and throat specialist, Dr. D., whose diagnosis was "loss of equilibrium function with no response to tests stimulating the inner ear." Dr. D. testified at length at the trial and was the patient's only medical witness. He said the patient had told him of a gradual and progressive hearing loss of five years' duration, and of a "tinnitus" or ringing sound in both ears which had been present for three years. The patient, said Dr. D., had worked around loud machinery for about twenty years, and in such work one can develop ringing in the ears, which is commonly called "boilermakers' deafness."

According to Dr. D., the patient had no more hearing loss than would be expected of a man of his age and work history, and there was no way he (Dr. D.) could say that the patient suffered any hearing loss while hospitalized. (There was evidence, however, that this witness was not aware at the time of how much Kantrex the patient had received, or what other drugs he had been given.) Dr. D. did testify that although the cause of the patient's deafness was "obscure" he (Dr. D.), wrote in "Kantrex" as the cause on the patient's insurance forms, mainly, he said, because he knew of medical literature that recognized deafness as one of the effects of Kantrex.

The defendant-physician's testimony was to the effect that he gave the patient Kantrex because he felt under the circumstances it was necessary. The possible outcome, without the drug, being bacterial septicemia, which could be fatal. Furthermore, the defendant said, in 1963 there was no other effective treatment available for a condition such as that presented by the patient. He added that if the same circumstances arose again, he would prescribe the same drug. He said that he had treated about 100 patients in his practice with Kantrex, all without "bad results."

The question of informed consent was raised, and the defendant said he was sure he had discussed possible hearing loss with the patient. While the defendant stated that he did not inform the patient of the specific risk of "damage to the vestibular portion of the eighth cranial nerve" from the use of Kantrex, he said that generally all necessary warnings and disclosures were carefully given, including the possibility of death or serious injury from the use of drugs.

The jury returned a verdict in favor of the defendant, and judgment was entered accordingly. The Court of Civil Appeals of Texas affirmed.

Bochum v. Sherman Hosp. (No. 70L-10196, Circuit Court, Kane County, Ill., Sept. 28, 1973).

Hearing loss—Possible synergistic action of several antibiotics—$675,000 judgment against manufacturer—Physicians and hospital not liable

The patient, a 62-year-old man, underwent a double operation: a hernia repair and a skin graft for an ulcer on his lower leg. Both operative sites became infected and the graft was unsuccessful. The patient was administered daily doses of a combination of 7 gm. of streptomycin, 2.85 gm. of Coly-Mycin (cholistimethate), and 13 gm. of Kantrex. The patient later developed vestibular paralysis of the inner ear and became totally deaf.

A lawsuit was brought against the two physicians who treated the patient, the hospital, and the manufacturer of Kantrex. It was alleged against the physicians that they should have known not to mix the antibiotics. Against the manufacturer, the patient charged that the current package insert did not contain information warning physicians about adverse reactions when three drugs such as these were combined, information that, according to the patient, was available from clinical research. It was further alleged that six years previously a physician had recommended eight guidelines for using Kantrex, but that the manufacturer had omitted some of these in its package inserts, including the one pertaining to combining the drug with other antibiotics. The patient also charged that the manufacturer had failed to investigate another researcher's report about possible adverse reactions. And, at the trial, one of the patient's physicians testified that, had he known about the possible adverse reactions from combining the antibiotics, he would not have prescribed Kantrex for the patient.

The jury found no liability on the part of the physicians and the hospital, but returned a verdict of $675,000 against the manufacturer.[21]

Bristol-Myers Co. v. Gonzales (Tex., 1978) 561 S.W.2d 801.

Hearing loss—$100,000 settlement with physician and $400,000 judgment against manufacturer—Judgment reversed for failure to disclose settlement

The plaintiff in this action was a 25-year-old male admitted to the hospital because of a severe pain in his leg caused by a hip infection. On discovering the source of the problem, his physician started him on Kantrex, first tablets, and then injection. Over the next two weeks he was given a total of 20.5 grams of the drug by this route. In addition, following surgical treatment of the infection, the physician started continuous irrigation of the wound with alternating solutions of Kantrex and neomycin. The total amount of these drugs which the plaintiff received through absorption into his body is not known, but at some time during his stay in the hospital he suffered irreversible hearing loss due to damage to the auditory nerve.

In his suit against his physician and the manufacturers of both drugs, the plaintiff settled with the physician shortly before trial for $100,000 under a "Mary Carter Agreement." He also dismissed as against Upjohn Company, the manufacturer of the neomycin because, according to his attorney, "he did not believe it was liable." His action against Bristol-Myers, manufacturer of Kantrex, went to the jury who found that the company had failed to give the plaintiff's physician "adequate warnings and specific instructions" in the 1970 edition of *Physicians' Desk Reference* regarding use of the drug. A verdict of $800,000 was returned against the company. This was later reduced to $400,000.

On appeal, the Supreme Court of Texas held that the evidence supported the jury's finding that the manufacturer's warning was inadequate, citing expert testimony that "the PDR entry should have warned a physician to treat the infection, if possible, with a drug less noxious than Kantrex and that the wound should be irrigated one time only, as a post-surgical wash, because significant amounts of the drug would otherwise be absorbed in continuous irrigation."

---

[21] AMA *The Citation* 28:112, 1974.

The reviewing court also found that Bristol-Myers had known that the warning was inadequate "long before" it was known to the Food and Drug Administration which approved the package insert.

The court reversed the judgment, however, because the existence of the settlement agreement between the plaintiff and his physician had not been made known to the jury.

Van Iperen v. Van Bramer (Iowa, 1986) 392 N.W.2d 480.

Hearing loss—Kanamycin and neomycin used in rectal flush—Insufficient evidence of lack of informed consent and hospital negligence

The plaintiff was treated with kanamycin and neomycin in the form of a "rectal flush" because of a fistula that developed in his bladder wall following intestinal surgery and an ileostomy. After periodic hospitalizations over a period of five months during which time he received from two to three flushes daily, the plaintiff developed hearing loss. There was a dispute as to whether the plaintiff was informed of this risk by his physicians, and the jury decided this issue in favor of the defendants. The reviewing court held that this decision was supported by substantial evidence.

Also at issue was the trial court's directed verdict in favor of the hospital despite the plaintiff's contention that the hospital had not met the standards of the Joint Commission on the Accreditation of Hospitals which require that, within the limits of available resources, a hospital should provide drug monitoring services through its pharmacy which includes a review of every patient's drug regimen for any potential adverse reactions. The Supreme Court of Iowa held that while hospital accreditation standards provide some evidence of the proper standard of care, the evidence presented by the plaintiff was insufficient "without additional reliable interpretative data" to generate a jury issue on this question.

Related cases

Hearing loss following extensive antibiotic therapy

In Schering Corp. v. Giesecke (Tex. Civ. App., 1979) 589 S.W.2d 516, a patient being treated for peritonitis following colon surgery was given extensive antibiotic therapy, including kanamycin and gentamicin sulfate (Garamycin). A week later he suffered total hearing loss. The case is summarized herein under GENTAMICIN SULFATE.

In Dillon v. Herren (No. C18319, Superior Court, Los Angeles County, Cal., April 5, 1977), a jury awarded a woman patient $950,000 when one of her physicians, unaware that a second physician had already prescribed sixteen grams of kanamycin, prescribed additional doses of the drug, bringing the total dosage to 56 grams, and causing the patient to suffer irreversible loss of hearing.

Loss of sight after Keflex and Kantrex therapy—No breach of warranty action against manufacturers

In McCarthy v. Bristol Laboratories Division of Bristol-Myers Co. (1982) 86 App. Div. 2d 279, 449 N.Y.S.2d 280, a plaintiff who suffered loss of sight following treatment of a kidney infection with Keflex and Kantrex had no cause of action for breach of warranty against the manufacturers of the drugs where there was no privity of contract between her and the defendants.

KANTREX
See KANAMYCIN

KEFLEX
See CEPHALEXIN MONOHYDRATE

KEFLIN
See CEPHALOTHIN SODIUM

KENACORT
See TRIAMCINOLONE ACETONIDE

KENALOG
See TRIAMCINOLONE ACETONIDE

KESSO-BAMATE
See MEPROBAMATE

KEVADON
See THALIDOMIDE

L

LAETRILE
See AMYGDALIN

LANIAZID
See ISONIAZID

LANOXIN
See DIGOXIN

LASIX
See FUROSEMIDE

LAZERSPORIN-C
See NEOMYCIN SULFATE

LEDERCILLIN VK
See PENICILLIN

LERITINE
See ANILERIDINE

LEVARTERENOL BITARTRATE
See NOREPINEPHRINE BITARTRATE

LEVOPHED BITARTRATE
See NOREPINEPHRINE BITARTRATE

LIBRAX
See CHLORDIAZEPOXIDE HYDROCHLORIDE

LIBRIUM
See CHLORDIAZEPOXIDE HYDROCHLORIDE

LIDOCAINE HYDROCHLORIDE
Anestacon
Embolex
Xylocaine

Lidocaine hydrochloride has cardiac antiarrythmic properties and is also used as a local anesthetic. The product is available in various strengths and solutions. Frequently it is combined with epinephrine, a vasoconstrictor.

Anestacon is manufactured by Webcon Pharmaceuticals (Ft. Worth, Tex.), Embolex by Sandoz Pharmaceuticals (East Hanover, N.J.), and Xylocaine by Astra Pharmaceutical Products Inc. (Worcester, Mass.). The drug is also produced by several manufacturers under the generic name.

Allergic reactions can be serious, and are characterized by cutaneous lesions, urticaria, edema or anaphylactoid reactions. The manufacturer of Xylocaine warns in the product literature that resuscitative equipment and drugs should be immediately available when Xylocaine (or any local anesthetic) is used.[21]

LeBeuf v. Atkins (1980) 28 Wash. App. 50, 621 P.2d 787.

**Possible subarachnoid hemorrhage in hypertensive patient—
Dentist fails to take patient's blood pressure—
Summary judgment reversed**

A patient was given Xylocaine by his dentist prior to an extraction. Immediately after the tooth was removed the patient became violently ill. He was admitted to the hospital the following day with a preliminary diagnosis of cerebral hemorrhage. His condition worsened, causing eventual total disability and death.

At trial it was revealed that the morning he was to have the tooth removed, the patient was suffering from a severe headache. An expert testified that in his opinion the patient was suffering from hypertension, and that the injection of Xylocaine, which contains the vasoconstrictor epinephrine, "probably caused the ensuing damage to Claude LeBeuf's central nervous system and it is more likely than not that this resulted in a subarachnoid hemorrhage."

It was also revealed that the dentist did not take the patient's blood pressure prior to administering the Xylocaine, although the manufacturer warns about its use with patients suffering from hypertension or cardiovascular disease.

A summary judgment for the defendant-dentist was reversed by the Court of Appeals of Washington.

Stalum v. Evangelical Hosp. Ass'n (No. 75-L-5981, Circuit Court, Cook County, Ill., Aug. 27, 1981).

**Allergic reaction during cystoscopy—Permanent mental retardation—
$1.5 million settlement by urologist and hospital**

The plaintiff, a sixteen-year-old boy, was admitted to the defendant hospital complaining of urinary retention. Attempts to

---

[21]*Physicians' Desk Reference,* 43th ed., pp. 537-538.

catheterize the plaintiff were unsuccessful, and he was scheduled for a cystoscopy. Upon learning that the hospital anesthesiologist was not available to administer general anesthesia, the urologist elected to proceed using Xylocaine. Immediately upon administration of the anesthetic, the plaintiff suffered cardiac arrest and convulsions which, because of the hospital personnel's delay in responding, were not controlled for forty-five minutes. The plaintiff suffered brain damage and is permanently mentally retarded.

Among other things, the urologist was charged with negligence in administering a local anesthetic on a "young, apprehensive patient whose urethra already had been traumatized by the unsuccessful catheterization attempts," and in failing to take proper precautionary measures including anesthesiological consultation. The hospital staff was also charged with negligence in failing to respond immediately to the plaintiff's cardiac arrest and convulsions. The case was settled for $1.5 million, with the urologist contributing $1.2 million of that amount.[22]

Morris v. Roseville Community Hospital (No. 49251, Superior Court, Placer County, Cal., July 27, 1982).

Mother given Xylocaine late in labor—Child born with brain damage—$677,500 settlement

The plaintiff was an eight-year-old boy who was born with brain damage resulting in cerebral palsy and spastic quadriplegia. The plaintiff claimed the condition was the result of his mother being administered Xylocaine for a paracervical block late in labor. The defendants were the physician who had administered the injection, the hospital, and the manufacturer of the drug, Astra Pharmaceutical, whom the plaintiff claimed failed to warn the medical profession adequately of the danger posed to the fetus in the event of an excessive dose to the mother. The parties settled for $677,500.[1]

Stanton by Brooks v. Astra Pharmaceutical Products, Inc. (C.A.-3 Pa., 1983) 718 F.2d 553.

Brain damage in infant from adverse reaction—$2.3 million award reversed for procedural errors

The eight-month-old female infant was hospitalized for anemia. A bone marrow aspiration was performed and Xylocaine was in-

[22] ATLA *Law Reporter* 25:90, 1982.
[1] Id., 25:375, 1982.

jected into the posterior iliac crest to anesthetize the area. Twenty minutes later, the infant convulsed and suffered two respiratory arrests and cardiac stoppage. She had permanent and severe brain damage.

At trial it was alleged, among other things, that the manufacturer of Xylocaine negligently failed to test it, and failed to file adverse reaction reports with the FDA between 1964 and 1971. The manufacturer denied knowledge of any adverse reactions. The jury found for the plaintiff and awarded $315,000. Because of a change in the Pennsylvania law regarding calculation of damages, however, the district court granted a new trial limited to computation of compensatory damages. This time the plaintiff obtained a $2.3 million verdict.

But on appeal this verdict was reversed, the Court of Appeals finding that it was error to retry the case only on the damage issue, because it could not be said that the questions of liability and damages "were so separable that the jury's determination of the one had no bearing on its determination of the other." The Court of Appeals did find, however, that the manufacturer should have filed the adverse reaction reports and that the evidence was sufficient to support a verdict for the plaintiff.

Hart v. Landers (No. 87-15921-H, 160th Judicial District Court, Dallas County, Tex., May 25, 1988).

Heart patient given excessive dosage—$1.1 million settlement with hospital

The patient, a commercial artist, was admitted to the hospital suffering from a heart attack. After initial treatment, he was placed in the intensive care unit where the standard procedure called for the administration of 50 mg. of lidocaine hydrochloride to control premature ventricular contractions. Instead, a nurse administered 1,000 mg. of lidocaine from a prepackaged syringe which was supposed to be diluted in IV fluid for drip administration. The patient suffered a cardiac arrest and died several hours later.

The plaintiffs alleged negligence on the part of the nurses in administering the excessive dosage, and on the part of the hospital for storing the two forms of dosages next to each other.

The parties entered into a structured settlement worth $1.1 million.[2]

---

[2] ATLA *Professional Negligence Law Reporter* 4:10, 1989.

Feldburg v. Sun Towers Hosp. (No. 87-8421, 65th Judicial District Court, El Paso County, Tex., March 1, 1989).

Emergency department patient given fatal overdose—Cause of death covered up—$2.02 million settlement

The patient was taken to the emergency department of the Sun Towers Hospital, El Paso, Texas, suffering from chest pains. An emergency department physician performed an EKG and ordered 100 mg. of lidocaine hydrochloride intravenously. The emergency department nurse, however, mistaken administered twenty times the prescribed dosage. The patient immediately went into convulsions and died.

The nurse did not inform the physician of her mistake, and he told the patient's wife that the patient had died from a heart attack. Two weeks later, as a result of an internal investigation, the physician learned of the overdose, but he did not inform the patient's family nor change the death certificate, which listed cardiac arrest as the cause of the death.

Seven years later an anonymous caller informed the patient's family of the true cause of his death. In their suit against the hospital, they sought punitive damages, alleging fraud, intentional and negligent infliction of emotional distress, and civil conspiracy. The hospital moved for summary judgment, which the trial judge denied. The plaintiffs then settled with the hospital's insurance company for $2.02 million.[3]

Related cases

Alleged allergic reaction—Jury case established against manufacturer

In Trebesch v. Astra Pharmaceutical Products, Inc. (D. Minn., 1980) 503 F. Supp. 79, the plaintiff, trustee for the heirs of a patient who died following an alleged adverse reaction to Xylocaine administered by a dentist, moved for partial summary judgment on the basis of the judgment in the Stanton case (see above) which, argued the plaintiff, collaterally estopped Astra Pharmaceutical Products from controverting its negligence in failing to file required adverse reaction reports and in failing to exercise reasonable care to monitor and investigate adverse reactions to Xylocaine. The plaintiff's motion was denied because post-trial motions in the Stanton case were still pending. The defendant's motion for partial summary

[3] ATLA *Professional Negligence Law Reporter* 4:132, 1989.

judgment was also denied with the court holding that Astra failed to show that there were no disputed issues of material fact as to whether it had a duty to report adverse reactions to Xylocaine to the FDA prior to 1971, as to whether there was evidence to support claims of overpromotion and false advertising, and as to whether the patient did experience an allergic reaction to the drug.

Fatal adverse reaction—No case against FDA

A Minnesota plaintiff was unsuccessful in an attempt to impose liability on the federal government for the death of a patient from an adverse reaction to Xylocaine on the theory that the Food and Drug Administration "negligently failed to withdraw its prior approval of Xylocaine and negligently failed to enforce the provisions of the Food, Drug and Cosmetic Act and its own regulations relating to information collection and labeling changes, thereby allowing Xylocaine to remain in interstate commerce in a misbranded and/or adulterated condition." Gelley v. Astra Pharmaceutical Products, Inc. (C.A.-8 Minn., 1979) 610 F.2d 558.

Overdose causes cardiac arrest—Action barred by statute despite cover-up

In Sharrow v. Archer (Alaska, 1983) 658 P.2d 1331, the plaintiff received a "massive overdose" of lidocaine by mistake following an operation. As a result she suffered cardiac arrest, but was resuscitated by the medical staff. The physician in charge later told the nurses they were not to report the mistake to the plaintiff and the hospital records were altered to delete any mention of the overdose. Another physician, however, told the plaintiff of the incident, and it was reported in the newspapers when the physician who ordered the cover-up was suspended. Despite this knowledge, the plaintiff failed to file her action within the two-year statute of limitations. Her case was dismissed and the Supreme Court affirmed, holding that the defendant could be estopped from raising the statute of limitations as a defense only if the plaintiff's delay in bringing suit was occasioned by reliance on his fraudulent concealment. This the plaintiff had failed to prove.

Excessive administration of Xylocaine and other drugs during office surgery

In Kemble v. Antonetti (No. 87-1002-B, 44th Judicial District Court, Dallas County, Tex., January 29, 1988), a plastic surgeon administered excessive Xylocaine and other drugs during breast augmentation surgery. The case is summarized herein under FENTANYL.

LIMBITROL
See AMITRIPTYLINE

LINCOCIN
See LINCOMYCIN

LINCOMYCIN
Lincocin

Lincomycin, manufactured by The Upjohn Company (Kalamazoo, Mich.) under the name Lincocin, is an antibacterial agent used primarily to treat infections caused by organisms that are resistant to the penicillins and erythromycin, or for patients who cannot tolerate other antibacterial agents.[4]

In the beginning, few serious reactions were observed during treatment with lincomycin. Hypersensitivity reactions occasionally seen with antibiotics occurred, but generally these were mild, most often consisting of pruritus, rash, urticaria, swelling, exfoliative dermatitis, and in some cases anaphylactic reactions and serum sickness.[5] There were some effects on the formation of blood cells, but this was rare, and usually reversible following withdrawal of the drug. Gastrointestinal disturbances were reported, including nausea, vomiting and abdominal cramps, and occasionally persistent and severe diarrhea.[6] These were not considered serious until 1975, when the Food and Drug Administration reported at least 26 fatalities in which lincomycin, or its semisynthetic derivative clindamycin (Cleocin — The Upjohn Company), "played a major or contributing role in the death."[7]

As a result, product literature, revised March 17, 1975, contained the following warning:

> Lincomycin can cause severe colitis which may end fatally. Therefore, it should be reserved for serious infections where less toxic antimicrobial agents are inappropriate.... It should not be used in patients with nonbacterial infections, such as most upper

---

[4] *AMA Drug Evaluations,* 2d ed., p. 534.
[5] Id.
[6] Id.
[7] *American Medical News,* February 10, 1975, p. 10.

respiratory tract infections.... The colitis is usually characterized by severe, persistent diarrhea and severe abdominal cramps and may be associated with the passage of blood and mucus. Endoscopic examination may reveal pseudomembranous colitis.

When significant diarrhea occurs, the drug should be discontinued or, if necessary, continued only with close observation of the patient. Large bowel endoscopy has been recommended.

Antiperistaltic agents such as opiates and diphenoxylate with atropine (Lomotil) may prolong and/or worsen the condition....

Diarrhea, colitis, and pseudomembranous colitis have been observed to begin up to several weeks following cessation of therapy with lincomycin.[8]

Johnston v. Upjohn Co. (Mo. App., 1969) 442 S.W.2d 93.

Patient hypersensitive to drug—Manufacturer's warning based on knowledge at time satisfactory—Physician not liable

A woman patient developed a "hurting in her ear" and consulted her physician who diagnosed the problem as otitis media. He recommended an antibiotic, but the patient told him that she had suffered reactions to both penicillin and streptomycin during the previous year, and that an internist whom she had consulted had advised her not to take any more antibiotics. She showed the physician a "medical alert bracelet" indicating an allergy to the two drugs. The physician told her that in view of her allergy, he would use Lincocin, from which she should have no "ill effects." The physician's nurse gave the patient an injection of Lincocin and a prescription for fifteen tablets to be taken at a rate of three per day. The patient took these as directed.

The patient received her injection on July 31, 1965. On August 8, she felt a little "under par" and was "tense." On August 10 or 11 she experienced a "breaking-out" on her face, and severe itching. She called her internist who prescribed corticotropin (ACTH) and cream for the rash. Her condition improved temporarily, but then worsened, with swelling, rash, itching and blistering over most of her body.

On August 20, the patient was hospitalized where she was given more ACTH and wrapped in saline packs. By this time, almost 95% of her body was affected. Her condition finally began to improve and she was discharged five days later. At the time of trial, however, she was not fully recovered and still suffered some itching, rash and swelling.

---

[8]*Physicians' Desk Reference,* 35th ed., p. 1824.

At the trial, evidence was introduced as to the development and testing of the drug Lincocin. The package insert was introduced which stated, with regard to the treatment of otitis media, that such patients "have been treated with good clinical results in the majority of cases" and that "Lincocin has been administered to over 460 persons with known allergies (including persons reported to be allergic to penicillin). No serious hypersensitivity reactions have been reported in these patients and many patients have received repeated courses of Lincocin without developing evidence of hypersensitivity." The insert also stated that cross-resistance has not been demonstrated with penicillin or streptomycin.

With regard to adverse reactions, the package insert stated:

> The most frequently observed side effect has been loose stools or diarrhea.... Other adverse reactions reported in a small per cent of patients have been nausea, vomiting, abdominal cramps or pain, skin rash, rectal irritation, vaginitis, urticaris, and itching. Angioneurotic edema, serum sickness, anaphylaxis or other serious hypersensitivity reactions have not been reported.

There was testimony that the package insert, which bore a date of May, 1965, was identical to the insert in use since late 1964, when the drug was first made available to the public. The plaintiff offered no evidence that the drug company was aware of any adverse reaction which was not contained in the package insert.

The jury returned a verdict in favor of the physician, but against the drug company. The trial judge, however, granted a new trial in favor of the company and the plaintiff appealed this order. The Kansas City Court of Appeals reversed the order granting a new trial, and remanded the case with directions to enter judgment in favor of the company. The reviewing court stated:

> There is no evidence that anyone had ever suffered a reaction to Lincocin different in nature or more serious than that described in the package insert. If such reaction had never occurred before, defendant [The Upjohn Company] could not know about it or in the exercise of the required degree of care, could not have found out about it, and absent knowledge of such reaction, there could be no duty to warn.

Barkan v. Upjohn Pharmaceutical Co. (No. 25-92-42, Superior Court, Orange County, Cal., Jan. 22, 1982).

Kidney failure after six weeks of treatment with Lincocin—Manufacturer failed to warn—$5.9 million jury verdict

A twenty-three-year-old premed student was placed on Lincocin in 1975 for acne. After six weeks on the drug he was admitted to the hospital for kidney failure. In 1977 both kidneys were removed, and in 1979, his spleen. At the time of trial he was required to spend four hours a day, three days a week, on a dialysis machine.

In his suit against the manufacturer, the plaintiff contended that the defendant knew as early as 1969 that the drug could cause kidney problems but failed to notify the FDA or the medical profession. Prior to trial, the plaintiff offered to settle for $3,000,000 plus funding for a kidney foundation. The defendant offered $50,000. The jury awarded $5.9 million.[9]

Mauldin v. Upjohn Co. (C.A.-5 La., 1983) 697 F.2d 644.

Ulcerative colitis following treatment with Cleocin and Lincocin—$570,000 verdict against manufacturer for inadequate warning affirmed

The plaintiff was given both Lincocin and Cleocin to guard against infection following a severe hand injury. He soon experienced diarrhea and eventually developed ulcerative colitis, requiring extensive surgery and hospital confinement. He filed suit against the Upjohn Company, manufacturer of both drugs, for failure to warn adequately of the side effect he experienced. The jury awarded him $570,000.

On appeal the defendant argued that the evidence on causation was strictly circumstantial, and that the plaintiff's physician testified that he would have prescribed the same two medications despite a stronger warning. In affirming the award, the Court of Appeal pointed out that proof of causation can be established by circumstantial evidence, and that the plaintiff's physician also testified that if he had known of the possible severity of the side effects, he would have followed a "different regimen" in using the drugs.

Rodriguez v. Nauenberg (No. 82 Civ. 5940, U.S. District Court, S.D. N.Y., March 10, 1983).

Choice of drug questioned—Improper injection—$182,000 obtained for partial loss of use of arm

The plaintiff, a twenty-seven-year-old male, received three daily injections of Lincocin from his family physician for an upper respiratory condition. On the third day he lost sensation in his arm and suffered wrist drop. He was diagnosed as having right radial nerve

---

[9] ATLA *Law Reporter* 25:226, 1982.

paralysis and ultimately sustained a permanent 20% loss of function of the wrist and arm. In his lawsuit the plaintiff alleged that the Lincocin was contraindicated because the manufacturer's package insert stated that the drug was not recommended for the treatment of upper respiratory infections. Also, the plaintiff contended that the injection was administered improperly in that it was given in the area below the deltoid muscle where the radial nerve lies just beneath the skin instead of the deltoid muscle area where the nerve lies beneath the bone. The parties settled for $182,500.[10]

Related cases

"Discovery rule" applicable in action against Lincocin manufacturer

In Bonney v. The Upjohn Company (1983) 129 Mich. App. 18, 342 N.W.2d 551, the Court of Appeals of Michigan held that the "discovery rule" applies to products liability claims against drug manufacturers, and the question of when a plaintiff discovered or should have discovered that he had a cause of action against the manufacturer of Lincocin for a "variety of psychological and physical disorders," should be decided by a jury.

LIQUAEMIN

See HEPARIN SODIUM

LIQUID PRED SYRUP

See PREDINISONE

LOESTRIN

See NORETHINDRONE ACETATE with ETHINYL ESTRADIOL

LOMOTIL

See DIPHENOXYLATE HYDROCHLORIDE with ATROPINE SULFATE

---

[10] Id., 26:473, 1983.

LOPURIN
See ALLOPURINOL

LORCET
See PROPOXYPHENE HYDROCHLORIDE

LOXAPINE SUCCINATE
Loxitane

Loxapine succinate is a major tranquilizer recommended for the management of manifestations of psychotic disorders. It is manufactured and marketed under the name Loxitane by Lederle Laboratories (Wayne, N.J.). As with virtually all major tranquilizers, there are numerous possible adverse reactions. The drug is issued with an extensive warning regarding the risk of tardive dyskinesia.[11]

American Cyanamid v. Frankson (Tex. App., 1987) 732 S.W.2d 648.

Tardive dyskinesia following treatment with Loxitane— $3.3 million jury award against manufacturer for failure to warn

The patient, who suffered a head injury when thrown from a horse, was given Loxitane at the hospital. He became combative, confused, incoherent and lethargic, and eventually was diagnosed as suffering from tardive dyskinesia.

In a lawsuit against the patient's psychiatrist and neurosurgeon, and Lederle Laboratories, the manufacturer of Loxitane, it was alleged that Lederle failed to give adequate warnings or instructions for the safe use of Loxitane, and that the physicians failed to obtain the patient's informed consent to being treated with the drug and failed to warn the patient or his family of its possible side effects.

The jury held Lederle 100% liable and awarded the patient, a veterinarian who had been earning $37,000 per year, a total of $2,695,000 in damages, which included $500,000 in punitive damages. No negligence was found on the part of the physicians. The verdict was affirmed on appeal.

---

[11] *Physicians' Desk Reference,* 41st ed., p. 1099.

Related cases

"Extremely small risk" of tardive dyskinesia sufficient to take case to jury on informed consent issue

In Barclay v. Campbell (Tex., 1986) 704 S.W.2d 8, the Supreme Court of Texas held that expert testimony that the risk of contracting tardive dyskinesia from the use of a drug was "small to extremely small" constituted "some evidence that the risk was material enough to influence a reasonable person in his decision to give or withhold consent to the procedure," and therefore a directed verdict in favor of the physician on the issue of informed consent was improper.

LOXITANE

See LOXAPINE SUCCINATE

M

MACRODANTIN

See NITROFURANTOIN

MAGNESIUM CARBONATE with ALUMINUM HYDROXIDE

Estomul

Estomul, formerly manufactured in tablet and liquid form by Riker Laboratories, Inc. (Northridge, Cal.), contained aluminum hydroxide, magnesium carbonate, bismuth aluminate and orphenadrine hydrochloride. It was used in the treatment of peptic ulcer, hyperacidity, and related disorders. Possible side effects included skin reactions (urticaria and other dermatoses), but these were considered rare.[12]

Dermatological reaction in patient receiving Estomul and five other drugs

In Slack v. Fleet (La. App., 1970) 242 So. 2d 650, a middle-aged woman patient who complained to her physician of "pain and cramping in the stomach, nausea, vomiting and nervousness" was given prescriptions for Estomul and five other drugs. She took the drugs simultaneously, as directed, and developed a severe rash. In the resulting lawsuit a question arose over the propriety of pre-

---

[12] *Physicians' Desk Reference*, 27th ed., pp. 1143-44.

scribing that particular combination of drugs in a case such as the plaintiff's. The defendant-physician offered two medical witnesses who testified that his choice of medication was within acceptable standards. The plaintiff offered no expert testimony. The trial court dismissed the action and was upheld on appeal. The case is summarized herein under PHENACETIN.

MAGNESIUM TRISILICATE with ALUMINUM HYDROXIDE
Gaviscon
Gelusil

Magnesium trisilicate is a weak antacid. It reacts with hydrochloric acid in the stomach to form hydrated silicon dioxide which may provide symptomatic relief from the pain of an ulcer by coating the crater. It also has absorbent properties.[13] The drug is frequently combined with aluminum hydroxide, also an antacid. A mixture of 500 mg. magnesium trisilicate and 250 mg. aluminum hydroxide (in both tablet and liquid form) was manufactured by Warner/Chilcott, a division of Warner-Lambert Company (Morris Plains, N.J.) under the brand name Gelusil.[14] (Today, Gelusil contains magnesium hydroxide instead of magnesium trisilicate[15] and is manufactured by Parke-Davis, a division of Warner-Lambert, Inc.) Gaviscon is manufactured by Marion Laboratories, Inc. (Kansas City, Mo.).

The most common adverse reactions associated with prolonged use of this antacid were constipation or diarrhea. Formation of fecal concretions (impactions) was also an occasional complication.[16]

O'Malia v. Oakes (No. 360174, Superior Court, Alameda County, Cal., 1971).

Impaction, bowel perforation and gangrene—Case against manufacturer dismissed—Two of three physicians found not liable

A 57-year-old male patient suffering from gastrointestinal bleeding was treated with Gelusil and other drugs. The patient's colon became impacted, resulting in obstruction and perforation of the

---

[13] *AMA Drug Evaluations,* 2d ed., p. 789.
[14] Id., p. 790.
[15] *Physicians' Desk Reference,* 35th ed., p. 1352.
[16] *AMA Drug Evaluations,* 2d ed., p. 786.

small bowel which led to peritonitis. A colostomy was performed, but gangrene had developed, and the patient died.

A lawsuit was brought against the physicians who had attended the patient, and against the manufacturer of Gelusil. It was contended that the Gelusil, together with the other drugs, caused a "complete shutdown of bowel motility." The plaintiff charged specifically that the defendants were negligent in not seeking consultation with a specialist in gastrointestinal disorders, and in failing to take steps to prevent the impaction.

The defendants contended that the risk of colon impaction in the patient's case had been remote, and that it could not have been the result of the Gelusil and the other drugs. They contended that while constipation was anticipated, and that laxatives were given to counteract this, the bowel obstruction was entirely unexpected and was due to other causes.

The manufacturer of Gelusil was granted a nonsuit, and after a two-day deliberation, the jury returned a verdict for two of the three physicians. The disposition of the charge against the third physician was not revealed in the report of the case.[17]

MARCAINE

See BUPIVACAINE HYDROCHLORIDE

MAXZIDE

See TRIAMTERENE

MEASLES VACCINE

Attenuvax

Measles virus vaccine (live) is used for immunization against measles in persons 15 months of age or older. At one time several drug companies manufactured and marketed the vaccine, but currently, only Merck, Sharp & Dohme (West Point, Pa.) offers the product (Attenuvax).[18]

Merck, Sharp & Dohme reports that "[e]xperience with more than 80 million doses of all live measles vaccine given in the U.S. through 1975 indicates that significant central nervous system reactions such as encephalitis and encephalopathy, occurring within 30 days after vaccination, have been temporarily associated with

---

[17] AMA *The Citation* 24:99, 1972.

[18] *Physicians' Desk Reference,* 41st ed., p. 1245.

measles vaccine approximately once for every million doses. In no case has it been shown that reactions were actually caused by vaccine." Other adverse reactions have been reported, including fever, convulsions, and forms of optic neuritis. Also, the manufacturer states "There have been isolated reports of ocular palsies and Guillain-Barre syndrome occurring after immunization with vaccines containing live attenuated measles virus. The ocular palsies have occurred approximately 3-24 days following vaccination. No definite causal relationship has been established between either of these events and vaccination."[19]

Carrao v. Heitler (1986) 117 App. Div. 2d 308, 502 N.Y.S.2d 424.

Reaction to injection—Brain damage—Summary judgments denied on failure to identify specific vaccine

A nine-month-old infant was given an injection of measles vaccine in September, 1970. She experienced seizure episodes, fever and rash, and subsequently was found to be suffering from epilepsy and to be mentally retarded.

In a lawsuit on the child's behalf against the two pediatricians in whose office she received the injection, and against four manufacturers of measles vaccine whom the plaintiffs claimed may have supplied the vaccine in question, three of the manufacturers (Philips Roxane Laboratories; Merck, Sharp & Dohme; and Eli Lilly & Company) moved for summary judgments when the pediatrician who administered the injection testified by affidavit that, to the best of his knowledge, the vaccine he used was Lirugen, manufactured by the Dow Chemical Company (the fourth named defendant). The motion was denied, however, when further testimony established that Lirugen was not the only measles vaccine used by the defendant pediatricians at the time, and that the form in which Lirugen was supplied at the time (pink in color and in solid tablet form) was not the form remembered by the second pediatrician as the one most often used.

MEASLES, MUMPS and RUBELLA VIRUS VACCINE M-M-R II

Merck, Sharp & Dohme manufactures M-M-R II, a combination of measles vaccine (Attenuvax), mumps vaccine (Mumpsvax) and ru-

[19] Id.

bella, or German measles, vaccine (Meruvax II). These are live virus vaccines. As with Attenuvax (see above), there are numerous precautions issued with the product, and it is contraindicated in: the presence of any febrile respiratory illness or infection, patients with active, untreated tuberculosis, patients receiving immunosuppressive therapy, patients with blood dyscrasias, leukemia, or other malignant neoplasms affecting the bone marrow or lymphatic systems, and patients with a family history of immunodeficiency. Further, it should not be given to pregnant patients, and when given to postpubital females, they should be instructed to avoid pregnancy for three months following vaccination.[20]

Walker v. Merck & Co. (M.D. Ga., 1986) 648 F. Supp. 931, aff'd (C.A.-11 Ga., 1987) 831 F.2d 1069.

Congenital blindness—Pregnant plaintiff sufficiently warned of risk to fetus

The plaintiff, a student at a rural Georgia public school, was pregnant when she received a county-sponsored vaccination with M-M-R II. Her child was born blind. In her action against the manufacturer of the vaccine, she claimed that the defendant did not sufficiently warn her of the potential risk.

The trial court granted the defendant's summary judgment, finding that the plaintiff's mother had signed a consent form which clearly delineated all potential risks connected with the vaccine, including a paragraph on potential effects on an unborn fetus. Also, the court found that the defendant manufacturer had fulfilled its duty to warn the licensed practical nurse who administered the vaccine, and that this nurse had questioned the plaintiff regarding her last menstrual period, whether or not she was sexually active, and whether or not she was pregnant at the time of vaccination. The Court of Appeals affirmed.

MEDICONE

See BENZOCAINE

[20] *Physicians' Desk Reference,* 42d ed., p. 1342.

MEDROXYPROGESTERONE ACETATE

Amen
Curretab
Depo-Provera
Provera

Medroxyprogesterone acetate is a derivative of progesterone which is used as adjunctive therapy and as palliative treatment of inoperable, recurrent, and metastatic endometrial carcinoma and renal carcinoma. It is contraindicated in cases of thromboembolic disorders, carcinoma of the breast, undiagnosed vaginal bleeding, missed abortion, and as a diagnostic test for pregnancy. Also, use of the drug as a contraceptive is still investigational.

Amen is manufactured by Carnrick Laboratories, Inc. (Cedar Knolls, N.J.), Curretab by Reid-Rowell, Inc. (Atlanta, Ga.), and Depo-Provera and Provera by The Upjohn Company (Kalamazoo, Mich.).[21]

Lynch v. Bay Ridge Obstet. & Gynec. Assoc. (1988) 72 N.Y.2d 632, 532 N.E.2d 1239.

Patient given Provera while pregnant has cause of action against clinic for psychological injury caused by having to undergo abortion

The plaintiff was given a prescription for Provera by an obstetrician-gynecologist at the defendant clinic to induce menstruation. The physician did not perform a pregnancy test first, nor did he warn the plaintiff of the danger to a fetus if a patient is pregnant when she takes Provera. The plaintiff later discovered that she was pregnant when she went on the drug, and she chose to undergo an abortion (prior to establishing whether or not the fetus had been harmed).

In her malpractice action against the defendant, the plaintiff alleged that because of her religious beliefs she suffered severe and permanent psychological injury as a result of the abortion. The court granted the defendant's motion to dismiss. On appeal, the appellate court affirmed, holding that the physician's alleged negligence in not performing a pregnancy test before prescribing Provera was not a "substantive causative factor in the sequence of

[21] *Physicians' Desk Reference,* 40th ed., pp. 1839-40.

events" that led to the plaintiff's decision to have an abortion (520 N.Y.S.2d 431).

On review, however, the Court of Appeals reversed, holding that the physician's negligent diagnosis and treatment were the precipitating causes of all that followed: that but for the physician's conduct, the plaintiff would not have been in the position of having to choose between two objectionable alternatives — undergo an abortion or risk having a baby with serious birth defects. That the plaintiff made the very choice forced upon her by the physician's negligence cannot insulate the clinic from legal responsibility for such conduct.

Rubin v. Bergman (No. 1934/82, Supreme Court, Queens County, N.Y., June 1, 1988).

Birth defects—Gynecologist fails to warn plaintiff to discontinue taking drug if she becomes pregnant—$900,000 settlement

The defendant, a gynecologist, prescribed Provera for the plaintiff because of irregular menstrual periods. He did not, however, warn her to stop taking the drug if she became pregnant. She continued taking the drug after she became pregnant and her child was born without a hand and part of a forearm. The defendant's defense was that there was no proof linking Provera to birth defects, and that in light of studies showing "insignificant adverse effects," an FDA subcommittee had recommended that the pregnancy warnings on Provera be removed.

According to the plaintiff's attorney, the parties settled for $900,000.[22]

Farley v. Upjohn Co. (No. C515 909, Superior Court, Los Angeles County, Cal., Nov. 8, 1988).

Patient pregnant when given drug—Manufacturer sued for failure to warn—$350,000 settlement

The patient was given Provera while pregnant to prevent miscarriage. Her baby was born with missing and shortened fingers on one hand, which apparently can be corrected to some extent by a series of operations.

In their suit against the manufacturer, the patient and her husband charged failure to warn of the drug's hazards, negligent mar-

[22] ATLA *Professional Negligence Law Reporter* 4:8, 1989.

keting of a dangerous product, breach of warranty, and strict liability.

The parties settled for $350,000.[1]

Upjohn Co. v. MacMurdo (Fla. App., 1988) 536 So. 2d 337.

Excessive menstrual bleeding—Manufacturer liable for inadequate warning—Patient not negligent for agreeing to unnecessary hysterectomy

The patient received two injections of Depo-Provera in 1974 for contraceptive purposes. Following the second injection, she experienced excessive, continuous, and prolonged menstrual bleeding. Because her physician failed to diagnose the true cause of her problem, she had to undergo an unnecessary hysterectomy. In her suit against the manufacturer, she claimed that the defendant failed to adequately warn the medical profession of this side effect. The jury returned a verdict for the patient, but found her 49% comparatively negligent in agreeing to the hysterectomy without first exploring alternative methods of treatment.

On appeal, the District Court of Appeal of Florida held that the evidence supported the verdict as to the defendant's failure to warn, but reversed the finding that the patient was negligent in agreeing to the hysterectomy.

Related cases

Vaginal bleeding—Plaintiff's evidence excluded—Directed verdict for physician and hospital affirmed

In Perez v. Mount Sinai Hosp. (1986) 7 Conn. App. 514, 509 A.2d 552, the trial court properly excluded the testimony of the plaintiff's treating physician, who offered to testify as to the "authoritative nature" of *Physicians' Desk Reference* with respect to the side effects of Depo-Provera, on grounds that the plaintiff had failed to answer the defendant's interrogatories relative to the identity of any expert witnesses which the plaintiff intended to call at trial. The plaintiff had claimed that the drug, given to her as a birth control measure, had caused heavy vaginal bleeding, dizziness and nervousness. The trial court's directed verdict for the physician and hospital was affirmed.

---

[1] ATLA *Products Liability Law Reporter* 8:87, 1989.

Adequacy of cancer warning questioned

In an action against the manufacturer of Depo-Provera, the New York Supreme Court, Appellate Division, held that there were triable issues concerning the adequacy of the defendant's warning, including whether or not it should have been reported that there were incidents of cancer in humans associated with the use of the drug and whether the defendant "undercut its warnings and nullified or eroded their adequacy." Popham v. Reyner (App. Div. 2d, 1986) 503 N.Y.S.2d 645.

Variety of disorders possibly related to Depo-Provera—Action against manufacturer time barred

Where the plaintiff knew for over two years before filing her complaint against the manufacturer of Depo-Provera that she was suffering from a variety of disorders that she believed could have been caused by the drug, including darkening of the skin, hair loss, Gray's disease, fibroid tumors, iritis, fatty breast deposits, arthritis, and depression, her action was time barred under Ohio law. Longmire v. The Upjohn Co. (S.D. Ohio, 1988) 686 F. Supp. 659.

Birth defects—Insufficient evidence of gynecologist's duty to warn of inappropriate prescriptions

A plaintiff's unsubstantiated allegations that a gynecologist committed malpractice by failing to advise the plaintiff, who gave birth to a deformed child, or her other doctors that their prior prescription of Provera and estrogens was inappropriate, were not sufficient to defeat the defendant's motion for summary judgment. Winje v. The Upjohn Co. (App. Div., 1989) 549 N.Y.S.2d 280.

MEFOXIN

See CEFOXITIN SODIUM

MELLARIL

See THIORIDAZINE

MEPERGAN

See MEPERIDINE HYDROCHLORIDE; PROMETHAZINE HYDROCHLORIDE

MEPERIDINE HYDROCHLORIDE
Demerol
Mepergan

Meperidine hydrochloride is an analgesic which is as effective as morphine if given in doses eight to ten times greater. However, it has considerably shorter duration of action than morphine. Meperidine hydrochloride is given both orally and parenterally. With some variation, the analgesic action is apparent in approximately fifteen minutes, reaching a peak in about an hour, and subsiding in two to four hours.[2]

The drug is used in diagnostic procedures, e.g., cystoscopy, retrograde pyelography, gastroscopy, pneumoencephalography, and in surgery as preanesthetic medication. It is also used postoperatively, to make the patient more comfortable and to reduce restlessness.[3]

Excessive doses of meperidine hydrochloride may cause respiratory depression, coma, and death. The recommended adult dose is in the range of 50 to 150 mg. administered intramuscularly, subcutaneously, or orally.[4] In most conditions the dose may be repeated at intervals of three or four hours. For children, the recommended dose is 0.5 to 0.8 mg. per pound of weight, administered intramuscularly, subcutaneously, or orally, and it may be repeated at three- or four-hour intervals.[5] If the intravenous route is used, the manufacturer recommends that the drug be administered very slowly.[6]

Meperidine hydrochloride should be used with great caution and in reduced dosage in patients who are also receiving other narcotic analgesics, general anesthetics, phenothiazines, other tranquilizers, sedative-hypnotics, tricyclic antidepressants, or other central nervous system depressants, including alcohol.[7]

Winthrop Laboratories (New York, N.Y.) manufactures meperidine hydrochloride under the brand name Demerol, and Wyeth Laboratories (Philadelphia, Pa.) produces Mepergan. It is also sold under the generic name.

---

[2] *United States Dispensatory,* 27th ed., p. 699.

[3] Id.

[4] Id.

[5] Id., p. 700.

[6] *Physicians' Desk Reference,* 35th ed., p. 1900.

[7] Id.

Schmite v. Ramos (No. 619271, Superior Court, San Francisco County, Cal., June 6, 1974).

Death after 25 mg. dose of Demerol—Evidence of Librium and alcohol—Verdict for physician

A physician was called to the home of a patient who was complaining of painful hemorrhoids, and gave him 25 mg. of Demerol. That night the patient died. The family brought suit against the physician, claiming that the Demerol had caused the patient's death. There was evidence at the trial, however, that the patient had also been taking Librium (chlordiazepoxide hydrochloride), which is a tranquilizer, and had been drinking. The jury returned a verdict for the physician.[8]

Hair v. County of Monterey (No. 67538, Superior Court, Monterey County, Cal., 1971).

Demerol given intravenously to child under general anesthesia—Cardiac arrest—$390,000 verdict

An eight-year-old child undergoing major dental work on a root canal was given 50 mg. of Demerol intravenously while already under general anesthesia. He suffered cardiac arrest which caused brain damage and left him partially blind, mentally retarded and a quadriplegic. The operation was being performed in a hospital and an anesthesiologist was in attendance.

The dental surgeon in charge, the anesthesiologist, and the hospital made a joint admission of liability (issues included faulty anesthesia technique), and the matter was tried only as to damages. Evidence was offered by the plaintiffs that the child's lifetime nursing care would cost over $1,700,000 and his loss of future earnings was estimated at $567,367. The defense countered with the argument that the sum of $256,893, invested at 7½%, would provide the boy with lifetime care. The jury returned a verdict for $390,000.[9]

Fuller v. Starnes (1980) 268 Ark. 476, 597 S.W.2d 88.

Respiratory failure resulting in brain damage—Plaintiff fails for want of expert medical evidence on physician's duty to disclose risks

An 86-year-old patient was seen at a hospital emergency department for pains in her left side and a temperature of 102°. The

---

[8] AMA *The Citation* 30:23, 1974.

[9] Id., 23:102, 1971.

emergency department physician concluded the patient was suffering from pleurisy, and told her daughter that he would give her penicillin and "something for pain," which turned out to be 25 mg. of Demerol plus 25 mg. of Phenergan[10] (promethazine hydrochloride) for nausea.

Prior to ordering the injections, the physician asked the patient if she was allergic to "any medication." Apparently she replied that she was not.

After the patient was treated, the physician told her to wait in the emergency room "to see if she might have a reaction to the medication." He did not mention any particular risks associated with the drugs.

Approximately twenty minutes after the injections, the patient began having difficulty breathing, and shortly thereafter she stopped breathing altogether. She was revived with emergency measures, but suffered brain damage. She was eventually discharged, but lived only two years.

In her complaint against the physician, the patient's daughter alleged that he was negligent in prescribing Demerol "without disclosing adequate information about the perils of its use." At the trial, however, she failed to produce expert medical testimony to support this charge, and the trial judge directed a verdict for the defendant.

On appeal, the Supreme Court of Arkansas affirmed, holding that, although the plaintiff established certain known risks associated with the use of Demerol, she presented no evidence concerning their incidence or the existence and feasibility of alternative treatment. Such evidence, said the court, was crucial to a jury's determination of the materiality of the defendant's failure to disclose.

Nieto v. Kurzner (No. 18457/76, Supreme Court, New York County, N.Y., Oct. 10, 1980).

Infant suffers brain damage at birth—Mother allegedly given excessive dose of Demerol—$1,000,000 settlement

An infant's mother was given an allegedly excessive dose of Demerol one-half hour before the child's birth, which slowed his heartbeat and depressed his respiration, resulting in brain damage. No oxygen was given to the mother before birth, and Narcan, an antidote for Demerol, was not given until an hour after delivery.

[10] In the reported opinion, this drug is spelled "Phenegran."

The lawsuit was brought on behalf of the infant who, at age six, was spastic, unable to talk, and required total care. It was contended that the Demerol "crossed the placenta," thus depressing the fetal respiration, and that Narcan should have been administered earlier.

According to the attorney for the infant, the obstetrician and the hospital contributed equally to a $1 million settlement.[11]

Fraijo v. Hartland Hosp. (1979) 99 Cal. App. 3d 331, 160 Cal. Rptr. 246.

Asthma patient suffers fatal reaction—Verdict for defendants

A thirty-nine-year-old asthma patient was admitted to the defendant hospital for tests. Her physician left orders for "Demerol 75, plus Phenergan 25 mg." every four hours as needed for pain. During the night the patient's pulse, respiration and blood pressure increased and she complained of chest pains. The medication nurse administered one injection of Demerol and Phenergan as ordered. Soon thereafter, the patient became cyanotic and went into convulsions. A "Code Blue" signal was given but attempts of resuscitation were unsuccessful.

At the trial the plaintiffs claimed the injection was contraindicated because of the patient's asthma condition and attempted to introduce the product literature which stated that the drug "should be used with extreme caution in patients having an acute asthmatic attack." The trial judge refused to admit the literature because no evidence was presented that it had accompanied the product and had been "distributed to the customers purchasing the product." The defense's position was that the patient died because of a rare idiosyncratic reaction.

Judgment was rendered for the defendants and the Court of Appeal affirmed.

Newitt v. Hospital Corp. of Louisiana (La. App., 1982) 417 So. 2d 391.

Patient's allergy to Demerol noted on chart—Injected anyway—Bench award of $1,500—Damages for resulting "phobia" of hospitals denied

The patient was allergic to Demerol and this fact was noted on her medical chart. Despite this, she was administered the drug (50

[11] ATLA *Law Reporter* 24:41, 1981.

mg.) and suffered a reaction which lasted twelve hours. At the trial she claimed the incident also triggered a "phobia" of hospitals for which she had to seek psychiatric help.

The trial judge awarded the patient $1,500 for "pain, suffering, mental anguish and medical costs," but rejected the claim for the phobia, even though the patient's expert medical testimony on this issue was uncontradicted. The Court of Appeal affirmed, holding that the trial judge was not bound by expert testimony and could substitute his own common sense and judgment for that of the expert where warranted by the evidence as a whole.

Shuttles v. Glasser (No. 83-7239-3, Superior Court, DeKalb County, Ga., June 13, 1984).

**Child suffers brain damage from cardiac arrest—
Dentist settles for $950,000**

The defendant dentist, a pedodontist, administered a combination of Demerol, Thorazine (chlorpromazine) and Phenergan (promethazine hydrochloride) to a two-year-old boy prior to a root canal. Shortly after the injection (intramuscular), the child suffered respiratory and cardiac arrest. He was revived by physicians from a nearby office, but remains comatose with permanent brain damage. The child's parents charged that the defendant was negligent in failing to monitor him adequately while under sedation, in administering an improper dose, and in failing to provide adequate equipment and trained personnel to handle an emergency. The defendant settled prior to trial for $950,000.[12]

Sanchez v. Flower & Fifth Avenue Hospital (No. 14073/79, Supreme Court, New York County, N.Y., Jan. 31, 1986).

Excessive narcotics during prolonged labor—Brain-damaged child—Jury awards $4 million

An obstetrical patient was admitted to the defendant hospital for delivery. Although her membranes had ruptured six hours earlier, she went into prolonged labor, during which time she received periodic doses of Demerol, Sparine (promazine hydrochloride) and Seconal (secobarbital sodium). After 22 hours, the patient's obstetrician performed a mid-forceps delivery. The infant's Apgar scores were 5 at one minute and 7 at five minutes, and he exhibited substantial

[12] ATLA *Law Reporter* 27:427, 1984.

forceps marks on his face and scalp. Within two days after birth, the child began to experience seizures, cyanosis and tremors. He was diagnosed as suffering from neonatal meningitis. There was severe diffuse brain damage, cerebral palsy, profound mental retardation and permanent seizure disorders. He always will require custodial care.

When the child was eight years old, a legal review of the case revealed that the original diagnosis of neonatal meningitis was unsupported, and that the boy's condition probably was the result of the obstetrician's excessive use of narcotics during the mother's labor. The boy's parents also charged that the neonatologist who made the diagnosis of neonatal meningitis did so to cover up the apparent negligence of the obstetrician.

A jury awarded the parents $4 million.[13]

Akuly v. Suburban Medical Center (No. 81L-28824, Circuit Court, Cook County, Ill., Nov. 25, 1986).

Brain damage at birth—Use of Demerol and Nisentil questioned—$5.3 million structured settlement

The mother of the plaintiff in this action was an obstetrical patient at the defendant hospital. After seven hours of labor, an internal fetal heart monitor revealed questionable patterns, including occasional severe variable decelerations and then decreased variability. During the monitoring, Demerol and Nisentil were administered to relieve pain. About twelve hours after admission, the defendant obstetrician arrived and took the patient to the delivery room where he unsuccessfully attempted a high-forceps delivery. A second obstetrician was called to perform the delivery. The plaintiff, now six, suffers cerebral palsy, mental retardation, and right hemiparesis.

In this action, the plaintiff alleged delayed delivery and negligent administration of the Demerol and Nisentil which were, according to the plaintiff, contraindicated in view of the plaintiff's questionable fetal heart patterns. The plaintiff also alleged negligent performance of the high-forceps delivery.

A structured settlement with a present value of $5.3 million was reached with both the hospital and the obstetrician participating. The plaintiff will receive $4.35 million cash, lifetime monthly payments of $4,000, increasing 3% annually, guaranteed for ten years,

[13] ATLA *Law Reporter* 29:324, 1986.

and additional lifetime monthly payments commencing at age 21 of $4,000, increasing 4% annually for life.[14]

Tolman v. Memorial Hosp. of Natrona County. (No. 59428, District Court, Natrona County, Wyo., May 9, 1988).

Blood clot and paralysis following spinal surgery—Alleged excessive use of Demerol and Vistaril—$563,665 structured settlement

The patient, a woman age 52, underwent spinal nerve root surgery. Following the operation, she was given several injections of Demerol and Vistaril for pain. Two days after the operation, she developed a problem evacuating her bowels and bladder. The following day, her legs became partially paralyzed. Her surgeon performed emergency surgery and found a blood clot pressing on her spinal cord. He removed it, but the patient still has pain, difficulty in walking, and only partial control of her bowels and bladder. She has not been able to return to her former job as a retail sales clerk.

In her suit against the surgeon and the hospital, she alleged numerous acts of negligence. She claimed the surgeon failed to advise the nursing staff to check her frequently for symptoms of neurologic deficits, failed to perform necessary postoperative examinations, and ordered an excessive amount of Demerol and Vistaril which caused an insufficient blood supply to her spinal cord. As to the hospital, she claimed the staff failed to monitor her sufficiently and failed to advise her surgeon of her postoperative symptoms.

According to the plaintiff's attorney, the parties agreed to a structured settlement with a present value of $563,665.[15]

Related cases

Addiction to Talwin, possibly Demerol

In Winthrop Laboratories Division of Sterling Drug, Inc. v. Crocker (Tex. Civ. App., 1973) 502 S.W.2d 850; revd. (Tex., 1974) 514 S.W.2d 429, a patient on Demerol and Talwin (pentazocine) became addicted to the Talwin and possibly also to the Demerol. Suit was filed against Winthrop Laboratories, manufacturer of both drugs, in which it was alleged that Talwin was introduced on the market without sufficient warnings about addiction. The plaintiff

---

[14] ATLA *Professional Negligence Law Reporter* 2:43, 1987.

[15] ATLA *Professional Negligence Law Reporter* 4:10, 1989.

obtained a jury verdict which was eventually affirmed by the Supreme Court of Texas. The case is summarized herein under PENTAZOCINE.

Respiratory depression and brain damage in newborn

The mother of a brain-damaged infant was unsuccessful in proving any violation of accepted medical standards or hospital regulations by her obstetrician when he administered 150 milligrams of Demerol to her shortly before delivery, allegedly causing narcotization of the fetus and the resulting injury. Gamell v. Mount Sinai Hosp. (1970) 34 App. Div. 2d 981, 312 N.Y.S.2d 629.

In Downing v. Manta (No. 79-21845, Circuit Court, Dade County, Fla., Oct. 17, 1980), a pregnant patient given oxytocin (Pitocin), Demerol and several other drugs prior to delivery, gave birth to twin fetuses suffering from severe respiratory depression and brain damage. The case is summarized herein under OXYTOCIN.

In a similar case, Lhotka v. Larson (1976) 307 Minn. 121, 238 N.W.2d 870, the drugs administered were secobarbital sodium (Seconal), Demerol and Phenergan. This case is summarized herein under SECOBARBITAL SODIUM.

Cardiac arrest during general anesthesia—Surgeon's selection of Demerol as preoperative medication not negligence

In Thompson v. Presbyterian Hosp., Inc. (Okla., 1982) 652 P.2d 260, a surgeon was not liable for choosing Demerol as premedication, which later combined with a general anesthetic caused the patient to suffer cardiac arrest during surgery, on the strength of a plaintiff's expert's testimony that he would not have selected that particular drug for preoperative medication. According to the court, the patient's brain damage could not have occurred except for the supervening negligence of the anesthesiologist.

Complications following tonsillectomy

In Alton v. Kitt (1982) 103 Ill. App. 3d 387, 59 Ill. Dec. 132, 431 N.E.2d 417, the patient either fainted or suffered respiratory arrest while his physician was attempting to stop post-tonsillectomy bleeding. The patient had just been given Demerol (50 mg.) intramuscularly, which the patient's expert testified was contrary to acceptable practice, and which probably caused the respiratory arrest due to the patient's already low blood pressure. The defendant's expert disagreed, claiming the dose was insufficient to cause respiratory arrest. Numerous other acts of malpractice were alleged. The jury found for the defendant physician and the verdict was affirmed.

Nerve injury after injection of Demerol and Vistaril

In Holbrooks v. Duke University, Inc. (1983) 63 N.C. App. 504, 305 S.E.2d 69, the jury was entitled to consider whether a nurse had violated the standard of care in administering an injection of Demerol and Vistaril three inches above the patient's knee which allegedly caused injury to a nerve.

MEPROBAMATE

Deprol
Equagesic
Equanil
Kesso-Bamate
Meprospan
Milpath
Milprem
Miltown
Miltrate
Pathibamate
PMB 200/400
SK-Bamate
T.M.C. Tablets

Meprobamate is a very popular tranquilizing agent, with anticonvulsant, muscle relaxant, and sedative actions. It is used to provide relief in anxiety and tension states, and as an adjunct in the treatment of various conditions in which anxiety and tension are manifested. It is used also in the treatment of musculoskeletal disorders, and sometimes as an anticonvulsant in petit mal epilepsy.[16] Since the effects of meprobamate and alcohol or meprobamate and other central nervous system depressants or psychotropic drugs may be addictive, the drug is issued with a warning that appropriate caution should be exercised with patients who take more than one of these agents simultaneously.[17]

Deprol, Meprospan, Milpath, Milprem, Miltown and Miltrate are manufactured by Wallace Laboratories (Cranbury, N.J.); Equagesic and Equanil by Wyeth Laboratories (Philadelphia, Pa.); PMB-200

[16] *United States Dispensatory,* 27th ed., pp. 705-06.
[17] *Physicians' Desk Reference,* 35th ed., p. 1871.

and PMB-400 (wich also contain estrogens) by Ayerst Laboratories (New York, N.Y.); Pathibamate by Lederle Laboratories (Wayne, N.J.); SK-Bamate (until 1987) by Smith Kline & French Laboratories (Philadelphia, Pa.), and T.M.C. Tablets by Zenith Laboratories (Northvale, N.J.). The product is also manufactured by several companies under the generic label.

Alleged interaction between meprobamate and carisoprodol

In Perkins v. Park View Hosp., Inc. (1970) 61 Tenn. App. 458, 456 S.W.2d 276, a woman hospital patient died, apparently from anaphylactic shock, after receiving meprobamate, carisoprodol (Soma), and several other drugs. Included in the plaintiff's charges was the allegation that there was an insidious interaction between the meprobamate and carisoprodol. Directed verdicts in favor of all defendants were sustained. The case is summarized under CARISOPRODOL herein.

MEPROSPAN

See MEPROBAMATE

MER/29

See TRIPARANOL

MERALLURIDE

Mercuhydrin

Meralluride is a mercurial diuretic used in edema accompanying congestive heart failure, nephrosis, certain liver disorders and for other conditions in which such a diuretic is indicated. In persons hypersensitive to the drug, adverse reactions can be serious and even fatal.[18]

Lakeside Laboratories, Inc. (Milwaukee, Wis.) has produced meralluride under the trade name Mercuhydrin, but the drug is no longer included in its product information list.

Depper v. Nakada (Mo. App., 1977) 558 S.W.2d 192.

Reaction to Mercuhydrin—Use of drug for obesity criticized—Jury verdict for patient

The patient in this action was an overweight female in her forties who also suffered from thrombophlebitis. In June, 1966, her physi-

---

[18] *United States Dispensatory,* 27th ed., p. 707.

cian prescribed medication for her obesity which included three injections of Mercuhydrin. Shortly after the first injection the patient's arm and shoulder became sore, "swollen, discolored and the skin looked kind of shiny like." A second injection a week later in the patient's leg produced a similar reaction, and a third necessitated her hospitalization.

In a suit against the physician's estate, the patient produced expert testimony that Mercuhydrin was not an appropriate drug for treatment of excessive weight, and that in view of the patient's reaction following the first injection, the physician, in administering such treatment, did not exercise that degree of skill and learning "normally exercised by other doctors in 1966 under the same or similar circumstances."

The jury returned a verdict for the patient (amount not reported) which was affirmed on appeal.

MERCUHYDRIN

See MERALLURIDE

METARAMINOL BITARTRATE

Aramine

Aramine, manufactured by Merck, Sharp & Dohme (West Point, Pa.), is a potent sympathomimetic amine that increases both systolic and diastolic blood pressure, and therefore is used to treat shock. According to the National Academy of Sciences-National Research Council, the drug is effective for the prevention and treatment of acute hypotensive state occurring with spinal anesthesia, as well as for adjunctive treatment of hypotension due to hemorrhage, reactions to medications, surgical complications and shock associated with brain damage due to trauma or tumor. It also is considered "probably" useful as an adjunct in the treatment of hypotension due to cardiogenic shock or septicemia.[19]

The drug is contraindicated with the use of cyclopropane or halothane anesthesia "unless clinical circumstances demand such use." Adverse reactions include the possibility of sinus or ventricular tachycardia, or other arrhythmias, especially in patients with myocardial infarction. Also, in patients with a history of malaria, Aramine may provoke a relapse. There is also the risk of tissue

---

[19] *Physicians' Desk Reference,* 42d ed., p. 1286.

necrosis, abscess formation or sloughing at the site of injection, but this is rare.[20]

Woodard v. HCA Health Services of Texas (No. 352-91150-85, 352d Judicial District Court, Tarrant County, Tex., March 6, 1987).

Excessive administration of Aramine and other alleged negligence—Brain damage—$4.1 million settlement

While undergoing an intravenous pyelogram, the plaintiff, age 37, suffered anaphylactic shock. To raise his blood pressure, the radiologist administered Aramine intravenously. When his blood pressure returned to normal, the plaintiff was left unattended in a hallway for an hour while the Aramine continued to drip. His blood pressure rose excessively until a blood vessel burst in his brain. He was rushed to the emergency room, where the radiologist told the emergency room physician that the plaintiff had reacted to the dye but failed to tell him that Aramine had been administered. The E.R. physician administered epinephrine, which can raise blood pressure when given with Aramine. Later, a CAT scan showed a subdural hematoma. The plaintiff is partially paralyzed and mentally impaired.

The plaintiff's lawsuit charged that the radiologist (1) was not competent to handle the emergency, (2) failed to have the plaintiff moved to intensive care or the emergency room when he diagnosed anaphylactic shock, and (3) failed to have him monitored while on the Aramine I.V. The hospital was sued for the negligence of its agents, the radiologist and the E.R. physician, and for failing to have policies and procedures for treating patients who have gone into anaphylactic shock. The E.R. physician was sued individually for failure to take a complete history.

The parties settled for $4.1 million: The radiologist is to pay $3.6 million, the hospital, $400,000, and the E.R. physician, $100,000.[21]

---

[20] Id.

[21] ATLA *Professional Negligence Law Reporter* 2:141, 1987.

METHADONE

Methadone is a synthetic analgesic with actions and analgesic potency similar to morphine. It is used to prevent or relieve acute withdrawal symptoms produced by morphine-like drugs, and is useful orally in the detoxification of patients dependent upon these agents. The withdrawal of methadone itself produces symptoms which are less intense but more prolonged than those of heroin or morphine withdrawal.[22]

Rebollal v. Payne (1988) 145 App. Div. 2d 617, 536 N.Y.S.2d 147.

Driver killed in accident involving patient on way home from methadone treatment center—County not liable

The plaintiff's decedent was killed in an automobile accident when the car she was driving was struck by one driven by the defendant. The defendant was driving home after having received a dose of methadone at a county-operated out-patient drug treatment center.

The plaintiff charged that the county had a duty to warn the defendant that he should not operate an automobile after ingesting methadone, and that the county is liable to third persons who are injured by out-patients such as the defendant as a result of their operation of a vehicle while under the influence of methadone.

The trial court dismissed the plaintiff's claim as to the county, and was upheld on appeal. The Supreme Court, Appellate Division, held that while physicians and health-related facilities, which would include a methadone treatment center, owe a duty of care to patients and to persons known to be relying on them for service to a patient, such physicians and facilities do not undertake a duty to the public at large, of which the plaintiff's decedent was a member. The same rule would be apply to the county.

METATENSIN

See RESERPINE

---

[22] AMA *Drug Evaluations,* 6th ed., pp. 61-62.

METHIMAZOLE
Tapazole

Methimazole is an antithyroid drug used to manage hyperthyroidism, to prepare hyperthyroid patients for thyroidectomy, and to treat thyrotoxic crisis. Frequent administration is necessary, especially initially, to achieve maximum clinical effectiveness. For adults with hyperthyroidism, the initial oral dose is 15 to 60 mg. daily divided into doses every six to eight hours. For maintenance, 10 to 30 mg. is given daily in one to three doses.[1]

The drug is manufactured and marketed under the brand name Tapazole by Eli Lilly & Company (Indianapolis, Ind.).

Carter v. Dunlop (1985) 138 Ill. App. 3d 58, 92 Ill. Dec. 418, 484 N.E.2d 1273.

Allegedly insufficient dosage—Patient's claim unsuccessful for failure to take medication

The plaintiff was suffering from an overactive thyroid. On March 2, the defendant physician placed her on 10 mg. of Tapazole three times a day. The defendant next saw the plaintiff on March 25 at which time blood tests indicated that she was "significantly better." Another appointment was scheduled for her in six weeks, but she did not keep it.

The plaintiff did return on June 3. She showed "significant symptoms" of hyperthyroidism and laboratory tests revealed that her thyroid was "markedly abnormal." She told the defendant that she had stopped taking the Tapazole two weeks before the visit and that before that, she had at times forgotten to take "quite a few" of the tablets. The defendant cautioned the plaintiff to take her medication and continued her on the same dosage.

On June 22, the plaintiff began seeing another physician who found her "extremely malnourished as a result of thyrotoxicosis." He placed her on 60 mg. of Tapazole daily, plus an iodine solution, and called in a surgeon for consultation. It was decided to remove her thyroid gland, after which her condition improved.

In her suit against the defendant, the plaintiff claimed his treatment was insufficient. She could not produce an expert witness, however, and had to rely on the affidavit of the physician who began treating her on June 22. This witness testified that a six-

---

[1] AMA *Drug Evaluations,* 6th ed., p. 808.

month Tapazole regimen of 30 mg. per day was proper initial treatment for an overactive thyroid if the patient was supervised during such period, specifically, if the patient's thyroid level was monitored monthly. He concluded that in the plaintiff's case, she had not been adequately treated.

Despite the above testimony, the trial court granted the defendant's motion for summary judgment, and the Appellate Court of Illinois affirmed, holding that in view of the plaintiff's own failure to take her medication, the second physician's opinion did not create an issue as to whether the defendant had been guilty of malpractice.

METHOTREXATE
Folex

Methotrexate is an anticancer drug, most frequently effective against acute lymphoblastic leukemia. It can be used singly to produce remissions of the disease, but it is more commonly used in combination with other drugs. It is also considered the drug of choice for choriocarcinoma in the female, and may be useful in Hodgkin's disease, mycosis fungoides, and squamous cell tumors of the head and neck, and uterine cervix.[2]

In 1951 it was discovered that methotrexate can also produce rapid clearing of psoriasis, which led to its wide use for this disease. The effectiveness of the drug for this purpose is now well established, but there is a danger of liver damage, and there have been some fatalities.[3] Because of this risk, methotrexate is indicated only in the "symptomatic control of severe, recalcitrant, disabling psoriasis which is not adequately responsive to other forms of therapy," and then, only when the diagnosis has been firmly established, by biopsy or after dermatologic consultation.[4] Furthermore, methotrexate should not be given to psoriatic patients who are pregnant, who have severe kidney or liver disorders, or who have preexisting blood dyscrasias.[5] The drug itself may produce marked depression of bone marrow, anemia, leukopenia, thrombocytopenia and bleed-

[2] *United States Dispensatory,* 27th ed., p. 735.
[3] Id.
[4] *Physicians' Desk Reference,* 35th ed., p. 1007.
[5] Id.

ing. There has also been some suggestion that methotrexate may cause cancer in psoriasis patients.[6]

Because of the drug's high potential for toxicity, it is issued with warnings that it must be used only by physicians experienced in antimetabolite chemotherapy; that before treatment is begun, the patient should be fully informed of the risks involved, and that during treatment, the patient should be under the physician's constant supervision.[7]

Methotrexate is marketed under the generic name by several companies, and Adria Laboratories (Columbus, Ohio) produces Folex, an injectable form of the drug.

Murray v. Teichmann (Circuit Court, Montgomery County, Md., Feb. 11, 1970).

Aplastic anemia—Failure to run blood tests during treatment—Lack of informed consent—$600,000 verdict against physician

A 25-year-old female patient under treatment with methotrexate for psoriasis developed aplastic anemia. In a malpractice action against the physician (a dermatologist), the patient's attorneys charged that at the time the drug was used it had not yet been cleared for the general treatment of skin conditions by the Food and Drug Administration.

The patient's attorneys introduced into evidence recommendations by the manufacturer that initial treatment with methotrexate should be undertaken only in hospital patients where there were adequate laboratory facilities for periodic blood counts and bone marrow biopsies. And, at trial, the patient testified that the defendant had not ordered blood tests, and had not warned her of the possible side effects of the drug.

The patient's medical expenses were reported to be just under $11,000; according to her attorneys, the jury returned a verdict in her favor for $600,000.[8]

---

[6] Craig, S. R. and Rosenberg, E. W., "Methotrexate-Induced Carcinoma?" *Archives of Dermatology* 103:505-506, 1971. Harris, C. C., "Malignancy During Methotrexate and Steroid Therapy for Psoriasis," *Archives of Dermatology* 103:501-504, 1971. Molin, L. and Larson, T. E., "Psoriasis, Methotrexate and Cancer," *Archives of Dermatology* 105:292, 1973. Bailin, P. L., et al., "Is Methotrexate Therapy for Psoriasis Carcinogenic? A Modified Retrospective-Prospective Analysis," *Journal of the American Medical Association* 232:359-362, 1975.

[7] *Physicians' Desk Reference,* 35th ed., p. 1006.

[8] ATLA *News Letter* 14:359, 1971.

Snell v. Curtis (No. 119586, Circuit Court, Wayne County, Mich., June 14, 1971).

Cirrhosis of the liver—Evidence that physician failed to monitor liver function—$200,000 award

A physician treated a patient with methotrexate for psoriasis over a period of 43 months. The dosage was usually two pills per day for five days, then two days off. On some occasions, the dosage was as high as 32.5 mg. per week. At the end of about thirty months, the patient began to develop "spider angiomas." These increased, but treatment was continued for another eleven months, until the patient was admitted to the hospital suffering from cirrhosis of the liver, presumably secondary to the effects of the methotrexate. The patient died four months later.

At the trial, there was evidence that the physician had been conducting studies for the manufacturer of methotrexate, and that he was aware that the drug might cause liver damage. The evidence disclosed that despite this knowledge the physician had monitored the patient's liver function only once during the three and one-half years of treatment.

A verdict of $200,000 was returned against the estate of the physician who had died prior to trial. The hospital where the patient had been treated was also named in the suit, but was not found liable. The drug manufacturer was also named a defendant, but apparently any question of sufficient warning on its part was resolved in its favor because of the study carried out by the physician.[9]

Kowalski v. Rees (No. 609709, Superior Court, San Francisco County, Cal., Jan. 9, 1974).

Cirrhosis of the liver—Patient charges drug not yet approved for psoriasis—Verdicts for physician and manufacturer

A patient being treated with methotrexate for psoriasis sued his physician and the manufacturer of the drug when he developed cirrhosis of the liver and esophageal varices. At the trial, the patient's position was that the drug had not been fully approved by the Food and Drug Administration for use in treating psoriasis, yet the manufacturer sold the drug knowing that it was being prescribed by physicians for this purpose. The manufacturer defended

---

[9] AMA *The Citation* 23:161, 1971; ATLA *News Letter* 14:419, 1971.

this argument on the ground that it had no control over a physician's use of its products. The defendant-physician contended that he merely was following the standard practice in the community in choosing methotrexate as one of the means of treating psoriasis. The jury found for the defendants.[10]

Related cases

Two additional cases involving reactions to methotrexate in which the courts dealt only with procedural matters are Miller v. Wells (1977) 58 App. Div. 2d 954, 397 N.Y.S.2d 183 (commencement of the action) and Bernstein v. Cheslock (1979) 171 N.J. Super. 566, 410 A.2d 271 (motion to add defendant).

METHOXSALEN
Oxsoralen

Methoxsalen is a constituent of an herb, *Ammi majus,* found in the Mediterranean countries. It is a "pigment stimulant," having the property of inducing the production of melanin pigment in the skin on exposure to the sun or other source of ultraviolet light, and is used in treating vitiligo, a condition characterized by patches of depigmentation. The effectiveness of the drug which is sold as Oxsoralen, and the closely related compound trioxsalen (Trisoralen), is uncertain, because of frequently contradictory reports and insufficient objective information.[11]

When these drugs are used to enhance pigmentation, extreme caution must be observed to assure that subsequent exposure to the sun is obtained in carefully increased increments. Otherwise the phototoxic effect may cause severe burning and blistering.[12] The drugs are contraindicated in patients with diseases such as lupus erythematosus and porphyria, which may in themselves be associated with photosensitivity.[13]

Topical use of methoxsalen can cause acute photosensitization in a high percentage of patients. High concentrations of the drug and overexposure of the treated site are the major factors contributing

---

[10] AMA *The Citation* 29:35, 1975.

[11] *United States Dispensatory,* 27th ed., p. 739.

[12] Fisher, W. C., "Dermatologic Diseases" in *Diseases of Medical Progress: A Study of Iatrogenic Disease,* 3rd ed., R. H. Moser, editor (Springfield, Ill.: Charles C Thomas, Publisher, 1969), p. 224.

[13] Id.

to severe erythema and blistering. Dilution of the lotion to concentrations of 1:10,000 or 1:1,000 has been recommended to avoid excessive reactions.[14]

Both Oxsoralen and Trisoralen are marketed by Paul B. Elder Company (Bryan, Ohio).

Tonnessen v. Paul B. Elder Co. (No. 286356, Superior Court, Santa Clara County, Cal., March 8, 1974).

Skin blotches—Patient given drug for home use—Warnings removed from bottle—Pharmacist and physician liable

A woman patient obtained a prescription from her physician for Oxsoralen lotion to treat vitiligo, a condition which causes patches of skin depigmentation. After applying the lotion, she went outside for approximately ten minutes and suffered first and second degree burns from the sun. After the burns healed, there remained permanent blotches on her skin where she had applied the lotion. The patient filed actions against the physician, the manufacturer of Oxsoralen, and the pharmacy where she purchased the lotion.

At the trial, the evidence revealed that the pharmacist, before dispensing the lotion to the patient, had disposed of the manufacturer's package insert, which had contained a warning about exposure to sunlight, and had placed the pharmacy's own label over the manufacturer's label, which had also contained a warning, including statements that the drug was very potent, should be applied only by a physician, and was not to be dispensed for home use.

The pharmacist defended his actions by offering evidence that covering up such labels and disposing of such information was common practice among pharmacists in the community because many physicians were reluctant to allow their patients to see instructions that might be contrary to their own. In this regard the defendant-physician testified that he had instructed the patient about exposure to sunlight, and furthermore, that even if the pharmacist had called his attention to the manufacturer's warning, he still would have had the pharmacist supply the drug directly to the patient. He then offered testimony by a local dermatologist who said it was common practice in the community for physicians to prescribe Oxsoralen for home use, with proper instructions, and that the defendant's actions were within acceptable standards.

---

[14] *AMA Drug Evaluations,* 2d ed., p. 669.

The jury didn't agree, and returned a verdict for $7,750 against the pharmacist and the physician. The action against the drug manufacturer was dismissed by the court.[15]

METHOXYFLURANE
Penthrane

Methoxyflurane is a potent general anesthetic with which a number of cases of impaired kidney function have been associated. High output renal failure and death have occurred in a few such instances.[16] It should be used cautiously in patients with preexisting kidney disease or abnormalities which may impair kidney function.[17] It may be unwise to administer the drug to patients receiving tetracyclines because the concurrent use of these agents has been associated with kidney failure.[18]

Methoxyflurane is also known to cause liver damage,[19] and it probably should not be given to patients who have developed jaundice and unexplained fever after previous administration of methoxyflurane or the anesthetic halothane.[20] (See HALOTHANE, herein.)

Abbott Pharmaceuticals (North Chicago, Ill.) manufactures methoxyflurane under the name Penthrane.

Perrone v. Abbott Laboratories, Inc. (Supreme Court, Broome County, N.Y., Nov., 1974).

Permanent kidney damage—Surgeon and anesthesiologist charged with failure to consult on choice of anesthetic—Manufacturer accused of insufficient warning—$100,000 settlement

A 45-year-old man with a history of kidney disease suffered permanent kidney damage during surgery for an ulcer, allegedly as a result of undergoing Penthrane anesthesia at high levels for several hours. In the subsequent lawsuit, the plaintiff charged that the surgeon failed to inform the anesthesiologist that the patient's kid-

---

[15] AMA *The Citation* 29:103, 1974.

[16] *AMA Drug Evaluations,* 2d ed., p. 230.

[17] *United States Dispensatory,* 27th ed., p. 740.

[18] *AMA Drug Evaluations,* 2d ed., p. 231.

[19] Klein, N. C. and Jeffries, G. H., "Hepatoxicity after Methoxyflurane Administration," *Journal of the American Medical Association* 197:1037-1039, 1966. Tornetta, B. J. and Boger, W. P., "Methoxyflurane and the Liver," *Archives of Surgery* 90:253-260, 1965.

[20] *AMA Drug Evaluations,* 2d ed., p. 231.

neys were not normal, and that the anesthesiologist failed to inform the surgeon that methoxyflurane was known to endanger patients with preexisting kidney disorders. The manufacturer of the anesthetic was also sued on the theory that its warnings were inadequate.

According to plaintiff's attorney, the plaintiff obtained a $100,000 settlement.[1]

Related cases

Renal failure resulting in fatal peritonitis—Verdict against anesthesiologist—Nonsuit in favor of manufacturer for plaintiff's failure to answer interrogatories

In Dion v. Graduate Hospital (1987) 360 Pa. Super. 416, 520 A.2d 876, the plaintiff, whose husband died as a result of acute peritonitis due to renal failure caused by Penthrane toxicity following surgery, obtained a verdict against the anesthesiologist but failed to recover damages against the manufacturer of Penthrane (Abbott Laboratories) because she failed to comply with the court's order to answer written interrogatories, which resulted in sanctions precluding her use of necessary expert testimony.

METHYCLOTHIAZIDE

Aquatensen
Diutensen
Enduron
Enduronyl
Eutron

Methyclothiazide is an oral diuretic-antihypertensive agent used in the management of hypertension and as adjunctive therapy in edema associated with congestive heart failure and cirrhosis of the liver.[2] Aquatensen and Diutensen (methyclothiazide plus cryptenamine) are manufactured by Wallace Laboratories (Cranbury, N.J.), Enduron, Enduronyl (methyclothiazide plus deserpidine), and Eutron (methyclothiazide plus pargyline hydrochloride) are manufactured by Abbott Pharmaceuticals (North Chicago, Ill.).

In the product literature for Enduron, the manufacturer cautions that methyclothiazide may deplete potassium reserves to an unpre-

---

[1] ATLA *News Letter* 18:115, 1975.

[2] *Physicians' Desk Reference,* 35th ed., p. 514.

dictable degree, and therefore periodic determinations of serum electrolytes should be performed at appropriate intervals for the purpose of detecting possible electrolyte imbalances.[3]

Sears v. Cooper (Tex. Civ. App., 1978) 574 S.W.2d 612.

Brain damage allegedly caused by Enduron aggravating electrolyte imbalance—Jury returns $500,000 award against physician

The patient in this case was suffering from edema. On October 12, 1972 her physician prescribed Enduron. Several days later she called his office, complaining that the drug was making her ill. The physician was out of the city, and his nurse told the patient to discontinue the medication until he returned. He returned on October 20. After examining her in his office, he instructed her to resume taking the drug.

On the evening of October 21, the patient began to feel worse. The following morning her husband called the physician and was told to have the patient discontinue solid foods, take only liquids, and come to the office the next morning. The patient's husband gave her a glass of tea, and shortly thereafter she fainted. She was rushed to the hospital in a coma and was later found to be suffering from brain damage. At the time of trial she was institutionalized, and would require custodial care for the remainder of her life.

The complaint charged that the physician was negligent in initially prescribing Enduron and in later having the patient resume taking it without having her tested for electrolyte imbalance. The plaintiffs produced a medical expert who testified that the patient suffered from electrolyte imbalance which was aggravated by the Enduron, and that this aggravation resulted in her brain damage. The physician produced several medical witnesses who testified that in their opinion the patient's condition could have been caused by "hepatic coma, meningial disease, cerebral hemorrhage, encephalomyelitis and stroke."

The jury awarded the plaintiffs $500,000. On appeal, the Court of Civil Appeals of Texas affirmed, holding that there was sufficient evidence to support the verdict.

---

[3] Id.

METHYLPHENIDATE HYDROCHLORIDE
Ritalin

Methylphenidate is a central nervous system stimulant that has been useful as an adjunct to remedial measures (psychological, educational, or social) in the management of children with attention deficit disorders (previously known as minimal brain dysfunction). According to the manufacturer, CIBA Pharmaceutical Company (Summit, N.J.), the drug is indicated as an integral part of a total treatment program for a stabilizing effect in children with a behavioral syndrome characterized by the following group of developmentally inappropriate symptoms: moderate-to-severe distractibility, short attention span, hyperactivity, emotional liability, and impulsivity.[4]

The mode of action of this drug is not completely understood, but presumably it activates the brain stem arousal system and cortex to produce its stimulant effect. The drug is contraindicated in patients with marked anxiety, tension, agitation, or glaucoma, and it should be used with caution in epileptic and hypertensive patients. It should be discontinued if seizures occur.[5]

There have been complaints about the drug's side effects, and plaintiffs began filing medical malpractice suits in the fall of 1987. Among the problems attributed to the product are increased hyperactivity and, upon withdrawal, depression and suicidal tendencies. In a criminal trial held in Boston in early March 1988, attorneys for the defendant, a 15-year-old boy accused of bludgeoning a classmate to death, claimed the defendant's treatment with Ritalin since age nine had "exacerbated his mental illness" and was partially responsible for his actions.[6]

Boston attorney Lawrence E. Lafferty, who has filed five medical malpractice actions involving Ritalin, reports that he is investigating about 200 other possible cases in Massachusetts, Rhode Island, Florida, Arizona, North Dakota and Washington state. According to Lafferty, from one to four million children have been administered Ritalin in the United States. There also is possible litigation

---

[4] *Physicians' Desk Reference,* 42d ed., p. 880; AMA *Drug Evaluations,* 6th ed., p. 165.

[5] Id.

[6] Blum, A., "Lawsuits Over Ritalin Spread to Massachusetts," *National Law Journal,* March 28, 1988, p. 41.

forthcoming in several cities over the involvement of school administrators in the use of Ritalin to control hyperactive children.[7]

METHYSERGIDE MALEATE
Sansert

Methysergide maleate is sold under the brand name Sansert by Sandoz Pharmaceuticals (East Hanover, N.J.). It is used in the management of migraine and cluster headaches, and is indicated in patients whose vascular headaches are of sufficient frequency and severity to warrant prophylactic therapy. The drug is related to the ergot alkaloid derivative, methylergonovine maleate, and is similar chemically to lysergic acid diethylamide (LSD).[8]

Adverse reactions to the drug occur frequently. Some are mild and disappear with continued use, but others are serious and require discontinuance of therapy. Central nervous system symptoms include insomnia, nervousness, euphoria, dizziness, rapid speech, difficulty in thinking, feeling of depersonalization, nightmares, and hallucinations. Drowsiness, lethargy, loss of initiative, and depression have also been observed.[9]

Fibrotic changes have been reported, as well as vascular insufficiency of the lower limbs with pain, swelling, and muscular atrophy. Thrombophlebitis from involvement of the aorta, vena cava, and the common iliac vessels may also occur.[10]

The manufacturer warns that with long-term, uninterrupted administration of Sansert, retroperitoneal fibrosis or related conditions, e.g., pleuropulmonary fibrosis and cardiovascular disorders with murmurs or vascular bruits, have been reported. Patients should be instructed to report immediately the following symptoms: cold, numb, and painful hands and feet; leg cramps on walking; any type of girdle, flank, or chest pain, or any associated symptoms. Should any of the foregoing symptoms develop, the drug should be discontinued.[11]

The manufacturer warns that continuous administration of Sansert should not exceed six months; that there must be a drug-

---

[7] Id.

[8] *AMA Drug Evaluations,* 2d ed., p. 284. See also *Physicians' Desk Reference,* 35th ed., p. 1581.

[9] Id.

[10] Id.

[11] *Physicians' Desk Reference,* 35th ed., p. 1581.

free interval of three to four weeks after each six-month period of treatment; and that during the last two to three weeks of a period of treatment the dosage should be gradually reduced.[12]

Mahaffey v. Sandoz, Inc. (No. C-20275, District Court, Sedgwick County, Kan., May, 1974).

Endocardial fibrosis—Failure to warn charged against manufacturer, physician and pharmacist—$350,000 settlement

A patient was given Sansert over a period of two years for treatment of migraine headache. When he developed endocardial fibrosis, which resulted in a blockage of the left coronary artery and required a coronary artery bypass operation, he brought suit against the manufacturer of the drug, the pharmacy where he obtained it, and the physician who prescribed it.

Against the manufacturer the patient charged failure to warn physicians sufficiently of the fibrotic side effects either by a "Dear Doctor letter," a supplementary notice in *Physicians' Desk Reference,* or through detailmen. The patient charged that the pharmacist had failed to call to the attention of the prescribing physician the drug's fibrotic side effects after he became aware of this information. Against the physician the patient alleged failure to warn of such side effects, failure to monitor the patient's drug intake, and failure to require that he undergo a "drug-free interval" every six months.

According to the attorneys for the patient, the case was settled for $350,000, with all defendants contributing.[13]

METICORTEN

See PREDNISONE

METOCLOPRAMIDE HYDROCHLORIDE

Octamide

Reglan

Metoclopramide is an agent used in disorders of the upper gastrointestinal tract. In the injectable form, the drug is classified as an antinauseant, and according to A.H. Robins Company (Richmond, Va.), manufacturer of Reglan, the tablet form is to be used "as a short-term (4 to 12 weeks) therapy for adults with symptomatic,

---

[12] Id.

[13] ATLA *News Letter* 17:351, 1974.

documented gastroesophageal reflux who fail to respond to conventional therapy." Adult dosage is from 10 mg. (1 tablet) to 15 mg. ($1^1/_2$ tablets) up to four times per day, thirty minutes before each meal and at bedtime, depending upon symptoms being treated and clinical response.[14]

In addition to A.H. Robins, several companies manufacture and market the product under the generic name, and Adria Laboratories (Columbus, Ohio) produces the drug under the brand name Octamide.

Lou v. Smith (1985) 285 Ark. 249, 685 S.W.2d 809.

Excessive dosage—Pharmacist liable for altering prescription—Damages for mental anguish and punitive award affirmed

The plaintiff obtained a prescription from her family doctor for her four-month-old daughter calling for one milligram of Reglan, four times a day. The pharmacist, thinking the doctor had meant to write "10 milligrams," the adult dosage, changed the "1" to a "10" by adding a zero. The doctor had not written in the patient's age on the prescription blank, and the pharmacist assumed the medication was for one of the parents. The child experienced "severe reactions" on being given the drug, but apparently suffered no permanent injury.

In her suit against the pharmacist, the plaintiff charged "willful and wanton misconduct" and claimed, in addition to damages for the child, damages for her own mental anguish. A jury awarded compensatory damages of $2,000 to the child, $1,250 to the mother, and an additional $3,750 in punitive damages to the mother, father and child.

On appeal, the Supreme Court of Arkansas affirmed, holding that medical evidence introduced by the plaintiff established that altering a prescription under the circumstances presented was a clear violation of the standards of pharmacy practice.

METRIC

See METRONIDAZOLE

---

[14] *Physicians' Desk Reference,* 41st ed., pp. 1634-36.

METRONIDAZOLE
Flagyl
Metric
Metryl
Protostat

Metronidazole is a synthetic antiprotozoal and antibacterial agent especially effective in treating serious anaerobic infections. Serious side effects include convulsive seizures and peripheral neuropathy, which demand prompt discontinuation of metronidazole therapy. The manufacturers also warn that alcoholic beverages should not be consumed during the course of treatment and for at least one day afterward because abdominal cramps, vomiting, and headaches may occur.

Flagyl is manufactured by Searle Pharmaceuticals, Inc. (Chicago, Ill.), Metric by The Fielding Company (St. Louis, Mo.), Metryl by The Lemmon Company (Sellerville, Pa.), and Protostat by Ortho Pharmaceutical Corporation (Raritan, N.J.). The product also is manufactured by numerous companies under the generic name.[15]

Perkins v. Windsor Hosp. Corp. (1982) 142 Vt. 305, 455 A.2d 810.

Adverse reaction to Flagyl after ingesting alcohol—Question of informed consent

The patient was given a prescription for Flagyl to determine the cause of atypical cells disclosed in a routine pap smear. Prior to taking the initial dose, she consumed some alcoholic beverage; later when she took the drug, she suffered a severe reaction (chest pains and shortness of breath) and had to be rushed to the hospital. Following her release from the hospital she continued to suffer chest pains and related problems.

At the trial the patient testified that her physician failed to warn her of any side effects of Flagyl, and in particular, the potential adverse reaction when the drug is combined with alcohol. The physician testified that although he did not recall actually warning the patient of this risk, it nevertheless was his "custom" to do so. The patient's expert testified that even if the physician had given his customary warning it would not have provided the patient with sufficient information concerning the dangers of the drug "to per-

---

[15] Id., 40th ed., pp. 1688-89.

mit plaintiff to make a knowledgeable evaluation to undergo the treatment."

Despite the above testimony the trial judge refused to instruct the jury on the standards pertaining to informed consent in medical malpractice cases. The Supreme Court of Vermont held that this was error and ordered a new trial.

METRYL
See METRONIDAZOLE

MICRhoGAM
See Rh_o (D) IMMUNE GLOBULIN (HUMAN)

MIGRAL
See ERGOTAMINE TARTRATE

MILPATH
See MEPROBAMATE

MILPREM
See MEPROBAMATE

MILTOWN
See MEPROBAMATE

MILTRATE
See MEPROBAMATE

MINI-GAMULIN Rh
See Rh_o (D) IMMUNE GLOBULIN (HUMAN)

MINTEZOL
See THIABENDAZOLE

MITOMYCIN
Mutamycin

Mitomycin is used in the palliative treatment of various solid tumors (gastric, non-small cell lung, cervical, colorectal, breast, bladder, pancreatic, and esophageal carcinomas). Its action is probably due to the inhibition of DNA synthesis. Reported adverse reactions include bone marrow, integument, mucus membrane, pulmonary and renal toxicity. Also, fever, loss of appetite, nausea and vomiting occur in about 14% of patients.[16]

Bristol-Myers Oncology Division (Evansville, Ind.) produces the agent under the brand name Mutamycin.

Weinberger v. Bristol-Myers Co. (D. Md., 1986) 652 F. Supp. 187.

Skin ulceration at sight of injection—
Manufacturer's warning adequate

The patient was undergoing treatment for cancer. His physician selected, among other drugs, Mutamycin. Shortly after the first intravenous injection into his right forearm, the plaintiff noticed some irritation, redness and soreness. The condition worsened, and by the sixth month, the plaintiff's skin had ulcerated to the point where it was necessary to perform a skin graft. The plaintiff filed suit, alleging that the manufacturer had not adequately warned the physician of this side-effect. Suit was brought under the theories of both negligence and strict liability.

The manufacturer moved for summary judgment, claiming the physician was sufficiently warned through the following statement contained in the package insert: "Integument and Mucous Membrane Toxicity — This has occurred in approximately 4% of patients treated with Mutamycin. Cellulitis at the injection site has been reported and is occasionally severe." Elsewhere in the package insert it was stated that "Mutamycin should be given intravenously only, using care to avoid extravasation of the compound. If extravasation occurs, cellulitis, ulceration, and slough may result." The manufacturer also submitted proof that substantially the same statements were published in the *Physician's Desk Reference.*

In granting the manufacturer's motion for summary judgment, the court held that the above warnings were legally adequate to avoid damages under both the theories of negligence and strict liability.

---

[16] AMA *Drug Evaluations,* 6th ed., p. 1202; *Physicians' Desk Reference,* 42d ed., p. 776.

M-M-R II
See MEASLES, MUMPS and RUBELLA VIRUS VACCINE

MORPHINE SULFATE
Astramorph
Duramorph
MS Contin Tablets
MSIR Tablets
RMS Suppositories
Roxanol

Morphine, the principal alkaloid of opium, is used mainly to relieve pain which it accomplishes by increasing the threshold for the perception of pain and by altering the psychic response so that the patient is better able to tolerate the pain.[17]

The major effects of narcotic analgesics such as morphine are produced on the central nervous system and the large intestines. Central nervous system effects include pain relief, drowsiness, mental clouding, and changes in mood. Narcotics cause decreased motility through the gastrointestinal system, and have been used to treat diarrhea and dysentery. (Constipation is a common side effect of treatment with narcotics.) Narcotics have also been proven useful for sedation, cough control, dyspnea, and anesthesia.

Acute toxicity may result from attempted suicide, a gross error in dosage, accidental overdose, or an abnormal response to an accepted therapeutic dose, especially if peripheral circulation is impaired or adequate respiration is already a problem (e.g., emphysema). Allergic manifestations rarely occur, however, anaphylactoid reactions after the administration of intravenous morphine and codeine have been reported. Urticaria, rashes, and contact dermatitis may also occur. Patients with decreased thyroid activity, those who have had severe head injury with increased pressure within the cranial vault, and those who suffer urinary retention due to enlargement of the prostate or a stricture of the urethra, may be adversely and seriously affected by the use of these analgesics. This is especially true in bronchial asthma, where the depression of the reflex mechanism of the bronchi (lung tubules) to eliminate secretions caused by narcotics may result in the patient's "drowning" in his own secre-

[17] *United States Dispensatory,* 27th ed., p. 760.

tions. Drug addicts show very little response to visual therapeutic doses.[18]

Astramorph is manufactured by Astra Pharmaceutical Products (Westboro, Mass.), Duramorph by Elkins-Sinn, Inc. (Cherry Hill, N.C.), MS Contin Tablets and MSIR Tablets by Purdue Frederick (Norwalk, Conn.), RMS Suppositories by Upsher-Smith Laboratories, Inc. (Minneapolis, Minn.), and Roxanol by Roxane Laboratories, Inc. (Columbus, Ohio). The product also is marketed by several companies under morphine sulfate.

Ballenger v. Crowell (1978) 38 N.C. App. 50, 247 S.E.2d 287.

Patient has cause of action against physician for addiction

The patient in this case was a victim of Charcot-Marie-Tooth disease, a debilitating neuromuscular disorder occasionally characterized by severe pain. From 1962 to 1974 the defendant physician treated the patient by prescribing morphine sulfate and other addictive drugs. By 1974, the patient was taking 35 half-grain morphine tablets a day, plus 25 other various tablets and capsules.

On several occasions the patient attempted to break his addiction. In 1967 he voluntarily entered the Federal Narcotics Addiction Hospital in Lexington, Kentucky, but he returned to the morphine on the defendant's advice "not to worry about the drugs," that he "would just always have to take them."

In 1974 he entered Appalachian Hall Hospital for treatment of the addiction, where consulting physicians told him that he did not need narcotics for his pain, that lesser drugs would do. Under the program there he successfully withdrew from the morphine.

In his suit against the defendant for causing his addiction, the patient produced an expert medical witness who testified that, while morphine in such doses as the plaintiff had received might be appropriate in terminal cases of the Charcot-Marie-Tooth disease, the dosage the patient was taking for his condition "was not normal." The witness would not say, however, that the dosage was in violation of approved medical standards. He did say that in such a case, "at some point, a doctor should intervene and either switch medication or break the addiction."

The trial judge granted the defendant's motion for summary judgment, but on appeal it was reversed, with the Court of Appeals of

[18] *Lawyers' Medical Cyclopedia,* § 6.12(D) (3rd ed., 1981).

North Carolina holding that "there was some evidence presented which tended to show that standard medical practice no longer considered addiction necessary and that defendant should have known more care was required than the mere writing of ever-increasing prescriptions."

Hoskie v. United States (C.A.-10 N.M., 1981) 666 F.2d 1353.

Child suffers brain damage from overdose—$25,000 award for pain and suffering inadequate

A two-year-old child was hospitalized at the Gallup Indian Medical Center in Gallup, New Mexico for a bronchoscopy to remove a sunflower seed that had become lodged in his bronchial tube. During the course of the treatment he was given an injection of morphine in the amount of ten milligrams, which was several times the amount recommended for a child his age and weight. He lapsed into a coma which lasted for several days. Tests determined he had suffered severe brain damage. He is spastic, mentally retarded and cannot speak.

The trial judge awarded $236,101 which included $25,000 for pain and suffering. The Court of Appeals held that the latter amount was inadequate and remanded the case for reconsideration.

Davis v. Washington University (No. 802-05960, Circuit Court, St. Louis County, Mo., Jan. 17, 1983).

Excessive postoperative injections—$2 million settlement

The patient was admitted to the defendant hospital for surgery on her foot. Following the operation, which was successful, she was given an intramuscular injection of morphine. Ten minutes later she received more morphine, intravenously. She suffered seizures and was comatose for over two months. She now has brain damage, suffers speech and memory impairment and is unable to care for herself. The hospital entered into a structured settlement calling for $100,000 annually for twenty-five years, a lump sum payment of $900,000 at the end of twenty-five years, and $431,000 to the patient's husband. The present value of the settlement was $2,000,000.[19]

---

[19] ATLA *Law Reporter* 26:231, 1983.

Rose v. Doctors Hospital (No. 84-4467-B, 44th Judicial District Court, Dallas County, Tex., Nov. 11, 1985).

Outpatient receives excessive dosage in emergency department—Dies five hours later—$4.46 million jury verdict

A 29-year-old man appeared at the defendant hospital's emergency department complaining of flu-like symptoms. Five hours later he died, according to the autopsy report, from morphine intoxication. In an action against the hospital it was alleged that emergency department personnel administered the decedent morphine without any orders from an attending physician. According to the testimony of the county medical examiner, the decedent's body contained .56 mg of morphine per liter of blood, and morphine was also found in bile and lung samples. This amount, according to the evidence, exceeded any known survivable level, which ruled out the possibility that the drug could have been present in the body prior to the decedent's arrival at the emergency department.

A jury returned a verdict of $4.46 million and the court added $1.35 million in prejudgment interest.[20]

St. Clair v. Doctors Med. Center (No. 215956, Superior Court, Stanislaus County, Cal., February 24, 1989).

Emergency department patient dies after apparent excessive dosage—$400,000 jury verdict

The plaintiff's wife injured her hip in a fall and was taken to the defendant hospital's emergency department. The patient's medical history included malnutrition, below-normal weight, chronic obstructive pulmonary disease, cardiac arrythmia, and rheumatoid arthritis. She also had a tracheostomy tube in place. An X-ray examination showed no fracture, however, and the emergency department physician ordered an injection of 50 mg. Demerol (meperidine hydrochloride) and 50 mg. Phenergan (promethazine hydrochloride) to relieve her pain. The patient was released, and the plaintiff took her to the car, where she fell asleep in about five minutes. When they arrived home, the plaintiff could not awaken her, and he called 911. The paramedics arrived and pronounced her dead.

---

[20] Id., 29:227, 1986.

On autopsy, in addition to the Demerol and Phenergan, the tests showed morphine in the patient's blood. In the plaintiff's suit against the hospital and the physician's medical group that operated the emergency department, he charged that the morphine had constituted an overdose of narcotics. Also, he claimed that in view of his wife's medical history, she was at high risk for an adverse reaction to narcotic medication, and she should have been observed for at least an hour after receiving her pain medication. The hospital records did not indicate that the patient had been given morphine.

The jury returned a verdict for $400,000 which the court reduced to $250,000 under California's statutory cap on noneconomic damages.[21]

Related cases

Stillbirth following use during labor—Action barred by statute

In Lutes v. Farley (1983) 113 Ill. App. 3d 113, 68 Ill. Dec. 695, 446 N.E.2d 866, the plaintiff delivered a stillborn infant in May, 1978. In April, 1982, she filed suit against the physician and midwife, alleging that the death was due to the negligent administration of morphine during labor. The complaint further alleged that the defendants' negligence was not known to the plaintiff until July, 1980, at which time the plaintiff's sister "embarked upon a nursing course and in the course of her studies, determined that morphine should not be administered to a pregnant mother." A summary judgment for the defendants was affirmed by the Appellate Court which held that the plaintiff's cause of action commenced on the death of the child because "the stillbirth of a child is a sudden traumatic event which should prompt some investigation by the injured party and trigger the application of the discovery rule."

MOTRIN

See IBUPROFEN

---

[21] ATLA *Professional Negligence Law Reporter* 4:128, 1989.

MS CONTIN
See MORPHINE SULFATE

MSIR
See MORPHINE SULFATE

MUDRANE
See AMINOPHYLLINE

MUTAMYCIN
See MITOMYCIN

MYAMBUTOL
See ETHAMBUTOL HYDROCHLORIDE

MYCOLOG
See NEOMYCIN SULFATE; TRIAMCINOLONE ACETONIDE

MYDRIACYL
See TROPICAMIDE

MYLERAN
See BUSULFAN

MYOCHRYSINE
See GOLD SODIUM THIOMALATE

MYSOLINE
See PRIMIDONE

MYSTECLIN
See TETRACYCLINE HYDROCHLORIDE

MYTREX
See TRIAMCINOLONE ACETONIDE

N

NALDECON
See CHLORPHENIRAMINE MALEATE

NALFON
See FENOPROFEN CALCIUM

NAQUIVAL
See RESERPINE

NARDIL
See PHENELZINE SULFATE

NEBCIN
See TOBRAMYCIN SULFATE

NEMBUTAL
See PENTOBARBITAL SODIUM

NEOBIOTIC
See NEOMYCIN SULFATE

NEODECADRON
See NEOMYCIN SULFATE—DEXAMETHASONE SODIUM PHOSPHATE

NEOMYCIN SULFATE
Bactine
Cortisporin
LazerSporin-C
Mycolog
Neobiotic
Neo-Polycin
Neosporin
Neo-Synalar
Octicair
Otocort
Topisporin

Neomycin is a broad spectrum antibiotic very similar to streptomycin. A cross resistance exists with the other aminoglycosides. The parenteral use of neomycin is not recommended due to the increased risk of toxicity. Orally, neomycin is indicated as an adjunct in the treatment of hepatic coma, in infectious diarrhea due to enteropathogenic E. Coli, and in preoperative bowel preparations. Neomycin is not used for systemic infections. In the treatment of chronic liver insufficiency or hepatic coma, a 1% neomycin retention enema may be administered if the drug cannot be taken orally. Concomitant administration with erythromycin base provides suppression of anaerobic microorganisms in preoperative bowel antisepsis.

Given orally, only negligible amounts, approximately 3% of neomycin, are absorbed through the intact intestinal mucosa. Significant amounts may be absorbed through ulcerated or denuded mucosa or if there is impaired gastrointestinal motility. Oral neomycin may cause diarrhea, nausea, vomiting and malabsorption. Nephrotoxicity, neurotoxicity and ototoxicity may occur as a result of parenteral administration or significant oral absorption. Patients should be kept well hydrated to prevent renal tubular damage.

Compared to all the other aminoglycosides, neomycin is probably the most potent neuromuscular blocking agent causing respiratory paralysis. The most important toxic effect of neomycin is its irreversible damage to the auditory branch of the eighth cranial nerve; in some cases complete hearing loss has occurred. Skin rashes have made up the majority of hypersensitivity reactions to neomycin.[1]

Bactine is manufactured by Miles, Inc. (Elkhart, Ind.); Cortisporin and Neosporin by Burroughs Wellcome Company (Research Triangle Park, N.C.); LazerSporin-C by Pedinol Pharmacal (Farmingdale, N.Y.); Mycolog by E. R. Squibb & Sons, Inc. (Princeton, N.J.); Neobiotic by the Pfipharmecs Division of Pfizer, Inc. (New York, N.Y.); Neo-Polycin by Dow Pharmaceuticals (Indianapolis, Ind.); Neo-Synalar by Syntex Laboratories, Inc. (Palo Alto, Cal.); Octicair and Topisporin by Pharmafair, Inc. (Hauppauge, N.Y.); and Otocort by Lemmon Company (Sellersville, Pa.).

Several companies also produce neomycin sulfate under the generic label.

Marchese v. Monaco (1958) 52 N.J. Super. 474, 145 A.2d 809.

Hearing loss—Choice of Mycifradin over other antibiotics questioned—$56,000 judgment for plaintiff affirmed

A male patient consulted his physician for fever, purple blotches under the skin on his legs, and swollen ankles. He was hospitalized

[1] *Lawyers' Medical Cyclopedia,* § 6.8(C) (3rd ed., 1981). For product information on neomycin sulfate, see the latest edition of *Physicians' Desk Reference.*

with an admitting diagnosis of "Nephritis, Diverticulitis of the large bowel." The usual tests were run, some of which suggested kidney disease and some of which did not. When no definite diagnosis could be established, the patient was released.

Several days later the patient returned to his physician's office complaining of passing blood. He was again hospitalized with the possible diagnosis of kidney stone. There was some swelling in his abdomen and legs, and apparently he was retaining fluids. After another battery of tests, a definite diagnosis of kidney disease with impaired kidney function was made.

During the first ten days of hospitalization the patient was treated with Terramycin. When it appeared that this drug was not handling the infection, the attending physician ordered neomycin sulfate (Mycifradin) injections intramuscularly. During the next eight days the patient received thirty such injections of 1/4 gram each. The injections were suspended for eight days and then renewed for another four days, during which time fourteen injections were given. There was some dispute as to the dosage during this second series of injections; some evidence suggests 1/8 gram, but the records were incomplete. Possibly, some injections were as much as one-half gram each.

At the end of a month, the patient was discharged. Several days later, however, he noticed an impairment in his hearing. It grew worse until there was no useful hearing in either ear.

The patient filed a malpractice suit against the attending physician; the main thrust being Mycifradin should not have been selected as the antibiotic. Evidence was introduced at the trial that there were more than fifty antibiotics on the market, and Mycifradin was one of the three or four most dangerous with regard to side effects. The package insert for Mycifradin was introduced. The defendant contended that he had read the brochure, and had followed the manufacturer's directions in substantially all respects. He admitted, however, that laboratory tests on the patient had not revealed any of the organisms named in the Mycifradin brochure for which the drug was recommended by the manufacturer. The closest was *staphylococcus albus,* which the defendant and his expert witnesses stated was a "first cousin" to *staphylococcus aureus,* an organism mentioned in the brochure. This argument was weakened, however, by the testimony of one of the defendant's experts who admitted that *aureus* "is far more pathogenic" than *albus.*

The jury found for the patient and awarded $56,000. On appeal, numerous issues were raised and the Appellate Division of the Superior Court of New Jersey delivered a lengthy opinion, setting out much of the evidence, including the pertinent portions of the drug brochure and testimony by the experts.

Among the defendant's contentions on appeal was the argument that he had called in two specialists, a urologist and an internist, to consult with him on the patient's case. This fact, argued the defendant, proved conclusively that he exercised reasonable care. To this argument the reviewing court responded by pointing out that the jury may consider that a general practitioner still has a primary duty to care for his patient regardless of advice from consulting specialists. Furthermore, the reviewing court observed that in the present case it was questionable whether the defendant actually had adequate consultation, i.e., the defendant had not shown the drug brochure to his consulting urologist, and the urologist had testified at trial that he was not familiar with the brochure at the time he was brought in on the case, and at the time he did not even know that Mycifradin could cause hearing impairment.

The Appellate Court affirmed the judgment for the patient.

Yetton v. Desert Hosp. Dist. of Palm Springs (No. 92756, Superior Court, Riverside County, Cal., May 25, 1972).

Hearing loss—Alleged excessive dose and intramuscular rather than oral administration—$60,000 settlement with physician and manufacturer—$675,000 verdict against hospital

A 36-year-old woman hospital patient being treated for kidney and liver difficulties suffered total hearing loss, allegedly as a result of negligence on the part of the hospital's nurses and pharmacist in administering an excessive dose of neomycin sulfate. In the resulting lawsuit the patient claimed in addition that the drug was negligently administered intramuscularly instead of orally, contrary to her physician's orders. The physician and the manufacturer of the drug were also named in the suit.

Prior to trial of the case, attorneys for the hospital offered $190,000 to settle. The patient's attorneys countered with a demand for $250,000. A settlement was made with the physician and drug company for $60,000. The case went to trial against the hospital and the jury returned a verdict of $675,000 for the patient and $30,000 for her husband.[2]

Thompson v. Kaiser Foundation Health Plan, Inc. (No. SOC 21485, Long Beach Superior Court, Los Angeles County, Cal., 1973).

Hearing loss—Neomycin and streptomycin administered at same time—$350,000 settlement

A seven-year-old girl with a ruptured appendix and peritonitis was given streptomycin and neomycin for the infection. The patient apparently recovered, but several weeks later developed symptoms of hearing loss.

The plaintiff's lawsuit charged, among other things, that both the streptomycin and neomycin should not have been prescribed at the same time and that the dosage of neomycin was excessive and unduly prolonged. The action went to trial, but before the case was given to the jury, it was settled for $350,000.[3]

Portis v. United States (C.A.-4 Va., 1973) 483 F.2d 670.

Hearing loss—Injections given instead of oral dosage—Statute of limitations failed to bar action

A fifteen-month-old girl was admitted to the United States Air Force Hospital at Maxwell Air Force Base, Alabama for corrective surgery of a bowel disorder. In preparation for the operation a staff physician prescribed one gram of neomycin sulfate every six hours. The drug was to be given orally, but by mistake an unidentified government nurse administered seven intramuscular injections. The child suffered immediate kidney toxicity but was treated successfully.

The parents were warned that the inadvertent injections could also cause damage to the auditory (eighth cranial) nerve resulting in hearing impairment. The child's hearing was tested before she left the hospital but no damage was found. The parents were cautioned, however, to have the child's hearing tested again at age three.

Over the next several years the child was ill frequently with ear, throat and respiratory infections, including pneumonia and tonsilli-

---

[2] ATLA *News Letter* 15:412, 1972; AMA *The Citation* 26:120, 1973.

[3] ATLA *News Letter* 16:267, 1973.

tis. During these illnesses the child's hearing began to deteriorate. This was first suspected by her mother within a year after the accidental injections, and was confirmed when she was given hearing tests at age three. The child then underwent treatment for the hearing difficulties for five years, during which time the actual cause of the loss was never determined. The parents were told that the child's deafness could have been caused by the neomycin injections, but also by ear infection or high fever. Finally, in 1969, six years after the injections, the child's hearing difficulty was definitely diagnosed as auditory nerve damage directly related to the neomycin toxicity. The parents brought an action under the Federal Tort Claims Act against the government.

The government defended by raising the statute of limitations, and was upheld by the trial judge who ruled that the parents knew soon after the injections that there was a "distinct possibility" of future hearing loss as a result of the neomycin. The Court of Appeals disagreed, however, finding that while the parents knew of the possibility of hearing loss and the likelihood that the injections had caused it, they could not have pursued a successful action against the government until there was sufficient evidence of proximate cause. This was not established until 1969 when a physician was willing to state definitely that there was auditory nerve damage related to the drug toxicity.

The judgment in the lower court was reversed.

DaRoca v. St. Bernard Gen. Hosp. (La. App., 1977) 347 So. 2d 933.

Hearing loss—Excessive dosage not in violation of prevailing medical standards

A female patient had a proctoscopic examination, and a premalignant growth was found inside her colon. Surgery was recommended. The patient asked the surgeon to avoid a colostomy unless it was absolutely necessary. To comply, the surgeon ordered that neomycin sulfate be given to the patient orally prior to surgery since it would sterilize the intestine but would not be absorbed in significant amounts into the bloodstream.

The surgery was performed and a colostomy was avoided. Three grams of neomycin sulfate were administered daily over the next four days following the operation. It was instilled periodically into a catheter leading to the site of the surgical union of the bowel. During this four-day period, there were no signs of infection and the patient's kidneys functioned normally, thus eliminating the drug by excretion.

The patient's wound was opened during a coughing spell eight days after the neomycin sulfate was stopped. The surgeon performed a secondary closure as an emergency procedure. Thereafter the patient developed peritonitis and became critically ill. Her family transferred her to another hospital with an intensive care unit. She was given extensive treatment and medication which included two other ototoxic drugs. The patient recovered, but with almost total loss of hearing.

The surgeon testified that he was aware that he had prescribed an amount of neomycin sulfate which exceeded the recommended dosage in medical reference books, but he pointed out that reference books "were merely guidelines intended to assist physicians in exercising medical judgment in given circumstances." He also contended that he had used an "irrigation dosage" which did not really exceed the recommended maximum because a large portion of the drug ran out through the drain and was not absorbed. Another surgeon testified that he would have used "a lot more" as long as renal function was normal. He also testified that he had used neomycin for surgery about 2,000 times over twelve years without one case of hearing loss. A specialist in colon-rectal surgery also stated that ototoxic reaction to neomycin was "extremely rare."

Judgment for the patient was reversed on appeal, the reviewing court finding the evidence insufficient to establish that the surgeon had violated prevailing medical standards.

Richards v. Upjohn Co. (1980) 95 N.M. 675, 625 P.2d 1192.

Hearing loss—Settlement with physicians—Summary judgment for manufacturer reversed on issue of sufficient warning

This is another case in which a patient suffered hearing loss following the irrigation of an open wound with neomycin. The treatment was rendered in October, 1973. At the time, *Physicians' Desk Reference* and package inserts accompanying neomycin no longer recommended the drug for irrigation purposes.

The physicians involved in the patient's treatment admitted that they were not aware of the dangers associated with the topical use of neomycin or that such usage was no longer recommended. On the fifth day of trial they settled with the patient for undisclosed sums.

A mistrial was then declared and Upjohn moved for a summary judgment, which was granted.

On appeal, the Court of Appeals of New Mexico reversed, holding that the patient had a cause of action against the manufacturer. According to the reviewing court, although Upjohn's product literature and the information provided in *Physicians' Desk Reference* contained warnings concerning the use of neomycin, the patient, said the court, presented evidence that these warnings were "inadequate." Neomycin had been on the market for over ten years before the recommendation to use it topically was withdrawn. The court apparently felt that a stronger warning should have been given in view of the danger presented and the fact that the medical profession had for so long relied upon the drug in irrigating wounds.

Van Iperen v. Van Bramer (Iowa, 1986) 392 N.W.2d 480.

Hearing loss—Kanamycin and neomycin used in rectal flush—Insufficient evidence of lack of informed consent and hospital negligence

The plaintiff was treated with kanamycin and neomycin in the form of a "rectal flush" because of a fistula that developed in his bladder wall following intestinal surgery and an ileostomy. After periodic hospitalizations over a period of five months during which time he received from two to three flushes daily, the plaintiff developed a hearing loss. There was a dispute as to whether the plaintiff was informed of this risk by his physicians, and the jury decided this issue in favor of the defendants. The reviewing court held that this decision was supported by substantial evidence.

Also at issue was the trial court's directed verdict in favor of the hospital despite the plaintiff's contention that the hospital had not met the standards of the Joint Commission on the Accreditation of Hospitals which require that, within the limits of available resources, a hospital should provide drug monitoring services through its pharmacy, which includes a review of every patient's drug regimen for any potential adverse reactions. The Supreme Court of Iowa held that while hospital accreditation standards provide some evidence of the proper standard of care, the evidence presented by the plaintiff was insufficient, "without additional reliable interpretative data" to generate a jury issue on this question.

Turner v. Peden (La. App., 1986) 496 So. 2d 515.

Loss of hearing and equilibrium following use of eardrops—Judgment for physician affirmed

The defendant physician, an otolaryngologist, treated the plaintiff for a punctured right eardrum. To prevent infection, he gave the plaintiff Cortisporin Otic Suspension in the form of liquid eardrops to be applied every six hours. On the sixth application, the plaintiff experienced an "extreme burning sensation throughout his entire body, accompanied by dizziness, nausea, and vertigo." He eventually permanently lost all hearing in the ear and suffers permanent equilibrium problems.

At the trial the defendant introduced evidence that the Cortisporin eardrops, although containing neomycin, were routinely prescribed for potential and actual infections of the middle ear, and that "billions of doses of Cortisporin have been used in people with perforations of the eardrum." The trial court found for the defendant and the Court of Appeal affirmed.

Pratt v. Stein (1982) 298 Pa. Super. 92, 444 A.2d 674.

Hearing loss—Excessive postoperative use when other antibiotics could have been used—$1,000,000 verdict affirmed

The patient was given neomycin for infection following a spinal fusion. The wound was either instilled, injected or irrigated with five grams of neomycin daily for ten days. During the first eight days the drug was administered in a 20 cc. solution of saline, and the last two days, in a 1,000 cc. solution of saline. On the eleventh day the drug was discontinued because of a "possible ototoxic reaction."

The *Physicians' Desk Reference* contains a warning that the maximum daily dosage for an *intramuscular* or *oral* injection of neomycin should not exceed one gram. The defendants argued that this warning did not apply in the present case because the drug was frequently *instilled* or the wound *irrigated* in which case less than *one fifth* of the dosage is absorbed by the body. This theory was disputed by the plaintiff's expert because of the "highly vascular" tissue in the spinal area. Evidence also was introduced that other less toxic antibiotics could have been used.

A $1,000,000 verdict for the plaintiff was affirmed by the Superior Court of Pennsylvania.

Callan v. Nordland (No. 80-L-372, Circuit Court, Will County, Ill., Mar. 26, 1982).

**Hearing loss after prolonged use of Neomycin—
$265,000 jury verdict against internist**

A sixty-eight-year-old woman consulted the defendant internist for treatment of ulcerative colitis. The defendant prescribed Neomycin which the patient took over a period of fourteen months. During that time the patient complained of ringing in her ears and some mild hearing loss, but the defendant attributed it to wax in the ears and performed no audiometric tests. The patient eventually was referred to an ear, nose and throat specialist who diagnosed profound hearing loss. A jury returned a verdict of $265,000,[4] which was affirmed on appeal (see "Related cases," below).

Marlar v. West (No. 17-56941-79, 17th Judicial District Court, Tarrant County, Tex., Mar. 18, 1983).

**Hearing loss and kidney failure following irrigation of
knee infection—Alleged failure to obtain informed
consent and to monitor toxicity levels—Orthopaedic surgeon settles for $600,000**

The patient suffered a postoperative infection following surgery to repair a torn medial meniscus in his knee. When the infection failed to respond to cephalexin monohydrate (Keflex), the orthopaedic surgeon irrigated the area with a solution of neomycin, and the patient was put on continuous irrigation for four days. Blood and hearing studies were not performed. On the fourth day the patient displayed symptoms of auditory and renal impairment and the irrigation was discontinued. The total dosage was 90 to 120 grams. The patient later suffered kidney failure, which was corrected, but he has permanent hearing loss and tinnitus.

Suit was brought based on failure to obtain informed consent, improper prescription of neomycin, excessive dosage and failure to order blood and hearing studies. The parties settled for $600,000.[5]

---

[4] ATLA *Law Reporter* 25:327, 1982.
[5] Id., 26:330, 1983.

Shrew v. Romond (No. F4-1329, Wisconsin Patient's Compensation Panel, Milwaukee County, Wis., Feb., 1984).

Hearing loss following irrigation of knee infection—Failure to monitor toxicity levels—Orthopaedic surgeon and hospital settle for $100,000

A twenty-five-year-old apprentice plumber suffered hearing loss (high tones) following irrigation of a knee infection with neomycin. The plaintiff's physician, an orthopaedic surgeon, prescribed the drug after checking with the hospital pharmacist. No blood or hearing tests were performed. The parties entered into a structured settlement agreement calling for an immediate payment of $35,000 and $4,800 annually for fifteen years. Lump sum payments of $10,000, $20,000 and $30,000 are also to be made at ten year intervals. The present value of the settlement was $100,000.[6]

Related cases

Hearing loss—Neomycin and kanamycin involved—Settlement with physician—Judgment against manufacturer reversed

In Bristol-Myers Co. v. Gonzales (Tex., 1978) 561 S.W.2d 801, a patient claiming hearing loss from neomycin and kanamycin obtained a $100,000 settlement with his physician and a $400,000 judgment against the manufacturer of kanamycin, but saw his judgment reversed because the jury was not informed of the settlement. The case is summarized herein under KANAMYCIN.

Hearing loss after prolonged use—Misunderstanding as to drug to be used—Brand name warnings held admissible

In affirming a $265,000 verdict against a physician whose patient suffered hearing loss after being treated with neomycin for colitis for over fourteen months (see Callan v. Nordland, above), the court held that, where the brand and generic name could not be distinguished by the pharmacist (the physician testified he called in a prescription for the Eli Lilly brand "Neomycin Sulfate" but the pharmacist assumed he meant the generic "neomycin sulfate"), and the pharmacist filled the prescription with Mycifradin (Upjohn's brand), the trial judge did not err in admitting into evidence the manufacturer's warning for Mycifradin. Callan v. Nordland (1983) 114 Ill. App. 3d 196, 69 Ill. Dec. 933, 448 N.E.2d 651.

---

[6] Id., 27:284, 1984.

Hearing loss—Claim barred by statute of limitations

In United States v. Kubrick (1979) 444 U.S. 111, 62 L. Ed. 2d 259, 100 Sup. Ct. 352, the plaintiff was treated with neomycin for an infected leg at a Veterans' Hospital in 1968 and soon thereafter suffered a hearing loss. In January, 1969 he was informed by a private physician that it was highly possible that the hearing loss was due to the neomycin. He filed a claim with the VA for benefits, but did not bring a civil action. Then, in June, 1971 he was told by another doctor that the neomycin should not have been administered. In 1972, he filed under the Federal Tort Claims Act, and the government raised the statute of limitations. The plaintiff prevailed in District Court and in the Court of Appeals, but the Supreme Court of the United States reversed, holding that a claim accrues when a plaintiff knows both the existence and the cause of his injury, and not at a later time when he also knows that the acts inflicting the injury may constitute medical malpractice.

NEOMYCIN SULFATE — DEXAMETHASONE SODIUM PHOSPHATE
Neodecadron

Neodecadron is an ophthalmic solution containing neomycin sulfate and dexamethasone sodium phosphate. (Neomycin sulfate and dexamethasone are both discussed herein.) This combined antibiotic-cortico-steroid preparation is designed for topical use in certain disorders of the anterior segment of the eye, i.e., for steroid-responsive inflammatory ocular conditions for which a corticosteroid is indicated and where bacterial infection or a risk of bacterial ocular infection exists. The side effects may be those of either component or a combination of the two. Prolonged use may result in glaucoma, with damage to the optic nerve, defects in visual acuity and fields of vision, and posterior subcapsular cataract formation. Also, prolonged use may suppress the host response and thus increase the hazard of secondary ocular infections.

The product is manufactured by Merck, Sharp & Dohme, a division of Merck and Company, Inc. (West Point, Pa.).[7]

---

[7] *Physicians' Desk Reference,* 40th ed., p. 1207.

Aetna Cas. & Sur. Co. of Illinois v. Medical Protective Co. of Ft. Wayne, Indiana (N.D. Ill., 1983) 575 F. Supp. 901.

Glaucoma following prolonged treatment—$1.5 million award

The patient, a young girl, was taken to her pediatrician in 1972 for conjunctivitis, an inflammation of the mucous membrane which lines the eyelids and the front portion of the eyeball. The pediatrician prescribed Neodecadron ointment, to be applied topically to the inside of the eyelid. The patient's mother continued to treat her child's eye problem off and on for two years, during which time the prescription for the Neodecadron was refilled six times. The child developed glaucoma, a known risk in continuous use of dexamethasone because of its tendency to elevate the pressure within the eyeball. The increased pressure damaged the child's optic nerves and she lost her sight.

At the trial, the plaintiffs introduced evidence that at no time during his treatment of the child did the pediatrician check her intraocular pressure. The jury awarded the plaintiffs $1.5 million. (Thurston v. Ninio (Docket No. 75 L 12065, Circuit Court, Cook County, Ill.) The case later reached the United States District Court in a suit by the defendant's excess liability insurer against the primary liability insurer to determine whether the defendant's failure to monitor the child's treatment constituted a single "occurrence" within the terms of the policy.

NEO-POLYCIN

See NEOMYCIN SULFATE

NEOSPORIN

See NEOMYCIN SULFATE

NEO-SYNALAR

See NEOMYCIN SULFATE

NEO-SYNEPHRINE

See PHENYLEPHRINE HYDROCHLORIDE

NICOTINYL ALCOHOL
Roniacol

Nicotinyl alcohol is used to treat conditions associated with deficient circulation. It acts by relaxing the musculature of peripheral blood vessels.[8] The drug was manufactured by Roche Laboratories (Nutley, N.J.) under the name Roniacol, but no longer is included on the company's product information list.

Adverse reactions include transient flushing of the face and neck, gastrointestinal disturbances, rash, and allergic reactions such as urticaria.[9]

Holland v. Stacy (Okla., 1972) 496 P.2d 1180.

Vision loss from retinal thrombosis—Judgment for physician affirmed

On October 18 the patient was hospitalized by an orthopedic surgeon for treatment of two infected toes. On October 24, while still hospitalized, he suddenly went totally blind. Specialists were brought in, and the cause of the blindness was diagnosed as "retinal central arterial thrombosis."

The patient brought suit against his surgeon, charging him with negligence. He attempted to establish that Roniacol, prescribed by the defendant along with other medications, had caused the thrombosis. He testified at the trial that for six days he was given a teaspoon of Roniacol three times a day, and an "alcoholic stimulant" four times a day. On October 23, he told the defendant that he was refusing to take any more because the medicines were making him ill.

At the trial, the attorney for the patient called the defendant to the stand and questioned him extensively about the drugs used, particularly Roniacol. The attorney sought to show by the defendant's own testimony that Roniacol was not recommended for persons with a medical history such as that of the patient, which apparently included at least one incident of possible cerebral vascular difficulties. Counsel asked the defendant about a statement on Roniacol appearing in the 1964 edition of the American Medical Association's *New and Nonofficial Drugs* which read: "the drug [Roniacol] should not be used on patients with cerebral vascular diseases since diminution of blood vessels which might occur could

---

[8] *Physicians' Desk Reference,* 35th ed., p. 1525.

[9] Id.

be harmful." The defendant answered that he was familiar with the statement, but that it referred to a person with "high blood pressure" (which, according to the defendant, the patient did not have) and with "suddenly lowering that high blood pressure with large doses of basal dilators, causing circulatory trouble."

The trial court rendered judgment in favor of the physician, and the patient appealed. The Supreme Court of Oklahoma affirmed, declaring there was no evidence that either the Roniacol or the alcoholic stimulant (referred to in the evidence as "spirits fermenti"), or a combination of the two, caused the patient's blindness.

NIPRIDE

See SODIUM NITROPRUSSIDE

NISENTIL

See ALPHAPRODINE HYDROCHLORIDE

NITROFURANTOIN

Furadantin
Macrodantin

Nitrofurantoin is an antibacterial drug used in the treatment of certain infections of the urinary tract. It is active against a variety of gram-positive and gram-negative organisms, and is effective in treating pyelonephritis, pyelitis, cystitis, and prostatitis caused by organisms susceptible to it.[10]

Adverse reactions include gastrointestinal disturbances (nausea, vomiting, diarrhea); dermatologic reactions (e.g., urticaria, eczematoid eruptions, pruritus); hematologic reactions, and various hypersensitivity reactions, including anaphylaxis, angioedema and pulmonary infiltration with pleural effusion.[11]

The manufacturer of Furadantin also warns:

> Acute, subacute and chronic pulmonary reactions have been observed in patients treated with nitrofurantoin products. If these reactions occur, the drug should be withdrawn and appropriate measures should be taken.
>
> An insidious onset of pulmonary reactions (diffuse interstitial pneumonitis or pulmonary fibrosis, or both) in patients on long-term therapy warrants close monitoring of these patients.

---

[10] *United States Dispensatory,* 27th ed., p. 786.

[11] Id.

There have been isolated reports giving pulmonary reactions as a contributing cause of death.[12]

Furadantin and Macrodantin are manufactured by Norwich-Eaton Pharmaceuticals (Norwich, N.Y.). Geneva Generics (Broomfield, Colo.) produces nitrofurantoin under the generic label.

McCue v. Norwich Pharmacal Co. (C.A.-1 N.H., 1972) 453 F.2d 1033.

Pulmonary fibrosis—Inadequate warning alleged—Manufacturer held liable

In an action against the Norwich Pharmacal Company (now Norwich-Eaton Pharmaceuticals), the evidence revealed that a woman patient sought treatment from her family physician for an apparent chronic urinary infection. Her physician was out of town, and she was referred to a locum tenens who gave her a prescription for Furadantin. She took the drug as directed, and when her own physician returned, she renewed the prescription, apparently open-endedly. (The physician's records did not reveal this, but the pharmacist's files did.)

The evidence further suggested that for some time prior to the date the patient had the prescription renewed, the manufacturer of Furadantin was aware that a possible side effect of long-term use was pulmonary fibrosis. Allegedly, however, the company did not give adequate warning of this danger to the medical profession. (Nor, apparently, did such information reach the patient's physician in any other manner.) The company did, however, recommend to physicians that patients taking the drug be kept under general observation, but this advice was not expressed in terms of a danger from pulmonary fibrosis.

The patient's physician kept a close check on her urinary difficulties, but did not connect worsening bronchial symptoms with the drug, and the patient developed pulmonary fibrosis.

A jury returned a verdict in favor of the patient, and the drug company appealed, contending that it was warranted in not anticipating "unsupervised taking" of its product, and consequently should not be held liable. This contention was rejected by the reviewing court, which said:

---

[12] *Physicians' Desk Reference,* 35th ed., pp. 1278-79.

If the doctor had been warned, and had nevertheless given such a prescription and forgotten about it, it is clear that defendant would not have been liable.... Correspondingly, having put a dangerous drug on the market without adequate warning defendant cannot be heard to say that the physician might have disregarded a proper one.

Related cases

Hepatitis—Issue of fact raised over wording of manufacturer's warning

In Kaplow v. Katz (1986) 120 App. Div. 2d 569, 502 N.Y.S.2d 216, an issue of fact was raised with respect to the adequacy of the manufacturer's warnings regarding the dangers of hepatitis following the use of Macrodantin in light of an expert's affidavit that the warnings understated the danger and mischaracterized it as a "dose-related toxicity reaction" when it really is an "allergic reaction" which cannot be avoided merely by limiting the dosage.

NITROGLYCERIN

Nitroglycerin is used to treat angina pectoris. When taken sublingually (below the tongue) at the onset of ischemic pain by patients with classic or variant angina, it usually provides relief within one to three minutes. Individual sensitivity varies, and the dose must be individualized to relieve symptoms with minimal adverse effects. It is usually preferable to initiate therapy with the lowest dose. Intravenous nitroglycerin relieves refractory chest pain caused by myocardial ischemia, and is useful in hospitalized patients with severe unstable angina.[13]

Nitroglycerin is manufactured by numerous companies under many brands, but in practice the drug is nearly always referred to generically.

DiGiovanni v. Sherman (No. 84-03161 CA 11, Circuit Court, Dade County, Fla., April 1986).

Bypass patient dies after injection of undiluted nitroglycerin—$1.2 million settlement

During coronary bypass surgery, the defendant surgeons intended to inject diluted nitroglycerin directly into a patient's coro-

---

[13] AMA *Drug Evaluations*, 6th ed., pp. 464-5.

nary arteries. On this particular occasion, however, the nitroglycerin was undiluted, and the patient died.

The nurses claimed that the surgeon in charge ordered "straight" nitroglycerin. The surgeon denied this, and claimed that the nurses erroneously gave him the undiluted drug. The plaintiff alleged that the routine use of intracoronary injections of nitroglycerin was unnecessary and that the surgeons had insufficient control over that practice. The surgeons contended that the routine was supported by medical literature, was beneficial to the patient, and that the patient's death was caused solely by nursing negligence.

The hospital settled before trial for $600,000 and the surgeons settled during trial for the same amount.[14]

NITROPRESS

See SODIUM NITROPRUSSIDE

NOREPINEPHRINE BITARTRATE

Levophed bitartrate

Norepinephrine bitartrate (formerly called levarterenol bitartrate) constricts the peripheral vessels, stimulates the heart, and dilates the coronary arteries. This results in an increase in systemic blood pressure and coronary blood flow.[15] The drug is used in the treatment of shock due to myocardial infarction, bacteriemia, and in anaphylactic shock after initial treatment with epinephrine. It is also given to control acute hypotension during general anesthesia if cardiac stimulation is not contraindicated.

The drug can cause tissue necrosis at the site of injection. The risk of injury is reduced if the drug is infused via a catheter in a deeply seated vein. The infusion site should be changed if prolonged administration is necessary. If extravasation and infiltration of tissue occurs, the site should be infiltrated with 10 ml. of a solution containing 0.5 to 1 mg. of phentolamine per milliliter.[16]

Norepinephrine bitartrate is manufactured by Breon Laboratories, Inc. (New York, N.Y.) under the brand name Levophed bitartrate.

---

[14] ATLA *Professional Negligence Law Reporter,* 2:10, 1987.

[15] *Physicians' Desk Reference,* 35th ed., p. 691.

[16] Id. Zucker, G., "Use of Phentolamine to Prevent Necrosis Due to Levarterenol," *Journal of the American Medical Association* 163:1477-1478, 1957.

Carpenter v. Campbell (1971) 149 Ind. App. 189, 271 N.E.2d 163.

Infiltration into tissue—Patient not attended during infusion—Intensive care unit available—Physicians held liable

Approximately a month after a Caesarean section, the patient was rushed back to the hospital for surgery to relieve a bowel obstruction. On the morning after the operation she received Levophed to raise her blood pressure. A quantity of the solution came in contact with her skin and subcutaneous tissue, causing scarring. Two operations were needed to correct this, and the patient filed suit against the physicians involved in her case.

The trial court rendered judgment for the patient, and the Appellate Court of Indiana affirmed, finding that the record contained ample testimony to the effect that "it was good medical practice to have someone in attendance at all times during introduction of such a caustic drug" and that the defendant-physicians did not see to it that a nurse or other properly trained personnel remained present during the infusion. It was pointed out that the intensive care area was available at the time, but that her physician decided not to place her there because "he felt she was receiving and would receive every protection without it."

Hundemer v. Sisters of Charity of Cincinnati, Inc. (1969) 22 Ohio App. 2d 119, 258 N.E.2d 611.

Infiltration into tissue—No evidence on standard of care offered—Directed verdicts for physician and hospital personnel affirmed

While recuperating from surgery the patient suddenly went into shock. Levophed was administered, and during the course of the infusion the solution infiltrated, resulting in necrosis, and sloughing of the skin, which eventually required skin grafts.

The patient brought suit against the physician and hospital personnel. At the trial there was no expert testimony introduced relative to the use of Levophed, nor as to the proper standard of care of a patient receiving Levophed. The trial court directed a verdict in favor of all defendants and the Court of Appeals of Ohio affirmed.

North Shore Hosp., Inc. v. Luzi (Fla. App., 1967) 194 So. 2d 63.

Infiltration into tissue—Private duty nurse in attendance negligent—Hospital held liable

A hospital patient was operated on for acute gallbladder disease. On the day of the operation, he was taken to the recovery room at

9:45 a.m. and returned to his room at 6:15 p.m. Approximately five hours later, the patient fell off the end of the bed. There was evidence that only the side rails near the patient's head were up.

The following day, approximately 21 hours after his fall, the patient went into shock, and he was administered Levophed. Although private duty nurses were ordered to attend the patient, the solution infiltrated the patient's leg, causing permanent partial disability.

The patient alleged negligence on the part of the hospital in failing to restrain him adequately when he was in a semiconscious condition, in failing to properly administer the Levophed, and in allowing infiltration of the solution for an estimated two hours.

The jury returned a verdict in favor of the patient, and the trial court entered judgment accordingly. The District Court of Appeals of Florida affirmed, declaring that the jury might have reasonably found that the fall and subsequent shock were caused by the hospital's negligence in failing to adequately restrain the patient, that there was sufficient evidence that there was negligence in the failure to detect the Levophed infiltration within a reasonable period of time, and that the private duty nurse in attendance was under the control of the hospital at the time.

Renrick v. City of Newark (1962) 74 N.J. Super. 200, 181 A.2d 25.

Infiltration into tissue—Plaintiff offers no expert testimony—Res ipsa loquitur refused—Dismissal upheld

A 36-year-old woman patient was admitted to the hospital for a gastric ulcer. She underwent surgery and during the postoperative period went into shock. She was given various stimulating drugs including Levophed intravenously. The solution infiltrated, causing necrosis of the skin on her forearms which later required grafting, and she brought suit.

At the patient's trial her attorney attempted to prove negligence on the part of the hospital personnel without the aid of expert medical testimony, relying instead on a request that the trial court apply the doctrine of *res ipsa loquitur*. Counsel argued that his patient "did not know what happened to her while she was being treated, and that she was entitled to know whether the infusions were properly done." The trial court refused to apply the doctrine and the case was appealed on this issue.

The Superior Court of New Jersey, Appellate Division, upheld the lower court's decision, finding that absent expert testimony there was no proof that the extent or quality of care, as revealed by the hospital records, was inadequate.

Sanchez v. Rodriguez (1964) 226 Cal. App. 2d 439, 38 Cal. Rptr. 110.

Probable gangrene and nerve injury—Dismissal of action against surgeon affirmed

The plaintiff brought suit against a surgeon for injuries to her arm sustained as the result of alleged negligence in performing certain emergency procedures, which included the administration of Levophed, after she suffered a vascular collapse following abdominal surgery.

At the trial the evidence disclosed that the plaintiff, 32 years old, had several operations during the preceding year, including an appendectomy, tubal ligation, cholecystectomy and hemorrhoidectomy, all performed by other doctors. As she was still suffering from severe abdominal pain and nausea, she was admitted to the hospital for observation and tests under the care of the defendant. The tests confirmed his preliminary diagnosis of pancreatitis due to biliary tract disease resulting in a partial intestinal obstruction, and several weeks later the defendant performed an operation to correct the condition.

Before the operation, the plaintiff was in good condition and had a blood pressure of 90-100/60, normal for a woman of her age and size. During the operation, she received one blood transfusion in her left arm. The operation lasted from 12:30 p.m. to 4:45 p.m. The anesthesiologist's records showed that at the conclusion of surgery, the plaintiff's condition was satisfactory, with a blood pressure of 90/60. The defendant left the hospital after placing the plaintiff in the care of the anesthesiologist in the recovery room.

The nurse's notes showed that at the time the plaintiff was removed to the recovery room at 4:45 p.m., her blood pressure was down to "60/?." At 4:46 p.m., on the orders of the anesthesiologist, the plaintiff received intravenously caffeine and Desoxyn, and was put on "shock blocks," (elevation of her feet). All of these measures were designed to raise blood pressure. At 4:48 p.m. the plaintiff was conscious and talking, and her blood pressure was 80/70. But at 4:55 p.m. her pressure dropped to "60/?," and at 5:00 p.m. she was given 500 cc. of whole blood under pressure. At 5:15 p.m., two cc. of Levophed were administered by the anesthesiologist and other staff physicians, and another four cc. were given at 5:50 p.m.

The plaintiff's blood pressure and pulse continued to recede, and the hospital got in touch with the defendant, who arrived at the hospital at 6:20 p.m. The plaintiff's condition continued to decline, and by 7:30 p.m., she had no blood pressure or pulse. The defendant did an arterial cut-down on her left wrist while fluids and other substances were intravenously fed through the right arm. After applying an antiseptic solution to the wrist, the surgeon performed the cut-down with a special kit provided by the hospital to introduce blood directly into the wrist artery to increase the pumping of the heart. The procedure involves various risks including gangrene and the loss of the hand because of the necessary ligation of the arteries and because the blood supply to the extremity is temporarily cut off. A special hollow needle is used, then closed with a stylet and left in the artery, with a corner of the wound open, pending further developments. Immediately after the cut-down, the plaintiff's condition improved, and by midnight she was out of danger.

The next day the plaintiff complained of pain at the cut-down site. The surgeon assumed that it was caused by the cut-down and the presence of the needle which, pursuant to the usual procedures, had been left in the artery. He so informed the plaintiff, and she was given painkillers. Antibiotics were administered on the second and third days, and after the removal of the needle, the wound was dressed. This was on December 12.

The plaintiff first noted discoloration of her left arm on the 13th and early in the morning asked a staff physician to look at it. On the 14th the defendant noted the discoloration and that evening prescribed drugs and heat treatments to the site. By December 16 the plaintiff's arm had improved, and appeared well-healed on December 21, the day before her discharge.

After the plaintiff returned home, her arm turned painful and became "leathery and black." It also began to drain. The defendant treated her in his office, and she saw several other physicians without success. The defendant readmitted her to the hospital on February 7, but before treatment was begun, she discharged herself and returned home.

On February 22 the plaintiff saw Dr. E., who treated her from February 27 to March 2. By March 29 the wound was completely healed but her finger sensations and movements were restricted.

Dr. E. stated that it was difficult to determine the cause of this neurological defect. For a period of time there was evidence that the nerve was recovering. Then the plaintiff fell on the stairs at her home, grabbing the banister rather forcefully. After this incident, Dr. E. concluded that the recovery of the nerve had apparently been arrested.

On July 12 the patient was readmitted to the hospital under the care of Dr. E., who performed exploratory surgery to ascertain the nature of the nerve difficulty. He exposed the median nerve, found it to be completely normal, and not damaged in the cut-down or buried in scar tissue. The cut-down site was one-half to one inch from the nerve. Dr. E. noted that the plaintiff was suffering from a clinical condition called "transverse carpal syndrome," i.e., a tightening of the ligament across the wrist which impairs the functioning of the nerve. He split the ligament and the wound healed, and the plaintiff recovered almost full use and sensation of her hand and fingers. She was discharged from the hospital on July 15 and saw Dr. E. only once more, on July 24.

The trial judge granted a nonsuit, and the plaintiff appealed. The District Court of Appeals of California affirmed the nonsuit, declaring:

> The record shows that both the administration of Levophed and the arterial cut-down are medical procedures of a complicated nature used in emergency situations and that their justification and the risks involved are entirely outside the realm of lay knowledge. Thus, the standard of care against which the acts of respondent [defendant surgeon] are to be measured is a matter peculiarly within the knowledge of experts and expert evidence is conclusive.... The only medical evidence presented was that of respondent ... and [Dr. E.] who subsequently treated the patient. Neither testified that the results here were such that medical men know ordinarily do not happen in absence of negligence. The only expert evidence in the record indicates that gangrene and loss or impairment of the hand were calculated risks of the use of Levophed and the arterial cut-down, which involved cutting off the blood supply to the hand and binding the artery. Respondent testified that these risks had to be balanced against saving the appellant's life. There was no evidence that the procedures were contrary to good medical practice or that those rare cases where tissue death occurs are more probably than not the result of negligence. The fact that a particular injury suffered by a patient as the result of an operation is something that rarely occurs does not in itself prove that the injury was probably caused by the negligence of those in charge of the operation.

Related cases

Death after electroshock therapy, chlorpromazine and Levophed

In Kosberg v. Washington Hosp. Center, Inc. (1968) 129 App. D.C. 322, 394 F.2d 947, a woman died after receiving electroshock therapy, chlorpromazine and Levophed. One medical witness said the death resulted from giving the shock therapy and chlorpromazine (a tranquilizer) to a person in the patient's weakened condition, but another said it was due to the combination of the therapy and the drugs, which brought on a bowel infarction. A directed verdict for the psychiatrist who ordered the shock therapy and chlorpromazine was reversed on appeal. For further details on the case see CHLORPROMAZINE herein.

NORETHINDRONE ACETATE with ETHINYL ESTRADIOL
Loestrin
Norlestrin

Norethindrone acetate with ethinyl estradiol is manufactured by Parke-Davis (Morris Plains, N.J.) under the brand names Loestrin and Norlestrin. It is a progestogen-estrogen combination oral contraceptive.

For an extensive discussion of the possible side effects of oral contraceptives, see NORETHINDRONE with MESTRANOL.

Looza v. Parke-Davis Co. (No. 94116, Superior Court, Butte County, Cal., April 28, 1972).

Stroke—$500,000 verdict against manufacturer despite conflicting medical testimony

The patient, a 33-year-old mother of twelve, was put on Norlestrin by her physician in November of 1967 after the birth of her twelfth child. She had taken two pills when she suffered a basilar artery occlusion, or stroke, which left her paralyzed, unable to speak, and confined to a wheelchair for life. In the subsequent lawsuit against the manufacturer of Norlestrin, a physician testifying for the patient stated that in his opinion the drug had caused the woman's stroke. On cross-examination, however, he admitted that the drug was only one possible cause. A second physician appearing for the patient also testified that the drug caused the stroke, but when he was cross-examined, he admitted that she had several conditions which were predisposing to stroke. These included cigarette smoking, obesity, and a vaginal infection known to cause blood clots.

The manufacturer of Norlestrin offered evidence by several physicians who had conducted studies on oral contraceptives. One stated that he had found no difference between the blood coagulation factors of women using oral contraceptives and those not using them. This witness testified also that in his opinion it was impossible for two Norlestrin pills to have caused a stroke. A second witness testified that he had conducted extensive clinical studies of oral contraceptives, and that he found that the incidence of stroke was actually lower in users of oral contraceptives than in nonusers. He testified further that in his opinion there was no established cause-and-effect relationship between oral contraceptives and thromboembolic conditions. This witness likewise stated that the two Norlestrin pills could not have been responsible for the woman's condition. A third physician offered by the drug manufacturer testified that it was his opinion the woman's stroke was due to a blood clot that had formed as a result of her vaginal infection.

After a lengthy trial, the jury returned a verdict against the drug manufacturer for just over $500,000.[17]

Decker v. Ortho Pharmaceutical Corp. (No. 120647, Superior Court, Contra Costa County, Cal., July 12, 1974).

Stroke—Conflicting medical testimony—Verdicts for manufacturers and physician

In 1967, a 37-year-old woman patient was put on Norlestrin (1 mg.). She was given the usual booklet distributed by the manufacturer which contained a recommendation that if a user suffers severe headaches or any changes in vision she should consult her physician immediately. The patient did experience blurred vision and told her physician. He suggested that she see an ophthalmologist — which she did not do. Later, when she developed severe headaches, she again consulted her physician, and he prescribed a sedative and pain reliever.

Approximately a year after she began taking Norlestrin she developed menstrual difficulties and her physician changed her to Ortho-Novum 1/80 (norethindrone with mestranol). Three months later, when her difficulties continued, she was changed again, this time to Ortho-Novum SQ. Two months after this, the patient suf-

[17] ATLA *News Letter* 15:373, 1972; AMA *The Citation* 26:137, 1973.

fered a stroke involving branches of the middle cerebral artery. She lost the use of her left hand and arm, and partial use of her left leg.

The patient filed suit against both drug manufacturers, alleging negligence (failure to warn of the possibility of stroke), strict liability, and breach of express and implied warranty. The patient also sued the physician, charging that he was negligent in failing to supervise her care after prescribing the contraceptives, specifically in failing to monitor her blood pressure. She also charged failure on the physician's part to inform her of the risk involved, and therefore failing to obtain her informed consent to the use of the particular contraceptive measures.

The patient introduced at the trial physicians who testified that the stroke was the result of a thrombosis which probably was caused by the contraceptives. They pointed out the low incidence of strokes in women of the patient's age, and that it was known that oral contraceptives did cause thrombophlebitis.

Medical witnesses testifying for the defendants countered that the oral contraceptives were safe and were marketed with proper directions. It was argued that the standard of care in 1967 did not require that a physician monitor the blood pressure of the patients on oral contraceptives, nor were physicians required to inform patients of the risk of stroke since such risk was considered extremely rare. Evidence was introduced also that the results of arteriograms performed on the patient after her stroke revealed the presence of at least two aneurysms, one in the middle cerebral artery and the other in the internal carotid artery. These aneurysms, the defense witnesses testified, probably caused embolisms which resulted in the stroke.

The jury returned a verdict in favor of the drug manufacturers and the physician.[18]

May v. Parke, Davis & Co. (1985) 142 Mich. App. 404, 370 N.W.2d 371.

Stroke—$2,275,000 award affirmed against manufacturer for failure to warn physician

The plaintiff's wife began taking Norlestrin on December 1, 1975. Nineteen days later she collapsed and lapsed into unconsciousness. Six days after that she died. On autopsy blood clots were found in the brain and lungs.

---

[18] AMA *The Citation* 30:51, 1974.

In his lawsuit, the plaintiff charged the manufacturer with failure to inform the prescribing physician of the danger of blood clots. The jury returned a verdict of $2,275,000. The Court of Appeals of Michigan affirmed, holding that whether the manufacturer of Norlestrin should have warned the physician that certain patients may be susceptible to blood clots, whether it should have recommended that the physician determine if the patient had a family history of strokes, and whether it should have recommended special tests and warnings for patients who, like the plaintiff's wife, had Type A blood and faced a higher risk of blood clots, were all proper questions for the jury.

NORETHINDRONE with MESTRANOL
Norinyl
Ortho-Novum

The combination of the hormones norethindrone and mestranol is an effective oral contraceptive, apparently through inhibition of ovulation from suppression of anterior pituitary gonadotropins, and possibly through other mechanisms.[19] Norinyl is manufactured by Syntex (F.P.) Inc. (Humacao, P.R.); and Ortho-Novum by Ortho Pharmaceutical Corporation (Raritan, N.J.).[20]

A note on oral contraceptives

Over the years the various oral contraceptives have been blamed for a number of disorders, some of which have been substantiated and some of which have not.

A possible cause-and-effect relationship between estrogen-progestogen oral contraceptives and thromboembolic phenomena was under investigation as early as 1961. Studies in Great Britain and the United States led to a general but not universal agreement that the use of oral contraceptives was associated with an increase in morbidity and mortality caused by peripheral venous thrombophlebitis, with or without pulmonary embolism. According to studies in the United Kingdom, this increase in morbidity and mortality varied from three- to tenfold. Studies in the United States suggested about a fourfold increase in morbidity. Insufficient data on the incidence of idiopathic thrombophlebitis and thromboembolism

---

[19] *United States Dispensatory,* 27th ed., p. 792.

[20] For a current list of norethindrone preparations on the market, see the latest edition of *Physicians' Desk Reference.*

in nonusers of oral contraceptives accounted in part for these variations in results.[1]

Cerebral arterial thrombosis was the most common occlusive disease of the cerebral vasculature reported in women taking oral contraceptives. About one-fourth of these cases involved occlusion of the vertebrobasilar artery, which formerly was considered a rare disorder in young persons. However, the incidence of cerebral thrombosis in users of oral contraceptives was not shown to be significantly increased over that in the general population in the United States.[2]

Other adverse reactions from estrogen-progestogen type oral contraceptives reported in the 1960's and early 1970's included vitamin deficiencies, disturbance in liver function, hypertension, alterations in glucose tolerance, changes in cervical erosion and cervical secretions, unpredictable menstrual bleeding, mood changes, neuro-ophthalmic disorders (particularly retinal disorders), skin blotching, and irregular loss of hair (or occasionally hirsutism). Also, because the carcinogenic potential of these preparations on the breast and other ovarian hormone-dependent tissues had not been determined, the American Medical Association's Department of Drugs warned that patients should be carefully examined periodically, and those who had a known or suspected hormone-dependent tumor should not use this method of contraception.[3]

As a result of complaints over side effects from these products, over 500 damage suits were on file against physicians and manufacturers by 1972. Most of these involved the "sequential" type of contraceptive. These products, which represented about 5-10% of all oral contraceptives used, were withdrawn voluntarily by their manufacturers after the Food and Drug Administration pointed out several known and suspected serious disadvantages of this type of drug, and asked the manufacturers to show that there was a population in whom well-defined benefits outweighed these disadvantages.[4]

Unlike the "combination" oral contraceptives, which provide a fixed combination of estrogen and progestogen for 20-21 days of the menstrual cycle, the sequentials provide estrogen alone for two weeks, then an estrogen-progestogen combination for the remain-

---

[1] *AMA Drug Evaluations,* 2d ed., p. 418.

[2] Id., p. 419.

[3] Id., pp. 418-20.

[4] *FDA Drug Bulletin,* June-July 1976, p. 26.

der of the 20-21 days. Although this dosage pattern was designed to imitate "natural" hormone production during the normal cycle more closely than the combination products, in practice the sequence provided little or no benefit. Instead, the sequentials appeared to be less satisfactory than the most commonly used combination oral contraceptives in three important ways: (1) They are less effective. (2) They may be associated with a greater risk of thromboembolism. (3) They may be associated with an increased risk of adenocarcinoma of the endometrium.[5]

In most studies, users of sequentials experienced higher pregnancy rates than users of combination products. The reason for this is not fully established. It is thought, however, to reflect the dependence of the sequentials on a single contraceptive mechanism (prevention of ovulation by suppression of pituitary gonadotropin release) in contrast to the combination products which in addition alter the endometrium and cervical mucus in ways unfavorable to conception.[6]

The risk of thromboembolism in women using oral contraceptives seems to increase with the estrogen content of the contraceptive. Since all sequentials contain a relatively large estrogen dose, it was thought that they are more likely to cause thromboembolism than most combination products. One study has detected such an increased hazard, although other studies have not.[7]

Cases reported to a registry of endometrial cancer in women under forty taking oral contraceptives were analyzed. Of the first 21 cases accepted into the registry, thirteen were users of sequentials. After elimination from the 21 cases of eight patients who had received oral contraceptives for less than one year or who had preexisting risk factors for adenocarcinoma of the endometrium (e.g., oral contraceptives administered because of abnormal bleeding, polycystic ovaries), eleven of the thirteen remaining patients were users of sequentials. In view of the ten- to twenty-fold greater use nationally of the combination products, only one or two of the cases would be expected to occur in users of sequentials. These data are in no way conclusive, but do suggest that the sequentials are associated with a greater risk of endometrial cancer than the combinations.[8]

---

[5] Id.
[6] Id.
[7] Id.
[8] Id.

Several investigators have reported that prolonged use of estrogens in postmenopausal women is associated with an increased risk of endometrial carcinoma. Possibly either the relatively large estrogen dose in the sequentials or the two weeks in every cycle of unopposed (by a progestogen) estrogen administration could also increase the risk for this cancer in premenopausal women.[9]

On the basis of these considerations, the Food and Drug Administration felt that, compared with combination oral contraceptives, the sequentials are less effective and may also be less safe. Moreover, no population of women was identified in whom the sequentials could be shown to have proven advantages sufficient to justify the possible increased risks. The FDA therefore asked manufacturers of the sequentials to withdraw these products from the market and they agreed to do so.[10]

In 1978 the FDA revised the labels on oral contraceptives to include the following warnings:[11]

> Cigarette smoking increases the risk of serious cardiovascular side effects from oral contraceptive use. This risk increases with age and with heavy smoking (15 or more cigarettes per day) and is quite marked in women over 35 years of age. Women who use oral contraceptives should be strongly advised not to smoke.
>
> Oral contraceptives containing both estrogen and progestogen are about 99% effective in preventing pregnancy when taken as directed. The "mini-pill," which contains only progestogen, is about 97% effective.
>
> Women who have had blood clotting disorders, cancer of the breast or sex organs, unexplained vaginal bleeding, a stroke, heart attack, or angina pectoris, or who suspect they may be pregnant should not take oral contraceptives.
>
> Women with scanty or irregular periods are strongly advised to use another method of contraception because if they use oral contraceptives they may have difficulty becoming pregnant or may fail to have menstrual periods after discontinuing the pill.
>
> Most side effects associated with oral contraceptives are not serious, and include nausea, vomiting, bleeding between menstrual periods, weight gain, and breast tenderness.
>
> The more serious side effects, while uncommon, can be fatal. They include blood clots in the legs, lungs, brain, heart or other organs, cerebral hemorrhage, liver tumors that may rupture and cause severe bleeding, birth defects (if the oral contraceptive is

---

[9] Id.

[10] Id.

[11] *FDA Drug Bulletin,* March-April, 1978, pp. 12-13.

taken during pregnancy), high blood pressure, stroke, and gallbladder disease.

Estrogen, an ingredient in the combination pill, causes cancer in certain animals and it may therefore also cause cancer in humans, though studies to date of women taking currently marketed oral contraceptives have not confirmed this. There is strong evidence that estrogen use increases the risk of endometrial cancer in postmenopausal women.

Oral contraceptives are of no value in prevention or treatment of venereal disease.

Women who stop using oral contraceptives should wait a few months before becoming pregnant to minimize the risk of birth defects associated with the use of sex hormones during pregnancy.

The patient should consult her physician before resuming use of the drug after childbirth, especially if she intends to breastfeed the baby, because the hormones in the oral contraceptives appear in the milk and may decrease the flow.

Studies continued on the risks of oral contraceptives, with the most extensive (a ten-year study of over 16,000 women) being the Walnut Creek Contraceptive Drug Study funded by the National Institute of Child Health and Human Development (NICHD). The following is a summary report of that study prepared by the National Institutes of Health, Bethesda, Maryland, and published in the September 4, 1981 issue of *The Journal of the American Medical Association* (246:1071-72).

The recently published *Walnut Creek Contraceptive Drug Study* (vol. 3)[12] is the latest in a series of reports from this long-term study of the effects of oral contraceptives (OCs) on various physiological and health outcome variables in a large population. The report concludes that women using OCs do not have an increased risk of breast cancer, benign ovarian tumors, or death from all causes, compared with nonusers. However, the Walnut Creek data also confirm that OC users who smoke or who are older than 30 years are at somewhat greater risk of serious side effects, particularly circulatory disorders.

These conclusions result from a ten-year study of 16,638 women. The research was conducted by the Kaiser-Permanente Medical Center in Walnut Creek, Calif., and was funded by the National Institute of Child Health and Human Development (NICHD).

---

[12] *The Walnut Creek Contraceptive Drug Study,* volume 3, published by the NICHD, was prepared by Drs. S. Ramcharan, F. A. Pellegrin, R. Ray, and J-P. Hsu. Volumes 1 and 2 of the study, which were published earlier, describe methodology and data collection.

The Walnut Creek investigation is one of three large cohort studies that started in 1968 in response to clinical reports in the United States and Europe of thromboembolism and other hazards possibly associated with OC use. Two of these investigations — by the Royal College of General Practitioners and the Oxford-Family Planning Association — gave primary attention to such matters as the return of fertility after discontinuation of birth control, outcome of pregnancy, or contraceptive efficacy. In contrast, the Walnut Creek study was concerned with patterns of hospitalization and death in users and nonusers of OCs.

Women entering the Walnut Creek study were much older than those in the two British studies. About 40% were aged 40 years or older, with a range of 18 to 54 years, and the majority were white, middle class, and healthy. The Walnut Creek study was also largely concerned with past use of OCs, an extremely important point in terms of the results relating to cardiovascular disease. Most of the existing evidence relates cardiovascular disease to OCs only in current users.

During the Walnut Creek study, the occurrences of death and disease in women who previously had used or were using OCs were compared with those in women who had never used OCs. When all of the causes of death under study were combined, it was found that OC users do not have an increased risk of death. In addition, results showed that use of OCs apparently does not lead to breast cancer or benign ovarian tumors and may even offer protection from fibrocystic breast disease and cancer of the endometrium. Researchers also noted that the risk of high blood pressure seems to be lower than previously reported.

Some health risks were detected, however. Walnut Creek results confirmed that the negative effects of smoking are intensified in women who use OCs. Heavy smokers in general have an increased risk for development of heart disease and other circulatory disorders, but those who also take OCs are even more vulnerable. According to the Walnut Creek report, "smoking should be considered a contraindication to oral contraceptive use, or at the very least, women wishing to use oral contraceptives should be strongly urged not to smoke."

The study also showed that certain life-style factors may predispose women to some health problems associated with OCs. For example, it is known that women who initiated sexual activity at an early age and have multiple partners are more likely to have development of cancer in situ of the cervix. Because of this known association, the role of OCs in this disorder could not be isolated.

A new finding to emerge from the study is the apparent increased risk of malignant melanoma in OC users. However, users in the study sunbathed more often, and from the data available it was not possible to separate the effects of OCs from exposure to the sun's ultraviolet rays. The NICHD is supporting further research on the tentative relationship between these drugs and malignant melanoma.

Although the study was not primarily designed to monitor relatively uncommon events, apparent links were found between OCs and such conditions as subarachnoid hemorrhage and thromboembolism. The report emphasized that study results "cannot be considered final, and must be weighed with evidence from other clinical and epidemiological studies." Oral contraceptives are effective when used properly, but they harbor measurable risks for certain women, and their use should be carefully weighed by a woman and her physician.

Leibowitz v. Ortho Pharmaceutical Corp. (1973) 224 Pa. Super. 418, 307 A.2d 449.

Thrombophlebitis—Warning at the time adequate—Cause-and-effect not proven—Judgment for manufacturer affirmed

A patient brought suit against the manufacturer of Ortho-Novum for a thrombophlebitic condition allegedly caused by the drug. Originally, the patient had been placed on Enovid (norethynodrel with mestranol) because of irregular menstrual periods. When she suffered breakthrough bleeding, the prescription was changed to Ortho-Novum. This was in February, 1964. The drug was apparently successful in regulating her menses until August, 1964, when she suffered acute thrombophlebitis in her leg.

At the trial, evidence was introduced that some fifteen years earlier she had experienced a brief period of thrombophlebitis following an unsuccessful pregnancy and tubal ligation.

With regard to the drug, evidence was introduced pertaining to the investigations which had begun in 1961 involving the possible connection between thrombophlebitis and oral contraceptives. Witnesses testified that as a result of the debate over the problem, the Food and Drug Administration had summoned a special committee to investigate the question. This committee, according to the witnesses, conducted a comprehensive study and concluded that, on the basis of available data, there was no significant increase in the risk of death from thrombophlebitis in the use of oral contraceptives. On the basis of the report of the committee, and with the approval of the Food and Drug Administration, the manufacturer, in 1963, inserted the following statement in the package insert accompanying Ortho-Novum:

> A few cases of thrombophlebitis have been reported on patients taking ORTHO-NOVUM. Although there is no evidence to sup-

> port a causal relationship between the use of ORTHO-NOVUM and the occurrence of venous thrombosis, a definite recent history of thrombophlebitis and/or pulmonary embolism is considered a contraindication to the use of ORTHO-NOVUM.

The statement was in effect when the plaintiff was placed on the drug.

Evidence was introduced also concerning subsequent studies on the problem, including a British report which appeared in 1968 suggesting a seven to tenfold increase in mortality and morbidity due to embolic diseases in women taking oral contraceptives. As a result of this study, the Food and Drug Administration required drug companies to revise their product literature to reflect the new findings.

Medical witnesses offered by the plaintiff, however, were less than certain in their testimony as to a cause-and-effect relationship. One physician testified that a "significant factor [in the development of thrombophlebitis] would have been taking the oral contraceptive." This witness, however, admitted that the plaintiff was predisposed to the disease, and that it could have resulted from other causes.

The best testimony offered by a second medical witness appearing for the plaintiff was that the contraceptive was the "most likely cause" of the thrombophlebitis.

The manufacturer of the drug produced two expert witnesses who testified that the studies to date offered little proof that there was a causal connection.

At the close of the evidence, judgment was rendered in favor of the manufacturer. On appeal, the judgment was affirmed by the Superior Court of Pennsylvania which stated:

> In reviewing the evidence presented at trial and in reading the insert itself and accompanying literature provided by Ortho, we believe that the warnings were adequate.
>
> It must be borne in mind that this was a prescription drug. It could not be obtained by anyone except on a doctor's prescription, presented at a drugstore.... 'Since the drug was available only upon prescription of a duly licensed physician, the warning required is not to the general public or to the patient, but to the prescribing doctor.' It is for the prescribing physician to use his own independent medical judgment, taking into account the data supplied to him from the drug manufacturer, other medical literature, and any other source available to him, and weighing that knowledge against the personal medical history of his patient, whether to prescribe a given drug....

> Appellee's insert did state that there were cases of thrombophlebitis reported from the use of Ortho-Novum. It stated that there were studies being conducted into the causal connection but that no evidence had established same. It further warned against the prescription of Ortho-Novum to patients having 'recent' cases of thrombophlebitis. Because said insert was directed to the practicing physician, who should have been aware of the literature pro and con, we cannot as a matter of law conclude that the insert was misleading or inadequate.

On the specific issue of proximate cause, the court said:

> We are unable to conclude that the trial court could not find defendant's experts more credible than plaintiff's. Both of defendant's experts were unequivocal and unwavering in their opinions that there was no causal link between thrombophlebitis and the use of Ortho-Novum. On the other hand, not only were plaintiff's experts ambiguous and shaken badly on the cross-examination, but their opinions as to medical causation reflect a lack of certainty.

Chambers v. Ortho Pharmaceutical Corp. (No. 195615, Superior Court, Pierce County, Wash., March 28, 1973).

Thrombophlebitis—Failure to take history—Prescription error—$94,000 award against physician and pharmacist

A 34-year-old woman who allegedly had once suffered from thrombophlebitis was given a prescription for Ortho-Novum (1 mg.). The physician also gave her a month's supply of the drug from samples left by the manufacturer's detail man. When the patient took the prescription to a pharmacy, she allegedly was given 10 mg. Ortho-Novum instead of 1 mg. This prescription was refilled on four occasions, each for a three months' supply.

Approximately one year after going on the drug, the patient developed thrombophlebitis with pulmonary involvement. She filed suit against the manufacturer, physician and pharmacy. At the trial there was conflicting evidence as to whether the physician authorized the refilling of the prescription, but apparently there was evidence that he had failed to take the patient's history, and had failed to warn her about the possibility of side effects from Ortho-Novum.

According to the attorney for the patient, she obtained a jury verdict of $94,000 against the physician and the pharmacy.[13]

---

[13] ATLA *News Letter* 16:221, 1973.

Harris v. Rosecrans Medical Group (No. SOC 26403, Superior Court, Los Angeles County, Cal., Jan. 25, 1974).

Thrombophlebitis and pulmonary embolism—$20,000 settlement with drug company—$150,000 award against physicians

A 35-year-old woman taking Ortho-Novum complained of pain in her lower legs. Her physician made an initial diagnosis of lower back involvement and hospitalized her with traction. On the twelfth day of hospitalization, the patient developed thrombophlebitis and a pulmonary embolism.

Claiming that her condition was caused by the Ortho-Novum, she filed suit against her physicians and the manufacturer. Her attorneys alleged that her condition had left her partially disabled and unable to engage in any strenuous physical activity. Before the case went to trial, the manufacturer settled with the patient for $20,000. The case against the physicians went to trial with the defendants arguing that the patient's condition was not as serious as she claimed. They contended that the patient had recovered pulmonary function, that her thrombophlebitis had been treated, and that any circulatory difficulty had been compensated for by collateral circulation. The jury found for the patient and awarded $150,000.[14]

Ostheller v. Syntex Laboratories, Inc. (No. 270723, Superior Court, Santa Clara County, Cal., May 15, 1972).

Thrombosis of anterior spinal artery—$262,500 settlement by manufacturer

A nineteen-year-old patient taking Norinyl developed moderately severe paralysis due to a thrombosis of the anterior spinal artery, allegedly as a result of the side effects of the contraceptive. A lawsuit was filed against the manufacturer. At the time of trial, the patient had recovered some use of her limbs, but was still required to use a wheelchair or walker. She was still severely restricted in performing useful functions, particularly with her hands.

According to her attorney, on the first day of trial, prior to selecting the jury, the case was settled for $262,500.[15]

---

[14] AMA *The Citation* 29:115, 1974.
[15] ATLA *News Letter* 15:324, 1972.

Decker v. Ortho Pharmaceutical Corp. (No. 120647, Superior Court, Contra Costa County, Cal., July 12, 1974).

Stroke—Conflicting medical testimony—Verdicts for manufacturers and physician

In 1967 a 37-year-old woman patient was put on Norlestrin (norethindrone acetate with ethinyl estradiol). She was given the usual booklet distributed by the manufacturer which contained a recommendation that if a user suffers severe headaches or any changes in vision she should consult her physician immediately. The patient did experience blurred vision and told her physician. He suggested that she see an ophthalmologist — which she did not do. Later, when she developed severe headaches, she again saw her physician and was put on a sedative and pain reliever.

Approximately a year after she began taking the Norlestrin, she developed menstrual difficulties and her physician changed her to Ortho-Novum 1/80. Three months later, when her difficulties continued, she was changed again, this time to Ortho-Novum SQ. Two months after this, the patient suffered a stroke involving branches of the middle cerebral artery. She lost the use of her left hand and arm, and partial use of her left leg.

The patient filed suit against both drug manufacturers, alleging negligence (failure to warn of the possibility of stroke), strict liability, and breach of express and implied warranty. The patient also sued the physician, charging that he was negligent in failing to supervise her care after prescribing the contraceptives, specifically in failing to monitor her blood pressure. She also charged failure on the physician's part to inform her of the risk involved, and therefore failing to obtain her informed consent to the use of the particular contraceptive measures.

The patient introduced at trial physicians who stated that the stroke was the result of a thrombosis which probably was caused by the contraceptives. They pointed out the low incidence of strokes in women of the patient's age, and that it was known that oral contraceptives did cause thrombophlebitis.

Medical witnesses testifying for the defendants countered with testimony that oral contraceptives were safe and were marketed with proper directions. It was argued that the standard of care in 1967 did not require that a physician monitor the blood pressure of patients on oral contraceptives, nor were physicians required to inform patients of the risk of stroke since such risk was considered extremely rare. Evidence was introduced also that the results of arteriograms performed on the patient after her stroke revealed the presence of at least two aneurysms, one in the middle cerebral artery and another in the internal carotid artery. These aneurysms, the defense witnesses testified, probably caused the embolisms which resulted in the stroke.

The jury returned a verdict in favor of the drug manufacturers and the physician.[16]

McEwen v. Ortho Pharmaceutical Corp. (1974) 270 Ore. 375, 528 P.2d 522.

Retinal hemorrhages—Manufacturer's warning insufficient—$281,000 verdict upheld

The patient began using Norinyl on December 3, 1966. In the following months she experienced severe headaches, nausea, falling hair, swollen ankles and feet, and a "constant backache." In July, 1967, she discontinued the drug for three months during which time her symptoms subsided. She resumed using Norinyl in October, and within a short time she began to experience difficulty with her vision. In November, 1967, she called the Kaiser Hospital in Portland and reported that she was losing the sight in her right eye. The next month she began to cough up blood, and on December 20, 1967, an examining physician at Kaiser changed her prescription from Norinyl to Ortho-Novum.

On January 2, 1968, another examination revealed that the patient's eyes did not focus properly, but the examining physician found no other abnormalities and diagnosed her condition as "nearsightedness." About eleven months later, on December 5, 1968, the patient noticed "two vivid black lines come across the field of vision in her right eye." When she blinked, the lines disappeared. Additional lines appeared a few days later, followed by "black dots" which seemed to "fill her right eye." An ophthalmologist examined her and found "a growth of abnormal new blood vessels extending out from the retina into the vitreous" of the right eye. He noted further, "a vitreous hemorrhage" in her right eye. On December 11, 1968, a second specialist essentially confirmed that she was suffering from retinal hemorrhages.

On December 21, 1968, she developed something which she called "streaks or [something like] looking through gelatin" in her left

[16] AMA *The Citation* 30:51, 1974.

eye. A specialist at the University of Oregon Medical School advised her to discontinue using any oral contraceptives. Treatment was commenced which included "photocoagulation operations" to stop the hemorrhaging. The damage could not be reversed, however, and the patient suffered total and permanent blindness in her right eye. Also, her left eye "tires more easily than before and bears the scars of photocoagulation."

A lawsuit was filed against Ortho Pharmaceutical Corporation, the manufacturer of Ortho-Novum and against Syntex Laboratories, Inc., the manufacturer of Norinyl. The sole theory of recovery was the defendants' alleged failure "to adequately warn the medical profession of the dangerous propensities of their oral contraceptives."

At the trial, a physician specializing in pharmacology appeared as a witness for the patient and testified as to articles published in the *British Medical Journal* in May, 1967, which established a cause-and-effect relationship between oral contraceptives and vascular disorders. Evidence was introduced also as to a cooperative two-year "oral drug safety study" conducted by Ortho and Syntex to determine the effects on rats of norethindrone and mestranol. According to this evidence, an interim report from the study indicated that these drugs did cause damage to the eyes of the rats examined, and that, according to the witness, "some of the lesions resemble, to me, very much the lesions found in the retinas of Mrs. McEwen." Furthermore, one of the rats treated with norethindrone experienced a "local retinal hemorrhage." The witness also testified to an article appearing in the *Archives of Ophthalmology* in 1965 in which approximately sixty patients taking oral contraceptives were studied. According to the witness, out of the sixty, nine patients had "ocular lesions which, in my opinion, resembled changes found in Mrs. McEwen."

In addition to the above, there was evidence introduced which tended to show that each defendant-company had "some knowledge during the relevant time periods of a connection between the use of its oral contraceptive and injuries such as those suffered by plaintiff."

The defense introduced package inserts for Norinyl and Ortho-Novum distributed during the period of time the patient was taking these drugs. As to Norinyl, under "Contraindications," the insert contained the following statement: "At this time Norinyl is not recommended in patients with thrombophlebitis or with a history of thrombophlebitis or pulmonary embolism." For the same drug, under "Warning," was the following: "Discontinue medication pending examination if there is sudden partial or complete loss of vision, or if there is a sudden onset of proptosis, diplopia or migraine. If examination reveals papilledema or retinal vascular lesions, medication should be withdrawn."

The above statements were also included with the Ortho-Novum package insert as of November, 1967, plus this additional precaution: "Because of the occasional occurrence of thrombophlebitis and pulmonary embolism in patients taking oral contraceptives, the physician should be alert to the earliest manifestations of the disease." This Ortho-Novum insert also noted thrombophlebitis, pulmonary embolism and "neuro-ocular lesions" among the side effects observed in patients receiving oral contraceptives. This insert stated further that the clinical laboratory results of coagulation tests indicated that Ortho-Novum "affected various characteristics of blood clotting."

In addition, in June, 1968, package inserts for Ortho-Novum included the conclusion of the studies reported in the *British Medical Journal* in 1967 which was "there is a seven to tenfold increase in mortality and morbidity due to thromboembolic diseases in women taking oral contraceptives." The insert further warned the physician to be on the alert for such diseases, including "retinal thrombosis, and to discontinue the drug immediately if such disorders occurred or were suspected." Finally, the insert stated that "available evidence is suggestive of an association" between Ortho-Novum and retinal thrombosis.

In his closing statement, the attorney for the plaintiff argued strenuously that all of these warnings were inadequate, since physicians still continued to prescribe the drugs.

The jury returned a verdict in the amount of $280,978 against the companies. On appeal to the Supreme Court of Oregon, the defendants contended that the "adequacy and timeliness" of their package insert warnings were beyond their control, since the warnings were actually written by the Food and Drug Administration. This argument was not accepted, however, the reviewing court holding that the defendants could have given additional warnings through "Dear Doctor" letters or through personal contact by company detail men.

The defendants also argued that even if further warnings had been given, the physicians involved in the patient's case would have continued to prescribe the oral contraceptives. In answer to this, the court said there was sufficient evidence to permit the jury to come to the opposite conclusion.

Syntex Laboratories made the specific argument that its product, Norinyl, could not have been a "substantial factor" in causing the patient's condition because her condition did not occur until a year after she had discontinued use of that drug. This contention was likewise rejected by the reviewing court, and the judgment in the trial court was affirmed.

Laura v. Jones (No. 240516, Superior Court, Sacramento County, Cal., April 23, 1977).

Myocardial infarction, quadriplegia and mental impairment—$2,000,000 settlement by manufacturer and physician group

The patient used Ortho-Novum for about fourteen weeks and suffered a serious myocardial infarction which resulted in quadriplegia, loss of speech functions and mental impairment.

The complaint against the Kaiser Permanente physician group which prescribed the drug was that in view of the patient's blood pressure reading of 150/96 and the known risk of thrombosis relating to the use of the drug, it should have stopped the prescription and investigated the cause of the hypertension. The plaintiff also claimed that, given the existing knowledge in 1972 regarding the propensity of the pill to cause thrombosis, the warnings given by the manufacturer were inadequate.

According to the attorneys for the patient, the defendants settled for $2,084,000, of which the manufacturer contributed $25,000.[17]

Ortho Pharmaceutical Corp. v. Chapman (1979) 180 Ind. App. 33, 388 N.E.2d 541.

Thrombophlebitis—$100,000 verdict against manufacturer set aside for court's failure to exclude FDA's subsequent "Patient Warning"

An Ortho-Novum user who developed severe thrombophlebitis while on the drug sued the manufacturer under theories of negligence, strict liability and breach of warranty for failure to warn of the risk of the disease.

The plaintiff was awarded $100,000 in trial court. On appeal, the Court of Appeals of Indiana held that she did offer evidence from

[17] ATLA *Law Reporter* 21:36, 1978.

which the jury could have found the defendant's warning inadequate and the proximate cause of her injury, but it also held the trial court committed reversible error in admitting evidence of the "Patient Warning" later mandated by the Food and Drug Administration which should have been excluded as a "post-occurrence remedial measure."

Brochu v. Ortho Pharmaceutical Corp. (C.A.-1 N.H., 1981) 642 F.2d 652.

Cerebral thrombosis—$600,000 and $100,000 verdicts upheld against manufacturer for failing to warn of higher estrogen contents in pills

A 27-year-old patient began taking Ortho-Novum by prescription in August of 1967, and continued to use the drug until November 14, 1971. The next day she suffered a cerebral thrombosis.

The patient claimed inadequate warning and fraudulent misrepresentation. She contended that the drug manufacturer misrepresented to the medical profession that the risks for each of its oral contraceptives were the same when in fact some were higher, and the one taken by the patient, the 2 mg. pill, was the highest. She contended that the estrogen in it was significantly greater inasmuch as it contained 100 mcg. (micrograms) of a synthetic estrogen. By comparison, she contended that the Ortho-Novum 10 mg. pill contained 10 mg. of progestogen, but only 60 mcg. estrogen; the Ortho-Novum sequential contained 2 mg. of progestogen, and 80 mcg. estrogen; the 1/80 pill contained 1 mg. progestogen, and 80 mcg. estrogen; and the 1/50 pill contained 1 mg. of progestogen, and 50 mcg. estrogen.

A jury awarded the patient $600,000, and her husband $100,000, which were affirmed on appeal.

Lukaszewicz v. Ortho Pharmaceutical Corp. (E.D. Wis., 1981) 510 F. Supp. 961.

Stroke—Manufacturer of oral contraceptives has duty to warn consumers of risks—Failure to do so is negligence per se

The patient suffered a stroke while taking Ortho-Novum and sued the manufacturer for failing to warn her directly of the possibility of this side effect.

In denying the manufacturer's motion for summary judgment, the court held that although the product was available only by prescription from a physician, the defendant had a duty to warn the user directly of possible side effects, and failure to do so constituted negligence per se under Wisconsin law in view of the federal regulation requiring that warnings pertaining to oral contraceptives be given to patients in the form of package inserts.

Schierz v. Dodds (No. 500-05-006363-798, Superior Court, Quebec, Can., May 19, 1981).

Ortho-Novum prescribed for patient with history of phlebitis—Stroke—$243,963 judgment against physician

The twenty-five-year-old patient had been on birth control pills since age eighteen. When she complained of what appeared to be phlebitis in her right calf, the defendant physician told her to discontinue taking the pill. When she returned two weeks later, the defendant found no evidence of phlebitis but advised her to wait before starting back on the pill. A year later, the defendant prescribed Ortho-Novum 150. Ten months later the patient suffered a stroke.

The patient's case was based upon the negligence of the defendant in prescribing oral contraceptives to a patient with a history of phlebitis, negligence in failing to investigate the patient's condition, and failure to obtain her informed consent to the oral contraceptives. At the time of trial, the patient was partially paralyzed on the right side with a marked limp and speech impairment. She had no function in her right hand and suffered fifteen percent permanent mental incapacity. The court awarded her $243,963.[18]

Taylor v. Wyeth Laboratories, Inc. (1984) 139 Mich. App. 389, 362 N.W.2d 293.

Pulmonary embolism—Manufacturer's duty to warn of higher risks among certain blood types—Directed verdict for defendant reversed

The plaintiff's wife was being treated for a broken ankle when she died suddenly from a pulmonary embolism. On autopsy the medical examiner reported that the Ortho-Novum she was taking was "a factor in the forming of the clot." The plaintiff sued the manufacturer, alleging that it had knowledge that women of certain blood types, of which the plaintiff's wife was one, might be at a

---

[18] ATLA *Law Reporter* 25:138, 1982.

higher risk of forming blood clots while taking Ortho-Novum, and that it was negligent in not conducting tests to determine if this was true, and in not advising the medical profession in the meantime of certain tests physicians could perform to determine if their patients were in these higher risk groups.

The trial court directed a verdict for the manufacturer, holding that there was no evidence that if the manufacturer had conducted further tests to determine if there were high risk blood types, the results would have changed the current warnings. Also, the court held that even if the warnings were inadequate, the plaintiff had failed to show proximate cause.

The Court of Appeals reversed, holding that there was sufficient evidence to submit both issues to the jury.

Wooderson v. Ortho Pharmaceutical Corp. (1984) 235 Kan. 387, 681 P.2d 1038.

Hemolytic uremic syndrome with eventual kidney failure—Manufacturer failed to warn—$4.75 million in damages, including $2.75 million punitive

The plaintiff began taking Ortho-Novum in the fall of 1972. Two years later her blood pressure had risen from 100/56 to 130/80 but her physicians did not connect this change to the contraceptive. The plaintiff's blood pressure continued to rise over the next two years. In July, 1976, she was diagnosed as suffering from hemolytic uremic syndrome, induced by the oral contraceptives. Later both kidneys had to be removed and she went on dialysis until a successful transplant could be achieved.

Included in the plaintiff's evidence at trial was testimony that there were twenty-one reported cases of women on oral contraceptives who had developed hemolytic uremic syndrome prior to the plaintiff's diagnosis, and by the time of trial, this number had reached thirty-nine. The jury returned a verdict of $4.75 million, including $2.75 in punitive damages. The Supreme Court of Kansas affirmed, holding that there was an abundance of evidence to support the jury's finding that the Ortho-Novum had caused the plaintiff's condition, and that the manufacturer had knowledge of this risk and had failed to warn the medical profession.

Jones v. Ortho Pharmaceutical Corp. (1985) 163 Cal. App. 3d 396, 209 Cal. Rptr. 456.

Carcinoma in situ of the cervix—Insufficient evidence of reasonable causal connection

In an action against the manufacturer of Ortho-Novum, a woman in her early twenties claimed that the pills caused her to develop a precancerous condition of the cervix. She had taken the product for six months, through January, 1971. Three months later a Pap smear disclosed "atypical squamous cells suggestive of mild dysplasia," and six months after that a biopsy revealed "carcinoma in situ."

At the trial the plaintiff's experts included a specialist in pharmacology who testified that "there is a reasonable medical possibility" that the drug contributed to the development of the disease. His opinion was based in part on a review of eighteen cases of carcinoma in situ which occurred during the premarketing clinical studies of Ortho-Novum. A second expert, an obstetrician-gynecologist, testified that he thought the pills "may have been a contributing factor for the progression of [plaintiff's] lesion from dysplasia ... to the end point of carcinoma in situ."

The trial court, however, held that the above evidence did not establish a "reasonable causal connection" between the development or aggravation of the disease and the pills, and the manufacturer was granted a nonsuit.

The Court of Appeals affirmed.

MacDonald v. Ortho Pharmaceutical Corp. (1985) 394 Mass. 131, 475 N.E.2d 65.

Stroke—Manufacturer has duty to warn consumer

The plaintiff suffered a stroke after having taken Ortho-Novum for three years. In her suit against the manufacturer she claimed that if she had been warned that the pills could cause a stroke she would not have taken them. At the time, the product contained a warning in the dispenser, as required by FDA regulations, that the pills should not be taken without a doctor's "continued supervision," and that the "most serious known side effect is abnormal blood clotting which can be fatal." The plaintiff claimed that she did not know that the risk of "abnormal blood clotting" encompassed the risk of stroke.

The jury returned a verdict in favor of the plaintiff but the trial court granted the defendant's motion for judgment n.o.v. on the ground that a drug manufacturer's duty to warn is satisfied by warning the prescribing physician.

The Supreme Court reversed and remanded the case, holding that the general rule governing warnings of side effects of prescription drugs does not apply to oral contraceptives; that a manufacturer of oral contraceptives has a direct duty to warn the consumer of the dangers inherent in their use.

> Oral contraceptives ... bear peculiar characteristics which warrant the imposition of a common law duty on the manufacturer to warn users directly of associated risks. Whereas a patient's involvement in decision-making concerning use of a prescription drug necessary to treat a malady is typically minimal or nonexistent, the healthy, young consumer of oral contraceptives is usually actively involved in the decision to use "the pill," as opposed to other available birth control products, and the prescribing physician is relegated to a relatively passive role.
>
> Furthermore, the physician prescribing "the pill," as a matter of course, examines the patient once before prescribing an oral contraceptive and only annually thereafter .... At her annual checkup, the patient receives a renewal prescription for a full year's supply of the pill. Thus, the patient may only seldom have the opportunity to explore her questions and concerns about the medication with the prescribing physician. Even if the physician, on those occasions, were scrupulously to remind the patient of the risks attendant on continuation of the oral contraceptive, the patient cannot be expected to remember all of the details for a protracted period of time.

Odgers v. Ortho Pharmaceutical Corp. (E.D. Mich., 1985) 609 F. Supp. 867.

Stroke—Under Michigan law manufacturer has duty to warn consumer

The plaintiff suffered a stroke while taking Ortho-Novum. In an action against the manufacturer, the United States District Court for the Eastern District of Michigan held that under Michigan law the manufacturer of an oral contraceptive has a duty to warn the user of the product, not just the prescribing physician, of possible side effects.

The Court based its holding on the fact that use of oral contraceptives is generally attributed to consumer demand rather than to advice from a physician; that consumers use the product for extended periods without medical assessment; and that FDA regulations require warnings to consumers.

Ortho Pharmaceutical Corp. v. Heath (Colo., 1986) 722 P.2d 410.

Kidney failure—Verdict for plaintiff reversed—Manufacturer entitled to "risk-benefit test" and "unavoidably unsafe product" instructions

The plaintiff first began taking Ortho-Novum in 1967. She became pregnant in the summer of 1970 and discontinued the drug until February, 1972. In March, 1972, the plaintiff's obstetrician-gynecologist increased her dosage from Ortho-Novum 1/50 to Ortho-Novum 1/80 because she reported an incident of "break-through bleeding." The plaintiff continued taking the 1/80 until November, 1974, at which time she became critically ill with acute kidney failure. She eventually required a kidney transplant and later a hysterectomy due to cervical dysplasia thought to be the result of immunosuppressant therapy she had received to minimize the risk of tissue rejection.

The plaintiff's suit against Ortho was based on its failure to warn physicians to monitor blood pressure for the possibility of kidney failure in patients taking the high dosage Ortho-Novum 1/80.

Following a battle of experts over whether the drug was the proximate cause of the plaintiff's kidney disorder, the jury returned a verdict for the plaintiff and awarded her $975,000 plus prejudgment interest of $506,500. On appeal, the Supreme Court of Colorado found that the plaintiff's evidence was sufficient on the issue of a design defect in the product, but it also found that the trial court had erred in not allowing a defense instruction based upon Comment k of Section 402A of the *Restatement (Second) of Torts* regarding "unavoidably unsafe products." The reviewing court also ruled that the trial court erred in not allowing the defendant's instruction on the "risk-benefit test" under which Ortho would have been permitted to show that the benefits of the extra thirty milligrams of estrogen in Ortho-Novum 1/80 outweighed the risks of the higher estrogen content because Ortho-Novum 1/80 was the only available product for patients who experienced break-through bleeding.

Rhoto v. Ribando (La. App., 1987) 504 So. 2d 1118.

Stroke while taking Ortho Novum SQ and other drugs for weight reduction—Manufacturers not liable for failure to warn

The patient, a 36-year-old woman who was slightly overweight and who smoked a half of a pack of cigarettes per day, was placed on a weight reduction program by her physician. The program consisted of taking (1) Ortho Novum SQ, (2) Thyrolar (liotrix), a thyroid medication, (3) Renese (polythiazide), a diuretic, (4) Eskatrol (dextroamphetamine sulfate and prochlorperazine), an amphetamine, and (5) human chorionic gonadotropin, a fertility hormone. The patient had been on the regime for two weeks when she suffered a stroke.

The patient and her husband brought suit against the physician and each of the manufacturers of the drugs in the prescribed combination. The plaintiffs made no attempt to show that the drugs were unreasonably dangerous or defective. Instead, their claim was grounded on the contention that the manufacturers failed to warn of the danger of stroke when their drugs were used individually or in combination with other drugs as part of a weight reduction program. The plaintiffs specifically argued that the ingestion of Ortho Novum SQ causes a restriction of the opening for the passage of blood through the arteries, thereby damaging the vascular system and contributing to the cause of a stroke. Against the manufacturer of this drug, the plaintiffs charged also that the risk of stroke was enhanced if a patient smoked.

During the trial, evidence was introduced as to the warnings issued by the manufacturers. At the close of evidence, the trial court rendered a directed verdict in favor of all defendants. The Court of Appeals affirmed, holding that all of the warnings adequately informed the patient's physician of known risks associated with the normal use of the drugs in the prescribed combination, and thus the manufacturers could not be held liable for the patient's injury.

Related cases

Stroke—Manufacturer's warnings adequate

In Dunkin v. Syntex Laboratories, Inc. (W.D. Tenn., 1977) 443 F. Supp. 121, the plaintiff, who suffered a stroke while taking Norinyl, was unsuccessful in her claim that the defendant-manufacturer's warnings concerning the possibility of cerebrovascular accidents were inadequate.

Stroke—$750,000 award reversed for insufficient evidence of failure to warn and proximate cause

In Lindsay v. Ortho Pharmaceutical Corp. (C.A.-2 N.Y., 1980) 637 F.2d 87, a stroke victim's $750,000 jury award was reversed for want of evidence of the manufacturer's failure to give an adequate warning to her physician of the risk involved in prescribing Ortho-Novum and that such failure was the cause of her injury. The trial court also committed error in admitting contents of warnings given after the plaintiff had received her last prescription.

Blood clot and paralysis—New trial ordered after $3.3 million verdict

In Odgers v. Ortho Pharmaceutical Corp. (No. 78-70543, Federal District Court, Eastern District, Detroit, Mich., July 7, 1980), an eighteen-year-old college student was awarded $3.3 million for paralysis resulting from a blood clot allegedly caused by taking Ortho-Novum prescribed by a physician at the student medical clinic. However, on November 4, 1980, the trial judge decided that he may have erred in instructing the jury, and ordered a new trial.

Thrombophlebitis—Warnings sufficient—No evidence of overpromotion of product

In Spinden v. Johnson & Johnson (1981) 177 N.J. Super. 605, 427 A.2d 597, a New Jersey court held that warnings in a 1970 package of Ortho-Novum were adequate with regard to the risk of thromboembolic disease, and that there was no evidence to support the user's claim that the manufacturer overpromoted the product.

Stroke—Manufacturer and physician share liability

In Skill v. Martinez (C.A.-3 N.J., 1982) 677 F.2d 368, the manufacturer of Ortho-Novum and the plaintiff's physician were held liable to the extent of 35% and 65%, respectively, for a stroke suffered by the plaintiff who took the product from 1969 to 1976. The plaintiff ceased taking the product in August and the stroke occurred the following January.

Stroke—Warnings sufficient

In Cobb v. Syntex Laboratories, Inc. (La. App., 1983) 444 So. 2d 203, a summary judgment for the manufacturer was affirmed in an action by a woman who suffered a stroke while using Norinyl, where her physicians were advised by the manufacturer of the risks and contraindications associated with the drug and the plaintiff herself received a pamphlet entitled "What You Should Know About Oral Contraceptives" which warned of the risk of stroke.

Stroke—Psychiatrist failed to warn of risk for smokers—Issue of fact raised

In Gitlin v. Cassell (1985) 107 App. Div. 2d 636, 484 N.Y.S.2d 19, the trial court erred in granting a summary judgment to a psychiatrist who was sued by a patient for failing to warn her when he prescribed Ortho-Novum of the risk of stroke in heavy smokers who take birth control pills.

Liver tumors—Plaintiff fails to show she received no warning

In Jordon v. Ortho Pharmaceuticals, Inc. (Tex. App., 1985) 696 S.W.2d 228, the plaintiff, who developed liver tumors while taking Ortho-Novum, failed to establish conclusively that she had not received warnings of this possible side effect, in view of evidence that she had read the defendant's booklet in her physician's office which contained the statement, "Tumors of the liver, sometimes fatal, have been reported in women taking the pill."

Stroke—Manufacturer not liable for failure to warn chiropractors of risk of treating oral contraceptive users

In Moore v. Vanderloo (Iowa, 1986) 386 N.W.2d 108, the plaintiff, who suffered a cerebral stroke following a neck manipulation by a chiropractor, failed to establish that in view of the medical knowledge at the time (1978), the manufacturer of Ortho-Novum had a duty to warn chiropractors of the risk of stroke in administering chiropractic manipulations to patients taking its oral contraceptives. (Medical literature warning of this risk was first published in late 1980.)

Visual impairment—Manufacturer's warning adequate

In Eiser v. Feldman (1986) 123 App. Div. 2d 583, 507 N.Y.S.2d 386, the appellate court reversed the trial court's dismissal of the manufacturer's motion for summary judgment, and held that the defendant had adequately warned the patient's physician through the *Physicians' Desk Reference,* and the patient through literature accompanying the drug, that visual impairment was a danger associated with the drug's use.

Question of manufacturer's duty to warn consumers of side effects left to legislature

The Supreme Court of Michigan was asked by the U.S. District Court for the Eastern District of Michigan to decide whether a manufacturer of oral contraceptives (Ortho Pharmaceutical Corporation, manufacturer of Ortho-Novum) and other prescription drugs has a duty to disclose the risks and potential side effects directly to the consumer. The Court declined to answer the question, holding instead that the legislature is in a better position to allocate the duties of a drug manufacturer regarding the hazards of its products. In re Certified Questions from the U.S. Dist. Court for the E. Dist. of Mich., So. Div. (1984) 419 Mich. 686, 358 N.W.2d 873.

No causal relationship between manufacturer's inadequate warning to physician and plaintiff's stroke—Question of duty to warn consumer not decided

In an action against the manufacturer of Ortho-Novum by a woman who suffered a stroke while taking the drug, the trial court dismissed the plaintiff's claim that she was entitled to be directly warned of the risk of stroke. The case then went to trial on the claim that the manufacturer failed to adequately warn the plaintiff's physician. The jury found that the warning to the physician was inadequate, but also found that there was no causal relationship between the inadequate warning and the plaintiff's stroke. On appeal, the District Court of Appeal of Florida held that the jury verdict mooted the claim that the trial court erred in dismissing the plaintiff's claim that she was entitled to a direct warning. Parker v. Ortho Pharmaceutical Corp. (Fla. App., 1989) 536 So. 2d 390.

Physician negligent for prescribing Ortho-Novum for patient with history of thrombophlebitis

In Witherell v. Weimer (1987) 118 Ill. 2d 321, 113 Ill. Dec. 259, 515 N.E.2d 68, a physician was found negligent for prescribing Ortho-Novum for a patient who had a history of thrombophlebitis.

California proper forum

In Holmes v. Syntex Laboratories, Inc. (1984) 156 Cal. App. 3d 372, 202 Cal. Rptr. 773, it was held that the trial court had abused its discretion in dismissing, on grounds of forum non conveniens, the actions of a group of British plaintiffs who claimed injuries from the side effect of Norinyl where there were facts suggesting a connection between the litigation and California, and where all three defendants (the parent corporation of the manufacturer and two subsidiaries) maintained offices there.

Statutes of limitation

For cases involving claims for damages resulting from the side effects of Ortho-Novum in which the action was barred by the statute of limitations, see Ramey v. Guyton (Ala., 1980) 394 So. 2d 2; Drazin v. Shanik (1979) 171 N.J. Super. 76, 407 A.2d 1274; Witherell v. Weimer (1981) 85 Ill. 2d 146, 52 Ill. Dec. 6, 421 N.E.2d 869 (as to the manufacturer). For cases in which the action was held not to be barred, see McKenna v. Ortho Pharmaceutical Corp. (C.A.-3 Pa., 1980) 622 F.2d 657; Witherell v. Weimer (1981) 85 Ill. 2d 146, 52 Ill. Dec. 6, 421 N.E.2d 869 (as to physicians).

NORETHYNODREL with MESTRANOL
Enovid
Enovid-E

Norethynodrel (a progestogen) with mestranol (an estrogen) is used most widely as an oral contraceptive, the belief being that in combination, these two hormones inhibit ovulation by suppressing pituitary gonadotropic hormones in the female. The combination is virtually completely effective when taken daily from the 5th through the 24th day of the menstrual cycle.[19]

The combination has other actions and uses as well. It often dramatically relieves the symptoms of painful menstruation, and can control dysfunctional uterine bleeding (although it generally does not correct the underlying cause of such bleeding). It may also be helpful in treating endometriosis, secondary amenorrhea, and possibly habitual abortion. Some physicians have reported using it with success in treatment of acne.[20]

Enovid and Enovid-E are manufactured by Searle & Company (San Juan, P.R.).

For an extensive discussion of the possible side effects of oral contraceptives, see NORETHINDRONE with MESTRANOL.

---

[19] *United States Dispensatory,* 27th ed., p. 793.
[20] Id.

Simonait v. G. D. Searle & Co. (No. 1916, Circuit Court, Kent County, Mich., May 26, 1965).

**Thrombophlebitis—Varicose veins possible cause—
Verdict for manufacturer**

This is reported to have been the first case to go to trial which involved side effects of an oral contraceptive. The patient claimed that she had developed thrombophlebitis as a result of taking Enovid. She based her action on the theories of breach of implied warranty and negligence, claiming that the manufacturer of Enovid had failed to warn of the possibility that the drug might cause the disorder from which she suffered.

At the trial, the manufacturer introduced strong testimony by its medical witnesses that the probable cause of the patient's condition was varicose veins and not Enovid. The jury found for the manufacturer.[1]

Black v. G. D. Searle & Co. (Civil No. 4082, U.S. District Court, N.D., Ind., May, 1969).

**Pulmonary embolism—Patient previously involved in accident—
Verdict for manufacturer**

A 29-year-old woman died in September of 1965 from a pulmonary embolism, allegedly as a result of taking Enovid. Her husband brought suit against the manufacturer alleging failure to issue adequate warnings in its instruction booklets distributed to physicians for use by patients. The attorneys for the plaintiff charged that at the time of the patient's death there were approximately 600 reports of thromboembolic phenomena, including some deaths, among women who were taking Enovid.

The plaintiff introduced several expert witnesses who testified that in their opinion Enovid was directly connected with the patient's death. One expert testified that the drug slows down circulation of the blood and dilates the veins in the genital organs and the chest. This, he said, can cause the blood to "congeal." He stated that in his opinion the risk involved in the use of Enovid for contraceptive purposes was not justified.

Experts for the manufacturer testified that the woman's death could have been caused either by inflammation from an upper res-

---

[1] Barrett, J., "Product Liability and the Pill," *Cleveland State Law Review* 19:468, 1970.

piratory infection or from injury to a vein possibly received in a minor automobile accident in which she had been involved approximately two months prior to her death. A gynecologist testifying for the manufacturer stated that he had supervised the use of the Enovid in five to six thousand women and had observed no evidence of thromboembolic disease. He added that he had performed surgery on a number of these women and had found nothing unusual in their pelvic organs, such as distended veins or evidence of blood clots. Other medical experts testifying for the defense stated that there was no relationship between the use of Enovid and emboli.

The cause of action had been brought on the theories of negligence, breach of implied warranty, and strict liability. The jury returned verdicts for the manufacturer on all three counts.[2]

Meinert v. Interboro Gen. Hosp. (No. 2549-65, Supreme Court, Kings County, N.Y., 1970), aff'd (1971) 323 N.Y.S.2d 1010.

Mesenteric thrombosis—Manufacturer held liable on three counts—$250,000 verdict affirmed

A thirty-year-old woman took Enovid for eight months in 1962 during which time she developed a mesenteric thrombosis which required surgery and necessitated removal of portions of the large and small intestines.

The Enovid was blamed as the cause of the thrombosis and a lawsuit was filed based on the express warranty, implied warranty, strict liability, and common-law negligence. Charges against the manufacturer included failure to test the drug properly before marketing and failure to warn of dangers which were known or which should have been known at the time of marketing.

The trial court rejected the theory of express warranty, but after a five-week trial submitted the case to the jury on the other three theories. The jury found the drug company liable on all three counts, and returned a verdict against the manufacturer in the amount of $250,000. The verdict was affirmed by the Supreme Court, Appellate Division.[3]

---

[2] Id.

[3] Id. See also ATLA *News Letter* 14:369, 1971.

Carmichael v. Reitz (1971) 17 Cal. App. 3d 958, 95 Cal. Rptr. 381.

Thrombophlebitis—Actions against physicians dismissed—Verdict for manufacturer on warning issue

The patient first consulted her physician, an obstetrics and gynecology specialist, on July 10, 1963. She complained of pain during intercourse and during her menstrual periods. She also suffered from premenstrual tension, bloating, and for over two years had been unsuccessful in attempts to become pregnant. After a thorough examination, the physician diagnosed a minimal case of endometriosis. He recommended that the patient continue to attempt to become pregnant, and prescribed a combination diuretic and tranquilizer for the bloating and premenstrual tension. He advised her to return in a year.

The patient returned on May 12, 1964. There had been no progression in her symptoms; in fact, they were slightly improved, although she still had been unable to become pregnant. She did say, however, that she had experienced some nausea and loss of appetite during the past several months, and that she had been suffering from "flu" for a few weeks prior to her visit. Apparently there had been some chest pains, and she had been seeing another doctor for these, but she did not complain of any chest pain on this visit.

The physician believed the patient's endometriosis had progressed from "minimal" to "moderate" even though the amount of pain she usually experienced had decreased slightly. A roentgenogram of the patient's uterus and fallopian tubes was taken which confirmed the diagnosis. The physician prescribed Enovid, which he considered the drug of choice, for the patient's problems.

The physician was aware, at the time, of a "statistical relationship" between thromboembolic episodes and Enovid, but he did not believe there was a "causal relationship" between the two. The *Physicians' Desk Reference* for 1964 (copyrighted in 1963), which he used, indicated no such contraindications. Certain product literature concerning Enovid, issued by the drug company on March 5, 1964 did state, however, under contraindications: "Previous Thrombophlebitis or Pulmonary Embolism. Enovid-E is contraindicated in these patients unless the reason for its use in the judgment of the physician is overwhelming."

The prescription was filled at a pharmacy on May 14, 1964. The directions on the label were: "One tablet daily for 14 days then one tablet 2 times a day." The patient waited until May 25th before she started taking the pills because she had had "a rather bad time" with her menstrual period and wanted to wait until it was over. The patient, who did not normally eat breakfast, took her first pill on the morning of May 25th, and within one hour became extremely nauseous. She "took it for one or two days" and then called the physician who advised her to continue taking the pills "if at all possible." By June 5th she was spitting up blood and experiencing chest pains and shortness of breath. Her pain alleviated the following morning, but it grew more intense as the day wore on. On the morning of June 7th she called the physician's office and was told to come in at 2:00 p.m. She did so and was seen by an associate. A roentgenogram of her chest was taken and reported as negative. This physician diagnosed the patient's complaints as bronchopneumonia and prescribed an antibiotic.

The patient was seen by her own physician on June 8, and was instructed to continue the antibiotic. Her pain continued to worsen and the physician examined her again on June 9, at which time he turned her over to a partner in the clinic, a specialist in internal medicine. He had her hospitalized, took a detailed history, and diagnosed her condition as "pneumonia with possible pulmonary embolism originating from a pelvic thrombophlebitis." When he learned that she had taken Enovid, he added on her chart: "possibility of Enovid-induced embolism." Later, a venogram disclosed large clots in the inferior vena cava, and a "plication" of the vein was performed.

The patient and her husband brought suit against the physician who had prescribed the Enovid, the internist, the clinic, and the company which manufactured Enovid. The trial court rendered judgment of nonsuit as to all the defendants except the drug company, and a jury verdict was returned in its favor. The patient appealed the verdict and the Court of Appeals of California affirmed, declaring:

> It is the general rule that the duty of adequate warning by the manufacturer of an ethical drug is discharged by its warning of hazards to doctors who may in the exercise of their medical judgments decide to use the drug as a part of their chemotherapy.... Absent special circumstances, known or foreseeable in the exercise of due care by the manufacturer, there is no duty to warn the patient.... It is the prescribing doctor who in reality stands in the shoes of 'the ordinary consumer'.

Schaefer v. Kaiser Foundation Hosp., Inc. (No. SEC 8395-S, Superior Court, Los Angeles County, Cal., Feb. 22, 1972).

Heart attack and stroke—Blood clots—Conflicting medical testimony on causation—Physicians not liable

A 42-year-old woman patient suffering from polycythaemia vera, a blood disease involving an excess of red blood cells, underwent a dilation and curettage, and was put on Enovid-E to regulate menstruation. Soon thereafter she suffered both a heart attack and a stroke, apparently due to the formation of blood clots, which resulted in the complete loss of the right field of vision.

In a malpractice action against the hospital and the medical group that treated her, the patient offered testimony by a physician that she should not have been given the birth control pills because of her preexisting blood disease. This witness testified also that the heart attack and stroke were the result of the effects of the pills. The defendants argued that the patient's problem was not due to the pills but to a myocardial infarction occurring about a week after her surgery. Physician witnesses testifying for the defense stated that the defendants had met the standard of care in treating the patient, and that her clotting problems were not due to the pills.

The court granted a nonsuit as to the hospital, and a jury returned a verdict in favor of the physicians.[4]

Brewer v. G. D. Searle & Co. (No. 69L-1276, Circuit Court, Cook County, Ill., Oct. 12, 1973).

Occlusion of carotid artery—Manufacturer charged with careless research methods—$100,000 verdict

A 21-year-old woman patient began taking Enovid soon after the birth of her child in 1963. She took 5 mg. pills until May, 1965 when she went on the 2.5 mg. Enovid-E. Soon after the change to Enovid-E the patient suffered headaches, blackouts, and seizures. She eventually became partially paralyzed, partially blind and unable to speak. On her death the diagnosis was occlusion of the left carotid artery.

A lawsuit was brought by the patient's estate against the manufacturer. Evidence was introduced that the patient's physicians had ruled out all possible causes for her death except the drug. The manufacturer denied this, arguing that the patient's condition had

---

[4] AMA *The Citation* 25:163, 1972.

been the result of a myocardial embolism brought on by taking reducing pills which contained digitalis and thyroid extract. At the trial, cross-examination of representatives of the manufacturer suggested that portions of the results of studies conducted on side effects of the drug had become misplaced, and that all reports of such studies had not been turned over to the Food and Drug Administration. It was also alleged that the manufacturer had withdrawn financial support from a researcher in its employ when his reports were not favorable, and that results of other research studies on the drug had not been reported accurately. The jury returned a verdict for the patient's estate in the amount of $100,000.[5]

McCurnin v. G. D. Searle & Co. (No. 70L-12887, Circuit Court, Cook County, Ill., Aug. 2, 1974).

Cancer of cervix—Patient not examined when drug prescribed—Issue over prescription renewal—Verdict for all defendants

A woman patient who began taking Enovid in 1962 developed cancer of the cervix in 1970. She brought suit against the physician who prescribed the drug, the manufacturer, and four pharmacies where she had the prescription filled.

There was evidence that when her physician prescribed Enovid, he had not examined the patient vaginally, because she had been menstruating. At the trial, this physician testified that the prescription he had given was not renewable, and, apparently, he had not seen her again until the lawsuit was filed. There was some evidence that there were other physicians involved in the patient's case, but this was not clear; there being confusion with regard to who, if anyone, renewed the prescription as the patient went from pharmacy to pharmacy obtaining the pills.

The jury denied recovery.[6]

Berry v. G. D. Searle & Co. (1974) 56 Ill. 2d 548, 309 N.E.2d 550.

Stroke—Patient held to have warranty claim under Uniform Commercial Code

A woman taking Enovid suffered a stroke which partially paralyzed her. She filed an action against the manufacturer alleging breach of implied warranty and strict liability in tort. She also

---

[5] Id., 28:112, 1974. See also ATLA *News Letter* 17:12, 1974.

[6] AMA *The Citation* 30:8, 1974.

named as a defendant the Planned Parenthood Association of Chicago where she had purchased the pills.

It was not reported in the decision how long the woman had been taking Enovid before she suffered her stroke, which occurred on May 30, 1965; her lawsuit, however, was not filed until May 29, 1969. The trial court dismissed the action, holding that it was barred because it had been instituted more than two years after the occurrence of the injury.

The plaintiff had filed her action under the Illinois Uniform Commercial Code to take advantage of the four-year statute of limitations established by section 2-725(1) of that act which governs actions brought for personal injury allegedly arising from a breach of implied warranty. The trial court, however, held the section inapplicable to the plaintiff's claim. On appeal, the Supreme Court of Illinois disagreed, holding that the four-year statute did apply. In doing so, the court rejected the Planned Parenthood Association's argument that the Code section was applicable only to claims alleging that products are not fit for the purpose for which they are purchased, and not to claims alleging that products are unsafe. Also rejected was the contention of the manufacturer that there was neither a sale nor privity between it and the plaintiff.

With regard to the claim of strict liability in tort, however, the court held that Illinois' general two-year statute of limitations applied, and the plaintiff's cause under this theory was barred by the late filing. Here, the court rejected the plaintiff's attorney's contention that her cause of action should be determined to have commenced on the date that she knew that the side effects of Enovid were the cause of her condition. This date, she claimed, was June 1, 1967. Disregarding this argument, the court stated: "From plaintiff's description of the severity of her condition in the complaint and her reply brief it is inconceivable that her injury was not occasioned by a traumatic event and that she knew of this injury more than two years prior to the filing of her complaint."

Accordingly, the reviewing court reversed the trial court's judgment which had dismissed the count alleging breach of implied warranty, and remanded that cause for further proceedings. The portion of the judgment dismissing the count charging strict liability was affirmed.

Lawson v. G. D. Searle & Co. (1976) 64 Ill. 2d 543, 1 Ill. Dec. 497, 356 N.E.2d 779.

Thromboembolic disorders—Conflicting evidence on relationship to use of Enovid—Verdict for manufacturer upheld

This case involves two users of Enovid. The first, Sarah Lawson, entered the hospital in September, 1962 suffering from a blood clot in the leg and died the following day from multiple pulmonary emboli. The second, Joanne Holmes, noticed in December, 1963 a "shortness of breath, numbness in her arm and fingers, and a pain in her right shoulder." She was hospitalized and treated with anticoagulants, on the theory that she, too, was suffering from a pulmonary embolism.

At the trial, the evidence was conflicting. The defendant-manufacturer offered proof which indicated that thromboembolic episodes could occur "idiopathically" (from an unknown origin), and that the incidence of such episodes increases with such factors as childbirth, obesity, vascular abnormalities, and restricted movement. The defendant also produced three expert witnesses who testified that there was no relationship between the use of Enovid and the occurrence of thrombophlebitis or pulmonary emboli. The plaintiffs, on the other hand, produced experts who were of the opposite opinion, and who were able to base their conclusions on various case reports and clinical studies which showed conclusively that there was a causal relationship between Enovid use and thromboembolic disorders.

After a lengthy trial, the jury found in favor of the defendant. On appeal to the Appellate Court of Illinois, the verdict was overturned. But on further appeal to the Supreme Court of Illinois, the Appellate Court's decision was reversed and the jury verdict reinstated.

The Supreme Court admitted that the "manifest weight of the evidence" supported the plaintiffs' position on the issue of a relationship between Enovid and the occurrence of thrombophlebitis, but, said the court, "even if the jury did find that defendant's product may cause blood clotting, under the instructions given, the jury could have refused to find that use of the drug was the proximate cause of the injuries involved in this case. There is credible evidence in the record which, if believed by the jury, would show that Mrs. Lawson's death was a result of predisposing causes, and that Mrs. Holmes' injuries did not result from a pulmonary embolism."

Mahr v. G. D. Searle & Co. (1979) 72 Ill. App. 3d 540, 28 Ill. Dec. 624, 390 N.E.2d 1214.

Thromboembolic disorder—Manufacturer's warning inadequate—$100,000 wrongful-death award upheld

A 25-year-old obese woman took Enovid and Enovid-E from March, 1963 to December, 1966. In January, 1967, she suffered an occlusion of the left internal carotid artery which resulted in her death.

In an action against the manufacturer, it was alleged that the defendant's warnings regarding the drug's side effects were inadequate. The plaintiffs produced expert witnesses who testified that oral contraceptives cause thromboembolic disorders, and that this was the cause of the woman's death. The manufacturer called on experts who testified that the woman's death was instead the result of a diseased arterial system brought about by the overuse of diet pills.

A jury found for the plaintiffs and awarded them $100,000. On appeal, the Appellate Court of Illinois affirmed, finding that there was sufficient evidence that Enovid does produce the disorders complained of, and that the manufacturer's warnings did not convey the true risk involved. The court was especially critical of the manufacturer's failure to make use of detail men to warn the medical community of the danger.

Chambers v. G. D. Searle & Co. (C.A.-4Md., 1977) 567 F.2d 269.

Cerebral thrombosis—No evidence of fraud, breach of implied warranty, strict liability or negligence

The plaintiff alleged that Enovid-E caused her to suffer a cerebral thrombosis. In her lawsuit against the manufacturer, she charged the defendant with fraud, breach of implied warranty, strict liability and negligence. At the conclusion of her case, the district court granted the defendant's motion for summary judgment, finding that the plaintiff failed to adduce sufficient evidence on any of her four theories.

On appeal, the reviewing court affirmed, holding that the evidence was insufficient to permit a jury to determine whether the defendant was negligent in not pursuing medical research to determine the possible consequences of ingesting the product, in warning physicians in light of the medical knowledge at the time, or in overpromoting the product.

NORGESTREL with ETHINYL ESTRADIOL
Ovral

This oral contraceptive, manufactured by Wyeth Laboratories (Philadelphia, Pa.) and distributed under the trade name Ovral, contains 0.5 mg. of norgestrel, a totally synthetic progestogen, and 0.05 mg. of ethinyl estradiol.[7]

For an extensive discussion of the possible side effects of oral contraceptives, see NORETHINDRONE with MESTRANOL.

Jurin v. Wyeth Laboratories, Inc. (No. 769855, Superior Court, King County, Wash., May 20, 1977).

Stroke causing paralysis—$400,000 verdict against manufacturer

A 35-year-old woman used Ovral for six weeks and then suffered a stroke which rendered her left arm permanently paralyzed and her left leg partially paralyzed. She brought suit against the manufacturer of the drug, alleging that there were inadequate warnings concerning its side effects, and contending that the estrogen content (ethinyl estradiol), was 114.4% of the amount specified on the label.

According to the attorneys for the plaintiff, she obtained a jury verdict in the amount of $400,000.[8]

Batiste v. American Home Products Corp. (1977) 32 N.C. App. 1, 231 S.E.2d 269.

Stroke—No implied warranty on part of physician or druggist—Druggist also free of negligence and not subject to claim of strict liability

The plaintiff, who suffered a stroke while taking Ovral, brought suit against her physician, the druggist from whom she purchased the pills, and the manufacturer of the product. Her complaint alleged several claims for relief against each of the defendants. Prior to trial, the court dismissed claims against the physician based on implied warranties and dismissed the cause of action entirely against the druggist.

On appeal, the reviewing court affirmed, holding that the physician's issuance of a prescription for the pills did not constitute a transaction covered by the Uniform Commercial Code applicable to implied warranties, and that persons who furnish professional med-

---

[7] *Physicians' Desk Reference,* 35th ed., p. 1939.

[8] ATLA *Law Reporter* 20:434, 1977.

ical services "for the guidance and assistance of others" are not liable in the absence of negligence or intentional misconduct. As to the druggist, the court held that since there was no allegation that he had added anything or selected anything for the plaintiff to take, the section covering implied warranties likewise did not apply. Said the court:

> Obviously the plaintiff patient did not rely on the druggist's skill or judgment in assuming that the drug would be fit for its intended purpose. This reliance had been properly placed with her physician. We are not willing to extend the applicability of implied warranties of fitness and merchantability to this situation.

Regarding charges of negligence and strict liability against the druggist, the court held that he could not be liable for negligence where he filled the prescription as directed and there was no allegation that the product was other than it was supposed to be, and he could not be held strictly liable for injuries resulting from the use of a drug which was sold in strict compliance with the physician's order, in the absence of any knowledge that would constitute negligence.

Garner v. Wyeth Laboratories, Inc. (D. S.C., 1984) 585 F. Supp. 189.

Myocardial infarction—Army doctors negligent in prescribing Ovral for patient with cardiovascular condition—$215,000 award—No recovery against manufacturer

The plaintiff, a retired member of the armed forces, was overweight, a heavy smoker and had high blood cholesterol, hypertension, and a family history of cardiovascular disease. Despite this medical history, when she was discharged from the obstetrical-gynecological clinic at Moncrief Army Hospital, Fort Jackson, South Carolina, where she had been admitted for a spontaneous abortion, she received a prescription for Ovral. Eighteen months later she suffered a severe myocardial infarction, which she attributed to the drug. She brought suit against the government, alleging negligence on the part of the Army doctor that had treated her in prescribing Ovral and in not monitoring her blood pressure. The district court, sitting without a jury, awarded her and her husband $215,000, which was paid.

The couple's later action against the manufacturer was dismissed on grounds that under South Carolina law once a judgment is satisfied the injured party is precluded from bringing another action.

Related cases

Warning adequate regarding pregnant patients

In Reeder v. Hammond (1983) 125 Mich. App. 223, 336 N.W.2d 3, the labeling on Ovral was found adequate with respect to warning physicians to test for pregnancy before prescribing. This case is discussed herein under AMPHETAMINE and DEXROAMPHETAMINE.

Determining the proper forum for British cases

In Harrison v. Wyeth Laboratories Div. of American Home Products Corp. (E.D. Pa., 1980) 510 F. Supp. 1, aff'd (C.A.-3 Pa., 1982) 676 F.2d 685, it was held that England rather than Pennsylvania was the more convenient forum for the trial of products liability cases brought by British citizens for injuries allegedly sustained from taking Ovram, a related product sold in the United Kingdom, and the suit would be transferred on the condition that the defendant accept process in the foreign suit, make witnesses and documents available, and agree to pay any judgment rendered in the plaintiffs' favor.

And in Bewers v. American Home Products Corp. (1984) 99 App. Div. 2d 949, 472 N.Y.S.2d 637, aff'd 64 N.Y.2d 630, 485 N.Y.S.2d 39, 474 N.E.2d 247, it was held that the doctrine of forum non conveniens required dismissal of three cases involving Ovram and related products brought by British plaintiffs in the New York courts where the drugs were allegedly "dumped" on foreign markets after the FDA required a label warning of possible severe side effects. The drugs were marketed by a wholly owned British subsidiary company of the defendant, American Home Products Corporation, and the vast majority of witnesses and documents were located in the United Kingdom.

NORINYL

See NORETHINDRONE with MESTRANOL

NORLESTRIN

See NORETHINDRONE ACETATE with ETHINYL ESTRADIOL

NOVAFED
See CHLORPHENIRAMINE MALEATE

NOVAHISTINE
See CHLORPHENIRAMINE MALEATE; PSEUDOEPHEDRINE HYDROCHLORIDE and CHLORPHENIRAMINE MALEATE

NOVOCAINE
See PROCAINE HYDROCHLORIDE

NUPRIN
See IBUPROFEN

NYSTATIN
See TRIAMCINOLONE ACETONIDE

O

OCTAMIDE
See METOCLOPRAMIDE HYDROCHLORIDE

OCTICAIR
See NEOMYCIN SULFATE

OMNIPEN
See AMPICILLIN; PENICILLIN

OPHTHOCHLOR
See CHLORAMPHENICOL

OPHTHOCORT
See CHLORAMPHENICOL

ORACON
See ETHINYL ESTRADIOL with DIMETHISTERONE

ORAFLEX
See BENZOXAPROFEN

ORASONE
See PREDNISONE

ORENZYME
See CHYMOTRYPSIN

ORIMUNE
See POLIOVIRUS VACCINE

ORNADE
See CHLORPHENIRAMINE MALEATE

ORTHO-GYNOL CONTRACEPTIVE JELLY
See p-DIISOBUTYLPHENOXYPOLYETHOXYETHANOL

ORTHO-NOVUM
See NORETHINDRONE with MESTRANOL

OTOCORT
See NEOMYCIN SULFATE

OVRAL
See NORGESTREL with ETHINYL ESTRADIOL

OVULEN
See ETHYNODIOL DIACETATE with MESTRANOL

OXALID
See OXYPHENBUTAZONE

OXIDIZED CELLULOSE
See CELLULOSE, OXIDIZED

OXSORALEN
See METHOXSALEN

OXYCEL

See CELLULOSE, OXIDIZED

OXYCODONE

Percocet
Percodan

Oxycodone is a semisynthetic narcotic analgesic and sedative with multiple actions similar to those of morphine, and is indicated for the relief of moderate to moderately severe pain. The product is manufactured and sold by Du Pont Pharmaceuticals (Wilmington, Del.) combined with either acetaminophen (Percocet) or aspirin (Percodan).

The product is sold with a warning that it can produce drug dependence of the morphine type. Psychic dependence, physical dependence, and tolerance can develop upon repeated administration. The physician is advised to prescribe the product with the "same degree of caution" appropriate to the use of other oral narcotic-containing medications.[9]

Adams v. Allen (1989) 56 Wash. App. 283, 783 P.2d 635.

Addiction and lack of informed consent—Prescriptions written for eleven years in allegedly excessive quantities—Action not barred by statute of limitations.

The defendant physician first prescribed Percodan for the patient in January 1974 because of a lower back pain. The prescription stated that the pills were to be taken every six to eight hours as need for pain. Later, according to the patient, when she contracted the "flu," the defendant said she could take the drug "every hour without ill effects."

The patient continued to take the drug in excessive doses, and on visits to the defendant's office for "check-ups," he would give her new prescriptions. Occasionally he also renewed the prescriptions over the phone. She did not tell him that she was exceeding the recommended written dosage, but according to the defendant's and pharmacist's records, the defendant had prescribed enough pills for an average dosage of five to six per day.

The patient's husband began using his wife's Percodan in 1974 because of pain in his legs and feet. He later became a patient of the

---

[9] *Physicians' Desk Reference,* 43rd ed., pp. 915-16.

defendant and obtained prescriptions directly. He claimed that the defendant never advised him of the possible side effects of the drug. The patient and her husband also sought the services of a second physician who also prescribed Percodan on an "occasional basis." This physician did advise the patient's husband that the drug was addictive. Neither the patient nor her husband told either physician that they were receiving Percodan prescriptions from the other.

In 1982, the patient had a portion of her stomach removed. Her surgeon suggested that she not take any more Percodan because it contains aspirin which "likely contributed" to the patient's gastrointestinal problems. The defendant switched the patient to Percocet, which contains acetaminophen instead of aspirin.

In April 1985, the patient was hospitalized for a severe kidney infection, at which time she was found to be addicted to oxycodone. She began treatment for drug abuse, and the following month her husband also entered the same program. In July 1986, they filed suit against the defendant for failing to inform them of the risk of addiction, and for fraudulent misrepresentation of the "reasonableness of their course of treatment."

The trial court dismissed the plaintiffs' actions for failure to inform on the ground that they were barred by the three-year statute of limitations. The court also dismissed the misrepresentation charge for want of evidence of the element of "intentional wrongdoing or intent to deceive."

The Court of Appeals upheld the dismissal of the misrepresentation charge, but reversed as to the alleged failure to inform, holding that each time the defendant wrote a prescription (the last of which was written sixteen months before the suit was filed), it was a separate allegedly wrongful act for purposes of the statute of limitations.

OXYMYCIN

See OXYTETRACYCLINE

OXYPHENBUTAZONE

Oxalid
Tandearil

Oxyphenbutazone has anti-inflammatory, antipyretic (fever reducing) and analgesic properties, and is used in treating rheumatoid arthritis, rheumatoid spondylitis, psoriatic arthritis, osteoarthritis, gout, acute superficial thrombophlebitis, and severe forms of local inflammatory conditions.[10] The drug is sometimes used in place of aspirin when the latter is ineffective or poorly tolerated.[11]

The most serious adverse reaction is bone marrow depression, which may lead to aplastic anemia. This occurs only rarely during a one-week trial with the drug (which is recommended). During prolonged treatment, blood counts should be performed regularly; however, these cannot always be depended upon to predict blood disorders, and physicians should advise patients that if they develop a fever, sore throat, or stomatitis they should discontinue the drug immediately.[12]

Oxalid is manufactured by USV Pharmaceutical Corporation (Tuckahoe, N.Y.), and Tandearil, now discontinued, by Geigy Pharmaceuticals (Ardsley, N.Y.). The product also is marketed by Schein Pharmaceutical, Inc. (Port Washington, N.Y.), under the generic name.

Cohen v. Sperling (No. L-3748-69, Superior Court, Essex County, N.J., June 6, 1972).

Aplastic anemia—Patient treated for two and one-half years with Tandearil—$140,000 settlement

A 56-year-old woman patient was treated with Tandearil for two and one-half years for arthritis. She developed aplastic anemia, a known side effect of the drug, and brought suit against her attending physician and the manufacturer, Geigy Pharmaceuticals. According to a report by the patient's attorney, the matter was settled for the sum of $140,000.[13]

Formella v. Ciba-Geigy Corp. (1980) 100 Mich. App. 649, 300 N.W.2d 356.

Aplastic anemia—Settlement with physician—Manufacturer protected by physician's intervening negligence

An elderly woman patient had been taking Tandearil for six weeks as treatment for osteoarthritis when she began to notice multiple bruises over her body and extreme tiredness. She called her physician who immediately suspected that she was suffering

---

[10] *Physicians' Desk Reference,* 35th ed., p. 912.

[11] *AMA Drug Evaluations,* 2d ed., p. 298.

[12] *Physicians' Desk Reference,* 35th ed., p. 912.

[13] ATLA *News Letter* 16:33, 1973.

from a blood dyscrasia brought on by the drug. He ordered her to stop taking the drug and to report to the hospital for tests. The diagnosis was aplastic anemia.

In her lawsuit against the physician and the drug manufacturer, the patient charged the former with negligence in prescribing the drug and the latter with overpromotion and failure to warn of the product's side effects. The physician settled with the patient prior to trial for an undisclosed amount. The trial court then directed a verdict for the manufacturer.

On appeal, the trial court's action was affirmed, the Court of Appeals of Michigan holding that the negligence of the physician was the intervening, independent and sole proximate cause of the patient's injuries, and that the patient had not produced evidence showing that the manufacturer had overpromoted the drug or had failed to warn physicians adequately of the drug's risks through package inserts and other means.

Related cases

Internal hemorrhage during treatment with Tandearil and other drugs

In Robinson v. Duszynski (1978) 36 N.C. App. 103, 243 S.E.2d 148, a woman being treated in the hospital for arthritis with Celestone (betamethasone), Tandearil and prednisone began hemorrhaging from the vagina and died following emergency surgery. The case is summarized herein under BETAMETHASONE.

OXYPHENCYCLIMINE HYDROCHLORIDE with HYDROXYZINE HYDROCHLORIDE
Enarax Tablets

This is an antispasmodic used as adjunctive therapy in peptic ulcer, irritable bowel syndrome and similar gastrointestinal disorders. The manufacturer at the time the case below arose, Roerig, a division of Pfizer Pharmaceuticals (New York, N.Y.), listed numerous adverse reactions, including urticaria and other skin manifestations. The manufacturer also warned that the potentiating action of hydroxyzine must be considered when the drug is used in combination with central nervous system depressants.[14] The drug is now produced by Beecham Laboratories (Bristol, Tenn.).

---

[14] *Physicians' Desk Reference,* 29th ed., pp. 1266-67.

Dermatological reaction in patient receiving Enarax tablets and five other drugs

In Slack v. Fleet (La. App., 1970) 242 So. 2d 650, a middle-aged woman patient who complained to her physician of "pain and cramping in the stomach, nausea, vomiting and nervousness" was given prescriptions for Enarax tablets and five other drugs. She took the drugs simultaneously, as directed, and developed a severe rash. In the resulting lawsuit a question arose over the propriety of prescribing that particular combination of drugs in a case such as the plaintiff's. The defendant-physician offered two medical witnesses who testified that his choice of medication was within acceptable standards. The plaintiff offered no expert testimony. The trial court dismissed the action and was upheld on appeal. The case is summarized herein under PHENACETIN.

OXYTETRACYCLINE
Oxymycin
Terramycin
Urobiotic-250

Oxytetracycline, a member of the tetracycline family of antibiotics, is effective against most gram-positive and many gram-negative bacterial pathogens, the rickettsiae, and certain members of other bacterial groups, including some protozoa.[15]

Major adverse results are due to irritant properties in the drug, hypersensitivity of the patient, metabolic effects, and overgrowth or "superinfection" by yeasts or by resistant bacteria. Most common complaints are gastrointestinal disturbances following oral administration, particularly an epigastric burning sensation, abdominal discomfort, nausea, vomiting and diarrhea.[16] Skin reactions include maculopapular and erythematous rashes, photosensitivity, and, according to current literature accompanying the drug, exfoliative dermatitis "has been reported but is uncommon."[17] Other reactions include those common to the tetracycline group. (See TETRACYCLINE, herein.)

Oxymycin is manufactured by Forest Pharmaceuticals, Inc. (St. Louis, Mo.), Terramycin by the Pfifpharmecs Division of Pfizer, Inc. (New York, N.Y.), and Urobiotic-250 by Roerig, also a division of Pfizer, Inc.

---

[15] *United States Dispensatory,* 27th ed., p. 825.

[16] Id.

[17] *Physicians' Desk Reference,* 35th ed., p. 1417.

Fisher v. Wilkinson (Mo., 1964) 382 S.W.2d 627.

Exfoliative dermatitis—Patient claims physician failed to diagnose reaction—Recovery denied for want of expert medical testimony

The plaintiff filed suit against two physicians for malpractice, alleging that they had been negligent in failing to discover her allergy to Terramycin before prescribing the drug, and in failing to diagnose her resulting allergic reaction within a reasonable time.

At the trial the evidence disclosed that the plaintiff had undergone gallbladder surgery. On the third day after her release from the hospital her son called her physician and informed him that his mother was "sick," that she had a "slowing" of urine, and that she appeared to have a fever. The physician told the son to take his mother's temperature and call back. By the time he had done so, it was after office hours, and the physician had gone home. The son talked to an associate who told him he believed his mother had a urinary infection. He suggested a sulfa drug, but the son said his mother was allergic to sulfa. He then prescribed Terramycin, which he later testified was the "commonly accepted medication" for such a condition. Neither the plaintiff nor the son requested the associate to make a house call.

The plaintiff testified that on the following day, which was a Sunday, she was "no better," and her skin was beginning to feel as though "someone had rubbed me with wire." On Monday she called the first physician and told him that she still had a temperature, and that she had a "sensation" in her face and eyes. She testified that she asked him if it was caused by the medicine she was taking and she said he replied that it was not.

On the following Wednesday, in response to a request from the plaintiff, the associate made a house call. He testified that at that time he did not notice anything unusual about the plaintiff's skin, and he diagnosed her condition as a "low-grade urinary infection." He obtained a urine specimen, and later reported by telephone that there was nothing "to worry about."

The plaintiff's son testified that his mother developed redness around her eyes and that they were "starting to puff and swell." However, it was not clear from his testimony when he first noticed this condition. A woman who was visiting the plaintiff testified that she was present when the physician called, and that the plaintiff then had "very small red spots" beneath the surface of the skin, and that her eyes "were swollen and puffy looking." The plaintiff testified that the physician "pulled my gown and housecoat down, and looked around a little" and said that he "could see no redness."

On the following Tuesday the associate returned and found the plaintiff "obviously sick," although not "critically ill." She "had a redness, a rash ... over her face and shoulder ... [and the] upper part of her trunk" which was "an allergic reaction to something." He told her that she "should be in the hospital immediately," but she "absolutely refused" because she said that she could not afford it and she did not think she was that ill. The associate prescribed a cortisone preparation which was recognized treatment for allergic reactions. On Thursday she finally had to enter the hospital, where her condition was diagnosed as "exfoliative-dermatitis."

The first physician testified that the only side effect of Terramycin of which he was aware was "pseudo-mucinous enterocolitis" which was a reaction that occurred in the bowel from the antibiotic killing off normal bacteria as well as the infection.

A medical doctor from New York who was associated with the drug company that manufactured Terramycin testified that dermatitis was not an expected or a common reaction to be looked for in Terramycin, and that the plaintiff's occurrence of exfoliative-dermatitis was the only case which could be traced to Terramycin. But the "package insert" supplied by the company with Terramycin contained a paragraph headed "Precautions" where it was stated that "Glossitis and dermatitis as reactions of an allergic nature may occur but are rare." It also stated "If adverse reactions occur or individual idiosyncrasy or allergy occur, discontinue medication." The company medical director testified that the term "dermatitis" in the brochure was used without the term "exfoliative" and with reference only "to dermatitis, meaning essentially a skin irritation" which did not include exfoliative, and the two were distinct conditions, the exfoliative-dermatitis being a "much more serious condition than dermatitis alone" and also being a "very rare condition."

The jury returned a verdict in favor of the physicians, and the plaintiff appealed. The Supreme Court of Missouri affirmed the judgment of the lower court, stating:

> Plaintiff offered no expert medical testimony, and her evidence consisted only of the testimony of herself, her son, her daughter-in-law, a family friend (none of whom qualified as a medical expert witness), the hospital records, and certain excerpts from the depositions of [the two physicians].... [T]he mode of treatment selected by a competent physician for the treatment of an injury or illness is largely a matter of professional judgment....

this case clearly is one where expert medical testimony is required.

Related cases

Discoloration of teeth following use of Terramycin and other tetracyclines

In Dalke v. Upjohn Co. (C.A.-9 Wash., 1977) 555 F.2d 245, a child was given Panalba, Declomycin (demeclocycline hydrochloride) and Terramycin from 1965 to 1973 for an upper respiratory condition. These drugs allegedly caused her teeth to become discolored. The case is summarized herein under DEMECLOCYCLINE HYDROCHLORIDE.

OXYTOCIN
Pitocin
Syntocinon

Oxytocin is a sterile, synthetic oxytocic (uterine stimulating) hormone recommended for the initiation or improvement of uterine contractions when such is necessary. It is not indicated for the *elective* induction of labor (i.e., the initiation of labor in an individual with a term pregnancy who is free of medical indications for the initiation of labor) because data are inadequate on benefit-risk considerations. According to the product literature (Pitocin), its use is indicated in the following cases:

> For the initiation or improvement of uterine contractions, where this is desirable and considered suitable, for the following purposes: induction of labor in patients with a medical indication for the initiation of labor, such as mild preeclampsia at or near term, when delivery is in the best interest of mother and fetus or when membranes are prematurely ruptured and delivery is indicated; stimulation or reinforcement of labor, as in selected cases of uterine inertia; as adjunctive therapy in the management of incomplete or inevitable abortion. In the first trimester, currettage is generally considered primary therapy. In second trimester abortion, oxytocin infusion will often be successful in emptying the uterus. Other means of therapy, however, may be required in such cases.
>
> Pitocin is also indicated to produce uterine contractions during the third stage of labor and to control postpartum bleeding or hemorrhage.[18]

[18] *Physicians' Desk Reference,* 35th ed., p. 1381.

The drug is contraindicated in the following cases:

> Significant cephalopelvic disproportion; unfavorable fetal positions or presentations which are undeliverable without conversion prior to delivery (as, for example, transverse lies); in obstetrical emergencies where the benefit-to-risk ratio for either the fetus or the mother favors surgical intervention; in cases of fetal distress where delivery is not imminent; prolonged use in uterine inertia or severe toxemia; hypertonic uterine patterns; patients with hypersensitivity to the drug; induction or augmentation of labor in those cases where vaginal delivery is contraindicated, such as cervical carcinoma, cord presentation or prolapse, total placentia previa, and vasa previa.[19]

The manufacturer of Pitocin also warns that when the drug is given for induction or stimulation of labor it must be administered only by the intravenous route and with adequate medical supervision in a hospital.

Excessive dosage or hypersensitivity to the drug may result in uterine hypertonicity, spasm, tetanic (sustained) contractions or rupture. In addition, anaphylactic reaction, postpartum hemorrhage, cardiac arrhythmia, and pelvic hematoma have been reported.[20]

Pitocin is manufactured by Parke-Davis (Morris Plains, N.J.) and Syntocinon by Sandoz Pharmaceuticals (East Hanover, N.J.).

Gonzales v. Fuchs (No. 4624/75, Supreme Court, Kings County, N.Y., May 12, 1977).

Brain damage at birth—Possible overstimulation of uterus—$1,030,000 verdict against physician and hospital

A male infant's mother was given Pitocin to strengthen her contractions. The infant was born with brain damage.

In a lawsuit against the hospital and the physician, it was alleged that giving the drug to the mother caused the infant's head to jam against her pelvic bones, and that the physician had not examined her to make sure that her pelvis could accommodate the head.

According to counsel for the infant, he obtained a jury verdict of $1,030,000, of which 70% was assessed against the hospital, and the remaining 30% against the physician.[21]

---

[19] Id.

[20] Id.

[21] ATLA *Law Reporter* 21:40, 1978.

Long v. Johnson (Ind. App., 1978) 381 N.E.2d 93.

Child born with cerebral palsy—Nurse found negligent in monitoring patient's contractions—$350,000 verdict against hospital

The main issue in this matter is a dispute over whether the patient, Wanda Long, was properly monitored while being given Pitocin to induce labor. Her child, a girl, was born with cerebral palsy which was attributed to being expelled from the patient's ruptured uterus into the abdomen at which time her oxygen supply was "compromised."

The patient was being administered Pitocin via intravenous drip to accelerate the labor process. The labor room nurse claims she closely monitored the patient during this time to determine the frequency and intensity of the patient's contractions, but the patient claims no one continuously monitored her contractions. The evidence showed there was "a sudden change in the contour of Wanda's abdomen," and according to Wanda she "experienced a terrible pain in the pit of her stomach." Her abdomen then resembled "the shape of an hourglass," a condition diagnosed as Bandl's ring, which is a strong contraction of the uterus which is not released, and "the precursor of a uterine rupture."

Expert testimony disclosed that to avoid this occurrence, i.e., to reverse abnormal contractions, the medical attendant should stop or slow down the flow of Pitocin.

A jury returned a verdict against the hospital for $350,000, finding negligence on the part of the nurse who was supposed to be monitoring the patient. The physician, who was not present during the patient's labor except for several brief vaginal examinations, was found not liable. Both verdicts were upheld on appeal.

Rutherford v. Zearfoss (1980) 221 Va. 685, 272 S.E.2d 225.

Child born with cerebral palsy—$1.5 million verdict against obstetrician held excessive

The patient, who was approximately nine months pregnant, was admitted to the hospital with mild labor contractions at about two in the morning. At 6:15 a.m. her physician determined that the baby's head had not descended into the pelvic canal. The contractions were every five minutes. He administered Tocosamine (sparteine sulfate) to stimulate the uterus and force the baby's head down through the canal. At 7 a.m. the contractions were moderate and every three minutes, but the baby's head had not descended.

The physician ordered another injection of Tocosamine. Forty-five minutes later the contractions were moderately hard and every two to three minutes, and the fetal heart rate was 160, the normal range being 120 to 160 beats per minute according to an expert. An attending nurse noted meconium, a bowel movement by the baby indicating possible oxygen deprivation in the baby's brain. By 9:45 there was no change in the patient's condition. Another injection of Tocosamine was given at 10:15, and five minutes later the patient was taken to the delivery room. At 10:45 Syntocinon was administered. Sometime within the next 35 minutes the baby boy was delivered through the use of a vacuum extractor and forceps.

The child had "marked molding of the head" and, while still in the hospital, suffered a number of seizures. A year later he was diagnosed as having spastic quadriparesis and ataxic cerebral palsy. By the age of three years, seven months, he tested at less than twelve months for motor skills. At the trial, expert testimony revealed that "he may learn to walk, but it is improbable that he will ever run, climb a tree, throw a ball, swim, or play a musical instrument."

An expert testifying for the plaintiff stated that the delivering physician had violated the standard of medical care as it existed in the community at the time by not performing a Caesarean section which would have prevented the oxygen deprivation which caused the cerebral palsy. It was also this expert's opinion that administering oxytocic drugs before the engagement of the baby's head and giving an intravenous injection of Syntocinon only one-half hour after administering a dose of Tocosamine also violated the standard of care required by obstetricians practicing in the community at the time and contributed to the child's oxygen deprivation.

Experts produced by the defendant testified that there was no medical reason for performing a Caesarean section, and that throughout the delivery there had been no deviation from the accepted standard of care. (There was also evidence which indicated that the mother had on at least one occasion expressed a desire not to have a Caesarean section.)

A jury returned a verdict for the plaintiff in the amount of $1.5 million, but on motion of the defendant the trial judge ruled it excessive and ordered a new trial on all issues. The Supreme Court of Virginia affirmed the ruling, holding that the verdict was excessive, and that the issue of liability was "hotly contested," and that although the evidence was sufficient to support a verdict for either party, there was no clear preponderance of evidence in favor of either.

Madrid v. Phelps-Dodge Corp. (No. 158601, Superior Court, Pima County, Ariz., Sept. 9, 1977).

Brain damage at birth—Use of drug in shoulder-arm presentation questioned—$300,000 settlement

A male infant's mother was given either one or two doses of Pitocin while she was in labor, the hospital records being inconsistent. The infant was born with severe brain damage. At age eleven he weighed only about forty pounds and had a mental age of about six months.

The plaintiff contended that the infant presented himself in a shoulder-arm position in which case Pitocin, according to *Physicians' Desk Reference*, is contraindicated. It was also alleged that the physician failed to determine the position of the fetus before administering the drug. According to counsel for the infant, he obtained a settlement in the amount of $300,000.[1]

Downing v. Manta (No. 79-21845, Circuit Court, Dade County, Fla., Oct. 17, 1980).

Brain damage at birth, quadriplegia, blindness, mental retardation—$1.5 million settlement

A pregnant patient who had not been diagnosed for multiple pregnancy went into premature labor at home and gave birth to the first child. It received neonatal care in a hospital and was normally developed. Still in labor, the patient was taken to another hospital and given two intramuscular administrations of Pitocin, even though it is more commonly given by IV drip or infusion pump. Also administered were Demerol, Sparine and scopolamine hydrobromide. The second fetus was in a transverse position and the obstetrician suspected partial placental separation, but he did not order a Caesarean section for an hour after admission, and the hospital did not provide an operating room for another hour. Both fetuses were delivered severely depressed and asphyxiated. One died after four days and the other suffered spastic quadriplegia, blindness, profound mental retardation and partial deafness.

---

[1] ATLA *Law Reporter* 21:40, 1978.

Among the allegations in the complaint were administering Pitocin by an uncontrollable method, and administering drugs shown to have depressing effects on fetuses.

According to the attorney representing the plaintiffs, there was a structured settlement for the parents with a present value of $1.5 million.[2]

Schiffer v. Central Gen. Hosp. (No. 3174/76, Supreme Court, Nassau County, N.Y., Nov. 21, 1980).

Uterine rupture and cardiac arrest—Use of Pitocin questioned—$761,320 settlement

The thirty-year-old patient was admitted to the hospital in early active labor, and her attending obstetrician administered Pitocin even though she did not have a history of prolonged or difficult labor. Three and one-half hours after admission, the obstetrician delivered a healthy infant. Immediately after delivery, problems developed for the patient. Four and one-half hours later she suffered cardiac arrest and sustained brain injury from which she died three days later.

Her husband brought suit against the hospital and the obstetrician alleging negligence in administering Pitocin unnecessarily which caused the patient's uterus to rupture. The obstetrician admitted that he routinely administered Pitocin without medical indication to avoid the possibility of prolonged labor. The defendants denied that the patient's uterus had ruptured.

According to the attorneys for the plaintiff, there was a settlement for $761,320.[3]

Fornoff v. Parke-Davis & Co. (1982) 105 Ill. App. 3d 681, 61 Ill. Dec. 438, 434 N.E.2d 793.

Prolapsed rectum following buccal Pitocin—$820,000 verdict against physician and hospital—Manufacturer not liable

The plaintiff was given 5,400 units of buccal Pitocin to induce labor because she wanted her physician to deliver her child and he would be out of town on her due date. Following delivery the plaintiff suffered "massive rectal prolapse" requiring major reconstructive surgery and a colostomy.

---

[2] Id., 24:233, 1981.

[3] Id., 24:186, 1981.

At the trial the plaintiff introduced the manufacturer's package insert which contained six pages of instructions, precautions, warnings and adverse reactions. Included in the instructions was the recommendation that the maximum dose be no greater than 3,000 units.

The jury returned awards for the plaintiff and her husband of $750,000 and $80,000, respectively, against the physician and the hospital, but found for the manufacturer on the issue of inadequate warnings. The verdict for the manufacturer was affirmed. The awards to the plaintiff and her husband were not appealed.

Haught v. Maceluch (C.A.-5 Tex., 1982) 681 F.2d 291.

Pitocin increased despite symptoms of fetal distress—Brain damage—$1.4 million award upheld

Despite symptoms of fetal distress (meconium staining and loss of fetal heart beat-to-beat variability) the defendant obstetrician ordered and later increased the administration of Pitocin, and then went to attend other patients. On delivery the baby was found with the umbilical cord wrapped around its neck, which caused severe deprivation of oxygen and brain damage.

After a jury trial the mother was awarded $1,160,000 for her child's medical expenses, $175,000 for her child's lost future wages, and $118,000 for her own (the mother's) mental suffering over her daughter's impaired condition. The trial judge, however, deleted the award for the mother's mental suffering. On appeal, this award was reinstated, with the Court of Appeals holding that although the mother was not conscious at the time the child was born and did not see its injury, because she was conscious during eleven hours of labor and was aware of the obstetrician's negligent acts, in particular his absence in a "near emergency situation" and his over-administration of Pitocin. Under these circumstances the mother had an "experimental perception" of the tragedy that befell her daughter.

Mayhorn v. Pavey (1982) 8 Ohio App. 3d 189, 456 N.E.2d 1222.

Child stillborn—Plaintiff instructed to take Pitocin at home—Directed verdict for physician affirmed

After her child was delivered stillborn, the plaintiff charged her obstetrician with negligence in failing to test her for diabetes, in instructing her to take Pitocin while she was not under medical supervision, and in failing to test "the well-being" of the fetus when it was suspected that her pregnancy was post-term.

With regard to the Pitocin, the defendant instructed the plaintiff to take the drug at home. He later testified that his purpose in doing this was to determine if the pregnancy was post-term; if it was, the Pitocin was supposed to produce contractions which would then develop into labor.

Despite testimony by the plaintiff's expert who criticized the defendant's use of the drug, the court directed a verdict for the defense. The Court of Appeals affirmed, holding that the expert's response to hypothetical questions did not constitute sufficient evidence to take the case to the jury because the questions themselves lacked facts critical to a showing of proximate cause.

Ray v. Steadman (No. 79-189, U.S. District Court, W.D. N.Y., Jan. 28, 1983).

**Infant's brachial plexus injury blamed on Pitocin—
Structured settlement worth $600,000**

The patient received Pitocin less than an hour into her labor and continued to receive it for eight hours. Her obstetrician attempted traction delivery of the fetus, which was in an unengaged brow position, but was unsuccessful. When cephalopelvic disproportion was determined, the infant was delivered by cesarean section. Later, the child experienced impairment of her hands which was attributed to bilateral brachial plexus injury. In her suit, the plaintiff alleged that the defendant obstetrician's use of Pitocin in the presence of an unengaged brow presentation had caused the fetal head to become wedged into the mother's pelvis, and that the defendant's attempt to dislodge it caused excessive traction on the child's arms. The parties agreed to a structured settlement with a present value of $600,000.[4]

Wilson v. Nealy (No. 81-10118-10, District Court, Pinellas County, Fla., March 1, 1983).

**Amount and method of administering Pitocin questioned—
Infant brain damaged—$2.3 million settlement**

The plaintiff's mother was admitted to the defendant hospital for delivery of twins. The first child was born without complications,

[4]ATLA *Law Reporter* 26:330, 1983.

but at that point the mother's contractions ceased. The defendant obstetrician administered Pitocin but monitored the patient only infrequently. The child remained in the birth canal for almost an hour, suffering fetal distress. Once delivered, the plaintiff was taken to the nursery where pediatricians administered dextrose by mouth instead of by I.V., causing him to remain hypoglycemic for several hours. He will require constant custodial care due to brain damage.

The charges included negligence in administering excessive Pitocin and in using the drip method instead of a pump. A $2.3 million settlement was reached with the obstetrician contributing $1,000,000, the hospital $100,000, two pediatricians $500,000 each, and a midwife who was assisting the obstetrician, $200,000.[5]

Neblett v. Protestant Hospital Builders Club, Inc. (No. 79-L-30, Circuit Court, St. Clair County, Ill., March 3, 1983).

Physician orders Pitocin without examining patient—Tetanic contractions—Failure to monitor—Hospital and physician settle for $1.3 million

The patient had been in labor approximately twelve hours when the defendant physician, who was not present at the hospital, ordered that Pitocin be administered. The drug was continued until after delivery about three hours later, although the record showed that the patient experienced tetanic contractions. The infant suffered brain damage and is severely retarded. The plaintiff's claim was based on negligence of the physician in ordering Pitocin without examining the patient and continuing its administration well beyond delivery. The hospital personnel were accused of failing to monitor the mother's progress and failing to record vital signs and fetal heart tone according to professional standards.

The case was settled for a present value of $3 million with the physician contributing $1.1 million.[6]

Hale v. Southwestern General Hospital (No. 82-7653, 65th Judicial District Court, El Paso County, Tex., June 17, 1983).

Need for Pitocin questioned—Improper monitoring—Brain damaged child lives four months—$324,000 settlement

The decedent's mother was admitted to the defendant hospital with a premature rupture of the membranes during her thirty-sec-

---

[5] Id., 26:473, 1983.
[6] Id., 26:428, 1983.

ond week of pregnancy. The defendant general practitioner, concerned with infection, induced labor by administering Pitocin. Labor was unsuccessful, and the child had to be delivered by caesarean section. The infant showed no brain wave activity and was placed on a respirator where she died four months later from septicemia. The plaintiffs alleged that the physician was unqualified, and that the hospital was negligent for allowing him to use its obstetrical facilities. They claimed he administered Pitocin without sufficient reason, and that its use caused "uteroplacental insufficiency." They also contended that the physician failed to use internal monitoring on the mother until it was too late. The hospital settled for $40,000 and the physician for $280,000.[7]

Coxon v. Casa Grande Valley Community Hospital (No. 32948, Superior Court, Pinal County, Ariz., June 22, 1983).

Induced labor not monitored—Severe brain damage—Hospital and obstetrician settle for $1.6 million

When a pregnant patient's labor did not progress after nine hours, her obstetrician administered Pitocin which allegedly caused rapid and hard contractions. These were not monitored, and the infant became anoxic during delivery, suffering severe brain damage. The child now has cerebral palsy, is unable to walk or communicate with others and requires 24-hour custodial care. The hospital and obstetrician entered into a structured settlement having a present value of $1.6 million. If the child lives to age sixty-five, the total payout is estimated at $31 million.[8]

James v. Kennebec Valley Medical Center (No. 80-CV-649, Superior Court, Kennebec County, Me., Aug. 26, 1983).

I.V. infusion of Pitocin without infusion pump—Inadequate monitoring—Infant brain damaged—$700,000 settlement

Pitocin was introduced through I.V. infusion without an infusion pump. Data received from the external monitor was unreadable, and the obstetrician continued Pitocin induction with stethoscopic evaluation of the fetal heart rate every fifteen minutes. The plaintiffs claimed the obstetrician was inexperienced in internal monitoring and the hospital was negligent in allowing him to preside

---

[7] ATLA *Law Reporter* 27:41, 1984.

[8] Id., 27:88, 1984.

over a patient whose labor was induced by Pitocin without adequate electronic monitoring and an infusion pump. A $700,000 settlement was reached on behalf of the infant who suffered brain damage, cerebral palsy, microcephaly and mental retardation.[9]

Goff v. Olson (No. F2-1512, Wisconsin Patient's Compensation Panel, Oct. 26, 1983).

Pitocin allegedly contraindicated—Infant born with brain damage—Structured settlement valued at $1.2 million

Suit was brought on behalf of a two and one-half-year-old boy who sustained brain damage at birth and is now profoundly retarded and a spastic quadriplegic. The plaintiff alleged that Pitocin, which was administered during labor, was contraindicated because the mother was over forty-two weeks into her pregnancy, and because monitor strips taken during labor indicated "repetitive late decelerations" of contractions, which should have alerted the defendant obstetrician to the possibility of fetal distress. The parties agreed upon a structured settlement with a present value of $1.2 million.[10]

Capaccio v. Neuman (No. 21831/81, Supreme Court, New York County, N.Y., Oct. 26, 1984).

Pitocin administered without physician present—Infant brain damaged and severely retarded—$10.9 million verdict against hospital

The patient was two weeks overdue when admitted. Although there was no physician present, a Pitocin drip was ordered. An external fetal heart monitor was attached, but no physician was notified of the readings, and the monitor was discontinued an hour and one-half before delivery. The child was born severely retarded and has the mental capabilities of a one-year-old. She requires complete custodial care. The plaintiffs charged that the labor room personnel violated a hospital rule that required the discontinuance of Pitocin in the absence of an obstetrician; that the Pitocin caused unusually rapid dilation and labor, resulting in excessive, long and frequent contractions and fetal hypoxia. The physician who should have been present settled with the plaintiff shortly after the open-

[9] Id.

[10] Id., 27:139, 1984.

ing statement for $1.35 million. The jury returned a verdict against the hospital for $10.9 million.[11]

Blackwell v. Southern Baptist Hospital (No. 78-2547-4, District Court, Orleans Parish, La., July, 1985).

Alleged inadequate monitoring during administration of Pitocin—$1.5 million settlement with obstetrician, $600,000 with hospital

The patient was admitted to the hospital for delivery at 8:20 a.m. She was examined and found to have a -2 fetal presentation and an intact membrane. Her obstetrician, by telephone, ordered intramuscular Pitocin, which was administered at 8:35 and 9:05 a.m. At 9:40 a.m., the obstetrician, again by telephone, ordered an IV drip of Seconal, Demerol, Largon (propiomazine HCL) and scopolamine plus one ampule of Pitocin added to the dextrose and water used for the drip.

Vital signs were next checked at 9:50 a.m. and thereafter on an average of every 45 minutes. The obstetrician arrived at 11:00 a.m. and examined the patient, but left the hospital shortly thereafter. He returned at 4:00 p.m., and at 6:00 p.m. the patient was delivered by Cesarean section, at which time it was discovered that the infant had suffered perinatal asphyxia causing seizures and severe global hypoxic eschemic encephalopathy. Because of the brain damage, he is profoundly retarded, has cerebral palsy, periodic seizures, and is functually blind and deaf.

The obstetrician was charged with inadequate monitoring of his patient during labor, negligent ordering of Pitocin and excessive analgesics, and failure to attend his patient properly. Similar allegations were made against the hospital personnel. For his evidence, the plaintiff was prepared to introduce standards published by the American College of Obstetricians and Gynecologists pertaining to the monitoring of patients during the administration of Pitocin, and JCAH standards relative to rules and protocols of hospital obstetric units.

The plaintiff settled with the obstetrician for $450,000 in cash and annual payments of $55,000 for 20 years. The hospital agreed to a $600,000 cash settlement.[12]

---

[11] ATLA *Law Reporter* 28:89, 1985.
[12] Id., 29:228, 1986.

Steele v. Seglie (No. 84-2200-0, U.S. District Court, D. Kan., Dec. 16, 1986).

Brain damage at birth—Excessive use of Pitocin and other negligence—$3.24 million jury verdict

The patient was admitted to the hospital to give birth. There was little progress in her labor and the defendant physician, a general practitioner, administered five times the normal dose of Pitocin. The fetal heart monitor, which was not attached internally, was removed temporarily for use on another patient. The monitoring that did take place either was not recorded or was of such poor quality as to be of no significance. An obstetrician was called in and performed a cesarean section. The infant is brain-damaged, suffers developmental delays, and will require institutionalized care the rest of her life.

At trial, the plaintiffs alleged negligence on the part of the physician in allowing the post-mature pregnancy to continue, in overdosing the mother with Pitocin, and in failing to document adequately the course of the labor. (There was little or no documentation of the fetal distress, of the infant's status after delivery, and of what, if any, resuscitative efforts were made.) The hospital was charged with negligence in failing to monitor and in failing to take steps to alleviate the fetal distress once it was discovered. The defendants contended that the condition was caused either by prenatal or post-delivery injuries.

The jury awarded $3.24 million, with the physician being found 75% at fault and the hospital, 25%.[13]

Clark v. Mitchell Clinic and Maternity Hospital (No. 86-238-199, 199th Judicial District Court, Collin County, Tex., Jan. 20, 1987)

Failure to order oxytocin challenge test and other alleged negligence—$1.9 million settlement

The defendant, a general practitioner, administered Pitocin to the patient during her nine-hour labor. Her child was delivered in a flaccid, cyanotic state with a heart rate of thirty beats per minute. He is brain-damaged, and suffers from cerebral palsy and seizures.

---

[13] *Professional Negligence Law Reporter* 2:60, 1987.

In her lawsuit, the patient, among other charges, alleged negligence (1) in prescribing hypertensive medications for treatment of her preeclampsia, (2) in allowing the pregnancy to continue three weeks past term, (3) in failing to order an oxytocin challenge test, (4) in administering excessive doses of Pitocin during labor, and (5) in failing to have a pediatrician available to assist with a high-risk baby. The parties settled for $1.9 million.[14]

Ewing v. Aubert (La. App., 1988) 532 So. 2d 876.

Ruptured uterus and fatal amniotic embolism—Nurse not negligent in administering Pitocin to patient in prolonged labor

The plaintiff's wife died during prolonged labor from a massive amniotic fluid embolism caused by the rupture of her uterus. Several counts of negligence were alleged against the obstetrician and the nurses in attendance, including a charge that a nurse was negligent in increasing the Pitocin drip from 12 to 14 drops per minute at a time when it appeared that the decedent's labor was progressing, and later failing to discontinue the Pitocin when it appeared that the decedent's labor was arrested.

Expert witnesses called by the plaintiff, including two physicians and two delivery room nurses, testified as to the nurse's negligence. One of these physicians admitted, however, that an increase in Pitocin is warranted when the level of the patient's contractions has not reached a desirable quality (the decedent's had not). Experts for the hospital testified that the increase of Pitocin by only two drops per minute was insignificant and unrelated to the uterine rupture, and one of these witnesses stated that if the increase had been too much, the effects would have been seen much sooner. (The decedent's uterine ruptured two hours later.)

The jury returned a verdict in favor of the hospital, which was affirmed on appeal. A medical review panel had earlier found that the obstetrician had failed to comply with the appropriate standard of care in supervising the decedent's labor, and the plaintiff was awarded the statutory maximum of $500,000 against his insurer and from the Louisiana Patients Compensation Fund.

---

[14] Id.

Underwood v. Kirk (No. 85-3806, Supreme Court, Ulster County, N.Y., May 2, 1989).

Brain damage—Pitocin allegedly contraindicated because of narrow birth canal and normally progressing labor—$500,000 settlement with obstetrician

Four hours after the plaintiff was admitted to the hospital in labor, her obstetrician ordered Pitocin to stimulate her contractions. Shortly before delivery he also gave her a general anesthetic and pain medication. At birth, the plaintiff's child seemed to be normal, but she was later found to be mentally retarded, and as an adult probably will never function intellectually beyond the eighth-grade level.

The plaintiff claimed the Pitocin and the depressive effects of the general anesthesia and pain medication caused the fetus to suffer anoxia and the resulting brain damage. She charged the obstetrician with negligence in administering the Pitocin. She claimed the drug was contraindicated because she had a narrow birth canal and because she had been in labor only four hours and was progressing normally. The obstetrician's defense was that the child's injury was not due to any negligence, that she was suffering from a genetic defect, which he claimed was evidenced by "a high palate and large nose."

According to the plaintiff's attorney, the obstetrician settled for his malpractice policy limit of $500,000.[15]

Related cases

Premature separation of placenta—Claim for anxiety over child's welfare allowable

In Friel v. Vineland Obstetrical & Gynecological Professional Assn. (1979) 166 N.J. Super. 579, 400 A.2d 147, a mother who was allegedly left unattended after being given oxytocin and suffered a premature separation of the placenta was entitled to claim damages "for fright, anxiety and shock sustained by the premature delivery and uncertainty as to the child's normality during the formative years of development to the stage where educational testing may be had."

---

[15] ATLA Professional Negligence Law Reporter 4:190, 1989.

Brain damage with blindness and quadriplegia—Mother has cause of action against manufacturer for breach of warranty—No strict liability

In Woodill v. Parke-Davis & Co. (1980) 79 Ill. 2d 26, 37 Ill. Dec. 304, 402 N.E.2d 194, a mother who claimed her child's brain damage, permanent blindness and quadriplegia was the result of the failure of the manufacturer of Pitocin to warn physicians and patients of the danger in using the drug while a fetus is in "a high station" was held to have a cause of action based on breach of warranty but no cause based on strict liability.

Brain damage at birth—Evidence of mother's prior abortions admissible

Where the obstetrician testified that had he known his patient had undergone three abortions he would not have administered Pitocin, the trial court did not commit reversible error in admitting evidence of the abortions. Davila v. Bodelson (1985) 103 N.M. 243, 704 P.2d 1119.

Pitocin allegedly given over plaintiff's objections—No claim for battery

In Kohoutek v. Hafner (Minn. App., 1985) 383 N.W.2d 295, where the plaintiff wanted her baby to be delivered by Caesarean and physicians allegedly induced labor with Pitocin over the plaintiff's objections, the trial court properly refused to submit a claim for battery to the jury. The jury found no evidence of "negligent nondisclosure" regarding the risks involved in the use of Pitocin, and this finding was affirmed on appeal.

Ruptured anal sphincter muscle—Verdict for physician reversed because of "locality rule" instruction

In Tirpak v. Weinberg (1986) 27 Ohio App. 3d 46, 499 N.E.2d 397, the reviewing court reversed a verdict for a physician who allegedly overused Pitocin, causing the fetus to "explode" out of the plaintiff's pelvis and rupture her anal sphincter muscle. The trial court had improperly instructed the jury on the standard of care "in this community," which gave the impression that the standard to be applied was to be limited to "locality."

Injury to uterus—Fact question presented on excessive use of Pitocin

In Yang v. Stafford (Ind. App., 1987) 515 N.E.2d 1157, genuine issues of material fact existed as to (1) whether hospital nurses breached the standard of care by increasing the Pitocin flow beyond the rate allowed by hospital protocols when the plaintiff's fetus' heart tones indicated overstimulation; (2) whether the nurses refused the plaintiff's request to discontinue the Pitocin after informing her that she had a right to do so; and (3) whether the nurses' acts proximately caused an extreme thinning of the plaintiff's uterus which ruptured on delivery.

Brain damage—Verdict for hospital reversed because of use of pediatrician's privileged testimony

In Moore v. Grandview Hospital (1986) 25 Ohio St. 3d 194, 495 N.E.2d 934, a jury returned a verdict for the hospital in an action on behalf of a child who suffered brain damage following the administration of Pitocin to the child's mother by delivery room nurses. The Supreme Court of Ohio reversed, however, because the trial court had admitted testimony, over the plaintiff's objections, of the pediatrician who had treated the child shortly after birth. This testimony, said the reviewing court, was inadmissible because the physician-patient privilege had not been waived.

Brain damage—Manufacturer not entitled to summary judgment on strength of codefendant physician's self-serving statements

In a combined medical malpractice and products liability action by the mother of a brain-damaged infant, the manufacturer of Pitocin was not entitled to a summary judgment on grounds that the prescribing physician, a codefendant, was fully aware of the risk of using the drug, where the manufacturer relied solely on the physician's self-serving statements to support its motion. Sacher v. Long Island Jewish-Hillside Medical Center (App. Div., 1988) 530 N.Y.S.2d 232.

Patient had no action for battery for physician's alleged misrepresentation of purpose of administering oxytocin

An obstetrical patient could not recover damages against her physician under the theory of battery for his alleged misrepresentation that the oxytocin he wanted to administer to her was necessary to prevent infection, when in fact its purpose was to induce labor. Freedman v. Superior Court (Cal. App., 1989) 263 Cal. Rptr. 1.

P

PANWARFIN

See SODIUM WARFARIN

PARALDEHYDE

Paraldehyde is an antiepileptic agent used to treat status epilepticus when other drugs are not effective. Intravenous administration must be slow or severe coughing results which may add to the difficulty of administration and may even cause pulmonary hemorrhage. Intramuscular injection can cause tissue necrosis and sterile abscess, but this method is relatively safe if care is taken to avoid peripheral nerves.[16]

Fatalities have occurred with the use of paraldehyde. Bronchopulmonary disease is a contraindication, since a significant amount of the drug is excreted by the lungs. The sedative effect of paraldehyde may be intensified and prolonged in patients with liver disease. Thrombophlebitis is a frequent complication of intravenous administration.[17]

Serota v. Kaplan (1987) 127 App. Div. 2d 648, 511 N.Y.S.2d 667.

Death allegedly due to synergistic action of paraldehyde and Mellaril

A 59-year-old woman, hospitalized in the psychiatric ward for depression, had been given her evening dosage of Mellaril, an antidepressant. Later that evening, a nurse entered the room with a glass of paraldehyde and orange juice which she intended to give to the patient's roommate. By mistake, she gave the solution to the patient. The following morning the patient was found cyanotic and unresponsive. A few minutes later she was pronounced dead.

At the trial, the defendant hospital did not deny that the nurse's act was a departure from accepted standards of medical practice, but challenged instead the plaintiffs' theory that the patient died as a result of the synergistic effect of Mellaril and paraldehyde. In cross-examining the defense experts on this question, the plaintiffs' counsel was permitted to impeach the witnesses' credibility regarding the lethal dosage of paraldehyde by referring to a medical book which the witnesses did not concede to be authoritative. Also, the opinion of one of the defense experts that the cause of the patient's

---

[16] AMA *Drug Evaluations,* 6th ed., p. 193.

[17] Id.

death was "undetermined" was stricken from the record by the trial judge as unresponsive.

The jury returned a verdict for the plaintiffs in the amount of $540,000. On appeal, however, the verdict was set aside, the reviewing court holding that both the plaintiffs' cross-examination and the striking of the defense expert's opinion were reversible error.

PARENOGEN

See FIBRINOGEN

PATHIBAMATE

See MEPROBAMATE

PATHOCIL

See PENICILLIN

PBZ

See TRIPELENNAMINE

PENICILLAMINE

Cuprimine
Depen

Penicillamine is a chelating agent recommended for the removal of excess copper in patients with Wilson's disease. It is also indicated in the treatment of cystinuria and in patients with severe, active rheumatoid arthritis who have failed to respond to an adequate trial of conventional therapy. The manufacturers report that available evidence suggests that the drug is not of value in treating ankylosing spondylitis.[18] Cuprimine is produced by Merck, Sharp and Dohme, a division of Merck and Company, Inc. (West Point, Pa.) and Depen by Wallace Laboratories (Cranbury, N.J.).

The use of penicillamine has been associated with fatalities due to diseases such as aplastic anemia, agranulocytosis, thrombocytopenia, Goodpasture's syndrome, and myasthenia gravis. Because of the potential for serious adverse reactions, routine urinalysis, white and differential blood cell count, hemoglobin determination, and direct platelet count should be done every two weeks for at

[18] *Physicians' Desk Reference,* 40th ed., pp. 1153-54.

least the first six months of penicillamine therapy and monthly thereafter.[19]

Reinhardt v. Colton (Minn., 1983) 337 N.W.2d 88.

Aplastic anemia after taking penicillamine six months—Plaintiff has prima facie case for nondisclosure of risk

The defendant physician prescribed penicillamine for the plaintiff in February, 1977 as treatment for rheumatoid arthritis. At the time the drug was approved by the FDA only for the treatment of Wilson's disease, and use in cases of rheumatoid arthritis was still experimental. The defendant, a rheumatologist, testified that he told the plaintiff this, but she denied it, claiming that he told her only that penicillamine was a "new drug."

The plaintiff was supposed to report for periodic blood tests while on the drug. She testified that the defendant told her that these were designed to "detect side effects." She denied that he told her that one of the side effects was aplastic anemia. The defendant testified that he did tell her of this risk.

The plaintiff developed aplastic anemia in August, 1977. In her lawsuit she charged the defendant with both negligent treatment and negligent nondisclosure of the risk involved. At the trial, her only expert witness was a pathologist who had never engaged in clinical practice and had never prescribed penicillamine. The trial judge ruled that he was not qualified to testify and directed a verdict for the defendant.

On appeal, the Supreme Court of Minnesota agreed and held that without this expert's testimony the plaintiff failed to establish a prima facie case of negligent treatment. On the issue of nondisclosure of the risk of aplastic anemia, however, the Supreme Court reversed the trial court, holding that the testimony of the plaintiff and defendant introduced sufficient evidence to create a jury question.

PENICILLIN

Benzathine Penicillin G

Bicillin; Bicillin C-R; Bicillin L-A

Potassium Penicillin G

Pentids

Pfizerpen G

---

[19] Id.

Procaine Penicillin G
- **Bicillin**
- **Crysticillin**
- **Duracillin**
- **Wycillin**

Oral Penicillin
- **Omnipen**
- **Pathocil**
- **Pentids**
- **Pen Vee K**
- **Principen**
- **SK-Penicillin VK**
- **Unipen**
- **Veetids**

Phenoxymethyl Penicillin (Penicillin V)
- **Betapen-VK**
- **Compocillin-V**
- **Veetids**

Potassium Phenoxymethyl Penicillin
- **Ledercillin VK**
- **Pen Vee K**
- **Pfizerpen VK**
- **Robicillin VK**
- **SK-Penicillin VK**
- **Uticillin VK**
- **V-Cillin K**

The penicillins comprise a large family of natural and semisynthetic antibiotics derived directly and indirectly from culture media fermented by species of *Penicillium* and other soil-inhabiting fungi. Literally hundreds of species and thousands of strains of *Penicillia* are known, and many of these are elaborate antibiotic substances.[20]

Pencillin G (benzyl penicillin) was the first antibiotic developed industrially for medicinal use in the "antibiotic era" of the early 1940's, and despite some shortcomings, this natural product remains in many respects the best agent available for infections caused by organisms susceptible to it.[21] Penicillin G is effective against most gram-positive organisms (streptococci, staphylococci, pneumococci); clostridia; some gram-negative organisms (gonococci,

[20] *United States Dispensatory,* 27th ed., p. 847.
[21] Id., p. 864.

meningococci); some spirochetes (*Treponema pallidum, Treponema pertenue*); and some fungi.[1]

Penicillin V (phenoxymethyl penicillin) is 6-phenoxyacetamido-penicillanic acid and can be produced biosynthetically via fermentation or semisynthetically from 6-amino-penicillanic acid.[2] Penicillin V is more resistant to gastric acidity and is better absorbed than penicillin G; therefore it is often given when oral administration is preferable.[3]

Like penicillin V, many of the numerous semisynthetic penicillins listed above have certain advantages over natural penicillin G, among which are better resistance to gastric juices and a broader antibacterial spectrum.[4] Dosage and route of administration depends upon the type of penicillin chosen.[5]

The penicillin brands Bicillin, Bicillin C-R, Wycillin, Omnipen, Pathocil, Pen Vee K, and Unipen are manufactured by Wyeth Laboratories (Philadelphia, Pa.); Pfizerpen G and Pfizerpen VK by Pfipharmecs Division of Pfizer, Inc. (New York, N.Y.); Pentids, Crysticillin, Principen, and Veetids by E. R. Squibb & Sons, Inc. (Princeton, N.J.); Duracillin and V-Cillin K by Eli Lilly and Company (Indianapolis, Ind.); SK-Penicillin VK (until 1987) by Smith, Kline & French Laboratories (Philadelphia, Pa.); Betaphen VK by Bristol Laboratories (Syracuse, N.Y.); Ledercillin by Lederle Laboratories (Wayne, N.J.); Uticillin VK by The Upjohn Company (Kalamazoo, Mich.); and Robicillin VK by A. H. Robins Company (Richmond, Va.). These brand names constitute only a partial list. For others, consult the latest edition of *Physicians' Desk Reference*.

Hypersensitivity reactions are the most serious consequence of penicillin therapy. It has been estimated that 5 to 6% of all individuals demonstrate varying degrees of hypersensitivity to the drug.[6] Fortunately, acute anaphylactic reaction, the most severe manifes-

---

[1]Falconer, M. W., et al., *Current Drug Handbook* (Philadelphia: W.B. Saunders Company, 1974).

[2]*United States Dispensatory,* 27th ed., pp. 878, 879.

[3]*The Merck Manual of Diagnosis and Therapy,* 12th ed. (Rahway, N.J.: Merck Sharp & Dohme Research Laboratories, 1972), p. 1564. *Current Drug Handbook,* p. 15; *United States Dispensatory,* 27th ed., pp. 855, 878.

[4]*The Merck Manual,* p. 1564; *Current Drug Handbook,* pp. 15-17.

[5]For dosages of the various penicillins, see *Merck Manual,* pp. 1562-1566. For manufacturers' recommendations, see *Physicians' Desk Reference,* 35th ed.

[6]Zurek, R. C., "Antibiotic-induced Diseases," in *Diseases of Medical Progress: A Study of Iatrogenic Disease,* 3rd ed., R. H. Moser, editor (Springfield, Ill.: Charles C Thomas, Publisher, 1969), p. 17.

tation of penicillin allergy, is uncommon. In one analysis of 25,550 patients treated with penicillin for venereal diseases, reactions were reported in only 248 (9.7 per 1,000). Urticaria was the most frequent reaction, occurring in 5.7 per 1,000. Anaphylaxis was observed in only 27 (1.1 per 1,000).[7]

Factors which influence the incidence of penicillin allergy include frequency of administration, dose, duration of treatment and route of administration.[8] As with other drugs, a patient with an "allergic disposition" is more prone to have a reaction to penicillin. The vast majority of reactions occur with parenteral administration, but severe reactions may follow oral dosage.[9]

There is disagreement regarding the clinical usefulness of any screening test in predicting hypersensitivity to penicillin, and they are of value only if positive.[10]

Tangora v. Matanky (1964) 231 Cal. App. 2d 468, 42 Cal. Rptr. 348.

Anaphylactic reaction—Question whether penicillin was necessary; also whether treatment following reaction was proper— Judgment for physicians affirmed

The patient was 32 years of age at the time of her death. She had been in good general health all of her life except for "some female conditions." She was first seen by the defendant-physician on January 23 for injuries received in an automobile accident. He diagnosed contusions, lumbosacral strain, whiplash and cerebral concussion, and prescribed physiotherapy and medicines for pain, muscle relaxation and sleep. On January 25, 26 and 27 the patient was given physiotherapy and cervical traction. On January 28 there was some slight improvement, but that night she began sneezing and coughing.

The morning of January 29 she went to the defendant's office complaining of severe, cramping abdominal pain, generalized discomfort and that her menstrual period had started. The defendant examined her and found her temperature elevated, tender lymph nodes, a reddened pharynx, and congestion in her bronchial tubes.

---

[7]Id., p. 18 (citing Brown, W. J., Simpson, W. G. and Price, E. V., "Reevaluation of Reactions to Penicillin in Venereal Disease Clinic Patients," *Public Health Reports* 76:189-198, 1961).

[8]Zurek, "Antibiotic-induced Diseases," p. 18.

[9]Id.

[10]Id., p. 19.

He made a diagnosis of "flu syndrome" and decided to give her penicillin, which he later said was not to combat the influenza virus, but any secondary infection, specifically strep and pneumococcus.

The defendant asked the patient whether she was allergic to penicillin to which she stated she had had penicillin several times without any signs of allergy. He asked her if she ever had asthma, hay fever or hives, to all of which she answered no. He then injected penicillin intramuscularly (either in the arm or buttock).

Within ten minutes the patient complained of feeling very ill, and then retched. While being taken to a treatment room she went into a convulsion and collapsed. She was placed on a table and within approximately one minute the defendant gave her an intramuscular injection of adrenalin. At this time she still had a pulse and was breathing. She was then given an injection of Benadryl intramuscularly and 100% oxygen was started by mask. But despite these efforts, her heart stopped. A physician assisting the defendant performed a chest incision and massaged the heart while the defendant gave artificial respiration. This was continued for twenty or thirty minutes, but with the exception of a few feeble contractions of the heart muscle, there was no response, and she was pronounced dead.

The jury returned a verdict in favor of the defendant, and the trial court entered judgment accordingly. The plaintiffs, the patient's survivors, appealed.

The District Court of Appeals of California affirmed the judgment of the trial court, declaring:

> Appellants' ... primary contention is that the symptomatology of the deceased did not warrant the diagnosis made by the respondent and, therefore, it was negligent to prescribe and administer penicillin. More specifically they contend that the deceased at most had the symptoms of a common cold and to give penicillin on a prophylactic basis is malpractice. While it is generally conceded that administration of penicillin prophylactically for a cold virus only is not indicated, yet the uncontradicted testimony of respondent of the various symptoms upon which he diagnosed a 'flu syndrome' sustained a diagnosis of infection for which the administration of penicillin is not malpractice.... [B]efore administering the penicillin respondent ascertained that prior administrations of penicillin had not resulted in any untoward results.... [A] well qualified expert, called by respondent, testified in answer to a comprehensive hypothetical question embracing de-

ceased's symptoms that it was within the standard of practice to administer penicillin.

Appellants' claim that to give penicillin intravenously, as distinguished from intramuscularly, is malpractice is answered by the uncontradicted testimony of respondent that the penicillin injection was in fact given deceased intramuscularly and not intravenously.

... From the evidence as a whole it appears that doctors live in deadly fear of anaphylactic shock and that when it happens it is a catastrophic event requiring immediate and drastic action to attempt to combat it. It further appears from the evidence that there is no one procedure in combating such a shock that may be said to be within the standard of practice but that varying procedures are acceptable as good practice. Here the respondent immediately and correctly diagnosed the shock and immediately undertook the procedures ... to combat it. The testimony ... was that the procedures undertaken and carried out by respondent were in accordance with the standard of practice of reputable physicians practicing in the community. We conclude there was substantial evidence to support the verdict.

Rotan v. Greenbaum (1959) 107 App. D.C. 16, 273 F.2d 830.

Anaphylactic reaction—Penicillin allegedly given for mumps—Directed verdict for physician reversed

A girl was seen at a physician's office, apparently suffering from mumps. The physician administered a penicillin injection, 600,000 units. Fifteen minutes later the patient died from anaphylactic shock.

At the trial of a malpractice suit brought by the girl's mother, the evidence included a report of the police who responded to the call on behalf of the coroner's office. This report read: "Died suddenly about 15 minutes after receiving an injection of penicillin, 600,000 units for mumps." The defendant admitted that penicillin is not a "therapeutic" for mumps, and that if a physician gave penicillin for mumps, per se, "it would not be good and approved practice."

Included in the evidence was the patient's record maintained by the defendant's office. It contained the following notation: "6/6/56 Expired after penicillin, 600,000 for ? mumps & pharangitis (sic). Expired 2:15 p.m." On the copy of this entry, however, the question mark preceding the word "mumps" and the words "& pharangitis [sic]" were written by a pen different from that which was used for the remainder of the notation. Also, the words "& pharangitis [sic]" were written in above the line.

The defendant admitted during testimony that part of the entry was probably made immediately after the injection was given, but other parts some time later, the exact time of which he could not specify.

The trial judge entered a directed verdict in favor of the defendant. On appeal, the reviewing court held this in error. The jury, said the court, could have found as a fact that the penicillin injection was given for mumps alone, that such treatment did not meet the standard of practice in the community, and that the defendant was therefore negligent. The judgment was reversed.

Campos v. Weeks (1966) 245 Cal. App. 2d 678, 53 Cal. Rptr. 915.

Anaphylactic reaction—Patient had taken penicillin before—Physician considered skin tests "unreliable"—No negligence found

A woman patient filed suit against her physician after suffering an anaphylactic reaction to a penicillin injection. At the trial the evidence disclosed that the patient had consulted the physician for a puncture-type cut on her finger. He mentioned tetanus antitoxin, but she said she was afraid of taking a tetanus shot because her father had nearly died from one. The physician then asked if she had any allergies to any medications, and she replied that she had taken penicillin without any reaction. He gave her 300,000 units by injection into the arm.

The physician testified at trial that he was aware that a patient could be given certain tests prior to taking medication, but that he considered such tests unreliable and that they were not ordinarily used with penicillin.

About five minutes after the injection, while the patient was still in the reception room, she began to complain of "pin pricks" in her hands and head. She looked pale and gradually became in acute distress. The physician suspected a reaction, and administered emergency treatment. She was taken to the hospital and put under the care of a specialist.

The jury returned a verdict in favor of the physician, and the trial court entered judgment accordingly. The patient appealed, and the District Court of Appeals of California affirmed, declaring:

> [T]he unfortunate reaction which plaintiff suffered ... was caused by the medicine injected.... The determinative question presented here is whether evidence was offered by expert testimony, that when reactions such as plaintiff suffered occur, they are

more probably than not caused by negligence. A review of the evidence ... dictates the conclusion that there was no evidence whatsoever that any negligence on defendant's [the physician's] part was involved. The ... doctors who testified concerning the question, all stated that penicillin can and does produce anaphylactic shock or reaction; none indicated that such occurrence could in any way be attributed to negligence on the part of anyone.

Brewer v. Trelle (No. NCC 6607-B, Superior Court, Los Angeles County, Cal., June 28, 1972).

Anaphylactic reaction—Patient had received injection previous month without reaction—Verdict for physician

A 54-year-old man suffering from a respiratory ailment was given an injection of penicillin by his physician, an internist. He was also given a prescription, and while at a pharmacy having it filled, he suffered a fatal anaphylactic reaction. In a lawsuit against the physician, the defendant testified that just one month earlier he had given the patient a penicillin injection without an adverse reaction, and at no time did the patient ever advise him that he was allergic to the drug.

The case went to trial and the jury returned a verdict of no liability.[11]

Saez v. Municipality (P.R., 1962) 84 P.R.R. 515.

Anaphylactic reaction—Eleven-year-old patient told intern she had previously taken drug without reaction—Judgment for defendant affirmed

An eleven-year-old girl complaining of a sore throat was examined by an intern at the Tricoche Hospital, a public-charity institution operated by the Municipality of Ponce, Puerto Rico. The examination revealed swollen tonsils and audible rales, but no wheezing sounds. In the presence of the girl's grandmother she was asked if she had ever been given penicillin. She said she had, and that she had never had any allergic reaction. No test was made to determine susceptibility.

The intern's final diagnosis was tonsillitis or bronchitis, and he prescribed aspirin, an expectorant, and a daily injection of 400,000 units of penicillin for three days. A nurse gave the first injection

[11] AMA *The Citation* 26:113, 1973.

(arm) and the girl was allowed to leave. Ten minutes later she collapsed and died at the gate of the hospital.

The evidence at the trial revealed that the girl was suffering from asthma and died from asphyxia resulting from a bronchial obstruction produced by thick secretions and atelectasis (incomplete expansion of the lungs). The evidence further showed that this bronchial obstruction was fatally aggravated by the administration of the 400,000 units of penicillin which produced an anaphylactic reaction.

The trial court rendered judgment in favor of the municipality, and the girl's legal guardian appealed. The Supreme Court of Puerto Rico affirmed the judgment of the trial court, stating:

> In order that an action to exact professional liability based on the administration of a drug to which the patient is allergic or hypersensitive may prosper, it is necessary to establish that the physician had knowledge of this anaphylactoid reaction.... In the instant case it has not even been intimated that the administration of penicillin was not the standard treatment for the symptoms which the minor presented upon examination. Regarding the knowledge of the anaphylactic condition, the trial court concluded that the standard practice in the community which is limited to asking the patient whether the drug in question has produced any reaction on previous occasions, had been observed. It thus resolved the conflict in the evidence. An examination of the transcript supports this conclusion.... The fact alone of prescribing the penicillin injection would not constitute negligence in the absence of proof that the physician had knowledge of the minor's hypersensitive condition.

Clausen v. Zizlis (No. SW C11067, Superior Court, Los Angeles County, Cal., 1970).

Anaphylactic reaction—Conflicting testimony whether patient was asked if allergic to drug—Jury finds no damages

During treatment for a hand laceration, a 43-year-old man was given a penicillin injection. He apparently suffered a reaction, including hives and general swelling. He later said he was disabled from this condition for three months. In an action against the clinic where he had received the injection, he testified that no one had asked him if he was allergic to penicillin. The clinic nurse, however, testified that she had asked the man if he was allergic, and that he told her he was not.

The attorneys for the clinic recommended a settlement of $1,500; the patient's attorneys, however, demanded over $6,000. The case was allowed to go to trial and the jury returned a verdict of no damages.[12]

Arzaga v. Southern California Permanente Medical Group (No. SOC 266 77, Superior Court, Los Angeles County, Cal., Sept. 13, 1973).

Anaphylactic reaction—Physician failed to consult patient's record containing note of possible penicillin sensitivity—Case settled at trial—Third party involved

A patient suffered an anaphylactic reaction after taking oral penicillin prescribed by his physician. He brought suit claiming brain damage with memory and emotional impairment.

The action was based on evidence that the patient's medical records at the physician's office contained earlier notations indicating a number of allergies, including the possibility of a sensitivity to penicillin. Apparently the physician had not looked at the records before prescribing for the patient. Evidence was introduced also that a year earlier the patient had suffered a severe allergic reaction from coming in contact with bags of swine feed additive which contained penicillin. He was treated for this condition for several months by the defendant-physician's medical group.

The patient's complaint included a charge that the physician failed to obtain the patient's informed consent to the treatment with penicillin, and, in a separate action, the patient sued the company that manufactured the swine feed additive, alleging that its product had increased his sensitivity to penicillin and had predisposed him to the anaphylactic reaction.

The case went to trial but on the first day was settled in the amount of $675,500.[13] According to the plaintiff's attorney, $50,000 of this was paid by the feed additive manufacturer.[14]

Yorston v. Pennell (1959) 397 Pa. 28, 153 A.2d 255, 85 A.L.R. 2d 872.

Delayed reaction—Patient claimed he advised hospital personnel of allergy—Conflicting evidence regarding entry on chart—Associate surgeon liable under respondeat superior doctrine

On September 13 the plaintiff was working for a construction company when a nail ricocheted from a ramset gun, entered his

[12] Id., 23:66, 1971.

[13] Id., 28:95, 1974; ATLA *News Letter* 16:463, 1973.

[14] ATLA *News Letter* 16:463, 1973.

right leg and fractured the fibula. He was brought to the hospital between 2:00 and 3:00 p.m. He later charged that the defendant-physician, an associate staff surgeon, negligently permitted his agents and servants to prescribe penicillin although they knew, or should have known, that he was allergic to the drug.

A few months before his accident the plaintiff had contracted a virus condition. His family physician had given him one injection of penicillin. The plaintiff developed a skin rash, whereupon his physician discontinued its use and wrote a note on one of his prescription blanks which stated that the plaintiff was allergic to penicillin and that he was never to receive the drug under any circumstances. The plaintiff put the note in his wallet and kept it with him. He had it with him when he arrived at the hospital on September 13.

While the plaintiff was in the receiving ward he showed the note to one of the nurses and to a "junior intern" (fourth-year medical student). The plaintiff's wife, who had arrived shortly after the plaintiff, also showed the note to one of the nurses, and she told a Dr. W., an intern, about the note, and that he had shown it to a nurse. She also told him that the plaintiff was allergic to tetanus antitoxin.

The plaintiff also advised the junior intern about his allergy to tetanus antitoxin, and a skin test for tetanus was made. This proved negative, and tetanus antitoxin was administered. No test was made for allergy to penicillin.

The plaintiff remained in the receiving ward about four hours. During this time the defendant appeared, and the plaintiff's wife spoke to him, complaining about the long time her husband was kept waiting.

While the plaintiff was still in receiving, Dr. H., a resident surgeon, was called to the ward. He examined the plaintiff, took a brief history of the manner in which the accident had happened and ordered roentgenograms. These disclosed the fracture and the presence of the nail in the fibula. Dr. H. took the roentgenograms to the defendant and together they reviewed a plan of treatment to be followed in repairing the injury. This plan included a general discussion of postoperative care in which antibiotics were mentioned but no specific reference to penicillin was made. (An insurance adjuster called by the plaintiff, however, testified that during a later investigation on behalf of the plaintiff's employer's compensation insurance carrier, the defendant told him that after the operation he had advised penicillin but at the time had no knowledge of the plaintiff's allergy, and that as soon as he found out about it he withdrew the drug.)

After the defendant and Dr. H. had agreed on the proper procedures, the defendant approved of Dr. H.'s operating, and the latter examined the plaintiff's heart and pulse. The plaintiff was then brought into the operating room. At that point the junior intern, who was outside, remembered that he had neglected to note that the plaintiff was allergic to penicillin in the written history. He went to the door of the operating room, but since he was improperly attired, hospital procedures prevented his entering. He called the nurse anesthetist to the door and asked her to make a notation on the history that the plaintiff was allergic to penicillin. She said she would. (Prior to the operation Dr. H. said he read the history. It was produced at the trial and showed a notation "Allergic to Penicillin." The junior intern denied that he had personally made the entry, and there was no evidence introduced to show who made it, or when it was made.)

The nail was successfully removed, a cast was placed on the leg, and the operation was completed. Dr. H., as the operation was drawing to a close, dictated the postoperative orders in which he prescribed 600,000 units of penicillin every four hours. The plaintiff was taken to the ward where he said he again advised a nurse that he was allergic to penicillin. Nevertheless, between 8:15 p.m. and 9:00 p.m. she administered penicillin in accordance with the directions on the chart. (She testified that as late as 11:00 p.m. that evening there was no notation of a penicillin allergy on the chart.) The plaintiff was again given 600,000 units of penicillin at midnight by another nurse, and again at 4:00 a.m. The plaintiff testified that he told all with whom he came into contact that he was allergic to penicillin, including two other men in the ward, and that on one occasion, according to the plaintiff, when Dr. H. and the defendant were present, Dr. H. said that he was giving the plaintiff "oremycin," but the defendant told Dr. H. to give him 25,000 units of penicillin. When the plaintiff protested to the defendant that he was allergic to penicillin, he said the latter "merely walked away." The plaintiff insisted that he protested so much that the nurses considered him a "pest."

On September 14, the morning after the operation, when a nurse tried to administer another injection, the plaintiff objected so strenuously that she called the defendant. He then canceled the order for penicillin and directed that Achromycin be given instead.

The plaintiff was discharged from the hospital on September 18. On the morning of September 20 he developed a skin reaction and called his own physician who had him readmitted to the hospital. The next morning the plaintiff suffered a cerebrovascular accident followed by severe physical and "personality changes" allegedly as a direct result of the penicillin reaction.

After an instruction by the judge on the doctrine of respondeat superior, the jury returned a verdict against the defendant-physician. He appealed, contending the doctrine should not have been applied. The Supreme Court of Pennsylvania affirmed the judgment, holding that regardless of where the negligence occurred — on the part of the junior intern, the resident physician, or the nurse anesthetist — they were all under his control and he therefore was responsible for their acts.

Rodriguez v. Columbus Hosp. (1971) 38 App. Div. 2d 517, 326 N.Y.S.2d 439.

Anaphylactic reaction—LPN allegedly intended to give intramuscular injection but injected intravenously—Judgment against hospital affirmed but $100,000 award held excessive

A licensed practical nurse injected penicillin into the buttock of a hospital patient being treated for a throat infection. She suffered an anaphylactic reaction and died. It was later alleged that the drug had been injected into a vein instead of muscle.

The patient was married, had three children, and was 49 years old at the time of her death. Her hospital expenses were $678.65 and her funeral expenses $600. A jury found the hospital liable and awarded the patient's husband $100,000. On appeal, the hospital's liability was affirmed, but the evidence on damages was held insufficient, and the case was remanded to the trial court for a new trial on the damage issue.

Wilson v. Mackenbrook (No. 390145, Superior Court, Alameda County, Cal., Jan. 16, 1974).

Possible anaphylactic reaction—Conflicting evidence that death due to cardiac condition—Verdict for physician

In 1968, after ingesting two penicillin tablets, a woman patient was admitted to the hospital suffering from brief loss of vision, nausea, low blood pressure, chest pain, shortness of breath and cardiac arrhythmia.

Approximately a week following her discharge from the hospital, the patient was seen at her physician's office because of a severe toothache. He gave her an injection of 1,200,000 units of penicillin. Five minutes later she went into shock and suffered fatal cardiovascular collapse. On autopsy, because of the absence of edema of the larynx, pharynx or glottis, the examining pathologist attributed the cause of death to a coronary condition. However, the patient's husband and children filed suit alleging that her death was due to a reaction to the penicillin, and that the physician was negligent in not considering her earlier hospitalization for an apparent sensitivity to the drug.

At the trial the plaintiff produced an allergy specialist who testified that, in his opinion, the patient's death was due to a reaction to penicillin, and that the defendant's injection of the drug, in view of a suspicion of sensitivity, was not within acceptable standards of practice. On cross-examination the witness admitted that the patient's hospital record showed symptoms consistent with a diagnosis of myocardial infarction, but stated that he believed this was secondary to the reaction.

The patient's husband testified that before the defendant gave the patient the injection he suggested to the defendant that she should be tested for sensitivity. He said that the defendant told him that such tests were not reliable.

The defendant produced a heart specialist who stated that, in his opinion, the patient died from the cardiac condition rather than a penicillin reaction, and he added that he believed that the defendant followed acceptable standards of care in administering the injection. On cross-examination, however, he admitted that he could not rule out the possibility that drug sensitivity was related to the patient's death.

The jury returned a verdict for the physician.[15]

Mann v. Michael Reese Hosp. & Medical Center (No. 65 L-21254, Circuit Court, Cook County, Ill., Dec. 16, 1970).

Hospital patient reacts to aerosol penicillin while visiting another patient's room—Suit against hospital unsuccessful

A male patient, hospitalized for injuries received in an automobile accident, visited a friend in another room who was being treated with aerosol penicillin. The visitor, who was allergic to

[15] AMA *The Citation* 29:67, 1974.

penicillin, suffered a reaction which allegedly persisted for nearly six months. A damage suit against the hospital was unsuccessful, with the hospital defending on the ground that the plaintiff's visit to another patient's room was unauthorized.[16]

Mirhosseiny v. Board of Supervisors of Louisiana State University (La. App., 1977) 351 So. 2d 1318.

Sciatic nerve irritation—No evidence of negligence

The plaintiff's cause of action arose out of an injection of Bicillin L-A he received in the right buttock. Soon after the injection, the plaintiff, a student at L.S.U., began to suffer intense pain in his right leg. He sought treatment at the university infirmary and was hospitalized for several weeks.

In his lawsuit, the plaintiff claimed the nurse who gave him the injection was negligent in that she injected the drug directly into the right sciatic nerve. The defendants offered medical testimony disputing this. According to their experts, if the Bicillin had been injected directly into the nerve, the plaintiff would have instantly reported severe pain. Instead, said the experts, the drug likely *infiltrated* the tissues over a period of time and some of it eventually reached the sciatic nerve area. This is not an uncommon occurrence in very thin persons, they said, and the plaintiff was a "very frail, emaciated individual."

The trial court entered judgment rejecting the plaintiff's claim, and the Court of Appeal of Louisiana affirmed.

Williams v. Lallie Kemp Charity Hosp. (No. 51,279, District Court, 21st Judicial District, La., Sept. 4, 1980).

Cardiac arrest, possibly from acute potassium intoxication, following potassium penicillin IV—$105,000 settlement

A sixteen-year-old patient delivered a healthy child by Caesarean section, but then developed an infection. Antibiotic therapy failed and a hysterectomy and removal of one ovary and fallopian tube was performed. At the close of the surgery, the anesthesiologist administered twenty million units of aqueous potassium penicillin intravenously. About ten minutes later the patient suffered a cardiac arrest and died. The autopsy report stated that acute potassium intoxication resulting from the potassium penicillin therapy

---

[16] Id., 22:187, 1971.

was indicated, but could not be documented because after death potassium leaks out of the dying cells into the blood and there are no morphologic changes associated with potassium intoxication which could be discovered.

The plaintiff's suit claimed that it was improper to administer so large a dose of potassium penicillin intravenously.

According to the attorneys representing the plaintiffs, the case was settled for $105,000.[17]

DiBona v. Chilton Memorial Hosp. (No. L 35391-78, Superior Court, Passaic County, N.J., Sept. 24, 1980).

Laryngeal edema following Bicillin injection and release from hospital emergency room—$375,000 verdict

A 39-year-old male patient was seen in the hospital emergency room with a fever and severe throat pain, which the defendant-physician diagnosed as tonsillitis. Ampicillin was prescribed and the patient was released. Later that day the patient returned, gasping for air, coughing up phlegm and unable to speak. The physician examined the patient's throat with a tongue depressor and a flashlight. He diagnosed the condition as tonsillopharyngitis, administered an injection of Bicillin and ordered the patient released (over objections of the patient and his wife). On returning home, the patient suffered respiratory arrest. The condition was relieved forty minutes later by a tracheotomy, but the patient's loss of oxygen resulted in hypoxic encephalopathy and blindness. Subsequent examination revealed laryngeal edema which had blocked respiration.

The patient's suit alleged that the physician had negligently failed to examine the laryngeal area, and was negligent in ordering the patient to leave the hospital.

According to the attorney for the patient, he obtained a jury verdict against the physician for $375,000.[18]

Cardiorespiratory arrest—Summary judgment for hospital and operator of emergency department reversed on agency issues

In an action by a hospital emergency department patient who experienced severe spasms and suffered cardiorespiratory arrest

---

[17] ATLA *Law Reporter* 24:91, 1981.
[18] Id.

after receiving penicillin and bicillin for a sore throat, a summary judgment for the hospital and the professional association that operated the emergency department was reversed on appeal because there were material issues of fact as to whether the physician who administered the injection was an ostensible agent of the hospital and as to whether the professional association could be held vicariously liable for the actions of the physician. Smith v. Baptist Memorial Hospital System (Tex. App., 1986) 720 S.W.2d 618.

Related cases

Seizure following injection of penicillin and chymotrypsin

In Moore v. Guthrie Hosp., Inc. (C.A.-4 W. Va., 1968) 403 F.2d 366, a hospital patient suffered a grand mal seizure immediately upon injection of a combined solution of penicillin and chymotrypsin, the latter a proteolytic enzyme sometimes used for inflammatory conditions. The plaintiff argued that the injection was given intravenously rather than intramuscularly and that this accounted for the seizure. The penicillin was ruled out as a probable cause by the plaintiff's medical expert who testified that enough time had not elapsed after an earlier injection of penicillin (his first), for his system to have produced antibodies sufficient to cause a reaction. The case is summarized herein under CHYMOTRYPSIN.

Patient allergic to penicillin reacts to ampicillin

In Walstad v. University of Minnesota Hospitals (C.A.-8 Minn., 1971) 442 F.2d 634, it was held that a hospital patient whose chart had been noted for penicillin allergy had a cause of action against the surgeon in charge of the case who had prescribed ampicillin daily for twelve days during which time the patient developed a skin rash on her arms and back. The case is summarized herein under AMPICILLIN.

Anaphylactic reaction—Evidence of negligent treatment

In Daniels v. Hadley Memorial Hosp. (1977) 185 App. D.C. 84, 566 F.2d 749, judgments for a hospital and physicians were reversed where there was evidence of improper respiratory ventilation of a patient following an anaphylactic reaction to a penicillin injection, and evidence that hospital personnel did not administer an intravenous injection of adrenalin as soon as possible.

Negligent treatment of reaction—$750,000 award against government

In Wright v. United States (E.D. La., 1981) 507 F. Supp. 147, the plaintiff suffered acute laryngeal edema after taking V-Cillin-K oral penicillin. Physicians at a VA hospital were negligent in not administering epinephrine and the plaintiff was left a spastic quadriplegic. A Louisiana federal district court awarded him $750,000.

Fatal reaction—Question of neurosurgeon's negligence in failing to advise internist of patient's allergy

There was a material issue of fact with respect to whether a neurosurgeon was negligent in failing to inform a patient's internist of the patient's known allergy to penicillin during the course of consultation on the patient's pulmonary infection. Tysinger v. Smisson (1985) 176 Ga. App. 604, 337 S.E.2d 49.

Kidney failure—Plaintiff aware of earlier reaction— Statute of limitations bars action

In Branch v. Hensgen (1988) 90 Or. App. 528, 752 P.2d 1275, the plaintiff, a college student, found her malpractice action barred by the statute of limitations when the evidence showed that she had failed to file her action within the required statutory period following the date she became aware that she had suffered a penicillin reaction.

Although the plaintiff had suffered a "rash, swollen joints, fever and prostration" within two months after receiving penicillin from the student infirmary for her chronic strep throat, she failed to advise the defendant of this fact when he began treating her several weeks later. She eventually developed kidney failure from the prolonged penicillin therapy.

PENTAZOCINE
Talacen
Talwin

Pentazocine, manufactured by Winthrop Laboratories (New York, N.Y.) under the brand names Talacen and Talwin, is a potent analgesic. It is administered orally (pentazocine hydrochloride) or by injection (pentazocine lactate). Both forms of administration are recommended for the relief of moderate to severe pain and the injection is indicated also for preoperative or preanesthetic medication and as a supplement to surgical anesthesia.[19]

The drug was introduced in 1967 as a "nonnarcotic analgesic" because it did not suppress the withdrawal symptoms in persons physically dependent on morphine. It can be used in place of morphine for relief of pain. Administered by injection, 30 mg. of pentazocine is usually as effective as 10 mg. of morphine. An oral dose of pentazocine is about one-fourth to one-third as potent as an injected dose.[20]

The adverse effects of pentazocine are similar to those of narcotic analgesics. Although it is claimed that there is less risk of severe respiratory depression with pentazocine than with morphine, the respiratory effect of pentazocine compared to that of narcotic analgesics generally remains in dispute.[1] The manufacturer warns that there have been instances of psychological and physical dependence on pentazocine (particularly when administration has been by injection) in patients with a history of drug abuse and, rarely, in patients without such a history. Physicians are warned to keep patients with a history of drug dependence "under close supervision" while receiving pentazocine, and to "take precautions to avoid increases in dose by the patient and to prevent the use of the drug in anticipation of pain rather than for the relief of pain."[2]

Winthrop Laboratories Division of Sterling Drug, Inc. v. Crocker (Tex. Civ. App., 1973) 502 S.W.2d 850, rev'd (Tex., 1974) 514 S.W.2d 429.

Addiction—Safety of drug deemed misrepresented when placed on market—Judgment for plaintiff reinstated

Suit was brought against the manufacturer of Talwin by a woman who alleged her husband had become addicted to the drug. At the trial the evidence disclosed that the patient had received medication for arthritis for many years and for diabetes since May of 1967. In June of 1967 he had an industrial accident while working in a cold storage facility. He suffered a hernia, and it was subsequently determined that he had received a severe frostbite to his thumb and finger. The hernia was surgically repaired in July of

[19] *Physicians' Desk Reference,* 35th ed., pp. 1908-09.
[20] *United States Dispensatory,* 27th ed., p. 883.
[1] Id.
[2] *Physicians' Desk Reference,* 35th ed., p. 1909.

1967, at which time morphine was administered and thereafter Demerol (meperidine hydrochloride) and Darvon (dextropropoxyphene) were used for post-surgical pain. Later, the condition of his finger and thumb caused his physician to refer him to an internal medical specialist, who hospitalized him for five days, beginning on September 18, 1967, for a thorough evaluation. On September 23, 1967 the referring physician gave him two prescriptions for Demerol and referred him to an orthopedist. The orthopedist referred the patient to a plastic surgeon and the latter hospitalized him for a skin graft on September 28, 1967. At that time he received more Demerol, and Talwin. The patient was again hospitalized in October of 1967 for skin graft, at which time both Demerol and Talwin were again administered. In November of 1967 the patient was hospitalized on two occasions during which time both Demerol and Talwin were administered again. The end of his thumb was amputated.

The patient continued to received prescribed doses of Talwin through February of 1968. Two physicians were prescribing the drug, and they attempted to reduce the doses, but the patient soon began buying Talwin in Juarez, Mexico, where it was available without prescription.

By June, 1968 the patient's wife persuaded him to undergo hospitalization for detoxification. He was hospitalized for six days, but then slipped out and went home. There, at the patient's insistence, his wife called one of his physicians who gave him a double dose of Demerol on June 10, and he died in his sleep.

The evidence at the trial revealed that Winthrop Laboratories had placed Talwin on the market in July, 1967 as a non-narcotic drug. While the accompanying product literature did not state that the drug would not cause addiction, it did indicate that patients with chronic pain had used the drug for prolonged periods (over 300 days) without experiencing withdrawal symptoms, even when administration was stopped abruptly. The literature did state, however, that patients dependent on narcotics who received Talwin might suffer some withdrawal symptoms, and that in such cases it should be administered with special caution.

The orthopedist who saw the patient in September testified that when Talwin came out he was told by the manufacturer's detail man that the drug was perfectly harmless and that he could prescribe all he wanted without fear of physical addiction. But this same witness expressed the opinion at the trial that the patient was addicted to Talwin when he was hospitalized in November. (In a pretrial deposition he said the patient was first addicted to Demerol.)

The manufacturer offered extensive testimony concerning the development and testing of Talwin before it was placed on the market. Laboratory tests had been performed on animals and the medication was turned over to the Committee on Drug Addiction and Narcotics, an independent organization composed of members of the National Academy of Science, for further testing. The drug was then tested by qualified physicians and by the United States Public Health Service. Eventually, the National Academy of Science's Committee on Drug Dependence recommended to the United States Bureau of Narcotics that Talwin be classified as a non-narcotic drug. This recommendation was accepted and application was made to the Federal Drug Administration for permission to market the drug. By the time of the application, Talwin had been tested in 17,000 patients with no report of addiction or drug dependency. The Federal Drug Administration approved the sale of Talwin to the public as a potent, non-narcotic, injectable analgesic to relieve pain of all types and degrees in patients with acute and chronic disorders.

By the time of the patient's death in 1968 the company had sold approximately 34,900,000 doses of Talwin. The evidence was conflicting as to the number of reported cases of addiction from the use of the drug at that time; witnesses for the company acknowledged they had received four reports of which three were possible dependencies. It was estimated that as of June 10, 1968 three-and-a-half million patients had been treated with Talwin. The proof established that after the death of the patient, but prior to the trial of the case, advertising materials had been amended to warn of psychological and physical dependence on Talwin in patients who were emotionally unstable or who had a history of drug abuse.

The jury returned a verdict in favor of the plaintiff, and the trial court entered judgment accordingly. The company appealed. The Court of Civil Appeals of Texas reversed the judgment of the trial court, declaring:

> [W]here the jury has found, as in this case, that the state of medical knowledge was not such that Appellant could reasonably have foreseen the addiction caused by the use of Talwin there would be no way to give any reasonable, meaningful warning.... Unfortunately for the Appellee in this case, the jury found both,

> that the state of medical knowledge was such that the Appellant could not have reasonably foreseen the resulting addiction in an appreciable number of persons ... and that the dependency on Talwin was an abreaction which could not have been reasonably foreseen in an appreciable number of potential users....

The case was then appealed by the plaintiff to the Supreme Court of Texas, which reversed the Court of Civil Appeals, finding that despite the rarity of a reaction such as that of the patient to the drug, the risk did exist, and the company's advertisement that the drug was perfectly safe was a misrepresentation. Citing Restatement, Torts, Second, § 402B, the court said:

> Liability of Winthrop Laboratories will be predicated upon the finding of misrepresentation that the drug would not cause physical dependence, a fact conceded by the attorney for the company in his jury argument, and upon the findings of reliance and causation. Whatever the danger and state of medical knowledge, and however rare the susceptibility of the user, when the drug company positively and specifically represents its product to be free and safe from all dangers of addiction, and when the treating physician relies upon that representation, the drug company is liable when the representation proves to be false and harm results.

Henry v. Winthrop Laboratories (No. 67248, Superior Court, San Francisco County, Cal., April 19, 1974).

**Addiction—Another claim for failure to warn—
Verdict for manufacturer**

This lawsuit was brought by a 53-year-old woman patient who had become addicted to Talwin. The patient had been given a prescription for the drug by an orthopedic surgeon in November, 1967. She took the drug daily and became addicted within a year. She had been placed on the drug because of chronic pain, the cause of which was not mentioned in the report of the case.

The patient's suit was against the manufacturer of Talwin, and in her complaint she contended that the company had wrongly advertised that there was little, if any, threat of addiction to the drug. In fact, her attorney claimed, Talwin was advertised as the first strong pain reliever for chronic pain patients which was without the danger of addiction. It was charged that the manufacturer was negligent in making such statements without reviewing the results of extensive clinical use by chronic pain sufferers.

The patient also argued that the manufacturer knew that Talwin was addictive in August, 1968, and so noted on the package insert in October, 1968, but did not inform the medical profession by a "Dear Doctor letter" until August, 1969. She claimed that by advertising that there was no danger of addiction to the drug, the manufacturer was liable on the theory of breach of express warranty.

At the trial, the manufacturer argued that before Talwin was placed on the market, it was tested on 17,000 people without any indication of addiction. The company contended further that its researchers had performed every possible test under the auspices of the National Research Council and these tests likewise showed no indication of addiction. The manufacturer did admit, however, that after the drug had been placed on the market, a few patients were reported to have become addicted, and this brought about the change in the package insert in October, 1968. The company defended the case also on the ground that if the patient had not used Talwin, she would, because of her chronic pain, have been treated with another drug which would have been even more addictive. Also, the manufacturer argued that the patient had a history of drug abuse and that she had in fact abused Talwin.

The patient's attorney had also pleaded the theories of strict liability and implied warranty, and had asked for punitive damages. Prior to giving the case to the jury, the trial judge ruled out punitive damages, and denied requests for instructions on strict liability and implied warranty. The jury was instructed on negligence and express warranty, and returned a verdict for the defendant.[3]

Profant v. Einstein (No. 122627, Superior Court, Kern County, Cal., March 7, 1975).

**Addiction—$20,000 settlement with manufacturer—
Verdict for physician**

A 39-year-old college professor sought treatment from his physician for chronic low back pain. The physician prescribed Talwin by injection. At the end of ten months, the physician suspected that the patient was abusing the drug, and refused to renew the prescription or administer further doses.

The patient had become dependent upon the drug, and was admitted for treatment at a state hospital. On release he had diffi-

---

[3] AMA *The Citation* 29:138, 1974.

culty functioning in his work, and ultimately lost his position as a professor.

Suit was brought against the manufacturer of Talwin and the physician. The manufacturer settled for $20,000. The case against the physician went to trial with the patient charging negligence in prescribing Talwin for the ten-month period without periodic examinations and close supervision to prevent addiction. The patient also charged that the physician should have put him on trial doses of other milder drugs with less risk of addiction, and should have tried physical therapy instead of drug therapy.

In his defense, the physician argued that his choice of Talwin in treating the patient was within acceptable standards, and that in the patient's case other medications were not suitable because of possible gastrointestinal complications. He contended that addiction to a drug such as Talwin was "an acceptable risk" in a case such as the patient's, because of the extreme need to relieve his pain.

The jury found in favor of the physician.[4]

Bikowicz v. Nedco Pharmacy (1987) 130 App. Div. 2d 89, 517 N.Y.S.2d 829.

Addiction—Issues exist as to accrual date of action and adequacy of manufacturer's warning—Punitive damages also jury question

The patient first began taking Talwin in 1968 for migraine headaches. Until 1973, she received the drug by intramuscular injection from her family physician. In February 1973, her physician issued her a prescription for 50 mg. ampules to take on a vacation to Florida. Although her physician claimed that the prescription was not to be refilled, the patient obtained many refills from 1973 through 1981 from the defendant pharmacy.

In 1980, the patient sought treatment for Talwin addiction from a neurologist who attempted to wean her off the drug with decreasing doses. This treatment was unsuccessful, however, and the patient renewed her Talwin intake by again obtaining refills of unrefillable prescriptions. She was finally hospitalized and successfully rehabilitated in April 1981.

---

[4]Id., 31:79, 1975.

The patient filed a lawsuit in July of 1981 against her physicians, the pharmacy that refilled the prescriptions, and the manufacturer of Talwin, Winthrop Laboratories. All defendants raised the statute of limitations as a defense. The court, however, held that a genuine issue of material fact existed as to whether the patient's action was time-barred. The defendant manufacturer also raised the doctrine of "informed intermediary," arguing that its duty to warn of any side effects of Talwin extended only to the physician and that that duty ended with the termination of treatment of the patient by her attending physician in 1977. Thus, argued the manufacturer, the action against it was time-barred. The court disagreed, holding that the informed intermediary doctrine is a substantive legal rule that pertains to the question of liability on the part of a drug manufacturer and to the substance of a warning itself, and it has nothing to do with the procedural question of when a patient's cause of action accrues.

As to the accrual date of the patient's action, the court held that a cause of action arising out of an injection or ingestion of a drug accrues on the date the substance is introduced into the body. When this occurs over a period of time, the cause of action accrues on the date of the last exposure to the drug which, in the patient's case, was in March 1981.

The court held also that a question of fact existed as to the adequacy of the warning of the drug's risks, thereby precluding the granting of a summary judgment in favor of the manufacturer. In the patient's case, the adequacy of the warnings depended upon the actual and constructive knowledge the defendants possessed before and during the time the patient was exposed to Talwin.

The court was impressed by testimony of an expert witness who conducted premarketing studies of Talwin on behalf of the manufacturer in connection with another trial. The witness stated that there is a "tremendous" number of people who develop addiction to Talwin. Furthermore, the patient alleged that despite its knowledge of the drug's addictive qualities, the manufacturer's sales representatives were instructed to assure doctors that Talwin was "nonaddictive." This was despite published articles on the effects of the drug which showed that the manufacturer was aware of the danger of addiction. The patient argued that if the manufacturer had disclosed all information they possessed concerning Talwin's potential to cause addiction, she would not have been administered the number of injections she received from her family physician and would not have been issued the number of prescriptions she obtained.

In light of the above, the court concluded that the patient had shown that the adequacy of the manufacturer's warnings presented questions of fact to be determined at trial and that it was for a jury to determine whether the manufacturer possessed actual or constructive knowledge of Talwin's potential to cause addiction. Also, said the court, a jury must determine whether the manufacturer failed to make a timely disclosure of the information they possessed on the drug and whether such failure was the proximate cause of the patient's injuries. Furthermore, the court refused to dismiss the patient's claim for punitive damages, holding that whether the manufacturer's conduct constituted reckless disregard of the public's safety was also essentially a jury question that could be answered only after the issue of the adequacy of the warning was resolved.

Related Cases

Addiction—Failure to warn—Verdict for plaintiff reversed for exclusion of evidence of earlier drug abuse

A verdict for a plaintiff who claimed she became addicted to Talwin because the manufacturer failed to warn the medical profession of this risk was reversed because the trial court excluded a deceased psychiatrist's deposition taken at an earlier workers' compensation hearing which disclosed the plaintiff's pre-existing drug abuse problem. DeLuryea v. Winthrop Laboratories (C.A.-8 Ark., 1983) 697 F.2d 222.

No evidence that excessive dosages caused plaintiff's injuries

In Paul v. Boschenstein (1984) 105 App. Div. 2d 248, 482 N.Y.S.2d 870, the plaintiff failed to establish that excessive dosages of Talwin were a proximate cause of her complaints. (Actions against physician and hospital dismissed, and jury verdict for manufacturer.)

Cancer at site of injections—Action not barred by statute of limitations

In Comstock v. Collier (Colo., 1987) 737 P.2d 845, the patient, on the advice of her physician, injected Talwin into her leg five times a day from 1967 to 1982 as treatment for "chronic phlebitis." In December 1982, the patient was found to be suffering cancer at the sites where the drug had been injected. The patient's claim for negligent diagnosis and treatment was not barred by the statute of limitations since the court held that the statute did not begin to run until the last injection, or in the words of the court, the "final act constituting the treatment."

Tissue necrosis and gangrene from subcutaneous injection

In Fleming v. Baptist General Convention of Oklahoma (Okla., 1987) 742 P.2d 1087, a hospital nurse administering an injection of Atarax and Talwin injected the solution subcutaneously rather than intramuscularly, causing tissue necrosis and gangrene. The case is summarized herein under HYDROXYZINE.

PENTHRANE

See METHOXYFLURANE

PENTIDS

See PENICILLIN

PENTOBARBITAL

See SODIUM PENTOBARBITAL

PENTOLINIUM TARTRATE

Ansolysen

Pentolinium tartrate is a potent ganglionic blocking agent used mainly for hypertension. It is also useful in some peripheral vascular disorders. Administration may be oral, subcutaneous or intramuscular. It is not administered intravenously. The initial dose by injection should not exceed 3.5 mg., and in patients known to be susceptible to the drug, the dose should not exceed 2.5 mg. Once established, dosage by injection usually ranges between 30 to 60 mg. daily at six- to eight-hour intervals. With oral administration, the initial dose is usually 20 mg. every eight hours. This is increased gradually until the minimum effective dose is reached. Daily oral dosage, once established, ranges from as low as 60 mg. to as high as 600 mg., in exceptional cases.[5]

The drug is contraindicated in patients with recent myocardial infarction, and in severe coronary insufficiency, cerebral arterio-

[5] *United States Dispensatory,* 27th ed., p. 884.

sclerosis, and organic pyloric stenosis. Furthermore, it should not be used where impairment of kidney function can lead to accumulation of the drug, or where lowered blood pressure intensifies kidney insufficiency.[6]

Adverse effects include postural hypotension, fainting, blurring of vision, dryness of mouth, urinary retention, constipation or diarrhea, and impotence in the male. Overdose may cause peripheral circulatory collapse.[7]

Pentolinium tartrate was manufactured by Wyeth Laboratories (Philadelphia, Pa.) under the name Ansolysen. It is no longer included on the company's product information list.

Larrimore v. Homeopathic Hosp. Assn. of Delaware (1962) 54 Del. 449, 181 A.2d 573.

Injection of 30 mg. mistakenly given during withdrawal process—$30,000 verdict against hospital—New trial ordered on damages

A hospital patient was suffering from chronic kidney disease and malignant hypertension. He was being given Ansolysen by injection for the hypertension, but it was determined that his case was terminal, and a decision was made to withdraw him from the drug. The withdrawal was to be carried out over a period of days by gradually decreasing the amount injected, and then placing him on oral administration.

On October 1, 1959, the patient's attending physician entered an order on his chart to discontinue the injections and begin oral dosage. The hospital nurses followed this procedure through October 4. On that date a nurse who had been off duty for three days, and who did not know the prescription had been changed to oral, overlooked the notation on the chart and gave the patient a 30 mg. injection. The patient suffered no major permanent effects from this dose, but it was necessary to give him emergency treatment, consisting mainly of glucose injections, for a period of about 36 hours, during which time he suffered violent headaches, loss of vision, and emotional upset.

In a negligence action brought by the patient's family against the hospital, it was claimed that the patient, prior to the erroneous injection, was in fairly good spirits, despite the knowledge that his illness was terminal. Testimony was introduced that after the injec-

---

[6] Id.

[7] Id.

tion the patient "degenerated physically, morally and spiritually." He had planned to go home as soon as the withdrawal process was completed, but the effects of the injection delayed this. The patient did get to go home on October 17, but he had to return to the hospital in a week, and four days later he died.

The jury rendered a verdict for $30,000. The trial judge denied the defendant's motion for a new trial on the liability question, but did order a new trial on the amount of damages. This order was affirmed on appeal.

PENTOTHAL

See SODIUM THIOPENTAL

PEN VEE K

See PENICILLIN

PERMITIL

See FLUPHENAZINE HYDROCHLORIDE

PERPHENAZINE

Etrafon
Triavil
Trilafon

Perphenazine is a member of the phenothiazine group of tranquilizers and is indicated for use in the management of the manifestations of psychotic disorders and for the control of severe nausea and vomiting in adults. It has not been shown effective in the management of behavioral complications in patients with mental retardation. In the product literature for Trilafon (Schering Corporation, Kenilworth, N.J.), the manufacturer warns that prolonged administration of doses exceeding 24 mg. daily should be reserved for hospitalized patients or patients under continued observation. The adverse reactions are those experienced generally with potent tranquilizers.[8]

Etrafon (also manufactured by Schering Corporation) and Triavil (Merck, Sharp and Dohme, a division of Merck and Company, Inc., West Point, Pa.) contain a combination of perphenazine and amitriptyline hydrochloride, an antidepressant with sedative effects.

---

[8] *Physicians' Desk Reference,* 40th ed., pp. 1217, 1617, 1655.

Speer v. United States (N.D. Tex., 1981) 512 F. Supp. 670.

Excessive supply of Etrafon prescribed for suicide victim—Government not liable

The patient was being treated as an outpatient at a Dallas, Texas VA facility for depression and paranoid schizophrenia. Over a period of time he built up a supply of Etrafon and consumed a fatal overdose in July, 1976. His wife filed suit against the government, alleging negligence on the part of the treating psychiatrist for prescribing an excessive supply of the drugs, and on the part of VA pharmacists for failing to monitor refill prescriptions.

The trial court held that under Texas law the psychiatrist did not breach acceptable standards of care, and if he did, any such negligence was not the proximate cause of the patient's death.

The court further held that although the VA pharmacists breached their duty to monitor refills of the patient's prescriptions, their negligence also was not the proximate cause of his death.

Related cases

Tardive dyskinesia—Question as to commencement of action

Where the plaintiff was advised that his tardive dyskinesia might be a temporary condition and that his symptoms were successfully controlled by medication, the evidence did not establish "beyond dispute" that he was aware, at that time, that his condition was possibly due to negligent treatment with Trilafon so as to bar his action under California's statute of limitations. Timmel v. Moss (C.A.-9 Cal., 1986) 803 F.2d 519.

PFIZERPEN G; PFIZERPEN VK

See PENICILLIN

PHENACETIN

This drug is a mild analgesic. It is approximately equivalent to aspirin in pain-relieving and fever-reducing effectiveness, but has little anti-inflammatory activity. It is used mainly in the treatment of headache and mild to moderate myalgia and arthralgia.[9]

Phenacetin was once used extensively in over-the-counter headache and sinus remedies until it was discovered that long-term use

---

[9] *AMA Drug Evaluations,* 2d ed., p. 266.

could damage the kidneys. Acetaminophen has now replaced phenacetin in most of these mixtures.

Phenaphen with Codeine, a mixture involved in the first case listed below, and manufactured by A.H. Robins Company (Richmond, Va.), formerly contained phenacetin along with aspirin, phenobarbital and codeine phosphate.[10] (The product now contains only acetaminophen and codeine phosphate.) When phenacetin was used, the manufacturer listed among possible adverse reactions "nausea, constipation and drowsiness."[11] However, both the AMA's Department of Drugs,[12] and Osol and Pratt[13] mentioned the possibility of skin rash. And, there were some reports then linking long-term use of phenacetin with serious kidney lesions.[14]

Slack v. Fleet (La. App., 1970) 242 So. 2d 650.

Dermatological reaction in patient taking Phenaphen with Codeine and five other drugs—Question of proper prescribing—Patient's action dismissed for want of medical evidence

A middle-aged woman patient saw her physician, complaining of "pain and cramping in the stomach, nausea, vomiting and nervousness." After an examination, the physician made a diagnosis of "acute cholecystitis with liver manifestations, possible gastric ulcer, hypertension and extreme nervousness." He prescribed six drugs: (1) Estomul (liquid);[15] (2) Donnatal Elixir;[16] (3) Butisol Sodium Elixir;[17] (4) Phenaphen with Codeine; (5) Enarax;[18] and (6) Pro-Banthine with Phenobarbital.[19]

The patient was instructed to take these drugs simultaneously, which she did. There are then two versions as to what happened.

---

[10] *Physicians' Desk Reference,* 29th ed., p. 1221.

[11] Id.

[12] *AMA Drug Evaluations,* 2d ed., p. 267.

[13] *United States Dispensatory,* 27th ed., p. 891.

[14] Id., p. 890.

[15] See MAGNESIUM CARBONATE with ALUMINUM HYDROXIDE, herein.

[16] Donnatal Elixir, manufactured by A.H. Robins Company (Richmond, Va.), is an antispasmodic containing hyoscyamine sulfate, atropine sulfate, scopolamine hydrobromide, and phenobarbital. According to the manufacturer, adverse reactions may include blurred vision, dry mouth, difficult urination, flushing, or dryness of the skin. These rarely occur with the usual dose, however. *Physicians' Desk Reference,* 35th ed., p. 1471.

[17] See BUTABARBITAL SODIUM, herein.

[18] See OXYPHENCYCLIMINE HYDROCHLORIDE with HYDROXYZINE HYDROCHLORIDE, herein.

[19] See PROPANTHELINE BROMIDE, herein.

According to the patient, on the third day she experienced "dizzy spells and a skin rash." She telephoned her physician, described her symptoms, and was told to continue the medication. Her symptoms persisted and two days later she had her daughter call the physician. The daughter testified that she told him that her mother's rash was more severe and was spreading over her body. She said the physician asked her to read the prescription numbers on the labels to him and the drugstore where they were purchased. She said the physician then told her to discontinue one of the drugs. (Apparently she could not remember which one.) The patient said her condition still persisted, and five days later, which was a full week after she had begun taking the drugs, her daughter again called the physician. This time he had her come to his office, examined her rash, and arranged to have her seen by a dermatologist.

The physician's version of this story was as follows: Two days after prescribing the drugs, an unidentified woman called him and told him that the patient was suffering from dizziness and rash. He said he instructed the caller to tell the patient to discontinue taking all of the prescribed drugs and drink "baking soda water" two to three times that day. He said he told the caller to see that the patient's condition was reported to him within the next day or two. Two days later he said he received another call, apparently from the same person, who told him that the patient still suffered from the rash. He asked if the patient had stopped taking the drugs and he was told that she had. He said he then prescribed two antihistamines. He said he received a third call, apparently from the same person, on the sixth day. She told him that the patient's rash had spread. He said he informed the caller to have the patient come to his office that afternoon or the next day. He said she did so the next day, and an appointment was made with the dermatologist.

In her lawsuit against the physician, the patient charged negligence in prescribing the six drugs simultaneously, in not ordering her to discontinue the medication sooner, and in not examining her immediately on learning of her symptoms. At the trial, the patient's attorneys offered no medical testimony on her behalf. A specialist in internal medicine appeared for the defendant and testified that according to medical standards, a physician would not have performed a skin test prior to prescribing such drugs; that although he himself might not have used exactly the same drugs as the defendant, the defendant's choice of drugs "represents a conscientious and enthusiastic effort to rid her of her symptoms"; and that the defendant prescribed "well-known frequently used medications" for treatment of the symptoms presented by the patient.

A second witness testifying for the defense, a general practitioner, stated that he likewise felt that the prescribing of the six drugs was acceptable medical practice. He added that "I think that his care was not only as good as the average but better than the average.... I can find no real fault with the use of the drugs of his program." This witness added that the use of such drugs in a case like the patient's was "pretty common" and that he would have prescribed the same drugs if he had been treating the patient. He did admit, however, that the drugs prescribed, especially the Phenaphen with Codeine, could "trigger off the reaction" suffered by the patient. He pointed out, however, that the components of these drugs were in "very mild doses" and reiterated that Phenaphen with Codeine is commonly used by physicians.

The first witness was also asked if, by prescribing more than one drug containing barbiturates, a physician increases the chances of an adverse reaction. To this the witness answered that, although the patient is taking an increased amount of the drug, it does not necessarily increase his chances of an adverse reaction. "If you are hypersensitive to it you are going to be hypersensitive to a small amount" he testified.

Both witnesses testified as to the impracticality of testing for possible drug reaction before prescribing the drugs in question. Both said that a physician must rely on the history given by the patient as to whether the patient is allergic to any drugs which are to be taken orally.

After hearing the evidence, the trial judge dismissed the action. The Court of Appeals reviewed the case and agreed with the trial judge that the patient failed to show that the defendant's prescription was not within the acceptable standards of the medical profession. As to the issue whether the defendant was negligent in not ordering the patient to discontinue the medication sooner, and in not examining the patient sooner upon learning of her symptoms, the reviewing court observed that if one accepts the defendant's version of what happened, the trial court committed no error in finding no negligence.

Michael v. Warner/Chilcott (1978) 91 N.M. 651, 579 P.2d 183.

Kidney failure—Adequacy of manufacturer's warning for jury to decide

The plaintiff in this case suffered from sinus congestion since about 1952. Over the years he took a variety of medicines for his condition. About 1965, his physician prescribed Sinutab, which at the time contained phenacetin.[20] The drug could be obtained over-the-counter without a prescription, and the plaintiff purchased it this way for five years, taking four tablets a day.

In 1970, when he was about to buy another supply of the medicine at his pharmacy, the cashier informed him that the drugstore carried its own house brand of the same medicine under the name Sinus Congestion Tablets. The plaintiff compared the labels of the two products and concluded that the ingredients were the same. He bought the house brand and took the tablets on a regular daily basis until 1973, when he suffered kidney failure.

When the plaintiff discovered that the tablets contained phenacetin, a drug which can cause kidney damage, he filed suit against the manufacturer of Sinutab, the manufacturer of the house brand of tablets and the drugstore.

At the trial, a label was introduced which showed that the Sinus Congestion Tablets the plaintiff had been buying contained the following warning: "This medication may damage the kidneys when used in large amounts or for a long period of time. Do not take more than the recommended dosage, nor take regularly for longer than 10 days without consulting your physician." Although it was not made clear in the report of the case, it is presumed the Sinutab package contained the same warning.

The defendants moved for summary judgment which the trial judge denied, and they appealed. On review of the evidence, the Court of Appeals of New Mexico affirmed, holding that there existed an issue of material fact as to whether the label gave adequate warning.

Related cases

Alleged interaction of drugs

In Perkins v. Park View Hosp., Inc. (1970) 61 Tenn. App. 458, 456 S.W.2d 276, a woman hospital patient died, apparently from ana-

[20] The phenacetin has since been replaced by acetaminophen.

phylactic shock, after receiving Phenaphen, Carisoprodol (or Soma Compound), meprobamate and hydromorphine over a two-day period. Directed verdicts in favor of all defendants were sustained. The case is summarized herein under CARISOPRODOL.

PHENDIMETRAZINE TARTRATE

Plegine

Phendimetrazine is a central nervous system stimulant used to treat obesity. It has not been established, however, that the action of the drug is primarily one of appetite suppression; other central nervous system actions or metabolic effects may be involved. The drug is indicated in the management of exogenous obesity as a short-term adjunt (a few weeks) in a regimen of weight reduction based on caloric restriction. The manufacturer of Plegine, Wyeth-Ayerst Laboratories (Philadelphia, Pa.), warns that the limited usefulness of agents of this class should be measured against possible risk factors inherent in their use. The drug is contraindicated in cases of advanced arteriosclerosis, symptomatic cardiovascular disease, moderate and severe hypertension, hyperthyroidism, glaucoma, highly nervous or agitated patients, patients with a history of drug abuse, and patients taking other central nervous system stimulants, including monamine oxidase inhibitors.[21]

McKee v. American Home Products Corp. (1989) 113 Wash. 2d 701, 782 P.2d 1045.

Addiction—Pharmacists not liable for failing to warn patient or to supply manufacturer's package insert

From 1974 through 1984, the plaintiff received prescriptions from her family physician for Plegine to control her weight problem. Sometime during this period she became addicted to the drug.

The plaintiff sued her physician, the manufacturer of Plegine, and the pharmacists who filled most of her prescriptions. As to the pharmacists, the plaintiff alleged negligence in selling her the product for such an extended period of time without warning her of its adverse effects, and in failing to give her the manufacturer's package insert which would have alerted her to the risk of addiction. The plaintiff also alleged strict liability and breach of express and implied warranties.

---

[21] *Physicians' Desk Reference,* 43rd ed., p. 2349.

Prior to trial, the pharmacists moved for summary judgment, contending that they had no duty to warn their customers of the potential hazards of a prescription drug. The trial court granted the motion and dismissed all claims against the pharmacists.

On appeal, the Supreme Court of Washington refused to consider the strict liability and breach of warranty claims because of the plaintiff's failure to assign error to the trial court's dismissal of these claims, as required by Washington's rules of appellate procedure. As to the claim of negligence, the court affirmed the trial court's decision, holding that the plaintiff failed to establish the standard of care of a pharmacist practicing in the state of Washington. (The plaintiff's only offer of evidence on this issue was an affidavit of an Arizona physician, which the court ruled was insufficient.)

Citing the majority rule from decisions in other states, the court held further that while pharmacists would have a duty to be alert for patent errors in a prescription (e.g., obvious lethal dosages, inadequacies in instructions, known contraindications, incompatible prescriptions), they do not have a duty to question the judgment of a physician as to the propriety of a prescription, warn customers of side effects, or provide customers with the manufacturer's package inserts because it would place an "unknown burden" on pharmacists, frighten the customer, and also abrogate the learned intermediary doctrine applicable to warnings given by manufacturers to physicians.

PHENELZINE SULFATE

Nardil

Phenelzine is a potent monoamine oxidase inhibitor (MAOI) used to treat depression in patients who are clinically characterized as "atypical," "monendogenous," or "neurotic." (Patients who often have mixed anxiety and depression, and phobic or hypocondriacal features.) There is no conclusive evidence of the drug's usefulness with severely depressed patients with endogenous features. The manufacturer of Nardil (Parke-Davis, Morris Plains, N.J.), states that the product should rarely be the first antidepressant drug used, and that it is more suitable for use with patients who have failed to respond to the drugs more commonly used for these conditions.[1]

---

[1]*Physicians' Desk Reference,* 42d ed., p. 1573.

As with MAOI antidepressants generally, there are many contra-indications and side effects. The most serious reactions reported involve changes in blood pressure. Also, there are many foods and other drugs one should avoid when taking Nardil.[2]

Death from butalbital intoxication while on Nardil and Fiorinal

In Whittle v. United States (C.A.-D.C., 1987) 669 F. Supp. 501, a psychiatric resident at a military hospital was found negligent in the death of patient from butalbital intoxication while on a regimen of Nardil and Fiorinal (butalbital). The case is summarized herein under BUTALBITAL.

PHENERGAN

See PROMETHAZINE HYDROCHLORIDE

PHENMETRAZINE HYDROCHLORIDE
Preludin

Phenmetrazine hydrochloride, manufactured by Boehringer Ingelheim Ltd. (Ridgefield, Conn.) under the trade name Preludin, is a stimulant related chemically and pharmacologically to the amphetamines. It is indicated for the management of certain cases of obesity as a short-term (a few weeks) adjunct in the regimen of weight reduction based on caloric restriction.[3]

In the product literature the manufacturer states that the drug should be given with caution where patients have even mild high blood pressure. Adverse reactions generally include heart palpitations, tachycardia, elevated blood pressure, insomnia, euphoria, and gastrointestinal disorders.[4]

Mendoza v. Varon (Tex. Civ. App., 1978) 563 S.W.2d 646.

Gastric irritation—Combination of drugs questioned—Verdict for physician upheld

The patient was a teenage girl who suffered from obesity. She was referred to the defendant-physician because of her weight problem and an elevated blood pressure reading. The defendant pre-

---

[2] Id.

[3] *Physicians' Desk Reference,* 35th ed., p. 666.

[4] Id.

scribed a combination of drugs designed to reduce the patient's weight without aggravating her blood pressure problem.

A few weeks after treatment was begun, the patient began to experience nausea attacks which gradually worsened until she would suffer violent vomiting and stomach spasms that lasted throughout the night. An examination eventually revealed inflammation and scarring of the sphincter valve between the patient's stomach and esophagus which permitted the contents of the stomach to enter the esophagus, causing regurgitation.

The drugs prescribed by the defendant were Preludin (phenmetrazine hydrochloride), Dyazide (triamterene), Aldactone (spironolactone) and Slow-K (potassium chloride). In her lawsuit against the physician, the patient's mother contended that this combination of drugs caused her daughter's condition.

The defendant, in support of his choice of treatment, testified at the trial that the combination of Dyazide, Preludin and Aldactone reduced both excess fluid and weight without stimulating the blood pressure, a common complication with weight-reducing therapy. The Slow-K, a potassium supplement, was added to replace potassium that might be lost with such a regimen.

The plaintiff produced expert witnesses who testified that the prescribed combination of drugs "violated community standards of practice," and that the Preludin, being a stimulant, in fact increases the blood pressure, which was to be avoided in the patient's case. An expert for the defendant, however, testified that while he did not totally agree with the defendant's treatment techniques, and that he considered the drug combination "unusual," he concluded that the overall approach was "reasonable."

Other issues at the trial were raised, including the correctness of the defendant's diagnosis, whether in fact the patient did have high blood pressure, alleged negligence in monitoring the treatment, and whether the defendant should have discontinued or reduced the therapy once the patient's symptoms arose.

The jury found the defendant free of negligence on all counts, and the verdict was upheld on appeal.

Argus v. Scheppegrell (La., 1985) 472 So. 2d 573.

Addiction and suicide—Physician negligent in continuing to prescribe drugs

The defendant, a general practitioner, was charged with negligence in continuing to prescribe Preludin and Tuinal for a nineteen-year-old girl who obviously was addicted to both drugs. Early in August, 1977, the girl's mother called the defendant and asked that he not furnish her daughter with any more prescriptions because she was addicted and might be suicidal. The defendant agreed, but two weeks later gave the girl a prescription for fifty tablets each of Preludin and Tuinal. Two days later she consumed three-fourths of the bottle of Tuinal and became comatose. She died one month later.

Finding the girl guilty of contributory negligence, a jury returned a verdict for the defendant. The Court of Appeals affirmed, but the Supreme Court of Louisiana reversed, holding that the defendant had breached his duty not to give the girl any more drugs upon learning of her addiction and possible suicidal tendencies, and that because of "the disparity of positions in the relationship between a trained and licensed physician and a nineteen-year-old uneducated patient whose drug addiction was known to the physician, and because of the vastly different duty required of each party under the circumstances, the patient's reasonably expected conduct did not constitute an absolute bar to her parents' recovery for her wrongful death."

Kinney v. Hutchinson (La. App., 1985) 468 So. 2d 714.

Manufacturer not liable for injuries inflicted by person under influence of Preludin and alcohol

The plaintiff was shot in the throat by a patient who was under the influence of a combination of Preludin and alcohol. The shooting occurred in a bar, and the two parties were total strangers. Among defendants in the plaintiff's lawsuit was the manufacturer of the Preludin, whom the plaintiff alleged failed to provide an adequate warning regarding the risks inherent in using the drug.

The trial court granted the manufacturer's motion for summary judgment, and the appellate court affirmed, holding that the warnings provided in the package insert, which reflected the state of medical knowledge at the time, put physicians on notice that the drug carried the possiblity of "psychosis" under normal dosage and the possibility of "confusion, assaultiveness, hallucinations, and panic states" with overdosages, and that these warnings were sufficient in the absence of evidence suggesting that combining Preludin with alcohol causes other side effects.

Related cases

Pharmacist has no duty to warn of adverse effect of mixing Preludin and alcohol

In Kinney v. Hutchinson (La. App., 1984) 449 So. 2d 696, it was held that a pharmacist had no duty to warn a customer of the effects of combining Preludin and alcohol.

PHENOBARBITAL

Phenobarbital is a barbiturate used in seizure disorders and occasionally as a daytime sedative or for mild anxiety. It generally is given orally, but it may be administered parenterally if necessary. (During intravenous injection, patients should be observed carefully). Phenobarbital is also used to treat barbiturate and other nonbenzodiazepine withdrawal syndromes. It is sometimes given to control signs and symptoms of withdrawal in infants of mothers addicted to opioids and short-acting barbiturates. Long-term use of the drug in larger than usual dosages may result in physical and psychological dependence.[5]

Guevara v. Dorsey Laboratories, Division of Sandoz (C.A.-1 P.R., 1988) 845 F.2d 364.

Skin reaction—Manufacturer's warning sufficient

The plaintiff suffered an adverse reaction to the phenobarbital contained in Bellergal-S, a product manufactured by Dorsey Laboratories for the treatment of conditions characterized by nervous tension. Three days after she began taking the drug, the plaintiff developed a skin rash and blisters that later became infected and left permanent scars. In her lawsuit against the manufacturer, she alleged failure to warn physicians adequately of the risk of this side effect.

The package insert contained a warning to physicians not to give the drug to persons with "a demonstrated hypersensitivity to any of its components." The plaintiff argued that this warning was insufficient in that it did not specifically warn of the kind of reaction she experienced.

The jury found for the plaintiff, but on appeal the verdict was reversed, the reviewing court holding that in light of the testimony of the expert witnesses, including the plaintiff's own expert, the

---

[5] *Drug Evaluations,* 6th ed., p. 104.

danger of an adverse reaction to phenobarbital was already well known to the medical community, and doctors who were warned about "hypersensitivity" to the drug should know that this could be manifested as a skin rash. In view of such evidence, the court added: "We conclude ... as a matter of law, that apprising physicians of the existence of phenobarbital in Bellergal-S and cautioning them not to prescribe Bellergal-S to persons allergic to phenobarbital is adequate, given the level of knowledge in the medical community as explained by the experts, to put doctors on notice that a skin rash, such as that suffered by the plaintiff ... could occur as a result of the ingestion of Bellergal-S."

Kempf v. University of North Dakota Family Practice Center (No. 87292, District Court, Grand Forks, N.D., Feb. 19, 1988).

Excessive administration of phenobarbital to distressed newborn—Brain damage—Death—$100,000 settlement

The plaintiff, a maternity patient, was admitted to the defendant facility for the delivery of her child and placed on an external fetal monitor. Although the monitor indicated that the fetus was in distress, the plaintiff was allowed to continue in labor for one and one-half hours.

The plaintiff's baby was born severely distressed, with an Apgar score of one at one minute and four at five minutes. Twenty hours after birth, the infant was administered phenobarbital in an amount three and one-half times the recommended dosage. She was in a coma for four days, and suffered severe brain damage. Three months later, she died.

In addition to being accused of over-medicating the child, the obstetrician and consulting family practitioner were charged with failing to perform an emergency cesarean at the first indication of fetal distress, and with failing to provide adequate resuscitation. According to the plaintiff's attorney, the case was settled for $100,000.[6]

Related cases.

Skin loss during treatment with phenobarbital and Tegretol (carbamazepine)

In Reeves v. Geigy Pharmaceutical, Inc. (Utah App., 1988) 764 P.2d 636, a patient being treated for epilepsy with phenobarbital

[6] ATLA *Professional Negligence Law Reporter* 3:127, 1988.

and Tegretol (carbamazepine) brought suit against his neurologist and the manufacturer of the two drugs when he suffered skin loss so severe that he was required to undergo grafts. The case is summarized herein under CARBAMAZEPINE.

Stevens-Johnson syndrome—Question of informed consent

In Shinn v. St. James Mercy Hosp. (W.D. N.Y., 1987) 675 F. Supp. 94, aff'd (C.A.-2 N.Y., 1988) 847 F.2d 836, a patient who developed Stevens-Johnson syndrome while taking Dilantin (phenytoin sodium) and phenobarbital charged his physician with failure to obtain his informed consent to the method of treatment selected. The case is summarized herein under PHENYTOIN SODIUM.

PHENOXYMETHYL PENICILLIN

See PENICILLIN

PHENYLBUTAZONE

Azolid
Butazolidin

Phenylbutazone is used primarily in the treatment of gout and rheumatoid arthritis. It has anti-inflammatory, fever-reducing and pain-relieving properties; however, its usefulness has been said to be limited by its potential toxicity.[7] The manufacturer of Butazolidin states in the product literature that the drug "cannot be considered a simple analgesic and should never be administered casually." The manufacturer emphasizes that each patient should be carefully evaluated before treatment is started and should constantly remain under the close supervision of the physician.[8]

The adverse effects of phenylbutazone include, but are not limited to, serious blood dyscrasias (including aplastic anemia), often of sudden onset; unexplained bleeding; toxic and nontoxic goiters; hepatitis; Stevens-Johnson syndrome; anaphylactic shock; kidney failure; optic neuritis, retinal hemorrhage, and retinal detachment; hearing loss; cardiac decompensation, pericarditis and myocarditis.[9]

---

[7] *AMA Drug Evaluations,* 2d ed., p. 298.
[8] *Physicians' Desk Reference,* 35th ed., p. 903.
[9] Id., p. 904.

Azolid is manufactured by USV Pharmaceutical Corporation (Tuckahoe, N.Y.), and Butazolidin by Geigy Pharmaceuticals (Ardsley, N.Y.).

Brown v. Geigy Pharmaceuticals (No. 68L 306, Circuit Court, Cook County, Ill., Nov., 1971).

Stevens-Johnson syndrome resulting in loss of sight—Manufacturer charged with delay in issuing warning—$500,000 settlement

A 53-year-old male patient was given Butazolidin by his physician for an arthritic condition. After two weeks, he developed a "Stevens-Johnson syndrome" reaction evidenced by blisters on his skin and a drying up of mucous membranes. The condition eventually affected the patient's eyes and he became totally blind. The patient retained an attorney who filed against the physician and the manufacturer of the drug.

According to the patient's attorney, his investigation in preparation for trial revealed that at the time the patient was placed on Butazolidin there were already cases reported in the medical journals of Stevens-Johnson syndrome being associated with the drug, and that some of these had resulted in loss of vision and others in death. The attorney reported that he was prepared to show that the manufacturer's medical librarian had access to these journals, and that therefore the company should have been aware of the dangers involved. He claimed additional information disclosed that at least six months before his client suffered the reaction to the drug, a product physician had recommended to the manufacturer that a warning about Stevens-Johnson syndrome should be included with the drug literature. This warning was issued, but not until two months after the patient suffered his loss of sight.

The attorney reported that the case was settled for $500,000, with the manufacturer contributing $495,000.[10]

Baldino v. Castagna (1982) 505 Pa. 239, 478 A.2d 807.

Aplastic anemia following twenty day treatment with drug—Physician negligent—Verdict for manufacturer upheld

The plaintiff took Butazolidin for twenty days (ten day prescription plus renewal by phone) for an "inflamed coccyx." Two weeks later she developed aplastic anemia, for which she has had to re-

---

[10] ATLA *News Letter* 15:71, 1972.

ceive blood transfusions (every two months) and male hormones. Her physicians give her a 20% chance of surviving the disease.

After a fifteen day trial, a jury found the plaintiff's physician negligent in prescribing the drug, or in failing to advise her to report any side effects to him, or in failing to comply with the prevailing medical standards for prescribing the drug (which would have included prior tests to determine a patient's propensity to develop blood dyscrasias). The jury did not find the manufacturer negligent, however, despite evidence introduced by the plaintiff that it encouraged physicians to prescribe the product in instances where it was not medically appropriate, and encouraged them to prescribe it without taking proper precautions. On review, the Superior Court disagreed. It found that the evidence introduced by the plaintiff, consisting of documents from the Ciba-Geigy Corporation files and testimony of practicing physicians, clearly showed that the manufacturer was guilty of negligently overpromoting the drug. The verdict in Ciba-Geigy's favor was reversed and the case was remanded for retrial on this issue.

The manufacturer appealed, and the Supreme Court of Pennsylvania reversed the Superior Court, reinstating the original judgment. It held that evidence consisting of: published warnings by Ciba-Geigy as to the use of the drug, contradictory testimony as to whether its detail men told the plaintiff's physician to ignore the warnings, and contradictory testimony as to whether new warnings regarding changes in prescribing information were effectively conveyed to physicians, was sufficient to support the jury's verdict that Ciba-Geigy was not negligent.

Boyer v. Smith (1985) 345 Pa. Super. 66, 497 A.2d 646.

Adverse reaction—Instruction on informed consent refused

The defendant orthopaedist prescribed a ten-day supply of Butazolidin (100 mg.) capsules for the plaintiff who was complaining of sciatic pain. He testified that he informed her that the drug could cause oral and gastrointestinal ulcers but did not inform her about the possibility of any other side effects. He did instruct her to have a complete blood count performed and told her to notify him if "any problems" arose.

After taking the medication for a week, the plaintiff suffered a severe adverse reaction. At trial she alleged lack of informed consent, but the judge refused to instruct the jury on this issue. The jury returned a verdict for the defendant and the Superior Court affirmed, holding that the doctrine of the law of informed consent as it is applied in Pennsylvania "should continue to be limited in its applicability to only those cases involving surgical or operative medical procedures."

Parks v. Maitland (No. 13807/85, Supreme Court, Bronx County, N.Y., Nov. 25, 1986).

Stevens-Johnson syndrome resulting in permanent disability—Failure to test, lack of warning and failure to monitor—$600,000 settlement

The plaintiff, age 52, sought treatment from the defendant physician for a swollen, discolored lower right leg. The defendant diagnosed superficial phlebitis and prescribed 200 mg. Butazolidin daily for two weeks. Without ordering any tests, and without warning the plaintiff of the drug's toxicity and side effects, the defendant renewed the prescription for another week. After she took the drug for eighteen days, the plaintiff suffered a severe reaction, resulting in Stevens-Johnson syndrome with significant permanent scarring over her body, blurred vision, and loss of 25% of her hair.

In her lawsuit, the plaintiff claimed the defendant failed to (1) do a necessary laboratory work-up before administering Butazolidin and before renewing the prescription; (2) warn her of the toxicity and potential side effects of the drug; and (3) monitor her while she was taking the drug. The parties settled for $600,000 prior to trial.[11]

Related cases

Bone marrow damage, anemia and other disorders—Action by Air Force Academy cadet against government

A former football player at the Air Force Academy had a cause of action under the Federal Tort Claims Act for bone marrow damage, chronic mononucleosis, chronic anemia and heartbeat irregularity allegedly caused by the side effects of Butazolidin with which he was treated for a knee injury during his junior and senior years. Fischer v. United States (E.D. N.Y., 1978) 451 F. Supp. 918.

---

[11] ATLA *Professional Negligence Law Reporter* 2:29, 1987.

Mental deterioration—Action by professional baseball player against club

A professional baseball player who claimed treatment with Butazolidin caused mental deterioration had no civil action for damages against his baseball club; his remedy, if any, being under the workmen's compensation act. Bayless v. Philadelphia Nat. League Club (C.A.-3 Pa., 1979) 615 F.2d 1352.

Stevens-Johnson syndrome—Jury verdict for physician upheld

In Boucheron v. Tilley (1982) 87 App. Div. 2d 983, 450 N.Y.S.2d 110, the reviewing court found no error in the trial court's exclusion from evidence of gratuitous opinions by physicians contained in the hospital record as to whether the plaintiff's Stevens-Johnson syndrome was caused by her ingestion of Butazolidin, nor in the exclusion from evidence of the manufacturer's package insert containing prescribing information for use by physicians.

Stevens-Johnson syndrome—Issue whether patient disclosed history of allergies—Verdict for physician affirmed

In Haynes v. Hoffman (1982) 164 Ga. App. 236, 296 S.E.2d 216, a verdict for the defendant orthopaedic surgeon was affirmed where the evidence supported the finding that the patient, who developed Stevens-Johnson syndrome after taking Butazolidin for two weeks for a painful wrist, did not disclose to the defendant that she had a history of allergies, including allergies to numerous medications.

PHENYLEPHRINE HYDROCHLORIDE
Neo-Synephrine

Phenylephrine hydrochloride is a vasoconstrictor and pressor (induces an elevation in the blood pressure) chemically related to epinephrine and ephedrine. Among its uses is maintenance of an adequate level of blood pressure during spinal and inhalation anesthesia and for the treatment of vascular failure in shock and drug-induced hypotension or hypersensitivity. It is also used as an ingredient in numerous over-the-counter cold remedies. For a complete list, consult the latest edition of *Physicians' Desk Reference*.

The injectable form (1% solution) of Neo-Synephrine is produced by Winthrop Laboratories (New York, N.Y.). Although it is advertised as a "well-tolerated" drug, the manufacturer warns that "physicians should completely familiarize themselves with the complete contents" of the package insert before prescribing the product. Caution is advised, particularly in the case of elderly patients and patients with hypertension and certain heart problems.[12]

Laurence v. Ambulatory Surgical Facility, Inc. (No. 82-418-CY, Circuit Court, Broward County, Fla., Jan. 11, 1983).

Use of Neo-Synephrine on patient under halothane anesthesia—Fatal cardiac arrhythmia—$700,000 settlement

A pediatrician who was surgically removing a foreign object from the nose of a three-year-old boy elected also to correct the patient's ankyloglossia (tongue-tie) during the same procedure. While the patient was still under general anesthesia (halothane), two drops of Neo-Synephrine were placed in each nostril. He immediately experienced cardiac irregularity. Cardiac massage was attempted, but not until after seven minutes. All attempts at resuscitation were unsuccessful and the boy died.

In the parents' suit against the pediatrician, anesthesiologist, nurse anesthetist and surgical facility, they alleged that the use of Neo-Synephrine was contraindicated in a patient under halothane general anesthesia, that the administration of Neo-Synephrine was excessive, and that the defendants employed inadequate resuscitation measures. The parties settled for $700,000, with the pediatrician, anesthesiologist and anesthetist each contributing $100,000, the surgical facility $50,000, and the state patients' compensation fund $350,000.[13]

Fabelo v. Mercy Hospital (No. 84-16463, Circuit Court, Dade County, Fla., July 29, 1985).

Excessive dose during surgery—Severe brain damage— $7.3 million settlement by hospital, $500,000 by surgeon, and $100,000 by anesthesiologist

During a tonsillectomy, two surgical nurses mistakenly injected an excessive dose of Neo-Synephrine into the plaintiff's tonsillar bed. The plaintiff underwent a severe hypotensive crisis and suffered brain damage. She is now in a semi-vegetative state and requires 24-hour nursing care.

Suit was brought on behalf of the plaintiff, a 33-year-old accountant, against the hospital for the nurses' negligence (they had used

---

[12] *Physicians' Desk Reference,* 35th ed., p. 1902.
[13] ATLA *Law Reporter* 26:229-30, 1983.

unmarked vials), against the surgeon for failing to check the drugs prior to the injection, and against the anesthesiologist for failing to recognize immediately that the plaintiff was suffering from a drug overdose. On the second day of trial the hospital settled for $7.3 million plus waiver of the plaintiff's $1.2 million hospital bill. The surgeon settled for $500,000 and the anesthesiologist, for $100,000.[14]

Related cases

Paralysis following renal arteriography—
Use of Neo-Synephrine questioned

In Medvecz v. Choi (C.A.-3 Pa., 1977) 569 F.2d 1221, a patient became paralyzed following a renal arteriogram as a result of the dye, sodium iothalamate, infiltrating the spinal canal. There was evidence that this may have been caused by an injection of Neo-Synephrine. The case is summarized herein under SODIUM IOTHALAMATE.

PHENYTOIN SODIUM
Dilantin

This drug was formerly called diphenylhydantoin sodium. It is an anti-convulsant used in the treatment of epilepsy. Dilantin is manufactured by Parke-Davis (Morris Plains, N.J.). The drug is also sold as phenytoin sodium by Elkins-Sinn, Inc. (Cherry Hill, N.J.) and other companies.

The product literature on Dilantin lists among adverse reactions various central nervous system disorders, skin disorders, hemopoietic complications, and conditions of the connective tissue system.[15]

There have also been reports of birth defects,[16] Stevens-Johnson syndrome, and toxic hepatitis leading to liver damage.[17]

---

[14] Id., 29:178, 1986.
[15] *Physicians' Desk Reference,* 40th ed., p. 1333.
[16] Id.
[17] *United States Dispensatory,* 27th ed., p. 1055.

Fritz v. Parke-Davis & Co. (1967) 277 Minn. 210, 152 N.W.2d 129, 30 A.L.R.3d 982.

Liver damage—Choice of drug questioned—Directed verdicts for physicians and manufacturer affirmed

Evidence in this lawsuit against three physicians and the manufacturer of Dilantin disclosed that on December 21, 1961, the patient, a twelve-year-old boy, was hospitalized for a severe form of epilepsy. To control his seizures, it was decided, on the advice of a consulting neurologist, that the patient be given one and one-half grains of Dilantin three times a day. The boy improved and was released from the hospital on December 30.

On January 13, 1962, the boy again became ill, this time with a high fever and rash over much of his body. On the basis of his symptoms and appropriate tests, his condition was diagnosed as measles. On January 31, he again became ill, and was brought to the defendant-physicians' office. On examination, he was "feverish," had a rash described as "morbilliform," was "jaundiced," and his "spleen and liver were enlarged and palpable." An allergic reaction to Dilantin was suspected, but tests suggested infectious mononucleosis. On being hospitalized, however, the Dilantin was discontinued to rule out the possibility of a reaction.

By February 6, the boy's condition had improved and he was again placed on Dilantin, at one-half the previous dosage. On February 16 he was discharged from the hospital, and the Dilantin was discontinued. The parents were told to have him return periodically to the office for observation.

The boy was seen again on February 26 and April 11, 1962. A year later, while in the care of other physicians, he died undergoing surgery of an undisclosed nature. Autopsy evidence revealed toxic damage to the liver, which brought on the lawsuit. At the trial, a pediatrician and neurologist testifying for the boy's parents offered the opinion that it was "highly probable" that the liver damage was the cause of death.

Further evidence revealed that there were at least five drugs on the market at the time, including Dilantin, which were commonly used by physicians to control epileptic seizures. It was established that all of these drugs could cause some allergic reactions in certain patients, but several of the medical witnesses, including the plaintiff's expert, were of the opinion that two of the other drugs, Luminal and Mysoline, were preferable to Dilantin because of a lesser risk of side effects. Other witnesses disagreed; a consulting neurologist testifying for the defense stated that he preferred Dilantin over the other drugs, and pointed out that it had demonstrated an ability to control certain types of epilepsy, and did in fact control the boy's seizures.

The trial court directed a verdict for the physicians and the drug company, and the Supreme Court of Minnesota affirmed, declaring:

> It is evident ... that the record is devoid of any evidence which would support a finding of negligence or breach of warranty in the manufacture and sale of [D]ilantin by defendant drug company. In medical malpractice actions of this type, a physician is not required to insure the successful outcome of his treatment, nor can he be held liable for honest mistakes of judgment where reasonable doubts and uncertainties as to the proper course of treatment exist. Liability rests upon proof of negligence judged by the standard of whether or not the physician brought and applied to the case at hand that degree of skill, care, knowledge, and attention ordinarily possessed and exercised by other physicians under like circumstances in the same or similar locality. Measured by this standard, the evidence in this case falls woefully short of establishing any negligence on the part of defendant physicians. They were clearly not negligent in their initial use of [D]ilantin, for a physician may properly adopt a method of treatment approved by a considerable number of other physicians in good standing in his community.

The court went on to say that it was:

> ... undisputed that [D]ilantin was in widespread use by physicians for controlling epileptic seizures in this state and elsewhere. Whether defendant physicians were negligent in continuing to use [D]ilantin is a technical medical question requiring expert testimony. Opinion evidence that it was highly probable that some toxic element contributed to cause William's death is not sufficient to establish such negligence. The only other evidence was the opinion expressed by the medical specialist called by plaintiffs that, based on one of defendant physician's testimony and the medical records, William manifested an allergic reaction to [D]ilantin. He was neither asked to give nor did his testimony reasonably imply an opinion that William's illness or death was caused by any failure to conform to the requisite skill and care required by defendant physicians. Defendants' expert testimony that the care and treatment by defendant physicians did conform stands uncontradicted. Viewing the record most favorably to plaintiffs, the evidence, both opinion and factual, requires the conclusion that the skill and care exhibited by defendant physicians' diagnosis and treatment of William's epilepsy were marked by devoted diligence and attention and were wholly

consistent with the professional skill and care ordinarily employed by other physicians in treating and controlling the effects of the complex disease of epilepsy.

Morris v. Children's Hosp. (U.S. District Court, D.C., April 18, 1973).

Stevens-Johnson syndrome—Loss of sight—$900,000 verdict set aside

A fourteen-year-old girl being treated with Dilantin for seizures developed Stevens-Johnson syndrome and became blind. In the resulting malpractice suit, the physician and hospital involved denied that the condition was caused by the Dilantin, claiming that other drugs had been administered to the girl, and that she had been suffering from several other conditions, including a virus infection.

A jury returned a verdict of $900,000 for the girl. This was set aside, however, and a new trial was ordered by the presiding judge because of a reference by the plaintiff's attorney to the hospital's insurance coverage.[18]

Mooney v. Parke-Davis & Co. (No. 77-355-NPZ, Circuit Court, Berrien County, Mich., Dec. 12, 1979).

Stevens-Johnson syndrome and blindness following sixteen days of treatment—$2.4 million verdict reported

When he was four years old, the patient was given Dilantin for sixteen days after tests indicated that he had epilepsy. Shortly thereafter he developed Stevens-Johnson syndrome which began as a rash and eventually caused scarring and blindness. Because the physician mistook the rash for measles, treatment was delayed.

The patient brought suit against the manufacturer of the drug when he was age sixteen and alleged that the defendant had failed to warn physicians to discontinue use if a rash develops when it was administered.

According to the attorney for the patient, he obtained a jury verdict of $2.4 million.[19]

---

[18] AMA *The Citation* 27:165, 1973.
[19] ATLA *Law Reporter* 23:86, 1980.

Harbeson v. Parke-Davis, Inc. (1983) 98 Wash. 2d 460, 656 P.2d 483.

Parents insufficiently warned of risk of birth defects from Dilantin have "wrongful birth" action against government—Children have "wrongful life" actions

A young airman's wife being treated with Dilantin for epilepsy inquired of Air Force physicians about the risk of birth defects in her children if she became pregnant. She was told that Dilantin could cause "a cleft palate and temporary hirsutism." She became pregnant and two of her children were born with "fetal hydantoin syndrome," from which they suffer growth deficiencies, developmental retardation, wide-set eyes, "drooping" eyelids, low-set hairline, broad nasal ridge, and other physical and developmental defects. On deposition the physicians admitted they did not check the medical journals for the possibility of reports of such Dilantin-related birth defects before advising the plaintiff.

The Supreme Court of Washington held that the parents had a cause of action against the government for "wrongful birth," and the children causes of action for "wrongful life." The ruling was made in response to questions of law certified to the Court by the United States District Court for the Western District of Washington which was hearing the plaintiff's case against the manufacturer and the government.

Harbeson v. Parke Davis, Inc. (C.A.-9 Wash., 1984) 746 F.2d 517.

Birth defects—Government liable for Air Force physician's failure to warn of risks

The plaintiffs in Harbeson v. Parke Davis, Inc. (1983) 98 Wash. 2d 460, 656 P.2d 483 (see above), proceeded against the manufacturer and the government in the United States District Court for the Western District of Washington. A jury heard the case against the manufacturer and found for the defendant, i.e., that the plaintiffs failed to prove that the Dilantin caused the child's birth defects. The court, however, found in favor of the plaintiffs against the government, holding that the Air Force physicians were negligent in failing to warn the plaintiffs of the risk of birth defects in children born of women taking Dilantin during pregnancy. The Court of Appeal allowed the judgment against the government to stand when attorneys failed to raise the jury verdict in the lower court as an affirmative defense.

Alboher v. Parke-Davis (No. 80 Civ. 0046, U.S. District Court, E.D. N.Y., Dec. 29, 1983).

Birth defects—Manufacturer charged with failure to warn and misrepresentation of drug's effectiveness—$7 million jury verdict

The plaintiff's mother was given Dilantin in 1970 for control of a non-convulsive Parkinson-type disorder. She became pregnant two months after going on the drug and continued to take it during her first trimester before discontinuing it at her obstetrician's suggestion. The plaintiff was born without eyes.

In the action against Parke-Davis, it was alleged that as early as 1964 the defendant was aware that Dilantin could cause birth defects, yet did not warn the medical profession or the public. The plaintiff also charged that although in August 1970, prior to the date the plaintiff's mother began taking the drug, Parke-Davis was informed that the drug was ineffective in the treatment of disorders such as that suffered by the plaintiff's mother, yet the company continued to market the product for that purpose.

A jury awarded the plaintiff $7 million.[20]

Peterson v. Parke-Davis & Company (Colo., 1985) 705 P.2d 1001.

Brain damage from excessive dosage—Manufacturer not liable on evidence of psychiatrist's misuse of product

The patient, a seventeen-year-old boy, was treated with Dilantin for epilepsy. His physician, a psychiatrist, prescribed the drug without referring to the dosage recommendations on the package insert or in *Physicians' Desk Reference.* The dosage was excessive and the boy suffered brain damage.

The psychiatrist settled with the plaintiff for an unreported amount as did the hospital where the treatment occurred. In a suit against the manufacturer, the plaintiff alleged that the company did not adequately warn of the possibility of permanent neurological damage from Dilantin toxicity as a result of excessive dosage. The manufacturer claimed "misuse of the product" as a defense and

[20] ATLA *Products Liability Law Reporter* 3:21, 1984.

also argued that its warning did state that if toxic effects occurred, the dosage should be reduced or discontinued.

The jury found for the manufacturer and the verdict was upheld on appeal.

Hendricks v. Charity Hosp. of New Orleans (La. App., 1987) 519 So. 2d 163.

Excessive dosage—Skin reaction and possible central nervous system injury—$130,000 judgment against physician

The plaintiff's physician, an employee of the state Department of Health and Human Resources, wrote the plaintiff a prescription for 500 mg. of Dilantin to be taken "every eight hours." He had intended to write "500 mg. daily." When the plaintiff presented the prescription to the pharmacist, an employee of the City of New Orleans, she sent the plaintiff back to the physician with a comment that he had prescribed enough Dilantin "to kill a horse." The physician, however, merely checked the plaintiff's medical record on which he had written that he had prescribed Dilantin "500 mg. daily," and he told the plaintiff the prescription was correct.

When the plaintiff returned to the pharmacy, the pharmacist tried to reach the physician by phone but was unsuccessful. The plaintiff, thinking the prescription was correct, became angry and insisted that the pharmacist fill it. The pharmacist reluctantly did so, but added a note on the label that "Patient should consult Physician about dosage." The plaintiff took the Dilantin as directed and suffered a severe skin reaction and possible central nervous system injury.

The case was tried before the judge who found the physician negligent and awarded the plaintiff $30,000 in special damages and $100,000 in general. The Louisiana Court of Appeal affirmed.

Shinn v. St. James Mercy Hosp. (W.D. N.Y., 1987) 675 F. Supp. 94, aff'd (C.A.-2 N.Y., 1988) 847 F.2d 836.

Stevens-Johnson syndrome—$625,000 jury verdict on informed consent issue set aside

The plaintiff was admitted to the hospital for recurrent seizures. His attending physician prescribed Dilantin and phenobarbital, but the drugs did not prove effective. Shortly after his second week of hospitalization, the plaintiff was diagnosed as suffering from Stevens-Johnson syndrome, which was attributed to the treatment.

A jury returned a verdict in the plaintiff's favor in the amount of $625,000 on a finding that the physician did not obtain his informed consent to the method of treatment selected. The physician testified that he did inform the plaintiff of the risks involved, including the possibility of Stevens-Johnson syndrome. The plaintiff denied this.

Following the verdict, the physician's attorney moved the trial court for a judgment n.o.v. The court granted it, holding that while the physician may not have informed the plaintiff of the risk of Stevens-Johnson syndrome in being treated with Dilantin and phenobarbital, the evidence led to the "inescapable conclusion" that, because of the plaintiff's serious condition when admitted to the hospital, a reasonably prudent person in the plaintiff's position would have elected to proceed with the treatment even if he had been informed of the risk of Stevens-Johnson syndrome. The Court of Appeals affirmed the lower court's holding without an opinion.

Related cases

Overdose—Damages for temporary pain and suffering only—Defense expert qualified to give opinion

In McCrory v. State (1981) 67 Ohio St. 2d 99, 423 N.E.2d 156, where damages were allowed in a Dilantin overdose case only for temporary pain and suffering, and nothing was allowed for permanent brain damage, the Supreme Court of Ohio held that the trial court did not abuse its discretion in permitting a defense expert to testify on the damage issue over the plaintiff's objection that over 85% of his time was devoted to work with a drug manufacturer and not in active clinical practice.

Whether discontinuing seizure patient's medication was negligence was for jury to determine

In Howard v. Piver (1981) 53 N.C. 46, 279 S.E.2d 876, the trial court erred in directing a verdict for physician who discontinued a patient's anti-seizure medication (Dilantin) to perform tests. The patient suffered six grand mal seizures, resulting in the breaking of both shoulders.

Birth defects—Canada proper forum

An action in a New York federal district court on behalf of an infant who allegedly suffered birth defects as a result of his mother taking Dilantin during pregnancy was subject to dismissal on grounds of forum non conveniens where the plaintiff's mother was a citizen and resident of Canada, where the majority of the evidence relating to causation and damages was located in Canada, and where public interest warranted litigating the case in Canada, notwithstanding that the plaintiff's potential award might be smaller there and that the litigation there might be more expensive and difficult. Ledingham v. Parke-Davis Division of Warner-Lambert Co. (E.D. N.Y., 1986) 628 F. Supp. 1447.

PHOSPHOLINE IODIDE

See ECHOTHIOPHATE IODIDE

PIROXICAM

Feldene

Piroxicam is an anti-inflammatory, analgesic, and antipyretic agent recommended for acute and long-term use in the relief of the signs and symptoms of osteoarthritis and rheumatoid arthritis. It is manufactured and marketed under the brand name Feldene by Pfizer, Inc. (New York, N.Y.).[1]

The manufacturer cautions that the drug should not be used in patients who have previously exhibited hypersensitivity to it, or in individuals with "the syndrome comprised of bronchospasm, nasal polyps, and angioedema precipitated by aspirin or other nonsteroidal anti-inflammatory drugs." Also, physicians are warned that peptic ulceration, perforation, and gastrointestinal bleeding, sometimes fatal, have been reported following use of the drug, and that patients with a history of upper gastrointestinal tract disease should be kept under close supervision.[2]

Leesley v. West (1988) 165 Ill. App. 3d 135, 116 Ill. Dec. 136, 518 N.E.2d 758.

Gastrointestinal hemorrhage—No duty on part of manufacturer or pharmacy to warn consumer

The plaintiff suffered severe gastrointestinal hemorrhage after taking Feldene. In his lawsuit against his physician, the manufacturer, and the pharmacy from which he purchased the drug, the plaintiff claimed that the manufacturer and the pharmacy were

---

[1] *Physicians' Desk Reference,* 42d ed., pp. 1614-15.

[2] Id.

negligent in not warning him of the risk of the side effect in question. The plaintiff did not, however, allege that the manufacturer failed to warn the medical community regarding such risk.

Included in the plaintiff's complaint were claims that the manufacturer and pharmacy were strictly liable because the product was "unreasonably dangerous," and a claim against the manufacturer for breach of an implied warranty of fitness.

The manufacturer and the pharmacy moved for summary judgment on all counts on grounds that they have no duty to warn a consumer of the potential hazards of a prescription drug. The trial court denied the motions except as to the claim for breach of implied warranty.

On appeal, the Appellate Court of Illinois reversed, holding that the trial court should have granted the defendants' motions for summary judgment on all counts. (The plaintiff's physician was not involved in the appeal.) The manufacturer, said the court, had no duty other than to warn the prescribing physician of the drug's hazards, and the pharmacy did not have an independent duty to warn a consumer of such dangers.

PITOCIN

See OXYTOCIN

PLACIDYL

See ETHCHLORVYNOL

PLEGINE

See PHENDIMETRAZINE TARTRATE

PMB 200/400

See ESTROGENS (CONJUGATED); MEPROBAMATE

PODOPHYLLUM RESIN

Podophyllum resin is obtained from the dried roots of the *Podophyllum peltatum,* an indigenous perennial herb, and is used both as a laxative and, more recently, as a topical agent for the treatment of certain warts, particularly venereal and plantar warts.[3] For topical application to venereal warts (condylomata

[3] *United States Dispensatory,* 27th ed., p. 930.

acuminata), podophyllum resin should be used in 25% concentration in compound benzoin tincture applied at weekly intervals.[4]

Occasional hypersensitivity to podophyllum resin is encountered and a reaction sometimes occurs, apparently as a result of liquefaction and separation of the base of the wart.[5] At least one death of a woman patient has been reported after application of an ointment containing 25% podophyllum resin to a large venereal wart of the vulva.[6]

Bowden v. Adami (No. 653125, Superior Court, San Francisco County, Cal., Nov. 6, 1974).

Patient suffered burns on penis after self-application for venereal warts—Verdict for physician

A 29-year-old patient sought treatment from the defendant-physician for venereal warts. He made several office visits and the physician applied podophyllum resin (brand name not given), but the warts recurred. He then gave the patient the drug (or prescribed it) for use at home. After several applications the patient suffered burns on his penis which, on healing, left a scar which the patient claimed was painful during erection and sexual intercourse.

In the resulting malpractice suit, a dermatologist supported the patient's claim for injuries. The patient testified that the defendant did not give him adequate instructions on how often to apply the drug nor information on the risks in using it. The defendant testified that he violated no standards of medical practice in issuing the drug for home use and that he informed the patient adequately with regard to application. He said he specifically told the patient not to apply the drug more than "once a week" and that "excessive use" could cause "extreme irritation and skin erosion." Testifying also for the defendant was a dermatologist who stated that in his opinion the patient's scar was so small that he could see no reason why he could not engage in normal sexual intercourse.

The jury returned a verdict for the physician.[7]

---

[4] *The Merck Manual of Diagnosis and Therapy,* 12th ed. (Rahway, N.J.: Merck Sharp & Dohme Research Laboratories, 1972), p. 1437.

[5] Id.

[6] *United States Dispensatory,* 27th ed., p. 930.

[7] AMA *The Citation* 30:141, 1975.

Phelps v. Blomberg Roseville Clinic (Minn., 1977) 253 N.W.2d 390.

Cancer of the penis following prolonged treatment—$79,500 verdict against clinic

During the summer of 1971 the plaintiff noticed some small growths on his penis. He was seen at the defendant-clinic and then referred to a dermatologist. The dermatologist took a biopsy of one of the growths and it was found to be a nonmalignant seborrheic keratosis. The dermatologist treated the lesions with a 20% solution of podophyllin on six occasions between August 18, 1971 and November 10, 1971.

When the plaintiff noticed no improvement he returned to the defendant-clinic on December 30. Treatment was resumed there and the plaintiff made periodic visits until June, 1973. After complaining of the time lost in visiting the clinic, the plaintiff was given a supply of podophyllin and some Q-tips and instructed on how to treat himself. He was told that "if the treatments were not successful" he should return to the clinic. The physician wrote on the plaintiff's chart "Recheck in one month."

The plaintiff did not return and continued to treat himself until the following March when he noticed a "dark brown spot" at the site of one of the lesions. A biopsy then revealed squamous cell carcinoma. A partial penectomy was performed and 100 lymph nodes were removed from the plaintiff's abdomen.

In a lawsuit against the clinic physicians, an expert testifying for the plaintiff commented that podophyllum resin might be carcinogenic.

A jury returned a verdict of $79,500 for the plaintiff, finding under Minnesota's comparative negligence law that the plaintiff was 25% negligent in not returning to the clinic sooner. The verdict was affirmed on appeal.

POLIOMYELITIS VACCINE

See POLIOVIRUS VACCINE

POLIOVIRUS VACCINE

Orimune

Immunization against poliomyelitis may be accomplished by either a vaccine of inactivated polio virus (administered by injection) or a vaccine of attenuated live virus (administered orally). The former is commonly called Salk vaccine and the latter Sabin, after the investigators chiefly responsible for their development.[8]

Dr. Jonas Salk reported active immunization of humans against poliomyelitis early in 1953, using a formaldehyde-inactivated vaccine preparation containing the three known strains of polio virus grown in cultures of monkey kidneys. The vaccine was soon put to wide use and contributed greatly to the decline of the disease. The oral Sabin vaccine has become preferred, however, because in contrast to the Salk vaccine it inhibits viral multiplication in the intestinal tract and appears to achieve longer-lasting immunity. Also, the oral dose is easier to administer, and requires no boosters, as did the Salk vaccine.

A problem has been encountered with the live oral vaccine, however. Poliomyelitis following ingestion of the vaccine has been reported, and in some instances, in persons who were in close contact with subjects who had been given the vaccine. Fortunately, these occurrences are rare; a total of only approximately thirty cases were reported for the eight-year period covering 1963 to 1970, during which time about 147 million doses of the vaccine were distributed nationwide.[9] From 1969 through 1980, approximately 290 million doses were distributed in the United States, during which time 25 "vaccine-associated" and 55 "contact vaccine-associated" paralytic cases were reported.[10]

Gottsdanker v. Cutter Laboratories (1960) 182 Cal. App. 2d 602, 6 Cal. Rptr. 320, 79 A.L.R.2d 290.

Poliomyelitis after vaccination by injection—Manufacturer liable on theory of implied warranty

Two children contracted poliomyelitis shortly after being given Salk poliovirus vaccine manufactured by Cutter Laboratories. Suit was brought on behalf of both children, and the actions were consolidated for trial. The evidence disclosed that the vaccine was purchased by a physician from a pharmacy in a sealed ampule. In one case the hypodermic injection of the vaccine was made by a physician, in the other by a nurse under a physician's direction. There

[8] *United States Dispensatory,* 27th ed., p. 931.

[9] *Physicians' Desk Reference,* 29th ed., p. 888.

[10] Id., 40th ed., p. 1023. See also Nikowane, et el., "Vaccine-Associated Paralytic Poliomyelitis: United States 1973 through 1984," *Journal of the American Medical Association* 257:1335, 1987.

was substantial evidence presented that the vaccine contained live virus of poliomyelitis, and that the injected vaccine caused the disease in each child.

The jury returned verdicts in favor of the plaintiffs, and the trial court entered judgments accordingly. The company appealed. The Court of Appeals affirmed the judgments, stating:

> In view of the established California rule that the consumer of a food product may recover from the manufacturer upon implied warranty, is there any reason to apply a different rule to the vaccine here involved? We think not. The vaccine is intended for human consumption quite as much as is food. We see no reason to differentiate the policy considerations requiring pure and wholesome food from those requiring pure and wholesome vaccine.... We can conceive of no reason for applying the rule to foodstuffs which does not equally extend to drugs. The vaccine here involved is, like food products, designed solely for introduction into the body of a human being. The fact that the entry is made by injection rather than ingestion in no way alters the premise that each is for human consumption — each enters the human system. In fact, the digestive system has means of rejecting or minimizing the effects of many toxic compounds taken orally. Such defenses are much less available as against harmful elements introduced into the system by hypodermic injection.

Berry v. American Cyanamid Co. (C.A.-6 Tenn., 1965) 341 F.2d 14.

Poliomyelitis after taking oral vaccine—Judgment for manufacturer on privity issue affirmed

The plaintiff contracted paralytic poliomyelitis about eight days after taking the Sabin oral polio vaccine Orimune. The plaintiff brought suit against the manufacturer, pleading breach of implied warranty, and alleging that the physician who administered the vaccine was but a "conduit" through which the manufacturer caused its product to reach the ultimate consumer. He alleged that the company consented and created privity by placing its product in the "stream of trade and commerce" knowing that it could only reach the ultimate consumer through a physician.

The trial court decided in favor of the company, and the plaintiff appealed. The United States Court of Appeals for the Sixth Circuit affirmed the trial court, declaring:

> We must reject the argument that there was privity of contract between the plaintiff and Lederle. Privity of contract, as we understand it, is the relationship which subsists between two con-

tracting parties. Clearly here, under the pleading, the plaintiff had no relationship with Lederle. He did not purchase the drug from Lederle. His only contact in the transaction was with his physician. The physician was not an agent of Lederle either in fact or by implication of law.... If the plaintiff's case is to be maintained on the theory of implied warranty, it must be upon the basis that Tennessee has joined those states that have abandoned the common law requirement of privity in products liability cases.... [P]rivity of contract between vendor and vendee is still a requirement in an action [suit] upon an express or implied contract in Tennessee.... We conclude that Tennessee has not abolished the requirement of privity under the facts of this case and that there was not privity of contract herein between plaintiff and Lederle.

Davis v. Wyeth Laboratories, Inc. (C.A.-9 Idaho, 1968) 399 F.2d 121.

Poliomyelitis after taking oral vaccine—Manufacturer should have warned public directly of risk—Strict liability applicable

The plaintiff took Sabin Type III oral polio vaccine at a mass immunization clinic conducted in West Yellowstone, Montana in March, 1963. Within thirty days he developed symptoms of poliomyelitis, and became paralyzed from the waist down. Suit was brought against the manufacturer, Wyeth Laboratories.

At the trial, extensive evidence was presented on the background of the development of the Sabin oral vaccine and the program leading to the immunization clinic where the plaintiff received his dose.

The use of a live virus polio vaccine (as opposed to immunization by the injection of a dead virus) that could be taken orally had been under study for a number of years. Finally, after worldwide clinical testing on between 700,000 to 1,000,000 people, it was determined in the early 1960's that the Sabin vaccine should be licensed for distribution in the United States. Three companies were licensed to manufacture the vaccine; the defendant, Wyeth Laboratories, received its license effective May 17, 1962.

The vaccine was licensed for sale as a prescription drug. It was usually manufactured in what were called "lots," each lot being prepared under extremely rigid standards devised by the Division of Biologic Standards of the National Institutes of Health. The virus used in the vaccine, regardless of the manufacturer, came from a common source. It was obtained from Dr. Sabin, the originator, from a so-called "seed virus," which was the parent of each separate lot of vaccine manufactured.

At the manufacturer's laboratory, the lot involved in the present case was run through a number of tests, as was customary, and then shipped to the Division of Biologic Standards for more tests. The Division was satisfied with the results, and the lot was released on January 31, 1963.

Earlier, in the fall of 1960, an advisory committee was established by the Surgeon General of the United States to review all phases of polio prevention. In February, 1962, the Communicable Disease Center of the U. S. Public Health Service issued recommendations of this committee. Included was a recommendation that community mass immunization clinics be established in various locations across the nation. The following month the Surgeon General issued specific recommendations for the use of oral vaccine during 1962 at these clinics.

That month, March of 1962, representatives of the Public Health Service held a meeting with Idaho public health officials and medical association officers at which a joint release was issued recommending the holding of community clinics in the area. This was later officially authorized by the Idaho Falls Medical Society which selected the defendant company's product as the vaccine to be administered. At a subsequent meeting it was decided to include West Yellowstone, Montana in the Eastern Idaho program since there were no physicians there and the residents relied on medical facilities in Ashton, Idaho. In the absence of a physician, the administration of the vaccine for the West Yellowstone clinic was delegated to a pharmacist.

The clinics in Eastern Idaho were originally scheduled for the fall of 1962. On September 14, 1962 a statement was issued by the Association of State and Territorial Health Officers through the subcommittee on epidemic intelligence of its committee on infectious diseases. It said:

> The Sub-committee ... has reviewed data showing a temporal association between the incidence of paralytic poliomyelitis and the administration of Type 3 [III] oral poliomyelitis vaccine. The Sub-committee believes that the data indicate a causal relationship and show that a small but definite risk attends the use of presently available Type 3 [III] oral polio vaccines. The data further suggest that the risk is almost exclusively limited to adult populations. While the Sub-committee acknowledges the presence of a small risk, it recognizes the tremendous value of oral poliomyelitis vaccines and the detrimental effect the unqualified withdrawal at this time would have on their future use. In view

of the very small magnitude of the risk and the enormous potential value of oral vaccines, the Sub-committee therefore recommends that the Surgeon General issue a statement which will:

1. Apprise the public of the nature of the risk.
2. Recommend that the non-epidemic use of Type 3 [III] oral vaccine be restricted to preschool and school age children.
3. Recommend that the vaccine continue to be available for epidemic use.
4. Reaffirm the desirability of restricting mass application to the late Fall, Winter and Spring.

The following day a statement was issued by the Surgeon General respecting his own special advisory committee's review of polio cases associated with the administration of the vaccine. It stated:

> The level of this risk can only be approximated but clearly is within range of less than 1 case per million doses. Since the cases have been concentrated among adults the risk to this group is greater; whereas, the risk to children is exceedingly slight or practically nonexistent.
>
> The Committee therefore recommends that the use of Type III vaccine in mass campaigns be limited to preschool and school age children. Plans for mass programs using Type I and II vaccines in all age groups should continue. Furthermore, Type III vaccine is still indicated for use among adults in high risk groups, which include tourists to hyperendemic areas and persons residing in epidemic areas.
>
> A special report is being prepared and will be sent to the members of the medical and public health profession within the next few days and will be made public.

The special report followed on September 21, 1962. It stated: "Present data indicate that for 1962, the paralytic poliomyelitis rate for those under 20 will be approximately 7.6 per million; for those over 20, about 0.9 per million. These rates will represent a record low for the 52-year period since the reporting began."

The special report reiterated the recommendation earlier made in the Surgeon General's statement:

> With the incidence of poliomyelitis at a low level in this country, the Committee therefore recommended that the Type III vaccine be restricted to preschool and school age children and to those adults in high risk groups, such as those traveling to hyperendemic areas or in areas where a Type III epidemic is present or impending. Since the vast majority of poliomyelitis cases occur among young children and since children are the principal disseminators of the virus, continued intensive immunization programs among this group are clearly indicated. If this

> group can be adequately immunized, the spread of the poliomyelitis viruses will be sharply restricted, if not essentially eradicated.

In December of 1962 a further report was issued. It stated:

> It is therefore recommended: (1) that community plans for immunization be encouraged, using all three types; and (2) that immunization be emphasized for children in whom the danger of naturally occurring poliomyelitis is greatest and who serve as the natural source of poliomyelitis infection in the community. Because the need for immunization diminishes with advancing age and because potential risks of vaccine are believed by some to exist in adults, especially above the age of 30, vaccination should be used for adults only with the full recognition of its very small risk. Vaccination is especially recommended for those adults who are at higher risk of naturally occurring disease; for example, parents of young children, pregnant women, persons in epidemic situations and those planning foreign travel. Of greatest importance is the continuing vaccination of oncoming generations.

With these recommendations before them the East Idaho officials postponed their clinics scheduled for the fall of 1962, but determined to proceed in the spring of 1963. Adults were included in their immunization program.

When Eastern Idaho chose the defendant-company's vaccine for its clinics, one of the company's salesmen was assigned to handle the sales and assist in establishing the clinics. He furnished books to those in charge of clinics, setting forth schedules and procedures to be followed and details of the physical manner in which the clinics were to be established and also showing sample promotional letters and advertising matter. He arranged for delivery of the vaccine from headquarters at Idaho Falls to the various clinics, including that at West Yellowstone. He arranged for the printing of forms and immunization cards and posters urging "KO Polio" and took charge of sending them to West Yellowstone. He organized meetings and conferred with those in charge of the separate clinics as to the procedures to be followed.

Each person who received the vaccine was charged 25¢ (although it was given free of charge if the recipient so requested). Funds collected from the clinics were used to pay the medical society's bill from the drug company for the vaccine, with the remainder retained by the society.

The vaccine when sold to the medical society had a printed insert with each bottle of 100 doses. This insert contained directions for use and pertinent excerpts from the Surgeon General's report. But apparently a fact sheet put out by the company and contained in the book it supplied to clinics was published prior to the Surgeon General's report, and represented the vaccine as completely safe for all ages. A collection of news clippings from Idaho newspapers introduced in evidence by the plaintiff showed not only a complete lack of warning but assurances that the vaccine was safe for all.

Evidence at the trial suggested also that no effort was made by the company's salesman or the medical society to inform the West Yellowstone pharmacist of the possible risk. The latter did not read the package insert, nor did the plaintiff. The advertising posters made no disclosure of risk and none was made directly to those who took the drug in West Yellowstone. The plaintiff testified that he had no knowledge of the risk, relied on the posters and was convinced by the campaign's advertising that it was his civic duty to participate.

The jury returned a verdict that the company was not negligent, and the District Court entered judgment accordingly. The plaintiff appealed, contending that it was error on the part of the District Court to fail to instruct the jury that the company was "strictly liable" if its vaccine caused him to contract polio and if his taking of the vaccine was without knowledge of risk. The plaintiff's contention was upheld by the United States Court of Appeals for the Ninth Circuit, which reversed the judgment of the District Court and remanded the case for a new trial.

The United States Court of Appeals, in a very lengthy opinion, stated among other things:

> We conclude that the facts of this case imposed on the manufacturer a duty to warn the consumer (or make adequate provision for his being warned) as to the risks involved, and that failure to meet this duty rendered the drug unfit in the sense that it was thereby rendered unreasonably dangerous. Strict liability, then, attached to its sale in absence of warning. Appellee [the manufacturer] contends that its duty to warn was met by [its salesman's] disclosures to the medical society. It points out that its only direct sale of vaccine was to the medical society and that it was the society's judgment and not appellee's to proceed with the clinics. Ordinarily in the case of prescription drugs warning to the prescribing physician is sufficient. In such cases the choice involved is essentially a medical one involving an assessment of medical risks in the light of the physician's knowledge of his patient's needs and susceptibilities. Further, it is difficult under such circumstances for the manufacturer, by label or direct communication, to reach the consumer with a warning. A warning to the

medical profession is in such cases the only effective means by which a warning could help the patient. Here, however, although the drug was denominated a prescription drug it was not dispensed as such. It was dispensed to all comers at mass clinics without an individualized balancing by a physician of the risks involved. In such cases (as in the case of over-the-counter sales of nonprescription drugs) warning by the manufacturer to its immediate purchaser will not suffice. The decision (that on balance and in the public interest the personal risk to the individual was worth taking) may well have been that of the medical society and not that of appellee. But just as the responsibility for choice is not one that the manufacturer can assume for all comers, neither is it one that he can allow his immediate purchaser to assume. In such cases, then, it is the responsibility of the manufacturer to see that warnings reach the consumer, either by giving warning itself or by obligating the purchaser to give warning. Here appellee knew that warnings were not reaching the consumer. Appellee had taken an active part in setting up the mass immunization clinic program for the society and well knew that the program did not make any such provision, either in advertising prior to the clinics or at the clinics themselves. On the contrary, it attempted to assure all members of the community that they should take the vaccine. We conclude that appellee did not meet its duty to warn. This duty does not impose an unreasonable burden on the manufacturer. When drugs are sold over the counter to all comers warnings normally can be given by proper labeling. Such method of giving warning was not available here, since the vaccine came in bottles never seen by the consumer. But other means of communication such as advertisements, posters, releases to be read and signed by recipients of the vaccine, or oral warnings were clearly available and could easily have been undertaken or prescribed by appellee.

Grinnell v. Charles Pfizer & Co. (1969) 274 Cal. App. 2d 424, 79 Cal. Rptr. 369.

Poliomyelitis after taking oral vaccine—Claims based on strict liability and express warranty—Vaccine ruled defective—$60,000 and $80,000 judgments affirmed

In May 1962 six San Francisco Bay area medical societies joined together to coordinate and publicize an area-wide polio immunization program. The date set for the campaign was September 23, and news releases began in late July. Vaccine manufacturers were invited to submit quotes, and the defendant-company was selected.

The plaintiff Grinnell and another, Bendetti, both adults, received the oral vaccine on the 23rd. Shortly thereafter both came down with poliomyelitis. In an action against the manufacturer, evidence was introduced showing that oral poliovirus vaccine, if produced properly, is free of virulent particles, i.e., all particles are attenuated or nonvirulent. The evidence showed further that in 1962 a special advisory committee was appointed by the Surgeon General of the United States to investigate several earlier cases of polio occurring after oral vaccination. The Chief of the Epidemiology Branch of the United States Communicable Disease Center, who had been a member of this committee, testified that in his opinion some recent cases had been induced by the vaccine, but the committee had concluded, and he was in agreement, that it was impossible to prove by any test that a particular case of polio was the result of the vaccine.

On the other hand, evidence was introduced that the plaintiffs in the present case were in a group considered "compatible" with the possibility of vaccine-induced disease. The subject of "compatibility" was widely discussed and variously defined by the numerous medical experts appearing at the trial. By one definition, if a case was compatible, the possibility of causation by the vaccine "could not be ruled out." Cases were judged compatible when three criteria were met: (1) the disease must occur from four to thirty days after ingestion of the vaccine; (2) the disease must be clinically consistent with paralytic polio; and (3) the laboratory findings must not exclude the possibility of a vaccine relationship. The plaintiffs' cases of polio met the criteria. In laboratory tests conducted by the federal agencies, stool and blood samples from both plaintiffs were found to contain Type I polio virus, ruling out infection by Types II and III. (The plaintiffs had been given Type I vaccine.) Also, the strains recovered from the plaintiffs indicated the infections were "recent" and "vaccine-like." None of the tests showed the presence of a "wild" virus strain of polio.

In addition, testimony was elicited from the physicians who had attended the plaintiffs. Grinnell's doctor testified that in his "own considered opinion" his patient's disease was "related to the oral polio vaccine which he ingested." Bendetti's physician testified that in terms of "reasonable probability" the polio contracted by his patient also was caused by the vaccine.

Introduced next was the package insert distributed by the manufacturer which quoted a February, 1962 report of the Surgeon General's advisory committee which indicated that, in light of knowledge at that time, there were "no known contraindications to oral polio virus vaccines." The manufacturer had distributed information containing this quote to over 200,000 physicians throughout the country, pointing out that the company was a "prime supplier" of polio vaccines and would continue "to keep the practicing physician well informed of new developments in this crucial area." It was revealed, however, that before the date of the San Francisco immunization the Surgeon General had issued new information indicating a possible risk of oral vaccine-induced polio to adults, particularly those over thirty years of age. Apparently the company did not change its package insert to reflect this revised information until after the San Francisco immunization.

At the close of the lengthy trial, the jury returned verdicts for the plaintiffs ($60,000 and $80,000), and the company appealed. The Court of Appeals of California affirmed, declaring:

> [W]e conclude that there was substantial circumstantial evidence from which the jury could infer that defendant's oral polio vaccine was the cause of the polio suffered by plaintiffs. They were also entitled to infer from the evidence that if the vaccine caused the polio, it was defective.... [T]he jury was entitled to reasonably infer that the material issued by defendant was not accurate when it excluded all possible contraindications. Moreover, since the jury was entitled ... to infer that the vaccine was defective and caused plaintiffs to contract polio, the jury was also entitled to conclude that the vaccine was not of the quality represented by defendant and that, therefore, defendant breached its express warranty.

Stahlheber v. American Cyanamid Co. (Mo., 1970) 451 S.W.2d 48.

Poliomyelitis after taking oral vaccine—Causal connection established—Manufacturer's liability affirmed

The plaintiff instituted suit against the defendant-company when she became afflicted with what appeared to be poliomyelitis after taking oral poliovirus vaccine manufactured by the defendant. The evidence introduced at the trial showed that City-County Charities, Inc. sponsored mass polio immunization programs in the St. Louis area in 1964 using Trivalent Orimune vaccine purchased from the defendant. The plaintiff, then 41 years of age, accepted a dose on April 5, 1964 at one of the immunization centers, the Crestwood School, where she had a child enrolled.

On April 16 the plaintiff noticed a stiffness on the right side of her neck, and the following day she developed pains in her lower back. She did not feel well over the weekend and, at her husband's insistence, called her physician on Monday to make arrangements to have a rectal fistula taken care of which had bothered her for several months. The physician told her to come to the Missouri Pacific Hospital on April 22. She did so and was admitted around noon on that date. Except for the cause of her admission, physical examination upon admission was negative. On the first night she complained to the nurse of severe back pain. She was given a sedative, but it did not relieve her pain. Sometime after midnight she was examined by a physician who tested the motion of her legs and suggested the possibility of a low back sprain.

Operative repair of the fistula was performed on the morning of April 23. When the patient returned to her room from surgery, pain in her back and legs became worse. She was able to walk to the bathroom in the afternoon, but the pain continued to become more severe in her back. Sometime after midnight she noticed that she was unable to move her right leg. A physician examined the patient early on the morning of April 24, and found "only minimal motor function of extensor and flexor groups, right lower extremity. Absent patellar reflex and very minimal ankle reflex.... No absence of sensation noted." The patient was examined by a neurosurgeon who called in a neurologist-psychiatrist. The latter found paralysis of the right leg and a moderate weakness in all muscular movements of the left leg. His tentative diagnosis at that time was meningoencephalomyelitis. Another physician also examined the patient on April 24 and made a note in her hospital record: "Think this is probably virus —? Poliomyelitis."

The patient's left leg became weaker and eventually both legs and both arms became involved. At the suggestion of the neurologist-psychiatrist, the patient was moved to Barnes Hospital on April 27 so that a respirator would be available should her breathing become involved. The discharge note stated that the patient was transferred to the Barnes Hospital "with (?) signs of Landry's paralysis (?)." The discharge diagnosis at the Missouri Pacific Hospital was: "Landry's paralysis, undetermined."

The patient's paralysis reached its peak about five days after her admission to Barnes Hospital. She lost the use of her right arm completely, could not turn her head and had no control of her bladder or bowel functions. She suffered excruciating pain, "like hot corkscrews in my legs and my back and my neck."

The patient was taken out of isolation at the Barnes Hospital after five to seven days, and physical therapy was begun. She was discharged from the Barnes Hospital on July 17, 1964. At that time she had no function in the muscles of her legs. Some function with weakness had returned to her arms and a slow gain in strength in those muscles was noted. She had regained bowel and bladder control. The discharge diagnosis at Barnes Hospital was "Post Infectious Myeloradiculopathy." At the trial, however, medical witnesses testifying for the plaintiff said she probably had suffered poliomyelitis.

A jury returned a verdict in favor of the plaintiff and the company appealed, contending that no submissible case was made because the plaintiff had failed to show a causal connection between the taking of the vaccine and the disease of which she complained. This contention was rejected by the Supreme Court of Missouri, which, in affirming the verdict, declared:

> On the issue of causation, the medical testimony offered by [the plaintiff] was that Mrs. Stahlheber's poliomyelitis was caused by the ingestion of defendant's vaccine. The opinion was based upon the appearance of [the plaintiff's] illness some 19 days after she took the polio vaccine. There was no known contact with another polio victim. There was no polio epidemic in the St. Louis area in April, 1964. The Reports of the Special Advisory Committee on Oral Poliomyelitis Vaccine to the Surgeon General, Public Health Service, of September 20, 1962 and December 18, 1962, upon which the duty to warn in this case was essentially based,[11] specified an onset of polio within a period of four to thirty days after feeding as one of the criteria upon which cases studied by the committee were deemed "'compatible" with the possibility of having been induced by the vaccine.' The plaintiff's medical witnesses testified that they considered that criterion in arriving at their conclusion as to the cause of Mrs. Stahlheber's illness. The opinions of the physicians as to the causal connection, demonstrated to have been based upon their medical knowledge, did constitute substantial evidence from which the jury could find the necessary element of causation.... In the present case, not one but four treating physicians, plus one other physician, testified positively as to the nature of plaintiff's illness and its cause. The qualifications of the medical witnesses were not questioned. They explained at length the facts which they considered in arriving at their opinion. There has been no demonstrated lack of consideration of essential facts in arriving at such opinion and no showing of such inconsistencies in the testimony of any of the witnesses as would destroy the probative value of their testimony. Their testi-

[11] Pertinent information contained in the Special Advisory Committee's reports to which the court refers is set out in Davis v. Wyeth Laboratories, Inc., supra.

mony did constitute substantial evidence on the nature and cause of plaintiff's illness and made a submissible case on such issues.

Griffin v. United States (E.D. Pa., 1972) 351 F. Supp. 10, rev'd in part (C.A.-3 Pa., 1974) 500 F.2d 1059.

Poliomyelitis after taking oral vaccine—Government liable for negligence in approving below-standard vaccine

The plaintiff and her husband filed suit under the Federal Tort Claims Act after she developed poliomyelitis subsequent to taking Sabin live virus vaccine. At the trial (nonjury) the evidence disclosed that in October, 1963 the plaintiff participated in a mass immunization campaign sponsored by the Montgomery County (Pennsylvania) Medical Society. The dose taken by the plaintiff was from "Lot 56," manufactured by Charles J. Pfizer & Company and approved after testing by the United States government.[12]

Much testimony was introduced on the government's role in maintaining the quality of the vaccine. The Division of Biologic Standards (DBS) of the Public Health Service was charged with the administration of regulations promulgated by the Secretary of Health, Education and Welfare and the Surgeon General of the United States. DBS was also in charge of testing and evaluation under these regulations, and had the power of approval or disapproval of each lot of vaccine. The DBS "in-house expert" on testing live virus preparations testified at the trial. She had primary responsibility for evaluating monkey neurovirulence tests, and she had signed the review approving Lot 56, despite certain reservations about its quality.

Evidence was introduced that no vaccine which was not at or under a specific level in neurovirulence was ever to reach the market, yet apparently Lot 56 did exceed such level and was approved. The trial judge awarded damages of $2,059,946, declaring:

> The clear mandate of the regulation[13] was that doubts be resolved against the lot under test. Dr. [the DBS "in-house expert"] testified that Lot 56 seriously troubled and gave her pause. At that point, her only options under the regulations were further testing to resolve doubts or rejection. Yet she signed the review of testing approval which led to the lot's release. Thus it is clear

---

[12] Charles J. Pfizer & Company settled with the plaintiffs prior to trial for $350,000.

[13] The court is referring to the federal regulation [42 CFR 73.114(b)(1)] which governed the evaluation of monkey neurovirulence.

> that at the time of the release of Pfizer Lot 56, the Lot 56 clearly did not meet the criteria of 73.114(b)(1)(iii) for release. The personnel of D.B.S. knew this or should have known it. It was released basically either because the personnel of D.B.S. charged with enforcing the regulation failed to read the regulation carefully, or because they did not understand or failed to take seriously the strict duty imposed upon them by the regulation. Either circumstance constitutes negligence.

The trial judge's decision was appealed to the Court of Appeals, Third District, on four issues: (1) failure to hold the action barred because the claim is based on the exercise or performance of a "discretionary function"; (2) insufficient evidence of negligence and proximate cause; (3) the award of excessive damages; and (4) the failure to give effect to a "joint tortfeasor release" given by the plaintiffs to Charles J. Pfizer & Company which settled with the plaintiffs prior to trial.

The Court of Appeals affirmed the judgment as to the first three issues, but reversed because of the failure to honor the terms of the manufacturer's release which called for a reduction, by the settlement amount agreed upon, in its pro rata share of any judgment against the government.

NOTE: On June 30, 1987, the United States Court of Appeals, Third Circuit, reconsidered its holding in this case as it applied to the discretionary function exception under the Federal Tort Claims Act. See Berkovitz v. United States (C.A.-3 Pa., 1987) 822 F.2d 1322 (summarized infra).

Reyes v. Wyeth Laboratories (C.A.-5 Tex., 1974) 498 F.2d 1264.

Poliomyelitis after taking oral vaccine—Manufacturer liable for failure to warn recipient of risk

In May, 1970, slightly more than two weeks after she had received a dose of the defendant-company's Sabin oral poliovirus vaccine, an eight-month-old girl developed paralytic poliomyelitis. The girl's father brought suit on her behalf, alleging the defendant was liable for failing to warn of this danger.

The child had been fed two drops of the vaccine by eyedropper at the Hidalgo County Department of Health Clinic in Mission, Texas. The vaccine had been administered by a registered nurse; there were no physicians present. The girl's mother testified at the trial that she had not been warned of any possible danger involved in her daughter's taking the vaccine. The mother had a seventh-grade education, but her primary language was Spanish. Prior to the vaccination she signed a form releasing the state of Texas from "all liability in connection with immunization." The form contained no warning of any sort, and it was apparent from her testimony that she either did not read the form or lacked the ability to understand its significance.

The vaccine given to the girl in the Mission clinic was part of a "Lot No. 15509," prepared by the defendant-company. This lot was trivalent oral polio vaccine that the company had titered (mixed) from Types I, II, and III monovalent vaccine provided by another company. In response to an order placed by the Texas State Department of Health on December 23, 1969 the defendant shipped 3,500 vials of Lot No. 15509 vaccine to the State Health Department which in turn transferred 400 vials to the Hidalgo County Health Department.

Included with every vial, each of which contained ten doses of vaccine, was a "package circular" provided by the defendant which was intended to warn physicians, hospitals, or other purchasers of potential dangers in ingesting the vaccine. The nurse who administered the vaccine to the girl testified that she had read the directions on this package insert, but that it was not the practice of the nurses at the Mission Health Clinic to pass on the warnings to the recipients or their parents. She testified that she gave the girl's mother no warning before she administered the vaccine to the girl.

The jury returned a verdict in favor of the girl's father, and the District Court entered judgment accordingly.

The company appealed, contending that if it had a duty to warn at all, that duty was discharged by the warning contained on the package insert which accompanied the vials of vaccine sold to the Texas State Department of Health. This was so, the drug company contended, because the Sabin trivalent oral polio vaccine in issue was a "prescription drug," and those who prepare such drugs are not required to warn the ultimate consumer.

The company's contention was rejected by the United States Court of Appeals for the Fifth Circuit, which affirmed the judgment of the District Court.

> Wyeth had ample reason to foresee the way in which its vaccine would be distributed. A drug manufacturer is held to the skill of an expert in his field, and is presumed to possess an expert's knowledge of the arts, materials, and processes of the pharmaceutical business. Included in such expertise must be a

> familiarity with practices and knowledge common in the drug industry as to distribution and administration of pharmaceutical products.... [I]t was common knowledge in the drug industry that "a great majority" of vaccinees receive their Sabin vaccine in mass administrations or county clinics manned at least in part by volunteers.... [I]t was well known that such clinics were stocked primarily by sale of vaccine to state health departments. These clinics, as Wyeth must be presumed to know, dispense Sabin vaccine to all comers in an "assembly line" fashion; there is often neither time nor personnel to make an "individualized medical judgment" of the vaccinee's needs or susceptibilities.... Viewed in this light, the present controversy ... invites ... the conclusion that Wyeth was under a duty to warn Anita Reyes' parents of the danger inherent in its vaccine. Wyeth knew or had reason to know that the vaccine would not be administered as a prescription drug, and therefore was required to warn foreseeable users, or see that the Texas Department of Health warned them.

The defendant petitioned the Supreme Court of the United States for writ of certiorari. The court accepted *amicus curiae* briefs from The American Academy of Pediatrics and The Conference of State and Territorial Epidemiologists but denied the defendant's writ on December 23, 1974.[14]

Cunningham v. Charles Pfizer & Co. (Okla., 1974) 532 P.2d 1377.

Poliomyelitis after taking oral vaccine—Jury should have been allowed to consider whether vaccine would have been refused had warning been given—Verdict for plaintiff set aside

A fifteen-year-old boy contracted polio five weeks after he was given Type I oral vaccine during a mass immunization program. Suit was filed against the manufacturer charging that it had failed to warn him or his parents of the risk involved in taking the vaccine. A jury awarded him $340,000.

On appeal, the Supreme Court of Oklahoma set the judgment aside for the trial judge's failure to allow the jury to consider whether the boy or his parents would have refused the vaccine if adequate warning had been given by the manufacturer. The court said that there was a rebuttable presumption that he would have heeded such a warning, but the fact that there was at the time a polio epidemic in Oklahoma tended to overcome the presumption.

---

[14] Wyeth Laboratories v. Reyes (1974) 419 U.S. 1096, 42 L. Ed. 2d 688, 95 Sup. Ct. 687.

The court agreed that in the case of a mass immunization program the physician does not assess the medical risks for each user and that it would not have been an unreasonable burden on the manufacturer to warn the public by means of advertisements, posters and press releases of the possibility of a recipient contracting polio after taking the vaccine.[15]

Givens v. Lederle (C.A.-5 Fla., 1977) 556 F.2d 1341.

Poliomyelitis after daughter given oral vaccine—$250,000 verdict against manufacturer upheld

This case involves a mother who contracted polio nine days after her daughter received the third of three Sabin oral polio vaccine dosages. As a result, the plaintiff suffered total paralysis in the lower part of her body and partial paralysis in the upper part.

At the first trial, a jury returned a verdict for the defendant-manufacturer. A new trial was granted, however, when the court ruled that it had erred in excluding records of other vaccine-induced polio cases. At the second trial, the plaintiff was awarded $250,000 in damages and her husband, $12,500.

On appeal, the reviewing court noted that Lederle's defense that its oral vaccine could not cause polio was weakened considerably by a warning contained in the vaccine package insert itself which stated: "Paralytic disease following the ingestion of live polio virus vaccines has been reported in individuals receiving the vaccine, and in some instances, in persons who were in close contact with subjects who had been given live oral polio virus vaccine."

The verdict for the plaintiff was affirmed, and the verdict for her husband was deemed inadequate as failing to take into account the trial court instructions that he could obtain damages for the lifetime loss of his wife's services, comfort, society and attention.

McNeary v. Lederle Laboratories (No. 86-3881, Superior Court, King County, Wash., April 15, 1982).

Poliomyelitis from contact with daughter—Plaintiff confined to wheelchair—$1,100,000 jury verdict against manufacturer

A thirty-six-year-old mother contracted poliomyelitis from washing the diapers of her infant daughter who had recently been vacci-

[15] AMA *The Citation* 30:150, 1975; *American Medical News*, July 14, 1975, p. 8.

nated with the Sabin oral polio vaccine. The disease left her confined to a wheelchair. The plaintiff charged that the manufacturer failed to give adequate warning of the risk of contracting the disease from a vaccinated person. The plaintiff also claimed that she should have been informed that Salk dead polio virus vaccine was a risk-free alternative to the live Sabin vaccine.

The jury returned a $1,100,000 verdict for the plaintiff. She also settled a claim against the county health service (which administered the vaccine) for $400,000.[16]

Dunn v. Lederle Laboratories (1983) 121 Mich. App. 73, 328 N.W.2d 576.

Poliomyelitis after daughter given oral vaccine—Judgment for manufacturer affirmed—Proximate cause not shown

The plaintiff contracted poliomyelitis from her daughter shortly after the child was given oral vaccine. In her suit against the manufacturer, she alleged failure to warn. The jury returned a verdict for the defendant and the Court of Appeals affirmed, holding that the jury could have reasonably found that any failure on the part of the manufacturer to warn of the risk of contracting poliomyelitis from a person recently vaccinated was not the proximate cause of the plaintiff's injuries, i.e., the plaintiff failed to show that such a warning would have altered the conduct of the physician who administered the vaccine in such a way that the plaintiff would not have been exposed.

Berry v. Pfizer, Inc. (No. 81-0280-C, U.S. District Court, Southern District, Ala., Jan. 8, 1985).

Poliomyelitis following vaccination—$275,000 settlement with manufacturer

An infant developed polio shortly after being given a dose of oral poliovirus vaccine in 1973. In the suit on her behalf it was alleged that the manufacturer, Pfizer, Inc., should have warned the child's parents that the vaccine carries an inherent risk of causing the disease in a small number of individuals so that they could have made an informed decision as to whether to have the vaccine administered. The manufacturer argued that the infant contracted polio from her father, a merchant seaman who had recently been

[16] ATLA *Law Reporter* 25:323, 1982.

aboard a ship which called at ports in countries where there were polio epidemics.

After a two-week trial, the jury failed to reach a decision on whether the parents would have heeded a warning by the manufacturer if one had been given. The jury was dismissed and a new trial date was set, but the parties settled the day before the new trial was to begin for $275,000.[17]

Johnson v. American Cyanamid Co. (1986) 239 Kan. 279, 718 P.2d 1318.

Poliomyelitis after daughter given vaccine—$12 million award overturned

The plaintiff, a 65-year-old farmer, developed poliomyelitis following the vaccination of his daughter with Sabin vaccine (Orimune). In an action against the manufacturer and the physician, a jury awarded the plaintiff $2 million in actual damages and $10 million in punitive, all against the manufacturer for inadequately warning of the risk. No negligence was found on the part of the physician.

The Supreme Court of Kansas reversed, finding that Orimune was an "unavoidably unsafe product" as described under Comment k of Section 402A of the *Restatement (Second) of Torts* (1963), and that the following warning, issued by the manufacturer with the product, was adequate.

> Individual patients have at times attributed symptoms or conditions to the vaccine by reason of time relationship, but these in general have been minor and apparently unrelated.
>
> Expert opinion is in agreement that the administration of live oral poliovirus vaccines is generally an effective and safe method of protecting populations against the natural disease. Paralytic disease following the ingestion of live poliovirus vaccines has been reported in individuals receiving the vaccine, and in some instances, in persons who were in close contact with subjects who had been given live oral poliovirus vaccine. Fortunately, such occurrences are rare, but considering the epidemiological evidence developed with respect to the total group of "vaccine related cases" it is believed by some that at least some of the cases were caused by the vaccine.
>
> The estimated risk of vaccine-induced paralytic disease occurring in vaccinees or those in close contact with vaccinees is extremely low. A total of approximately 30 of such cases were re-

---

[17] ATLA *Products Liability Law Reporter* 4:104, 1985.

ported for the 8 year period covering 1963 to 1970, during which time about 147,000,000 doses of the vaccine were distributed nationally. Even though this risk is low, it should always be a source of consideration.

Plummer v. Lederle Laboratories (C.A.-2 N.Y., 1987) 819 F.2d 349.

Poliomyelitis from contact with granddaughter after inoculation—$3.2 million verdict set aside—Manufacturer's warning adequate

A 43-year-old building contractor developed poliomyelitis following contact with his infant granddaughter after she had been given Orimune. In an action against the manufacturer based on inadequate warning, the plaintiff was awarded a $3.2 million jury verdict. On appeal, however, the U.S. Court of Appeals, Second Circuit, reversed, holding that given the fact that the probability of contracting polio in such an instance was extremely remote, the warnings issued by the manufacturer in the package inserts were adequate as a matter of law even though they might be viewed as minimizing such risk, and even though they did not include specific precautions.

In addition, the court held that the plaintiff had failed to establish proof of proximate cause in light of testimony by the physician who administered the inoculation that he was aware of the risk of a third person contracting polio in such cases, but that he did not warn parents for fear of discouraging immunization.

Berkovitz v. United States (1988) 108 Sup. Ct. 1954.

Poliomyelitis after taking oral vaccine—Suit against government barred by discretionary function exception to FTCA

The plaintiff, a minor, developed poliomyelitis within a month after receiving a dose of Orimune. The plaintiff filed suit against the United States government under the Federal Tort Claims Act for negligence of the Division of Biologic Standards, a division of the National Institute of Health, in licensing Lederle Laboratories, manufacturer of the vaccine, to produce a vaccine using live virus.

The government moved for dismissal on grounds that the acts complained of fell within the discretionary function exception to the United States' waiver of sovereign immunity under the FTCA. The district court granted the government's motion, relying on the decision in Griffin v. United States (C.A.-Pa., 1974) 500 F.2d 1059 (summarized supra). The Court of Appeals reversed, however (822

F.2d 1322), citing a 1984 decision of the Supreme Court, United States v. S.A. Empresa De Viacao Aerea Rio Grandense (Varig Airlines) (1984) 467 U.S. 797, in which it was held that the discretionary function exception barred an FTCA suit based on the negligence of the Federal Aviation Administration in certifying an aircraft that did not comply with applicable safety regulations. In light of the Varig Airlines case, the Court of Appeals held that it was necessary to reevaluate the holding in the Griffin case. While it would not "disturb the portions of Griffin that hold that an agency's violation of its own mandatory regulation is not a discretionary act," said the court, the Varig case "instructs that a court must determine whether 'the basic responsibility for satisfying [the agency's] safety standards rests with the manufacturer'" and whether the role of the agency "is merely to police the conduct of private individuals by monitoring their compliance with [the applicable] regulations." The Varig case, said the court, requires that this determination be made by examining agency regulations as a whole.

On grant of certiorari, the Supreme Court of the United States reversed the Court of Appeals, holding that the discretionary function exception did not bar the plaintiff's claim against the government. Justice Marshall, speaking for a unanimous court, held that the Division of Biologic Standards, under the circumstances, had no discretion in issuing a license to produce the vaccine, and, in fact, had it exercised such discretion, it would have violated specific statutory and regulatory directives.

Related cases

Poliomyelitis after nephew given vaccine—Claim against government not barred under FTCA

The discretionary function exception to the Federal Tort Claims Act did not bar the claim of a plaintiff who contracted poliomyelitis after his nephew was inoculated with trivalent, live, oral poliovirus vaccine. The plaintiff claimed that the Department of Health, Education and Welfare was negligent in failing to require mandatory tests prior to issuing a license to Lederle Laboratories to manufacture the vaccine. Baker v. United States (C.A.-9 Cal., 1987) 817 F.2d 560. (But see Berkovitz v. United States, supra.)

Poliomyelitis after son given oral vaccine—Government charged with increasing risk

An Arkansas mother who contracted polio following her infant son's inoculation was unsuccessful in her claim in the U.S. District

Court that the government increased the risk of such a result by licensing the live vaccine and undertook the duty owed by the drug manufacturer to those who would be affected. But on review the Eighth Circuit Court of Appeals held that because the plaintiffs were Arkansas residents the law of that state should apply and not the law of the District of Columbia, which the lower court had applied, and under Arkansas law the plaintiffs' allegations stated a claim. Loge v. United States (C.A.-8 Ark., 1981) 662 F.2d 1268.

Poliomyelitis following vaccination—Action barred by statute

Once the plaintiff knew of the injury and its cause, the two-year statute of limitations applicable to FTCA actions began to run and the statute was not tolled until the plaintiff discovered the government's negligence, nor did the government's failure to ascertain and publish the fact of its negligence constitute fraudulent concealment so as to toll the statute. Davis v. United States (C.A.-9 Idaho, 1981) 642 F.2d 328.

Poliomyelitis following receipt of vaccine—Pre-existing immunity deficiency—Directed verdicts for manufacturer and American Academy of Pediatrics

In Schindler v. Lederle Laboratories (C.A.-6 Mich., 1983) 725 F.2d 1036, the manufacturer of poliovirus vaccine and the American Academy of Pediatrics were both found to have issued adequate warnings to the medical profession regarding the risk of administering poliovirus vaccine to persons with pre-existing immunity deficiencies.

Poliomyelitis after taking vaccine—Manufactuers not liable for failure to warn public—"Market share," "enterprise liability," and related theories not applicable

In an action on behalf of a child who contracted poliomyelitis following an injection of Salk anti-polio vaccine, it was held that the defendant manufacturers had no duty to warn the public of the danger from defective vaccine and the theories of "market share liability," "enterprise liability," "concert of action," and related theories were not applicable. Also, the plaintiff could not recover by coupling res ipsa loquitur with an alternative theory of liability. Sheffield v. Eli Lilly & Co. (1983) 144 Cal. App. 3d 583, 192 Cal. Rptr. 870.

Poliomyelitis after daughter given vaccine—Jury could not presume that parents would have refused vaccine if risk were known

In affirming a verdict for a county health department, the Court of Appeals of Arizona held that the trial court did not err in refusing to instruct the jury that it could presume that if the parents of a child who was to receive poliovirus vaccine had been warned about the possibility of contracting polio from the child, they would not have allowed her to receive the vaccine. Sheehan v. Pima County (1983) 135 Ariz. 235, 660 P.2d 486.

Poliomyelitis after child given vaccine—Standard of care of pediatricians not relevant—Physician's conduct could insulate manufacturer

In Fraley v. American Cyanamid Co. (D. Colo., 1984) 589 F. Supp. 826, the mother of a six-month old child who contracted polio from her child after she received vaccine was entitled to an order excluding evidence of the standard of practice and duties of pediatricians during the period in question because the acts of the pediatrician who gave the plaintiff's child the vaccine were the only acts relevant to proximate cause. The court also held that the physician's conduct could insulate the vaccine manufacturer from liability for failure to provide an adequate warning of the risk in using the vaccine if it was established that the physician would not have heeded an adequate warning.

Poliomyelitis after daughter given vaccine—Adequacy of warning to be determined at trial

In Williams v. Lederle Laboratories, Div. of American Cyanamid Co. (S.D. Ohio, 1984) 591 F. Supp. 381, the question of the adequacy of the manufacturer's warnings that a person could contract poliomyelitis from coming in contact with a person recently vaccinated with its poliovirus vaccine could not be disposed of by summary judgment and was a question of fact to be determined by the preponderance of the evidence.

Poliomyelitis following vaccination—Evidence on "unavoidable dangerous product" should have been admitted

In Kearl v. Lederle Laboratories (1985) 172 Cal. App. 3d 812, 218 Cal. Rptr. 453, the trial court erred in not taking evidence to determine whether the "unavoidably dangerous product" exemption applied to oral poliovirus vaccine. Also, evidence established that the plaintiff's mother was warned regarding the risk of contracting polio from vaccine.

POLYCILLIN
See AMPICILLIN

POLYCOSE
See GLUCOSE POLYMERS

POLY-HISTINE-D
See TRIPELENNAMINE

PONTOCAINE HYDROCHLORIDE
See TETRACAINE HYDROCHLORIDE

POTASSIUM CHLORIDE

Potassium chloride is recommended for therapeutic use in patients with hypokalemia (abnormally low potassium content of the blood) and in certain cases for prevention of potassium depletion when the dietary intake of potassium is inadequate. There are numerous other potassium chloride products in various forms and strengths. For a complete list, consult the latest edition of *Physicians' Desk Reference.*

Because of reports of intestinal and gastric ulceration and bleeding with slow-release potassium chloride preparations, there are warnings in the product literature that these drugs should be reserved for those patients who cannot tolerate or refuse to take liquid or effervescent potassium preparations or for patients in whom there is a problem of compliance. The package circular also notes that these preparations have also produced esophageal ulceration in certain cardiac patients.

Peltier v. Franklin Foundation Hospital (No. 73-142-F, 16th Judicial District Court, St. Mary Parish, La., Jan. 19, 1985).

Elderly patient suffers fatal tachycardia after being given potassium chloride—$240,000 settlement

Hospital nurses administered potassium chloride to a seventy-six-year-old woman patient who immediately suffered tachycardia (rapid heart beat) and died. It was later discovered the patient's physician had not ordered the drug. The hospital settled for $240,000.[18]

---

[18] ATLA *Law Reporter* 28:183, 1985.

Related cases

Gastric injury attributed to combination of potassium chloride and other drugs prescribed for weight reduction

In Mendoza v. Varon (Tex. Civ. App., 1978) 563 S.W.2d 646, a physician was sued for malpractice for prescribing a combination of Preludin (phenmetrazine hydrochloride), Dyazide (triamterene), Aldactone (spironolactone) and potassium chloride for a teenage girl who was overweight and suffered from high blood pressure. The patient experienced violent episodes of vomiting brought on by inflammation and scarring of the stomach and esophagus. The case is summarized herein under PHENMETRAZINE HYDROCHLORIDE.

Excessive dosage—Nurse's testimony admissible

In Maloney v. Wake Hosp. Systems, Inc. (1980) 45 N.C. App. 172, 262 S.E.2d 680, the Court of Appeals held that the trial court erred in excluding testimony of a nurse who specialized in intravenous therapy in an action involving alleged negligence in injecting undiluted potassium chloride into a patient's I.V. tube.

POTASSIUM PENICILLIN G

See PENICILLIN

POTASSIUM PHENOXYMETHYL PENICILLIN

See PENICILLIN

PREDNEFRIN

See PREDNISOLONE ACETATE and PHENYLEPHRINE HYDROCHLORIDE

PREDNISOLONE ACETATE and PHENYLEPHRINE HYDROCHLORIDE

Prednefrin

Prednisolone is an adrenal corticosteroid derived from hydrocortisone. Prednisolone acetate is applied topically to treat inflammations of the eye. It was at one time mixed in various strengths with phenylephrine hydrochloride, a potent vasoconstrictor similar to epinephrine, in the eyedrop preparation Prednefrin, formerly marketed by Allergan Pharmaceuticals, Inc. (Irvine, Cal.).[19] The company no longer includes this preparation on its product information list.

The possible adverse effects of Prednefrin were those common to adrenal corticosteroids. (See PREDNISONE.) As an ophthalmic preparation, repeated administration of the drug could raise the intraocular pressure leading to eventual visual loss (from glaucoma) in some patients. The condition was usually reversible, however, if detected before damage to the optic nerve occurred. The drug had to be used with extreme caution, and long-term use avoided in patients with primary open-angle glaucoma (and in their relatives), in myopic individuals, and in diabetics.[20]

Ortiz v. Allergan Pharmaceuticals (Tex. Civ. App., 1972) 489 S.W.2d 135.

Glaucoma and cataracts after prolonged use—Prescriptions refilled without authorization—Physician and pharmacist settle—Manufacturer not liable for failure to warn

On February 5, 1965 the patient consulted an ophthalmologist who fitted her with glasses. The patient was also suffering from conjunctivitis and the ophthalmologist prescribed Prednefrin 0.12% eyedrops.

About a month later a pharmacist called the ophthalmologist and asked if he could refill the patient's prescription in two bottles, since she wanted one for home and another for work. The ophthalmologist gave his permission, but said nothing about future refills. Apparently without authorization the pharmacist continued to refill the prescription over a period of five months, from April 20 to September 15, 1965. In doing so, the pharmacist dispensed the drug with the physician's original instructions as to dosage, but without the manufacturer's package insert.

In January, 1966 the patient was hospitalized for migraine headaches. The following September her eyes were examined and she was found to have increased intraocular pressure and corneal edema. The patient eventually developed both glaucoma and cataracts, and in July, 1967 underwent surgery for the cataracts.

---

[19] *United States Dispensatory,* 27th ed., p. 951; *AMA Drug Evaluations,* 2d ed., pp. 717, 718.

[20] *AMA Drug Evaluations,* 2d ed., p. 715.

Suit was filed against the ophthalmologist, the pharmacist and the manufacturer of Prednefrin. During the trial the patient settled with the ophthalmologist and the pharmacist.

The drug company offered the testimony of its director of clinical research, an ophthalmologist himself, who testified that the average period of treatment with Prednefrin was two to four weeks, and that adverse reactions during such time were, according to the history of the drug, "negligible." According to the witness, the manufacturer recommended the drug not be used in excess of six weeks. He admitted that if the drug was used over a long period of time it could cause increased intraocular pressure in susceptible persons, but he insisted that it could not damage the eyes unless improperly used. Evidence was introduced that over a million bottles of Prednefrin had been dispensed by 1965 without any report of cataracts.

The company introduced into evidence the package insert and warning issued with Prednefrin during the period of April, 1965 through July, 1966. It read as follows:

> Warning: (1) In diseases due to microorganisms, infection may be masked, enhanced or activated by the steroid. (2) Extended use may cause increased intraocular pressure in susceptible individuals. It is advisable that the intraocular pressure be checked frequently. (3) In those diseases causing thinning of the cornea, perforation has been known to have occurred with the use of topical steroids. (4) Since PREDNEFRIN contains no anti-microbial, if infection is present appropriate measures must be taken to counteract the organisms involved. (5) Should be used with caution in the presence of narrow angle glaucoma. (6) If sensitivity to any of the constituents of this medication is present or develops, it should not be used, or it should be discontinued immediately.

The jury found for the drug company on all material issues submitted, including a finding that the patient had misused the drug. It found also in a cross-action by the company that the pharmacist was negligent in dispensing the drug without authorization by the patient's physician. Judgments on these findings were affirmed on appeal.

PREDNISONE
Deltasone
Liquid Pred Syrup
Meticorten
Orasone
Sterapred

Prednisone is a synthetic glucocorticoid derivative of the hormone cortisone, an adrenal corticosteroid which itself can be produced synthetically. Prednisone is effective in the treatment of inflammatory and allergic conditions and other diseases that respond to glucocorticoids.[1]

As with other glucocorticoids the possible adverse reactions of prednisone are many; they include, but are not limited to: congestive heart failure in susceptible patients, hypertension, bone deterioration, peptic ulcer, impaired wound healing, suppression of growth in children, manifestations of latent diabetes mellitus and glaucoma.[2]

Deltasone is manufactured by The Upjohn Company (Kalamazoo, Mich.), Meticorten by Schering Corporation (Kenilworth, N.J.), Liquid Pred Syrup by Muro Pharmaceuticals (Tewksbury, Mass.), Orasone by Reid-Rowell (Marietta, Ga.) and Sterapred by Mayrand, Inc. (Greensboro, N.C.). The drug is also marketed under the generic name by several companies.

Graham v. Kaiser Foundation Hosp. (No. 633484, Superior Court, San Francisco County, Cal., Aug. 22, 1972).

Drug-induced diabetes—Alleged congestive heart failure—Condition misdiagnosed but treatment same in either case—Verdict for physicians

A 69-year-old woman patient was treated by the Kaiser group for four years with prednisone. The patient had been thought to have been suffering from some form of muscular weakness (myopathy), but at the end of the four-year period it was discovered that she actually had been suffering from polymyositis, a disorder of the collagenous tissues involving inflammation of the voluntary muscles. Suit was filed against the group, wherein it was also alleged that as a result of the four-year treatment with prednisone the

---

[1] Id., p. 398. For a complete list of indications for prednisone see the latest edition of *Physicians' Desk Reference.*

[2] *Physicians' Desk Reference,* 35th ed., p. 1817.

patient had developed congestive heart failure and drug-induced diabetes.

The defendants argued at the trial that the patient's diabetes had cleared up under proper medication, and that it was highly questionable whether her alleged congestive heart failure had really ever existed. Also, the defendants offered proof that even though they had diagnosed the patient's case as a myopathy rather than polymyositis, the standard treatment for polymyositis was prednisone and, in fact, prednisone was at the time the only drug used for this disease. Finally, they argued that any side effect occurring from this drug was caused by an idiosyncratic reaction.

The jury returned a verdict for the defendants.[3]

Nelson v. Stadner (No. 10148, Superior Court, San Joaquin County, Cal., June 28, 1974).

Allergic reaction—Physician charged with negligence in choice of drug and supervision—Pharmacist accused of improper labeling—Verdict for defendants

A patient was given a prescription for prednisone to treat a reaction to previous allergy treatments. He suffered a reaction to the drug, which brought on alleged loss of memory, tremors, facial swelling, drowsiness, and personality change. He filed suit against the physician and the pharmacist from whom he obtained the drug.

The physician was charged with negligence in prescribing prednisone and in supervising the patient's treatment. The pharmacist was accused of failing to set forth properly the physician's instructions on the drug label. The physician defended on grounds that he had not violated any standard of care in choice of treatment or management of the patient. The pharmacist denied that the prescription was improperly labeled, and contended that even if it was improper, this was not the proximate cause of the patient's condition, because of separate instructions given by the physician to the patient regarding use of the drug.

The jury found for the defendants.[4]

---

[3] AMA *The Citation* 26:113, 1973.

[4] Id., 30:24, 1974.

Precourt v. Frederick (1985) 395 Mass. 689, 481 N.E.2d 1144.

Aseptic necrosis—Ophthalmologist's failure to disclose risk did not violate duty to patient

The patient had been on prednisone for three and one-half years to control inflammation of his eye following surgery to remove a piece of metal from his retina and a second operation to remove scar tissue. When he developed aseptic necrosis of both hips he brought suit against his ophthalmologist for failing to disclose this risk in taking the drug over an extended period.

At the trial the defendant testified that he had practiced ophthalmology for nearly twenty years and never had a patient develop aseptic necrosis from long-term prednisone therapy. He did admit that he knew that there was "an association" between the use of the drug and the disease, and that *Physicians' Desk Reference* reported it as one of the more "prominent" complications of using the drug. He also admitted that he did not tell the patient that he could develop the disease.

Two experts for the plaintiff testified that physicians should inform a patient of the risk of aseptic necrosis before prescribing prednisone.

The jury found that the defendant did not obtain the patient's informed consent to being treated and awarded the patient and his wife $1,000,000. But the Supreme Court of Massachusetts reversed, holding that the plaintiff had not proven that the defendant had information about the risk that he (the defendant) "should have recognized Precourt would consider important" in deciding to undergo the treatment.

> In this case, there was no evidence of the likelihood that a person would develop aseptic necrosis after taking prednisone or that Frederick knew or should have known that the likelihood was other than negligible. Therefore, as a matter of law, the plaintiffs failed to show that Frederick recognized or reasonably should have recognized that the undisclosed risk was material to Precourt's decision. Characterization of Precourt's Prednisone dosage as "high" and the course of treatment as "long," in combination with the evidence that the probability of aseptic necrosis increases as the exposure to Prednisone increases, does not permit the inference that Frederick reasonably should have recognized that the possibility that Precourt would develop aseptic necrosis was material to Precourt's decision. Nor is such an inference made possible by the evidence of Precourt's preexisting medical condition or by the evidence that aseptic necrosis is one of the most prominent musculoskeletal complications of Prednisone, or

that the risk was "high" is a relative word. It could mean one in ten, but it could just as well mean one in a million.

The evidence did not warrant a finding that Frederick violated a duty he owed to Precourt. A contrary result is not required by the testimony of the expert witnesses with respect to their essentially legal conclusion that Frederick "should have" made a disclosure that he did not make.

Hutchison v. United States (C.A.-9 Cal., 1988) 841 F.2d 966.

Aseptic necrosis—Burden on physicians to prove why risk not disclosed

In 1981, the plaintiff developed aseptic necrosis after being treated for asthma with prednisone at a U.S. Health Services Hospital. In his suit, the plaintiff charged that the physicians who treated him should have warned him of the risk of this side effect.

At the trial, the district court ruled against the plaintiff, concluding that he had not met the burden of proving that a reasonable person in his position would not have undergone treatment with prednisone if he had known of the risk involved.

On appeal, however, the Court of Appeals reversed, holding that the district court had erroneously based its conclusion on a finding that in 1981 asthma patients were routinely warned of the risk of aseptic necrosis in being treated with prednisone. The record, said the court, did not support such a finding. Instead, the record revealed that asthma patients were rarely warned of the risk of aseptic necrosis from prednisone. Under the circumstances, said the court, California law required that the defendant satisfy the burden of providing evidence that would justify not disclosing this risk to the plaintiff.

Related cases

Osteoporosis—Claim not barred by statute of limitation

In Kraus v. Cleveland Clinic (N.D. Ohio, 1977) 442 F. Supp. 310, a patient who developed osteoporosis following prolonged treatment with prednisone for erythema nodosum prevailed against the defendant-physicians' motion for summary judgment in which they claimed the action was barred by Ohio's statute of limitation. The court found a genuine issue of fact as to whether the patient-physician relationship was terminated in view of the patient's failure to keep her last appointment.

Aseptic necrosis—Claim barred by statute of limitation

In Gray v. Reeves (1978) 76 Cal. App. 3d 567, 142 Cal. Rptr. 716, a patient who had been taking prednisone since 1968 was informed in January, 1971 that he was suffering from aseptic necrosis and it was probably caused by the drug. He did not, however, file suit until August, 1973 and his claim was barred by California's one-year statute of limitations on malpractice actions, the Court of Appeals holding that the statute was applicable not only to the physician but the drug company as well.

Skin discoloration—FTCA claim barred by statute of limitations

Although the plaintiff, the son of a member of the United States Air Force, may have thought that the marks, or "stria," which developed on the skin of his thighs, back and groin while taking prednisone for psoriasis were only temporary, it did not excuse his failure to file his claim against the government within the two-year period required by the Federal Tort Claims Act. Robbins v. United States (C.A.-10 N.M., 1980) 624 F.2d 971.

Internal hemorrhage during treatment with prednisone and other drugs

In Robinson v. Duszynski (1978) 36 N.C. App. 103, 243 S.E.2d 148, a woman being treated in the hospital for arthritis with prednisone, Celestone (betamethasone) and Tandearil (oxyphenbutazone) began hemorrhaging internally and died following emergency surgery. The case is summarized herein under BETAMETHASONE.

Aseptic necrosis blamed on ampicillin or prednisone

In Leary v. Rupp (1979) 89 Mich. App. 145, 280 N.W.2d 466, the patient suffered a reaction to ampicillin for which she was given prednisone. When she later developed aseptic necrosis she claimed her condition was caused by one or both of these drugs. The case is summarized herein under AMPICILLIN.

Cataracts—Claim not barred by statute of limitations

Where the plaintiff could have reasonably believed that his deteriorating eyesight and resulting cataracts were the result of long-time prednisone therapy, rather than his physician's failure to treat his lupus condition properly, a jury could reasonably conclude that he was not placed on notice to investigate a malpractice claim.

Skoglund v. Blankenship (1985) 134 Ill. App. 3d 628, 89 Ill. Dec. 695, 481 N.E.2d 47.

PRELUDIN
See PHENMETRAZINE HYDROCHLORIDE

PREMARIN
See ESTROGENS (CONJUGATED)

PRIMATINE
See EPINEPHRINE

PRIMIDONE
Mysoline

Primidone is an anticonvulsant which is used either alone or in combination with other anticonvulsants in the control of grand mal, psychomotor, and focal epileptic seizures. The drug is contraindicated in patients with porphyria and in patients who are hypersensitive to phenobarbital. Also, the manufacturer of Mysoline (Ayerst Laboratories, a division of American Home Products Corporation, New York, N.Y.) states that "[r]ecent reports suggest an association between the use of anticonvulsant drugs by women with epilepsy and an elevated incidence of birth defects in children born to these women."[5]

The product is also manufactured and marketed under the generic name by Danbury Pharmacal, Inc. (Danbury, Conn.) and Schein Pharmaceutical, Inc. (Port Washington, N.Y.).

Dillashaw v. Ayerst Laboratories, Inc. (1983) 141 Cal. App. 3d 35, 190 Cal. Rptr. 68.

Birth defects—Plaintiff's counsel fails to pursue claim within time period—Statute bars action

The plaintiff was born with birth defects in October, 1971. His mother, an epileptic, had taken Mysoline during pregnancy. In 1973 the plaintiff's attorney filed a complaint against the manufacturer claiming that it was responsible for the plaintiff's injuries. The plaintiff's attorney, however, conducted no discovery. No interrogatories were propounded, no admissions were sought from the

---

[5] *Physicians' Desk Reference,* 40th ed., pp. 631-32.

defendant, and no depositions were taken. In 1975 the plaintiff's attorney did seek to amend the complaint, specifying the drug Mysoline as the guilty product, and alleging that the drug was "negligently and carelessly manufactured" and that it was "inherently dangerous, defective and hazardous for the purposes of human consumption." Nothing more was done until June, 1978, at which time the parties stipulated to an extension of the time in which to bring the matter to trial to July 12, 1979. The matter failed to come to trial and the action was dismissed on July 20, 1979.

The plaintiff's attorney refiled a short time later. When the defendant moved for a summary judgment on grounds that the action was barred by the six-year statute of limitations applicable to minors, the plaintiff's attorney claimed that the action was filed within six years after "discovery" of the defendant's negligence, i.e., the date (1975) the defendant published in *Physicians' Desk Reference* a warning that there was a strong association between the use of Mysoline during pregnancy and birth defects. The trial court, however, did not accept this as a valid argument for tolling the statute and granted the defendant's summary judgment.

The Court of Appeal affirmed, holding that the plaintiff's complaint filed in 1973 demonstrated that his attorney recognized a cause of action against the manufacturer at that time.

PRINCIPEN; PRINCIPEN/N

See PENICILLIN

PRO-BANTHINE; PRO-BANTHINE with PHENOBARBITAL

See PROPANTHELINE BROMIDE

PROCAINE HYDROCHLORIDE

Novocaine

Procaine hydrochloride is used for infiltration, nerve block, peridural and spinal anesthesia. It is considered a fairly safe drug if suitable precautions are observed. However, as with any anesthetic, idiosyncrasy may be encountered. Slow administration and avoidance of accidental intravenous injection are advisable. In local administration, if increased sensitivity to procaine is suspected, as in patients with cardiac disease or endocrine disorders (such as hyperthyroidism), an initial small dose to test tolerance is recommended.[6]

In spinal anesthesia, several serious adverse reactions may occur, including hypotension, paralysis, and respiratory impairment.[7]

Winthrop Breon Laboratories, Inc. (New York, N.Y.) manufactures Novocaine, and Elkins-Sinn, Inc. (Cherry Hill, N.J.) produces the drug under the generic label.

Ball Memorial Hosp. v. Freeman (1964) 245 Ind. 71, 196 N.E.2d 274, 9 A.L.R.3d 567.

Tissue injury at site of procaine injection—Defective solution—Hospital liable for negligent preparation—Res ipsa loquitur applied

The plaintiff underwent outpatient surgery for removal of loose cartilage from his thumb. In preparation for the operation an anesthetic was injected into his hand. The solution was taken from a container labeled "Novocaine Anesthetic." The injection caused unusual pain and swelling in the plaintiff's hand and arm, and eventually caused an ulcer at the base of his thumb which failed to heal properly and required skin grafting and the removal of a nerve.

The evidence disclosed that the container did not contain a proper solution of procaine hydrochloride crystals. Hospital personnel, after obtaining the crystals from the manufacturer, had changed their nature entirely by putting them into an improper saline solution. Investigation revealed that the plaintiff's injury was one of eight occurring within a two-week period, all apparently the result of the improper preparation.

The hospital was found negligent on the theory of *res ipsa loquitur,* and the judgment was affirmed on appeal.

Gravis v. Parke-Davis & Co. (Tex. Civ. App., 1973) 502 S.W.2d 863.

Paralysis and other complications—Ingredients of spinal anesthetic solution claimed defective—Directed verdicts for manufacturers affirmed

In 1963 the patient underwent a one-hour exploratory operation. She was given a spinal anesthetic solution containing Novocaine, dextrose and Adrenalin. Each was manufactured by a different

[6] *Physicians' Desk Reference,* 35th ed., p. 695.

[7] Id.

company. She also received Pentothal Sodium. The surgeons found an intestinal obstruction and corrected it. Later, after she had been taken back to her room, the patient became ill and could not move her legs. She eventually developed a series of other disabilities, including bladder trouble, phlebitis, and hypertension.

The patient and her husband brought the present action against the three companies that had manufactured the drugs contained in the spinal anesthetic, claiming that one or more of the drugs were defective.[8]

At the trial the testimony showed that the surgeon had directed the anesthetist to use Novocaine, dextrose, and Adrenalin in the spinal anesthetic solution, following a formula previously worked out by the surgeon. This formula called for two cc.'s of Novocaine, .5 cc.'s of dextrose solution, and one cc. of Adrenalin. The anesthetist testified that she had examined the drugs for any defects before preparing the solution. She said that there were no cracks in the drug ampules and no discoloration. She said the ampules, which came in a box of 100, were sterilized overnight before use, and that the drugs she used were used in two other operations that day without incident. Prior to that time, 75 ampules had been used out of the box with no untoward results.

A diagnostician and specialist in internal medicine, a Dr. Fordtran, testified for the patient. He had been asked to see the patient when she began developing complications. He said that there is a hazard in the administration of any kind of anesthetic that could in some cases cause death; that bad results do occur from use of bad anesthetics and occur sufficiently enough that manufacturers warn of that possibility in their literature. He added that it was his opinion that the patient's condition was related somehow to the spinal anesthetic, but his specific testimony on this point went as follows:

> "Q. Okay. And when you say that, you mean to say that like one of those cases that just happens once in every 200,000 times, this just happened, is that what you mean?

[8] An earlier suit against the manufacturer of Pentothal Sodium resulted in a summary judgment for the company; see Abbott Laboratories v. Gravis (Tex., 1971) 470 S.W.2d 639. The patient and her husband also sued the physicians, anesthetist and the hospital; see Gravis v. Physicians & Surgeons Hosp. of Alice (Tex. Civ. App., 1967) 415 S.W.2d 674, rev'd (Tex., 1968) 427 S.W.2d 310. It was reported that this case was settled. See Abbott Laboratories v. Gravis (Tex., 1971) 470 S.W.2d 639, at 640.

"A. Yes, sir. Because like I say, this is something people have knowledge of, but it's extremely rare and I personally have never seen [it] before.

"Q. And indicates no wrongdoing on anybody's part?

"A. It doesn't indicate any wrongdoing on anybody's part as far as I can tell.

"Q. Or any defect in any of the procedures or the medication?

"A. According to the information I have."

The witness said that the patient's type of complications was described in the Novocaine warning:

In isolated instances one or several of the following complications or side effects may be observed during or after spinal anesthesia.... *Cauda equina and lumbosacral cord complications* (usually consisting of arachnoiditis and demelinization) *result in loss or impairment of motor and sensory function of the saddle area (bladder, rectum) and one or both legs. These complications have occurred after the use of most, if not all, spinal anesthetics. The loss or impairment of motor function may be permanent, or partial recovery may slowly occur.* Various explanations for such complications have been advanced, such as hypersensitivity or intolerance to the anesthetic agent with a resultant myelolytic or neurotoxic effect; pooling or relatively high concentrations of anesthetic solution around the cauda equina and spinal cord before diffusion; and accidental injection of irritating antiseptics or detergents (as when syringes are incompletely cleansed or when the ampule storage solution enters a cracked ampule). Hence, many anesthesiologists prefer to autoclave ampules in order to destroy bacteria on the exterior before opening.

In an article on the hazards of lumbar puncture, Dripps and Vandam (J.A.M.A. 147:1118, Nov. 17, 1951) pointed out that prolonged and occasionally permanent sensory or motor abnormalities may result from direct trauma to nerve roots when the puncture is performed. In some of the reported cases of neurologic sequelae it was found that the disturbance was due to preexisting disease of the vertebral column or central nervous system (for example, cord tumors, malignant metastases, multiple sclerosis). (Emphasis supplied)

These warnings were directed to the attending physician because, as the brochure pointed out under "Contraindications and precautions":

With the exception of infection in or about the lumbar area and certain serious diseases of the central nervous system or of the lumbar vertebral column, most anesthesiologists consider the following conditions to be only relative contraindications. The decision whether or not to use spinal anesthesia in an individual case depends on the physician's appraisal of the advantages as opposed to the risk and on his ability to cope with the complications that may arise.

The witness testified that a result such as the one involved in this case was extremely rare ("... once in 200,000 times ...") but it was known to happen after spinal anesthetic. He testified further that Adrenalin had nothing to do with the patient's condition.

At the close of the plaintiffs' evidence the drug companies moved for a directed verdict. It was granted, and the plaintiffs appealed. The Court of Appeals of Texas affirmed, declaring:

> Proof (either direct or circumstantial) that a drug in the anesthetic was defective is the prime requirement for recovery in this case.... The crux of this case, then, is proof of the existence of a defect in the drugs furnished by the appellees [the three drug companies]. There is no evidence that the drugs were impure or defective. All of the evidence indicates the contrary. The drugs were clear when visually inspected. Ninety-nine out of 100 that were in the original carton did not cause any injury. All sterilization processes were observed. There was no evidence that the drugs were administered improperly. Testimony showed that ampules from the same carton before and after the one used on Mrs. Gravis were administered without ill effects. The plaintiffs, on the other hand, did not rule out all of the other possible causes of the injury which could establish circumstantially at least, that the defective drug was the only cause. Although Dr. Fordtran testified that in his opinion the injury ... was related (somehow) to the spinal anesthetic, he does not testify that the drugs were defective and hence the cause. Evidence on the critical issue of the existence of a defect in the drugs was not established. Dr. Fordtran admitted that the same results could occur from a hypersensitive reaction (abreaction) where there was no defect in the drugs administered.

PROCAINE PENICILLIN G

See PENICILLIN

PROCHLORPERAZINE

Compazine

Prochlorperazine has a tranquilizing effect and is used to control severe nausea and vomiting, the manifestations of psychotic disorders, and severe to moderate anxiety, tension and agitation.[9]

The drug is contraindicated in comatose or greatly depressed patients due to central nervous system depressants, in the presence of

[9] *Physicians' Desk Reference,* 35th ed., p. 1672.

bone marrow depression, and should not be used in pediatric surgery.[10]

Adverse reactions include, but are not limited to: blurred vision, hypotension, jaundice, muscle spasms, and Parkinsonian-type tremors. Also, there have been occasional reports of sudden death in patients taking phenothiazine derivatives. In some of these cases the cause has appeared to be asphyxia due to failure of the cough reflex. In others the cause has not been determined.[11] In the product literature for Compazine, however, it is stated: "There is not sufficient evidence to establish a relationship between such deaths and the administration of phenothiazines."[12]

Compazine is manufactured by Smith, Kline & French Laboratories (Philadelphia, Pa.).

Smith v. United States (C.A.-5 Miss., 1968) 394 F.2d 482.

Compazine reaction in surgical patient—Conflicting evidence on whether drug should have been given—Judgment for physicians affirmed

The three minor children and the husband of a deceased patient brought suit against the United States government under the Federal Tort Claims Act for her death at the Keesler Air Force Base Hospital on December 6, 1965. At the trial (nonjury) the evidence disclosed that the patient entered the hospital on November 30, 1965 and was operated on for a gallbladder disorder on the morning of December 1. The operation was successful, but that evening, about 10:00 o'clock, the patient became very nauseated. The physician in charge ordered ten milligrams of Compazine. The patient's medical history revealed no untoward experience or idiosyncrasy with regard to the drug.

The first dose resulted in side effects at about 1:30 a.m. on December 2, which were noticed by the nurse on duty in the intensive care ward. The patient was frothing at the mouth and experiencing a "spasm." Various tests were made in an effort to determine the cause of her condition. Her attending physician was called at 3:30 a.m. and arrived in about fifteen minutes. He concluded she was having a reaction to Compazine and gave her phenobarbital. Ap-

[10] *United States Dispensatory,* 27th ed., p. 962.

[11] *Physicians' Desk Reference,* 35th ed., pp. 1673-74.

[12] Id., p. 1674.

parently it did not work, and the patient died early in the morning of December 6.

At the trial, a medical witness testified that Compazine should never be given a patient under any circumstances within 24 hours after an operation such as the patient had; that the drug was lethal when given within that time; and that this fact is recognized by most informed physicians and hospital personnel. In the present case, however, the surgeon, the assistant surgeon, and the anesthesiologist had all concurred in the order giving the patient Compazine the evening of the operation.

The amount of the dosage was not criticized. The government physicians said that they had used Compazine many times in the same manner, and for the same purpose on many patients with no side effects. The literature on the drug accompanying the package did not contain any warning that it might be lethal if given within a certain time after an operation. And the evidence did not reveal any known method of determining in advance as to the idiosyncrasies of a patient to Compazine.

The attending physician admitted that a delay longer than twenty minutes in administering an antidote after a reaction to Compazine would be dangerous and probably result in fatality. The record showed the patient was not given an antidote until about 4:00 a.m., which was two and one-half hours after her first symptoms of a reaction.

The autopsy report on the patient said in effect that death was *possibly* due to side effects of Compazine.

The District Court rendered judgment in favor of the defendants and the plaintiffs appealed. The United States Court of Appeals affirmed the judgment, declaring:

> The expert testimony was conflicting regarding (1) the propriety of administering Compazine to combat nausea after a gall bladder operation, and (2) the reasonableness of the delay in administering the antidote.... [T]he findings of the District Court are subject to being overturned only if 'clearly erroneous.' While the opinion evidence is conflicting, it cannot be said that the court's findings were unsupported.

Vincent v. Smith, Kline & French Laboratories (Docket No. 34117, First Circuit Court, Hawaii, 1973).

Brain damage in infant from excessive dosage—$160,000 settlement

An eight-month-old infant became ill with fever, nausea and vomiting. The child's parents described the symptoms over the telephone to the family physician and he prescribed Compazine suppositories. While the child was still under treatment, the physician went on vacation and the parents consulted a second physician who, without determining what had already been prescribed, ordered Compazine syrup.

The infant's condition worsened, and she was admitted to the hospital where yet additional doses of Compazine were administered. A diagnosis of "Compazine intoxication" was finally made by a pediatrician, but by this time the infant had suffered irreversible cerebral dysfunction which permanently affected her learning powers, verbal motor coordination, and personality.

The parents brought suit against the two physicians and the manufacturer of the drug. The physicians were charged with negligence in failing to heed the manufacturer's recommendations that Compazine not be given to children who weighed under twenty pounds or who were under two years of age, except where "potentially lifesaving." The manufacturer was charged with negligence in not fully warning the medical profession of the permanent disabilities which could occur when Compazine is used in treatment of children under the weight and age specified, and in cases where the dosage exceeds that which is recommended.

The case was settled prior to trial for $160,000, with all three defendants participating in the settlement.[13]

Tielis v. Smith, Kline & French Laboratories (Supreme Court, Kings County, N.Y., April 12, 1973).

Neuromuscular damage after reaction to Compazine—$409,500 settlement

Compazine was given to a fourteen-year-old child by a summer camp doctor for upset stomach. About an hour after the injection, the child suffered severe nerve and muscle reaction, and then paralysis which lasted for eight weeks. A partial recovery was made, but the child still walks with a "shuffling gait," has poor arm coordination, and suffers a speech defect. Actions were filed against the drug manufacturer, the physician and the camp administrators. The charge against the manufacturer was failure to include a warning on the label regarding possible neuromuscular damage. The case was settled for $409,500.[14]

---

[13] ATLA *News Letter* 16:315, 1973.
[14] Id., 16:271, 1973.

PRODROX
See HYDROXYPROGESTERONE CAPROATE

PROGESTERONE

Progesterone is an important hormone produced in the body in the testis and adrenal cortex. It has been used to treat a variety of menstrual disorders, although the availability of orally effective synthetic hormones has reduced its use in recent years.[15] It is currently produced by Legeve Pharmaceuticals (Costa Mesa, Cal.).

Mincey v. Blando (Mo. App., 1983) 655 S.W.2d 609.

Use of progesterone for pelvic pain and uterine bleeding question for jury

The patient saw the defendant general practitioner for pelvic pain and excessive uterine bleeding. He prescribed daily injections of progesterone for four days. At the end of the four days he examined the patient's uterus, determined that it was slightly enlarged, and suspecting a fibroid tumor, referred her to a specialist.

Although the patient introduced expert medical testimony that the use of progesterone was contraindicated in the case of undiagnosed genital bleeding, the trial court did not submit this question of negligence to the jury. The Court of Appeal reversed as to this issue and remanded the case for a new trial.

Shultz v. Rice (C.A.-10 Kan., 1986) 809 F.2d 643.

Progesterone administered to pregnant patient—Physician not liable for plaintiff's mental anguish

The plaintiff, aged 25, was treated by the defendant, a specialist in internal medicine, for various female-related problems, including amenorrhea. When the plaintiff informed the defendant that she had not had a menstrual period for two months, he administered 200 milligrams of progesterone in sesame oil. He later testified that before he administered the injection, he asked the plaintiff, who was unmarried, whether she had engaged in sexual intercourse recently and that he had noted in his records that she had "denied exposure." The plaintiff later claimed that the defendant had never inquired concerning her sexual activity.

---

[15] *United States Dispensatory,* 27th ed., pp. 963-4.

The afternoon of the day she received the injection, a laboratory report revealed that the plaintiff was pregnant. On learning of this fact, the defendant counseled the plaintiff concerning various options available to her, including abortion. He later testified that he did not mention any possible risk of fetal damage from the progesterone because he did not want to alarm the plaintiff about what he considered a "non-threatening situation."

The plaintiff testified that she consulted several other physicians and was told that an injection of progesterone was very dangerous to a fetus, and that it would likely cause birth defects in a child. She testified that one physician had told her that "it would be like shooting craps to keep the baby, because of the birth defects."

Twelve days after receiving the injection, the plaintiff was hospitalized for abdominal pains and bleeding which, upon examination, were found to be unrelated to the progesterone. Five days later, however, the plaintiff was notified that her fetus was dead.

In her lawsuit against the defendant, the plaintiff charged him with failing to ascertain whether pregnancy was the cause of her menstrual irregularity before injecting her with the progesterone, and with failing to inform her of the risks involved in administering progesterone to pregnant women. The plaintiff made no claim for personal injury, nor did she claim that the progesterone injection caused any harm to her fetus. She claimed only that the defendant's actions caused her mental anguish during the two-week period from the confirmation to the termination of her pregnancy.

The jury returned a verdict for the defendant. On appeal, the reviewing court, after finding no merit to numerous claims of procedural errors during trial, affirmed the lower court's judgment.

Related cases

No evidence that progesterone caused heart defects in children

In Fontenot v. Upjohn Co. (C.A.-5 La., 1986) 780 F.2d 1190, the mother of two children born with heart defects (one child had a ventricle septal defect and the other had both a ventricle septal defect and valve problems) failed to offer "a scintilla of evidence" that her children's conditions were the result of taking progesterone before the birth of each child.

PROLOPRIM

See TRIMETHOPRIM and SULFAMETHOXAZOLE

PROLOXIN

See FLUPHENAZINE HYDROCHLORIDE

PROMAZINE HYDROCHLORIDE

Sparine

Promazine hydrochloride, marketed as Sparine by Wyeth Laboratories (Philadelphia, Pa.), is a tranquilizing agent used in the treatment of acute and chronic abnormalities of the central nervous system characterized by emotional disturbances and hyperactivity. In obstetrics the drug is used in the management of labor, frequently as an analgesic-sedative combination with meperidine and scopolamine.[16]

When injected intravenously the concentration of promazine hydrochloride should not be greater than 25 milligrams per milliliter, and the dose should be administered slowly, with care to avoid perivascular extravasation (infiltration) into the surrounding tissues, which can lead to tissue destruction.[17]

Buchanan v. Downing (1964) 74 N.M. 423, 394 P.2d 269.

Reaction at injection site—Directed verdicts for physician and manufacturer—Physician's verdict affirmed on appeal

The patient had suffered from vomiting and diarrhea for about three days. A physician came to his home, examined him, and administered an injection of Sparine into the deltoid muscle of his arm. An "instant reaction" to the injection occurred, and the injection site "immediately reddened." A "festering" wound developed, and the patient ultimately had to undergo a skin graft.

The patient brought suit against the physician and the manufacturer of the drug. After depositions were taken, the defendants moved for a summary judgment, claiming there were no genuine issues of material facts. The motion was sustained.

The patient's attorneys appealed as to the physician, alleging that the theory of *res ipsa loquitur* should apply because of a statement made by the physician shortly after the incident: "This is not

[16] *United States Dispensatory,* 27th ed., p. 966.
[17] Id.

a natural reaction to such an injection." The patient's attorneys argued that this response sufficiently showed that the accident would not have occurred but for negligence. The Supreme Court of New Mexico did not agree, however, finding that even though the injury may not have been a natural reaction, "it does not follow that an unnatural reaction was the result of negligence."

Schrib v. Seidenberg (1969) 80 N.M. 573, 458 P.2d 825.

Gangrene—Sparine allegedly injected into artery—Judgment of $51,200 for plaintiffs affirmed

The patient and her husband brought suit against their physician after the patient developed gangrene following an injection of Sparine.

The trial court, hearing the case without a jury, found that the physician had failed to follow generally accepted standards to prevent arterial injection of the drug; i.e., after inserting the needle, he failed "to make adequate observations to determine whether the needle had been inadvertently introduced into an artery." Judgment was for the plaintiffs for $51,200.

The physician appealed, contending there was no evidence to support the findings of the court. He relied on testimony that (a) the drug could be properly injected into the vein and then leak into the artery and (b) in giving intravenous injections one can get into an artery even while exercising the best of precautions and the best medical practice. "This testimony expresses no more than 'possibilities'," stated the Court of Appeals of New Mexico, which affirmed the judgment. The court continued:

> Opposed to this testimony is the testimony of at least two of the expert medical witnesses. Their testimony directly supports the findings made by the trial court. If the 'possibilities' relied on by [the physician] can be considered as raising a conflict in the evidence, they do not aid [the physician] on appeal. Conflicts are resolved in favor of the successful party and in support of the judgment. [The physician] also relies on testimony to the effect that '... there is no way in the world to know in this particular case ...' exactly what happened. Thus, he attacks the finding that the injection was the proximate cause of the gangrene. In addition to testifying that in injecting the Sparine, [the physician] departed from recognized medical standards, the expert medical witnesses gave their opinion, as a reasonable medical probability, that this improper injection was the proximate cause of the gangrene and resultant consequences.... The evidence of the expert

medical witnesses substantially supports the findings as to [the physician's] malpractice in injecting the Sparine.

Nolan v. Dillon (1971) 261 Md. 516, 276 A.2d 36.

Gangrene at injection site—Excessive intravenous dosage alleged—$72,500 verdict for patient affirmed—Manufacturer's warning deemed adequate

The evidence disclosed that in January, 1968 the defendant physician, an obstetrician, admitted the patient, then nineteen years of age, to the hospital for the delivery of her first child. The patient was given two injections: the first, in preparation of delivery, at 12:45 a.m., and the second, just prior to delivery, at 1:50 a.m., when she became unmanageable and had to be restrained. The first injection contained Sparine, meperidine and scopolamine, and the second only Sparine.

Immediately after the second injection the patient's left hand became discolored and cyanotic. Ultimately gangrene set in, and it became necessary to amputate the distal phalanges of the index, ring and little fingers.

There was testimony at the trial that Sparine, prepared by Wyeth Laboratories, was available in the hospital delivery suite in two concentrations: one a ten cubic centimeter ampule containing 25 milligrams of the drug per cubic centimeter, and the other, also a ten cubic centimeter ampule, containing fifty milligrams of the drug per cubic centimeter. The second one was clearly labeled in large red letters, "For Intramuscular Use Only." Each package contained an insert which described the drug, its uses, and dosage and administration. The insert read, in part:

> *It is important to make sure that intramuscular injections are given deeply into large muscle masses, i. e., gluteal region, and intravenous injections are given in diluted solutions (25 mg./cc. or less) into the lumen of the vein. Under no circumstances should intra-arterial injections be given.*
>
> *Sparine (Promazine Hydrochloride ...) when used intravenously should be used in a concentration no greater than 25 mg. per cc. The injection should be given slowly.* Suitable dilution of the more concentrated solution, 50 mg. per cc., with an equivalent volume of physiological saline is advised if used intravenously. Under such circumstances of use, the parenteral administration of Sparine (Promazine Hydrochloride ...) is well tolerated. Its use is not usually attended by local discomfort or irritation provided correct techniques are employed to insure injection into the lumen of the vein; care should be exercised during intravenous

administration not to allow perivascular extravasation since under such circumstances chemical irritation may be severe. The intravenous administration of Sparine (Promazine Hydrochloride ...) in a concentration of 50 mg. per cc. has resulted in localized thrombophlebitis or vascular spasm and localized cellulitis in an extremely small number of cases. In nine cases, arteriolar spasm of the digital vessels with resulting gangrene has been reported, some of which have required amputation of the digits. Hazards such as this may be avoided provided that: 1) A concentration of no greater than 25 mg. per cc. be used; 2) The whole contents of the syringe be injected into the lumen of the vein; 3) That injections be made only into vessels previously undamaged by multiple injections or trauma.

In his pretrial deposition the physician said that he had injected Sparine "just as I got it from the ampule, (50 mgs)" using a two and one-half cubic centimeter syringe, clearly implying that he had used the fifty-milligram concentration. The note on the hospital record, signed by the physician, "Sparine 100 mgm I.V. at 1:50 a.m.," although not a contemporaneous one, would seem, if read in the light of the deposition, to bear this out.

The physician testified at the trial, however, that he had used the 25 milligram concentration in a five cubic centimeter syringe to inject 100 milligrams of Sparine. He and the attending nurse testified that the first injection, a "cocktail" of meperidine, scopolamine and Sparine, was given the patient at 12:45 a.m. in her right arm. (In his pretrial deposition the physician had been much less certain about this.) And the physician was sure that the second injection of Sparine was given at 1:50 a.m. in the antecubital vein of the left arm. The patient testified that she remembered only one injection, the first, and said it had been given in her left arm. (This contradiction was said to be of consequence because, had both injections been given in the same arm, the chances of extravasation of the drug, or escape from the vein, would have increased.)

In his deposition and in the clinical note he dictated for the hospital record the physician attributed the patient's reaction to the possibility that the drug had extravasated or that some of the medication had been injected outside the vein. He explained this by saying that the patient was "thrashing about" in bed while he was giving the injection.

A medical witness called by the physician testified that the warnings given on the package insert provided reasonable directions as to dosage and concentration of Sparine and represented the standard of care followed by physicians practicing in the community. He said that the same instructions appeared in the *Physicians' Desk Reference to Pharmaceutical Specialties and Biologicals* (PDR) published annually and distributed among physicians. The physician admitted that PDR was available to him, that he was familiar with it, and that it was "a good volume."

A physician called as a witness by the patient testified that an injection of Sparine in a 25 milligram concentration could cause a vascular spasm and cyanosis if injected into an artery, into the wall of an artery, or into a vein in such fashion that it extravasated.

The jury returned a verdict of $72,500 in favor of the patient against the physician,[18] and the trial court entered judgment accordingly. The physician appealed. The Court of Appeals of Maryland affirmed the judgment, declaring:

> On the testimony as a whole, whether [the physician] was negligent, and whether his negligence caused Mrs. Dillon's injury were clearly jury questions.... [T]here was ample testimony that a failure to observe the manufacturer's warnings did not conform to the standards of practice in the field of obstetrics in [the community]. The package insert ... does not standing alone establish a standard of care, but rather, prima facie proof of proper use.... Whether there was a failure to use properly, and whether such a failure proximately caused the injury, were jury questions.

Ohligschlager v. Proctor Community Hospital (1973) 55 Ill. 2d 411, 303 N.E.2d 392.

Infiltration into tissue—Directed verdicts for attending physician and hospital reversed on appeal

The patient was admitted to the hospital at 4:30 p.m. on September 15, 1966 because of persistent vomiting and diarrhea. Her physician (defendant) had ordered intravenous feeding when he arranged for her admission, but when he arrived at 6:30 it had not been started. He later testified that someone had "tried to insert a needle prior to my arrival" but apparently was unsuccessful. He inserted the needle into a vein near her right elbow, started the I.V., and added fifty milligrams of Sparine.

A nurse was present when the defendant started the I.V., but he gave her no special instructions. He left for dinner, and returned to

[18] The jury found Wyeth Laboratories free of liability. On review, the Court of Appeals commented that it was clear that the company's package insert and label on the 50-milligram concentration fully discharged its duty to warn. The company's duty, said the court, "is to give a reasonable warning, not the best possible one."

the patient's room about 10:00 p.m. By then the patient was on her second I.V. The needle appeared to be in place, and the fluid was running at the proper rate. The defendant added another 75 mg. of Sparine. In neither instance was the Sparine mixed with the I.V. solution, but added to the tube a few inches above the needle.

The patient testified that soon after visiting hours ended, she experienced severe pain in her right elbow. Another patient in the room called for a nurse by turning on a light. A nurse's aide came and the patient told her about the pain. The aide said she would see what she could do and left. No one came to the room, and the light was again turned on. The patient said she did not remember anyone responding to her complaint until 7:00 o'clock the next morning, although the hospital chart showed that the second I.V. was completed at 1:00 a.m. and at that time she asked for medicine for pain.

The nursing supervisor on the 7:00 a.m. to 4:00 p.m. shift testified that she received a report at 7:00 a.m. that the patient had been quite ill during the night and she went immediately to her room. In her "incident report" the supervisor wrote: "Apparently the I.V. solution infiltrated as the next morning her arm at the site of I.V. injection was discolored (white). Ice bags applied per [the defendant's] order." She also wrote: "The area on the right arm (inner aspect of elbow) where the first solution was started turned bluish black, became swollen, hard and the outer edges were red. Ice bags applied as ordered. Doctors [the defendant and a medical colleague] are aware of this situation." Sometime after this report was made, the defendant's medical partner examined the patient and wrote: "Medical findings — large ecchymotic area — extending over entire ulno-volar aspect of arm 3 inches above elbow to 2 inches above wrist. Etiology — infiltration from IV medication."

The testimony at the trial established that with intravenous feeding there is a risk of infiltration or extravasation, which is the escape of fluid from the vein into surrounding tissue. The defendant's medical partner testified that it occurs in connection with 5% to 10% of intravenous feedings.

The manufacturer's instructions that came with the Sparine cautioned:

> Sparine (Promazine Hydrochloride, Wyeth) when used intravenously should be used in a concentration no greater than 25 m.g. per c.c. The injection should be given slowly. Suitable dilution of the more concentrated solution, 50 m.g. per c.c., with an equivalent volume of physiological saline is advised if used intrave-

> nously ... care should be exercised during intravenous administration not to allow perivascular extravasation since under such circumstances chemical irritation may be severe. The intravenous administration ... in a concentration of 50 m.g. per c.c. has resulted in localized thrombophlebitis ... in an extremely small number of cases.... That injection be made only into vessels previously undamaged by multiple injections or trauma.

The plaintiff introduced a physician who had practiced medicine for 32 years in the hospitals in the area, including the Proctor Community Hospital. He testified that he was familiar with the practice in the community concerning the ordering of intravenous feedings, and that in his own practice he gave no special instructions when an ordinary intravenous solution was used, but when an additive was used he instructed the nurse to watch the patient more carefully. He stated that if Sparine was injected directly into the tubing during an intravenous feeding it could cause a reaction and might cause a thrombosis or breakdown of the blood vessel wall, and fluid in the vein would leak into surrounding tissue. He explained that this breakdown would not happen immediately, that it took time for the substance to corrode the inside wall of the blood vessel, and that the length of time depended on the concentration and solutions used, the particular blood vessel, and the individual anatomy of the person involved.

A plastic surgeon testified that the patient was referred to him by the defendant on October 10, 1966. His examination of her right arm revealed an area of skin necrosis and ulceration in the antecubital area. The affected area was about 32 square inches, being basically four inches by eight inches and running from above the elbow to below the elbow. On October 27th he surgically removed the dead tissue, and took a four-inch-by-eight-inch graft from her abdomen and applied it to her arm. She was released on November 17th.

The trial court directed a verdict and entered judgment in favor of the physician and the hospital. The patient appealed, and the Appellate Court of Illinois affirmed the judgment of the trial court. The patient then appealed to the Supreme Court of Illinois.

The Supreme Court reversed the judgment and remanded the case for a new trial. The court stated:

> It is true that except in the so-called 'common knowledge' or 'gross negligence' situations ... expert testimony is essential to the proof of the standard of professional care against which due care must be measured. In our opinion, however, this record

presents an appropriate state of facts for applying an exception to the rule. Under the circumstances shown, the explicit instructions furnished by the manufacturer for the proper manner of intravenous injection of the Sparine and the warning of the hazards accompanying its improper administration provide the proof of the proper professional standards which would ordinarily be shown by expert medical testimony.... Here the manufacturer's instructions contained specific instructions for the use of Sparine and warned of the hazards that could result from its improper administration; [the defendant-physician] was familiar with the recommendation that Sparine be used 'in a concentration of no greater than 25 m.g. per c.c.' and that intravenous administration 'in a concentration of 50 m.g. per c.c. has resulted in localized thrombophlebitis' and nevertheless ordered concentrations of 50 m.g. and 75 m.g. injected directly into the intravenous tubing. Although [the defendant-physician] was familiar with the manufacturer's *caveat* that 'care should be exercised during intravenous administration not to allow perivascular extravasation since under such circumstances chemical irritation may be severe' he did not instruct the nurse to watch more carefully than normal for extravasation. We hold that there was sufficient evidence of deviation from the manufacturer's recommendations and instructions for the issue of [the defendant-physician's] negligence to have been submitted to the jury.... We are also of the opinion that there was sufficient evidence adduced from which the inferences could be drawn that defendant Proctor was negligent, and that its negligence contributed to cause plaintiff's injury. Plaintiff testified that the gauze around her arm became tight because of swelling and she suffered terrible pain. Although a nurse's aide was told of the pain and swelling shortly after 8:30 P.M. the intravenous feeding was not discontinued until 1:00 A.M. The testimony of ... the nursing supervisor, shows that it was the duty of the nurses to make periodic checks and observe the condition of the needle and whether the fluid was flowing. She stated that in the 'in service' orientation programs at the hospital the problem of infiltration or extravasation is discussed and the nurses are warned of the dangers which accompany the administering of certain types of intravenous fluids. She testified that 'if a patient complained of pain at the injection site the I.V. feeding should be discontinued immediately. Pain and swelling are symptoms of extravasation.' ... [T]he evidence was sufficient to require submission of the issues to the jury and the circuit court erred in directing a verdict.

Magee v. Wyeth Laboratories (1963) 214 Cal. App. 2d 40, 29 Cal. Rptr. 322.

Fatal agranulocytosis—Physicians' failure to monitor patient exonerates manufacturer

The patient, an attorney suffering from "emotional depression," entered Las Encinas Sanitarium on October 7, 1958. He was placed on Sparine on admission and received the drug until November 17, 1958, when he died from severe infections brought about as a result of agranulocytosis, a blood disorder which deprives the body of the ability to fight infection. It was determined that the patient had developed the blood disorder on or about November 13, and that it was caused by the Sparine.

Evidence at the trial established that certain individuals are sensitive to promazine hydrochloride, and that in rare cases, agranulocytosis can result. The manufacturer was aware of this risk and the package insert contained a warning to this effect. Treating physicians were cautioned that "patients should be observed frequently and asked to report immediately any sudden appearance of any signs of infection," and that "if white blood counts and differential smears give an indication of severe cellular depression the drug should be discontinued and antibiotic and other suitable therapy should be initiated." According to the evidence, the patient's physicians had not ordered blood tests when the patient developed obvious signs of infection.

The patient's widow settled with the physicians at the sanitarium for $23,000, and the jury returned a verdict for the manufacturer. The Court of Appeal of California affirmed, finding the patient's physicians' failure to follow the instructions on using the drug constituted a break in causation which exonerated the manufacturer from liability.

Related cases

Respiratory depression and brain damage in newborn

In Downing v. Manta (No. 79-21845, Circuit Court, Dade County, Fla., Oct. 17, 1980), a pregnant patient given oxytocin (Pitocin), Sparine and several other drugs prior to delivery gave birth to twin fetuses suffering from severe respiratory depression and brain damage. The case is summarized herein under OXYTOCIN.

Excessive medication during prolonged labor

In Sanchez v. Flower & Fifth Avenue Hospital (No. 14073/79, Supreme Court, New York County, N.Y., Jan. 31, 1986), a jury awarded $4 million to an eight-year-old brain damaged boy whose mother was given repeated doses of Demerol (meperidine hydrochloride), Sparine and Seconal (secobarbital sodium) during 22 hours of prolonged labor. The case is summarized herein under MEPERIDINE HYDROCHLORIDE.

PROMETHAZINE HYDROCHLORIDE
Mepergan
Phenergan

Promethazine hydrochloride is a phenothiazine derivative used for the prevention of motion sickness, as an antihistamine, as a sedative, and as an adjunct to analgesics. It is available in an injectable form, sometimes in combination with meperidine hydrochloride (Demerol), and in tablet form, usually in combination with analgesics, mainly aspirin.[19]

Mepergan (25 mg. Demerol, 25 mg. promethazine hydrochloride) is manufactured by Wyeth Laboratories (Philadelphia, Pa.) as is Phenergan. The drug is also produced by several companies under the generic name.

Adverse reactions include, but are not limited to, drowsiness, dizziness, convulsive seizures, fluctuations in blood pressure, nausea and vomiting, and asthma.[20]

Facciolo v. Peoples Drug Stores, Inc. (No. 5C88CV-13333, Superior Court, Muscogee County, Ga., Nov. 29, 1989).

Plaintiff falls asleep at wheel after taking Phenergan—Pharmacist charged with failure to warn—$2 million settlement

Between one and two hours after taking a Phenergan, the plaintiff, a systems engineer, fell asleep while driving his automobile and struck the rear-end of a truck. He suffered a brain concussion, extensive facial lacerations, including the loss of the tip of his nose, and the loss of one eye. His medical expenses were nearly $100,000, he was off work for three months, and continuing memory loss, decreased stamina, and headaches threatened future employment.

He brought suit against the pharmacy that filled his prescription, alleging that the pharmacist failed to inform him, either orally or by placing a warning on the label, that Phenergan could cause drowsiness.

The parties settled for $2 million.[21]

---

[19] *Physicians' Desk Reference,* 35th ed., p. 1946.

[20] Id.

[21] *Professional Negligence Law Reporter* 5:34, 1990.

Respiratory failure during surgery—Interaction between promethazine hydrochloride and Nembutal blamed

In Schleichart v. St. John's Smithtown Hosp. (Docket No. 74/2532, Supreme Court, Suffolk County, N.Y., Sept. 27, 1979), a patient suffered respiratory failure during a tracheotomy, allegedly the result of the potentiating effects of promethazine hydrochloride and Nembutal (sodium pentobarbital). The case is summarized herein under SODIUM PENTOBARBITAL.

Respiratory failure and brain damage following Phenergan and Demerol injection

In Fuller v. Starnes (1980) 268 Ark. 476, 597 S.W.2d 88, an 86-year-old patient stopped breathing following an administration of 25 mg. of Demerol (meperidine hydrochloride) and 25 mg. of Phenergan. The case is summarized herein under MEPERIDINE HYDROCHLORIDE.

Respiratory distress and brain damage in newborn—Mother given Phenergan, Seconal and Demerol

In Lhotka v. Larson (1976) 307 Minn. 121, 238 N.W.2d 870, a newborn whose mother had been given Seconal (secobarbital sodium), Phenergan and Demerol (meperidine hydrochloride) suffered respiratory distress and brain damage. The case is summarized herein under SECOBARBITAL SODIUM.

PROPANTHELINE BROMIDE
Pro-Banthine
Pro-Banthine with Phenobarbital

Propantheline bromide inhibits gastrointestinal motility and diminishes gastric acid secretion. It is used as adjunctive therapy in the treatment of peptic ulcer.[1] Phenobarbital, a sedative, has been added to the preparation for patients who are also nervous, apprehensive or anxious.

Adverse reactions include varying degrees of drying of salivary secretions and blurred vision. Also, the following reactions have been reported: nervousness, drowsiness, dizziness, insomnia, headache, loss of the sense of taste, nausea, vomiting, constipation, impotence and allergic dermatitis.[2]

---

[1] Id., p. 1665.
[2] Id.

Searle & Company (San Juan, P.R.), manufactures Pro-Banthine, and several companies market the drug under the generic name.

Dermatological reaction in patient receiving Pro-Banthine with Phenobarbital and five other drugs

In Slack v. Fleet (La. App., 1970) 242 So. 2d 650, a middle-aged woman patient who complained to her physician of "pain and cramping in the stomach, nausea, vomiting and nervousness" was given prescriptions for Pro-Banthine with Phenobarbital and five other drugs. She took the drugs simultaneously, as directed, and developed a severe rash. In the resulting lawsuit a question arose over the propriety of prescribing that particular combination of drugs in a case such as the plaintiff's. The defendant-physician offered two medical witnesses who testified that his choice of medication was within acceptable standards. The plaintiff offered no expert testimony. The trial court dismissed the action and was upheld on appeal. The case is summarized herein under PHENACETIN.

PROPOXYPHENE HYDROCHLORIDE

Darvon
Dolene
Lorcet
SK-65; SK-65 Compound
Wygesic

Propoxyphene hydrochloride is a mild analgesic used orally to relieve mild to moderate pain.[3] The Darvon preparations are manufactured by Eli Lilly and Company (Indianapolis, Ind.), Dolene by Lederle Laboratories (Wayne, N.J.), Lorcet by UAD Laboratories (Jackson, Miss.), SK-65 and SK-65 Compound (until 1987) by Smith, Kline & French Laboratories (Philadelphia, Pa.), and Wygesic by Wyeth Laboratories (Philadelphia, Pa.).

The most frequent adverse reactions are dizziness, drowsiness, nausea, and vomiting. Less common are constipation, abdominal pain, rashes, headache, euphoria, dysphoria, and minor visual disturbances have been reported.[4]

In 1977 statistics released by the National Institute on Drug Abuse listed 5,580 abuse cases involving propoxyphene during the

[3] *Physicians' Desk Reference,* 35th ed., p. 1052.
[4] Id., p. 1053.

period between May, 1976 and April, 1977. About half of the cases involved suicide attempts. Measured by emergency room experience, propoxyphene was determined to be the sixth most abused drug in the nation. The following year the Food and Drug Administration ordered all manufacturers to include a warning in the package inserts that the drug can be poisonous or fatal in overdoses, that the majority of propoxyphene-related poisons and fatalities occurred in patients with histories of suicidal tendencies, emotional disturbances or misuse of alcohol, tranquilizers or other central nervous system depressants, and therefore "caution should be exercised in prescribing unnecessarily large amounts of propoxyphene for such patients."[5]

It was also discovered that newborn infants could experience propoxyphene withdrawal symptoms if their mothers took the drug during pregnancy, and a warning was issued on this hazard.[6]

In the fall of 1979 the warnings were revised to include a Patient Information Sheet highlighting these hazards.[7]

Shaugnessy v. Spray (No. A7905-02395, Circuit Court, Multnomah County, Ore., Feb. 16, 1983).

Drug addict dies from overdose—Physician charged with overprescribing—$250,000 jury verdict

The defendant physician treated a twenty-year-old patient for heroin and morphine addiction. After picking up a prescription at the defendant's office for sixty propoxphene hydrochloride capsules (65 mg.), the patient was found dead of an overdose. In their lawsuit, the patient's survivors alleged that the defendant was negligent in prescribing more than eight capsules at one time for an outpatient, in prescribing a drug in an amount sufficient to cause death, in failing to take an adequate medical history which would have revealed the patient's suicide tendencies, and in failing to hospitalize the patient. The jury awarded the plaintiffs $250,000 which was reduced by 25% for the patient's negligence, and by $3,500 for an earlier settlement with two drug companies.[8]

---

[5] *FDA Drug Bulletin,* March-April, 1978, pp. 14-15.
[6] Id.
[7] *FDA Drug Bulletin,* September, 1979, pp. 22-24.
[8] ATLA *Law Reporter* 26:331, 1983.

Eldridge v. Eli Lilly & Co. (1985) 138 Ill. App. 3d 124, 92 Ill. Dec. 740, 485 N.E.2d 551.

Pharmacist has no duty to warn of excessive dosage

The plaintiff alleged that his decedent died from an overdose of Darvon and several other drugs as a result of the defendant pharmacist's negligence in filling the prescriptions. According to the plaintiff, the defendant filled the prescriptions for quantities beyond those normally prescribed by physicians. The defendant had a duty, the plaintiff claimed, to warn the decedent's physician that his prescriptions were for an excess quantity.

The trial court granted the pharmacist's motion for summary judgment and the Appellate Court of Illinois affirmed, holding that the physician must evaluate a patient's needs, assess the risks and benefits of available drugs, prescribe them, and supervise their use, and a pharmacist has no common-law or statutory duty to refuse to fill a prescription simply because it is for a quantity beyond that normally prescribed, nor a duty to warn the patient's physician of that fact.

Related cases

Traces of propoxyphene hydrochloride in stomach of child who died after taking worm medicine

In Holbrook v. Rose (Ky. App., 1970) 458 S.W.2d 155, a pharmacist and the manufacturer of Jayne's P-W Vermifuge tablets (containing hexylresorcinol) were sued by the parents of a three-year-old child who died two days after being given the medicine for worms. A toxicologist's report showed traces of propoxyphene hydrochloride in the child's stomach contents, and during cross-examination, a pediatrician testifying for the plaintiffs admitted that the propoxyphene hydrochloride, if given in sufficiently large doses or over a long period of time, could have caused the symptoms from which the child suffered just prior to her death. The pharmacist was awarded a directed verdict and the manufacturer of the vermifuge was granted a judgment n.o.v. For further discussion of this case, see HEXYLRESORCINOL herein.

Addiction—Employee's complaint against company doctors not barred by Workers' Compensation Act

The exclusivity provisions of the Maryland Workers' Compensation Act did not bar an action by an employee who claimed his addiction to Darvon was the result of being supplied drugs and prescriptions by his employer's doctors for treatment of a work-related injury. Sterry v. Bethlehem Steel Corp. (1985) 64 Md. App. 175, 494 A.2d 748.

PROPOXYPHENE NAPSYLATE

Darvocet-N

Darvon-N

Propoxyphene napsylate differs from propoxyphene hydrochloride (see above) in that it allows more stable dosage forms and tablet formulations. Because of differences in molecular weight, a dose of 100 mg of propoxyphene napsylate is required to supply an amount of propoxyphene equivalent to that present in 65 mg of propoxyphene hydrochloride. The product is indicated for the relief of mild to moderate pain, either when pain is present alone or when it is accompanied by fever. Darvocet-N is also available with acetaminophen (Darvocet-N 100).[9] The manufacturer is Eli Lilly and Company (Indianapolis, Ind.).

Bourne v. Seventh Ward General Hosp. (La. App., 1989) 546 So. 2d 197.

Fatal hepatitis following overdose—Negligent care by internist and hospital

On February 10, 1978, the patient, a 20-year-old woman, was in an automobile accident and suffered a painful cervical strain. On February 14, she consulted her family physician who prescribed two drugs for her pain: Darvocet-N 100 and Flexeril (cyclobenzaprine hydrochloride). On February 17, the patient attempted suicide by swallowing the pills remaining in the two bottles.

At the hospital emergency room the family physician ordered the patient's stomach pumped, and recommended that her case be turned over to the defendant, a specialist in internal medicine. By the next day, the patient appeared to be progressing well, and she was transferred to a semi-private room. The following day, the defendant ordered a series of blood tests, and the day after that, she ordered a liver profile study. Neither set of tests could be performed at the Seventh Ward General Hospital, which was a small facility, and the samples were sent out to laboratories.

---

[9] *Physicians' Desk Reference,* 43rd ed., p. 1171.

Around noon on February 20, the patient began exhibiting bizarre and violent behavior, and the defendant summoned a psychiatrist. Since the hospital was not equipped to handle psychiatric cases, the patient was transferred to the Southeast Louisiana State Hospital. The results of the blood and liver tests had not yet been received. Also, the patient's records were not sent with her because the defendant and the psychiatrist each thought the other was going to do so.

The records of the receiving hospital noted that on admission the patient's skin was jaundiced. During the morning of the 21st, she began vomiting and was incontinent, and her temperature varied between 100.1 and 104.6 degrees Fahrenheit. That afternoon she aspirated vomitus, her condition worsened, and at 6:30 p.m. she was pronounced dead. The autopsy report listed the cause of death as "acute necrotizing toxic hepatitis with jaundice probably secondary to overdose of Flexeril and Darvocet deliberately ingested by the patient with suicidal intent."

In her suit against the internist and the two hospitals where her daughter was confined, the patient's mother claimed that the defendants deprived her daughter of a reasonable chance of surviving the overdose because of substandard care. The plaintiff introduced an expert who testified that the defendant internist should have known the potential of liver toxicity from the drugs the patient swallowed, especially the acetaminophen contained in Darvocet-N. He stated that the defendant should have watched carefully for the possibility of the patient developing hepatitis, and that she should have been supported properly through that illness with intravenous fluids to "rest" the liver. (The patient had been given a regular diet.)

The plaintiff's expert also faulted the defendant internist for failing to detect that the patient was hypoglycemic, which he claimed to be the probable cause of her bizarre behavior immediately before her transfer to the state hospital.

The case was heard by the trail judge without a jury who found the internist negligent as charged. He also found the Seventh Ward General Hospital personnel negligent in not having in effect a procedure whereby abnormal test results would be reported immediately to the physician. He held also that the Southeast Louisiana State Hospital was negligent in not ordering pertinent laboratory tests on the patient's admission nor making any attempt to follow-up with the Seventh Ward General Hospital concerning tests performed there.

On appeal, the Court of Appeal affirmed as to the internist and Southeast Louisiana State Hospital, and reversed as to Seventh Ward, holding that there was a procedure whereby the internist could have obtained the results of the patient's tests immediately, and that the use of outside laboratories for some studies was a common practice among hospitals.

Harrington v. Rush Presby. St. Lukes Hosp. (No. 79 L 11578, Circuit Court, Cook County, Ill., October 3, 1988).

Patient dies from while being treated for Darvocet addiction—$4 million verdict against hospital

After suffering injuries in an automobile accident, the patient, a 24-year-old woman, was treated by several physicians who prescribed several forms of pain medication, including Darvocet. She eventually became addicted to the Darvocet and was admitted to the defendant hospital's psychiatric unit for treatment of the addiction and for depression.

A week after she was hospitalized, the patient's attending psychiatrist prescribed Darvocet for her, but at a dosage twice that she was taking before her hospitalization. The following morning she was found dead in her bed.

In his suit against the hospital for negligence of the nursing staff, the patient's husband introduced evidence that the night before she died, after she had been administered the Darvocet, the patient was found unconscious on the floor, but the nurses returned her to bed without calling a physician.

According to the plaintiff's attorney, the hospital offered to settle for $500,000, which was refused, and the jury returned a verdict for $4 million.[10]

PROPRANOLOL HYDROCHLORIDE
Inderal
Inderide

Propranolol hydrochloride is a nonselective beta-adrenergic receptor blocking agent used in the management of hypertension, angina pectoris due to coronary atherosclerosis, cardiac arrythmias,

[10] ATLA *Professional Negligence Law Reporter* 4:50, 1989.

myocardial infarction, and for the prevention of common migraine headache. In the product literature for Inderal (Ayerst Laboratories, a division of American Home Products Corporation, New York, N.Y.), the manufacturer states that the drug is contraindicated in cases of (1) cardiogenic shock, (2) sinus bradycardia and greater than first degree block, (3) bronchial asthma, and (4) congestive heart failure unless the failure is secondary to a tachyarrhythmia treatable with Inderal.[11]

Ayerst Laboratories also manufactures Inderide, and several companies produce propranolol hydrochloride and market it under the generic name. Inderide contains propranolol hydrochloride and hydrochlorothiazide, a benzothiadiazine (thiazide) diuretic.

Muniz Nunez v. American Home Products Corp. (D. P.R., 1984) 582 F. Supp. 459.

**Peyronie's disease following treatment with Inderal—
Insufficient evidence on causation**

The plaintiff, a physician, developed Peyronie's disease, a disorder causing painful deformity of the penis, following treatment for six months with Inderal for hypertension. In his suit against the manufacturer, he produced as evidence three reports published in *The Medical Letter on Drugs and Therapeutics* of patients who developed the same disease while taking the drug. The defendant moved for a directed verdict, claiming this was insufficient evidence that the drug was the cause of the disorder, and the motion was granted.

Labbe v. Mangan (No. 31634, Superior Court, Clallam County, Wash., Oct. 3, 1984).

**Fatal asthma attack allegedly induced by propranolol—
Jury verdict for $500,000 against physicians**

The patient was a forty-one-year-old bank manager being treated with propranolol for hypertension. Five months after starting treatment he died from an asthma attack. His survivors claimed the defendant physicians failed to ascertain the patient's history of asthma and failed to obtain his informed consent prior to prescribing propranolol. A jury returned a verdict for $500,000.[12]

---

[11] *Physicians' Desk Reference,* 40th ed., pp. 622, 627.
[12] ATLA *Law Reporter* 27:472, 1984.

Albee v. Glesmann (1987) 23 Mass. App. 972, 503 N.E.2d 677.

Heart patient advised to discontinue use of Inderal—Later collapses and dies

A wrongful death action was brought against an internist whose nineteen-year-old heart patient collapsed and died after the defendant told him to discontinue using Inderal. The defendant had consulted a pediatric cardiologist who advised him that the patient "probably will not need to continue the Inderal" but that the "final decision" as to use of the drug was for the defendant to make after he had a further opportunity to evaluate the patient. Without further consultation with the cardiologist and without conducting any tests, the defendant advised the patient to discontinue the Inderal, avoid strenuous activity and rest "at the first sign of any trouble." He then told the patient to arrange for another appointment in thirty days. The patient, a musician, collapsed and died six weeks later after performing with his band at a social event.

At the trial, a cardiologist testified for the plaintiff that in his opinion the discontinuance of the Inderal without a complete knowledge of the family and personal history of the patient was not in compliance with the standard of care of a qualified internist. This opinion was based upon information in the notes of the pediatric cardiologist which stated that in the past, at times when the patient had not been taking his Inderal, he had on occasion suffered brief periods of loss of consciousness which apparently were brought on by emotional or physical stress.

The jury returned a verdict for the physician; however, the Appeals Court of Massachusetts reversed, holding that the trial court had erred in instructing the jury on the standard of care, in that the defendant was to be judged "in the light of facts which were known to him in 1979. Hindsight is not a proper basis for your evaluation." This instruction, said the Appeals Court, was erroneous because it confused the issues of what the defendant knew or should have known professionally at that time.

Related cases

Alleged excessive dosage

In Geibel v. United States (W.D. Pa., 1987) 667 F. Supp. 215, aff'd (C.A.-3 Pa., 1988), 845 F.2d 1011, a VA hospital patient being treated for hypertension claimed her physician "over-drugged" her with hydrochlorothiazide and Inderal during a two-week hospitalization. The case is summarized herein under HYDROCHLOROTHIAZIDE.

PROPYLTHIOURACIL

Propylthiouracil inhibits the synthesis of thyroid hormones and thus is used in the treatment of hyperthyroidism. It is manufactured under the generic name by several companies.

Major adverse reactions are rare, but include agranulocytosis, drug fever, hepatitis, periarteritis and a lupus-like syndrome.[13]

Agranulocytosis—Cause of action not barred by statute of limitations

In Brown v. Mary Hitchcock Memorial Hosp. (1977) 117 N.H. 739, 378 A.2d 1138, the plaintiff, who developed agranulocytosis while taking propylthiouracil, was not aware of any possible negligent conduct on the part of her physicians until one doctor suggested that there may have been some permanent damage caused by taking the drug. Her cause of action, therefore, did not accrue until that date, and her claim was not barred by the statute of limitations.

Related cases

Myocardial infarction following reduction of dosage

Whether reduction of a patient's dosage of Inderal from 40 m.g. three times a day to 20 m.g. three times a day and the withholding of two doses because of a decline in the patient's blood pressure were deviations from recognized medical standards presented a factual question precluding summary judgment for the defendant. Hearon v. Burdette Tomlin Mem. Hosp. (1986) 213 N.J.Super. 98, 516 A.2d 628 (shortly after the patient's medication was reduced, he suffered an acute myocardial infarction).

PROSTIN F2 ALPHA

See DINOPROST TROMETHAMINE

---

[13] *Physicians' Desk Reference,* 35th ed., p. 1089.

PROTAMINE SULFATE

Protamines are proteins that occur in the sperm of salmon and certain other species of fish. When administered alone, protamine sulfate has an anticoagulant effect; however, when given in the presence of the anticoagulant heparin, it causes the loss of anticoagulant activity of both drugs. Therefore, protamine sulfate is used in the treatment of heparin overdosage. Protamine sulfate is contraindicated in patients who have shown previous intolerance to the drug, and patients with a history of allergy to fish may develop hypersensitivity reactions to protamine. Also, reports of the presence of antiprotamine antibodies in the serums of infertile or vasectomized men suggest that some of these persons may react to protamine sulfate. There have been anaphylactic reactions following use of the drug, and intravenous injections of protamine sulfate may cause a sudden fall in blood pressure, bradycardia, or pulmonary hypertension. The manufacturer (Eli Lilly & Co., Indianapolis, Ind.) warns that the drug should be given only when resuscitation techniques and the means to treat anaphylactoid shock are readily available.[14]

White v. Weiner (Pa. Super., 1989) 562 A.2d 378.

Postvasectomy patient has possible anaphylactoid reaction--Bulk supplier of drug has no duty to warn final manufacturer beyond federal labeling requirements

The plaintiff's husband died in August 1982 allegedly from complications following a triple bypass surgery. The plaintiff claimed that her husband's death was caused by an anaphylactoid reaction to protamine sulfate which had been given to her husband shortly after the operation. The patient had undergone a vasectomy ten years earlier, and the plaintiff claimed that vasectomy patients are prone to reactions to protamine sulfate because the drug is derived from the semen of the male salmon, and vasectomy patients develop antibodies to sperm.

The plaintiff filed suit against her husband's physicians, the hospital, and also Eli Lilly & Company, which supplied protamine sulfate in bulk to The Upjohn Company, manufacturer of the drug administered to the plaintiff's husband. (Upjohn was not a party to this action, but was sued separately in federal court.) The plaintiff's

---

14. *Physicians' Desk Reference, 43rd ed., p. 1197.*

action against Lilly was based on the claim that as a bulk supplier of the drug, it had a duty to provide an adequate warning of the possibility of such a reaction on the packaging supplied to Upjohn. Lilly moved for summary judgment, arguing that it had no duty to warn other than that required by the federal government in its labeling requirements, with which Lilly had complied. The trial court granted the motion.

On appeal, the Superior Court of Pennsylvania affirmed, holding that a bulk supplier of a drug which satisfies federal labeling requirements does not have an additional common-law duty to warn final manufacturers of pharmaceutical products. Such manufacturers, together with the medical community, are in a better position to assess the risks associated with the administration of prescription drugs.

PROTOSTAT
See METRONIDAZOLE

PROVERA
See MEDROXYPROGESTERONE ACETATE

PSEUDOEPHEDRINE HYDROCHLORIDE and CHLORPHENIRAMINE MALEATE

Contac
CoTylenol
Novahistine
Sinutab
Sudafed
Teldrin

This product, a combined decongestant and antihistamine, is designed to relieve nasal and sinus congestion associated with the common cold, plus sneezing and other upper respiratory allergy symptoms.

The product may cause drowsiness, and with higher doses, dizziness or sleeplessness. Also, the label (Sudafed) contains the warning that the product should not be taken if the user has "high blood pressure, heart disease, diabetes, thyroid disease, asthma, glaucoma or difficulty in urination due to enlargement of the prostate gland except under the advice and supervision of a physician." Also, the label warns that if the purchaser is pregnant or nursing a baby, she should seek the advice of a health professional before using the product.[15]

Contac and Teldrin are manufactured by Menley & James Laboratories (Philadelphia, Pa.), CoTylenol by McNeil Consumer Products Co. (Fort Washington, Pa.), Novahistine by Merrell Dow Pharmaceuticals (Cincinnati, Ohio), Sinutab by Warner-Lambert Company (Morris Plains, N.J.) and Sudafed by Burroughs Wellcome Company (Research Triangle Park, N.C.).

Kelley v. Wiggins (1987) 291 Ark. 280, 724 S.W.2d 443.

Death from eclampsia—Clinic negligent in administering Sudafed—$2 million verdict

The patient, who was pregnant with her second child, was seen by the defendant physician and other personnel at his clinic for prenatal care during 1978. In May of that year, the patient began to suffer from edema in her legs, arms, hands and face. She also complained of headaches and nausea, and pain in her upper abdomen. Despite her problems, she was given no dietary advice nor a diuretic. On July 10, when the patient was in her seventh month of pregnancy, her symptoms became especially severe, and she returned to the clinic. She was not seen by the defendant physician, however, and was not hospitalized. Instead she was instructed to take Sudafed, apparently for her edema. Her condition did not improve, and several days later she experienced convulsions. She was hospitalized and diagnosed as suffering from eclampsia. She experienced additional seizures, and following the birth of her child several weeks later, she lapsed into a coma and died.

Medical testimony at the trial established that the defendant physician and his clinic personnel were negligent in failing to identify the patient as a "high risk patient," in failing to provide a physician to examine her on July 10, and in administering the drug Sudafed which constricts blood vessels and thereby worsened her condition. The jury returned a verdict of $2 million which was affirmed on appeal.

---

[15] *Physicians' Desk Reference for Nonprescription Drugs,* 6th ed., p. 53.

PYELOKON-R
See SODIUM ACETRIZOATE

Q

QUELIDRINE
See CHLORPHENIRAMINE MALEATE

QUINACRINE HYDROCHLORIDE
Atabrine Hydrochloride

Quinacrine was the principal antimalarial drug of World War II. It is now infrequently prescribed for that purpose, but it has been used with considerable success in the treatment of several other conditions, including tapeworm infestations, giardiasis, amebiasis, and lupus erythematosus.

Atabrine hydrochloride is manufactured by Winthrop Breon Laboratories (New York, N.Y.). Adverse reactions include nausea, vomiting, abdominal cramps, diarrhea, headache, vertigo, fever, excessive sweating, pruritus, muscle and joint pains and insomnia. Yellow pigmentation of the skin is common. Agranulocytosis and aplastic anemia have occurred occasionally.[16]

Watkins v. United States (M.D. Tenn., 1980) 482 F. Supp. 1006.

Atabrine hypersensitivity—VA physician not negligent in choice of treatment or failure to warn

The patient was diagnosed as suffering from discoid lupus erythematosus, a chronic skin disorder. He was seen at a local Veteran's Administration Hospital where a physician prescribed 100 mg. quinacrine hydrochloride (Atabrine) three times a day for seven days, then 100 mg. two times a day for seven days, and finally 100 mg. once a day. He was also given prednisone. At the time the drugs were prescribed, the physician told the patient that his skin would probably turn yellow but that he should not be alarmed by this. He did not warn of any other side effects.

Three days later the patient noticed a worsening of his skin condition and general swelling. On the fifth day he was hospitalized with a diagnosis of "Atabrine hypersensitivity — characterized by excoriative dermatitis." He was hospitalized several more times

---

[16] *United States Dispensatory,* 27th ed., pp. 989-90.

over a two-year period until he was finally treated with antibiotics which seemed to improve his skin eruptions.

Suit was filed against the government under the Federal Tort Claims Act. The specific charges were negligence on the part of the VA physician in prescribing Atabrine without attempting to determine whether the patient was allergic to the drug; negligence in failing to warn of the drug's possible side effects; and negligence in prescribing Atabrine for use as an outpatient rather than under controlled conditions at the hospital.

The trial judge found for the defendant on all counts. The evidence showed that there are no practical tests available to a physician to determine whether a patient will suffer side effects from a drug such as Atabrine which he has never taken before. As to a warning, the reactions suffered by the patient, said the court, "are distinctly uncommon side effects of Atabrine and a physician is not required under accepted medical practice to warn a patient about the possibility of these diseases as a side effect." As to hospitalizing the patient, the court held that the evidence disclosed that it is "very uncommon" to do so in the case of a patient suffering from discoid lupus erythematosus, and that a physician should not hospitalize a patient simply to see how he will react to the medicine.

Cross v. Huttenlocher (1981) 185 Conn. 390, 440 A.2d 952.

Loss of sight following treatment with Atabrine—Pediatric neurologist's failure to warn a jury question

The patient was placed on Atabrine at age three for myoclonic and occasional grand mal seizures. She took the drug for five years (1965-70) at the end of which time she suffered loss of her sight. In a suit against two physicians who treated the patient, a pediatrician and a pediatric neurologist, the plaintiffs claimed lack of informed consent, in that the patient's parents were not warned of the risk of blindness in prolonged Atabrine therapy.

The jury returned a verdict for the defendants on the Court's instructions to disregard the allegations in the plaintiffs' complaint that the defendants were negligent in failing to warn. On appeal the Supreme Court of Connecticut affirmed as to the pediatrician, finding that the plaintiffs failed to establish a standard of care by which to measure his conduct. But as to the pediatric neurologist, the court held that the plaintiff had offered sufficient evidence for the jury to consider negligence for failure to warn: in the form of disputed testimony of another pediatric neurologist who testified that the standard of care for his specialty with respect to administering Atabrine in 1965 included advising of the potential side effects of the drug, one of which was visual damage.

R

RABIES VACCINE

Imovax

Rabies vaccine (duck embryo, dried killed virus), formerly produced by Eli Lilly and Company (Indianapolis, Ind.) for both post-exposure and pre-exposure immunization, is now produced by Merieux Institute, Inc. (Miami, Fla.) under the generic name and under the brand name Imovax. The product literature supplied by Lilly contained the following information on when the vaccine should be used.[17]

> *Post-exposure Immunization* — Indications for and against giving rabies vaccine are difficult to define. In favor of giving it is the fact that, if rabies develops, it will almost certainly have fatal results. Against giving it is the danger of development of severe side effects involving the central nervous system when vaccine contains brain tissue. Experiments have shown that duck-embryo tissue contains little or none of the "paralytic factor," and the incidence of neurologic side effects has been low with the use of duck-embryo vaccine. The following factors also should be taken into consideration: (1) Approximately 40 percent of persons who are bitten by animals known to be rabid have developed rabies if not treated with rabies vaccine, and (2) rabies rarely occurs unless the individual actually has been bitten by the animal.
>
> The World Health Organization Expert Committee on Rabies has considered various types of exposure to rabies and made the following recommendations:
>
> I. If contact with the rabid animal has been indirect or if there has been only a lick on unabraded skin, no exposure is considered to have occurred and vaccine is not recommended.
>
> II. If the exposure was mild, i.e., a lick on abraded skin or on mucosal surfaces, or for single bites *not* on the head, neck, face, or arm:
>
> A. If the animal is healthy at the time of exposure, withhold vaccine, but observe the animal for ten days.

[17] This product information was taken from *Physicians' Desk Reference,* 35th ed., pp. 1091-93 (1981). Although the product is still available, this information is no longer published in *Physicians' Desk Reference.*

B. If during the ten-day observation period the animal is proved to have rabies or becomes clinically suspicious, start vaccine immediately.

C. If the animal has signs suspicious of rabies at the time of exposure, start vaccine immediately, but stop injections if the animal is normal on the fifth day after exposure.

D. If the animal is rabid, if it escapes or is killed, or if it is unknown, give complete course of vaccine. If the biting animal is wild, also give rabies antiserum.

III. If exposure was severe (multiple bites or single bites on the head, neck, face, or arm), the indications for giving vaccine are the same as in mild exposure (*see* II above). In addition, in every category, the administration of rabies antiserum is recommended.

The most recent report of the U.S. Public Health Service Advisory Committee on Immunization Practices recommends the use of passive antibody for treatment of ALL BITES by animals suspected of having rabies and for nonbite exposures inflicted by animals suspected of being rabid. There is evidence that, when antibody is administered concurrently with vaccine, it can interfere with the development of active immunity. If passive antibody is used, this committee recommends supplementary doses of vaccine ten and twenty days after the last usual dose.

When considering the above recommendations, physicians should consult local health officials to obtain information on the presence of rabies in the region.

Preexposure Immunization — Vaccination with duck-embryo rabies vaccine before exposure occurs may be desirable for certain high-risk individuals. These include veterinarians, deliverymen, meter readers, spelunkers, laboratory personnel working with rabies virus, and perhaps others.

The package insert also contains the following precautions:

Caution should be used in administering the vaccine to persons with a history of allergy, especially when the allergy is to chicken or duck eggs or proteins.

Adrenocorticotropin and adrenal corticosteroids may reduce host resistance to certain infectious agents either through suppression of antibody response or through other and as yet poorly understood mechanisms. Therefore, they should not be administered following exposure to infectious agents (such as rabies) for which no satisfactory antimicrobial therapy is available. To do so may alter the host-parasite relationship sufficiently to cause severe or fatal illness in spite of prophylactic administration of a vaccine. Under these circumstances, the occurrence of disease, actually due to the altered pattern of resistance, might be attributed to a vaccine failure.

Safety of this product for use during pregnancy has not been established; however, when postexposure rabies immunization is indicated, pregnancy has not been considered to be a contraindication to use of this killed virus vaccine.

Adverse reactions to rabies vaccine are varied.

Local reactions to the injected material have been observed to be fewer and somewhat less severe than those seen with vaccines of brain origin.[18] Tenderness at the injection site is common. Varying degrees of local erythema and induration have been observed; these reactions tend to appear from the sixth to the tenth day of treatment but may occur after each inoculation. Subsequent injections are likely to cause flare-ups at the sites of previous inoculations. Regional lymphadenopathy may also be encountered. Since this material is protein and foreign to the human body, systemic sensitivity to the vaccine may be encountered. Urticaria, respiratory distress (including dyspnea and bronchospasm), and gastrointestinal disorders (e.g., abdominal cramps, nausea, vomiting, and diarrhea) have occurred. Anaphylactic reactions have been reported. In one prospective study, anaphylaxis was observed in 0.5 to 0.9 percent of recipients. Epinephrine may be helpful in controlling these situations. Patients with a history of allergy should be tested for hypersensitivity before the vaccine is administered.

Constitutional reactions are difficult to evaluate because of the patient's tendency to be apprehensive about the situation, but the development of fever, malaise, and drowsiness calls for careful observation. Minor neurologic reactions, such as headache, photophobia, paresthesias, listlessness, malaise, and increased fatigability, have been reported. Major neurologic reactions temporally associated with vaccine therapy have been reported rarely. These include transverse myelitis, cranial or peripheral palsy, and encephalitis. If symptoms appear that indicate central-nervous-system involvement, vaccine injections should be discontinued.

Hitchcock v. United States (D. D.C., 1979) 479 F. Supp. 65, aff'd (C.A.-D.C., 1981) 665 F.2d 354.

"Demyelinating disease" following inoculation—
$519,051 awarded against government

The plaintiff in this case was the wife of a foreign service officer who, together with her husband, underwent inoculation in 1972 with rabies vaccine preparatory to an assignment in Buenos Aires,

[18] Rabies vaccine of duck-embryo origin was developed to circumvent the use of brain tissue, since it has been demonstrated that duck embryos contain little or none of the "paralytic factor" said to be present in brain tissue. Myelin, contained in conventional vaccines of brain origin, has been implicated as the causative factor in rabies treatment paralysis.

Argentina. After the first injection the plaintiff noted a "tiredness" and a "heaviness" in her legs. This worsened after the second injection and was followed by a numbness and difficulty in walking. Over the next several years her condition deteriorated to the point where she could no longer perform the functions of a Foreign Service Officer's wife. She was eventually diagnosed as suffering from a progressive "demyelinating disease" similar to multiple sclerosis in which there was paralysis, pain, numbness and limitation of physical movement.

In her lawsuit against the government she alleged that she was not informed of the risks involved in receiving the rabies vaccine nor the fact that she was not fully protected from rabies even with the inoculation. She thus argued that if this information had been disclosed to her she would not have agreed to the inoculation.

The District Court awarded the plaintiff and her husband $519,051, and the Court of Appeals affirmed.

Related cases

Neurological disorder—Expert testimony not required to prove failure to warn

In Calabrese v. Trenton State College (1980) 82 N.J. 321, 413 A.2d 315, the plaintiff, who suffered a neurological disorder following the administration of rabies vaccine, was not required to produce expert witnesses to prove allegations that he received no warnings concerning possible hazards involved in taking the vaccine, and he could rely on medical literature for such proof.

Vaccine contaminated by defective surgical gloves

In Travenol Laboratories, Inc. v. Bandy Laboratories, Inc. (Tex. App., 1980) 608 S.W.2d 308, aff'd (Tex. App., 1982) 630 S.W.2d 484, a rabies vaccine manufacturer recovered damages from the manufacturer of surgical gloves for contamination of the vaccine caused by microscopic holes in the gloves which permitted bacteria to pass from the hands of an employee into the vaccine during processing.

REGLAN

See METOCLOPRAMIDE HYDROCHLORIDE

REGROTON
See RESERPINE

RELA
See CARISOPRODOL

RENESE-R
See RESERPINE

RENOGRAFIN
See SODIUM DIATRIZOATE

RENO-M-60
See DIATRIZOATE MEGLUMINE

RESERPINE
Demi-Regroton
Diupres
Diutensen-R
Hydromox
Hydropres
Hydroserpine
Metatensin
Naquival
Regroton
Renese-R
Salutensin
Ser-Ap-Es
Serpasil

Reserpine is a cardiovascular preparation used orally with a diuretic to treat mild or moderate hypertension. The drug is a member of the rauwolfia alkaloid family and is the most commonly used drug in this group.[19]

Demi-Regroton and Regroton are manufactured by USV Pharmaceutical Corp. (Fort Washington, Pa.); Diupres and Hydropres, by Merck, Sharp & Dohme (West Point, Pa.); Diutensen-R, by Wallace Laboratories (Cranbury, N.J.); Hydromox-R, by Lederle Laboratories (Wayne, N.J.); Hydroserpine, by Zenith Laboratories (Ramsey, N.J.); Metatensin, by Merrell Dow Pharmaceuticals (Cincinnati,

[19] AMA *Drug Evaluations,* 6th ed., p. 519.

Ohio); Naquival, by Schering Corp. (Kenilworth, N.J.); Renese-R, by Pfizer Laboratories (New York, N.Y.); Salutensin, by Bristol Laboratories (Evansville, Ind.); and Ser-Ap-Es and Serpasil, by CIBA Pharmaceutical Co. (Summit, N.J.). The drug also is manufactured and marketed by several companies under the generic name.

The American Medical Association's Department of Drugs lists the following adverse reactions and precautions for reserpine: [20]

> ADVERSE REACTIONS AND PRECAUTIONS. Lethargy, dryness of the mouth, nasal congestion, and bradycardia may occur with therapeutic doses; fluid retention may develop if a diuretic is not given concomitantly. Other adverse effects include diarrhea, nausea, vomiting, anorexia, sexual dysfunction (decreased libido, impotence, and impaired ejaculation), stress incontinence, and nightmares. Mental depression may be severe enough to require hospitalization or, rarely, may result in attempted suicide; this can occur with any amount but is most common with high-dose regimens (0.5 to 1 mg or more daily). Small doses of reserpine (less than 0.125 mg daily), combined with a diuretic, often control blood pressure and may produce fewer side effects than larger doses (Participating VA Medical Centers, 1982). The rauwolfia alkaloids should not be given to patients with a history of depression; if depressive symptoms appear, the drug should be discontinued. Barbiturates enhance the central nervous system depressant effects of rauwolfia alkaloids.
>
> Gynecomastia has occured rarely in patients receiving rauwolfia alkaloids. An association between long-term therapy and breast cancer was reported in three retrospective studies, but many subsequent investigations have shown no relationship, and the weight of evidence is now against any such association.
>
> Rauwolfia alkaloids may adversely affect sinus node function in patients with sinus node disorders.
>
> Reserpine may increase gastric acid secretion and should be used cautiously in patients with a history of peptic ulcer. If symptoms suggest recurrence of the ulcer, the drug should be discontinued. Because rauwolfia alkaloids increase gastrointestinal tone and motility, they should not be given to patients with a history of ulcerative colitis.
>
> Reserpine passes through the placental circulation. When given parenterally (parenteral preparation no longer available) to treat eclampsia, it caused drowsiness, nasal congestion, cyanosis, and anorexia in the newborn infant.
>
> Because rauwolfia alkaloids lower the convulsive threshold, they should be used cautiously in patients with epilepsy. Large doses may cause extrapyramidal reactions.

---

[20] Id., pp. 519-20.

McFadden v. Haritatos (1982) 86 App. Div. 2d 761, 448 N.Y.S.2d 79.

Optic nerve damage—Mental depression—Statement that adverse reactions are reversible raises question of adequacy of warning

The plaintiff had been taking reserpine for just over a year as treatment for hypertension when he experienced a variety of illnesses, the most serious of which were optic nerve injury and severe and possibly permanent mental depression. In the plaintiff's action against his physician for negligent treatment and against the manufacturer (Purepac Pharmaceutical Company) for failure to warn, the trial court granted the manufacturer's motion for summary judgment.

The Supreme Court, Appellate Division, reversed, holding that while the package insert that accompanied the drug did warn, among other things, that persons suffering mental depression should not use the drug, there appeared on the same package insert, under "ADVERSE REACTIONS," a statement that "These reactions are usually reversible and disappear when the drug is discontinued." This statement, said the court, "tends to qualify and dilute the whole of the section's admonition" and prevents a finding that the manufacturer's warnings were adequate as a matter of law.

Rubin v. Aaron (No. 1615/81 Supreme Court, Nassau County, N.Y., June 5, 1989).

Patient treated with Ser-Ap-Es for three years despite depression and impotence—Commits suicide—$1.09 million jury verdict against internist

The patient was a 59-year-old salesman. In 1979, the defendant, an internist, prescribed Ser-Ap-Es for the patient's high blood pressure. During the following winter, the plaintiff's family noticed a change in his emotional state, and that he was often depressed. Although the defendant saw the patient several times during this period, he did not change his medication.

The defendant saw the patient only once in 1978, at which time he was markedly depressed and complained of impotence. He saw him again in June 1979, the same month he was fired from his job. He had developed a rectal abscess and fecal incontinence. Several months later the patient committed suicide.

In the family's lawsuit against the defendant, they claimed that he was negligent in prescribing the Ser-Ap-Es for the patient, in failing to discontinue the drug by at least June 1978 when its effects became apparent, and in failing to schedule more frequent visits during 1978 and 1979. At trial, the plaintiffs introduced the package insert which warned that Ser-Ap-Es had been associated with severe depression and suicide, and that it should be discontinued if a patient became despondent or impotent. A psychiatrist testifying for the plaintiffs was of the opinion that the patient should have been taken off the drug in June 1978.

The jury returned a verdict for $1.09 million.[21]

RH$_o$ (D) IMMUNE GLOBULIN (HUMAN)

Gamulin Rh
MICRhoGAM
Mini-Gamulin Rh
Rhesonativ
RhoGAM

Rh$_o$ (D) Immune Globulin (Human) is a sterile solution used for preventing Rh immunization in Rh negative individuals exposed to Rh positive red blood cells. In pregnancy, the product is indicated whenever it is known or suspected that fetal red cells have entered the circulation of an Rh negative mother unless the fetus or the father can be shown conclusively to be Rh negative.[22]

Gamulin Rh is manufactured by Armour Pharmaceutical Company (Tarrytown, N.Y.), as is Mini-Gamulin Rh. MICRhoGAM and RhoGAM are manufactured by Ortho Diagnostic Systems, Inc. (Raritan, N.J.), and Rhesonativ by Kabivitrum, Inc. (Alameda, Cal.). The product is also manufactured by Cutter Biological, a division of Miles Laboratories, Inc. (Emeryville, Cal.) under the generic name.

Goga v. Ortho Diagnostics, Inc. (1982) 90 App. Div. 2d 874, 456 N.Y.S.2d 476.

**RhoGAM fails to prevent hemolytic disease in newborn—
No express warranty by manufacturer in pamphlet**

Following the birth of her third child, the plaintiff received an injection of RhoGAM to prevent hemolytic disease of the newborn

---

21. ATLA *Professional Negligence Law Reporter* 5:10, 1990.

22. *Physicians' Desk Reference,* 40th ed., p. 1291.

in a subsequent pregnancy. A few months later, she became pregnant with her fourth child, Kristie. Kristie was born prematurely with hemolytic disease, but fully recovered within four or five months. The plaintiff brought an action for, among other things, breach of express warranty based on the manufacturer's RhoGAM explanatory pamphlet which the plaintiff had been given by her obstetrician prior to her injection with the drug. After the jury returned a verdict finding express warranty, the trial court granted the defendant's motion to set aside the verdict on the ground that the defendant's pamphlet does not contain an express warranty.

The Appellate Court held that the trial court correctly found that as a matter of law no express warranty existed. The pamphlet states that the drug "provides virtually complete protection" against hemolytic disease. The plaintiff alleged that she understood this language to mean that the drug gave "100%, absolute protection." The Appellate Court, however, disagreed, finding that virtually means "almost entirely" and merely alerted users that a few people might have an idiosyncratic reaction to RhoGAM.

Church v. Ortho Diagnostic Systems (Tex. Civ. App., 1985) 694 S.W.2d 552.

RhoGAM not given following birth of Rh positive child—Manufacturer not negligent in instructing physicians

The plaintiff gave birth to her first child in July 1976. The plaintiff had Rh negative blood and her baby had Rh positive. The plaintiff's physician, however, did not administer RhoGAM or another Rh immune globulin, even though the drug was available at the hospital. The reason later given by the physician was that the manufacturer's instructions that accompanied the drug stated that it should not be given to patients with certain disorders, one of which the physician had diagnosed in the patient. This diagnosis was later determined to be in error.

In 1978, the plaintiff became pregnant with her second child. Because of her exposure to Rh positive blood, the plaintiff had a difficult pregnancy and the child, an Rh positive girl, died several days after birth.

In her complaint against the manufacturer of RhoGAM (the physician was not a party to this suit), the plaintiff contended that had she been given RhoGAM in July 1976, it would have prevented her problems with the second pregnancy and her daughter's death. She alleged the manufacturer was negligent in instructing physicians on the administration of its product and it had breached express and implied warranties concerning use and nonuse.

The trial court granted the defendant's motion for summary judgment and the Court of Appeals of Texas affirmed, holding that there was no evidence of negligence. As to breach of warranty, the court stated that under Texas law a "warranty" contemplates that a sale or contract has been made. This did not exist in the plaintiff's case; her only connection with the product was that she did *not* use it.

In re Mitchell (No. 20,415, Chancery Court, Sunflower County, Miss., April 25, 1985).

RhoGAM not administered after first childbirth—Second child born with brain damage—Mother sensitized and sterile—$3.5 million structured settlement with physician

The plaintiff's mother experienced Rh isoimmunization following the birth of her first child but was not given RhoGAM. On the plaintiff's birth four years later, he suffered erythroblastosis fetalis and hydrops fetalis secondary to Rh isoimmunization. He will develop motor and language development deficits and will require extensive therapy during his lifetime. Suit was brought on his behalf against his mother's physician, a general practitioner, for failing to administer the RhoGAM. The mother also sued because she became permanently sensitized from the second birth and is now sterile.

The parties agreed to a structured settlement under which the plaintiff will receive $225,000 in cash and lifetime monthly payments of $1,500 which increase $500 every five years to a maximum of $3,500 at age 21. The mother settled for cash and periodic payments totalling $658,000. Total projected payout is estimated at $3.5 million.[23]

Related cases

Question of hospital's duty to Rh negative patient precludes summary judgment

Whether hospital personnel breached their duty to see that a patient with Rh negative blood received an injection of RhoGAM

[23] ATLA *Law Reporter* 29:82, 1986.

following delivery of her stillborn child raised a question of fact and precluded a summary judgment in favor of the hospital. Lucchesi v. Frederic N. Stimmell, M.D. (1985) 149 Ariz. 85, 716 P.2d 1022.

Rh immunization—Plaintiff fails to show when she became sensitized

Where there was a three to five percent chance that the plaintiff could have become sensitized by Rh positive cells after a 1971 miscarriage, and a twenty percent chance that she could have become sensitized after a 1972 pregnancy, and the plaintiff's expert had no way of determining at which time she did become sensitized, the trial court did not err in granting summary judgments in favor of the plaintiff's gynecologists who were accused of negligence in not administering RhoGAM to the plaintiff following the miscarriage. Howard v. Mitchell (Ala., 1986) 492 So. 2d 1018.

RHESONATIV
See Rh_o (D) IMMUNE GLOBULIN (HUMAN)

RHINOLAR
See CHLORPHENIRAMINE MALEATE

RhoGAM
See Rh_o (D) IMMUNE GLOBULIN (HUMAN)

RIFAMATE
See ISONIAZID

RITALIN
See METHYLPHENIDATE HYDROCHLORIDE

RMS SUPPOSITORIES
See MORPHINE SULFATE

ROBICILLIN VK
See PENICILLIN

ROBITET
See TETRACYCLINE HYDROCHLORIDE

RONIACOL
See NICOTINYL ALCOHOL

ROXANOL
See MORPHINE SULFATE

RUFEN
See IBUPROFEN

S

SABIN VACCINE
See POLIOVIRUS VACCINE

SALICYLAZOSULFAPYRIDINE
See SULFASALAZINE

SALK VACCINE
See POLIOVIRUS VACCINE

SALPIX
See SODIUM ACETRIZOATE

SALUTENSIN
See RESERPINE

SANSERT
See METHYSERGIDE MALEATE

SCOPOLAMINE HYDROBROMIDE
Donnagel
Donnatel
Donnazyme

Scopolamine is a parasympathetic blocking agent used primarily as a sedative. At one time it was also popular as a means of preventing motion sickness but now has been largely replaced by newer, less toxic drugs.

The drug is contraindicated in patients with asthma, hepatitis or toxemia of pregnancy. Adverse reactions include marked disturbances of intellect, somnolence, laryngeal paralysis and delirium in persons particularly susceptible to the drug.[24] Donnagel, Donnatel and Donnazyme are all produced by A. H. Robins Company (Richmond, Va.).

Bronchospasm and cardiac arrest during surgery

In Siegel v. Mt. Sinai Hosp. of Cleveland (1978) 62 Ohio App. 2d 12, 403 N.E.2d 202, an asthmatic patient was given numerous drugs, including scopolamine hydrobromide, prior to surgery. He suffered a bronchial spasm and cardiac arrest during the operation and later died. The case is summarized herein under SODIUM THIOPENTAL.

Respiratory depression and brain damage in newborn

In Downing v. Manta (Docket No. 79-21845, Circuit Court, Dade County, Fla., Oct. 17, 1980), a pregnant patient given oxytocin (Pitocin), scopolamine hydrobromide and several other drugs prior to delivery gave birth to twin fetuses suffering from severe respiratory depression and brain damage. The case is summarized herein under OXYTOCIN.

SECOBARBITAL SODIUM
Seconal
Tuinal

Secobarbital sodium is a short-acting barbiturate which has a depressing effect on the central nervous system. It is used as a sedative. When prescribed for insomnia, it is not recommended for prolonged use since it has not been shown to be effective for more than fourteen days. Also, it may be habit-forming.[1]

Seconal and Tuinal are manufactured by Eli Lilly and Company (Indianapolis, Ind.). Wyeth Laboratories (Philadelphia, Pa.) markets the product under the generic label.

Lhotka v. Larson (1976) 307 Minn. 121, 238 N.W.2d 870.

Respiratory distress and brain damage in newborn—No evidence that physicians deviated from manufacturers' instructions

This is a suit on behalf of a child born with severe respiratory distress who was later diagnosed as being severely mentally retarded and suffering from spastic quadriparesis and cerebral palsy.

---

[24] *United States Dispensatory,* 27th ed., p. 1036.

[1] *Physicians' Desk Reference,* 35th ed., p. 1092.

The child's mother was admitted to the hospital around 2:15 a.m. Her obstetrician immediately ordered three grains of Seconal orally. At 5 a.m. he diagnosed her condition as "polyhydramnios" (excessive amniotic fluid) and ordered 50 mg. of Demerol and 25 mg. of Phenergan. This was given intramuscularly at 5:10 a.m.

By 7 a.m. the patient was fully dilated, and because delivery was premature, the obstetrician ordered a local rather than a general anesthetic. At 7:22 he ruptured the amniotic sac and delivered the child. Ten minutes later, 0.2 mg. of Nalline were administered to the child.

The child could not breathe on her own, and she was connected to a resuscitator. Later, when voluntary breathing was attempted, she suffered several "cyanotic episodes." She was transferred to another hospital and placed in a Newborn Intensive Care unit where she remained for eighty days.

At the trial, the heart of the plaintiffs' argument was that the obstetrician knowingly deviated from the drug manufacturers' instructions on the use of the products. More specifically, the charges were that (1) use of Seconal was absolutely contraindicated in cases of premature labor, (2) that the dosages of Demerol and Phenergan were excessive under the circumstances, and (3) that the Nalline might have increased rather than decreased the child's respiratory distress. The plaintiffs contended that the drugs administered to the mother "crossed the placental barrier" and caused the depression of the child's central nervous and respiratory systems which in turn caused the cyanotic episodes and the resulting brain damage.

The trial court, however, refused to instruct the jury that a doctor's deviation from a drug manufacturer's recommendations is prima facie evidence of negligence. Verdicts were directed for the hospital and the anesthesiologist, and the jury found in favor of the obstetrician and his associate. On appeal, all verdicts were upheld. As to the trial court's failure to give the requested instruction, the Supreme Court of Minnesota said:

> The manufacturer's instructions concerning Seconal contained no warning against its *oral* use in premature delivery cases. Fetal immaturity constituted a contraindication only if the drug was administered parenterally (by injection). The manufacturer's instructions also called for a reduction of at least 50 percent in the dosage of barbiturates administered "in the presence of" Phenergan. But here the barbiturate Seconal was administered *before* the Phenergan, and the instructions are silent on whether a reduction in the dosage of Phenergan is necessary in such cir-

cumstances. Despite the ambiguity, the dosage of Phenergan which Mrs. Lhotka [plaintiff] received was only one-half the normal dosage. The reduced dosage was ordered even though the Seconal had undoubtedly metabolized by the time the Phenergan was administered. As for Nalline, one instruction cautioned against the use of more than one dosage; another exhibit stated that no more than three doses should be given. Tina [infant] received only a single dose.

The foregoing suggests the ambiguity of the instructions which the Doctors Larson [the obstetrician and his associate] allegedly failed to follow. Where the instructions were clear, sufficient testimony was introduced to justify the jury's conclusion that the doctors had not deviated from them. For example, the manufacturer's instructions called for a one-quarter to one-half reduction in the dosage of Demerol when it was administered with Phenergan. The usual dosage of Demerol was 100 mg.; Mrs. Lhotka received 50 mg. The recommended dosage of Nalline was 0.2 mg.; that was the amount administered to the child.

The reviewing court's conclusion was that if this were a case in which the manufacturers' instructions were "clear and unambiguous," or were this a case in which deviations from them clearly took place, then the requested jury instruction might have been appropriate. But this, said the court, was not such a case.

Webb v. Lightburn (No. C-82849, District Court, Colo., Feb. 12, 1980).

Prescribing Seconal for suicidal patient questioned—$100,000 settlement

The 31-year-old female patient was diagnosed as having a "passive-aggressive personality disorder with depressive and hysterical features." She was under the care of a psychiatrist for almost six years during which time he prescribed a great number of drugs. The patient was prone to take overdoses. In March of 1978, she attempted suicide. Shortly thereafter the psychiatrist renewed two of her prescriptions for Seconal. In May she took all of the sedatives and died.

Two minor children of the patient brought suit against the psychiatrist, claiming that he was negligent in prescribing Seconal for a suicidal patient. The psychiatrist contended that it was important to the patient's mental health and emotional stability that she be trusted with the drugs, but that she was hopelessly suicidal and, with or without the Seconal, the suicide was inevitable.

According to the attorney for the patient's survivors, the case was settled for the policy limits of all available coverage, $100,000.[2]

Argus v. Scheppegrell (La., 1985) 472 So. 2d 573.

Addiction and suicide—Physician negligent in continuing to prescribe drugs

The defendant, a general practitioner, was charged with negligence in continuing to prescribe Preludin and Tuinal for a nineteen-year-old girl who obviously was addicted to both drugs. Early in August, 1977, the girl's mother called the defendant and asked that he not furnish her daughter with any more prescriptions because she was addicted and might be suicidal. The defendant agreed, but two weeks later gave the girl a prescription for fifty tablets each of Preludin and Tuinal. Two days later she took three-fourths of the bottle of Tuinal and became comatose. She died one month later.

Finding the girl guilty of contributory negligence, a jury returned a verdict for the defendant. The Court of Appeals affirmed, but the Supreme Court of Louisiana reversed, holding that the defendant had breached his duty not to give the girl any more drugs upon learning of her addiction and possible suicidal tendencies, and that because of "the disparity of positions in the relationship between a trained and licensed physician and a nineteen-year-old uneducated patient whose drug addiction was known to the physician, and because of the vastly different duty required of each party under the circumstances, the patient's reasonably expected conduct did not constitute an absolute bar to her parents' recovery for her wrongful death."

Related cases

Excessive medication during prolonged labor

In Sanchez v. Flower & Fifth Avenue Hospital (Docket No. 14073/79, Supreme Court, New York County, N.Y., Jan. 31, 1986), a jury awarded $4 million to an eight-year-old brain damaged boy whose mother was given repeated doses of Demerol (meperidine hydrochloride), Sparine (promazine hydrochloride) and Seconal during 22 hours of prolonged labor. The case is summarized herein under MEPERIDINE HYDROCHLORIDE.

---

[2] ATLA *Law Reporter* 23:285, 1980.

SECONAL
See SECOBARBITAL SODIUM

SEFFIN
See CEPHALOTHIN SODIUM

SENSORCAINE
See BUPIVACAINE HYDROCHLORIDE

SEPTRA
See TRIMETHOPRIM and SULFAMETHOXAZOLE

SER-AP-ES
See RESERPINE

SEROMYCIN
See CYCLOSERINE

SEROPHENE
See CLOMIPHENE CITRATE

SERPASIL
See RESERPINE

SINEQUAN
See DOXEPIN HYDROCHLORIDE

SINULIN
See CHLORPHENIRAMINE MALEATE

SINUTAB
See CHLORPHENIRAMINE MALEATE; PSEUDOEPHEDRINE HYDROCHLORIDE and CHLORPHENIRAMINE MALEATE

SK-BAMATE
See MEPROBAMATE

SK-LYGEN
See CHLORDIAZEPOXIDE HYDROCHLORIDE

SK-PENICILLIN VK
See PENICILLIN

SK-PRAMINE
See IMIPRAMINE HYDROCHLORIDE

SK-65; SK-65 COMPOUND
See PROPOXYPHENE HYDROCHLORIDE

SMALLPOX VACCINE

Smallpox vaccine is a live-virus vaccine prepared from vaccinia virus-infected calf lymph. The virus multiplies at the site of inoculation and produces a local skin lesion that subsequently resolves. This elicits the production of virus-neutralizing antibodies and creates an active immunity to smallpox.[3]

In 1980, the World Health Organization (WHO), as the result of worldwide immunization programs, declared the world free of smallpox in the natural state. By 1986, all but four member nations of the WHO had officially discontinued routine smallpox vaccination. In the United States, general distribution of the vaccine to the civilian population was discontinued in May 1983. Today, smallpox vaccination is indicated only for laboratory workers directly involved with smallpox or closely related orthopox viruses (e.g., monkeypox, vaccinia), and for military personnel.[4]

Rozier v. Department of Public Health (1987) 161 Mich. App. 591, 411 N.W.2d 786.

Vaccine given to immune-deficient child—Tissue necrosis and loss of arm—$590,260 award affirmed for failure to warn

The plaintiff was vaccinated for smallpox in October 1963, when he was just over a year old. The vaccination site did not heal, and he developed a fever. His condition worsened, and he was finally diagnosed as suffering from an immune deficiency condition, agammaglobulinemia, which prevents the body from putting up an

---

[3] *Drug Evaluations,* 6th ed., p. 1134.
[4] Id.

adequate defense against live viruses such as those used in smallpox vaccine. The smallpox virus spread throughout the plaintiff's body, destroying tissue. Eventually, his arm had to be amputated at the shoulder.

The Department of Health, which was responsible for providing the smallpox vaccinations at the time, was found negligent in failing to warn of the danger of administering the vaccine to immune-deficient children. The court awarded the plaintiff $590,260, and the Court of Appeals of Michigan affirmed.

SNAKEBITE ANTIVENOM

See ANTIVENIN

SODIUM ACETRIZOATE

Cystokon
Pyelokon-R
Salpix
Urokon

Sodium acetrizoate, a water-soluble organic iodine compound derived from triiodobenzine, was introduced in 1951 by Mallinckrodt, Inc. (St. Louis, Mo.) as a significant step toward achieving an ideal contrast agent in diagnostic radiology.[5] However, the preparation (Urokon) was soon connected with serious reactions, including paralysis, and was eventually abandoned for use in intravascular studies.[6]

Salgo v. Leland Stanford Jr. University Board of Trustees (1957) 154 Cal. App. 2d 560, 317 P.2d 170.

Paralysis after aortogram—Alleged departure from manufacturer's recommendations on use of Urokon 70—Plaintiff's verdict reversed on erroneous instructions

The defendant-surgeon performed an aortogram using Urokon 70. The procedure was uneventful, but the following morning the patient awoke paralyzed in the lower extremities.

Prior to the aortogram, one cubic centimeter of the solution was injected into a vein in the patient's arm. The results were negative,

---

[5] Hess, R. J. and McDonald, H. B., "Diseases of Diagnostic Procedures," in *Diseases of Medical Progress: A Study of Iatrogenic Disease,* 3rd ed., R. H. Moser, editor (Springfield, Ill.: Charles C Thomas, Publisher, 1969), p. 729.

[6] Id., p. 743.

and it was concluded that he was not sensitive to the drug. The patient was then injected with 30 cc.'s at a fairly rapid rate, and the series of X-rays was taken. The pictures showed the descending aorta in the abdomen just below the vessels leading to the kidneys was blocked. The defendant consulted with several other specialists and decided to take additional X-rays to determine the extent of the blockage. During this time the patient remained under anesthesia and the needle through which the solution had been injected was kept in place. For the second series of X-rays another 20 cc.'s of Urokon 70 was injected. The test was completed and the patient was returned to his room.

At the trial, the patient's attorneys proceeded on the theory of *res ipsa loquitur,* and the patient received a jury verdict of $250,000. This was reversed, however, by the California District Court of Appeals, which held that the trial judge was in error in instructing the jury that an inference of negligence existed as a matter of law. The court said the jury should have been instructed on "conditional" *res ipsa loquitur,* i.e., that they should apply the doctrine only if they found that the facts justified doing so — in this case, if they found the needle had been inserted in the wrong place.

The reviewing court was also asked to consider the propriety of a jury instruction that stated, in effect, that if Urokon 70 was injected in a greater amount than that recommended by the manufacturer's drug brochure, and if the jury found that such injection constituted "experimentation," then the defendants should be found guilty of negligence unless the patient was first warned of such experimentation and consented to it. In connection with this question, the court was also requested to rule on the admissibility of the brochure itself.

The manufacturer's brochure issued with Urokon 70 stated that for an adult translumbar aortography (the test performed in the present case) "10 to 15 cc.'s of 70% Urokon is adequate," and that "aortography should not be repeated within 24 hours." The parties to the case differed as to the meaning of this language: the patient's attorneys contended that the statement negates a second injection, while the defendants argued that it negates only a second insertion of the needle, and that a second injection, if the needle is kept in place, does not contravene the manufacturer's recommendations.

The patient had received 50 cc.'s of Urokon 70, having been given 30 cc.'s for the first series of X-rays and 20 cc.'s for the second. A specialist appearing for the defense testified that "it was customary to use 50 cc.'s on the first run." A second witness testified that the customary dosage was from 30 to 70 cc.'s. A third said 30 cc.'s was customary for the first run and a fourth said frequently the custom was 50 cc. followed by another 50 cc. There was no testimony that the amount given to the patient in the present case was improper. Also, the manufacturer's brochure recommended 50 cc. of Urokon 70 in another procedure involving injection of the contrast solution for visualization of the heart.

The defendants urged that the manufacturer's brochure was not admissible in evidence and did not establish a standard of care for the physician. They argued that drug manufacturers' recommendations "are always conservative and are quickly outdated, that they expect and the custom is that after a material has been available for a period of time, physicians using it rely primarily on their own experience and the published literature of colleagues concerning its use in actual practice." The defendants contended further that "miraculous developments which have taken place in the effective use of antibiotics and other drugs might never have been accomplished if physicians were required to follow blindly the suggestions of the manufacturers who prepare but do not use them."

The reviewing court rejected the defendants' arguments and held that the Urokon 70 brochure was admissible. While the brochure "cannot establish as a matter of law the standard of care required of a physician in the use of the drug," said the court, it "may be considered by the jury along with the other evidence in the case to determine whether the particular physician met the standard of care required of him." The court added that the trial judge's instruction on the subject should have been limited to this effect.

The court went on to hold that the mere fact of a departure from the manufacturer's recommendations where such a departure is customarily followed by physicians of standing in the locality does not make that departure an "experiment." There was in this case no evidence of experiment, said the court, and the instructions to the jury in this regard should not have been given.

Ball v. Mallinckrodt Chemical Works (1964) 53 Tenn. App. 218, 381 S.W.2d 563, 19 A.L.R.3d 813.

Paralysis during aortogram—Choice of Urokon 70 questioned—Verdicts for physician and manufacturer affirmed

In January the plaintiff underwent a translumbar aortogram to determine the cause of her high blood pressure. Urokon 70 was the contrast medium used, and almost immediately after she was injected the plaintiff experienced excruciating pain in her chest and abdomen, followed shortly by numbness and paralysis of both legs. X-rays taken during the procedure showed that some of the solution escaped outside the aorta, and apparently had migrated to the spinal cord.

In the resulting lawsuit against the surgeon who had conducted the test and the manufacturer of Urokon 70, the issues included among other things, the question as to whether Urokon 70 was the proper choice in the plaintiff's case in view of other contrast media that were reportedly safer.

The main thrust of the defense was that there was a danger inherent in such procedures despite all precautions and regardless of the contrast medium chosen. Untoward results, it was argued, were to be expected in approximately 1% of the cases.

The jury returned verdicts in favor of the defendants, and the plaintiff appealed. The Court of Appeals of Tennessee affirmed, holding:

> Urokon 70 was the contrast agent chosen by at least half the surgeons performing aortograms in the United States. This choice was made despite the existence of other available agents considered by some to be less toxic because the use of Urokon 70 permitted the taking of better X-rays of the renal arteries. There is material evidence, however, that no contrast agent is completely safe. Some of the foremost practicing and teaching surgeons testified that, knowing its toxic nature, they have used Urokon 70 because it gives the best picture and, since the test is a severe and somewhat dangerous procedure used only in extreme cases when all else has failed, it is deemed unwise to have the patient undergo the test without a reasonable expectation that a satisfactory picture can be obtained. It is well settled that where the treatment or procedure is one of choice among competent physicians a physician cannot be held guilty of malpractice in selecting the one which, according to his best judgment, is best suited to the patient's needs.

The court added that there was abundant evidence from which the jury might conclude that the physician in the exercise of his best judgment chose the proper contrast agent for making the test, and that its use was approved by competent medical authorities. "We are also of opinion under the same evidence it was for the jury to say whether there was a breach of an implied warranty of fitness or negligence on the part of Mallinckrodt Chemical Works in making Urokon 70 available for use by competent and skilled surgeons in the performance of aortograms."

Nishi v. Hartwell (1970) 52 Haw. 188, 473 P.2d 116.

Paralysis after aortogram—Hazards of Urokon not discussed with patient—Dismissal affirmed for want of medical evidence establishing standard

The patient, a dentist, and his wife filed suit against a cardiovascular specialist and a thoracic surgeon primarily on the ground that they had not obtained his informed consent to thoracic aortography during which he suffered paralysis, apparently as a side effect of Urokon. The patient alleged that neither defendant had apprised him of the danger of Urokon, although both were fully aware of it.

The patient had a history of hypertension and chronic kidney ailments dating back many years. On the morning of October 18, 1959 he had severe attacks of chest pain, and was hospitalized. X-ray examinations indicated he might be suffering from an aneurysm, and the thoracic aortography was decided upon. After consulting with the thoracic surgeon, the cardiovascular specialist recommended the procedure to the patient.

In making the recommendation, the physician explained the procedure but said nothing about the attendant hazard. His reasons for the omission appeared in the following excerpts of his testimony:

> He had chronic kidney disease, having been operated on, either two or three times since 1929, for kidney stone, with a good deal of chronic infection resulting therefrom and some kidney damage.... [H]e was gravely ill — because the pain was so severe, he required Demerol injections ...; he was literally riding with it, at times.... Each person is different. This man was very well-educated, a fine man, but, in addition, he was very frightened about his condition, he was apprehensive, and this actually guided our hand in much of what we did because if a man has a serious heart disease, with hypertension, and you thereupon frighten him further, you have a problem which you have created.... I mentioned he had high blood pressure, he had pain in his chest which we were trying to find an answer to, and if I had ... said, 'We are about to inject something into you which has a remote chance of causing you to be paralyzed, you may get an immediate reaction which will cost you your life,' if I had said these things ... I think it would have been a terrible mistake.... [H]e's a dentist. I would dare say he's given thousands of injections of novocaine and he knows, as well as I ... that every time you inject anything into somebody, a hazard exists, so that it didn't seem necessary to tell this professional man, 'Now is it a hazard?' He knows it. And,

> therefore, not very much was said to him by me about the dangers of the procedure. I wished to reassure him that we were doing everything we could to find the cause of his pain and so I think, in talking to him, I said 'This is a fairly simple procedure, it simply is an injection of material into your circulation so we can outline the swelling or widening of your aorta'.

The thoracic surgeon also explained the procedure to the patient. He went into the technical aspects in greater detail than he would have done with average layman, but, like his codefendant, omitted any mention of attendant collateral hazard. At the trial he gave two reasons for the omission: one was that he thought that full disclosure would not be in the patient's best medical interest in view of his psychological condition; the other was that Urokon was practically the only satisfactory contrast medium then available for the procedure and he was of the opinion that the chance of a hazard materializing from its use was "relatively minimal."

The evidence indicated that from the explanations given to him, the patient had an understanding of the general nature of the procedure. He stated in his deposition that he knew that his femoral artery would be opened; that a tube would be placed in the artery and a dye would be injected through the tube; that he was not told, and did not inquire, about the kind of dye which would be used; and that he did not make any detailed inquiry because he relied on his physicians.

The trial judge granted the defendants' motion to dismiss. The plaintiffs appealed, and the Supreme Court of Hawaii affirmed, holding that the plaintiffs had failed to offer any evidence establishing a medical standard from which the defendants deviated.

SODIUM BUTABARBITAL

See BUTABARBITAL SODIUM

SODIUM BUTISOL

See BUTABARBITAL SODIUM

SODIUM DIATRIZOATE

Hypaque Sodium
Renografin

Sodium diatrizoate is one of the better tolerated and less toxic of the contrast media used in diagnostic radiology.[7] The agent comes in various strengths, mixtures and preparations. Winthrop Laboratories (New York, N.Y.) offers Hypaque Sodium in various strengths. E. R. Squibb & Sons, Inc. (Princeton, N.J.) markets similar mixtures under the Renografin label.

In the product literature, Hypaque 50% (the preparation involved in the litigation below) is indicated only for "excretory urography."[8]

Serious or fatal reactions are associated with contrast media generally. It is important that a course of action be carefully planned in advance for the immediate treatment of serious reactions and that appropriate treatment facilities be readily available. Before injecting a contrast medium, the patient should be questioned for a history of allergy, which, if present, implies a greater than usual risk (although it does not arbitrarily contraindicate the use of the medium).[9]

The untoward results associated with the use of sodium diatrizoate include, but are not limited to: hypotension (occasionally leading to renal shutdown), cardiac arrest, asthmatic attacks, anaphylactoid shock, pulmonary edema, and convulsions.[10]

All contrast media may produce adverse reactions, the nature and severity of which depend upon a number of things, especially the agent and diagnostic procedure involved. The physician performing the procedure should have a thorough understanding of what is involved, including the indications for specific media and the associated risks. The final criterion for administering the medium must depend upon the calculated risk and the extent of the need for the diagnostic information sought.[11]

Haven v. Randolph (D. D.C., 1972) 342 F. Supp. 538, aff'd (1974) 161 App. D.C. 150, 494 F.2d 1069.

Allergic reaction, apparently anaphylactoid, resulting in paralysis—Choice and method of use of agent questioned, lack of informed consent—Directed verdicts for physicians and hospital upheld

A child suffered an allergic reaction (apparently anaphylactoid) to Hypaque 50% during a retrograde femoral arteriogram which

---

[7] *United States Dispensatory,* 27th ed., p. 1054.

[8] *Physicians' Desk Reference,* 35th ed., p. 2044.

[9] Id.

[10] Id.

[11] *AMA Drug Evaluations,* 2d ed., p. 754.

left him paralyzed. His parents filed suit against the surgeon who had performed the test, the referring pediatrician, and the hospital. The action was in two counts: negligence and improperly obtained consent.

Included among the specific charges of negligence against the surgeon were: (1) use of Hypaque 50% in view of the child's medical history and physical condition; (2) use of Hypaque 50% in excessive dosages; (3) use of repeated injections; (4) failing to use the medium according to the manufacturer's specifications and warnings; (5) failure to apprise himself of the proper use, technique, precautions, dosage, dangers and contraindications of the medium, or disregarding same without sufficient justification; (6) failure to employ premedication to avoid or minimize an allergic reaction; (7) failure to use Hypaque 50% at body temperature; and (8) failure to use the medium in a manner consistent with the standards of the medical community.

Similar charges were made against the referring pediatrician, plus abandonment.

In their second count the plaintiffs alleged that the pediatrician represented to them that the test was "no more risky than taking an aspirin," and that both physicians had failed to inform them of the potential dangers involved.

To support the charge of negligence, the plaintiffs' attorney attempted to introduce package inserts supplied by the manufacturer of Hypaque 50%. The trial judge ruled several of these inadmissible; one because it did not address itself to the kind of procedure performed, and another because it was not in effect at the time of the accident. A third brochure was admitted, but the trial judge commented that it did not provide "any insight into what might constitute the standard of care in these circumstances." The plaintiffs offered no other medical evidence on standard of care.

The trial judge granted the defendants' motions for directed verdicts on both counts, citing want of expert medical testimony supporting the plaintiffs' charges. He pointed out that the surgeon did not discuss the risk of paralysis because the evidence showed there had been no known instance of a child under nine years who had become paralyzed as a result of undergoing the procedure. He added that the pediatrician had admitted that when he stated that he believed an arteriogram was "no more harmful than taking an aspirin" he in fact had no experience with such a procedure. Also, the judge commented that there was no evidence to show that the plaintiffs would have refused to allow the test had more facts concerning the risks been disclosed to them. The hospital was absolved of liability when the court failed to accept application of the doctrine of *respondeat superior*.

The judgment of the trial court was affirmed on appeal.

E. R. Squibb & Sons, Inc. v. Heflin (Tex. Civ. App., 1979) 579 S.W.2d 19.

Fatal reaction during discogram—Evidence that medium entered subarachnoid space—$25,000 judgment against manufacturer

The patient in this case died three hours after a myelogram and discogram during which he suffered an apparent anaphylactic reaction to the contrast medium used in the discogram, Renografin. Suit was brought against the manufacturer of the solution.

The evidence suggested that somehow the medium entered the subarachnoid space surrounding the spinal canal. The radiologist who performed the discogram testified that he "put the needle where it was supposed to be" and not in the subarachnoid space. The evidence also showed that the substance could have found its way into the subarachnoid space without actually being injected into it.

According to the radiologist, if he had known that the Renografin was "toxic and dangerous" when present in the subarachnoid space, he would have used another contrast medium. The product information accompanying the solution did not contain a warning to this effect.

The jury awarded the patient's survivors $50,000 which was reduced to $25,000 by the trial court. This judgment was upheld on appeal.

Related cases

Fatal reaction during intravenous pyelogram—Verdicts for defendants

In Smith v. E. R. Squibb & Sons, Inc. (1979) 405 Mich. 79, 273 N.W.2d 476, a jury returned verdicts for all defendants in an action against a hospital, various physicians and the manufacturer of Renografin brought by the husband of a woman who suffered a fatal reaction during an intravenous pyelogram. Appeal was against the manufacturer only, whom the jury found had adequately warned the physicians of the risk involved through package inserts accompanying the product. The Supreme Court of Michigan affirmed.

SODIUM FLUORESCEIN

Sodium fluorescein is a dye used in various diagnostic examinations. In some it is injected intravenously and in others it is applied locally.

A sterile 2% solution is used for diagnosis of lesions of the cornea. Also, during surgery for strangulated hernia, the dye may be injected intravenously to differentiate normal intestine, which will fluoresce, from nonviable bowel, which fails to do so. It has also been found useful in delineating the gallbladder and bile ducts in surgery on these organs.[12]

Fatal reaction during eye examination—$77,500 jury verdict

In Clark v. University Hosp. of Jacksonville (No. 802246CA, Circuit Court, Duval County, Fla., Jan. 15, 1981), hospital personnel used an excessive amount of sodium fluorescein in performing an eye examination on an 85-year-old male patient. He suffered a reaction, developed laryngeal edema and hypoxia, and died in twenty minutes allegedly as a result of resuscitation measures being delayed. A jury awarded the plaintiff $77,500.

SODIUM HEPARIN

See HEPARIN SODIUM

SODIUM IOTHALAMATE

Angio-Conray
Conray-60/400

Sodium iothalamate is a contrast medium used for intravascular angiography. Solutions of various strengths are sold under the names Angio-Conray, Conray 60, Conray 400 and others, by Mallinckrodt, Inc. (St. Louis, Mo.). The product can cause acute allergic reactions, including anaphylaxis.[13]

---

[12] *United States Dispensatory,* 27th ed., pp. 1056-57.
[13] Id., p. 1066.

Medvecz v. Choi (C.A.-3 Pa., 1977) 569 F.2d 1221.

Infiltration of spinal canal causing paralysis—$200,000 award against surgeon and anesthesiologist

This action arose when the plaintiff became paralyzed from the waist down within 48 hours after an injection of Angio-Conray dye during a renal arteriogram.

The parties conceded that the dye has neurotoxic properties, and that the plaintiff, a middle-age woman, suffered the paralysis as a result of movement of the solution from her blood vessels, where it had been injected, into her spinal canal. The plaintiff maintained that the dye infiltrated the spinal canal because the defendant-surgeon continued to administer injections despite a precipitous drop in the plaintiff's blood pressure. The surgeon argued that the anesthesiologist, also a defendant, did not inform him of the drop in blood pressure.

The plaintiff also produced evidence that her condition may have been caused by the administration of Neo-Synephrine (phenylephrine hydrochloride), designed to raise the blood pressure, because the consequence of administering this drug is to constrict the blood vessels, and therefore its injection "squeezed" the dye into the spinal canal. Evidence was introduced that a qualified anesthesiologist would have known that the use of Neo-Synephrine in such a case was improper.

There was also evidence that the anesthesiologist may have left the operating room at about the time the plaintiff's blood pressure dropped.

A jury returned verdicts of $150,000 for the plaintiff and $50,000 for her husband against the surgeon and the anesthesiologist. The plaintiff had previously settled with the surgeon and the manufacturer of Angio-Conray for $160,000, and this amount was deducted from the awards.

Because the trial court had refused to instruct the jury on (1) the anesthesiologist's alleged abandonment and (2) the issue of punitive damages, the plaintiff and her husband appealed and won a new trial.

Pardy v. United States (C.A.-7 Ill., 1986) 783 F.2d 710.

Reaction during IVP—Brain damage—No liability for failure to obtain informed consent

In November, 1978, the plaintiff's husband underwent an intravenous pyelogram (IVP) to determine if he was suffering from a urinary obstruction. The test was administered at the hospital at Scott Air Force base near East St. Louis, Illinois. As part of the test, the radiologist injected the patient with Conray 60. The radiologist did not discuss the risks of the injection nor request the patient's written consent. He merely asked the patient if he was allergic to any drugs, to which the patient answered no.

Shortly after the injection, the patient became ill and began to vomit. When the vomiting subsided, the radiologist began taking the X-rays but noticed that the patient was having difficulty breathing. The patient then went into convulsions and required emergency treatment. He recovered but suffered permanent brain damage.

In the lawsuit against the government, it was alleged that the IVP was performed without the patient's informed consent. As evidence, the plaintiff introduced a manual published by the American Hospital Association entitled *Patient's Bill of Rights*. In this manual it was stated:

> The patient has a right to obtain from his physician complete, current information concerning his diagnosis, treatment and prognosis in terms the patient can reasonably understand. When it is not medically advisable to give such information to the patient, the information should be made available to an appropriate person in his behalf.
>
> The patient has the right to receive from his physician information necessary to give informed consent prior to the start of any procedure and/or treatment. Except in emergencies, such information for informed consent should include but not necessarily be limited to the specific procedure and/or treatment, and medically significant risks involved, and the probable duration of the incapacitation.

The Chief of Hospital Services at the Air Force base admitted in his testimony that the above statement is part of hospital policy. He added, however, that the failure to inform the patient in question of the remote risk of an allergic reaction in connection with the IVP test did not deviate from the "reasonable, acceptable standard of medical care." In support of the claim that the patient's reaction was a rare occurrence, the defense introduced evidence that only one in 40,000 patients dies from a reaction to the contrast material used in an IVP. The defense also introduced other medical witnesses who supported the argument that it was not standard medical practice to inform IVP patients of the remote risk of a reaction.

Judgment was entered in favor of the government, and the plaintiff appealed. On review, the Court of Appeals affirmed, holding that the "broad, ambiguous language surrounding the Bill of Rights statements is not controlling," and that the plaintiff failed to meet the burden of providing expert medical testimony to support his position.

SODIUM NITROPRUSSIDE
Nipride
Nitropress

Sodium nitroprusside is a potent, immediate-acting, intravenous hypotensive agent indicated for the immediate reduction of blood pressure of patients in hypertensive crisis. The drug is also used to produce controlled hypotension during anesthesia to reduce bleeding in surgical procedures. The manufacturer of Nipride (Roche Laboratories, a division of Hoffmann-La Roche, Inc., Nutley, N.J.) warns that the drug should not be used in the treatment of compensatory hypertension, e.g., arteriovenous shunt or coarctation of the aorta.[14]

Nitropress is manufactured by Abbott Laboratories (North Chicago, Ill.).

Davis v. Regents of the University of California (No. 314826, Superior Court, Sacramento County, California, Feb. 1, 1985).

Postoperative use of Nipride allegedly excessive—Hospital and manufacturer settle for structured $36.5 million

The patient was a three-month-old infant admitted to the hospital for correction of coarctation of the aorta. In response to postoperative hypertension, the child was given Nipride. Complications developed and the child suffered brain damage, leaving it microcephalic, moderately retarded and with a severe seizure disorder. The plaintiffs alleged the administration of Nipride was excessive and that fluids were negligently administered, causing fluid overload. The drug company was charged with failing to provide adequate data on the safety of the product in infants. The defendants claimed

[14] *Physicians' Desk Reference,* 40th ed., pp. 1492-93.

the child had a pre-existing porencephalic cyst which caused the brain damage.

A structured settlement was reached, calling for the defendants to pay $900,000 immediately and $4,000 monthly, increasing at 4% and compounded annually with a ten-year guarantee. At age twenty-one the child's monthly payments will increase to $6,000 and at age thirty, to $8,000. At age thirty-five a lump payment of $100,000 is to be made. Assuming a normal life expectancy, total payment will reach $36.5 million.[15]

SODIUM PENTOBARBITAL
Nembutal

Nembutal, manufactured by Abbott Pharmaceuticals (North Chicago, Ill.), is a short-acting barbiturate indicated for use as a sedative or hypnotic. The onset of action, which is as a general depressant mainly to the central nervous system, is from fifteen to thirty minutes. The duration of action ranges from three to six hours.

The manufacturer recommends caution when the drug is administered to patients with any respiratory difficulty. Possible adverse reactions listed in the product literature include respiratory depression, apnea, circulatory collapse, skin rash, allergic reaction, severe depression of the central nervous system, lethargy, hangover effect, nausea, vomiting and paradoxical excitement.[16]

Schleichart v. St. John's Smithtown Hosp. (No. 74/2532, Supreme Court, Suffolk County, N.Y., Sept. 27, 1979).

Respiratory failure during surgery—$1.5 million verdict

A sixty-year-old female patient undergoing cobalt treatments for cancer developed edema in her neck and upper airway obstruction. A tracheotomy was ordered, and prior to surgery the patient was given Nembutal and Phenergan (promethazine hydrochloride), an antihistamine, to prepare her for the operation. During the surgery she became hypoxic, experienced bradycardia and lapsed into a coma. Five weeks later she died.

In a lawsuit against the physicians and the hospital it was alleged that they were negligent in administering the Nembutal and promethazine hydrochloride because they each potentiate the

[15] ATLA *Law Reporter,* 28:226, 1985.

[16] *Physicians' Desk Reference,* 40th ed., p. 533.

other's effect of depressing respiration, and the patient was already "struggling to breathe."

According to the attorneys for the plaintiff, the jury returned a verdict of $1.5 million.[17]

Related cases

Child overdosed because of pharmacist's mistake—$2,000 awarded

In Richard v. Walgreen's Louisiana Co. (La. App., 1985) 476 So. 2d 1150, a pharmacist mistakenly filled a prescription for a child's antinausea suppository preparation with 100 mg. of sodium pentobarbital and 50 mg. of pyrilamine maleate instead of 30 mg. and 25 mg. respectively as called for by the physician. The child, age two, became heavily sedated and temporarily lost muscle control and the ability to speak. Liability was assumed and the case was tried on damages only. The trial court awarded the child $4,000 but this was reduced to $2,000 on appeal.

SODIUM PENTOBARBITAL with CARBROMAL
Carbrital

Sodium pentobarbital (see above) is one of the most widely used short to intermediate-acting barbiturates. Being a sedative and a hypnotic, it is used for insomnia and in a wide variety of ailments, including functional gastrointestinal disorders, anxiety neuroses, preoperative apprehension, hypertension, and coronary artery disease.[18]

Carbromal is also a sedative and hypnotic and is used to allay excitement and anxiety, and for nervous insomnia, hysteria, chorea, and other conditions of hyperirritability of the central nervous system.[19] The two drugs were marketed as a mixture under the label Carbrital by Parke-Davis (Morris Plains, N.J.), but the product is no longer on that company's list.

Drowsiness and lethargy are the untoward effects commonly observed in sensitive individuals or in those who have taken excessive doses of sedative-hypnotics. Also, residual sedation, or hangover, is common. Other reactions noted less frequently include skin eruptions and gastrointestinal disturbances. Prolonged use may result

---

[17] ATLA *Law Reporter* 23:185, 1980.

[18] Id.; *United States Dispensatory,* 27th ed., p. 235.

[19] *United States Dispensatory,* 27th ed., p. 235.

in psychic or physical dependence. In susceptible individuals, such dependence may lead to frequent self-administration until compulsive abuse of the drug becomes an established pattern.[20]

Runyon v. Reid (Okla., 1973) 510 P.2d 943, 58 A.L.R.3d 814.

Suicide by overdose of Carbrital—Summary judgments for physicians, clinic and pharmacist affirmed

This action was brought by the widow of a psychiatric patient who died from an overdose of Carbrital. Named as defendants were his family physician, a psychiatrist, a psychiatric foundation which operated a clinic where he had received treatment, and the pharmacist who had refilled prescriptions for the drug.

Interrogatories and depositions revealed that the patient had been suffering from a serious emotional disorder for some time. He had been hospitalized three times, in 1947, 1955 and 1956. On each occasion the confinement was for more than six months, the second being after he had threatened suicide.

In August, 1957 he became a patient at an outpatient clinic operated by the private psychiatric foundation named in the suit. He visited the clinic periodically until 1963. In June, 1963 his symptoms became more severe, and the foundation referred him to Dr. R., a psychiatrist, for in-hospital treatment. He was hospitalized from June 4 through June 28. Dr. R. then saw him at his office on five occasions between October, 1963 and February, 1964.

Between December, 1959 and March, 1964, the patient was also treated by Dr. T., a general practitioner, for a variety of physical ailments. This physician, the foundation, and Dr. R. all prescribed various drugs. Dr. T. was aware of the patient's emotional disorder, and that he was receiving treatment from Dr. R. and the foundation.

Dr. R. was of the opinion that the patient was suffering from a mild to moderate form of schizophrenia, that he was "harmless, frightened, scared and dependent." He prescribed several common "psychiatric" drugs, including tranquilizers, to calm his nerves, and antidepressants to combat his depression. He was "generally aware" of the kinds of drugs being prescribed by the foundation and Dr. T.

One of the drugs prescribed by Dr. T. was Carbrital, to help the patient sleep. He prescribed sixty tablets on August 2, 1961, twelve

[20] *AMA Drug Evaluations,* 2d ed., p. 306.

tablets on January 21, 1964, twelve tablets on January 27, 1964, sixty tablets on January 30, 1964, and sixty tablets on February 27, 1964. Dr. R. was aware of these prescriptions.

In his deposition, Dr. R. said that he would have agreed with Dr. T.'s decision to prescribe sixty Carbrital tablets at one time because this constituted only a month's supply, and the patient had never given any indication that he would exceed the prescribed dosage (one or two a night). Also, despite the patient's earlier medical history, Dr. R. felt people with schizophrenia do not have strong suicidal tendencies, although he admitted this was a possibility. He did not recall the patient ever mentioning suicide to him.

There was evidence that the pharmacist who had been filling the patient's prescriptions had refilled a sixty-tablet order of Carbrital without the physician's approval.

The patient was found dead on March 19, 1964. A container for sixty Carbrital tablets which he had filled on March 18 was found empty near his body. An autopsy revealed a massive overdose of sodium pentobarbital. It was brought out that the patient had been depressed for several weeks, and that he had stayed home from work the two days preceding his death.

The defendants moved for summary judgments, which the trial judge granted, and the plaintiff appealed. The Supreme Court of Oklahoma affirmed, stating:

> We do not construe the statutory provision as imposing an affirmative duty upon a pharmacist to protect his customer from the customer's voluntary act of suicide. Therefore, we conclude that a pharmacist who refills a 'non-refillable' drug prescription should not in all circumstances be liable for the death of a purchaser who uses the drugs so obtained to commit suicide.... Here it is not alleged that there was anything in the circumstances of the sale which should have made [the pharmacist] aware that decedent intended to use the Carbrital to commit suicide.... The facts presented indicate that neither [Dr. R., Dr. T.] nor the Foundation prescribed the particular pills which caused decedent's death. Further, the facts indicate that the Foundation did not treat or care for decedent after October, 1963, and that the Foundation never prescribed Carbrital for decedent. [Dr. T.] did prescribe Carbrital for decedent. He was a general practitioner treating decedent's physical ailments. [Dr. R.] never prescribed Carbrital for decedent. However, he was aware that [Dr. T.] had prescribed a sleeping pill for decedent. He could not be held liable under this theory unless he, as decedent's psychiatrist, had a duty to contact [Dr. T.] and direct [Dr. T.] to limit the number of sleeping pills prescribed for decedent. Furthermore, we are of the

opinion that there should be no liability under this theory unless a reasonably skillful psychiatrist using customary methods would have regarded decedent as a suicidal risk who should not have been given a large quantity of sleeping pills at any one time. Plaintiff does not allege that decedent exhibited strong suicidal tendencies. Plaintiff stated that he had only threatened suicide on one occasion, some nine years before his death. The record indicates that he had never previously attempted suicide. [Dr. R.'s] testimony implies that a reasonably skillful psychiatrist, using customary methods, would not have regarded decedent as a suicidal risk who should not have been allowed to possess sixty Carbrital pills at one time. The only reasonable inferences which can be drawn from the evidence presented are that these defendants did not prescribe the particular pills which caused decedent's death and that a reasonably skillful psychiatrist would not have regarded decedent as a suicidal risk who should not have been allowed to possess large quantities of sleeping pills.

SODIUM PHOSPHATE

Fleet Phospho-Soda

Each 100 ml. of Phospho-Soda contains 48 g. of sodium biphosphate and 18 g. of sodium phosphate in a buffered aqueous solution. It is used for the relief of occasional constipation or for preparing the colon for X-ray or other endoscopic examination. It produces a bowel movement in from one-half an hour to six hours. As a laxative, the recommended dosage is four teaspoonsful, diluted as directed. As a purgative, the dose is doubled.[1] The product is manufactured by C. B. Fleet Company (Lynchburg, Va.).

Hernandez v. Kaiser Foundation Health Plan (No. 85-4335, First Circuit Court, Hawaii, July 12, 1986).

Cardiac arrest following overdose—$990,000 settlement with hospital

The patient was to undergo a CAT scan for chronic abdominal pain. Prior to the test, a surgical resident ordered that Fleet Phospho-Soda be administered. Confusing the correct dosage (approximately 1 oz.) with the dosage of magnesium citrate, she mistakenly ordered 8 oz. of Fleet Phospho-Soda. After ingesting 3½ oz., the patient developed hyperphosphatemia and hypocalcemia, causing seizures and cardiac arrest. She died the next day.

In his lawsuit, the patient's husband claimed several errors led to the patient's death. First, he alleged that the resident confused the

---

[1] *Physicians' Desk Reference,* 42 ed., p. 958.

dosage amounts and, when questioned about the order by a nurse, told the nurse to administer the cathartic as ordered. Second, the pharmacist failed to recognize the overdose. Third, another resident contacted by telephone erroneously ordered Compazine, an antiemetic, which prevented expulsion of the overdose. Fourth, after a nurse discovered the patient was unresponsive, there was a forty minute delay before a physician arrived. By that time, the patient could not be saved. The plaintiff also offered to show that (1) any cathartic was contraindicated by the patient's abdominal pain, and (2) if it was to be administered, no more than 1 oz. of the Fleet Phospho-Soda should have been given.

The case was settled for $990,000.[2]

SODIUM TETRADECYL SULFATE
Sotradecol

Sotradecol (Elkins-Sinn, Inc., a subsidiary of A.H. Robins Company, Cherry Hill, N.J.) is a mild sclerosing agent which acts by irritating of the vein intimal endothelium. The drug is indicated in the treatment of small uncomplicated varicose veins of the lower extremities.

Contraindications include patients with acute superficial thrombophlebitis, underlying arterial disease, varicosities caused by abdominal and pelvic tumors, uncontrolled diabetes mellitus, thyrotoxicosis, tuberculosis, neoplasms, asthma, sepsis, blood dyscrasias, acute respiratory or skin diseases, and any condition which causes the patient to be bedridden.[3]

Rosario v. New York City Health & Hospitals Corp. (1982) 87 App. Div. 2d 211, 450 N.Y.S.2d 805.

Use of drug for temporomandibular joint disorder questioned—Award set aside for erroneous admission of PDR

The plaintiff suffered from a bilateral temporomandibular disorder resulting in an inability to open her mouth fully. In January, 1970, February, 1970 and August, 1971, physicians at the defendant hospital injected Sotradecol into the capsule of the tissue around the plaintiff's condyles, to cause "scarring" of the tissue under the belief that it would "tighten the capsules and prevent the

---

[2] ATLA *Professional Negligence Law Reporter* 2:11, 1987.
[3] *Physicians' Desk Reference,* 40th ed., p. 874.

condyles from slipping out." The treatment was not successful and surgery had to be performed which also was unsuccessful and led to serious complications.

With regard to the Sotradecol injections, an expert for the plaintiff testified that as early as 1969 experts in the field recognized that such treatment was ill-advised and could cause an "eroding of the cartilage that covered the jaw bone." The plaintiff introduced pages from the 1965, 1970, 1971 and 1981 editions of *Physicians' Desk Reference* to show that the manufacturer of Sotradecol recommended the product for treatment of "small uncomplicated varicose veins of the lower extremities" only and did not recommend it in connection with disorders of the jaw.

The jury found for the plaintiff and awarded her $350,000, but the Appellate Division reversed, holding that admission of *PDR* was error, as was the plaintiff's cross-examination of defense experts using *PDR*. The material in *PDR* was hearsay, said the court, and "tainted" the jury's finding that use of the drug was a deviation from acceptable medical practice.

SODIUM THIOPENTAL

Pentothal

Sodium thiopental is structurally similar to sodium pentobarbital. It is an ultra-short-acting depressant of the central nervous system which induces hypnosis and anesthesia, but not analgesia.[4]

The drug is indicated as the sole anesthetic agent for brief (fifteen minute) procedures, for induction of anesthesia prior to administration of other anesthetic agents, to supplement regional anesthesia, to provide hypnosis during balanced anesthesia with other agents for analgesia or muscle relaxation, for the control of convulsive states during or following anesthesia, and for narcoanalysis and narcosynthesis in psychiatric disorders. It is also indicated for use in neurosurgical patients with increased intracranial pressure if adequate ventilation is provided.[5]

Pentothal is manufactured by Abbott Pharmaceuticals (North Chicago, Ill.).

The drug is contraindicated in certain situations, including "status asthmaticus" (persistent and intractable asthma). Also, the manufacturer issues the following warning in the product litera-

---

[4] Id., 35th ed., p. 555.

[5] Id.

ture: "Keep Resuscitative and Endotracheal Intubation Equipment and Oxygen Readily Available. Maintain Patency of the Airway at All Times."[6]

Siegel v. Mt. Sinai Hosp. of Cleveland (1978) 62 Ohio App. 2d 12, 403 N.E.2d 202.

Bronchial spasm and cardiac arrest in asthmatic surgery patient—Choice of sodium thiopental questioned—Verdict for anesthesiologist overturned

The patient, a vigorous and athletic man in his mid-forties, suffered a severe bronchial spasm and cardiac arrest during surgery to repair a torn Achilles tendon.

The patient had a history of asthma, of which the surgeon and anesthesiologist were aware, yet, during the operation, when various sedatives and anesthetics did not appear to be calming the patient's restlessness, he was administered sodium thiopental which, according to conflicting expert testimony at the trial, is thought to produce bronchoconstriction in surgery patients.

At the close of the plaintiff's evidence the surgeon and the hospital were granted directed verdicts. The trial proceeded against the anesthesiologist, and the jury returned a verdict in his favor. On appeal, however, this was reversed, the Court of Appeals of Ohio, Cuyahoga County, holding that the medical evidence did not support the verdict, and that the consent form signed by the patient prior to surgery was not conclusive evidence (as ruled by the trial judge) that the patient had consented "to the added degree of risk of which he may not have been adequately informed, namely the special danger involved in administering anesthesia to an asthmatic."

Barth v. Rock (1984) 36 Wash. App. 400, 674 P.2d 1265.

Cardiac arrest during surgery—Issues involve role of Pentothal and lack of informed consent

The patient was a five-year-old girl who was undergoing surgery to correct a misaligned fracture of the arm. While under general anesthesia the patient began to move and the nurse anesthetist administered an additional dose of Pentothal. Immediately the patient's blood pressure dropped and she went into cardiac arrest. She was placed in intensive care and never regained consciousness. She

---

[6] Id.

was eventually determined to be brain dead, and life support systems were removed.

At the trial an expert for the defense testified that in his opinion the girl had suffered an unavoidable adverse reaction to the Pentothal. (All the other experts laid the blame on either the nurse anesthetist for negligent administration of the general anesthesia, or the surgeon for continuing the operation instead of immediately administering cardiac massage.) The defense witness further testified that he was familiar with a chapter in the Fourth Edition of Grey's and Nunn's *General Anesthesia* in which the authors reported fifty-five cases of allergic reactions to Pentothal. Later, the plaintiff's attorney obtained a copy of the book and found that this information was incorrect, that the fifty-five cases involved "barbiturates in general" and not Pentothal. This was in accord with other expert testimony that reactions to Pentothal are extremely rare (only nine reported cases in forty years of surgery).

Also, it was found that the child's parents had never signed a consent form: both the surgeon and the anesthetist had thought the other had given the form to the parents to sign.

The trial court vacated a jury verdict for the defendants and ordered a new trial, and the Appellate Court affirmed.

Related cases

Laryngospasm—Anesthesiologist guilty of abandoning patient

In Ascher v. Gutierrez (1976) 175 App. D.C. 100, 533 F.2d 1235, an anesthesiologist was found guilty of malpractice in abandoning a patient suffering from a laryngospasm brought on by a reaction to an injection of sodium thiopental.

Fatal reaction—Res ipsa loquitur not applicable

Where a healthy eighteen-year-old man in the hospital for minor surgery suffered a fatal reaction to an injection of Pentothal, the doctrine of res ipsa loquitur was not applicable where the only evidence to be presented was the fact that the injection terminated in the patient's death. Thomas v. St. Francis Hosp., Inc. (Del., 1982) 447 A.2d 435.

SODIUM WARFARIN
Coumadin
Panwarfin
Sofarin

Sodium warfarin (also called warfarin sodium) is a potent anticoagulant used in prophylaxis and treatment of thromboembolic disorders, including pulmonary embolism and coronary thrombosis with myocardial infarction.[7] Coumadin is manufactured by DuPont Pharmaceuticals, Inc. (Manati, P.R.), Panwarfin by Abbott Pharmaceuticals (North Chicago, Ill.), and Sofarin by Lemmon Company (Sellersville, Pa.).

The drug is contraindicated in patients with visceral ulceration or bleeding granulomatous lesions; subacute bacterial endocarditis; impaired liver or kidney function; threatened abortion; brain or spinal surgery; and continuous tube drainage of the stomach, small intestine, or urinary bladder. Also, it should be used with caution in poorly nourished patients, after any extensive surgical operation, and in the presence of vomiting.[8]

As in the case of other anticoagulants, hemorrhage is a danger in the use of sodium warfarin. Hypersensitivity has also been reported. Other adverse effects include hair loss, skin rash, fever, nausea, and diarrhea.[9]

Rusk v. Santa Ana Community Hosp. (No. 161561, Superior Court, Orange County, Cal., May 17, 1973).

Hemorrhage—Choice of drug questioned—Verdict for physician

After surgery for a knee injury, the patient, a 45-year-old man, developed thrombophlebitis. His surgeon referred him to a second physician who prescribed Coumadin. Complications developed, including internal bleeding on two occasions and, eventually, subarachnoid hemorrhage.

A malpractice suit was filed against the physician charging that Coumadin was improper treatment in the patient's case, because his blood already "was too thin." In his complaint, the patient's attorney included allegations that his client suffered brain injury,

---

[7] *United States Dispensatory,* 27th ed., p. 1081.

[8] Id.

[9] Id.

respiratory problems, kidney damage, and hearing difficulties, all of which resulted in permanent disability.

At the trial, the physician defended on the ground that he had followed the proper standard of care in the community applicable to a man in the patient's condition. He offered testimony by a neurologist and a general surgeon that the patient's condition at the time of trial was not caused by the drug, and that any complications from the drug had cleared without residual disability. The defendant urged further that the patient's condition had no physiological basis.

The jury returned a verdict for the physician.[10]

McIntyre v. Endo Laboratories, Inc. (No. 78-0077, U.S. District Court, D. Hawaii, Oct. 28, 1981).

Birth defects blamed on mother's use of Coumadin during pregnancy—Manufacturer allegedly failed to warn—Structural settlement

This action was brought on behalf of an eight-year-old girl born with birth defects allegedly caused by her mother's use of Coumadin during all three trimesters of her pregnancy. The child, born in 1973, suffers from spinal scoliosis and nasal hypoplasia. The plaintiffs charged that Endo Laboratories, then the manufacturer of Coumadin, failed to warn of the risk of birth defects in children born of mothers who used the drug during pregnancy. They claimed that as early as 1966 articles in medical journals reported that Coumadin could cause birth defects, but that the package inserts for the drug did not contain a warning until 1975.

The manufacturer agreed to a structured settlement calling for an immediate payment of $25,000 and $500 per month to the child until she reaches age eighteen at which time the monthly payments will increase to $750. The child is also to receive $25,000 in cash at age eighteen and $50,000 at ages twenty-five and thirty-three.[11]

Geleynse v. E.I. duPont de Nemours & Co. (No. C83-610R, U.S. District Court, W.D., Wash., Nov. 26, 1984).

Patient treated with Coumadin during pregnancy—Child born with birth defects—$475,000 cash payment and structured settlement of $1,080 per month

A pregnant patient who developed phlebitis following an automobile accident was given Coumadin. When her child was born, it

---

[10] AMA *The Citation* 28:95, 1974.

[11] ATLA *Law Reporter* 25:181, 1982.

suffered from neurological, orthopaedic and intellectual disorders, including Dandy-Walker syndrome and scoliosis. In a suit against E.I. duPont, parent company of Endo Laboratories, manufacturer of the drug, it was alleged that at the time the patient was given the drug the manufacturer was aware that it could cause birth defects in children of pregnant users, and that it had failed to warn physicians of this risk. The manufacturer, however, argued that the package insert contained a sufficient warning in that it stated that the drug could cause *fetal hemorrhage death* when administered to pregnant patients.

The parties settled for $475,000 cash and a structured settlement which called for the payment of $1,080 to the child monthly on attainment of the age of eighteen. The payments would increase 5% annually and be guaranteed for thirty years.[12]

Falls v. Endo Laboratories, Inc. (No. 96, 104-B, 146th District Court, Bell County, Tex., March 11, 1986).

Pregnant patient given excessive dose of Coumadin—Child born with birth defects—$1 million cash and $8 million structured settlement with manufacturer, hospital and physician

A pregnant patient's physician prescribed Coumadin to treat the patient's phlebitis. While hospitalized, the patient was accidently given a double dose of the drug, which caused an in utero hemorrhage. The patient's baby was born with brain damage and was partially paralyzed. By age ten, the child had developed difficulty in walking and running, and suffered severe spasticity and a "leveling off of intellectual skills."

In a suit on behalf of the child, the plaintiff charged Endo Laboratories, then manufacturer of the drug, with failure to warn of the risk to pregnant women, charged the hospital with negligently administering the drug, and charged the physician with negligence in prescribing Coumadin for a patient who was pregnant.

The parties entered into a structured settlement agreement which called for $1 million in cash and lifetime payments in excess of $8 million. Endo Laboratories contributed $600,000 to the cash payment, the hospital, $250,000 and the physician, $150,000.[13]

---

[12] ATLA *Products Liability Law Reporter* 4:42, 1985.
[13] Id., 5:72, 1986.

Mazurek v. Livas (No. 79 L 1624, Circuit Court, Cook County, Ill., Dec. 27, 1983).

Cerebral hemorrhage attributed to Coumadin therapy—$600,000 settlement by hospital and physician

A forty-nine-year-old man was admitted to the defendant hospital for phlebitis and placed on Coumadin. His condition improved, but three weeks after he was discharged he was readmitted for gross hematuria, anemia, infection, internal bleeding and kidney failure. He later suffered a cerebral hemorrhage, went into a coma and died. His survivors sued the hospital and the general practitioner who had treated him, alleging that the death was caused by uremia which in turn resulted from kidney failure and the Coumadin therapy. The defendants settled for $600,000, with the hospital contributing $500,000.[14]

Chelos v. Endo Laboratories, Inc. (No. 77 L 21775, Circuit Court, Cook County, Ill., March 19, 1986).

"Coumadin necrosis" following bypass surgery—Jury award of $13 million compensatory and $26 million punitive damages on evidence that manufacturer suppressed information on side effects

The patient was given two doses of Coumadin following a successful coronary artery bypass operation. Several days later he developed pain in his legs. They became discolored, later gangrenous, and eventually had to be amputated. In his lawsuit against the manufacturer of the drug, the patient alleged that his condition was the result of a side effect known as "Coumadin necrosis." He claimed that the manufacturer was aware of this danger but had concealed such information from the FDA. The manufacturer produced medical experts who testified that the patient's condition was the result of a form of deep vein thrombosis and unrelated to Coumadin. The jury found for the patient and awarded him $13 million in compensatory and $26 million in punitive damages.[15]

Eiss v. Lillis (Va., 1987) 357 S.E.2d 539.

Death from intracranial bleeding—Question of proper monitoring and treatment—No contributory negligence on part of patient

The patient, a 46-year-old male, was placed on Coumadin on January 25, 1979, following a mild heart attack. During his 12-day

---

[14] ATLA *Law Reporter* 27:186, 1984.

[15] ATLA *Products Liability Law Reporter* 5:72, 1986.

hospitalization, the patient was given three tests for prothrombin time, which is a test to determine the amount of time it takes the blood to clot.

On returning to the hospital's cardiac treatment center on February 23, the patient mentioned that he was suffering from pain in one of his legs. One of the physicians at the center told him to take aspirin. During the next several days the patient apparently took at least twelve aspirin. He began feeling "weak," and by the second day there was some bleeding from his gums and he had a "horrible headache." On returning to the hospital emergency room, he seemed a "little bit disoriented." At the hospital, the patient was treated with Vitamin K, but he received no blood transfusions and no tests for prothrombin time were administered. On the second day of hospitalization, the patient went into a coma and died from intracranial bleeding.

In a lawsuit against the attending physician, the patient's wife produced an expert witness who testified that the defendant was negligent in not having a prothrombin time test performed on the patient following his first hospitalization. This witness also testified that the defendant was negligent in failing to treat the patient "aggressively to counteract the bleeding" on his readmission to the hospital. According to the witness, the patient should have been put into an intensive care unit, given blood transfusions and should have been monitored carefully.

The jury returned a verdict for the defendant, but the Supreme Court of Virginia reversed because the trial judge had permitted the jury to consider the question of the patient's contributory negligence in taking aspirin which, according to the medical evidence, had contributed to his bleeding problem. The aspirin, said the reviewing court, was merely a factor that the defendant should have taken into consideration in treating the patient.

Kaval v. Kurucz (No. 3378/82, Supreme Court, Rockland County, N.Y., April 21, 1988).

Death from stroke—Patient's dosage accidently increased—Pharmacy, internist, and medical laboratory all deny fault—Parties settle for $515,000

The patient, age 50, had been taking Coumadin for five years following a heart valve replacement. Her maintenance dose by that time was 2.5 mg. daily. On one of her periodic trips to the pharmacy for a refill, the pharmacist refilled the prescription for 5 mg. per day dosage. Six weeks later, the patient noticed small ecchymotic areas around her knees and thighs, which is evidence of internal hemorrhaging, and she consulted her internist. He advised her to go have a blood test taken, which she did. Two days later, before she was advised of the test results, she suffered a stroke, which caused temporary one-sided paralysis. Twenty months later, she suffered another stroke, which was fatal.

In a suit against the internist, the pharmacist, and the medical laboratory, her personal representative charged that her strokes were caused by the excessive dosage. The internist claimed that he had called for the usual 2.5 mg. dosage on the prescription. The pharmacist claimed that he difficulty reading the prescription, but called the internist's office where someone confirmed the 5 mg. dosage. The internist denied that such conformation had been given. The medical laboratory personnel claimed that they had notified the internist's office that the patient's blood test showed that her blood was "dangerously thin," but the internist claimed that his office had never received the results of the blood test.

According to the plaintiff's attorney, the parties settled for $515,000, with the pharmacy contributing $300,000, the internist, $150,000 and the medical laboratory, $65,000.[16]

Related cases

Interaction between Coumadin and erythromycin not proven

In Armstrong v. Weiland (1976) 267 S.C. 12, 225 S.E.2d 851, a woman was unsuccessful in a suit against her deceased husband's physician in which she charged that erythromycin prescribed by the defendant interacted with Coumadin being taken by the patient for a heart condition and caused "numerous heart attacks as well as extensive prolonged and severe internal bleeding." On the stand, the plaintiff's medical witness admitted under cross-examination that he was not aware of any instance in which there had been an adverse reaction between the two drugs.

Birth defects—Mother had taken Coumadin during first trimester—Manufacturer's insurer liable

In Endo Laboratories v. Hartford Insurance Group (C.A.-9 Cal., 1984) 747 F.2d 1264, the liability insurer of Endo Laboratories, manufacturer of Coumadin, was liable for Endo's contribution to a

[16] ATLA *Professional Negligence Law Reporter* 3:158, 1988.

settlement of $500,000 paid to the parents of a child born with birth defects after the mother had been given the drug during pregnancy. The court held that the fetus was a "person" for purposes of the policy language, and that the injury occurred during the first trimester, before the policy lapsed.

Stroke—Discontinuation of Coumadin did not constitute "occurrence" under statute of limitations

The increased probability of the formation of a blood clot (that apparently led to a patient's stroke) as a result of a physician's discontinuance of a patient's Coumadin therapy following heart surgery was "too attenuated an 'occurrence' to give rise to a viable cause of action such as would activate a statute of limitations." Werner v. American-Edwards Laboratories (1987) 113 Idaho 434, 745 P.2d 1055.

Fatal intracerebral hemorrhage while on Coumarin and heparin sodium

In Leenheer v. Feliciano (No. L-071788-85MM, Superior Court, Passaic County, N.J., June 14, 1988), a jury awarded $388,000 to the survivors of a patient who died from intracerebral hemorrhage while taking Coumadin and heparin sodium for bilateral pulmonary emboli. The case is summarized herein under HEPARIN SODIUM.

SOLGANAL

See AUROTHIOGLUCOSE

SOMA

See CARISOPRODOL

SOMA COMPOUND

See CARISOPRODOL

SOMOPHYLLINE

See AMINOPHYLLINE

SOTRADECOL

See SODIUM TETRADECYL SULFATE

SPARINE

See PROMAZINE HYDROCHLORIDE

SPARTEINE SULFATE

Tocosamine

Sparteine sulfate is the salt of an alkaloid obtained from the scoparius plant. The drug was introduced many years ago as a substitute for digitalis in the treatment of cardiac conditions. Later, it came into use as an oxytocic agent for induction of labor at term and for the treatment of primary and secondary uterine inertia following the onset of labor. It has now generally been replaced by oxytocin (see herein).

Untoward effects of sparteine sulfate include an increase in uterine tonicity and tetanic (sustained) uterine contractions with or without fetal distress; also, partial premature separation of the placenta and at least one case of uterine rupture have been reported.[17]

Rosenberg v. Savel (No. L-72462-80 MM, Superior Court, Essex County, N.J., Oct. 26, 1983).

Need for drug questioned—Infant born with cerebral palsy—Jury verdict for $3.2 million

The plaintiff, a twenty-one-year-old cerebral palsy victim, brought suit against the obstetrician who delivered her twenty-one years earlier, claiming that his negligence was the cause of her disorder. The plaintiff charged that the defendant administered Tocosamine to her mother during labor even though she was not experiencing any difficulties and no abnormalities were noted. She claimed the Tocosamine caused abnormally long contractions and deprived the plaintiff of oxygen. The defendant denied administering the drug, but when confronted with the plaintiff's medical records, testified that there must have been justification for its use. The defendant's own records, however, showed that the labor was "uneventful." The jury awarded the plaintiff $3.2 million.[18]

---

[17] *United States Dispensatory,* 27th ed., p. 1082.

[18] ATLA *Law Reporter* 27:188, 1984.

Child born with cerebral palsy

In Rutherford v. Zearfoss (1980) 221 Va. 685, 272 S.E.2d 225, a patient given Tocosamine and oxytocin to induce contractions delivered an infant later diagnosed as suffering from spastic quadriparesis and cerebral palsy. The case is summarized herein under OXYTOCIN.

SPIRONOLACTONE
Aldactazide
Aldactone

Spironolactone acts both as a diuretic and as an antihypertensive drug. It is a specific pharmacologic antagonist of aldosterone, a hormone secreted by the adrenal cortex, and therefore is used in the treatment of hyperaldosteronism. It is also indicated for patients with congestive heart failure, cirrhosis of the liver accompanied by edema, certain kidney syndromes and certain cases of hypertension.[19]

Aldactazide and Aldactone are manufactured by Searle & Company (San Juan, P.R.), and the drug is produced by several companies under the generic name.

Possible adverse reactions include gynecomastia (male breast enlargement), menstrual disorders, mental confusion and gastrointestinal complaints.[20]

Monaco v. G.D. Searle Co. (No. 79-1513, U.S. District Court, D. N.J., July 16, 1982).

Irreversible gynecomastia in male patient—Insufficient warning by manufacturer—$7,775,000 verdict

The plaintiff, a fifty-two-year-old dentist, was given Aldactone by his physician for hypertension. He developed gynecomastia (enlargement of breast) and had to undergo surgery. He also developed severe psychological problems because of fear of breast cancer. In his action against the manufacturer he alleged that its warnings were insufficient, that it failed to inform the medical profession of the frequency of gynecomastia and that it could be irreversible in some cases. The plaintiff introduced testimony of an FDA investigator who stated that the manufacturer's reports on test results on

[19] *Physicians' Desk Reference,* 35th ed., pp. 1648-49.
[20] Id.

Aldactone were not submitted in a timely fashion, and he introduced an FDA investigative report stating that some of the testing was unreliable. The jury awarded the plaintiff $7,775,000, $5,775,000 of which were punitive damages.[21]

Gastric injury attributed to combination of Aldactone and other drugs prescribed for weight reduction

In Mendoza v. Varon (Tex. Civ. App., 1978) 563 S.W.2d 646, a physician was sued for malpractice for prescribing a combination of Preludin (phenmetrazine hydrochloride), Dyazide (triamterene), Aldactone and Slow-K (potassium chloride) for a teenage girl who was overweight and suffered from high blood pressure. The patient experienced violent episodes of vomiting brought on by inflammation and scarring of the stomach and esophagus. The case is summarized herein under PHENMETRAZINE HYDROCHLORIDE.

STELAZINE

See TRIFLUOPERAZINE

STERAPRED

See PREDNISONE

STREPTOKINASE-STREPTODORNASE

Varidase

This preparation is a mixture of enzymes of bacterial origin used to dissolve blood clots.[1] The product was manufactured and marketed in the 1960s and 1970s under the name Varidase by Lederle Laboratories (Wayne, N.J.), but is no longer listed by that company as an available drug. Streptokinase, however, is still manufactured by several companies for use as a thrombolytic (agent that dissolves thromboses).

Mulligan v. Lederle Laboratories (C.A.-8 Ark., 1986) 786 F.2d 859.

Mouth ulcers following injections of Varidase—Punitive award against manufacturer for failing to warn

The plaintiff received seven injections of Varidase in 1960 to break up blood clots caused by the episiotomy performed following

---

[21] ATLA *Law Reporter,* 26:227, 1983.

[1] AMA *Drug Evaluations,* 6th ed., p. 898.

the delivery of her first child. Two years later she began to develop lesions in and around her mouth known as "aphthous stomatitis." These have continued to occur off and on since that time. The plaintiff, a medical laboratory technician, assumed her trouble stemmed from a bladder problem until, in 1976, she came across a medical journal article on drug-induced kidney disease which suggested that her condition might be related to the Varidase injections. She pursued this and wrote to Lederle Laboratories which denied any knowledge of such a relationship.

At trial, however, the plaintiff introduced evidence showing that in the 1950s, batches of Varidase were found to be "unpredictably pyrogenic," that is, fever-causing. Internal documents obtained from Lederle files revealed that a majority of patients given Varidase from these batches suffered some sort of fever and other conditions, including nephritis and "mouth ulcers" of the type experienced by the plaintiff. Yet, the company did not include this information in its package inserts.

A jury returned a verdict of $50,000 compensatory and $100,000 punitive damages, and the Court of Appeals affirmed.

STREPTOMYCIN

Streptomycin is a generic name for several chemically and biologically related antibiotics biosynthesized by strains of the actinomycete microorganism *Streptomyces griseus*. The drug is widely used in the treatment of tuberculosis and plague, for which it may be the drug of choice. It is also used to treat brucellosis and tularemia, often in conjunction with a sulfa drug or a tetracycline. Combined with penicillin, it is often the most efficient method of treatment for subacute bacterial endocarditis.[2]

In other infections, streptomycin has generally been replaced with the newer antibiotics, mainly because of its toxicity, particularly damage to the eighth cranial nerve, which can cause hearing loss. Usually this is not a problem in treatment of acute infections that require only five to seven days of therapy if adequate doses are administered; however, it is a risk in prolonged treatment. Dysfunction of the optic nerve, leading to blurred vision, is also a hazard with streptomycin.[3]

According to the American Medical Association's Department of Drugs, the usual dosage (intramuscular) for adults is 15 to 25 milli-

[2] *United States Dispensatory,* 27th ed., p. 1109.

[3] Id.

grams per kilogram of body weight daily (in two divided doses) for seven to ten days and one gram daily thereafter. For children, 20 to 30 milligrams daily (in two divided doses).[4]

Streptomycin is marketed under the generic name by several companies.

Koury v. Follo (1968) 272 N.C. 366, 158 S.E.2d 548.

Hearing loss—Dosage given to nine-month-old child claimed excessive—Contrary to manufacturer's label and "Clark's Rule"—Nonsuit for pediatrician reversed on appeal

The plaintiff, the father of a nine-month-old girl, brought suit against a pediatrician alleging the defendant caused his daughter to suffer loss of hearing because of excessive doses of an antibiotic mixture containing penicillin and streptomycin. The plaintiff claimed the defendant knew or should have known the drug was hazardous for a child of his daughter's age, and that he had prescribed it without disclosing such danger to him or the girl's mother.

At the trial the defendant testified that he had prescribed the antibiotic in the amount of 1.5 cc.'s each twelve hours, and that five injections were given. He denied, however, that any deafness which may have resulted was caused by any negligence on his part.

According to the girl's mother, she developed a bronchial condition and fever. On admission to the hospital, the defendant ordered her placed in a croupette and instructed the nurses to administer the antibiotic. She underwent tests, including a chest X-ray, and was discharged the second day.

An ear, nose and throat specialist examined her seven weeks later and found total nerve deafness, a condition which he said could have been caused by disease or by a drug such as streptomycin.

A recognized expert in the use of antibiotics testified that damage to the hearing apparatus occurs frequently with streptomycin when administered above a certain dosage. The upper safe limit, he said, is normally forty milligrams per kilogram of body weight each 24 hours. The child's weight at the time of her treatment was less than ten kilograms; therefore, according to the expert's opinion, the upper safe limit for her was 400 milligrams of streptomycin every 24 hours. The dosage she actually received amounted to 750 milli-

[4] *AMA Drug Evaluations,* 2d ed., p. 573.

grams. In response to a hypothetical question, this witness said that, in his opinion, a dosage such as that received by the child could have caused her deafness.

The label on the bottle from which the solution was taken was introduced into evidence. In red letters it stated: "NOT FOR PEDIATRIC USE." On the other side it gave the recommended adult dosage.

Nelson's *Textbook of Pediatrics*[5] was accepted by the parties as a standard textbook in the field. Passages were introduced by the plaintiff, including a statement of "Clark's Rule" for estimating dosages for children in reference to the adult dosage. Under this rule a child's dosage is determined by multiplying the adult dosage by a fraction, of which the child's body weight in pounds is the numerator and 150 is the denominator. Following this rule, the girl's recommended dosage would have been approximately 13% of the adult dose. The dosage actually given to the girl, under this formula, was 75% of the adult dosage.

The defendant testified that he was aware that streptomycin can cause damage to the eighth cranial nerve which results in hearing loss, but that this and other adverse reactions to the drug were, in his opinion, rare, and that he did not regard the mixture dangerous in the amount he prescribed. There was evidence introduced that other pediatricians in the area used the same drug for children as young as nine months, and that they prescribed the same amount. The defendant admitted, however, that at the time he prescribed the drug for the plaintiff's daughter, he did not know that the manufacturer's label bore the statement "NOT FOR PEDIATRIC USE."

At the close of evidence the trial judge granted the defendant's motion for nonsuit, and the plaintiff appealed. The Supreme Court of North Carolina reversed the judgment, declaring:

> [T]he plaintiff's evidence is amply sufficient, if true, to support a finding that the defendant prescribed for his tiny patient a powerful drug without reading, or in disregard of, express warnings printed by the manufacturer upon the container and upon a leaflet packaged with each container of the drug. It is sufficient, if true, to show that he prescribed a dosage far in excess of that recommended for so small a child by a standard textbook in his own special field of medicine. It was his duty to exercise reason-

[5]Nelson, W. E., et al., editors, *Textbook of Pediatrics,* 9th ed. (Philadelphia: W. B. Saunders Company, 1969). At the time of trial the treatise was in the 8th edition.

able care, not only in his diagnosis of his patient's disease, but also in ascertaining the probable effects of the drug he prescribed and to observe appropriate precautions in its use.... Upon the motion for judgment of nonsuit ... the plaintiff's evidence is to be taken as true and interpreted in the light most favorable to him. So interpreted, it is sufficient to justify the jury in finding that the defendant knew, or should have known, that to administer this powerful drug in so large a dose to so small a patient could well result in the precise catastrophe which such evidence indicates did result therefrom. The illness for which the drug was so administered was not such as to create an emergency calling for hazardous measures. It was an illness from which most children have suffered and from which most of them have recovered in due time without such treatment.

Thompson v. Kaiser Foundation Health Plan, Inc. (No. SOC 21485, Long Beach Superior Court, Los Angeles County, Cal., 1973).

Hearing loss—Neomycin and streptomycin administered at same time—$350,000 settlement

A seven-year-old girl with a ruptured appendix and peritonitis was given streptomycin and neomycin.[6] The patient apparently recovered from the infection, but several weeks later developed symptoms of hearing loss.

The plaintiff's lawsuit charged, among other things, that the streptomycin and neomycin should not have been prescribed at the same time, and that the dosage of neomycin was excessive and unduly prolonged. The action went to trial, but before the case was given to the jury, it was settled for $350,000.[7]

Rodriguez v. Jackson (1977) 118 Ariz. 13, 574 P.2d 481.

Vestibular dysfunction and eighth cranial nerve damage—Excessive dosage charged—Plaintiff fails for want of testimony on standard of care

An elderly male patient was administered streptomycin after a diagnosis of "probably tuberculosis." Dosage was begun at one gram intramuscularly twice a day. After six days, when the patient displayed symptoms of vestibular nerve injury, the dosage was reduced to one gram per day. The drug was given four more days and

---

[6] Neomycin can also damage the hearing apparatus. See NEOMYCIN SULFATE herein.

[7] ATLA *News Letter* 16:267, 1973.

then stopped when clear signs of eighth cranial nerve damage was noticed.

In his lawsuit against the physicians involved in his case, the patient charged that he was given an excessive dose of the drug. In opposition to the defendant's motion for summary judgment, the patient submitted the drug manufacturer's package insert which stated that the dosage for treating tuberculosis should be only one gram daily. Also submitted were affidavits from a professor of biology, a pharmacologist, and a registered nurse, all of whom stated, in effect, that the physicians were negligent or violated accepted standards of medical care in prescribing the two grams of streptomycin daily for six days.

The trial judge, however, granted the defendants' motion, and was upheld on appeal, with the Court of Appeals of Arizona holding that the experts testifying for the patient by affidavit were not medical doctors and therefore could not testify as to the standard of care required of the defendants in treating the patient. As to the package insert, the court held that while it would be admissible into evidence, "it does not establish conclusive evidence of the standard or accepted practice in the use of the drug by physicians and surgeons, nor that a departure from such directions is negligence."

The patient also contended that there was lack of informed consent, in that the defendants failed to inform him of the dangers of streptomycin and failed to obtain his consent to the administration of the drug. The court disagreed, holding that "whether or not a physician or surgeon has a duty to warn a patient of the possibility of a specific adverse result of the proposed treatment depends upon the circumstances of the particular case and of the general practice followed by the medical profession in such cases," and that the patient presented no testimony by a medical doctor as to the custom of the medical profession relative to these warnings.

SUBLIMAZE

See FENTANYL

SUCCINYLCHOLINE CHLORIDE
Anectine

Succinylcholine chloride is a neuromuscular blocking agent used as an adjunct in anesthesia. It is used primarily to produce brief relaxation for such procedures as endotracheal intubation, endoscopy, orthopedic manipulation, and electroconvulsive therapy.[8] Anectine is manufactured by Burroughs Wellcome Company (Research Triangle Park, N.C.).

Holley v. Burroughs Wellcome Co. (N.C., 1986) 348 S.E.2d 772.

Malignant hyperthermia—Jury case against manufacturers for failure to warn

In this action on behalf of a patient who suffered oxygen deprivation and brain damage due to malignant hyperthermia which occurred during elective knee surgery, genuine issues of material fact existed as to whether the negligence of the manufacturers of Fluothane (halothane) and Anectine was the proximate cause of the patient's injuries in view of an affidavit of a pharmacologist that failure of the patient's anesthesiologist and other medical personnel to recognize and immediately treat the patient's malignant hyperthermia was due in part to the manufacturers' inadequate warnings and overpromotion of the products.

Reynolds v. Munroe Regional Medical Center (No. 83-3460D, Circuit Court, Marion County, Fla., Oct. 30, 1987).

Succinylcholine administered against surgeon's instructions—Other alleged negligence—Heart attack and brain damage—$1.33 million settlement

The plaintiff, age 35, was taken to the defendant hospital for a broken femur. He was treated by emergency room physicians and then by an orthopaedist. A fat embolism developed within two hours of admission, and the plaintiff lapsed into a coma. At least twenty minutes passed before a "code" was called.

Several weeks later, his orthopaedist thought the plaintiff had sufficiently recovered to have surgery on the leg. Because of its complex cardiovascular effects, the surgeon told the anesthesiologist not to administer succinylcholine during the operation under any circumstances. However, while the surgeon was out of the operating room, the anesthesiologist gave the plaintiff succinylcholine. The plaintiff suffered a heart attack on the operating table. He remained in the coma for about six weeks and in a partial coma for

---

[8] *AMA Drug Evaluations*, 2d ed., p. 245. See also *Physicians' Desk Reference*, 35th ed., p. 744.

another six weeks. He is now institutionalized from brain damage and suffers from severely impaired speech and aggressive behavior.

In his lawsuit against the orthopaedist, the plaintiff alleged failure to administer prophylactic steroids and appropriate oxygenation to prevent or diminish the effects of the fat embolism. Suit against the anesthesiologist alleged negligent administration of succinylcholine after the surgeon had warned the anesthesiologist specifically against its use. Suit against hospital alleged nursing negligence for not notifying physicians of the plaintiff's distress after he was first admitted. The parties settled for $1.33 million.[9]

Related cases

Choice of drugs questioned

In Chapman v. Argonaut-Southwest Ins. Co. (La. App., 1974) 290 So. 2d 779, Anectine was given to a three-year-old girl undergoing major dental restoration. Edrophonium chloride (Tensilon) was administered to reverse the effects of the drug, respiratory distress developed, and the patient died. An issue arose over whether the edrophonium chloride was properly used in connection with the Anectine. The case is summarized herein under EDROPHONIUM CHLORIDE.

Reaction during cystoscopic examination—No negligent treatment

No negligence was found on the part of the physician or the nurse-anesthetist in treating a 55-year-old man who suffered an adverse reaction to Anectine during a cystoscopic examination. Brown v. Allen Sanitarium, Inc. (La. App., 1978) 364 So. 2d 661.

SUDAFED

See CHLORPHENIRAMINE MALEATE; PSEUDOEPHEDRINE HYDROCHLORIDE and CHLORPHENIRAMINE MALEATE

SUFENTA

See SUFENTANIL CITRATE

---

[9] ATLA *Professional Negligence Law Reporter* 2:92, 1987.

SUFENTANIL CITRATE
Sufenta

Sufentanil citrate is a potent opioid analgesic which, when used in balanced general anesthesia, has been reported to be as much as ten times as potent as fentanyl. When administered as a primary anesthetic with 100% oxygen, is approximately five to seven times as potent as fentanyl. As a primary anesthetic, it is indicated for patients undergoing major surgical procedures such as cardiovascular surgery or neurosurgical procedures in the sitting position, to provide a favorable myocardial and cerebral oxygen balance, or when extended postoperative ventilation is anticipated. The agent should be administered only by persons specifically trained in the use of intravenous anesthetics and management of the respiratory effects of potent opioids, and it should be used only when resuscitative and intubation equipment and oxygen is readily available. Also, because the duration of sufentanil citrate may be longer than the duration of the opioid antagonist used to reverse its effects, appropriate surveillance should be maintained postoperatively.[10]

Sufenta is manufactured by Janssen Pharmaceutica, Inc. (Piscataway, N.J.).

Stewart v. Janssen Pharmaceutica, Inc. (Tex. App., 1989) 780 S.W.2d 910.

Respiratory arrest—Claim against manufacturer for inadequate warning dismissed because of anesthesiologist's knowledge of risk

The patient suffered respiratory arrest while in the recovery room following a hernia operation. He claimed it was the result of the anesthesiologist having used Sufenta which "renarcotized," a process in which a narcotic effect appears to have "worn off," but later reappears, sometimes causing respiratory depression. The patient sued the manufacturer, claiming that it did not adequately warn physicians of this hazard, and the anesthesiologist, charging that his use of Sufenta was inappropriate, that he failed to monitor the patient sufficiently, and that he failed to have sufficient personnel and resuscitation equipment on hand for such an emergency.

The manufacturer moved for summary judgment as to the adequacy of the warning, claiming no material issue of fact existed.

---

[10] Physicians' Desk Reference, 43rd ed., p. 1055.

The trial court granted the manufacturer's motion. On appeal, the Court of Appeals affirmed, holding that any deficiency in the warning was not the producing cause of the patient's injury because the anesthesiologist was familiar with Sufenta and fully aware of the possible hazards associated with the drug.

SULFACETAMIDE SODIUM
Blephamide

Sulfacetamide sodium is an antibacterial agent for ophthalmic therapy that is effective against some gram-positive and gram-negative organisms. It may be useful for mild acute bacterial conjunctivitis, and is also commonly used to treat chronic blepharitis and chronic conjunctivitis, but its efficacy in these last two conditions is questionable. The drug is contained in several ophthalmic preparations. In Blephamide (Allergan Optical, Irvine, Cal.), it is combined with prednisolone acetate and benzalkonium chloride.[11]

McMickens v. Callahan (Ala., 1988) 533 So. 2d 581.

Cataracts—Standard of care not established—Summary judgment for ophthalmologist affirmed

The plaintiff's ophthalmologist prescribed Blephamide "as needed" for an eyelid infection for a two-year period in 1980-82. In September 1982, the plaintiff was found to be suffering from early cataracts in both eyes, which she claimed were caused by the drug.

The ophthalmologist moved for a summary judgment. In response, the plaintiff submitted an affidavit by a pharmacist on the required standard of care in treating a patient with Blephamide. The court, however, ruled that under Alabama law a pharmacist was not qualified to establish such evidence. The plaintiff also submitted an affidavit by an ophthalmologist who stated that if he had prescribed Blephamide on an "as needed" basis, he would have examined the patient every three to six months for the possibility of side effects (the defendant had examined the plaintiff four times during the two years she had taken the drug). The ophthalmologist did not, however, testify as to the standard of care in the community regarding the monitoring of a patient on Blephamide.

The trial court granted the defendant's summary judgment, and the Supreme Court of Alabama affirmed.

---

[11] *Drug Evaluations,* 6th ed., pp. 356, 1486.

SULFAMETER
Sulla

Sulfameter is an antibacterial sulfonamide effective in urinary tract infections caused by susceptible strains of bacteria, especially *Escherichia coli.* It is contraindicated in persons hypersensitive to sulfonamide derivatives, including antibacterials, oral hypoglycemics, and thiazides. It is also contraindicated in persons with marked kidney or liver impairment. Fatalities have occurred due to the development of Stevens-Johnson syndrome following use of the drug; therefore patients should be closely observed, and should a rash develop during therapy the drug should be discontinued immediately.[12]

Sulfameter was manufactured by the A. H. Robins Company (Richmond, Va.) and marketed under the name Sulla, but it no longer appears on the company's product information list.

Roman v. A. H. Robins Co. (C.A.-5 Tex., 1975) 518 F.2d 970.

Stevens-Johnson syndrome—Instructed verdict for company because of late filing

In June, 1968 the patient was given a prescription for Sulla because of a recurring kidney infection. On July 16, 1968 she began having difficulties with her eyes. According to the evidence she was advised at this time that her problems "probably" resulted from an adverse reaction to the drug. Her condition worsened, she eventually developed Stevens-Johnson syndrome, and despite numerous operations she became totally blind by the summer of 1973.

A lawsuit was filed against the manufacturer in September, 1973 for failing to issue adequate warnings with the drug. At the close of the plaintiff's evidence the district trial judge instructed a verdict for the defendant, apparently on the ground that the claim was barred by Texas' two-year statute of limitations. Assuming this was the basis of the verdict below, the United States Court of Appeals affirmed, rejecting the plaintiff's argument that the running of the statute should have been tolled because the cumulative effect of the drug caused her to become a person of "unsound mind." The court held that under the law the statute could be deemed tolled only if the plaintiff's "unsound mind" had arisen on the same day she suffered injury from the drug.

---

[12]*Physicians' Desk Reference,* 29th ed., p. 1229.

SULFAMETHIZOLE
Thiosulfil
Urobiotic-250

Sulfamethizole is a sulfonamide compound used principally to treat urinary tract infections. The drug is occasionally mixed with an antibiotic, e.g., Urobiotic-250 (oxytetracycline), however, it cannot be used with all antibiotics.[13]

Adverse reactions from sulfonamide therapy are numerous, including, but not limited to: serious blood disorders, hepatitis, kidney disease, mental depression and psychoses. Nausea, vomiting and malaise occur frequently.[14]

Thiosulfil is manufactured by Ayerst Laboratories (New York, N.Y.); and Urobiotic-250 by Roerig (New York, N.Y.).

Cronin v. Hagan (Iowa, 1974) 221 N.W.2d 748.

Allergic reaction to sulfa—Diagnosis of ureter blockage allegedly delayed—Loss of kidney—Proximate cause not proven in action against surgeon

The patient, a mother of five, underwent a vaginal hysterectomy. The following day she became nauseous, unable to retain liquids and developed pain in the right flank. Subsequent surgery revealed ligatures and adhesions blocking the ureter which caused a fistula. A kidney later became diseased and had to be removed.

A malpractice suit was filed and the defendant-surgeon was found free of liability with regard to the blocked ureter. Also at issue was the defendant's choice of drug immediately after the original operation.

The defendant had prescribed Urobiotic postoperatively. When the patient's nausea failed to clear up after three days, the defendant checked her records and found that she was allergic to sulfa. The Urobiotic was withdrawn, she was put on a nonsulfa drug, and her nausea ceased. It was then that the blocked ureter was discovered.

At the trial the patient charged that the defendant was negligent in prescribing a drug containing sulfa, and that the nausea it produced prevented a prompt diagnosis of the blockage of the ureter which in turn led to the loss of the kidney. The only medical testi-

---

[13] *United States Dispensatory*, 27th ed., pp. 1114, 1119.

[14] *AMA Drug Evaluations*, 2d ed., p. 559.

mony on this issue, however, was by a urologist who had been consulted during the patient's hospitalization. He testified that during the period of the patient's nausea it was true that "less fluid would go to the kidneys," but he added that "after the nausea ceased there would be a greater thirst and probably plaintiff would ingest a greater amount of liquids." When asked whether "the taking of the drug and its results ... would have made it less able for her ultimate ureteral problem to be discovered," he answered "perhaps very slightly."

On appeal, the Supreme Court of Iowa agreed with the trial court that the urologist's testimony did not constitute sufficient evidence of proximate cause to submit the drug issue to the jury. The judgment in the lower court for the defendant was affirmed.

SULFANILAMIDE
AVC Suppositories
Vagimide

This product is a vaginal preparation designed to relieve symptoms of certain bacterial infections, including trichomoniasis, vulvovaginal candidiasis and vaginitis due to *Hemophilus vaginalis*. AVC Suppositories are manufactured by Merrell-National Laboratories, Inc. (Cayey, P.R.), and Vagimide by Legere Pharmaceuticals (Costa Mesa, Cal.). It is contraindicated in persons known to be sensitive to the sulfonamides.[15]

Hawkins v. Greenberg (1983) 166 Ga. App. 574, 304 S.E.2d 922.

Reaction to drug—Possibly anaphylactic—Question whether gynecologist aware of patient's allergy to sulfa—Verdict for defendant affirmed

The plaintiff had a history of allergies and was taking desensitization shots. In November, 1973 her gynecologist gave her AVC Suppositories for a vaginal infection. The following afternoon, after taking her desensitization shot that morning, she suffered what appeared to be an anaphylactic reaction.

At the trial the plaintiff testified that she had informed her gynecologist of her allergies, and of a particular allergy to sulfa. He testified, however, that she did not so inform him, and introduced her medical file which contained a notation "no drug allergies."

---

[15] *Physicians' Desk Reference*, 35th ed., pp. 1238-39.

The plaintiff also attempted to show that the defendant was negligent in not informing her of the contents of the AVC Suppositories before he prescribed them; in particular, that they contained sulfa. The trial judge, however, refused to instruct the jury that a physician has such a duty. The jury returned a verdict for the defendant, which was affirmed on appeal.

Related cases

Allergic reaction—Manufacturer not liable under strict liability theory or duty to warn patient of hazards

The plaintiff in the above case was unsuccessful in an earlier action against the manufacturer of AVC Suppositories based on the theories of strict liability and duty to warn the patient of potential dangers that may result from the drug's use. Hawkins v. Richardson-Merrell, Inc. (1978) 147 Ga. App. 481, 249 S.E.2d 286.

SULFASALAZINE
Azulfidine

Sulfasalazine, also referred to as salicylazosulfapyridine, is an antibacterial sulfonamide derivative used for the treatment of ulcerative colitis. Although favorable experience with the drug has been reported, there is a high incidence of recurrence of the disease. Also, toxic reactions are common.[16]

Adverse reactions include, but are not limited to: vomiting and gastric distress, pancreatitis, hepatitis, blood disorders, Stevens-Johnson syndrome, anaphylaxis, mental depression and hallucinations.[17]

Azulfidine is manufactured by Pharmacia Laboratories, Inc. (Piscataway, N.J.).

Bitterman v. Pharmacia Laboratories of New Jersey (U.S. District Court, Ga., June, 1973).

Stevens-Johnson syndrome and paralysis—$650,000 settlement with manufacturer

The plaintiff in this case was being treated with Azulfidine for ulcerative colitis. He was reported to have developed Stevens-Johnson syndrome, a condition accompanied by fever and erosive lesions

---

[16] *United States Dispensatory*, 27th ed., p. 1034.

[17] *Physicians' Desk Reference*, 35th ed., pp. 1424-25.

which form on the mucosa of the mouth, anus, penis, etc. Later, the plaintiff also developed inflammation of the spinal cord from which he allegedly became paralyzed.

A lawsuit was brought against the drug manufacturer charging that the plaintiff's condition was a result of adverse reactions to the Azulfidine. The defendant argued at trial that over one and one-half million people have taken the drug without showing this kind of reaction. According to the attorneys for the plaintiff, the case was settled for $650,000 after one week of trial.[18]

SULFATRIM

See TRIMETHOPRIM and SULFAMETHOXAZOLE

SULFONAMIDES

See SULFAMETHIZOLE

SULINDAC

Clinoril

Sulindac, manufactured under the name Clinoril by Merck, Sharp & Dohme (West Point, Pa.), is a nonsteroidal, anti-inflammatory agent used for the relief of the symptoms of osteoarthritis, rheumatoid arthritis, ankylosing spondylitis and acute gouty arthritis. Numerous adverse reactions have been reported, mainly gastrointestinal (pain, dyspepsia, nausea, diarrhea, constipation, flatulence, anorexia and cramps) and dermatological (rash, pruritus). There also have been reports of pancreatitis and, especially in patients with marginal cardiac function or congestive heart failure.[19]

Smith v. Weaver (1987) 225 Neb. 569, 407 N.W.2d 174.

Adverse reaction—Summary judgment for physician on question of physician's failure to warn

In August, 1979, the patient's physician prescribed Clinoril for treatment of what the physician believed to be systemic lupus erythematosus, a disorder of the connective tissue which produces, among other symptoms, fatigue, itching, loss of hair and sores and

[18] ATLA *News Letter* 16:230, 1973.

[19] *Physicians' Desk Reference,* 42d ed., 1293.

bumps on the skin. The following day, the patient called the physician to tell him that after taking two Clinoril tablets, she had become sick, had vomited, and her whole body was now "swollen and itched." The physician believed that the symptoms were from her disease process and advised the patient to continue taking the Clinoril, but to come to the office if her condition did not improve.

The patient took two more tablets and came to the office the following day. Her hands and feet were still swollen and itched. The physician still thought that her symptoms were the result of the lupus but on the chance that they might be a reaction to the Clinoril, he took her off the drug and put her on other medication. Her condition improved somewhat, but she still suffered pain, and the skin on her hands began to peel.

In her lawsuit against the physician, she complained that she still "lacks energy, has pain, develops sores, has white spots on her head, her cuticles grew over her nails and were pussy, and her mouth has become dry, as a result of which her ability to speak has been adversely affected, as has her ability to eat and sleep." Also, she claims she could "no longer work or enjoy life."

In her complaint, the patient claimed that the physician was negligent in not warning her of the side effects of Clinoril. In his motion for summary judgment, however, the physician stated that he told the patient of the "primary," or "common," side effects of the drug which, he said were "dermatologic and gastrointestinal in character," and that he instructed the patient to call him if she experienced any problems. The patient denied this in her statement, and testified that the defendant told her only that the drug was new and that it was "good and strong," and that he wanted her to try it.

The trial court granted the physician's motion for summary judgment. On appeal, the Supreme Court of Nebraska affirmed, holding that under the law of Nebraska, a duty of a physician to warn a patient of risks of treatment and obtain the patient's informed consent to such treatment is measured by the standard of the reasonable medical practitioner under the same or similar circumstances, and must be determined by expert medical testimony establishing the prevailing standard and the defendant's departure therefrom. Also, by statute in Nebraska, before a plaintiff may recover in a medical negligence case based upon the failure of a physician to obtain informed consent, the plaintiff must establish that a "reasonably prudent person in the plaintiff's position would not have undergone the treatment had he or she been properly informed and that the lack of informed consent was the proximate cause of the injury and damages claimed."

The summary judgment for the defendant physician was affirmed.

SULLA
See SULFAMETER

SUMYCIN
See TETRACYCLINE HYDROCHLORIDE

SURFACAINE
See CYCLOMETHYCAINE

SURGICEL
See CELLULOSE, OXIDIZED

SUS-PHRINE
See EPINEPHRINE

SWINE FLU VACCINE
See INFLUENZA VACCINE

SYNTOCINON
See OXYTOCIN

T

TAGAMET
See CIMETIDINE HYDROCHLORIDE

TALACEN
See PENTAZOCINE

TALWIN
See PENTAZOCINE

TANDEARIL
See OXYPHENBUTAZONE

TAPAZOLE
See METHIMAZOLE

TEDRAL
See THEOPHYLINE and EPHEDRINE

TEGRETOL
See CARBAMAZEPINE

TELDRIN
See CHLORPHENIRAMINE MALEATE; PSEUDOEPHEDRINE HYDROCHLORIDE and CHLORPHENIRAMINE MALEATE

TENSILON
See EDROPHONIUM CHLORIDE

TERRAMYCIN
See OXYTETRACYCLINE

TETANUS ANTITOXIN

Tetanus antitoxin is a sterile solution of concentrated antibody proteins obtained from the blood of horses (occasionally cattle) hyperimmunized with tetanus toxin or toxoid. It has been used for tetanus-prone wounds in persons who have not been immunized against tetanus. There is a serious risk of reaction, and tests for sensitivity should always precede use of the antitoxin.[20]

With the development of tetanus immune globulin obtained from the plasma of hyperimmunized humans, tetanus antitoxin is no longer preferred, and should not be used when immune globulin is available.[21] Human immune globulin presents very little risk of reaction.[22] Also, immune globulin protects the patient longer.[1]

---

[20] *AMA Drug Evaluations,* 2d ed., p. 882.
[21] Id. See also *Merck Manual,* 12th ed., p. 135.
[22] *AMA Drug Evaluations,* 2d ed., p. 883.
[1] *United States Dispensatory,* 27th ed., p. 1148.

Neely v. St. Francis Hosp. & School of Nursing, Inc. (1961) 188 Kan. 546, 363 P.2d 438.

Reaction to antitoxin—Alleged failure to allow time for skin test results—Verdict for patient upheld

The patient, a 37-year-old woman, cut her finger at work and was sent to the hospital. She was accompanied by a fellow employee and arrived at the emergency room at approximately 8:30 a.m. A nurse and intern cleaned the wound and sutured the cut. The patient was then given a penicillin injection followed by a skin sensitivity test (in the upper right arm) to determine her susceptibility to horse serum and tetanus antitoxin. Shortly thereafter she received 1,500 units of antitoxin and was told by the intern to call her own physician when she returned to work.

Soon after the patient and her companion left the hospital the area on her arm where the test had been made became "red and puffy" and increased in size "from a nickel to that of a half dollar." The reddening worsened, a rash broke out over her body, and she became ill and feverish. She was hospitalized, and eventually suffered 50-55% permanent hearing loss in both ears.

According to the evidence at the trial, the prescribed waiting time after a skin test for tetanus antitoxin is administered is fifteen to twenty minutes. An expert testifying for the plaintiff said that throughout the country he knew "the universal practice was to wait not less than ten minutes" but that in his own practice, when he was giving a tetanus shot to a person for the first time, he waited fifteen minutes and if the test was given in the upper arm "one should probably wait a minimum of thirty minutes." He added that a positive skin test was a "warning" and should "put one on guard" that a reaction, either "immediate or delayed," might occur. This witness stated that in his opinion the hospital, in allowing the medical procedures followed by the intern and nurse "had not met the approved standards of medical practice in the community."

The patient and her coworker both testified that "no more than five minutes" could have elapsed between the time the skin test was given by the nurse and the time the intern injected the antitoxin. The nurse and intern could only point to the hospital records which showed that the skin test was made at 9:10 a.m. and the antitoxin was injected at 9:45 a.m.

The jury returned a verdict for the plaintiff for just over $79,000. Judgment was entered accordingly and the hospital appealed. The Supreme Court of Kansas affirmed, stating:

> ... [T]here was no conflict regarding a skin test being given and plaintiff's testimony, along with that of the woman who took her to the hospital, that only five minutes elapsed between the test shot and the tetanus shot. Under such circumstances the purpose of the skin test would be totally defeated because there would not have been enough time for a reaction to take place from which a doctor could judge the advisability of giving the horse serum. In other words, the patient would not have had an opportunity to react and thus warn the doctor that some injurious result would occur in that particular patient if the tetanus shot were given.

Wilson v. St. Francis Hosp. & School of Nursing, Inc. (1962) 190 Kan. 150, 373 P.2d 180.

Delayed reaction to antitoxin—Question of positive skin test—Judgment for patient reversed—"Defendant could be negligent in not giving antitoxin even if skin test positive"

According to the patient he had slipped on some ice and cut his right index finger. He went to the emergency room of the defendant hospital where X-rays showed no fractures. The Sister in charge of the emergency room, however, informed him he would need tetanus antitoxin (TAT). She told him that first she would administer a sensitivity test by injecting a small needle under the skin on the inside of his forearm. The patient had never had a TAT test and knew nothing of the process. The injection was administered at 6:00 p.m., and the patient was told it would be checked in twenty minutes.

A "welt" appeared and there was "burning" on the patient's arm. By 6:20 p.m. the red area had "little peppery spots" and was a "little larger than a silver dollar." The patient testified that he told the Sister when the twenty minutes had expired and that she told him that he "would have to be patient." At 6:30 p.m. he again spoke to the Sister and received the same answer. The burning by then was "something terrible." About 7:00 p.m. he heard the Sister say she had not yet had dinner, and she left the emergency room.

The patient said his arm hurt so much he "could not sit there any more," and he began walking the hall. At 7:30 p.m. he saw the Sister returning and told her, "This thing is absolutely setting me afire." He said she asked his name again, but kept on walking, and he followed her. He told her he was interested in something to ease the burning and she directed him back to the emergency room. When he got there the Sister came in with a syringe and gave him a shot in the "big muscle on the outside of his upper left arm." She did not tell him what the shot was for. She told him to go home, that he would be "all right" and if it still hurt, to apply cold packs or hot packs.

This second injection caused a "great deal of hurting." In a short time his hand felt "dead and numb" like something had hit him "real hard." He applied ice packs throughout the night and over the weekend. He was able to return to work on Monday, but at times during the day he would feel nauseated. While at work on Tuesday he had a "little prickly sensation" on his legs and felt a "little woozy" once in a while. This continued through Wednesday and the first aid department at the plant suggested ointments, but on Thursday "little blotches came out" and salt and soda baths were then suggested for relief. This continued through Friday and Saturday, and on the next Monday he kept "feeling like he was being shot with something such as a dart." Monday night he went to see his doctor. He looked at the arm and asked him if they had given him a TAT shot in the hospital. The patient said he had been given a shot, but he did not know what it was called. The physician told him he was having a violent reaction to tetanus. The physician administered a shot in the patient's hip, gave him a prescription, and told him if he did not feel better by the next day he was to report back. By Tuesday evening the patient had swelling in his joints and arms, could not "shut his hands," and had difficulty walking. He called his doctor who made arrangements to send him to a hospital in another town where he remained for ten weeks.

The patient's doctor testified that according to the hospital record the patient had received the TAT injection after a "negative" skin test, and that if the skin test was indeed negative, in his opinion the hospital was not at fault in administering the TAT shot. On the other hand, if the test was positive, and the patient had developed a "red welt and inflammation," the hospital would be at fault if a TAT shot was administered. The witness said that he did not think the patient had a positive reaction, however, and if the hospital waited twenty minutes from the time the skin test was given, and there was no positive reaction, it would have been proper to go ahead and give the TAT. He said delayed serum sickness is very rare and the patient's case was of such unusual character it was presented for study to a group of physicians. The witness said he had gone to the hospital and had personally read the emergency room record card which stated "TAT test approximately 6:00-6:20

neg 1,500 U given." He testified that it was from this record card that he determined the skin test had shown a negative result.

Another medical expert testified that the sensitivity test in question, consisting of a small diluted portion of horse serum, was standard procedure for the defendant-hospital. However, the more modern method is to use a diluted portion of the actual tetanus antitoxin by itself. If a patient is very sensitive, the reaction should definitely show in twenty or thirty minutes and if there is any suspicion, the time should be extended to an hour. If the sensitivity test registers positive, the immediate administration of 1,500 units of TAT would probably be "inviting trouble and might be disastrous." He also testified there was a direct correlation between a positive reaction on the sensitivity test and a reasonable expectation of delayed serum sickness or reaction. The witness concluded by adding that it would definitely be negligence on the part of a physician *not* to give TAT even in the face of a positive reaction; the TAT could be given with precautions although some calculated risks were involved.

A clinical pathologist testified that he would have wanted to have made an actual examination of the place where the sensitivity test was administered before giving the 1,500 units of TAT. But he added that the main dose could be given, and if an anaphylactic result developed, the physician could start controlling it with adrenalin.

An allergy specialist also testified. He said the reason for the skin test was to detect "immediate reaction" and it could not be relied on to detect delayed serum sickness because it was impossible to predict how a person was going to "metabolize" and handle foreign protein over a period of several days. He said a patient having a positive reaction would more likely have an anaphylactic shock.

The jury returned a verdict in favor of the patient, and the trial court entered judgment accordingly. The hospital appealed. The Supreme Court of Kansas reversed the judgment of the trial court, declaring:

> All of the medical testimony established that the accepted standards of doctors and hospitals require tetanus antitoxin to be administered wherever there is a possibility that lockjaw may result from an injury, and on that basis and where a skin test for TAT is negative, it not only was not negligence for defendant to administer the 1,500 units of TAT but, as noted from the testimony of one of the experts, defendant would have been negligent in not so administering it.

Anderson v. Martzke (1970) 131 Ill. App. 2d 61, 266 N.E.2d 137.

Reaction after possible positive test—Directed verdict for physician reversed

The plaintiff stepped on a nail and sought treatment from her family physician, the defendant. He treated the foot and dressed it, then had his nurse administer a tetanus "test shot" under the skin. About fifteen minutes later, according to the plaintiff, there was a "redness and a raised area" on her arm, about the size of a "dime" and resembling a "mosquito bite." The defendant looked at it, and instructed his nurse to administer the tetanus shot.

That evening the plaintiff developed a fever. Her arm became painful, swollen and blistered, and eventually turned black. She was taken to the hospital where she underwent surgery. At the trial the surgeon who operated on her testified that she had suffered an allergic reaction to the tetanus injection.

The defendant was asked to testify to the proper procedure for a sensitivity test prior to administering tetanus antitoxin. He said he performs a common test which involves the injection of a microscopic amount of serum beneath the superficial layer of the skin. In this test, if a "wheal" forms on the skin, it indicates a positive reaction, and suggests that the patient should be given a lesser dose of antitoxin or none at all.

The defendant testified that a wheal could be likened to a "mosquito bite which had been scratched." He said he administered such a test to the plaintiff, and some minutes later observed a "minute elevation" caused by the needle and an area of redness about the "size of a dime." He considered the reaction to be negative, and had the remainder of the antitoxin administered to the plaintiff.

The trial judge directed a verdict in favor of the physician, and the plaintiff appealed. The Appellate Court of Illinois reversed the decision, declaring:

> Defendant established that it would be improper to administer the antitoxin to anyone who demonstrated a positive reaction to the preliminary test. He also established that such a reaction would be indicated by the formation of a wheal on the skin, and described a wheal as an elevated portion on the skin, which could be likened to a large mosquito bite which had been scratched. Plaintiff testified that after the test was given, there was a raised and red area on her arm about the size of a dime which resembled a mosquito bite. That description of the arm was a matter of simple observation on the part of plaintiff, and did not require that she have any expertise or special medical training. We be-

lieve that plaintiff's testimony was sufficient to create an issue of fact for the jury as to whether there had been a positive reaction to the test, and thus whether defendant had been negligent in administering the full dosage of the antitoxin.... In the present case, after the proper standard of care had been established, plaintiff's description of her arm was not beyond the scope of common knowledge so as to require expert testimony. We find that plaintiff's evidence was sufficient to establish a prima facie case as to whether she had a positive reaction to the test, and that the trial court erred in directing a verdict in favor of defendant.

Related cases

Tetanus, typhoid and cholera inoculations—Manufacturers required to warn of Guillain-Barre syndrome but no proximate cause established

In refusing to apply the "informed intermediary" doctrine in an action by a 44-year-old man who developed Guillain-Barre syndrome after receiving separate injections of tetanus toxoid, typhoid vaccine, and cholera vaccine, a New York trial court held that where the inoculations had been performed at the plaintiff's employer's clinic in preparation for intended overseas travel, the manufacturers of the products should have known that the inoculations would have been administered without "meaningful appraisal" by an informed intermediary, and the jury was properly instructed that the manufacturers had a duty to inform the plaintiff of the attendant risks. The jury, however, returned a verdict for the manufacturers, finding that the evidence did not establish that one of the vaccines caused the plaintiff's injuries. Samuels v. American Cyanamid Co. (1985) 130 Misc. 2d 175, 495 N.Y.S.2d 1006.

TETRACAINE HYDROCHLORIDE

Cetacaine Topical Anesthetic
Pontocaine Hydrochloride

Tetracaine, a derivative of aminobenzoic acid, is used for surface, nerve block, infiltration, caudal, and spinal anesthesia. It is approximately ten times more potent (and toxic) than procaine when injected, and five to eight times more potent than cocaine when applied topically. When injected, its onset of action is slow (approximately five minutes), but the duration of anesthesia may be up to two to three hours, more than twice as long as procaine.[2]

---

[2] *AMA Drug Evaluations,* 2d ed., p. 221.

As all local anesthetics, tetracaine should be used sparingly on open lesions and in patients with allergy, cardiac and liver disorders, emaciation, hyperthyroidism and other endocrine disorders associated with diminished tolerance. With regard to adverse effects, tetracaine, in spinal anesthesia, may cause vasomotor paralysis, respiratory paralysis, meningitis, palsies, headache, and nausea and vomiting. Used as a nerve block, infiltration or caudal analgesia, or as a surface anesthetic, it may cause muscular twitching, convulsions, central respiratory failure, thoracic muscular spasm, pallor, hypertension or circulatory collapse.[3]

In the product literature, the manufacturer of Pontocaine (Winthrop Breon Laboratories, Inc., New York, N.Y.) sets out a table of suggested dosage for spinal anesthesia, based upon the area to be anesthetized and the strength of the solution used.[4]

Cetacaine Topical Anesthetic is manufactured by Cetylite Industries, Inc. (Pennsauken, N.J.).

Ross v. St. Lukes Hosp. (No. 835261, Common Pleas Court, Cuyahoga County, Ohio, April 25, 1973).

Brain damage—Alleged excessive dosage—$450,000 settlement by physicians and hospital

An obstetrical patient with a history of toxemia was injected with seven milligrams of Pontocaine during delivery despite precautionary statements in the manufacturer's product literature that medium and high doses are dangerous for vaginal deliveries. The manufacturer recommended doses from two to five milligrams. The patient suffered permanent brain damage from cerebral anoxia allegedly induced by a severe drop in blood pressure and respiratory difficulty experienced immediately after the injection.

Suit was brought against the hospital and physicians. In his deposition, the head of the department of anesthesia conceded that, according to the standard procedure at the hospital, six milligrams was considered the maximum dose for Pontocaine in such cases. The injection had been given by a beginning obstetrical resident.

The case was settled just prior to trial for $450,000, with the hospital contributing $250,000.[5]

---

[3] *United States Dispensatory*, 27th ed., p. 1150.
[4] *Physicians' Desk Reference*, 35th ed., p. 699.
[5] ATLA *News Letter* 16:266, 1973.

Leiker v. Gafford (No. 83C2129, District Court, Sedgwick County, Kan., Feb. 25, 1988).

Excessive dosage during cesarean section—Brain damage—$4.25 million verdict against obstetrician and nurse anesthetist

The patient, a 22-year-old woman scheduled for a cesarean section, was administered an epidural injection of 15 mg. of tetracaine hydrochloride by a nurse anesthetist. Shortly after receiving the drug, the patient complained of "shortness of breath."

After the delivery of the patient's baby, she again complained of difficulty in breathing. A few minutes later, she lost consciousness and went into respiratory arrest. For the next fifteen minutes the nurse anesthetist administered oxygen by mask and injected the patient with several resuscitative drugs. The nurse anesthetist did not, however, advise the obstetrician, who had left the delivery room, of the patient's problem. When the obstetrician returned, he found the nurse anesthetist attempting intubation. The patient was cyanotic and her abdomen was distended. The obstetrician immediately called a "Code Blue" and began resuscitation, but the patient had suffered severe brain damage. She lived six years, during which time she required constant nursing care.

In the suit against the obstetrician and the nurse anesthetist, the plaintiff alleged improper and excessive administration of the tetracaine, claiming that the proper dose was 8 to 9 mg. The plaintiff also charged the defendants with failure to administer an adequate amount of fluids to the patient before she was given the anesthetic, and with failure to render proper emergency treatment. The defense argued that the patient's death was not due to negligence but to an unforeseeable "massive pulmonary embolism."

At the end of a six-week trial, the jury awarded the plaintiff $4.24 million. The nurse anesthetist was found to be 90% negligent and the obstetrician, 10%, with the obstetrician being liable for the entire award under Kansas law.[6]

TETRACYCLINE HYDROCHLORIDE

Achromycin
Mysteclin
Robitet
Sumycin

---

[6] ATLA *Professional Negligence Law Reporter* 3:89, 1988.

Tetrastatin
Topicycline

Tetracycline hydrochloride is a potent antibiotic active against a wide range of gram-negative and gram-positive organisms.[7] Achromycin is manufactured by Lederle Laboratories (Wayne, N.J.), Mysteclin and Sumycin by E. R. Squibb & Sons, Inc. (Princeton, N.J.), Robitet by A. H. Robins Company (Richmond, Va.), Tetrastatin by Pfizer Laboratories (New York, N.Y.), and Topicycline by Proctor & Gamble (Cincinnati, Ohio).

The drug is issued with a warning that use during the last half of pregnancy through childhood (to the age of eight years) may cause permanent discoloration of teeth. Also, with regard to use during pregnancy, animal studies indicate that tetracycline can cross the placental barrier and have a possible toxic effect on the developing fetus.[8]

See also DEMECLOCYCLINE HYDROCHLORIDE.

Donigi v. American Cyanamid Co. (1977) 57 App. Div. 2d 760, 394 N.Y.S.2d 422, aff'd 403 N.Y.S.2d 894.

Staining of teeth—Jury verdict for manufacturer upheld

The plaintiff in this action claimed that Achromycin administered when she was an infant caused permanent staining of her teeth, and that the drug's manufacturer was aware of such a hazard at the time but failed to warn physicians in its product literature and advertising material.

The matter was tried by a jury which found for the defendant. The trial judge, however, set the verdict aside. This order was appealed, and the Supreme Court of New York, Appellate Division, reversed the trial judge and reinstated the verdict.

The reviewing court held that the trial court's decision dwelt only on the evidence that favored the plaintiff, and ignored countervailing evidence substantial enough to have created a question of fact for the jury. For example, the trial court cited experiments prior to 1958 that revealed discoloration in the bones of animals treated with tetracycline, but ignored evidence that the dosages given were four to twenty times larger than the maximum children would receive. The trial court also cited a medical report that children suf-

[7] *Physicians' Desk Reference,* 35th ed., p. 982.
[8] Id., p. 983.

fering from cystic fibrosis and treated experimentally with tetracycline developed tooth stains, but overlooked the report's evidence that the children were also treated with many other antibiotics and that it was not known which may have caused the staining. Also, there was evidence that it may have been caused by the cystic fibrosis itself, and that the plaintiff may have been suffering from cystic fibrosis. Furthermore, in its decision, the trial court also failed to consider the extensive evidence of premarketing testing by the defendant that gave no indication of tooth staining, the testimony of its continuous work with the Food and Drug Administration to keep its publication of newly obtained information up to date, and contradictory testimony whether the plaintiff was ever treated with Achromycin after the time she claimed the defendant should have given warning.

Miller v. Upjohn Co. (La. App., 1985) 465 So. 2d 42.

Discoloration of teeth—Manufacturer liable for failure to warn—Awards of $75,000 and $65,000 upheld

The plaintiffs were two sisters who were given tetracycline in December, 1963 for one week's duration. When their adult teeth developed they were discolored.

The plaintiffs established that the possibility of teeth discoloration from tetracycline was known as early as 1960, and that Upjohn made no effort to obtain a warning label until early 1964. The plaintiffs were awarded judgments in the amounts of $75,000 and $65,000, and the Court of Appeal affirmed as against the manufacturer, but reversed as against Upjohn's salesman, whom the court refused to hold personally liable.

Wallace v. Upjohn Co. (La. App., 1988) 535 So. 2d 1111.

Discoloration of teeth—Manufacturers' liability for failure to warn affirmed—Detailmen not liable

This case was a consolidation of four actions against five manufacturers of tetracycline and three of their detailmen for discoloration of children's teeth. The plaintiffs charged that the defendant companies knew as early as the 1940s that the drug chelated with calcium which caused the discoloration in some children, and that in 1956 the Upjohn Company circulated an internal memorandum calling attention to a medical journal article on the subject, but that neither Upjohn nor the other defendants warned physicians or the public of this side effect. The court found all defendants joint and severally liable and awarded $395,000 to the four plaintiffs.[9]

On appeal, the Court of Appeal of Louisiana affirmed the liability of the manufacturers, finding that the testimony of the plaintiffs' experts established that in 1956 the companies should have warned of the tooth-staining side effects of the drug. As to the detailmen, however, the reviewing court reversed, holding that even though their duties included distribution of product samples, delivery of package inserts, and communication of warnings contained in the package inserts, they could not be held personally liable to the plaintiffs in view of their testimony that they were unaware of the danger at the time.

Barnette v. E.R. Squibb & Sons (E.D. Va., 1987) 670 F. Supp. 650.

Discoloration of teeth—Manufacturer's warning sufficient

The plaintiff brought suit against the manufacturer of tetracycline for discoloration and structural damage to his teeth, allegedly the result of being given the drug as a child.

The manufacturer, in moving for summary judgment, submitted affidavits and exhibits showing that since 1963 the company has issued warnings to physicians that tooth discoloration was a possible side effect associated with the use of tetracycline in early childhood. The plaintiff did not dispute these facts, but contended that it was possible that his physician did not receive such information. The plaintiff offered no proof of this fact, however, and the court granted the summary judgment.

Related cases

Class action not appropriate for tooth discoloration claims

A class action was not a superior method for handling claims for tooth discoloration because the issues would require creation of numerous subclasses which the jury would find difficult to keep separate, and because of the problem of allocating fault among various manufacturers and physicians. In re Tetracycline Cases (W.D. Mo., 1985) 107 F.R.D. 719.[10]

---

[9] ATLA *Products Liability Law Reporter* 5:135, 1986.

[10] Following the court's denial of class status for these claimants, the trial judge did agree to consolidate the cases for discovery purposes. In August 1986, after the

Discoloration of teeth—No claim under Magnuson-Moss Warranty Act—Question whether action barred by statute of limitations

In Cowan v. Lederle Laboratories (D. Kan., 1985) 604 F. Supp. 438, a claim on behalf of a child whose teeth allegedly were discolored by tetracycline failed to state a cause of action under the Magnuson-Moss Warranty Act (21 U.S.C. §§ 2301 et seq.), but did present factual issues as to when the child last ingested the drug, and when discoloration first became ascertainable to the parents, which precluded summary judgment under Kansas' two-year statute of limitations.

Discoloration of teeth—Claims stated under concert of action theory

Although plaintiffs who claimed tetracycline had stained their teeth during childhood could not maintain an action based on the "alternate liability theory," "enterprise liability theory," or the "market share theory," because Kentucky did not recognize such causes of action, they could maintain an action under the "concert of action theory." Dawson v. Bristol Laboratories (W.D. Ky., 1987) 658 F. Supp. 1036.

Achromycin allegedly cause of birth defects

An action involving a child born with severe birth defects (bilateral photocomelia), allegedly as a result of her mother's ingestion of Achromycin during the first trimester of pregnancy, is yet to be decided upon the merits. See DeMaio v. Coppola (1981) 80 App. Div. 2d 551, 435 N.Y.S.2d 360.

TETRASTATIN

See TETRACYCLINE HYDROCHLORIDE

---

jury was selected for the trial of the first of the consolidated cases, which by then involved more than 1,000 claimants, the five drug companies named in the lawsuits reportedly reached a tentative agreement with the plaintiffs. The trial judge, however, refused to confirm this report and issued an "order regarding noncommunication of any aspect, including the fact of settlement." *National Law Journal,* Sept. 15, 1986, p. 4.

THALIDOMIDE
Kevadon

Thalidomide was developed in the 1950's by a West German manufacturer, Chemie Grunenthal, as a mild sedative and hypnotic. In 1958 that company licensed Richardson-Merrell, Inc. (Cincinnati, Ohio) to manufacture and distribute the product in North America. The drug was not approved by the Food and Drug Administration for sale in the United States, but arrangements were made between Richardson-Merrell and physicians in 43 states for its use in clinical investigations. The drug was sold by Richardson-Merrell in Canada under the name Kevadon. The product was also widely marketed in Europe by the original manufacturer.[11]

In 1961 thalidomide was associated with severe congenital deformities in infants born of women who had taken it during pregnancy. The product was withdrawn by the manufacturer and its sale was banned in Germany, England and Canada.[12] There were over ninety known cases of deformity in Canada.[13] In a 1973 case filed on behalf of one such child, who by then was eleven years old, it was held that the statute of limitations of New Jersey, where Richardson-Merrell conducted manufacturing and some testing of the product, was applicable.[14] The New Jersey law provides for a tolling of the statute until a child reaches 21 years of age, whereas the law of Quebec, the residence of the plaintiff, does not contain such a provision.

By July, 1975, virtually all of the Canadian cases were settled, the last 28 for an amount reported to be $15 million.[15] In a 1971 California case, a jury returned a $2,700,000 verdict ($1,125,000 in punitive damages), which included $250,000 to the mother. The mother's judgment was set aside on the statute of limitations issue, and the child's recovery was reduced by $500,000 to conform to the

---

[11] Hall, W., "Congenital Diseases," in *Diseases of Medical Progress: A Study of Iatrogenic Disease,* 3rd ed., R. H. Moser, editor (Springfield, Ill.: Charles C Thomas, Publisher, 1969), p. 173. Henry v. Richardson-Merrell, Inc. (D. N.J., 1973) 366 F. Supp. 1192.

[12] Id.

[13] *American Medical News,* July 28, 1975, p. 2.

[14] Henry v. Richardson-Merrell, Inc. (D. N.J., 1973) 366 F. Supp. 1192.

[15] *American Medical News,* July 28, 1975, p. 2. "Thalidomide Maker Settles Damage Suits," *Business Insurance,* July 28, 1975, p. 1. A few Canadian cases, however, are still pending. See Haddad v. Richardson-Merrell, Inc. (N.D. Ohio, 1984) 588 F. Supp. 1158.

pleadings.[16] Settlements in England and Germany have been reported to top $60 million.[17]

THEOPHYLINE and EPHEDRINE

Tedral

Tedral (Parke-Davis, Morris Plains, N.J.) combines theophylline and ephedrine, both widely accepted oral bronchodilators having differing modes of action, with the sedative phenobarbital. A sustained action form (Tedral SA) is also marketed. The preparation is used for the symptomatic relief of bronchial asthma, asthmatic bronchitis and other bronchospastic disorders. The adult dosage for Tedral SA is one tablet on arising and one tablet 12 hours later. For Tedral SA, there is no dosage established for children under twelve years of age.[18]

Baas v. Hoye (C.A.-8 Iowa, 1985) 766 F.2d 1190.

Child dies after ingesting tablets from non-childproof container—Pharmacists liable under Consumer Product Safety Act

The plaintiff purchased a bottle of Tedral SA by prescription from the defendant's pharmacy in July 1981. The defendant's employee placed the tablets in a non-childproof container. A month later, the plaintiff returned to have the prescription refilled. He handed the defendant the empty container and the defendant refilled it. Later, at the plaintiff's home, his daughter (age unknown) ingested a number of the tablets and died. The plaintiff filed suit, claiming the defendant and his employee violated a Consumer Product Safety Act rule (16 C.F.R. § 1700 14(a)(10)) by dispensing the Tedral SA in a non-childproof container.

A jury awarded the plaintiff $205,000, which included $100,000 in punitive damages. After applying comparative negligence principles, the trial court reduced the compensatory portion to $60,000.

On appeal, the defendant argued that the trial court erred in allowing the action to be brought under the Consumer Product Safety Act, in that it was not a violation of the act to dispense

---

[16] McCarrick v. Richardson-Merrell (Superior Court, Los Angeles County, Cal., June 18, 1971); reported in ATLA *News Letter* 14:410, 1971.

[17] "Thalidomide Maker Settles Damage Suits," *Business Insurance,* July 28, 1975, p. 1.

[18] *Physicians' Desk Reference,* 41st ed., p. 1642.

Tedral SA in a non-childproof container because all three ingredients of Tedral SA (theophylline, ephedrine and phenobarbital), could be purchased *individually* in the defendant's store without prescription. The Court of Appeals did not accept this argument.

Also, the defendant argued that by handing him the non-childproof container to refill, the plaintiff, by implication, *requested* another non-childproof container. The court disagreed with this argument, too. The court did, however, rule that punitive damages were not recoverable under the Consumer Product Safety Act.

THEREVAC

See BENZOCAINE

THIABENDAZOLE

Mintezol

Thiabendazole is a vermicide used to kill parasites such as the common roundworm, hookworm and pinworm. The manufacturer of Mintezol (Merck, Sharp & Dohme, a division of Merck & Company, Inc., West Point, Pa.) cautions that the drug should be used only in patients in whom susceptible worm infestation has been diagnosed and should not be used prophylactically.[19]

There can be numerous adverse reactions, including convulsions, hypotension, hyperglycemia, hematuria and anaphylaxis.[20]

Baylis v. Wilmington Medical Center, Inc. (Del., 1984) 477 A.2d 1051.

Propriety of using thiabendazole questioned—Possible excessive dosage—Summary judgment for physician reversed

The patient was admitted to the hospital with skin rash, severe muscle pains, fever, and a high white blood cell count. A parasitic infestation was suspected, possibly hookworm contracted from the patient's dog. The defendant physician prescribed thiabendazole and several other drugs.

The patient's condition worsened and she came close to death. When she finally recovered sufficiently to be discharged she sued both her physician and the hospital, alleging numerous acts of negligent care. Among her complaints were charges that the defendant

---

[19] *Id.,* 40th ed., p. 1200.

[20] Id.

physician should not have prescribed thiabendazole, and that he prescribed excessive amounts which caused her skin to peel off and her hair to fall out. She offered an affidavit of a specialist in internal medicine which stated that at the time her physician prescribed thiabendazole it was not approved by the FDA for human use, and that it must have been obtained from a veterinary source. Also, he stated that thiabendazole is not effective against parasites when they are in the early stage, as they were in the patient's case.

Despite this affidavit the trial court granted the physician a summary judgment. The Supreme Court of Delaware reversed, holding that the question of whether the thiabendazole was properly prescribed raised a genuine issue of material fact for trial.

THIOPENTAL SODIUM

See SODIUM THIOPENTAL

THIORIDAZINE

Mellaril

Thioridazine is a tranquilizer derived from phenothiazine and used in the management of the symptoms of a variety of psychopathological conditions, including anxiety and tension states, acute and chronic psychoneuroses, acute and chronic schizophrenia, and manic psychoses.[1] It is contraindicated in severe central nervous system depression or comatose states, and in hypertensive or hypotensive heart disease.[2]

According to the manufacturer of Mellaril, Sandoz Pharmaceuticals (East Hanover, N.J.), dosage must be individualized depending on the degree of mental and emotional disturbance. In all cases the smallest effective dosage should be determined for each patient.[3]

Carter v. Metropolitan Dade County (Fla. App., 1971) 253 So. 2d 920.

Death from allegedly excessive dosage—
Verdicts for defendants affirmed

The mother of a fourteen-year-old girl sued the county, Jackson Memorial Hospital, two staff physicians, and Sandoz Pharmaceuti-

---

[1] *United States Dispensatory,* 27th ed., p. 1186.
[2] Id.
[3] *Physicians' Desk Reference,* 35th ed., p. 1576.

cals, the manufacturer of Mellaril, for the death of her daughter while hospitalized, allegedly from excessive dosages of the drug.

At the trial, the evidence disclosed that the girl was committed to Jackson Memorial by juvenile authorities because of a suicide attempt. While there, she began to respond favorably to 100 mg. per day of Mellaril, and the physicians, members of the hospital's psychiatric staff, increased the daily dosage to 2,400 mg., reportedly "three or four times" the manufacturer's recommended dosage. On the date of the girl's death, she was receiving 2,000 mg. per day.

The jury returned verdicts for all defendants, and the District Court of Appeals affirmed. In its opinion, the reviewing court commented that the physician in charge of the case was apparently aware of a so-called "sudden death phenomenon" associated with the drug, reported in 1965 in the *Journal of the American Medical Association.*[4] Issues unsuccessfully raised on appeal included the trial judge's refusal to instruct as to informed consent (the parents charged they were not informed regarding the risk of heavy dosages of thioridazine), and his refusal to admit into evidence portions of the "incident report" of a resident physician and the summary of the "Grand Round" presentation allegedly containing admissions against interest on the part of the defendants.

Hatfield v. Sandoz-Wander (1984) 124 Ill. App. 3d 780, 80 Ill. Dec. 122, 464 N.E.2d 1105.

Loss of vision—No liability on part of manufacturer—Evidence that plaintiff took excessive doses

The plaintiff took Mellaril from August 1969 to January 1974, sometimes at a dosage of up to 1,600 milligrams per day, and possibly higher. (During June and July 1973 her prescription records showed that she *purchased* an amount equal to 3,157 milligrams per day, almost eight times the amount allowed under her prescription.) In January 1974, she suffered nearly total blindness from pigmentary retinopathy.

In her lawsuit against the manufacturer, the plaintiff charged strict liability, alleging that the defendant's warnings were inadequate because they did not warn of the risk to total loss of sight. The manufacturer did mention under "Precautions" in both the

---

[4]Hollister, L. E. and Kosek, J. C., "Sudden Death During Treatment with Phenothiazine Derivatives," *Journal of the American Medical Association* 192:1035-1038 (June 21), 1965.

package insert and in *Physicians' Desk Reference* that pigmentary retinopathy had been observed in some patients "taking larger than recommended doses over long periods of time" and that the condition is characterized by, among other things, "diminution of visual acuity, browning coloring of vision, and impairment of night vision."

Despite expert medical testimony that the manufacturer should have included warnings about the possibility of more severe retinal problems, the jury found for the manufacturer and the Appellate Court of Illinois affirmed.

Flading v. Hill (No. 85-C-115, Circuit Court, Ohio County, W. Va., Dec. 4, 1987).

Partial loss of vision—Excessive dosage claimed—Psychiatrist settles for $150,000

The patient, a 25-year-old woman, was under the care of the defendant, a psychiatrist, for several problems, one of which was anxiety. The defendant prescribed Mellaril at a dosage that ranged from 800 to 1,200 mg. per day. When the patient complained of visual problems, the defendant attributed them to hallucinations, and advised the patient to continue taking the drug. A week later, the patient developed retinitis pigmentosa, which resulted in permanent partial vision loss in one eye.

In her malpractice suit against the defendant, the patient's attorney claimed that the defendant prescribed an excessive amount of Mellaril; that the patient's dosage should not have been more than 800 mg. per day. According to the patient's attorney, the defendant settled for $150,000.[5]

Related cases

Tardive dyskinesia following five years of treatment—Retarded state hospital-school inmate awarded $760,185

In Clites v. State (Docket No. 46274, District Court, Pottawattamie County, Iowa, Aug. 7, 1980), a 28-year-old retarded inmate of a state hospital-school who developed tardive dyskinesia (slow, rhythmical, automatic stereotyped movements) after being placed on Mellaril and similar tranquilizers for five years was awarded $760,185. In his suit, he charged negligence in improper use of the

[5] ATLA *Professional Negligence Law Reporter* 3:91, 1988.

drugs, failure to moderate dosage levels, and that he was given the drugs merely for the convenience of the medical staff.[6]

"Extremely small risk" of tardive dyskinesia sufficient to take case to jury on informed consent issue

In Barclay v. Campbell (Tex., 1986) 704 S.W.2d 8, the Supreme Court of Texas held that expert testimony that the risk of contracting tardive dyskinesia from the use of a drug was "small to extremely small" constituted "some evidence that the risk was material enough to influence a reasonable person in his decision to give or withhold consent to the procedure," and therefore a directed verdict in favor of the physician on the issue of informed consent was improper.

Tardive dyskinesia—County health clinic psychiatrist immune under statute

A Michigan community mental health psychiatrist's decision to treat a paranoid schizophrenic patient with Mellaril and Haldol, which allegedly caused the patient to develop tardive dyskinesia, was a discretionary act and thus immune from any claim of malpractice under the state's governmental immunity statute. Coen v. Oakland County (1986) 155 Mich. App. 662, 400 N.W.2d 614.

Loss of vision—Cause of action for excessive doses of Mellaril

In Chasse v. Banas (1979) 119 N.H. 93, 399 A.2d 608, a mental patient committed to a state hospital who was given excessive doses of Mellaril, allegedly causing vision loss, had a cause of action against the individual physicians who treated her, and her claim was not barred by the doctrine of sovereign immunity in view of a 1973 statute which provided that every mentally ill patient has a right to adequate and humane treatment.

Fatal heart attack—Question of manufacturer's duty to warn left to Michigan legislature

In Grainger v. Sandoz Pharmaceuticals (No. 79-40075, E. D. Mich. Oct. 30, 1980), a case involving a claim that a patient's death from a heart attack was brought on by her use of Mellaril, the U.S. District Court certified to the Supreme Court of Michigan the question of whether the manufacturer of the drug had a duty to disclose its risks directly to the consumer. The Supreme Court, however, declined to answer the question and held that the legislature is in a

---

[6] ATLA *Law Reporter* 24:43, 1981.

better position to allocate the duties of a drug manufacturer regarding the hazards of its products. In re Certified Questions from the U.S. Dist. Court for the E. Dist. of Mich., So. Div. (1984) 419 Mich. 686, 358 N.W.2d 873.

Death from synergistic action of Mellaril and paraldehyde

A 59-year-old hospital patient who had recently received a dose of Mellaril was mistakenly administered paraldehyde intended for her roommate. She died the following morning. The case, Serota v. Kaplan (1987) 127 App. Div. 2d 648, 511 N.Y.S.2d 667, is summarized herein under PARALDEHYDE.

Tardive dyskinesia—Informed consent doctrine available to involuntarily committed mental patient

In an action on behalf of patient confined to a state hospital for a manic-depression disorder who developed tardive dyskinesia while being treated with Mellaril and Proloxin (fluphenazine hydrochloride), the Supreme Court of Alabama held that, absent a finding of incompetency or an emergency situation, a person involuntarily committed to a mental hospital is not *ipso facto* barred from the invocation of the "informed consent" doctrine. Nolen v. Peterson (Ala., 1989) 544 So. 2d 863.

THIOSULFIL

See SULFAMETHIZOLE

THORAZINE

See CHLORPROMAZINE

THORIUM DIOXIDE

Thorotrast

Radioactive thorium dioxide was a popular diagnostic X-ray contrast medium in the 1940s and 1950s. It was discovered, however, that in some patients the agent induced latent cancer and granulomas,[7] and it was withdrawn from the market.

---

[7] *Lawyers' Medical Cyclopedia*, § 38.45e, citing Barry and Rominger, "Thorotrast Granulomas," *American Journal of Roentgenology* 92:584, 1964; Horta, et al., "Malignancy and Other Late Effects Following Administration of Thorotrast," *Lancet* 2:201, 1965; Person, et al. "Thorotrast-Induced Carcinoma of the Liver," *Archives of Surgery* 88:503, 1964.

Allrid v. Tenneco Chemicals, Inc. (No. C-56346, Superior Court, Fulton County, Ga., Aug. 14, 1986).

Granuloma formation in neck over 20 years after Thorotrast injection—15 operatons required—Death from complications—$600,000 settlement

The patient underwent diagnostic X-ray examinations in 1956 during which Thorotrast was used as the contrast medium. Apparently some of the medium leaked outside the patient's carotid artery and caused a latent granuloma formation. In 1979 the patient developed severe "neck problems" that required fifteen operations. He eventually died from complications which arose out of his condition and his surgery.

In a lawsuit by the patient's wife against Tenneco Chemicals, Inc., successor to Heyden Chemical Corporation, the manufacturer of the Thorotrast in 1956, the plaintiff charged that Heyden failed to warn the medical profession and the public about known latent dangers of the product. The plaintiff secured documents under the Freedom of Information Act which showed that the FDA had ordered Heyden to change its package inserts to warn of the dangers of extravasated Thorotrast solution during contrast studies or to stop manufacturing and distributing the product. According to the evidence, the warnings were not added to the package inserts until more than two years after the FDA order.

The parties settled for $600,000.[8]

Karibjanian v. Thomas Jefferson Univ. Hosp. (E.D. Pa., 1989) 717 F. Supp. 1081.

Patient's death attributed to use of Thorotrast during cerebral arteriogram—Plaintiff's complaint challenged

The plaintiff claimed that her husband died as a result of exposure in 1956 to Thorotrast injected during a cerebral arteriogram. She alleged that at the time of the procedure, the defendant hospital knew or should have known that Thorotrast was an inherently unsafe product.

The hospital moved to dismiss several paragraphs of the plaintiff's complaint, one of which was that the hospital was negligent for "failing to undertake or support research to find a remedy or palliative procedure for the conditions, symptoms or untoward ef-

---

[8] ATLA *Products Liability Law Reporter* 5:139, 1986.

fects caused by Thorotrast." The trial court granted the motion, holding that such a duty would have been "burdensome" and possibly fruitless.

The plaintiff also alleged that the hospital failed to warn the plaintiff's husband or his family of the dangerous propensities, risks and consequences of administering Thorotrast, and failed to obtain her husband's informed consent to the procedure. The court refused to dismiss these allegations.

The hospital's final challenge was to the plaintiff's allegation that the hospital supplied a defective and dangerous product which was administered to the plaintiff's husband substantially unchanged from the form in which it was received, and therefore the hospital is strictly liable under the *Restatement (Second) of Torts*. The court also let this paragraph stand.

Related cases

Thorotrast granuloma—Conflict of laws question

In an action brought in a Texas federal court by a plaintiff who developed "thorotrast granuloma" and other disorders in the 1960s and 1970s, allegedly as a result of having been administered Thorotrast during an arteriogram in North Carolina in 1943, the court held that the substantive law of North Carolina should apply, but as to procedural matters, including the statute of limitations, the law of Texas should apply. Hines v. Tenneco Chemicals (S.D. Tex., 1982) 546 F. Supp. 1229, *aff'd,* (C.A.-5 Tex., 1984) 728 F.2d 729.

THOROTRAST

See THORIUM DIOXIDE

THYROID (Medicinal)

Thyroid hormones are used for the treatment of hypothyroidism and certain other disorders involving the thyroid gland.[9]

Since thyroid increases the metabolic rate, it is sometimes used in the treatment of obesity when this is believed to be associated with hypometabolism resulting from thyroid deficiency. However, the majority of obese persons show no sign of hypometabolism. Injudicious use of thyroid can be dangerous because of its potential for

---

[9] *United States Dispensatory,* 27th ed., p. 1197.

cardiac disturbance; it is known to increase heart rate. Moreover, the weight lost rapidly under treatment with thyroid is often as rapidly regained when treatment is discontinued because the habitual excessive food intake has not been corrected. In some patients the intake of food may increase in consequence of nervousness and irritability developed during the induced hyperthyroid state.[10]

Ades v. Perloff (No. 1896, Court of Common Pleas, Philadelphia County, Pa., Dec. 18, 1972).

Possible hyperthyroidism—Use of thyroid hormone for weight control—Verdict for physician

A 29-year-old woman patient developed abnormal protrusion of the eyeballs (exophthalmos) and double vision while taking diet pills (Neo-Barine) containing thyroid extract. She filed a malpractice action against the physician who had prescribed the pills, claiming they had caused her to develop hyperthyroidism.

At trial, the patient introduced two physicians who testified that it was considered bad medical practice for a physician to prescribe thyroid extract for obesity unless the patient was suffering from hypothyroidism. Also, evidence was introduced that the pills taken by the patient had later been ordered off the market by the Food and Drug Administration because of possible dangerous side effects.

The patient's medical evidence suggested that her condition was caused by the pills, but the defendant introduced evidence disputing this. He also offered evidence that there was conflicting medical opinion on the use of thyroid extract, and that reputable physicians were at the time prescribing it for weight control.

The jury found for the defendant.[11]

TIMILOL MALEATE
Blocadren
Timolide
Timoptic

Timolol maleate (Timoptic), when applied topically to the eye reduces elevated as well as normal intraocular pressure, whether or not the condition is accompanied by glaucoma. Timilol maleate is also used to treat hypertension (Blocadren and Timolide). Merck,

---

[10] Id.
[11] AMA *The Citation* 27:50, 1973.

Sharp & Dohme (West Point, Pa.) manufactures all three products.[12]

As to Timoptic, Merck lists among adverse reactions: headache, chest pain, arrhythmia, hypotension, heart block, cerebral vascular accident, cardiac arrest, cardiac failure and broncospasm. The drug is contraindicated in patients with bronchial asthma (or a history of bronchial asthma), severe chronic obstructive pulmonary disease, sinus bradycardia, and related cardiac disorders.[13]

Cornell v. Merck & Co. (1987) 87 Ore. App. 373, 742 P.2d 667.

Unspecified side effects—Action against physician barred by statute of limitations—Products liability complaint fails to state claim

In July 1980, the plaintiff was diagnosed by his physician as suffering from glaucoma. The physician prescribed Timoptic, and the plaintiff apparently applied it for four years. In November 1984, he claimed he discovered that the medication was causing "various adverse side effects." He filed suit against his physician for failing to warn him about these side effects, and against the manufacturer, Merck, claiming that the drug was "unreasonably dangerous." In his suit against the physician, he also claimed that the defendant misdiagnosed his problem, that he did not suffer from glaucoma.

The plaintiff's claim against the physician was dismissed for failing to comply with the Oregon two-year statute of limitations in malpractice cases. The complaint against the manufacturer was also dismissed for failing to state a claim. The court found that the plaintiff did not allege any defective condition that made the drug unreasonably dangerous, and that a drug manufacturer cannot be held liable for damages merely because a drug causes side effects. The decision was affirmed on appeal.

TIMOLIDE

See TIMILOL MALEATE

---

[12] *Physicians' Desk Reference,* 42d ed., pp. 1391-96.
[13] Id., p. 1397.

TIMOPTIC
See TIMILOL MALEATE

T.M.C. TABLETS
See MEPROBAMATE

TOBRAMYCIN SULFATE
Nebcin

Tobramycin sulfate is a powerful antibiotic indicated for the treatment of a number of serious infections. The manufacturer, Eli Lilly and Company (Indianapolis, Ind.), warns in the package insert that patients should be carefully monitored because of the drug's potential for causing both kidney damage and auditory nerve damage with permanent hearing loss.[14]

Hamilton v. Barnes Hosp. (No. 802-02352, Circuit Court, St. Louis, Mo., April 22, 1981).

Auditory nerve damage—$166,667 settlement with hospital and medical school

The plaintiff, a 65-year-old woman, underwent a vulvectomy for a low-grade vaginal infection. She was given tobramycin sulfate postoperatively to prevent further infection. Creatinine tests were performed several days following the operation, but then no tests were run for ten days. By then, the plaintiff's creatinine level was ten times the normal level and she was suffering from temporary kidney failure and auditory nerve damage which rendered her permanently deaf.

Suit was brought against the hospital and the medical school whose personnel cared for the plaintiff. She charged negligence in failing to monitor her blood and urine levels during the antibiotic therapy.

The hospital settled for $100,000 and the medical school for $66,667.[15]

---

[14] *Physicians' Desk Reference,* 35th ed., pp. 1084-85.
[15] ATLA *Law Reporter* 24:378, 1981.

Garvey v. O'Donoghue (D.C. App., 1987) 530 A.2d 1141.

Permanent tinnitus—Choice of drug and duration of treatment questioned—Verdict for physician affirmed

The patient was diagnosed as suffering from a severe strep infection. While she was hospitalized, her internist, the defendant, prescribed Tobramycin: an initial dose of 80 mg. followed by 60 mg. every eight hours for 14 days. During this period of treatment, the patient's infection improved. Blood tests were conducted to monitor for side effects; however, the last test was conducted eight days before the treatment was concluded. A few weeks after being discharged from the hospital, the patient noticed a "sound" in her ears. At the time of trial, she claimed this condition was permanent.

At trial, the patient sought to prove that Tobramycin was a highly toxic drug likely to cause auditory nerve damage, and that more suitable, less dangerous drugs were available. Also, she attempted to show that both the dosage level and the duration of treatment exceeded the recommended standards for a person of her size and weight. She produced two medical experts who testified to this effect. She also attempted to introduce pages from the *Physician's Desk Reference* and the package insert which accompanied Tobramycin. Both were rejected by the trial judge. The plaintiff's medical witnesses were, however, allowed to refer to these documents during their testimony.

The plaintiff also attempted to admit the testimony of a pharmacologist on the issue of the proper dosage of Tobramycin and whether it was the proper choice of drug to treat the patient. The court refused this testimony, reasoning that since he was not a medical doctor, to allow him to testify on this question would be tantamount to allowing a nonmedical expert to testify to a medical standard of care.

The defense introduced several medical experts who testified that the defendant's choice of drug and method of treatment were within acceptable standards. Also, on cross-examination of the patient, there was some information elicited that she may have suffered a similar problem with her ears prior to her treatment by the defendant physician.

The jury returned a verdict for the defendant which was affirmed on appeal. The Court of Appeals did acknowledge, however, that the trial court erred in refusing the admission into evidence of the pertinent pages of the *Physician's Desk Reference* and the

Tobramycin package insert. Also, the reviewing court held that it was error to have excluded the testimony of the plaintiff's pharmacologist. But in the reviewing court's opinion, in light of the other evidence, neither error warranted reversal.

TOCOSAMINE
See SPARTEINE SULFATE

TOFRANIL
See IMIPRAMINE HYDROCHLORIDE

TOLECTIN
See TOLMETIN SODIUM

TOLMETIN SODIUM
Tolectin

Tolmetin sodium is a nonsteroidal anti-inflammatory agent indicated for the relief of signs and symptoms of rheumatoid arthritis, osteoarthritis, and juvenile rheumatoid arthritis. Anaphylactoid reactions have been reported with the use of this drug as with other nonsteroidal anti-inflammatory agents. The drug is not to be used in conjunction with aspirin and other salicylates because a greater benefit from the combination is unlikely, and the potential for adverse reactions is increased. The drug should not be given to persons in whom aspirin and other nonsteroidal anti-inflammatory agents induce symptoms of asthma, rhinitis, urticaria or other symptoms of allergic or anaphylactoid reactions.[16]

Tolmetin sodium is manufactured and marketed under the brand name Tolectin by McNeil Pharmaceutical (Spring House, Pa.).

Brown v. McNeil Laboratories (No. K87-388, U.S. District Court, D. Mich., June 29, 1988).

Allergic reaction—Failure to warn—Action under state law not preempted by federal law

The plaintiff filed suit against McNeil Laboratories after suffering a severe allergic reaction on taking Tolectin DS. He based his claim on an inadequate warning of the risk of such a reaction. The manufacturer moved for a summary judgment on grounds that the

---

[16] *Physicians' Desk Reference*, 42d ed., p. 1142.

plaintiff's claim was preempted by the federal Food, Drug and Cosmetic Act, and FDA regulations, in that the FDA had approved the drug and the package insert, thus indicating that the manufacturer's labeling complied with federal requirements.

The United States District Court, in denying the manufacturer's motion, held that in the absence of any express preemption of state law by federal law, one must look to the entire federal scheme to see if there was implied preemption. No such preemption existed, said the court. Even though the FDA had approved the drug and the package insert, thereby indicating its belief that the manufacturer met its obligations under the Act, this was not conclusive evidence that the manufacturer had satisfied its duty to warn under state law. The federal regulations merely set minimum standards as to design and warnings, and in a tort action under state law, FDA approval was only one factor to be considered.[17]

TOPICYCLINE
See TETRACYCLINE HYDROCHLORIDE

T-QUIL
See DIAZEPAM

TOPISPORIN
See NEOMYCIN SULFATE

TRAZODONE HYDROCHLORIDE
Desyrel

Trazodone hydrochloride is an antidepressant which has proved effective in both inpatient and outpatient settings for patients with or without prominent anxiety. Under the American Psychiatric Association's classifications, the drug is appropriate for "Major Depressive Episode," which implies a prominent and relatively persistent "depressed or dysphoric mood that usually interferes with daily functioning, and includes at least four of the following eight symptoms: change in appetite, change in sleep, psychomotor agitation or retardation, loss of interest in usual activities or decrease in sexual drive, increased fatigability, feeling of guilt or worthless-

[17] ATLA *Products Liability Law Reporter* 7:153, 1988.

ness, slowed thinking or impaired concentration, and suicidal ideation or attempts."[18]

Desyrel is marketed by Mead Johnson Pharmaceuticals (Evansville, Ind.). Several companies market the product under the generic name.

Gowan v. United States (D. Ore., 1985) 601 F. Supp. 1297.

Attempted suicide—Dosage and discontinuance of Trazodone questioned—No psychiatric malpractice

The patient was being treated with Trazodone at a V.A. hospital for depression. When it appeared that he was developing liver problems, he was taken off Trazodone and put on another drug. His mental condition apparently worsened and he attempted to hang himself.

The V.A. psychiatrists were charged with negligence in taking the patient off Trazodine. It was claimed that it is well known that the drug does not cause liver damage. The plaintiff also charged that while the patient was on Trazodone the dosage was insufficient.

The trial judge ruled in favor of the defendant on evidence that the dosage prescribed was that called for in *Physicians' Desk Reference.* As to withdrawing the drug, the court commented that the patient's physicians "properly believed that it [Trazodone] might have an unfortunate and secondary effect on the liver."

TRIAMCINOLONE ACETONIDE

Aristocort
Azmacort
Cinonide
Kenacort
Kenalog
Mycolog
Mytrex
Nystatin
Trymex

Triamcinolone acetonide is a synthetic adrenocorticosteroid, being a derivative of prednisolone. It has the potent anti-inflammatory, hormonal and metabolic effects common to cortisone-like

---

[18] *Physicians' Desk Reference,* 40th ed., p. 1123.

drugs.[19] It is used in a variety of disorders, including rheumatoid arthritis; acute rheumatic fever; allergies; bronchial asthma; skin conditions, including contact dermatitis; pulmonary emphysema; and lymphatic leukemia.[20]

The dosage requirements are variable and must be individualized on the basis of the disease being treated and the response of the patient.[1]

As with all adrenocorticosteroids the possible adverse effects are many. They include, but are not limited to: congestive heart failure in susceptible patients, muscle disorders, pathologic fracture of long bones, peptic ulcer and hemorrhage, pancreatitis, and Cushing's syndrome.[2]

Aristocort is manufactured by Lederle Laboratories (Wayne, N.J.); Azmacort by Rorer Pharmaceuticals (Fort Washington, Pa.); Cinonide by Legere Pharmaceuticals (Costa Mesa, Cal.); Kenacort and Kenalog by E. R. Squibb & Sons, Inc. (Princeton, N.J.); Mycolog by E.R. Squibb & Sons, Inc. (Princeton, N.J.); Mytrex and Trymex by Savage Laboratories (Melville, N.Y.); and Nystatin by E. Fougera & Company (Melville, N.Y.). Several companies also produce the drug under the generic label.

Malone v. Sunnyvale Medical Clinic (No. 201229, Superior Court, Santa Clara County, Cal., April 11, 1972).

Cushing's syndrome in patient receiving prolonged triamcinolone therapy—$460,358 verdict against physician and clinic

A forty-year-old man developed a rash on his hands, apparently as a result of a reaction to materials handled in his work. His employer sent him to a clinic where a physician prescribed Aristocort tablets and several other medicines. Apparently the rash cleared up, but it continued to appear on and off over the years, and during such time the patient was treated intermittently with Aristocort. At the end of four years, when the rash flared up again, the employer sent him to a different clinic. A physician at that clinic reviewed his medical history, and continued prescribing Aristocort.

---

[19] Id., 35th ed., p. 988.

[20] *United States Dispensatory,* 27th ed., p. 1206.

[1] *Physicians' Desk Reference,* 35th ed., p. 990.

[2] Id.

Three years later, due to an inquiry into his case by the employer's workmen's compensation carrier, the patient was examined by another physician. It was discovered that the patient was suffering from Cushing's syndrome, apparently brought on by the prolonged Aristocort therapy.

The patient filed a malpractice action against the physician and the clinic which continued the Aristocort therapy three years earlier. At the trial he offered testimony by an endocrinologist and a toxicologist who said that prolonged treatment with Aristocort is improper without periodic blood tests to determine possible side effects of the drug. They further testified that patients who needed such therapy should receive the smallest doses possible over the shortest period of time. Testimony was introduced that at times the patient had been taking four milligrams of Aristocort as often as every four hours.

Other medical witnesses introduced on behalf of the patient testified that as a result of the continued treatment with Aristocort he had developed diabetes, loss of teeth, loss of the use of his arm and hand, permanent muscle and joint pain, chronic weakness, and severe mental and psychological impairment.

The defendants testified that they had followed the proper standard of care in treating the patient. They argued that since they had not originally prescribed the Aristocort therapy, and since the patient had been taking the drug for four years without apparent side effects when they began treating him, they were not required to conduct blood tests. They also argued that the amount of Aristocort they prescribed was not enough to cause the injury claimed by the patient.

A neurologist testifying for the defendants stated that he found nothing wrong neurologically with the patient, and a psychiatrist testified that the patient's problems were actually related to a preexisting personality disorder rather than the effects of the drug, and that he was suffering from "litigation neurosis," motivated by "secondary gain."

After seventeen days of trial, the jury returned a verdict for the patient in the amount of $460,358.[3]

---

[3] AMA *The Citation* 25:147, 1972.

Hill v. Squibb & Sons, E.R. (Mont., 1979) 592 P.2d 1383.

Cataracts and osteoporosis—Verdicts for physician and manufacturer upheld

The plaintiff was a mechanic who suffered from contact dermatitis due to an allergy to petroleum-based products. In 1965, his physician began treating him with Kenalog-40 injections together with oral and topical steroids, at approximately two-week intervals. The treatment was continued until 1971, when a dermatologist recommended that the Kenalog-40 be discontinued immediately, and the steroids be tapered off. Two months later, it was discovered that the plaintiff was suffering from cataracts, and two years after that, it was found that he had osteoporosis, both of which conditions were attributed to the drugs, particularly the Kenalog-40.

In his lawsuit against the physician and the manufacturer of Kenalog-40, the plaintiff testified that the physician had never told him of the side effects of the treatment. The physician and his nurse disputed this, stating that the plaintiff was told many times that "steroid treatment was dangerous" and that the physician "hesitated to continue using it, and that [the plaintiff] should get another job."

Against the manufacturer, the plaintiff charged that the warnings contained in the package insert were inadequate. However, the plaintiff failed to produce any expert testimony on the issue of the warnings, and the trial court directed a verdict for the manufacturer.

The case against the physician was given to a jury, which decided in his favor. Both verdicts were upheld on appeal.

Related cases

Anaphylactic reaction—Res ipsa loquitur not applicable

In Bakos v. Russell (1977) 49 Ill. App. 3d 539, 7 Ill. Dec. 420, 364 N.E.2d 581, the doctrine of res ipsa loquitur was held not applicable where the plaintiff suffered an anaphylactic reaction following an injection of a combination of Aristocort, a vitamin and a hormone.

Undisclosed side effects—Manufacturer's duty to warn discharged

Since a drug manufacturer's duty to warn is discharged by its warning to the physician who administers the product, the manufacturer of Kenalog-40 could not be held liable for a Puerto Rican patient's injuries, allegedly caused by an injection of the drug, on the theory that warnings of the drug's side effects in the product literature were printed in English and the patient could read only Spanish. Pierluisi v. E. R. Squibb & Sons, Inc. (D. P.R., 1977) 440 F. Supp. 691.

TRIAMCINOLONE HEXACETONIDE
Aristospan

Triamcinolone hexacetonide is an anti-inflamatory agent containing the hexacetonide ester of the potent glucocorticoid triamcinolone (see also TRIAMCINOLONE ACETONIDE herein). It is recommended for certain localized inflammatory lesions and as short-term adjunctive therapy in synovitis of osteoarthritis, acute and subacute bursitis, Epicondylitis, posttraumatic osteoarthritis, rheumatoid arthritis, acute gouty arthritis and acute nonspecific tenosynovitis.

The manufacturer of Aristospan (Lederle Laboratories, a division of American Cyanamid Company, Wayne, N.J.) warns that the drug, as with other corticosteroids may mask some signs of infection, and new infections may appear during use. Also, there may be decreased resistance and inability to localize infection when the drug is used. Local injection into a previously infected joint is to be avoided.[4]

Crain v. Allison (D.C. App., 1982) 443 A.2d 558.

Osteomyelitis following injections in finger for arthritis—Lack of informed consent—Verdict for plaintiffs affirmed

The defendant physician injected Aristospan into the patient's right index finger for an arthritic condition. In all, nine injections were given: four into the distal interphalangeal joint and five into the proximal interphalangeal joint. The pain and swelling in her hand worsened, a cyst developed, and eventually the area was found to be infected with osteomyelitis.

In her suit against the defendant, the patient claimed she was not warned of the risk of infection, and had she been so warned, she would not have agreed to the injections. At trial the patient introduced evidence that both the Aristospan package insert and *Physicians' Desk Reference* warn physicians of the problems of infection associated with the use of Aristospan and similar glucocorticoid

---

[4]*Physicians' Desk Reference,* 40th ed., pp. 1003-14.

injections. The defendant admitted that Aristospan should never be injected into a joint in the presence of infection because it might reduce the body's resistance to the infection, and that before such an injection is administered, a diagnosis should be established and specific infectious arthritis should be ruled out. The defendant testified that he had warned the patient of the risk of infection before he began the injections and to support this claim he pointed out that after each injection he prescribed penicillin.

The jury chose to believe the patient's testimony over the defendant's and returned a verdict for her and her husband. The Court of Appeals affirmed, holding that the jury could properly decide the issue of informed consent.

TRIAMINIC

See CHLORPHENIRAMINE MALEATE

TRIAMTERENE

Dyazide
Dyrenium
Maxzide

Triamterene is a diuretic sold under the brand name Dyrenium. It is manufactured by Smith, Kline & French Laboratories (Philadelphia, Pa.) and is indicated for the treatment of edema associated with congestive heart failure, cirrhosis of the liver, and certain kidney syndromes. When combined with hydrochlorothiazide, it has the added effect of an antihypertensive.[5] This combination is sold under the name Dyazide, also by Smith, Kline & French, and under the name Maxzide by Lederle Laboratories (Wayne, N.J.).

Gastric injury attributed to combination of Dyazide and other drugs prescribed for weight reduction

In Mendoza v. Varon (Tex. Civ. App., 1978) 563 S.W.2d 646, a physician was sued for malpractice for prescribing a combination of Preludin (phenmetrazine hydrochloride), Dyazide, Aldactone (spironolactone) and Slow-K (potassium chloride) for a teenage girl who was overweight and suffered from high blood pressure. The patient experienced violent episodes of vomiting brought on by inflammation and scarring of the stomach and esophagus. The case is summarized herein under PHENMETRAZINE HYDROCHLORIDE.

---

[5] Id., 35th ed., pp. 1678-79.

TRIAVIL

See AMITRIPTYLINE; PERPHENAZINE

TRIFLUOPERAZINE

Stelazine

This tranquilizer, a derivative of phenothiazine, is used in the management of the manifestations of psychotic disorders, especially excessive anxiety, tension and agitation as seen in neuroses or associated with somatic conditions.[6]

As with all phenothiazine derivatives, there are many possible side effects of trifluoperazine, including but not limited to: muscle spasms or rigidity, tardive dyskinesia, pseudo-Parkinsonian symptoms such as drooling, tremors and shuffling gait, hypotension, blood disorders, eczema and related skin disorders, asthma, and, in rare instances, sudden death, apparently in some cases from asphyxia due to failure of the cough reflex.[7] All of these reactions have not been reported in connection with trifluoperazine, however.

Smith, Kline & French Laboratories (Philadelphia, Pa.), markets trifluoperazine under the name Stelazine.

Lesser v. Farbe (No. L-44353-67, Superior Court, Essex County, N.J., 1971).

Neurological disorder—Physician charged with continuing drug after appearance of side effects—Manufacturer accused of insufficient warning—Judgment for $180,000

Suit was filed on behalf of a thirty-year-old woman patient who had been given Stelazine for treatment of depression. It was alleged that as a result of taking the drug the patient suffered severe neurological disorders, including Parkinsonian symptoms.

The physician who had prescribed Stelazine was charged with negligence in continuing the therapy even after the patient manifested side effects which included "grimacing, blinking, and tremors." The plaintiff also sued the manufacturer of the drug, claiming that the information it provided the medical profession at the time Stelazine was prescribed for the patient, including package inserts and information forwarded to the publishers of *Physicians' Desk Reference,* suggested that such neurological side effects

---

[6] Id., p. 1686.

[7] Id., p. 1687.

were "rare and readily reversible." The patient's attorney offered to submit evidence of a newspaper article which mentioned similar such side effects experienced by a patient taking the drug, and evidence of reports in the medical journals for the past ten years stating that Stelazine could cause permanent neurological disorders if administered indiscriminately.

The trial court awarded the plaintiff $180,000.[8]

Collins v. Cushner (No. 48751, Circuit Court, Montgomery County, Md., Oct. 20, 1980).

Tardive dyskinesia following prolonged treatment—Settlement with physician for $125,000

A 55-year-old female patient was treated for six years with Stelazine for anxiety and "spastic colon." For 2½ years during that period she was not seen by her physician who merely renewed her prescription by telephone. When she developed "jerking movements" in her arm she was taken off the drug for two months but was returned to it when the symptoms subsided. Six months later she developed permanent tardive dyskinesia (involuntary, rhythmical, stereotyped movements).

In her lawsuit against the physician she alleged negligence in his continually prescribing Stelazine despite warnings in the product literature that tardive dyskinesia could result.

According to the attorney representing the patient, the physician settled prior to trial for $125,000.[9]

Lindley v. Hamilton (C.A.-5 Miss., 1989) 883 F.2d 360.

Tardive dyskinesia following prolonged treatment—Judgment for psychiatrist—Action against manufacturer barred by statute of limitations

From 1969 to 1973, the patient was treated by the defendant, a psychiatrist, for depression. Her medication was Stelazine. During that period, the patient complained of "eye tics," but the defendant dismissed them as a mimic reaction to a similar problem experienced by the patient's husband. In 1973, however, the patient was diagnosed as suffering from tardive dyskinesia. The defendant changed her medication to another drug, and the symptoms sub-

---

[8] ATLA *News Letter* 14:424, 1971; American Medical Association, *The Citation* 24:88, 1972.

[9] ATLA *Law Reporter* 24:185, 1981.

sided. The patient claims that no one told her that she had developed tardive dyskinesia in 1973, or that Stelazine can cause that condition. She claims she learned of this fact only in 1983, after seeing other physicians.

The patient sued both the defendant and the SK & F Co., Inc., the manufacturer of Stelazine. The manufacturer moved for summary judgment, claiming that Mississippi's six-year statute of limitations barred the action. The trial court granted the motion and dismissed SK & F Co., Inc., from the proceedings. The case against the defendant went to the jury, which returned a verdict for the plaintiff in the amount of $400,000. The trial court, however, after submitted special interrogatories to the jury, granted the defendant's motion for judgment notwithstanding the verdict, on grounds that the jury had erred on both the statute of limitations and negligence issues.

As to negligence, the trial court held that the plaintiff had failed to establish that the defendant's treatment breached the applicable standard of care. Although the plaintiff presented three expert witnesses, none was of the opinion that Stelazine itself or the dose she received was improper. Only one of her experts criticized the defendant's treatment. He was critical of his failure to specify "drug-free" weekends or holidays for the plaintiff, but this expert later admitted that this decision did not deviate from the proper standard of care. Instead, he merely stated that *he* would have required drug-free holidays for the plaintiff if he had been treating her.

On appeal, the trial court's decision was affirmed.

Related cases

Urinary difficulties

In Miller v. United States (S.D. Miss., 1976) 431 F. Supp. 988, a V.A. hospital patient, apparently allergic to antihistamines, suffered urinary difficulties following treatment with Stelazine and Vistaril (hydroxyzine pamoate). The case is summarized herein under HYDROXYZINE.

TRI-IMMUNOL

See DIPHTHERIA and TETANUS TOXOIDS with PERTUSSIS VACCINE

TRILAFON
See PERPHENAZINE

TRIMETHOPRIM and SULFAMETHOXAZOLE
Bactrim
Comoxol
Cotrim
Proloprim
Septra
Sulfatrim
Trimpex

Trimethoprim, an antibiotic, and sulfamethoxazole, a sulfonamide, constitute a synthetic antibacterial combination produced by many manufacturers. The drug is indicated for the treatment of urinary tract infections, acute otitis media, acute exacerbations of chronic bronchitis in adults, shigellosis, and *Pneumocystis carinii* pneumonitis. The product is issued with a warning that fatalities associated with sulfonamides, although rare, have occurred due to severe reactions, including Stevens-Johnson syndrome, toxic epidermal necrolysis, fulminant hepatic necrosis, agranulocytosis, aplastic anemia and other blood dyscrasias.

Bactrim and Trimpex are manufactured by Roche Laboratories, a division of Hoffmann-La Roche, Inc. (Nutley, N.J.), Comoxol by E.R. Squibb and Sons, Inc. (Princeton, N.J.), Cotrim by Lemmon Company (Sellersville, Pa.), Poloprim and Septra by Burroughs Wellcome Co. (Research Triangle Park, N.C.), and Sulfatrim by Schein Pharmaceutical, Inc. (Port Washington, N.Y.). The product also is manufactured and marketed by several companies under the generic names of both drugs.[10]

Ullman v. Grant (1982) 114 Misc. 2d 220, 450 N.Y.S.2d 955.

**Pharmacist substitutes drug as authorized by physician—
Adverse reaction—Case dismissed**

The plaintiff obtained a prescription from her physician for Bactrim D.S. When she presented to her pharmacist, however, he substituted Septra D.S., the same drug manufactured by a different company. The plaintiff allegedly suffered an adverse reaction after taking the first dose.

---

[10] *Physicians' Desk Reference,* 40th ed., pp. 1476-77.

On the prescription the physician had signed the "Substitute permitted" portion, thereby authorizing the pharmacist, under New York law, to substitute a less expensive drug containing the same ingredients, dosage and strength.

The defendant was granted a motion for summary judgment.

Gutwein v. Roche Laboratories (U.S. District Court, Southern District, N.Y., Jan. 14, 1985).

Loss of sight—Summary judgment denied in view of sulfa compound-related optic neuritis mentioned in medical literature

The plaintiff suffered loss of sight in both eyes after using Bactrim which was prescribed for a urinary infection. In response to the defendant manufacturer's motion for summary judgment, the plaintiff's medical expert stated in an affidavit that according to the medical literature, the drug sulfamethoxazole, being one of the sulfa compounds, can cause optic neuritis. In view of this statement, the trial judge ruled that there was sufficient evidence for a jury regarding the manufacturer's failure to warn even though there may be no reported incidents of optic neuritis caused specifically by sulfamethoxazole.[11]

Related cases

Stevens-Johnson syndrome—Trial court erred in excluding package insert and testimony of pharmacologist-toxicologist—Directed verdict for physician reversed

In a malpractice action by a patient who developed Stevens-Johnson syndrome a month after she began receiving Bactrim, the trial court erred in excluding from the evidence the package insert and the testimony of the plaintiff's expert, a pharmacologist-toxicologist. The package insert, although not conclusive evidence of the standard of care, was prima facie evidence of the proper method of using the drug as determined by the manufacturer, and was admissible if it could be shown that it was used by the physician as a source of information, and that it was accepted generally by the medical profession in the area as the standard for administering the drug. The pharmacologist was qualified to testify as to causation and standard of care upon showing that he possessed the neces-

---

[11] ATLA *Products Liability Law Reporter* 4:84, 1985.

sary medical knowledge to offer such testimony. It was not necessary that he possess a medical degree. Thompson v. Carter (Miss., 1987) 518 So. 2d 609.

Stevens-Johnson syndrome—Manufacturer's warnings found adequate

The manufacturer of Bactrim was entitled to a summary judgment in an action by a plaintiff who developed Stevens-Johnson syndrome after using the product, in view of unchallenged affidavits by two experts who concluded the manufacturer's warnings were adequate, and in view of the wording of the warnings themselves which listed Stevens-Johnson syndrome as one of the possible allergic reactions. Serna v. Roche Laboratories (1984) 101 N.M. 522, 684 P.2d 1187.

TRIPARANOL
MER/29

MER/29 was marketed in 1960 by the Wm. S. Merrell Company (Cincinnati, Ohio), to reduce high cholesterol. It was used by about 500,000 persons for a two-year period before being withdrawn because of an association with cataracts, hair loss, dermatitis and other side effects. It has been estimated that nearly 1,300 lawsuits were filed against the manufacturer, nearly all of which have been settled. A few went to trial and some have been appealed. For an extensive discussion of the MER/29 problem and summaries of the early decisions, see *Drug Liability: A Lawyers Handbook,* edited by Richard M. Goodman and Paul D. Rheingold (New York: Practicing Law Institute, 1970).

TRIMPEX

See TRIMETHOPRIM and SULFAMETHOXAZOLE

TRIPELENNAMINE
PBZ
Poly-Histine-D

Tripelennamine is a potent antihistamine, the major untoward effect of which is drowsiness.[12]

Geigy Pharmaceuticals (Ardsley, N.Y.) manufactures PBZ and Bock Pharmacal Company (St. Louis, Mo.), Poly-Histine-D. In the

[12] *Physicians' Desk Reference,* 35th ed., p. 911.

1960's and early 1970's CIBA-GEIGY produced the drug under the brand name Pyribenzamine.

Kaiser v. Suburban Transportation System (1965) 65 Wash. 2d 461, 398 P.2d 14, mod. 401 P.2d 350.

"Groggy" bus driver on Pyribenzamine involved in accident—Passenger sues physician for failure to warn of side effect—Dismissal reversed and new trial ordered

A bus driver suffering from a nasal condition was given a prescription for Pyribenzamine. He took a tablet before going to work and while driving "felt groggy and drowsy" and "noticed that his lips and tongue were dry." He continued to drive for a "few miles" and then "blacked out or went to sleep." His bus left the road and struck a telephone pole, injuring a passenger.

The passenger brought suit against the driver and bus company, and, in the alternative, against the driver's physician and the group health clinic where he was employed. The physician was charged with negligence in failing to warn the patient of the possible side effects of the drug.

At the trial the defense attorneys defended on the grounds that the driver was hypersensitive to Pyribenzamine. At the conclusion of the plaintiff's evidence, they moved for dismissal on grounds that the evidence did not show a standard of care to which the physician was bound, and that even if their client was found to be negligent in failing to warn his patient about the drug, the patient's negligence in continuing to drive the bus after he began to feel drowsy was "an intervening cause" which freed their client from liability. Their motion was sustained by the trial judge.

On appeal, the dismissal of the physician was held in error. The reviewing court found that the record did contain evidence on standard of care, in the testimony of a local physician who, in answer to questions regarding prescribing Pyribenzamine, had stated "it would appear reasonable to ascertain or at least to inform a patient of side effects that may occur from any drug."

With regard to the defense of "intervening cause," the reviewing court held that even if a jury found the bus driver negligent, the physician could also be held liable if the jury found that he had failed to warn of the side effects of the drug since "the harm resulting to the plaintiff was in the general field of danger, which should reasonably have been foreseen by the doctor when he administered the drug." A new trial was ordered with instructions that the jury should be directed that in the event it found no warning was given to the bus driver as to the side effects of the drug, it should bring a verdict against the physician.

TROPICAMIDE
Mydriacyl

Tropicamide is an anticholinergic drug used in ophthalmic practice to relax the sphincter muscle of the iris and permit dilation of the pupil. The patient experiences "minimal blurring" and is supposed to be able to return to work "within 2 hours." Apparently there are few local allergic reactions to the drug but it must be used with great caution in patients with glaucoma, in older patients and in those with a shallow anterior chamber or a narrow angle of the anterior chamber.[13]

The drug was manufactured by Alcon (Puerto Rico), Inc. (Humacao, P.R.) but is no longer on the company's product information list.

Graham v. Whitaker (1984) 282 S.C. 393, 321 S.E.2d 40.

Blurred vision causing fall—$87,500 award against ophthamologist

The plaintiff was having her eyes examined for glaucoma. She was called into an examining room where the defendant put some "drops" (Mydriacyl) in her eyes. She was not informed of any possible side effects of the drug. She was placed in the care of one of the defendant's assistants and given a seat. Her eyes soon began to "blur." Later, when her name was called, she stood up and fell. She struggled to rise and fell two more times, fracturing a hip.

At the trial the defense experts testified that while Mydriacyl would blur "near" vision, it would not affect "distance" vision, and that it "should not hinder walking and only rarely would more serious side effects occur."

The jury returned a verdict for $10,000 actual and $10,000 punitive damages. The trial judge, considering the award too small, ordered a new trial unless the defendant agreed to an additur of $67,500. The Supreme Court of South Carolina affirmed.

---

[13] *United States Dispensatory*, 27th ed., pp. 1226-27.

TRYMEX
See TRIAMCINOLONE ACETONIDE

TUINAL
See SECOBARBITAL SODIUM

TYLENOL
See ACETAMINOPHEN

TUSSAR
See CHLORPHENIRAMINE MALEATE

TYMPAGESIC
See BENZOCAINE

U

UNIPEN
See PENICILLIN

UROBIOTIC-250
See OXYTETRACYCLINE; SULFAMETHIZOLE

UROKON
See SODIUM ACETRIZOATE

UTICILLIN
See PENICILLIN

V

VAGIMIDE
See SULFANILAMIDE

VAGISIL
See BENZOCAINE

VALIUM
See DIAZEPAM

VALRELEASE
See DIAZEPAM

VANQUISH
See ASPIRIN

VARIDASE
See STREPTOKINASE—STREPTODORNASE

V-CILLIN K
See PENICILLIN

VEETIDS
See PENICILLIN

VERMIFUGE
See HEXYLRESORCINOL

VISTARIL
See HYDROXYZINE

VITAMIN B-17
See AMYGDALIN

VITAMINS

Vitamins are essential for normal metabolism and maintenance of health. Food is the best source, and healthy persons consuming an adequate balanced diet will not benefit from additional vitamins. However, individuals on low-calorie diets (less than 1,200 calories/day) often do not ingest adequate vitamins and may require a supplement. Purified or synthetic products are available individually or in various combinations. Products intended for prophylactic use should be distinguished from those preparations suitable only for therapeutic purposes.[14]

Despite the few valid indications for vitamin supplements, almost 40% of adults in the United States are thought to take such

[14] AMA *Drug Evaluations,* 6th ed., p. 853.

preparations. Approximately 4% of those taking Vitamin A ingest more than five times the RDA; 25% of Vitamin E users and 21% of Vitamin C users ingest more than ten times the RDA.[15]

Falk v. Puritan Pride, Inc. (No. L-00867-84, Superior Court, Middlesex County, N.J., Feb. 20, 1986).

Neuropathy from megadoses of Vitamin B_6—$71,500 settlement with distributor of product

The plaintiff brought suit against the defendant, a distributor of Vitamin B_6, when she developed a neuropathic syndrome due to taking megadoses of the product. Although Vitamin B_6 (pyridoxine) can cause sensory neuropathy when taken in doses exceeding 500 mg. to 2 grams per day over a prolonged period, the defendant advised the plaintiff to begin with a dosage of 500 mg. per day and increase it gradually to 5 grams per day (as treatment for premenstrual edema). The plaintiff took the product for two months when she began to feel a "tingling" in her neck, legs and soles of her feet. Eventually, she developed difficulty in walking. On discontinuing the product, the plaintiff's condition improved.

In her suit, the plaintiff charged that the defendant had failed to conduct scientific research on the product, test it for adverse effects, and warn users of its potential dangers. The parties settled prior to trial for $71,500.[16]

Barry v. Don Hall Laboratories (1982) 56 Or. App. 518, 642 P.2d 685.

Tooth decay—Jury question whether plaintiff should have been warned of high sugar content in Vitamin C tablets

The plaintiff charged Don Hall Laboratories, a manufacturer of Vitamin C tablets, with negligence, breach of warranty, and strict liability. The plaintiff claimed that after taking the defendant's product for over a year, he developed tooth decay which was the result of the tablets containing over 78 percent sugar. In his complaint, the plaintiff claimed that the defendant should have warned purchasers of the product's high sugar content.

At trial, the court granted the defendant's motion to strike the plaintiff's cause of action for negligence. The case went to trial on the remaining causes, and the jury found for the defendant.

---

[15] Id.

[16] ATLA *Products Liability Law Reporter* 5:154, 1986.

On appeal, the Court of Appeals of Oregon reversed, holding that even though the defendant may have complied with FDA requirements for labeling vitamins, and that at the time no other vitamin manufacturer listed the ingredients of its product, a jury question was presented as to whether the defendant was negligent in failing to inform users of the sugar content of the product.

Related cases

No cause of action against Vitamin E manufacturer under FDCA or RICO

A mother suing on behalf of her child whom she claimed was injured as a result of being given E-Ferol Aqueous Solution, a Vitamin E preparation, had no private right of action against the manufacturer and supplier of the product under the Federal Food, Drug and Cosmetic Act, nor did she have a civil action under the Organized Crime Control Act (RICO). Griffin v. O'Neal, Jones & Feldman (S.D. Ohio, 1985) 604 F. Supp. 717.

W

WARFARIN
See SODIUM WARFARIN

WIGRAINE
See ERGOTAMINE TARTRATE

WYCILLIN
See PENICILLIN

WYGESIC
See PROPOXYPHENE HYDROCHLORIDE

X

XYLOCAINE
See LIDOCAINE HYDROCHLORIDE

Z

ZOMAX

See ZOMEPIRAC SODIUM

ZOMEPIRAC SODIUM

Zomax

Zomepirac sodium, manufactured and distributed by McNeil Pharmaceutical (Spring House, Pa.) under the brand name Zomax in the 1970s and early 1980s, was a popular nonsteroidal anti-inflammatory agent used for the relief of mild to moderately severe pain. As with many similar agents, the drug was issued with numerous precautions and a generous list of possible adverse reactions.[17] The drug is no longer listed by the company among its available products.

Johnson v. McNeil Laboratories, Inc. (No. Civ-83-829-BT, U.S. District Court, W.D. Okla., Sept. 20, 1983).

Anaphylactic shock—Manufacturer accused of insufficient warning—$400,000 jury verdict

The plaintiff, a thirty-year-old warehouseman, was given Zomax for the relief of pain from an undisclosed injury. Six months later, due to another injury, he got out the bottle, ingested one pill, and suffered anaphylactic shock which resulted in one week of hospitalization. He eventually recovered, except for some residual "psychological injuries."

In his lawsuit against the manufacturer, McNeil Laboratories, the plaintiff alleged that the defendant had failed to warn of the dangers associated with the use of the drug. The jury agreed and awarded $400,000.[18]

Wooten v. Johnson & Johnson Products (N.D. Ill., 1986) 635 F. Supp. 799.

Alleged allergic reaction—Manufacturer's warning found sufficient

One day after taking Zomax and several other medications for sinusitis and rhinitis, a middle-aged male patient "collapsed" while talking to his wife and was rushed to the hospital. There physicians

---

[17] *Physicians' Desk Reference,* 36th ed., p. 1165.

[18] ATLA *Products Liability Law Reporter* 3:10, 1984.

found him "totally unresponsive" and concluded he was "clinically dead."

An autopsy report showed the decedent had died from a "ruptured berry aneurysm," but according to a medical expert hired by the decedent's estate in a product liability action against Johnson & Johnson, death was caused by an allergic reaction to the Zomax.

A summary judgment for the defendant manufacturer was sustained on introduction of the package insert and a copy of *Physicians' Desk Reference,* both of which included a specific warning of the risk of "allergic reactions," and upon introduction of an affidavit by the prescribing physician that although he was fully aware of the risks involved in prescribing Zomax, it was the appropriate medication to treat the decedent's condition at the time.

Anderson v. McNeilab (C.A.-5 La., 1987) 831 F.2d 92.

Adverse reaction—Possible heart damage—Manufacturer's warning sufficient

The plaintiff claimed that she experienced a severe adverse reaction to one dose of Zomax, and that as a result she suffered "residual damage" to her heart. Her lawsuit against McNeilab, manufacturer of the drug, was based on an inadequate warning of this side effect.

The manufacturer was granted a summary judgment on showing that the package insert contained a warning to physicians against prescribing the drug for persons who, like the plaintiff, were sensitive to aspirin. The Court of Appeals affirmed, finding that the warning was sufficient as a matter of law.

ZYLOPRIM

See ALLOPURINOL

SELECTED REFERENCES

"The Application of a Due Diligence Requirement to Market Share Theory in DES Litigation," *University of Michigan Journal of Law Reform* 19:771-796 (Spring), 1986.

Atkinson, L. M., "Pharmaceutical Litigation: Promoting Product Safety," *Trial* 17:50-53 (Nov.), 1981.

Averbach, A. "Physician's Liability for Prescription Drugs," *St. John's Law Review* 43:535-556, 1969.

Balkon, J., et al., "Immunofluorescense of Detection of Drugs in Postmortem Tissues: A New Technique with Potential for Assessment of Drug Influence in Cause of Death," *Journal of Forensic Sciences* 25:88, 1980.

Barnett, F. J., "Liability for Adverse Drug Reactions: The Role of the Package Insert," *Journal of Legal Medicine* 1:19-27 (March-April); 47-52 (May-June); 38-42 (July-August), 1973.

Brackins, L. W., "Liability of Physicians, Pharmacists, and Hospitals for Adverse Drug Reactions," *Defense Law Journal* 34:273-344, 1985.

Brushwood, D. B., "Drug-Induced Birth Defects: Difficult Decisions and Shared Responsibilities," *West Virginia Law Review* 91:51-90, 1988-89.

Brushwood, D. B., and Simonsmeier, L. M., "Drug Information for Patients: Duties of the Manufacturer, Pharmacist, Physician, and Hospital," *Journal of Legal Medicine* 7:279-340, 1986.

Brushwood, D. B., and Abood, R. R., "Strict Liability in Tort: Appropriateness of the Theory for Retail Pharmacists," *Food Drug Cosmetic Law Journal* 42:269-284, 1987.

"Can a Prescription Drug Be Defectively Designed? (Brochu v. Ortho Pharmaceutical Corp., 642 F.2d 652 (1st Cir. 1981)," *De Paul Law Review* 31:247-72 (Fall), 1981.

Carleton, R., "Physician Liability for Adverse Drug Reactions," *Medical Trial Technique Quarterly* 24:184-187, 1977.

Cohn, S. D., "Prescriptive Authority for Nurses," *Law, Medicine & Health Care* 12:72-5 (April), 1984.

Cooper, R. M., "Drug Labeling and Products Liability: The Role of the Food and Drug Administration," *Food Drug Cosmetic Law Journal* 41:233-240, 1986.

Crumley, M. G., "Professional Liability of Pharmacists," *Defense Law Journal* 22:471-489, 1973.

David, A. B., and Jalilian-Marian, A., "DTP: Drug Manufacturers' Liability in Vaccine-Related Injuries," *Journal of Legal Medicine* 7:187-233, 1986.

"Diminishing Role of Negligence in Manufacturers' Liability for Unavoidably Unsafe Drugs and Cosmetics," *St. Mary's Law Journal* 9:102-117, 1977.

DeMarco, M., and Andros, C. D., "Federal Preemption and State Failure to Warn Claims," *Federation of Insurance & Corporate Counsel Quarterly* 40:101-6, 1990.

Dixon, M. G., "Drug Product Liability: Information for Safety," *Trial* 16:62-67 (Nov.), 1980.

DPT Vaccine-Related Injury Actions: Federal Pre-emption Reconsidered,: *Rutgers Law Review* 41:373-98, 1988.

"The Drug Manufacturer's Duty to Warn — To Whom Does It Extend?" *Florida State University Law Review* 13:135-57 (Spring), 1985.

"Drug Synergism and Potential Medical Liability," *Case Western Reserve Journal of International Law* 3:207-212, 1971.

"The Duty of Drug Manufacturers to Warn of Newly Discovered Side Effects of Marketed Drugs," *Rutgers Camden Law Journal* 2:145-160, 1970.

"Evidence — Admissibility of Evidence — Products Liability — A Subsequent Warning of a Drug's Dangerous Side Effects Is Not Admissible as Evidence to Prove

Negligence or Culpable Conduct Under Federal Rule of Evidence 407 in a Negligence Action, or to Prove an Inadequate Warning Making the Drug Unreasonably Dangerous in a Strict Liability Action Against the Manufacturer," *University of Cincinnati Law Review* 50:176-187, 1981.

Faich, G. A., "Adverse Drug Experience Reporting and Product Liability." *Food Drug Cosmetic Law Journal* 41:444-449, 1986.

"The Failure to Warn Defect: Strict Liability of the Prescription Drug Manufacturer in California," *University of San Francisco Law Review* 17:743-62 (Summer), 1983.

Forde, K. M. and Kennelly, J. J., "Preparation of a Drug-Caused Injury Case," *Trial Lawyers Guide* 20:409-475, 1977.

Gilhooley, M., "Learned Intermediaries, Prescription Drugs, and Patient Information," *St. Louis University Law Journal* 30:633-702 (Aug.), 1986.

Goldstein, E. M., "Drug Warnings—Who Reads Them?" *Trial* 9:45-46 (March/April), 1973.

Grant. K. E. "'Misuse' Defense in Drug Products Liability Cases," *Pace Law Review* 8:535-70, 1988.

Hirsh, H. L., "Medicolegal Significance of the Package Insert," *Medical Trial Technique Quarterly* 23:143-150, 1976.

"Industry-Wide Liability and Market Share Allocation of Damages," *Georgia Law Review* 15:423, 1981.

Irey, N. S., "Validating Adverse Drug Reaction Cases," *Journal of Legal Medicine* 1:49 (September/October), 1973.

Junewicz, J. J., "Physicians' Liability for Failure to Anticipate and Control Reactions and Interactions Precipitated by Prescribed or Administered Drugs," *Medical Trial Technique Quarterly* 26:8-41, 1979.

Land, S. J. and Mehlman, M. J., "New California 'Market Share' Theory in Drug Liability Cases," *Food Drug Cosmetic Law Journal* 36:39-46, 1981.

Lawrence, V. I., "Drug Manufacturers' Recommendations and the Common Knowledge Rule to Establish Medical Malpractice," *Nebraska Law Review* 63:859-87 (Fall), 1984.

"Liability of Pharmaceutical Manufacturers for Unforeseen Adverse Drug Reactions," *Fordham Law Review* 48:735-763, 1980.

McClellan, F. M., "Strict Liability for Drug Induced Injuries: An Excursion Through the Maze of Products Liability, Negligence and Absolute Liability," *Wayne Law Review* 25:1-36, 1978.

"Market Share Liability Adopted to Overcome Defendant Identification Requirement in DES Litigation. (Sindell v. Abbott Laboratories 607 P.2d 924 (Cal. 1980)," *Washington University Law Quarterly* 571-84 (Summer), 1981.

Mobilia, M. A., "Allergic Reactions to Prescription Drugs: A Proposal for Compensation," *Albany Law Review* 48:343-81 (Winter), 1984.

Morgan, B.G., "Pharmacist Liability," *Medical Trial Technique Quarterly* 33:315-34, 1987.

Newdick, C., "Strict Liability for Defective Drugs in the Pharmaceutical Industry," *The Law Quarterly Review* 101:405-431 (July), 1985.

"Package Inserts for Prescription Drugs as Evidence in Medical Malpractice Suits," *University of Chicago Law Review* 44:398-456, 1977.

"Products Liability: Drug Manufacturer Found Liable for 'Overpromotion' by Detail Men — A Diminution in the Standard of Proof," *Temple Law Quarterly* 45:134140, 1971.

"Products Liability: Drug Manufacturers' Liability for Latent Defects in Drugs," *Washburn Law Journal* 20:468-478, 1981.

"Products Liability — Food, Drug and Cosmetic Law — Birth Control — A Drug Manufacturer Who Voluntarily Distributed Patient Pamphlets Has a Duty to Warn Patients of Dangers Associated with Use of the Drug," *University of Cincinnati Law Review* 49:517-530, 1980.

"Products Liability: The Continued Viability of the Learned Intermediary Rule as It Applies to Product Warnings for Prescription Drugs," *University of Richmond Law Review* 20:405-423 (Winter), 1986.
"Proof of Causation in Multiparty Drug Litigation," *Texas Law Review* 56:125-133, 1977.
"Refusing Psychotropic Drugs: Whose Day in Court?" *University of Kansas Law Review* 37:657-77, 1989.
Rheingold, P. D., "The Expanding Liability of the Drug Manufacturer to the Consumer," *Food Drug Cosmetic Law Journal* 40:135-144 (Apr.), 1985.
Schwartz, T. M., "Consumer Warnings for Oral Contraceptives: A New Exception to the Prescription Drug Rule," *Food Drug Cosmetic Law Journal* 41:241-256 (July), 1986.
Schwartz, V. E., "Unavoidably Unsafe Products: Clarifying the Meaning and Policy Behind Comment K," *Washington and Lee Law Review* 42:1139-48, 1985.
"Sindell [Sindell v. Abbott Laboratories, 607 P.2d 924 (Cal.)] and Beyond: A Case for Imposing Punitive Damages in Market Share Litigation," *Pacific Law Journal* 17:1445-1475 (July), 1986.
Smith, J. T. and Simon, R. I., "Tardive Dyskinesia Revisited: A Major Public Health Crisis," *Medical Trial Technique Quarterly* 31:342-49 (Winter), 1985.
Tietz, G. F., "Informed Consent in the Prescription Drug Context: The Special Case," *Defense Law Journal* 36:153-211, 1987.
"Tort Liability for DPT Vaccine Injury and the Preemption Doctrine," *Indiana Law Review* 22:655-705, 1989.
"Torts: Drug Manufacturer Held Negligent for Failure to Use Detail Men to Warn Physicians of Dangerous Side Effect," *Minnesota Law Review* 55:148-155, 1970.
"Torts — Market Share Liability — The California Roulette of Causation Eliminating the Identification Requirement," *Seton Hall Law Review* 11:610-628, 1981.
"Torts — Products Liability — FDA Required Warning Nullified by Manufacturer's Overpromotion of Drug," *University of Cincinnati Law Review* 43:224-231, 1974.
"Vaccine-Related Injuries: Alternatives to the Tort Compensation System," *St. Louis University Law Journal* 30:919-948 (Aug.), 1986.
Vandall, F. J., "Applying Strict Liability to Pharmacists," *University of Toledo Law Review* 18:1-49 (Fall), 1986.
"Warnings and the Pharmaceutical Companies: Legal Status of the Package Insert," *Houston Law Review* 16:140-164, 1978.
Yacura, M., "Inside the PDR: A Volume of Considerations," *Trial* 20:64-7 (June), 1984.
Zajc, M., "Antipsychotic Drugs: Their Pharmacology," *Medical Trial Technique Quarterly* 33:265-73, 1987.
Zugibe, F. T., "Sudden Death Related to the Use of Psychotropic Drugs," *Legal Medicine Annual* 75-90, 1980.

TABLE OF CASES

A

Abbot v. American Cyanamid Co. (C.A.-4 Va., 1988) 844 F.2d 1108—DTP
Abbott Laboratories v. Gravis (Tex., 1971) 470 S.W.2d 639—PROCAINE HCL
Abel v. Eli Lilly & Co. (1979) 94 Mich. App. 59, 289 N.W.2d 20, aff'd (1984) 418 Mich. 311, 343 N.W.2d 164—DIETHYLSTILBESTROL
Abner v. Pediatric Care P.S.C. (No. 87-CI-729, Circuit Court, Kenton County, Ky., June 27, 1989)—DTP
Adams v. Allen (1989) 56 Wash. App. 283, 783 P.2d 635—OXYCODONE
Addison v. Emfinger (Ala., 1989) 551 So. 2d 375—HYDROCHLOROTHIAZIDE
Addison v. Health & Hosp. Governing Comm. of Cook County (1977) 56 Ill. App. 3d 533, 14 Ill. Dec. 7, 371 N.E.2d 1060—CEPHALOTHIN
Ades v. Perloff (No. 1896, Court of Common Pleas, Philadelphia County, Pa., Dec. 18, 1972)—THYROID
Adkins v. Mong (1988) 168 Mich. App. 726, 425 N.W.2d 151—DIAZEPAM
Adleson v. United States (N.D. Cal., 1981) 523 F. Supp. 459—INFLUENZA VIRUS VACCINE
Aetna Cas. & Sur. Co. of Illinois v. Medical Protective Co. of Ft. Wayne, Indiana (N.D. Ill., 1983) 575 F. Supp. 901—DEXAMETHASONE
Akuly v. Suburban Med. Center (No. 81L-28824, Circuit Court, Cook County, Ill., Nov. 25, 1986)—ALPHAPRODINE HCL; MEPERIDINE HCL
Albee v. Glesmann (1987) 23 Mass. App. 972, 503 N.E.2d 677—PROPRANOLOL HCL
Albers v. Aycinena (No. 170062, Superior Court, San Mateo County, Cal., Aug. 16, 1974)—GENTAMICIN SULFATE
Albertson v. Richardson-Merrell, Inc. (Fla. App., 1983) 441 So. 2d 1146—DOXYLAMINE SUCCINATE
Alboher v. Parke-Davis (No. 80 Civ. 0046, U.S. District Court, E.D. N.Y., Dec. 29, 1983)—PHENYTOIN SODIUM
Allen v. Kaiser Foundation Hospital (1985) 76 Or. App. 5, 707 P.2d 1289—CHLORPROMAZINE; HALOPERIDOL
Allrid v. Tenneco Chemicals, Inc. (No. C-56346, Superior Court, Fulton County, Ga., Aug. 14, 1986)—THORIUM DIOXIDE
Alton v. Kitt (1982) 103 Ill. App. 3d 387, 59 Ill. Dec. 132, 431 N.E.2d 417—MEPERIDINE HCL
American Cyanamid v. Frankson (Tex. App. 1987) 732 S.W.2d 648—LOXAPINE SUCCINATE
Anderson v. Martzke (1970) 131 Ill. App. 2d 61, 266 N.E.2d 137—TETANUS ANTITOXIN
Anderson v. McNeilab (C.A.-5 La., 1987) 831 F.2d 92—ZOMEPIRAC SODIUM
Andrews v. Eli Lilly & Co. (N.D. Ill., 1983) 97 F.R.D. 494—DIETHYLSTILBESTROL
Anthony v. Abbott Laboratories (R.I., 1985) 490 A.2d 43—DIETHYLSTILBESTROL
Argus v. Scheppegrell (La., 1985) 472 So. 2d 573—SECOBARBITAL SODIUM
Armstrong v. Weiland (1976) 267 S.C. 12, 225 S.E.2d 851—SODIUM WARFARIN
Arzaga v. Southern California Permanente Medical Group (No. SOC 266 77, Superior Court, Los Angeles County, Cal., Sept. 13, 1973)—PENICILLIN
Ascher v. Gutierrez (1976) 175 App. D.C. 100, 533 F.2d 1235—SODIUM THIOPENTAL
Ashman v. SK & F LabCo. (N.D. Ill., 1988) 702 F. Supp. 1401—CIMETIDINE HCL

Axler v. E.R. Squibb & Sons, Inc. (No. 2888, Court of Common Pleas, Philadelphia County, Pa., Mar. 25, 1982)—DIETHYLSTILBESTROL
Ayres v. United States (C.A.-5 Tex., 1985) 750 F.2d 449—EPINEPHRINE

B

Baas v. Hoye (C.A.-8 Iowa, 1985) 766 F.2d 1190—THEOPHYLINE and EPHEDRINE
Bacardi v. Holzman (1981) 182 N.J. Super. 422, 442 A.2d 617—ACETAZOLAMIDE
Bailey v. Eli Lilly Co. (M.D. Pa., 1985) 607 F. Supp. 660—BENZOXAPROFEN
Baker v. St. Agnes Hospital (1979) 70 App. Div. 2d 400, 421 N.Y.S.2d 81—BISHYDROXYCOUMARIN
Baker v. United States (C.A.-9 Cal., 1987) 817 F.2d 560—POLIOVIRUS VACCINE
Bakos v. Russell (1977) 49 Ill. App. 3d 539, 7 Ill. Dec. 420, 364 N.E.2d 581—TRIAMCINOLONE ACETATE
Baldino v. Castagna (1982) 505 Pa. 239, 478 A.2d 807—PHENYLBUTAZONE
Ball v. Mallinckrodt Chemical Works (1964) 53 Tenn. App. 218, 381 S.W.2d 563, 19 A.L.R.3d 813—SODIUM ACETRIZOATE
Ball Memorial Hospital v. Freeman (1964) 245 Ind. 71, 196 N.E.2d 274, 9 A.L.R.3d 567—PROCAINE HCL
Ballenger v. Crowell (1978) 38 N.C. App. 50, 247 S.E.2d 287—MORPHINE SULFATE
Banda v. Danbury (La. App., 1985) 469 So. 2d 264—ISONIAZID
Barclay v. Campbell (Tex., 1986) 704 S.W.2d 8—LOXAPINE SUCCINATE; THIORIDAZINE
Barkan v. Upjohn Pharmaceutical Co. (No. 25-92-42, Superior Court, Orange County, Cal., Jan. 22, 1982)—LINCOMYCIN
Barnes v. St. Francis Hospital & School of Nursing, Inc. (1973) 211 Kan. 315, 507 P.2d 288—DIMENHYDRINATE
Barnes v. United States (M.D. Ala., 1981) 525 F. Supp. 1065—INFLUENZA VIRUS VACCINE
Barnes v. United States (W.D. Pa., 1981) 516 F. Supp. 1376, aff'd (C.A.-3 Pa., 1982) 685 F.2d 66, p. 316—INFLUENZA VIRUS VACCINE
Barnette v. E.R. Squibb & Sons (E.D. Va., 1987) 670 F. Supp. 650—TETRACYCLINE HCL
Barraza v. Vasquez (No. 85-485, Law Court, El Paso County, Feb. 16, 1987)—HERPARIN SODIUM
Barry v. Don Hall Laboratories (1982) 56 Or. App. 518, 642 P.2d 685—VITAMINS
Barson v. E.R. Squibb & Sons, Inc. (Utah, 1984) 682 P.2d 832—HYDROXYPROGESTERONE CAPROATE
Barth v. Rock (1984) 36 Wash. App. 400, 674 P.2d 1265—SODIUM THIOPENTAL
Basko v. Sterling Drug, Inc. (C.A.-2 Conn., 1969) 416 F.2d 417—CHLOROQUINE
Bass v. Barksdale (Tenn. App., 1984) 671 S.W.2d 476—ETHAMBUTOL HCL
Batiste v. American Home Products Corp. (1977) 32 N.C. App. 1, 231 S.E.2d 269—NORGESTREL with ETHINYL ESTRADIOL
Batteast v. St. Bernard's Hosp. (1985) 134 Ill. App. 3d 843, 89 Ill. Dec. 561, 480 N.E.2d 1304—AMITRIPTYLINE
Batteast v. Wyeth Laboratories (1988) 172 Ill. App. 3d 114, 122 Ill. Dec. 189, 526 N.E.2d 428—AMINOPHYLLINE
Baum v. United States (M.D. Pa., 1982) 541 F. Supp. 1349—INFLUENZA VIRUS VACCINE
Bayless v. Philadelphia Nat. League Club (C.A.-3 Pa., 1979) 615 F.2d 1352—PHENYLBUTAZONE

Buckner v. Allergan Pharmaceuticals, Inc. (Fla. App., 1981) 400 So. 2d 820—CORTISONE

Bulthuis v. Rexall Corp. (C.A.-9 Cal., 1986) 789 F.2d 1315—DIETHYLSTILBESTROL

Burgon v. Kaiser Foundation Hospitals (1979) 93 Cal. App. 3d 813, 155 Cal. Rptr. 763—DAPSONE

Burleson v. Mead Johnson & Co. (C.A.-5 Tex., 1972) 463 F.2d 180—ETHINYL ESTRADIOL with DIMETHISTERONE

Burlison v. Warner-Lambert Co. (C.A.-8 Iowa, 1988) 842 F.2d 991—EUCALYPTUS OIL and MENTHOL

Burnham v. Tabb (Miss., 1987) 508 So. 2d 1072—FENOPROFEN CALCIUM

Burnside v. Abbott Laboratories (1985) 351 Pa. Super. 264, 505 A.2d 973—DIETHYLSTILBESTROL

Burnside v. Golden State Memorial Hospital (No. NWC 10962, Superior Court, Los Angeles County, Cal., July 13, 1972)—DEXAMETHAZONE

Burroughs v. Board of Trustees of Alachua General Hosp. (Fla. App., 1979) 377 So. 2d 801—CHLORDIAZEPOXIDE HCL

C

Calabrese v. Trenton State College (1980) 82 N.J. 321, 413 A.2d 315—RABIES VACCINE

Callan v. Nordland (No. 80-L-372, Circuit Court, Will County, Ill., Mar. 26, 1982)—NEOMYCIN SULFATE

Callan v. Nordland (1983) 114 Ill. App. 3d 196, 69 Ill. Dec. 933, 448 N.E.2d 651—NEOMYCIN SULFATE

Campos v. Weeks (1966) 245 Cal. App. 2d 678, 53 Cal. Rptr. 915—PENCILLIN

Cannon v. Strauss (No. 49428, Superior Court, Suffolk County, Massachusetts, Jan. 4, 1985)—DTP

Capaccio v. Neuman (No. 21831/81, Supreme Court, New York County, N.Y., Oct. 26, 1984)—OXYTOCIN

Carmichael v. Reitz (1971) 17 Cal. App. 3d 958, 95 Cal. Rptr. 381—NORETHYNODREL with MESTRANOL

Carpenter v. Campbell (1971) 149 Ind. App. 189, 271 N.E.2d 163—NOREPINEPHRINE BITARTRATE

Carrao v. Heitler (1986) 117 App. Div. 2d 308, 502 N.Y.S.2d 424—MEASLES VACCINE

Carroll v. St. Paul Ins. Co. (La. App., 1989) 550 So. 2d 787—BETAMETHASONE

Carter v. Dunlop (1985) 138 Ill. App. 3d 58, 92 Ill. Dec. 418, 484 N.E.2d 1273—METHIMAZOLE

Carter v. Metropolitan Dade County (Fla. App., 1971) 253 So. 2d 920—THIORIDAZINE

Castrignano v. E. R. Squibb & Sons (R.I., 1988) 546 A.2d 775—DIETHYLSTILBESTROL

Cavanaugh v. Abbott Laboratories (1985) 145 Vt. 516, 496 A.2d 154—DIETHYLSTILBESTROL

Cazes v. Raisinger (La. App., 1983) 430 So. 2d 104—DIGOXIN

Chambers v. G.D. Searle & Co. (C.A.-4 Md., 1977) 567 F.2d 269—NORETHYNODREL with MESTRANOL

Chambers v. Merrell Dow Pharmaceuticals (1988) 35 Ohio St. 3d 123, 519 N.E.2d 370—DOXYLAMINE SUCCINATE

Chambers v. Ortho Pharmaceutical Corp. (No. 195615, Superior Court, Pierce County, Wash., Mar. 28, 1973)—NORETHINDRONE with MESTRANOL

Cook v United States (N.D. Cal., 1982) 545 F. Supp. 306—INFLUENZA VIRUS VACCINE
Cooper v. Bowser (Tex. Civ. App., 1980) 610 S.W.2d 825—INDOMETHACIN
Cornell v. Merck & Co. (1987) 87 Or. App. 373, 742 P.2d 667—TIMILOL MALEATE
Cornfeldt v. Tongen (Minn., 1977) 262 N.W.2d 684—HALOTHANE
Cowan v. Lederle Laboratories (D. Kan., 1985) 604 F. Supp. 438—TETRACYLINE
Coxon v. Casa Grande Valley Community Hospital (No. 32948, Superior Court, Pinal County, Ariz., June 22, 1983)—OXYTOCIN
Coyle v. Richardson-Merrell, Inc. (Pa. Super., 1988) 538 A.2d 1329—DOXYLAMINE SUCCINATE
Crain v. Allison (D.C. App., 1982) 443 A.2d 558—TRIAMCINOLONE HEXACETONIDE
Croft v. York (Fla. App., 1971) 244 So. 2d 161—EPINEPHRINE
Cronin v. Hagan (Iowa, 1974) 221 N.W.2d 748—SULFAMETHIZOLE
Crooks v. Greene (1987) 12 Kan. App. 2d 62, 736 P.2d 78—DIAZEPAM
Cross v. Huttenlocher (1981) 185 Conn. 390, 440 A.2d 952—QUINACRINE HCL
Crouch v. Most (1967) 78 N.M. 406, 432 P.2d 250—ANTIVENIN
Cunningham v. Charles Pfizer & Co. (Okla., 1974) 532 P.2d 1377—POLIOVIRUS VACCINE

D

Dalke v. Upjohn Co. (C.A.-9 Wash., 1977) 555 F.2d 245—DEMECLOCYCLINE HCL
Daniels v. Hadley Memorial Hospital (1977) 185 App. D.C. 84, 566 F.2d 749—PENICILLIN
Daniels v. Universal Health Servs. (No. A 233563, District Court, Clark County, Nev., Apr. 23, 1987)—HALOPERIDOL
DaRoca v. St. Bernard General Hospital (La. App., 1977) 347 So. 2d 933—NEOMYCIN SULFATE
Daubert v. Merrell Dow Pharmaceuticals, Inc. (S.D. Cal., 1989) 711 F. Supp. 546—DOXYLAMINE SUCCINATE
Davila v. Bodelson (1985) 103 N.M. 243, 704 P.2d 1119—OXYTOCIN
Davis v. Regents of the University of California (No. 314826, Superior Court, Sacramento County, California, Feb. 1, 1985)—SODIUM NITROPRUSSIDE
Davis v. United States (C.A.-9 Idaho, 1981) 642 F.2d 328—POLIOVIRUS VACCINE
Davis v. Washington University (No. 802-05960, Circuit Court, St. Louis County, Mo., Jan. 17, 1983)—MORPHINE SULFATE
Davis v. Wyeth Laboratories, Inc. (C.A.-9 Idaho, 1968) 399 F.2d 1210—POLIOVIRUS VACCINE
Davison v. Mobile Infirmary (Ala., 1984) 456 So. 2d 14—ASPIRIN
Dawson v. Bristol Labs. (W.D. Ky., 1987) 658 F. Supp. 1036—TETRACYCLINE HCL
Dawson v. Eli Lilly & Co. (D.D.C., 1982) 543 F. Supp. 1330—DIETHYLSTILBESTROL
Decker v. Ortho Pharmaceutical Corp. (No. 120647, Superior Court, Contra Costa County, Cal., July 12, 1974)—NORETHINDRONE ACETATE with ESTRADIOL; NORETHINDRONE with MESTRANOL
Deitch v. E.R. Squibb & Sons, Inc. (C.A.-7 Ill., 1984) 740 F.2d 556—DIETHYLSTILBESTROL
DeLuryea v. Winthrop Laboratories (C.A.-8 Ark., 1983) 697 F.2d 222—PENTAZOCINE
DeMaio v. Coppola (1981) 80 App. Div. 2d 551, 435 N.Y.S.2d 360—TETRACYCLINE HCL

E

F

Fleming v. Prince George's County (1976) 277 Md. 655, 358 A.2d 892—DIETHYLSTILBESTROL
Flood v. Wyeth Laboratories (1986) 183 Cal. App. 3d 1272, 228 Cal. Rptr. 700—DTP
Fontenot v. Upjohn Co. (C.A.-5 La., 1986) 780 F.2d 1190—PROGESTERONE
Formella v. Ciba-Geigy Corp. (1980) 100 Mich. App. 649, 300 N.W.2d 356—OXYPHENBUTAZONE
Fornoff v. Parke-Davis & Co. (1982) 105 Ill. App. 3d 681, 61 Ill. Dec. 438, 434 N.E.2d 793—OXYTOCIN
Fox v. Sterling Drug, Inc. (No. 687-394, Circuit Court, Milwaukee County, Wis., Aug. 11, 1989)—ASPIRIN
Fraijo v. Hartland Hosp. (1979) 99 Cal. App. 3d 331, 160 Cal. Rptr. 246—MEPERIDINE HCL
Fraley v. American Cyanamid Co. (D. Colo., 1984) 589 F. Supp. 826—POLIOVIRUS VACCINE
Franklin v. Gupta (No. 85242052/CL39375, Circuit Court, Baltimore, Md., March 3, 1988)—FENTANYL
Frasier v. Department of Health & Human Resources (La. App., 1986) 500 So. 2d 858—CHLORPROMAZINE
Fraysier v. United States (S.D. Fla., 1983) 566 F. Supp. 1085, aff'd (C.A.-11 Fla., 1985) 766 F.2d 478—INFLUENZA VIRUS VACCINE
Freedman v. Superior Court (Cal. App., 1989) 263 Cal. Rptr. 1—OXYTOCIN
Friel v. Vineland Obstetrical & Gynecological Professional Assn. (1979) 166 N.J. Super. 579, 400 A.2d 147—OXYTOCIN
Fritz v. Parke-Davis & Co. (1967) 277 Minn. 210, 152 N.W.2d 129, 30 A.L.R.3d 982—PHENYTOIN SODIUM
Frost v. Mayo Clinic (D. Minn., 1969) 304 F. Supp. 285—CELLULOSE, OXIDIZED
Fuller v. Starnes (1980) 268 Ark. 476, 597 S.W.2d 88—MEPERIDINE HCL
Funston v. United States (M.D. Pa., 1981) 513 F. Supp. 1000—INFLUENZA VIRUS VACCINE
Fykes v. Chatow (No. 976896, Superior Court, Los Angeles County, Cal., Oct. 29, 1974)—ECHOTHIOPHATE IODIDE

G

Galiardo v. St. Vincent's Hospital & Medical Center of New York (1979) 70 App. Div. 2d 563, 417 N.Y.S.2d 60—DIAZEPAM
Gallimore v. United States (E.D. Pa., 1982) 530 F. Supp. 136—INFLUENZA VIRUS VACCINE
Galvan v. Fedder (Tex. Civ. App., 1984) 678 S.W.2d 596—CHLORPROPAMIDE
Gamell v. Mount Sinai Hosp. (1970) 34 App. Div. 2d 981, 312 N.Y.S.2d 629—MEPERIDINE HCL
Ganczewski v. Smith (No. 52055, Superior Court, Ventura County, Cal., 1971)—HALOTHANE
Garner v. Wyeth Laboratories, Inc. (D. S.C., 1984) 585 F. Supp. 189—NORGESTREL with ETHINYL ESTRADIOL
Garron v. State of New York (No. 68209, Court of Claims, N.Y., Dec. 15, 1986)—EPINEPHRINE
Garvey v. O'Donoghue (D.C. App., 1987) 530 A.2d 1141—TOBRAMYCIN SULFATE
Gassmann v. United States (C.A.-11 Fla., 1985) 768 F.2d 1263—INFLUENZA VIRUS VACCINE
Gates v. United States (C.A.-10 Okla., 1983) 707 F.2d 1141—INFLUENZA VIRUS VACCINE
Gatts v. Lederle Laboratories (No. 25505, District Court, Plymouth County, Iowa, June 27, 1989)—DTP

Gaul v. United States (D. Del., 1984) 582 F. Supp. 1122—INFLUENZA VIRUS VACCINE

Geibel v. United States (W.D. Pa., 1987) 667 F. Supp. 215, aff'd (C.A.-3 Pa., 1988) 845 F.2d 1011—HYDROCHLOROTHIAZIDE

Geleynse v. E.I. duPont de Nemours & Co. (No. C83-610R, U.S. District Court, Western District, Wash., Nov. 26, 1984)—SODIUM WARFARIN

Gelley v. Astra Pharmaceutical Products, Inc. (C.A.-8 Minn., 1979) 610 F.2d 558—LIDOCAINE HCL

George v. Parke-Davis (1987) 107 Wash. 2d 584, 733 P.2d 507—DIETHYLSTILBESTROL

Getty v. Hoffman-LaRoche (1987) 189 Cal. App. 3d 1294, 235 Cal. Rptr. 48—DIAZEPAM; ETHCHLORVYNOL; FLURAZEPAM HCL

Gicas v. United States (E.D. Wis., 1981) 508 F. Supp. 217—INFLUENZA VIRUS VACCINE

Gitlin v. Cassell (1985) 107 App. Div. 2d 636, 484 N.Y.S.2d 19—NORETHINDRONE with MESTRANOL

Givens v. Lederle (C.A.-5 Fla., 1977) 556 F.2d 1341—POLIOVIRUS VACCINE

Glass v. Philips Roxane (No. C0270-762, Superior Court, Los Angeles County, Cal., Dec. 12, 1983)—DYDROGESTERONE

Goff v. Olson (No. F2-1512, Wisconsin Patient's Compensation Panel, Oct. 26, 1983)—OXYTOCIN

Goga v. Ortho Diagnostics, Inc. (1982) 90 App. Div. 2d 874, 456 N.Y.S.2d 476—RH$_{o}$ (D) IMMUNE GLOBULIN (HUMAN)

Goldstein v. G.D. Searle & Co. (1978) 62 Ill. App. 3d 344, 19 Ill. Dec. 208, 378 N.E.2d 1083—ETHYNODIOL DIACETATE with MESTRANOL

Gonzales v. Fuchs (No. 4624/75, Supreme Court, Kings County, N.Y., May 12, 1977)—OXYTOCIN

Gonzales v. Lovelace Medical Center (No. CV-84-02215, District Court, Bernalillo County, N.M., Feb. 2, 1986)—DTP

Goodson v. Searle Laboratories (D. Conn., 1978) 471 F. Supp. 546—ETHYNODIOL DIACETATE with ETHINYL ESTRADIOL

Gordon v. Roche Laboratories, Division of Hoffman-La Roche (1981) 116 Misc. 2d 688, 456 N.Y.S.2d 291—DIAZEPAM

Gottsdanker v. Cutter Laboratories (1960) 182 Cal. App. 2d 602, 6 Cal. Rptr. 320, 79 A.L.R.2d 290—POLIOVIRUS VACCINE

Goulet v. Smith Kline & French (No. 43 03 94, Superior Court, Orange County, Cal., June 2, 1989)—CHLORPHENIRAMINE MALEATE

Gowan v. United States (D. Ore., 1985) 601 F. Supp. 1297—TRAZODONE HCL

Graham v. Kaiser Foundation Hospital (No. 633484, Superior Court, San Francisco County, Cal., Aug. 22, 1972)—PREDNISONE

Graham v. Whitaker (1984) 282 S.C. 393, 321 S.E.2d 40—TROPICAMIDE

Graham v. Wyeth Laboratories (D. Kan., 1987) 666 F. Supp. 1483—DTP

Grainger v. Sandoz Pharmaceuticals (No. 79-40075, E.D. Mich. Oct. 30, 1980)—THIORIDAZINE

Granado v. Madsen (Tex. App., 1987) 729 S.W.2d 866—HALOTHANE

Grassis v. Retik (1988) 25 Mass. App. 595, 521 N.E.2d 411—GENTAMICIN SULFATE

Gravis v. Parke-Davis & Co. (Tex. Civ. App., 1973) 502 S.W.2d 863—PROCAINE HCL

Gravis v. Physicians & Surgeons Hosp. of Alice (Tex. Civ. App., 1967) 415 S.W.2d 674, rev'd (Tex., 1968) 427 S.W.2d 310—PROCAINE HCL

Gray v. Reeves (1978) 76 Cal. App. 3d 567, 142 Cal. Rptr. 716—PREDNISONE

Gray v. United States (S.D. Tex., 1978) 445 F. Supp. 337—DIETHYLSTILBESTROL

Greene v. Abbott Laboratories (1987) 137 Misc. 2d 424, 521 N.Y.S.2d 382, aff'd (1989) 148 App. Div. 2d 403, 539 N.Y.S.2d 351—DIETHYLSTILBESTROL

H

Hodge v. Crafts-Farrow Hosp. (S.C., 1985) 334 S.E.2d 818—DIAZEPAM

Hodge v. Fenderson (Superior Court, Kern County, Cal., 1974)—FIBRINOGEN

Hoffman v. Sterling Drug, Inc. (C.A.-3 Pa., 1973) 485 F.2d 132—CHLOROQUINE

Hoffman v. Sterling Drug, Inc. (M.D. Pa., 1974) 374 F. Supp. 850—CHLOROQUINE

Hofherr v. Dart Industries (C.A.-4 M.D., 1988) 853 P.2d 259—DIETHYLSTILBESTROL

Holbrook v. Rose (Ky. App., 1970) 458 S.W.2d 155—HEXYLRESORCINOL

Holbrooks v. Duke University, Inc. (1983) 63 N.C. App. 504, 305 S.E.2d 69—MEPERIDINE HCL

Holden v. United States (Civil No. 69-CV-57, U.S. District Court, N.D., N.Y., Dec. 27, 1973)—ASPIRIN

Holder v. Eli Lilly & Co. (E.D. Pa., 1989) 708 F. Supp. 672—DIETHYLSTILBESTROL

Holland v. Stacy (Okla., 1972) 496 P.2d 1180—NICOTINYL ALCOHOL

Holley v. Burroughs Wellcome Co. (N.C., 1986) 348 S.E.2d 772—HALOTHANE; SUCCINYLCHOLINE CHLORIDE

Holmes v. Syntex Laboratories, Inc. (1984) 156 Cal. App. 3d 372, 202 Cal. Rptr. 773—NORETHINDRONE with MESTRANOL

Horney v. Lawrence (1988) 189 Ga. App. 376, 375 S.E.2d 629—DIAZEPAM

Hoskie v. United States (C.A.-10 N.M., 1981) 666 F.2d 1353—MORPHINE SULFATE

Howard v. Mitchell (Ala., 1986) 492 So. 2d 1018—RH_o (D) IMMUNE GLOBULIN (HUMAN)

Howard v. Piver (1981) 53 N.C. 46, 279 S.E.2d 876—PHENYTOIN SODIUM

Hull v. Merrell Dow Pharmaceuticals (S.D. Fla., 1988) 700 F. Supp. 28—DOXYLAMINE SUCCINATE

Hundemer v. Sisters of Charity of Cincinnati, Inc. (1969) 22 Ohio App. 2d 119, 258 N.E.2d 611—NOREPHINEPHRINE BITARTRATE

Hurley v. Lederle Laboratories Division of American Cyanamid Co. (C.A.-5 Tex., 1989) 863 F.2d 1173—DTP

Hutchison v. United States (C.A.-9 Cal., 1988) 841 F.2d 966—PREDNISONE

Hymowitz v. Eli Lilly & Co. (Misc. 1987) 518 N.Y.S.2d 996, aff'd (73 N.Y.2d 487, 539 N.E.2d 1069—DIETHYLSTILBESTROL

I

Incollingo v. Ewing (1971) 444 Pa. 299, 282 A.2d 225—CHLORAMPHENICOL

Ingram v. Hook's Drugs (Ind. App., 1985) 476 N.E.2d 881—DIAZEPAM

In re Bendectin Litigation (C.A.-6 Ohio, 1988) 857 F.2d 290—DOXYLAMINE SUCCINATE

In re Bendectin Products Liability Litigation (No. 84-3710, 6th Cir. Ohio, Oct. 26, 1984)—DOXYLAMINE SUCCINATE

In re Certified Questions from the Court for the E. Dist. of Mich. S. Div. (1984) 419 Mich. 686, 358 N.W.2d 873—NORETHINDRONE with MESTRANOL; THIORIDAZINE

In re Mitchell (No. 20,415, Chancery Court, Sunflower County, Miss., April 25, 1985)—RH_o (D) IMMUNE GLOBULIN (HUMAN)

In re Richardson-Merrell, Inc. (Jud. Pan. Mult. Lit., 1982) 533 F. Supp. 489—DOXYLAMINE SUCCINATE

In re Richardson-Merrell, Inc. "Bendectin" Products Liability Litigation (S.D. Ohio, 1983) 624 F. Supp. 1271—DOXYLAMINE SUCCINATE

In re [Swine Flu Immunization] Products Liability Litigation (D. Colo., 1980) 495 F. Supp. 1188—INFLUENZA VIRUS VACCINE

In re Tetracycline Cases (W.D. Mo., 1985) 107 F.R.D. 719—TETRACYCLINE HCL

J

Jackson v. State (La. App., 1983) 428 So. 2d 1073—ISONIAZID
Jacobi v. Rexall (No. 636-624, Circuit Court, Milwaukee County, Wis., Aug. 21, 1986)—DIETHYLSTILBESTROL
Jacobs v. Dista Products Co. (D. Wyo., 1988) 693 F. Supp. 1029—CEPHALEXIN MONOHYDRATE
James v. Kennebec Valley Medical Center (No. 80-CV-649, Superior Court, Kennebec County, Me., Aug. 26, 1983)—OXYTOCIN
Javitz v. Slatus (1983) 93 App. Div. 2d 830, 461 N.Y.S.2d 44—CLINDAMYCIN HCL
Johnson v. American Cyanamid Co. (1986) 239 Kan. 279, 718 P.2d 1318—POLIOVIRUS VACCINE
Johnson v. Eli Lilly & Co. (W.D. Pa., 1983) 577 F. Supp. 174, aff'd (C.A.-3 Pa., 1984) 738 F.2d 422—DIETHYLSTILBESTROL
Johnson v. McNeil Laboratories, Inc. (No. Civ-83-829-BT, U.S. District Court, W.D. Okla., Sept. 20, 1983)—ZOMEPIRAC SODIUM
Johnston v. Upjohn Co. (Mo. App., 1969) 442 S.W.2d 93—LINCOMYCIN
Jolly v. Eli Lilly & Co. (1988) 44 Cal. 3d 1103, 751 P.2d 923, 245 Cal. Rptr. 658—DIETHYLSTILBESTROL
Jones v. Irvin (S.D. Ill., 1985) 602 F.2d 399—ETHCHLORVYNOL
Jones v. Lederle Laboratories (E.D. N.Y. 1988) 695 F. Supp. 700—DTP
Jones v. Ortho Pharmaceutical Corp. (1985) 163 Cal. App. 3d 396, 209 Cal. Rptr. 456—NORETHINDRONE with MESTRANOL
Jones v. Searle Laboratories (1983) 93 Ill. 2d 366, 67 Ill. Dec. 118, 444 N.E.2d 157—ETHYNODIOL DIACETATE with MESTRANOL
Jones v. Superior Court for City of Alameda (1981) 119 Cal. App. 3d 534, 174 Cal. Rptr. 148—DIETHYLSTILBESTROL
Jones v. Wyeth Laboratories, Inc. (C.A.-8 Ark., 1978) 583 F.2d 1070—INFLUENZA VIRUS VACCINE
Jordon v. Ortho Pharmaceuticals, Inc. (Tex. App., 1985) 696 S.W.2d 228—NORETHINDRONE with MESTRANOL
Jorgensen v. Meade Johnson Laboratories, Inc. (C.A.-10 Okla., 1973) 483 F.2d 237—ETHINYL ESTRADIOL with DIMETHISTERONE
Jurin v. Wyeth Laboratories, Inc. (No. 769855, Superior Court, King County, Wash., May 20, 1977)—NORGESTREL with ETHINYL ESTRADIOL

K

Kaiser v. Suburban Transportation System (1965) 65 Wash. 2d 461, 398 P.2d 14, mod. 401 P.2d 350—TRIPELENNAMINE
Kaplow v. Katz (1986) 120 App. Div. 2d 569, 502 N.Y.S.2d 216—NITROFURANTOIN
Karibjanian v. Thomas Jefferson Univ. (E.D. Pa., 1989) 717 F. Supp. 1081—THORIUM DIOXIDE
Kaufman v. Eli Lilly & Co. (1985) 65 N.Y.2d 449, 492 N.Y.S.2d 584, 482 N.E.2d 63—DIETHYLSTILBESTROL
Kaval v. Kurucz (No. 3378/82, Supreme Court, Rockland County, N.Y., April 21, 1988)—SODIUM WARFARIN
Kearl v. Lederle Laboratories (1985) 172 Cal. App. 3d 812, 218 Cal. Rptr. 453—POLIOVIRUS VACCINE
Kehr v. Simfam RX, Inc. (No. N39746, Superior Court, San Diego County, Cal., June 16, 1989)—DIGOXIN

Keil v. Eli Lilly & Co. (E.D. Mich., 1980) 490 F. Supp. 479—DIETHYLSTILBESTROL

Keith-Popp v. Eli Lilly & Co. (W.D. Wis., 1986) 639 F. Supp. 1479—DIETHYLSTILBESTROL

Kelley v. Wiggins (1987) 291 Ark. 280, 724 S.W.2d 443—PSEUDOEPHEDRINE HCL and CHLORPHENIRAMINE MALEATE

Kemble v. Antonetti (No. 87-1002-B, 44th Judicial District Court, Dallas County, Tex., Jan. 29, 1988)—FENTANYL

Kempf v. University of North Dakota Family Practice Center (No. 87292, District Court, Grand Forks, N.D., Feb. 19, 1988)—PHENOBARBITAL

Kensinger v. Abbott Laboratories (1985) 171 Cal. App. 3d 376, 217 Cal. Rptr. 313—DIETHYLSTILBESTROL

Kershaw v. Sterling Drug, Inc. (C.A.-5 Miss., 1969) 415 F.2d 1009—CHLOROQUINE

Killeen v. Reinhardt (1979) 71 App. Div. 2d 851, 419 N.Y.S.2d 175—HYDROMORPHONE HCL

Kim v. Hoffman-LaRoche (Nos. WEC 077655 & WEC 075943, Superior Court, Los Angeles County, Cal., Dec. 5, 1986)—ALPHAPRODINE HCL

Kirk v. Michael Reese Hospital & Medical Center (1987) 117 Ill.2d 507, 111 Ill. Dec. 944, 513 N.E.2d 387—FLUPHENAZINE HCL

Kinney v. Hutchinson (La. App., 1984) 449 So. 2d 696—PHENMETRAZINE HCL

Kinney v. Hutchinson (La. App., 1985) 468 So. 2d 714—PHENMETRAZINE HCL

Klink v. G.D. Searle & Co. (1980) 26 Wash. App. 951, 614 P.2d 701—ETHYNODIOL DIACETATE with MESTRANOL

Knudsen v. United States (M.D. Fla., 1987) 691 F. Supp. 1346—DTP

Kohoutek v. Hafner (Minn. App., 1985) 383 N.W.2d 295—OXYTOCIN

Kong v. Clay-Grant Pharmacy (No. 619350, Superior Court, San Francisco County, Cal., 1972)—HYDROCORTISONE

Kortenhaus v. Eli Lilly & Co. (1988) 228 N.J. Super. 162, 549 A.2d 437—DIETHYLSTILBESTROL

Kosberg v. Washington Hospital Center, Inc. (1968) 129 App. D.C. 322, 394 F.2d 947—CHLORPROMAZINE

Koury v. Follo (1968) 272 N.C. 366, 158 S.E.2d 548—STREPTOMYCIN

Kowalski v. Rees (No. 609709, Superior Court, San Francisco County, Cal., Jan. 9, 1974)—METHOTREXATE

Kraus v. Cleveland Clinic (N.D. Ohio, 1977) 442 F. Supp. 310—PREDNISONE

Kress v. United States (E.D. Pa., 1984) 587 F. Supp. 397, aff'd (C.A.-3 Pa., 1985) 762 F.2d 993—INFLUENZA VIRUS VACCINE

Krug v. Sterling Drug, Inc. (Mo., 1967) 416 S.W.2d 143—CHLOROQUINE

Kubs v. United States (E.D. Wis., 1982) 537 F. Supp. 560—INFLUENZA VIRUS VACCINE

L

Labbe v. Mangan (No. 31634, Superior Court, Clallam County, Wash., Oct.3, 1984)—PROPRANOLOL HYDROCHLORIDE

Laboy v. United States (D. P.R., 1985) 626 F. Supp. 105—FLURAZEPAM HCL

Lackey v. Bressler (1987) 86 N.C. App. 486, 358 S.E.2d 560—CHLORPROMAZINE

Lanczki v. Providence Hosp. (1977) 77 Mich. App. 732, 258 N.W.2d 238—AMPICILLIN

Larrimore v. Homeopathic Hospital Assn. of Delaware (1962) 54 Del. 449, 181 A.2d 573—PENTOLINIUM TARTRATE

Latinovich v. United States (E.D. Wis., 1982) 537 F. Supp. 671—INFLUENZA VIRUS VACCINE

M

N

O

Odgers v. Ortho Pharmaceutical Corp. (No. 78-70543, Federal District Court, Eastern District, Detroit, Mich., July 7, 1980)—NORETHINDRONE with MESTRANOL

Odgers v. Ortho Pharmaceutical Corp. (E.D. Mich., 1985) 609 F. Supp. 867—NORETHINDRONE with MESTRANOL

O'Gara v. United States (E.D. Pa., 1983) 560 F. Supp. 786—INFLUENZA VIRUS VACCINE

Ohligschlager v. Proctor Community Hospital (1973) 55 Ill. 2d 411, 303 N.E.2d 392—PROMAZINE HCL

Oksenholt v. Lederle Laboratories (1981) 51 Ore. App. 419, 625 P.2d 1357, aff'd (1982) 294 Ore. 213, 656 P.2d 293—ETHAMBUTOL HCL

O'Malia v. Oakes (No. 360174, Superior Court, Alameda County, Cal., 1971)—MAGNESIUM TRISILICATE with ALUMINUM HYDROXIDE

Oppenheimer v. Sterling Drug, Inc. (1964) 7 Ohio App. 2d 103, 219 N.E.2d 54—CHLORQUINE

Ornoff v. Kuhn and Kogan, Chartered (D.C. App., 1988) 549 A.2d 728—ASPIRIN

Ortho Pharmaceutical Corp. v. Chapman (1979) 180 Ind. App. 33, 388 N.E.2d 541-NORETHINDRONE with MESTRANOL

Ortho Pharmaceutical Corp. v. Heath (Colo., 1986) 722 P.2d 410—NORETHINDRONE with MESTRANOL

Ortiz v. Allergan Pharmaceuticals (Tex. Civ. App., 1972) 489 S.W.2d 135—PREDNISOLONE ACETATE and PHENYLEPHRINE HCL

Ostheller v. Syntex Laboratories, Inc. (No. 270723, Superior Court, Santa Clara County, Cal., May 15, 1972)—NORETHINDRONE with MESTRANOL

Oukrop v. Wasserburger (Wyo., 1988) 755 P.2d 233—ATROPINE SULFATE

Overton v. United States (C.A.-8 Mo., 1980) 619 F.2d 1299—INFLUENZA VIRUS VACCINE

Oxendine v. Merrell Dow Pharmaceuticals (D.C., 1986) 506 A.2d 1100—DOXYLAMINE SUCCINATE

P

Pardy v. United States (C.A.-7 Ill., 1986) 783 F.2d 710—SODIUM IOTHALAMATE

Parham v. United States (E.D. Tenn., 1980) 503 F. Supp. 70—INFLUENZA VIRUS VACCINE

Parke, Davis & Co. v. Mayes (1971) 124 Ga. App. 224, 183 S.E.2d 410—CHLORAMPHENICOL

Parke-Davis & Co. v. Stromsodt (C.A.-8 N.D., 1969) 411 F.2d 1390—DTP

Parker v. Ortho Pharmaceutical Corp. (Fla. App., 1989) 536 So. 2d 390—NORETHINDRONE with MESTRANOL

Parks v. Maitland (No. 13807/85, Supreme Court, Bronx County N.Y., Nov. 25, 1986)—PHENYLBUTAZONE

Patten v. Lederle Laboratories (D. Utah, 1987) 655 F. Supp. 745—DTP

Patten v. Lederle Laboratories (D. Utah, 1987) 676 F. Supp. 233—DTP

Paul v. Boschenstein (1984) 105 App. Div. 2d 248, 482 N.Y.S.2d 870—PENTAZOCINE

Pauscher v. Iowa Methodist Med. Center (Iowa, 1987) 408 S.W.2d 355—DIATRIZOATE MEGLUMINE

Payton v. Abbott Labs (D. Mass., 1981) 512 F. Supp. 1031—DIETHYLSTILBESTROL

Payton v. Abbott Labs (1982) 386 Mass. 540, 437 N.E.2d 171—DIETHYLSTILBESTROL

Payton v. Abbott Labs (C.A.-1 Mass., 1985) 780 F.2d 147—DIETHYLSTILBESTROL

R

Ramey v. Guyton (Ala., 1980) 394 So. 2d 2—NORETHINDRONE with MESTRANOL
Ramirez v. Richardson-Merrell (E.D. Pa., 1986) 628 F. Supp. 85—DOXYLAMINE SUCCINATE
Ramon v. Farr (Utah, 1989) 770 P.2d 131—BUPIVACAINE
Ratkovich v. Smith Kline & French Laboratories (N.D. Ill., 1989) 711 F. Supp. 436—DEXTROAMPHETAMINE SULFATE
Ray v. Steadman (No. 79-189, United States District Court, W.D. N.Y., Jan. 28, 1983)—OXYTOCIN
Raynor v. Richardson-Merrell, Inc. (D. D.C., 1986) 643 F. Supp. 238—DOXYLAMINE SUCCINATE
Raynor v. Richardson-Merrell, Inc. (No. 83-3506, U.S. District Court, D. D.C., May 20, 1987)—DOXYLAMINE SUCCINATE
Rebollal v. Payne (1988) 145 App. Div. 2d 617, 536 N.Y.S.2d 147—METHADONE
Reeder v. Hammond (1983) 125 Mich. App. 223, 336 N.W.2d 3—AMPHETAMINE and DEXROAMPHETAMINE
Reeves v. Geigy Pharmaceutical, Inc. (Utah App., 1988) 764 P.2d 636—CARBAMAZEPINE
Rein v. United States (E.D. N.Y., 1982) 531 F. Supp. 67—INFLUENZA VIRUS VACCINE
Reinhardt v. Colton (Minn., 1983) 337 N.W.2d 88—PENICILLAMINE
Renfroe v. Eli Lilly & Co. (C.A.-8 Mo., 1982) 686 F.2d 642—DIETHYLSTILBESTROL
Renfroe v. Eli Lilly & Co. (E.D. Mo., 1982) 541 F. Supp. 805, aff'd (C.A.-8 Mo., 1982) 686 F.2d 642—DIETHYLSTILBESTROL
Renrick v. City of Newark (1962) 74 N.J. Super. 200, 181 A.2d 25—NOREPINEPHRINE BITARTRATE
Renzulli v. Ortho Pharmaceutical Corp. (No. 82-0469B, U.S. District Court, D. R.I., July 5, 1983)—p-DIISOBUTYLPHENOZYPOLYETHOXYETHANOL
Revallion v. Parke, Davis & Co. (No. 602920, Superior Court, Boston, Mass., Nov., 1972)—CELLULOSE, OXIDIZED
Reyes v. Wyeth Laboratories (C.A.-5 Tex., 1974) 498 F.2d 1264—POLIOVIRUS VACCINE
Reynolds v. Munroe Regional Med. Center (No. 83-3460D, Circuit Court, Marion County, Fla., Oct. 30, 1987)—SUCCINYLCHOLINE CHLORIDE
Rhoto v. Ribando (La. App., 1987) 504 So. 2d 1118—NORETHINDRONE with MESTRANOL
Richard v. Walgreen's La. Co. (La. App., 1985) 476 So. 2d 1150—SODIUM PENTOBARBITAL
Richards v. Upjohn Co. (1980) 95 N.M. 675, 625 P.2d 1192—NEOMYCIN SULFATE
Richardson v. Richardson-Merrell (C.A.-D.C., 1988) 857 F.2d 823—DOXYLAMINE SUCCINATE
Riff v. Morgan Pharmacy (1986) 353 Pa. Super. 21, 508 A.2d 1247—ERGOTAMINE TARTRATE
Robbins v. United States (C.A.-10 N.M., 1980) 624 F.2d 971—PREDNISONE
Robinson v. Duszynski (1978) 36 N.C. App. 103, 243 S.E.2d 148—BETAMETHASONE
Robinson v. United States (E.D. Mich., 1982) 533 F. Supp. 320—INFLUENZA VIRUS VACCINE
Rochester v. United States (Cl. Ct., 1989) 18 Cl. Ct. 379—DTP
Rodriguez v. Columbus Hospital (1971) 38 App. Div. 2d 517, 326 N.Y.S.2d 439—PENICILLIN

Rodriguez v. Jackson (1977) 118 Ariz. 13, 574 P.2d 481—STREPTOMYCIN
Rodriguez v. Nauenberg (No. 82 Civ. 5940, United States District Court, S.D. N.Y., Mar. 10, 1983)—LINCOMYCIN
Rohrbough v. Wyeth Laboratories, Inc. (N.D. W.Va., 1989) 719 F. Supp. 470—DTP
Roman v. A.H. Robins Co. (C.A.-5 Tex., 1975) 518 F.2d 970—SULFAMETER
Rosario v. New York City Health & Hospitals Corp. (1982) 87 App. Div. 2d 211, 450 N.Y.S.2d 805—SODIUM TETRADECYL SULFATE
Rose v. Doctors Hospital (No. 84-4467-B, 44th Judicial District Court, Dallas County, Tex., Nov. 11, 1985)—MORPHINE SULFATE
Rosenberg v. Savel (No. L-72462-80 MM, Superior Court, Essex County, N.J., Oct. 26, 1983)—SPARTEINE SULFATE
Rosenstein v. St. Peter's Hosp. (No. 14834/83, Supreme Court, Albany County, N.Y., Dec. 9, 1986)—HEPARIN SODIUM
Ross v. Jacobs (Okla. App., 1984) 684 P.2d 1211—ETHAMBUTOL HCL
Ross v. St. Luke's Hospital (No. 835261, Common Pleas Court, Cuyahoga County, Ohio, April 25, 1973)—TETRACYCLINE HCL
Ross Labs v. Thies (Alaska, 1986) 725 P.2d 1076—GLUCOSE POLYMERS
Rotan v. Greenbaum (1959) 107 App. D.C. 16, 273 F.2d 830—PENICILLIN
Rothering v. DePaul Rehabilitation Hospital (F1-1785, Wisconsin Patient's Compensation Panel, June 28, 1985)—DISULFRAM
Rowland v. Lederle Laboratories (No. 365072, Superior Court, Alameda County, Cal., 1970)—DEMECLOCYCLINE HCL
Rozier v. Department of Public Health (1987) 161 Mich. App. 591, 411 N.W.2d 786—SMALLPOX VACCINE
Rubel v. Eli Lilly & Co. (S.D.N.Y., 1987) 681 F. Supp. 151—DIETHYLSTILBESTROL
Rubin v. Aaron (No. 1615/81 Supreme Court, Nassau County, N.Y., June 5, 1989)—RESERPINE
Rubin v. Bergman (No. 1934/82, Supreme Court, Queens County, N.Y., June 1, 1988)—MEDROXYPROGESTERONE ACETATE
Runyon v. Reid (Okla., 1973) 510 P.2d 943, 58 A.L.R.3d 814—SODIUM PENTOBARBITAL with CARBROMAL
Rusk v. Santa Ana Community Hospital (No. 161561, Superior Court, Orange County, Cal., May 17, 1973)—SODIUM WARFARIN
Rutherford v. United States (C.A.-10 Okla., 1986) 806 F.2d 1455—AMYGDALIN
Rutherford v. Zearfoss (1980) 221 Va. 685, 272 S.E.2d 225—OXYTOCIN
Ryan v. Eli Lilly & Co. (D. S.C., 1981) 514 F. Supp. 1004—DIETHYLSTILBESTROL

S

Sacher v. Long Island Jewish-Hillside Medical Center (App. Div., 1988) 530 N.Y.S.2d 232—OXYTOCIN
Saez v. Municipality (1962) 84 P.R.R. 515—PENICILLIN
Sagor v. Beverly Enterprises (No. C 449288, Superior Court, Los Angeles, Cal., Jan. 27, 1988)—HALOPERIDOL
Salgo v. Leland Stanford Jr. University Board of Trustees (1957) 154 Cal. App. 2d 560, 317 P.2d 170—SODIUM ACETRIZOATE
Salmon v. Parke, Davis & Co. (C.A.-4 N.C., 1975) 520 F.2d 1359—CHLORAMPHENICOL
Samuels v. American Cyanamid Co. (1985) 130 Misc. 2d 175, 495 N.Y.S.2d 1006—TETRACAINE HCL
Sanchez v. Flower & Fifth Avenue Hospital (No. 14073/79, Supreme Court, New York County, N.Y., Jan. 31, 1986)—MEPERIDINE HCL

Shirkey v. Eli Lilly & Co. (C.A.-7 Wis., 1988) 852 F.2d 227—DIETHYLSTILBESTROL

Shrew v. Romond (No. F4-1329, Patients Compensation Panel, Milwaukee County, Wis., Feb., 1984)—NEOMYCIN SULFATE

Shuttles v. Glasser (No. 83-7239-3, Superior Court, DeKalb County, Ga., June 13, 1984)—MEPERIDINE HCL

Siegel v. Mt. Sinai Hospital of Cleveland (1978) 62 Ohio App. 2d 12, 403 N.E.2d 202—SODIUM THIOPENTAL

Siehr v. Stern (No. 82-16527 F, Circuit Court, Hillsborough County, Fla., Jan. 31, 1984)—GENTAMICIN SULFATE

Simi v. Hoffmann-LaRoche (No. A8605 02536, Circuit Court, Multnomah County, Ore., July 29, 1988)—ISOTRETINOIN

Simon v. Hoffman-LaRoche (No. CJ-81-1267, District Court, Oklahoma County, Okla., Sept. 9, 1982)—DIAZEPAM

Simonait v. G. D. Searle & Co. (No. 1916, Circuit Court, Kent County, Mich., May 26, 1965)—NORETHYNODREL with MESTRANOL

Simonetti v. United States (E.D. N.Y., 1982) 533 F. Supp. 435—INFLUENZA VIRUS VACCINE

Sindell v. Abbott Laboratories (1980) 26 Cal. 3d 588, 163 Cal. Rptr. 132, 607 P.2d 924—DIETHYLSTILBESTROL

Singer v. Sterling Drug, Inc. (C.A.-7 Ill., 1972) 461 F.2d 288—CHLOROQUINE

Skill v. Martinez (C.A.-3 N.J., 1982) 677 F.2d 368—NORETHINDRONEwith MESTRANOL

Skoglund v. Blankenship (1985) 134 Ill. App. 3d 628, 89 Ill. Dec. 695, 481 N.E.2d 47—PREDNISONE

Slack v. Fleet (La. App., 1970) 242 So. 2d 650—PHENACETIN 515, 595

Smith v. Baptist Mem. Hosp. Sys. (Tex. App., 1986) 720 S.W.2d 618—PENICILLIN

Smith v. Eli Lilly & Co. (1988) 173 Ill. App. 3d 1, 122 Ill. Dec. 835, 527 N.E.2d 333—DIETHYLSTILBESTROL

Smith v. E.R. Squibb & Sons, Inc. (1979) 405 Mich. 79, 273 N.W.2d 476—SODIUM DIATRIZOATE

Smith v. United States (C.A.-5 Miss., 1968) 394 F.2d 482—PROCHLORPERAZINE

Smith v. United States (C.A.-8 Ark., 1984) 726 F.2d 428—INFLUENZA VIRUS VACCINE

Smith v. Weaver (1987) 225 Neb. 569, 407 N.W.2d 174—SULINDAC

Snell v. Curtis (No. 119586, Circuit Court, Wayne County, Mich., June 14, 1971)—METHOTREXATE

Sparks v. Wyeth Laboratories, Inc. (W.D. Okla., 1977) 431 F. Supp. 411—INFLUENZA VIRUS VACCINE

Speer v. United States (N.D. Tex., 1981) 512 F. Supp. 670—PERPHENAZINE

Spencer v. United States (W.D. Mo., 1983) 569 F. Supp. 325—INFLUENZA VIRUS VACCINE

Spinden v. Johnson & Johnson (1981) 177 N.J. Super. 605, 427 A.2d 597—NORETHINDRONE with MESTRANOL

St. Clair v. Doctors Med. Center (No. 215956, Superior Court, Stanislaus County, Cal., Feb. 24, 1989)—MORPHINE SULFATE

Stafford v. Nipp (Ala., 1987) 502 So. 2d 702—ETHYNODIOL DIACETATE with MESTRANOL

Stahlheber v. American Cyanamid Co. (Mo., 1970) 451 S.W.2d 48—POLIOVIRUS VACCINE

Stalum v. Evangelical Hosp. Ass'n (No. 75-L-5981, Circuit Court, Cook County, Ill., Aug. 27, 1981)—LIDOCAINE HCL

Stanton by Brooks v. Astra Pharmaceutical Products, Inc. (C.A.-3 Pa., 1983) 718 F.2d 553—LIDOCAINE HCL

Starr v. Wasner (1988) 93 Or. App. 48, 760 P.2d 900—IBUPROFEN

Stavro v. Upjohn (No. 77-1761, United States District Court, E.D. Mich., Mar. 17, 1982)—CLINDAMYCIN HCL

Stebbins v. Concord Wrigley Drugs (1987) 164 Mich. App. 204, 416 N.W.2d 831—IMIPRAMINE HCL

Steele v. Seglie (No. 84-2200-2, U.S. District Court, D. Kan., Dec. 16, 1986)—OXYTOCIN

Stephens v. G.D. Searle & Co. (E.D. Mich., 1985) 602 F. Supp. 379—ETHYNODIOL DIACETATE with MESTRANOL

Sterling Drug, Inc. v. Cornish (C.A.-8 Mo., 1966) 370 F.2d 82—CHLOROQUINE

Sterling Drug, Inc. v. Yarrow (C.A.-8 S.D., 1969) 408 F.2d 978—CHLOROQUINE

Sterry v. Bethlehem Steel Corp. (1985) 64 Md. App. 175, 494 A.2d 748—PROPOXYPHENE HCL

Stevens v. Parke, Davis & Co. (1973) 9 Cal. 3d 51, 507 P.2d 653, 107 Cal. Rptr. 45, 94 A.L.R.3d 1059—CHLORAMPHENICOL

Stewart v. Bay Minette Infirmary (Ala., 1986) 501 So. 2d 441—DIAZEPAM

Stewart v. Janssen Pharmaceutica (Tex. App., 1989) 780 S.W.2d 910—SUFENTANIL CITRATE

Stich v. United States (D. N.J., 1983) 565 F. Supp. 1096, aff'd (C.A.-3 N.J., 1984) 730 F.2d 115 (1984)—INFLUENZA VIRUS VACCINE

Stokes v. Dailey (N.D., 1959) 97 N.W.2d 676—CYCLOMETHYCAINE

Stone v. Smith, Kline & French Laboratories (C.A.-11 Ala., 1984) 731 F.2d 1575—CHLORPROMAZINE

Stone v. Smith, Kline & French Laboratories (Ala., 1984) 447 So. 2d 1301—CHLORPROMAZINE

Stottlemire v. Cawood (D. D.C., 1963) 213 F. Supp. 897, 215 F. Supp. 266—CHLORAMPHENICOL

Strickland v. Board of Supervisors of Louisiana State University (La. App., 1983) 432 So. 2d 964—DIAZEPAM

Sulesky v. United States (S.D. W.Va., 1982) 545 F. Supp. 426—INFLUENZA VIRUS VACCINE

Sullivan v. Henry (1982) 160 Ga. App. 791, 287 S.E.2d 652—AMYGDALIN

Swanson v. Williams (1975) 303 Minn. 433, 228 N.W.2d 860—CEPHALOTHIN SODIUM

Swayze v. McNeil Labs (C.A.-5 Miss., 1987) 807 F.2d 464—FENTANYL

Swiss v. Eli Lilly & Co. (D. R.I., 1982) 559 F. Supp. 621—DIETHYLSTILBESTROL

T

Tangora v. Matanky (1964) 231 Cal. App. 2d 468, 42 Cal. Rptr. 348—PENICILLIN

Tate v. Eli Lilly & Co. (M.D. Tenn., 1981) 522 F. Supp. 1048—DIETHYLSTILBESTROL

Tatum v. Karst (No. CV-83-988-G, Circuit Court, Montgomery County, Ala., Oct. 30, 1984)—GOLD SODIUM THIOMALATE

Tatum v. Schering Corp. (C.A.-11 Ala., 1986) 795 F.2d 925—AUROTHIOGLUCOSE

Taylor v. Wyeth Laboratories, Inc. (1984) 139 Mich. App. 389, 362 N.W.2d 293—NORETHINDRONE with MESTRANOL

Terrell v. United States (N.D. Tex., 1981) 517 F. Supp. 374—INFLUENZA VIRUS VACCINE

Thomas v. Ferndale Laboratories, Inc. (1980) 97 Mich. App. 718, 296 N.W.2d 160—DIETHYLSTILBESTROL

Thomas v. St. Francis Hosp., Inc. (Del., 1982) 447 A.2d 435—SODIUM THIOPENTAL

Thompson v. Carter (Miss., 1987) 518 So. 2d 609—TRIMETHOPRIM and SULFAMETHOXAZOLE

U

V

W

Watkins v. United States (M.D. Tenn., 1980) 482 F. Supp. 1006—QUINACRINE HCL

Watson v. Eli Lilly & Co. (No. 82-0951, United States District Court, D. D.C., Feb. 10, 1983)—DIETHYLSTILBESTROL

Watson v. Merrell Dow Pharmaceuticals (C.A.-6 Ohio, 1985) 769 F.2d 354—DOXYLAMINE SUCCINATE

Webb v. Claus (No. SEC 4312, Superior Court, Los Angeles County, Cal., Feb. 9, 1973)—INDOMETHACIN

Webb v. Lightburn (No. C-82849, District Court, Colo., Feb. 12, 1980)—SECOBARBITAL SODIUM

Weinberger v. Bristol-Myers Co. (D. Md., 1986) 652 F. Supp. 187—MITOMYCIN

Wells v. Ortho Pharmaceutical Corp. (C.A.-11 Ga., 1986) 788 F.2d 741—pDIISOBUTYLPHENOXYPOLYETHOXYETHANOL

Werner v. American-Edwards Laboratories (1987) 113 Idaho 434, 745 P.2d 1055—SODIUM WARFARIN

Werner v. Upjohn Co. (C.A.-4 Md., 1980) 628 F.2d 848—CLINDAMYCIN HCL

Wetherill v. University of Chicago (N.D. Ill., 1981) 518 F. Supp. 1387—DIETHYLSTILBESTROL

Wetherill v. University of Chicago (N.D. Ill., 1983) 565 F. Supp. 1553—DIETHYLSTILBESTROL

Wetherill v. University of Chicago (N.D. Ill., 1983) 570 F. Supp. 1124—DIETHYLSTILBESTROL

White v. Weiner (Pa. Super., 1989) 562 A.2d 378—PROTAMINE SULFATE

White v. Wyeth Laboratories (1988) 40 Ohio St. 3d 390, 533 N.E.2d 748—DTP

Whitley v. Cubberly (1974) 24 N.C. App. 204, 210 S.E.2d 289—CHLORAMPHENICOL

Whittington v. Eli Lilly & Co. (S.D. W. Va., 1971) 333 F. Supp. 98—CHLORMADINONE ACETATE MESTRANOL

Whittle v. United States (C.A.-D.C., 1987) 669 F. Supp. 501—BUTALBITAL SODIUM

Wilabay v. Herbeck (No. 86-2751-A, 188th Judicial District Court, Gregg County, Tex., June 13, 1988)—INTRAVENOUS SOLUTIONS

Wilkins v. Rueger (No. 76-630-889NM, Circuit Court, Wayne County, Mich., May 8, 1980)—INDOMETHACIN

Will v. Richardson-Merrell Inc. (S.D. Ga., 1986) 647 F. Supp. 544—DOXYLAMINE SUCCINATE

Williams v. Ciba-Geigy Corp. (W.D. La., 1988) 686 F. Supp. 573, aff'd (C.A.-5 La., 1988) 864 F.2d 789—CARBAMAZEPINE

Williams v. City of New York (No. 23503/83, Supreme Court, New York County, N.Y., Sept. 7, 1988)—DTP

Williams v. Lallie Kemp Charity Hospital (No. 51,279, District Court, Twenty-First Judicial District, La., Sept. 4, 1980)—PENICILLIN

Williams v. Lederle Laboratories, Div. of American Cyanamid Co. (S.D. Ohio, 1984) 591 F. Supp. 381—POLIOVIRUS VACCINE

Wilson v. Mackenbrook (No. 390145, Superior Court, Alameda County, Cal., Jan. 16, 1974)—PENICILLIN

Wilson v. Merrell Dow Pharmaceuticals, Inc. (C.A.-10 Okla., 1990) 893 F.2d 1149—DOXYLAMINE SUCCINATE

Wilson v. Nealy (No. 81-10118-10, District Court, Pinellas County, Fla., Mar. 1, 1983)—OCXYTOCIN

Wilson v. St. Francis Hospital & School of Nursing, Inc. (1962) 190 Kan. 150, 373 P.2d 180—TETANUS ANTITOXIN

Winje v. Upjohn Co. (App. Div. 1989) 549 N.Y.S.2d 280—MEDROXYPROGESTERONE ACETATE

Winkjer v. Herr (N.D., 1979) 277 N.W.2d 579—ECHOTHIOPHATE IODIDE

Y

Z

Index

A

INDEX

ANTIBIOTICS AND ANTIBACTERIALS—Cont'd

C

D

E

F

H

I

J

K

L

N

O

S

T

U

V